PHYSIOLOGICAL PSYCHOLOGY

Readings from

**SCIENTIFIC
AMERICAN**

PHYSIOLOGICAL PSYCHOLOGY

with introductions by
Richard F. Thompson,
University of California, Irvine

W. H. Freeman and Company
San Francisco

Most of the SCIENTIFIC AMERICAN articles
in *Physiological Psychology* are available as
separate Offprints. For a complete list of more
than 800 articles now available as Offprints,
write to W. H. Freeman and Company, 660
Market Street, San Francisco, California 94104.

Printed in the United States of America

Library of Congress Catalog Card Number:
72–190435

Standard Book Number: 0–7167–0851–5 (cloth)
0–7167–0850–7 (paper)

9 8 7 6 5 4

PREFACE

Physiological psychology, or psychobiology, is an enormously exciting field at the frontier of our understanding of the biological bases of behavior and experience. We are well on our way to comprehending some of the classic problems in psychology—for example, how it is that we experience our visual world as we do—because of recent research on how neurons function to encode stimuli. Indeed, we are even beginning to approach the most fundamental of human problems, such as the nature of consciousness, using the new tools of physiological psychology. The field of psychobiology cuts across many areas and disciplines: biochemistry, anatomy, neurophysiology, biology, psychology, and sociology, to name a few. Scientists have coined many names for the field, including biopsychology, behavioral biology, and neuropsychology. These all reflect the basic goal of unveiling the physical and biological mechanisms that underlie behavior and experience. In the final analysis, there can be no other approach to an ultimate understanding of ourselves and our fellow humans.

This collection of forty-six articles from SCIENTIFIC AMERICAN surveys our current knowledge at the interface of biology and psychology. The articles, prepared by outstanding scientists in many fields ranging from chemistry to the social sciences, share the important features of clarity and accessibility: they are understandable to an interested reader who may have no special background or training. Characteristic of SCIENTIFIC AMERICAN is the almost unique way in which work on the forefronts of scientific knowledge is presented with accuracy and, at the same time, in a highly readable and interesting manner.

Psychobiology represents the common ground of psychology and biology. As such, it is incorporated in courses and programs both in biology and in psychology. This reader is designed to meet the needs of students and teachers in both disciplines. It is divided into ten sections, which treat the most important topics in the field. The first section presents man in an evolutionary context, dealing specifically with genetics and human evolution, including the critically important issue of current human evolution. Section II focuses on the evolution and development of behavior—on how behavior patterns have evolved under the control of innate genetic factors interacting with environment and experience. The first portion of the section is a bird's-eye view of *ethology,* the biological analysis of natural behavior. The remainder deals with growth and development: the development of behavior and experience as the individual organism or person grows from conception to adulthood is fundamental to the biology of behavior. Section III presents the brain, the supreme organ of behavior and experience. The organization of the brain is described, together with some of the more important aspects of its functions, including brain waves and conscious experience.

The basic processes of information conduction and transfer in individual nerve cells—the mechanisms underlying integration and plasticity in the brain—are dealt with in Section IV. Section V reviews the new and exciting field of "psychochemistry"—hormone control of (and drug influences on) the brain and behavior. Sensory processes and perception, the phenomena that form the basis of our immediate experience, are sampled in Section VI. The forces that energize and drive behavior—the mechanisms of motivation and emotion—are reviewed in Section VII. Sleep, dreaming, and arousal, an area that has recently occasioned much excitement with the discovery of the "dream state," is covered in Section VIII. The physical basis of learning and memory, a topic fundamental to the biology of behavior, is treated in Section IX. Finally, Section X deals with the most complex and least understood aspects of brain function—thought, language, and attention.

A brief bibliography is provided at the end of the book that should be of help to those desiring to pursue a topic further. Cross-references within the articles are according to the following convention: references to articles included in this book are noted by the title of the article and the page on which it begins; references to articles that are available as SCIENTIFIC AMERICAN Offprints, but are not included here, are noted by the article's title and Offprint number; and references to articles published by SCIENTIFIC AMERICAN, but not available as Offprints, are noted by the title of the article and the month and year of its publication.

December 1971   Richard F. Thompson

CONTENTS

PHYSIOLOGICAL PSYCHOLOGY

I

GENETICS AND HUMAN EVOLUTION

I

GENETICS AND HUMAN EVOLUTION

INTRODUCTION

Man is an animal. This obvious fact is all too often overlooked in psychology. Human characteristics and abilities have been shaped by the pressures of evolution: the properties that define *Homo sapiens* evolved because they had survival value. The sole criterion of biological success is survival of the species, and man is, judging by his numbers, the most successful primate to inhabit the earth.

Man's nature cannot be understood without some appreciation of how *Homo sapiens* evolved. This section, together with the next section on the evolution of behavior, provides a brief introduction to the new and growing field of behavior genetics. Genes obviously do not produce or control behavior directly, but do so, rather, through the genetically determined structural and functional properties of the organism, particularly those of the brain. We are still probing the most elementary genetic aspects of behavior. There are indications that genetic control of behavior is far more profound than we had earlier thought possible, even in *Homo sapiens.*

Theodosius Dobzhansky, a leading geneticist, is the author of "The Genetic Basis of Evolution," the first article in this section. The unbelievable variety of living and extinct species of organisms, from viruses to man, is the result of a subtle interplay between the hereditary mechanism—the DNA that forms the genes—and a widely diversified environment. The basis for evolution is variation and mutation of the genetic material, which provides the diversity of individuals within a species necessary for them to respond differently to environmental pressures—some of them more successfully than others.

Sherwood L. Washburn, a noted anthropologist, discusses the recent evolution of man in "Tools and Human Evolution." He traces our descent from the early anthropoid ancestors of monkeys, apes, and men. A critical aspect of this evolution was the use of tools: evidence suggests that a very early ancestor of the human line, discovered by L. S. B. and Mary Leakey in Tanganyika and now called *Australopithecus,* may have used crude chipped-pebble "tools" more than a million years ago. Comparing the skull and brain of man with those of apes, Washburn emphasizes that the modern human brain did not appear *de novo*, but that its development was gradual, and was affected by interaction with the development of other human traits — the increased use of the hands, particularly the thumb, and increased mental powers associated with skills, social organization, and language. The human aspects of human nature did not develop by accident; they developed because they possessed survival value.

The Harvard anthropologist William W. Howells provides a more detailed account of our recent past in "The Distribution of Man." Although evidence is still somewhat sketchy, it is most probable that the modern races of man diversified within the past 100,000 years or so from a more-or-less common *Homo sapiens* stock. Several genetic mechanisms can produce racial diversity: natural selection, genetic drift, mutation, and interbreeding. Howells discusses these factors in relation to modern human races. Not all racial characteristics need have survival value — the often prominent noses of Caucasians being a case in point. Skin color is not so much a racial characteristic as a function of ultraviolet radiation in sunlight, ranging among Caucasians, for example, from very light in northern regions to dark brown in hot equatorial countries. Mongoloid facial characteristics seem a particularly clear adaptation to extreme cold. Perhaps the most important point, however, is that racial differences in modern men reflect recent and minor variations from a common ancestral stock.

This survey of human evolution concludes with another article by Dobzhansky, this one entitled "The Present Evolution of Man." It is a common but erroneous belief that *Homo sapiens* stopped evolving biologically when society and civilization removed man from the primitive "jungle" struggle for survival. Man, in fact, is still evolving; the forces of natural selection have merely changed. For the individual, survival potential is measured by "fitness," which means reproductive success. Many mutations and abnormalities can influence the number of children an individual has. Dobzhansky discusses these issues and indicates the directions in which mankind is still evolving.

1

THE GENETIC BASIS OF EVOLUTION

THEODOSIUS DOBZHANSKY
January 1950

THE living beings on our planet come in an incredibly rich diversity of forms. Biologists have identified about a million species of animals and some 267,000 species of plants, and the number of species actually in existence may be more than twice as large as the number known. In addition the earth has been inhabited in the past by huge numbers of other species that are now extinct, though some are preserved as fossils. The organisms of the earth range in size from viruses so minute that they are barely visible in electron microscopes to giants like elephants and sequoia trees. In appearance, body structure and ways of life they exhibit an endlessly fascinating variety.

What is the meaning of this bewildering diversity? Superficially considered, it may seem to reflect nothing more than the whims of some playful deity, but one soon finds that it is not fortuitous. The more one studies living beings the more one is impressed by the wonderfully effective adjustment of their multifarious body structures and functions to their varying ways of life. From the simplest to the most complex, all organisms are constructed to function efficiently in the environments in which they live. The body of a green plant can build itself from food consisting merely of water, certain gases in the air and some mineral salts taken from the soil. A fish is a highly efficient machine for exploiting the organic food resources of water, and a bird is built to get the most from its air en-

vironment. The human body is a complex, finely coordinated machine of marvelously precise engineering, and through the inventive abilities of his brain man is able to control his environment. Every species, even the most humble, occupies a certain place in the economy of nature, a certain adaptive niche which it exploits to stay alive.

The diversity and adaptedness of living beings were so difficult to explain that during most of his history man took the easy way out of assuming that every species was created by God, who contrived the body structures and functions of each kind of organism to fit it to a predestined place in nature. This idea has now been generally replaced by the less easy but intellectually more satisfying explanation that the living things we see around us were not always what they are now, but evolved gradually from very different-looking ancestors; that these ancestors were in general less complex, less perfect and less diversified than the organisms now living; that the evolutionary process is still under way, and that its causes can therefore be studied by observation and experiment in the field and in the laboratory.

The origins and development of this theory, and the facts that finally convinced most people of its truth beyond reasonable doubt, are too long a story to be presented here. After Charles Darwin published his convincing exposition and proof of the theory of evolution in 1859, two main currents developed in evolu-

tionary thought. Like any historical process, organic evolution may be studied in two ways. One may attempt to infer the general features and the direction of the process from comparative studies of the sequence of events in the past; this is the method of paleontologists, comparative anatomists and others. Or one may attempt to reconstruct the causes of evolution, primarily through a study of the causes and mechanisms that operate in the world at present; this approach, which uses experimental rather than observational methods, is that of the geneticist and the ecologist. This article will consider what has been learned about the causes of organic evolution through the second approach.

Darwin attempted to describe the causes of evolution in his theory of natural selection. The work of later biologists has borne out most of his basic contentions. Nevertheless, the modern theory of evolution, developed by a century of new discoveries in biology, differs greatly from Darwin's. His theory has not been overthrown; it has evolved. The authorship of the modern theory can be credited to no single person. Next to Darwin, Gregor Mendel of Austria, who first stated the laws of heredity, made the greatest contribution. Within the past two decades the study of evolutionary genetics has developed very rapidly on the basis of the work of Thomas Hunt Morgan and Hermann J. Muller of the U. S. In these developments the principal contributors have been C. D.

Darlington, R. A. Fisher, J. B. S. Haldane, J. S. Huxley and R. Mather in England; B. Rensch and N. W. Timofeeff-Ressovsky in Germany; S. S. Chetverikov, N. P. Dubinin and I. I. Schmalhausen in the U.S.S.R.; E. Mayr, J. T. Patterson, C. G. Simpson, G. L. Stebbins and Sewall Wright in the U. S., and some others.

Evolution in the Laboratory

Evolution is generally so slow a process that during the few centuries of recorded observations man has been able to detect very few evolutionary changes among animals and plants in their natural habitats. Darwin had to deduce the theory of evolution mostly from indirect evidence, for he had no means of observing the process in action. Today, however, we can study and even produce evolutionary changes at will in the laboratory. The experimental subjects of these studies are bacteria and other low forms of life which come to birth, mature and yield a new generation within a matter of minutes or hours, instead of months or years as in most higher beings. Like a greatly speeded-up motion picture, these observations compress into a few days evolutionary events that would take thousands of years in the higher animals.

One of the most useful bacteria for this study is an organism that grows, usually harmlessly, in the intestines of practically every human being: *Escherichia coli*, or colon bacteria. These organisms can easily be cultured on a nutritive broth or nutritive agar. At about 98 degrees Fahrenheit, bacterial cells placed in a fresh culture medium divide about every 20 minutes. Their numbers increase rapidly until the nutrients in the culture medium are exhausted; a single cell may yield billions of progeny in a day. If a few cells are placed on a plate covered with nutritive agar, each cell by the end of the day produces a whitish speck representing a colony of its offspring.

Now most colon bacteria are easily killed by the antibiotic drug streptomycin. It takes only a tiny amount of streptomycin, 25 milligrams in a liter of a nutrient medium, to stop the growth of the bacteria. Recently, however, the geneticist Milislav Demerec and his collaborators at the Carnegie Institution in Cold Spring Harbor, N. Y., have shown that if several billion colon bacteria are placed on the streptomycin-containing medium, a few cells will survive and form colonies on the plate. The offspring of these hardy survivors are able to multiply freely on a medium containing streptomycin. A mutation has evidently taken place in the bacteria; they have now become resistant to the streptomycin that was poisonous to their sensitive ancestors.

How do the bacteria acquire their

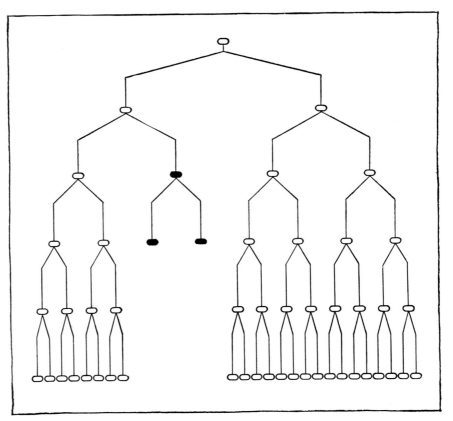

IN NORMAL ENVIRONMENT the common strain of the bacterium *Escherichia coli* (*white bacteria*) multiplies. A mutant strain resistant to streptomycin (*black bacteria*) remains rare because the mutation is not useful.

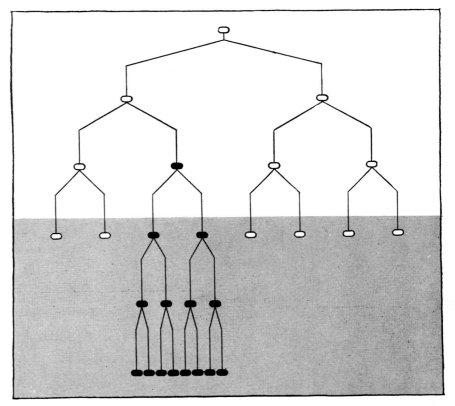

IN CHANGED ENVIRONMENT produced by the addition of streptomycin (*gray area*) the streptomycin-resistant strain is better adapted than the common strain. The mutant strain then multiplies and the common one dies.

CONTROLLED ENVIRONMENT for the study of fruit-fly populations is a glass-covered box. In bottom of the box are cups of food that are filled in rotation to keep food a constant factor in environment.

resistance? Is the mutation caused by their exposure to streptomycin? Demerec has shown by experimental tests that this is not so; in any large culture a few resistant mutants appear even when the culture has not been exposed to streptomycin. Some cells in the culture undergo mutations from sensitivity to resistance regardless of the presence or absence of streptomycin in the medium. Demerec found that the frequency of mutation was about one per billion; *i.e.*, one cell in a billion becomes resistant in every generation. Streptomycin does not induce the mutations; its role in the production of resistant strains is merely that of a selecting agent. When streptomycin is added to the culture, all the normal sensitive cells are killed, and only the few resistant mutants that happened to be present before the streptomycin was added survive and reproduce. Evolutionary changes are controlled by the environment, but the control is indirect, through the agency of natural or artificial selection.

What governs the selection? If resistant bacteria arise in the absence of streptomycin, why do sensitive forms predominate in all normal cultures; why has not the whole species of colon bacteria become resistant? The answer is that the mutants resistant to streptomycin are at a disadvantage on media free from this drug. Indeed, Demerec has discovered the remarkable fact that about 60 per cent of the bacterial strains derived from streptomycin-resistant mutants become dependent on streptomycin; they are unable to grow on media free from it!

On the other hand one can reverse the process and obtain strains of bacteria that can live without streptomycin from cultures predominantly dependent on the drug. If some billions of dependent bacteria are plated on nutrient media free of the drug, all dependent cells cease to multiply and only the few mutants independent of the drug reproduce and form colonies. Demerec estimates the frequency of this "reverse" mutation at about 37 per billion cells in each generation.

Evolutionary changes of the type described in colon bacteria have been found in recent years in many other bacterial species. The increasing use of antibiotic drugs in medical practice has made such changes a matter of considerable concern in public health. As penicillin, for example, is used on a large scale against bacterial infections, the strains of bacteria that are resistant to penicillin survive and multiply, and the probability that they will infect new victims is increased. The mass application of antibiotic drugs may lead in the long run to increased incidence of cases refractory to treatment. Indications exist that this has already happened in some instances: in certain cities penicillin-resistant gonorrhea has become more frequent than it was.

The same type of evolutionary change has also been noted in some larger organisms. A good example is the case of DDT and the common housefly, *Musca domestica*. DDT was a remarkably effective poison for houseflies when first introduced less than 10 years ago. But already reports have come from places as widely separated as New Hampshire, New York, Florida, Texas, Italy and Sweden that DDT sprays in certain localities have lost their effectiveness. What has happened, of course, is that strains of houseflies relatively resistant to DDT have become established in these localities. Man has unwittingly become an agent of a selection process which has led to evolutionary changes in housefly populations. Similar changes are known to have occurred in other insects; *e.g.*, in some orchards of California where hydrocyanic gas has long been used as a fumigant to control scale insects that prey on citrus fruits, strains of these insects that are resistant to hydrocyanic gas have developed.

Obviously evolutionary selection can take place only if nature provides a supply of mutants to choose from. Thus no bacteria will survive to start a new strain resistant to streptomycin in a culture in which no resistant mutant cells were present in the first place, and housefly races resistant to DDT have not appeared everywhere that DDT is used. Adaptive changes are not mechanically forced upon the organism by the environment. Many species of past geological epochs died out because they did not have a supply of mutants which fitted changing environments. The process of mutation furnishes the raw materials from which evolutionary changes are built.

Mutations

Mutations arise from time to time in all organisms, from viruses to man. Perhaps the best organism for the study of mutations is the now-famous fruit fly, Drosophila. It can be bred easily and rapidly in laboratories, and it has a large number of bodily traits and functions that are easy to observe. Mutations affect the color of its eyes and body, the size and shape of the body and of its parts, its internal anatomical structures, its fecundity, its rate of growth, its behavior, and so on. Some mutations produce differences so minute that they can be detected only by careful measurements; others are easily seen even by beginners; still others produce changes so drastic that death occurs before the development is completed. The latter are called lethal mutations.

The frequency of any specific mutation is usually low. We have seen that in colon bacteria a mutation to resistance to streptomycin occurs in only about one cell per billion in every generation, and the reverse mutation to independence of streptomycin is about 37 times more frequent. In Drosophila and in the corn plant mutations have been found to range in frequency from one in 100,000 to one in a million per generation. In man, according to estimates by Haldane in England and James Neel in the U. S., mutations that produce certain hereditary diseases, such as hemophilia and Cooley's anemia, arise in one in 2,500 to one in 100,000 sex cells in each generation. From this it may appear that man is more mutable than flies and bacteria, but it should be remembered that a generation in man takes some 25 years, in flies two weeks, and in bacteria 25 minutes. The frequency of mutations per unit of time is actually greater in bacteria than in man.

A single organism may of course produce several mutations, affecting different features of the body. How frequent are all mutations combined? For technical reasons, this is difficult to determine; for example, most mutants produce small changes that are not detected unless especially looked for. In Drosophila it is estimated that new mutants affecting one part of the body or another are present in between one and 10 per cent of the sex cells in every generation.

In all organisms the majority of mutations are more or less harmful. This may seem a very serious objection against the theory which regards them as the mainspring of evolution. If mutations produce incapacitating changes, how can adaptive evolution be compounded of them? The answer is: a mutation that is harmful in the environment in which the species or race lives may become useful, even essential, if the environment changes. Actually it would be strange if we found mutations that improve the adaptation of the organism in the environment in which it normally lives. Every kind of mutation that we observe has occurred numerous times under natural conditions, and the useful ones have become incorporated into what we call the "normal" constitution of the species. But when the environment changes, some of the previously rejected mutations become advantageous and produce an evolutionary change in the species. The writer and B. A. Spassky have carried out certain experiments in which we intentionally disturbed the harmony between an artificial environment and the fruit flies living in it. At first the change in environment killed most of the flies, but during 50 consecutive generations most strains showed a gradual improvement of viability, evidently owing to the environment's selection of the better-adapted variants.

This is not to say that every mutation will be found useful in some environment somewhere. It would be difficult to imagine environments in which such human mutants as hemophilia or the absence of hands and feet might be useful. Most mutants that arise in any species are, in effect, degenerative changes; but some, perhaps a small minority, may be beneficial in some environments. If the environment were forever constant, a species might conceivably reach a summit of adaptedness and ultimately suppress the mutation process. But the environment is never constant; it varies not only from place to place but from time to time. If no mutations occur in a species, it can no longer become adapted to changes and is headed for eventual extinction. Mutation is the price that organisms pay for survival. They do not possess a miraculous ability to produce only useful mutations where and when needed. Mutations arise at random, regardless of whether they will be useful at the moment, or ever; nevertheless, they make the species rich in adaptive possibilities.

The Genes

To understand the nature of the mutation process we must inquire into the nature of heredity. A man begins his individual existence when an egg cell is fertilized by a spermatozoon. From an egg cell weighing only about a 20-millionth of an ounce, he grows to an average weight at maturity of some 150 pounds—a 48-billionfold increase. The material for this stupendous increase in mass evidently comes from the food consumed, first by the mother and then by the individual himself. But the food becomes a constituent part of the body only after it is digested and assimilated, i.e., transformed into a likeness of the assimilating body. This body, in turn, is a likeness of the bodies of the individual's ancestors. Heredity is, then, a process whereby the organism reproduces itself in its progeny from food materials taken in from the environment. In short, heredity is self-reproduction.

The units of self-reproduction are called genes. The genes are borne chiefly in chromosomes of the cell nucleus, but certain types of genes called plasmagenes are present in the cytoplasm, the part of the cell outside the nucleus. The chemical details of the process of self-reproduction are unknown. Apparently a gene enters into some set of chemical reactions with materials in its surroundings; the outcome of these reactions is the appearance of two genes in the place of one. In other words, a gene synthesizes a copy of itself from nongenic materials. The genes are considered to be stable because the copy is a true likeness of the original in the overwhelming majority of cases; but occasionally the copying process is faulty, and the new gene that emerges differs from its model. This is a mutation. We can increase the

frequency of mutations in experimental animals by treating the genes with X-rays, ultraviolet rays, high temperature or certain chemical substances.

Can a gene be changed by the environment? Assuredly it can. But the important point is the kind of change produced. The change that is easiest to make is to treat the gene with poisons or heat in such a way that it no longer reproduces itself. But a gene that cannot produce a copy of itself from other materials is no longer a gene; it is dead. A mutation is a change of a very special kind: the altered gene can reproduce itself, and the copy produced is like the changed structure, not like the original. Changes of this kind are relatively rare. Their rarity is not due to any imperviousness of the genes to influences of the environment, for genic materials are probably the most active chemical constituents of the body; it is due to the fact that genes are by nature self-reproducing, and only the rare changes that preserve the genes' ability to reproduce can effect a lasting alteration of the organism.

Changes in heredity should not be confused, as they often are, with changes in the manifestations of heredity. Such expressions as "gene for eye color" or "inheritance of musical ability" are figures of speech. The sex cells that transmit heredity have no eyes and no musical ability. What genes determine are patterns of development which result in the emergence of eyes of a certain color and of individuals with some musical abilities. When genes reproduce themselves from different food materials and in different environments, they engender the development of different "characters" or "traits" in the body. The outcome of the development is influenced both by heredity and by environment.

In the popular imagination, heredity is transmitted from parents to offspring through "blood." The heredity of a child is supposed to be a kind of alloy or solution, resulting from the mixture of the paternal and maternal "bloods." This blood theory became scientifically untenable as long ago as Mendel's discovery of the laws of heredity in 1865. Heredity is transmitted not through miscible bloods but through genes. When different variants of a gene are brought together in a single organism, a hybrid, they do not fuse or contaminate one another; the genes keep their integrity and separate when the hybrid forms sex cells.

Genetics and Mathematics

Although the number of genes in a single organism is not known with precision, it is certainly in the thousands, at least in the higher organisms. For Drosophila, 5,000 to 12,000 seems a reasonable estimate, and for man the figure is, if anything, higher. Since most or all genes

suffer mutational changes from time to time, populations of virtually every species must contain mutant variants of many genes. For example, in the human species there are variations in the skin, hair and eye colors, in the shape and distribution of hair, in the form of the head, nose and lips, in stature, in body proportions, in the chemical composition of the blood, in psychological traits, and so on. Each of these traits is influenced by several or by many genes. To be conservative, let us assume that the human species has only 1,000 genes and that each gene has only two variants. Even on this conservative basis, Mendelian segregation and recombination would be capable of producing 2^{1000} different gene combinations in human beings.

The number 2^{1000} is easy to write but is utterly beyond comprehension. Compared with it, the total number of electrons and protons estimated by physicists to exist in the universe is negligibly small! It means that except in the case of identical twins no two persons now living, dead, or to live in the future are at all likely to carry the same complement of genes. Dogs, mice and flies are as individual and unrepeatable as men are. The mechanism of sexual reproduction, of which the recombination of genes is a part, creates ever new genetic constitutions on a prodigious scale.

One might object that the number of possible combinations does not greatly matter; after all, they will still be combinations of the same thousand gene variants, and the way they are combined is not significant. Actually it is: the same gene may have different effects in combinations with different genes. Thus Timofeeff-Ressovsky showed that two mutants in Drosophila, each of which reduced the viability of the fly when it was present alone, were harmless when combined in the same individual by hybridization. Natural selection tests the fitness in certain environments not of single genes but of constellations of genes present in living individuals.

Sexual reproduction generates, therefore, an immense diversity of genetic constitutions, some of which, perhaps a small minority, may prove well attuned to the demands of certain environments. The biological function of sexual reproduction consists in providing a highly efficient trial-and-error mechanism for the operation of natural selection. It is a reasonable conjecture that sex became established as the prevalent method of reproduction because it gave organisms the greatest potentialities for adaptive and progressive evolution.

Let us try to imagine a world providing a completely uniform environment. Suppose that the surface of our planet were absolutely flat, covered everywhere with the same soil; that instead of summer and winter seasons we had eternally constant temperature and humidity; that instead of the existing diversity of foods there was only one kind of energy-yielding substance to serve as nourishment. The Russian biologist Gause has pointed out that only a single kind of organism could inhabit such a tedious world. If two or more kinds appeared in it, the most efficient form would gradually crowd out and finally eliminate the less efficient ones, remaining the sole inhabitant. In the world of reality, however, the environment changes at every step. Oceans, plains, hills, mountain ranges, regions where summer heat alternates with winter cold, lands that are permanently warm, dry deserts, humid jungles —these diverse environments have engendered a multitude of responses by protoplasm and a vast proliferation of distinct species of life through the evolutionary process.

Some Adaptations

Many animal and plant species are polymorphic, *i.e.*, represented in nature by two or more clearly distinguishable kinds of individuals. For example, some individuals of the ladybird beetle *Adalia bipunctata* are red with black spots while others are black with red spots. The color difference is hereditary, the black color behaving as a Mendelian dominant and red as a recessive. The red and black forms live side by side and interbreed freely. Timofeeff-Ressovsky observed that near Berlin, Germany, the black form predominates from spring to autumn, and the red form is more numerous during the winter. What is the origin of these changes? It is quite improbable that the genes for color are transformed by the seasonal variations in temperature; that would mean epidemics of directed mutations on a scale never observed. A much more plausible view is that the changes are produced by natural selection. The black form is, for some reason, more successful than the red in survival and reproduction during summer, but the red is superior to the black under winter conditions. Since the beetles produce several generations during a single season, the species undergoes cyclic changes in its genetic composition in response to the seasonal alterations in the environment. This hypothesis was confirmed by the discovery that black individuals are more frequent among the beetles that die during the rigors of winter than among those that survive.

The writer has observed seasonal changes in some localities in California in the fly *Drosophila pseudoobscura*. Flies of this species in nature are rather uniform in coloration and other external traits, but they are very variable in the structure of their chromosomes, which can be seen in microscopic preparations. In the locality called Piñon Flats, on Mount San Jacinto in southern Califor-

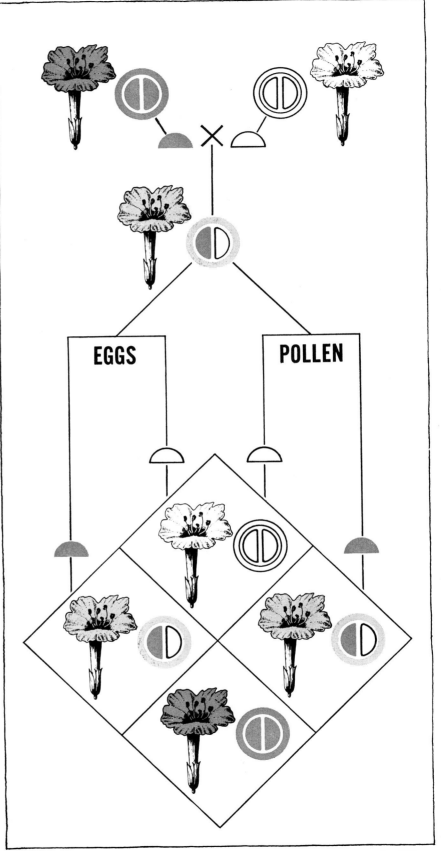

MENDELIAN SEGREGATION is illustrated by the four o'clock (*Mirabilis jalapa*). The genes of red and white flowers combine in a pink hybrid. Genes are segregated in the cross-fertilized descendants of pink flowers.

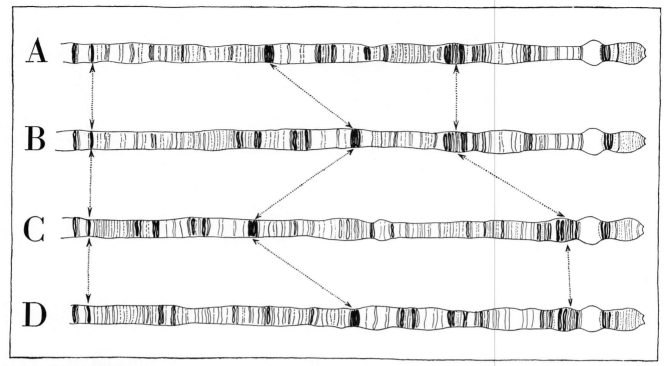

FOUR VARIETIES of the species *Drosophila pseudo-obscura* are revealed by differences in the structure of their chromosomes. Under the microscope similar markings may be observed at different locations (*arrows*).

nia, the fruit-fly population has four common types of chromosome structure, which we may, for simplicity, designate as types A, B, C and D. From 1939 to 1946, samples of flies were taken from this population in various months of the year, and the chromosomes of these flies were examined. The relative frequencies of the chromosomal types, expressed in percentages of the total, varied with the seasons as follows:

Month	A	B	C	D
March	52	18	23	7
April	40	28	28	4
May	34	29	31	6
June	28	28	39	5
July	42	22	31	5
Aug.	42	28	26	4
Sept.	48	23	26	3
Oct.-Dec.	50	26	20	4

Thus type A was common in winter but declined in the spring, while type C waxed in the spring and waned in summer. Evidently flies carrying chromosomes of type C are somehow better adapted than type A to the spring climate; hence from March to June, type A decreases and type C increases in frequency. Contrariwise, in the summer type A is superior to type C. Types B and D show little consistent seasonal variation.

Similar changes can be observed under controlled laboratory conditions. Populations of Drosophila flies were kept in a very simple apparatus consisting of a wood and glass box, with openings in the bottom for replenishing the nutrient medium on which the flies lived—a kind of pudding made of Cream of Wheat, molasses and yeast. A mixture of flies of which 33 per cent were type A and 67 per cent type C was introduced into the apparatus and left to multiply freely, up to the limit imposed by the quantity of food given. If one of the types was better adapted to the environment than the other, it was to be expected that the better-adapted type would increase and the other decrease in relative numbers. This is exactly what happened. During the first six months the type A flies rose from 33 to 77 per cent of the population, and type C fell from 67 to 23 per cent. But then came an unexpected leveling off: during the next seven months there was no further change in the relative proportions of the flies, the frequencies of types A and C oscillating around 75 and 25 per cent respectively.

If type A was better than type C under the conditions of the experiment, why were not the flies with C chromosomes crowded out completely by the carriers of A? Sewall Wright of the University of Chicago solved the puzzle by mathematical analysis. The flies of these types interbreed freely, in natural as well as in experimental populations. The populations therefore consist of three kinds of individuals: 1) those that obtained chromosome A from father as well as from mother, and thus carry two A chromosomes (AA); 2) those with two C chromosomes (CC); 3) those that re-ceived chromosomes of different types from their parents (AC). The mixed type, AC, possesses the highest adaptive value; it has what is called "hybrid vigor." As for the pure types, under the conditions that obtain in nature AA is superior to CC in the summer. Natural selection then increases the frequency of A chromosomes in the population and diminishes the C chromosomes. In the spring, when CC is better than AA, the reverse is true. But note now that in a population of mixed types neither the A nor the C chromosomes can ever be entirely eliminated from the population, even if the flies are kept in a constant environment where type AA is definitely superior to type CC. This, of course, is highly favorable to the flies as a species, for the loss of one of the chromosome types, though it might be temporarily advantageous, would be prejudicial in the long run, when conditions favoring the lost type would return. Thus a polymorphic population is better able than a uniform one to adjust itself to environmental changes and to exploit a variety of habitats.

Races

Populations of the same species which inhabit different environments become genetically different. This is what a geneticist means when he speaks of races. Races are populations within a species that differ in the frequencies of some genes. According to the old concept of race, which is based on the notion that

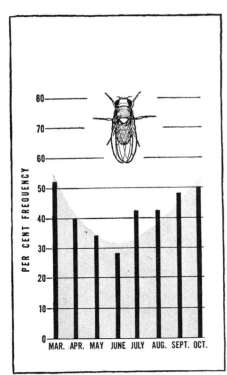

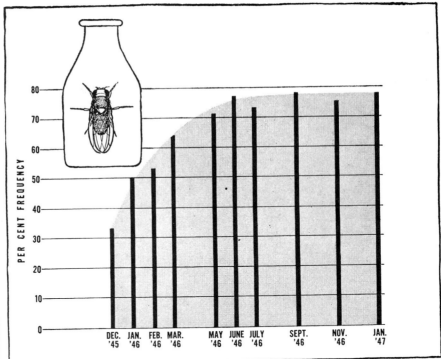

NUMBER OF FLIES of one chromosomal type varies in nature (*left*) and in the laboratory. In seasonal environ- ment of nature the type increases and decreases regular- ly; in constant environment of laboratory it levels off.

heredity is transmitted through "blood" and which still prevails among those ignorant of modern biology, the hereditary endowment of an isolated population would become more and more uniform with each generation, provided there was no interbreeding with other tribes or populations. The tribe would eventually become a "pure" race, all members of which would be genetically uniform. Scientists misled by this notion used to think that at some time in the past the human species consisted of an unspecified number of "pure" races, and that intermarriage between them gave rise to the present "mixed" populations.

In reality, "pure" races never existed, nor can they possibly exist in any species, such as man, that reproduces by sexual combination. We have seen that all human beings except identical twins differ in heredity. In widely differing climatic environments the genetic differences may be substantial. Thus populations native in central Africa have much higher frequencies of genes that produce dark skin than do European populations. The frequency of the gene for blue eye color progressively diminishes southward from Scandinavia through central Europe to the Mediterranean and Africa. Nonetheless some blue-eyed individuals occur in the Mediterranean region and even in Africa, and some brown-eyed ones in Norway and Sweden.

It is important to keep in mind that races are populations, not individuals. Race differences are relative and not absolute, since only in very remote races

do all members of one population possess a set of genes that is lacking in all members of another population. It is often difficult to tell how many races exist in a species. For example, some anthropologists recognize only two human races while others list more than 100. The difficulty is to know where to draw the line. If, for example, the Norwegians are a "Nordic race" and the southern Italians a "Mediterranean race," to what race do the inhabitants of Denmark, northern Germany, southern Germany, Switzerland and northern Italy belong? The frequencies of most differentiating traits change rather gradually from Norway to southern Italy. Calling the intermediate populations separate races may be technically correct, but this confuses the race classification even more, because nowhere can sharp lines of demarcation between these "races" be drawn. It is quite arbitrary whether we recognize 2, 4, 10, or more than 100 races—or finally refuse to make any rigid racial labels at all.

The differences between human races are, after all, rather small, since the geographic separation between them is nowhere very marked. When a species is distributed over diversified territories, the process of adaptation to the different environments leads to the gradual accumulation of more numerous and biologically more and more important differences between races. The races gradually diverge. There is, of course, nothing fatal about this divergence, and under some circumstances the divergence may

stop or even be turned into convergence. This is particularly true of the human species. The human races were somewhat more sharply separated in the past than they are today. Although the species inhabits almost every variety of environment on earth, the development of communications and the increase of mobility, especially in modern times, has led to much intermarriage and to some genetic convergence of the human races.

The diverging races become more and more distinct with time, and the process of divergence may finally culminate in transformation of races into species. Although the splitting of species is a gradual process, and it is often impossible to tell exactly when races cease to be races and become species, there exist some important differences between race and species which make the process of species formation one of the most important biological processes. Indeed, Darwin called his chief work *The Origin of Species*.

Races of sexually reproducing organisms are fully capable of intercrossing; they maintain their distinction as races only by geographical isolation. As a rule in most organisms no more than a single race of any one species inhabits the same territory. If representatives of two or more races come to live in the same territory, they interbreed, exchange genes, and eventually become fused into a single population. The human species, however, is an exception. Marriages are influenced by linguistic, religious, social, economic and other cultural factors.

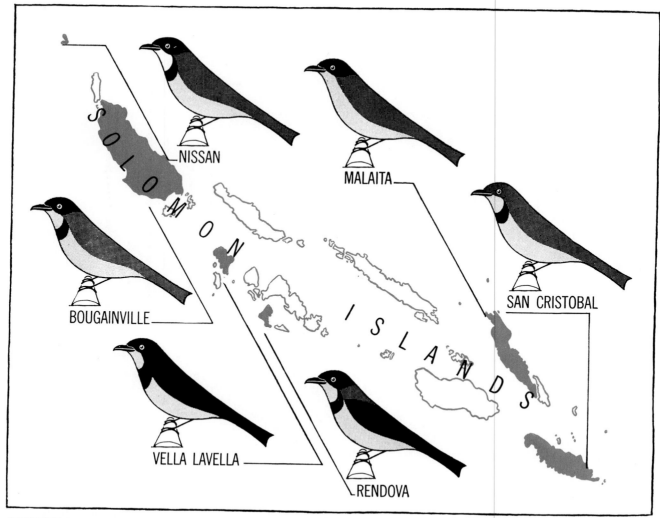

CONCEPT OF RACE is illustrated by the varieties of the golden whistler (*Pachycephala pectoralis*) of the Solomon Islands. The races are kept distinct principally by geographical isolation. They differ in their black and white and colored markings. Dark gray areas are symbol for green markings; light gray for yellow.

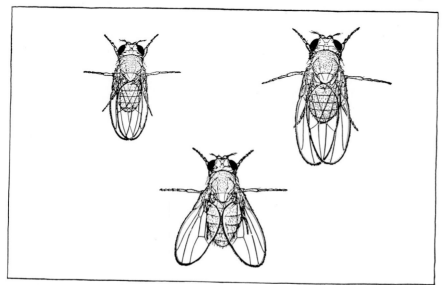

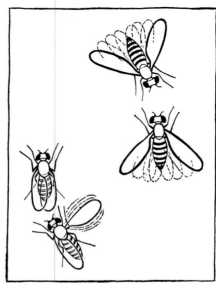

SPECIES OF DROSOPHILA and some other organisms tend to remain separate because their hybrid offspring are often weak and sterile. At left is *D. pseudoobscura*; at right *D. miranda*. Their hybrid descendant is at bottom.

RITUALS OF MATING in *D. nebulosa* (*top*) and *D. willistoni* are example of factor that separates species.

Hence cultural isolation may keep populations apart for a time and slow down the exchange of genes even though the populations live in the same country. Nevertheless, the biological relationship proves stronger than cultural isolation, and interbreeding is everywhere in the process of breaking down such barriers. Unrestricted interbreeding would not mean, as often supposed, that all people would become alike. Mankind would continue to include at least as great a diversity of hereditary endowments as it contains today. However, the same types could be found anywhere in the world, and races as more or less discrete populations would cease to exist.

The Isolationism of Species

Species, on the contrary, can live in the same territory without losing their identity. F. Lutz of the American Museum of Natural History found 1,402 species of insects in the 75-by-200-foot yard of his home in a New Jersey suburb. This does not mean that representatives of distinct species never cross. Closely related species occasionally do interbreed in nature, especially among plants, but these cases are so rare that the discovery of one usually merits a note in a scientific journal.

The reason distinct species do not interbreed is that they are more or less completely kept apart by isolating mechanisms connected with reproduction, which exist in great variety. For example, the botanist Carl C. Epling of the University of California found that two species of sage which are common in southern California are generally separated by ecological factors, one preferring a dry site, the other a more humid one. When the two sages do grow side by side, they occasionally produce hybrids. The hybrids are quite vigorous, but their seed set amounts to less than two per cent of normal; *i.e.*, they are partially sterile. Hybrid sterility is a very common and effective isolating mechanism. A classic example is the mule, hybrid of the horse and donkey. Male mules are always sterile, females usually so. There are, however, some species, notably certain ducks, that produce quite fertile hybrids, not in nature but in captivity.

Two species of Drosophila, *pseudoobscura* and *persimilis*, are so close together biologically that they cannot be distinguished by inspection of their external characteristics. They differ, however, in the structure of their chromosomes and in many physiological traits. If a mixed group of females of the two species is exposed to a group of males of one species, copulations occur much more frequently between members of the same species than between those of different species, though some of the latter do take place. Among plants, the flowers of related species may differ so much in structure that they cannot be pollinated by the same insects, or they may have such differences in smell, color and shape that they attract different insects. Finally, even when cross-copulation or cross-pollination can occur, the union may fail to result in fertilization or may produce offspring that cannot live. Often several isolating mechanisms, no one of which is effective separately, combine to prevent interbreeding. In the case of the two fruit-fly species, at least three such mechanisms are at work: 1) the above-mentioned disposition to mate only with their own kind, even when they are together; 2) different preferences in climate, one preferring warmer and drier places than the other; 3) the fact that when they do interbreed the hybrid males that result are completely sterile and the hybrid females, though fertile, produce offspring that are poorly viable. There is good evidence that no gene exchange occurs between these species in nature.

The fact that distinct species can co-exist in the same territory, while races generally cannot, is highly significant. It permits the formation of communities of diversified living beings which exploit the variety of habitats present in a territory more fully than any single species, no matter how polymorphic, could. It is responsible for the richness and colorfulness of life that is so impressive to biologists and non-biologists alike.

Evolution v. Predestination

Our discussion of the essentials of the modern theory of evolution may be concluded with a consideration of the objections raised against it. The most serious objection is that since mutations occur by "chance" and are undirected, and since selection is a "blind" force, it is difficult to see how mutation and selection can add up to the formation of such complex and beautifully balanced organs as, for example, the human eye. This, say critics of the theory, is like believing that a monkey pounding a typewriter might accidentally type out Dante's *Divine Comedy*. Some biologists have preferred to suppose that evolution is directed by an "inner urge toward perfection," or by a "combining power which amounts to intentionality," or by "telefinalism" or the like. The fatal weakness of these alternative "explanations" of evolution is that they do not explain anything. To say that evolution is directed by an urge, a combining power, or a telefinalism is like saying that a railroad engine is moved by a "locomotive power."

The objection that the modern theory of evolution makes undue demands on chance is based on a failure to appreciate the historical character of the evolutionary process. It would indeed strain credulity to suppose that a lucky sudden combination of chance mutations produced the eye in all its perfection. But the eye did not appear suddenly in the offspring of an eyeless creature; it is the result of an evolutionary development that took many millions of years. Along the way the evolving rudiments of the eye passed through innumerable stages, all of which were useful to their possessors, and therefore all adjusted to the demands of the environment by natural selection. Amphioxus, the primitive fishlike darling of comparative anatomists, has no eyes, but it has certain pigment cells in its brain by means of which it perceives light. Such pigment cells may have been the starting point of the development of eyes in our ancestors.

We have seen that the "combining power" of the sexual process is staggering, that on the most conservative estimate the number of possible gene combinations in the human species alone is far greater than that of the electrons and protons in the universe. When life developed sex, it acquired a trial-and-error mechanism of prodigious efficiency. This mechanism is not called upon to produce a completely new creature in one spectacular burst of creation; it is sufficient that it produces slight changes that improve the organism's chances of survival or reproduction in some habitat. In terms of the monkey-and-typewriter analogy, the theory does not require that the monkey sit down and compose the *Divine Comedy* from beginning to end by a lucky series of hits. All we need is that the monkey occasionally form a single word, or a single line; over the course of eons of time the environment shapes this growing text into the eventual masterpiece. Mutations occur by "chance" only in the sense that they appear regardless of their usefulness at the time and place of their origin. It should be kept in mind that the structure of a gene, like that of the whole organism, is the outcome of a long evolutionary development; the ways in which the genes can mutate are, consequently, by no means indeterminate.

Theories that ascribe evolution to "urges" and "telefinalisms" imply that there is some kind of predestination about the whole business, that evolution has produced nothing more than was potentially present at the beginning of life. The modern evolutionists believe that, on the contrary, evolution is a creative response of the living matter to the challenges of the environment. The role of the environment is to provide opportunities for biological inventions. Evolution is due neither to chance nor to design; it is due to a natural creative process.

2

TOOLS AND HUMAN EVOLUTION

SHERWOOD L. WASHBURN
September 1960

A series of recent discoveries has linked prehuman primates of half a million years ago with stone tools. For some years investigators had been uncovering tools of the simplest kind from ancient deposits in Africa. At first they assumed that these tools constituted evidence of the existence of large-brained, fully bipedal men. Now the tools have been found in association with much more primitive creatures, the not-fully bipedal, small-brained near-men, or man-apes. Prior to these finds the prevailing view held that man evolved nearly to his present structural state and then discovered tools and the new ways of life that they made possible. Now it appears that man-apes—creatures able to run but not yet walk on two legs, and with brains no larger than those of apes now living—had already learned to make and to use tools. It follows that the structure of modern man must be the result of the change in the terms of natural selection that came with the tool-using way of life.

The earliest stone tools are chips or simple pebbles, usually from river gravels. Many of them have not been shaped at all, and they can be identified as tools only because they appear in concentrations, along with a few worked pieces, in caves or other locations where no such stones naturally occur. The huge advantage that a stone tool gives to its user must be tried to be appreciated. Held in the hand, it can be used for pounding, digging or scraping. Flesh and bone can be cut with a flaked chip, and what would be a mild blow with the fist becomes lethal with a rock in the hand. Stone tools can be employed, moreover, to make tools of other materials. Naturally occurring sticks are nearly all rotten, too large, or of inconvenient shape; some tool for fabrication is essential for the efficient use of wood. The utility of a mere pebble seems so limited to the user of modern tools that it is not easy to comprehend the vast difference that separates the tool-user from the ape which relies on hands and teeth alone. Ground-living monkeys dig out roots for food, and if they could use a stone or a stick, they might easily double their food supply. It was the success of the simplest tools that started the whole trend of human evolution and led to the civilizations of today.

From the short-term point of view, human structure makes human behavior possible. From the evolutionary point of view, behavior and structure form an interacting complex, with each change in one affecting the other. Man began when populations of apes, about a million years ago, started the bipedal, tool-using way of life that gave rise to the man-apes of the genus *Australopithecus*. Most of the obvious differences that distinguish man from ape came after the use of tools.

The primary evidence for the new view of human evolution is teeth, bones and tools. But our ancestors were not fossils; they were striving creatures, full of rage, dominance and the will to live. What evolved was the pattern of life of intelligent, exploratory, playful, vigorous primates; the evolving reality was a succession of social systems based upon the motor abilities, emotions and intelligence of their members. Selection produced new systems of child care, maturation and sex, just as it did alterations in the skull and the teeth. Tools, hunting, fire, complex social life, speech, the human way and the brain evolved together to produce ancient man of the genus *Homo* about half a million years ago. Then the brain evolved under the pressures of more complex social life until the species *Homo sapiens* appeared perhaps as recently as 50,000 years ago.

With the advent of *Homo sapiens* the tempo of technical-social evolution quickened. Some of the early types of tool had lasted for hundreds of thousands of years and were essentially the same throughout vast areas of the African and Eurasian land masses. Now the tool forms multiplied and became regionally diversified. Man invented the

STENCILED HANDS in the cave of Gargas in the Pyrenees date back to the Upper Paleolithic of perhaps 30,000 years ago. Aurignacian man made the images by placing hand against wall and spattering it with paint. Hands stenciled in black (*top*) are more distinct and apparently more recent than those done in other colors (*center*).

OLDUVAI GORGE in Tanganyika is the site where the skull of the largest known man-ape was discovered in 1959 by L. S. B. Leakey and his wife Mary. Stratigraphic evidence indicates that skull dates back to Lower Pleistocene, more than 500,000 years ago.

bow, boats, clothing; conquered the Arctic; invaded the New World; domesticated plants and animals; discovered metals, writing and civilization. Today, in the midst of the latest tool-making revolution, man has achieved the capacity to adapt his environment to his need and impulse, and his numbers have begun to crowd the planet.

The later events in the evolution of the human species are treated in other articles in the September 1960 issue of SCIENTIFIC AMERICAN. This article is concerned with the beginnings of the process by which, as Theodosius Dobzhansky says in "The Present Evolution of Man" [*page 38*], biological evolution has transcended itself. From the rapidly accumulating evidence it is now possible to speculate with some confidence on the manner in which the way of life made possible by tools changed the pressures of natural selection and so changed the structure of man.

Tools have been found, along with the bones of their makers, at Sterkfontein, Swartkrans and Kromdraai in South Africa and at Olduvai in Tanganyika. Many of the tools from Sterkfontein are merely unworked river pebbles, but someone had to carry them from the gravels some miles away and bring them to the deposit in which they are found. Nothing like them occurs naturally in the local limestone caves. Of course the association of the stone tools with man-ape bones in one or two localities does not prove that these animals made the tools. It has been argued that a more advanced form of man, already present, was the toolmaker. This argument has a familiar ring to students of human evolution. Peking man was thought too primitive to be a toolmaker; when the first manlike pelvis was found with man-ape bones, some argued that it must have fallen into the deposit because it was too human to be associated with the skull. In every case, however, the repeated discovery of the same unanticipated association has ultimately settled the controversy.

This is why the discovery by L. S. B. and Mary Leakey in the summer of 1959 is so important. In Olduvai Gorge in Tanganyika they came upon traces of an old living site, and found stone tools in clear association with the largest man-ape skull known. With the stone tools were a hammer stone and waste flakes from the manufacture of the tools. The deposit also contained the bones of rats, mice, frogs and some bones of juvenile pig and antelope, showing that even the largest and latest of the

SKULL IS EXAMINED *in situ* by Mary Leakey, who first noticed fragments of it protruding from the cliff face at left. Pebble tools were found at the same level as the skull.

SKULL IS EXCAVATED from surrounding rock with dental picks. Although skull was badly fragmented, almost all of it was recovered. Fragment visible here is part of upper jaw.

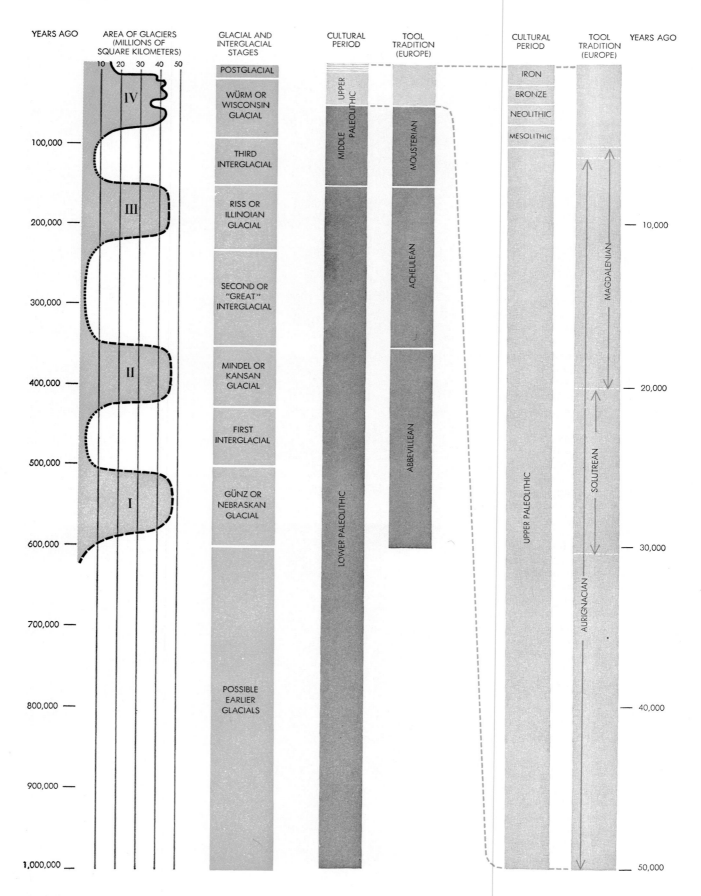

TIME-SCALE correlates cultural periods and tool traditions with the four great glaciations of the Pleistocene epoch. Glacial advances and retreats shown by solid black curve are accurately known; those shown by broken curve are less certain; those shown by dotted curve are uncertain. Light gray bars at far right show an expanded view of last 50,000 years on two darker bars at center. Scale was prepared with the assistance of William R. Farrand of the Lamont Geological Observatory of Columbia University.

man-apes could kill only the smallest animals and must have been largely vegetarian. The Leakeys' discovery confirms the association of the man-ape with pebble tools, and adds the evidence of manufacture to that of mere association. Moreover, the stratigraphic evidence at Olduvai now for the first time securely dates the man-apes, placing them in the lower Pleistocene, earlier than 500,000 years ago and earlier than the first skeletal and cultural evidence for the existence of the genus Homo [see illustration on next two pages]. Before the discovery at Olduvai these points had been in doubt.

The man-apes themselves are known from several skulls and a large number of teeth and jaws, but only fragments of the rest of the skeleton have been preserved. There were two kinds of man-ape, a small early one that may have weighed 50 or 60 pounds and a later and larger one that weighed at least twice as much. The differences in size and form between the two types are quite comparable to the differences between the contemporary pygmy chimpanzee and the common chimpanzee.

Pelvic remains from both forms of man-ape show that these animals were bipedal. From a comparison of the pelvis of ape, man-ape and man it can be seen that the upper part of the pelvis is much wider and shorter in man than in the ape, and that the pelvis of the man-ape corresponds closely, though not precisely, to that of modern man [see top illustration on page 23]. The long upper pelvis of the ape is characteristic of most mammals, and it is the highly specialized, short, wide bone in man that makes possible the human kind of bipedal locomotion. Although the man-ape pelvis is apelike in its lower part, it approaches that of man in just those features that distinguish man from all other animals. More work must be done before this combination of features is fully understood. My belief is that bipedal running, made possible by the changes in the upper pelvis, came before efficient bipedal walking, made possible by the changes in the lower pelvis. In the man-ape, therefore, the adaptation to bipedal locomotion is not yet complete. Here, then, is a phase of human evolution characterized by forms that are mostly bipedal, small-brained, plains-living, tool-making hunters of small animals.

The capacity for bipedal walking is primarily an adaptation for covering long distances. Even the arboreal chimpanzee can run faster than a man, and any monkey can easily outdistance him.

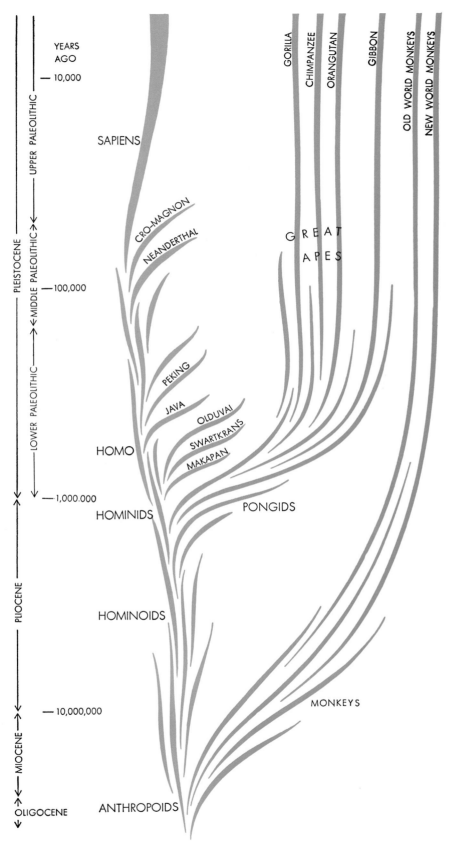

LINES OF DESCENT that lead to man and his closer living relatives are charted. The hominoid superfamily diverged from the anthropoid line in the Miocene period some 20 million years ago. From the hominoid line came the tool-using hominids at the beginning of the Pleistocene. The genus *Homo* appeared in the hominid line during the first interglacial (*see chart on opposite page*); the species *Homo sapiens*, around 50,000 years ago.

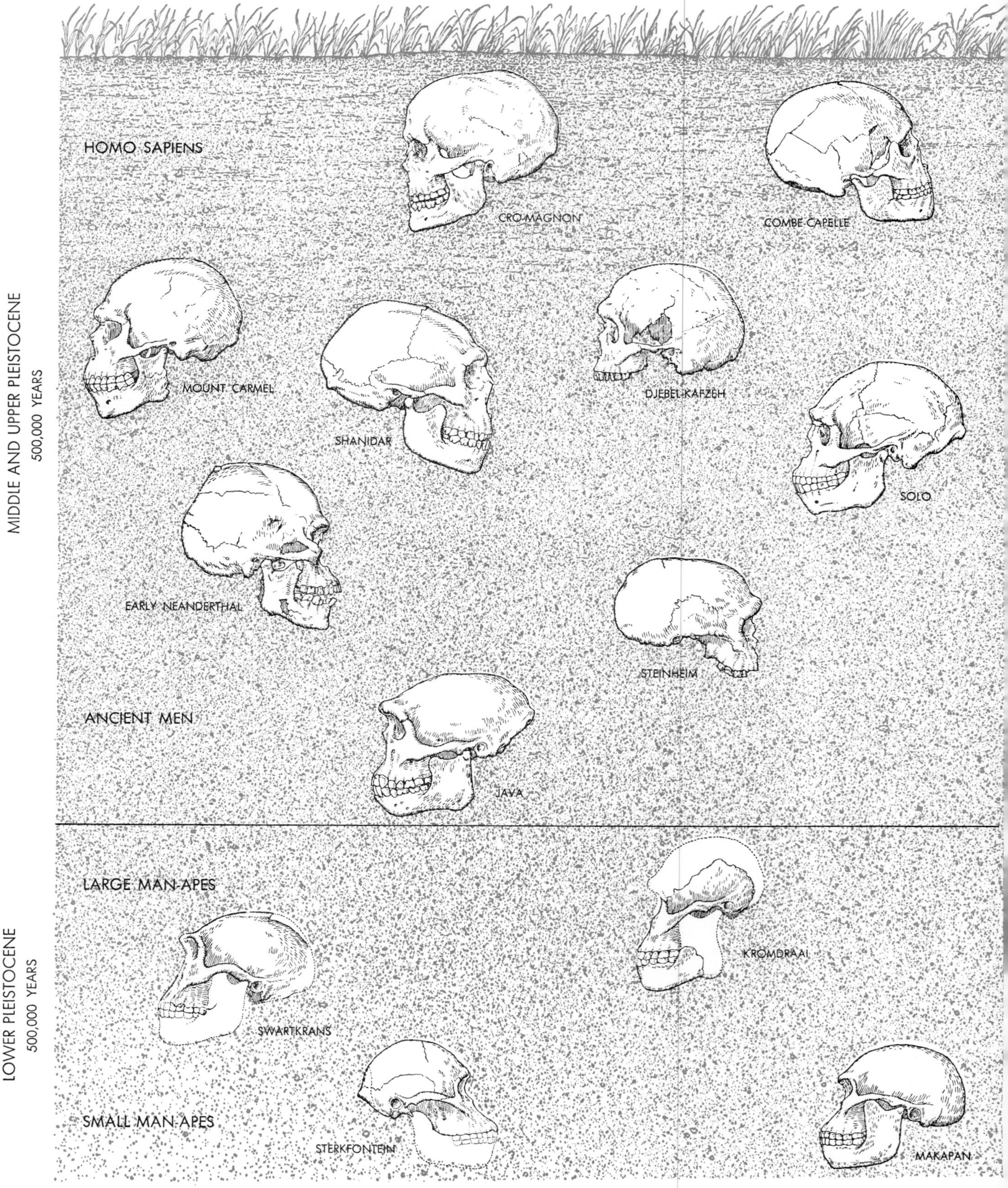

HOMO SAPIENS

CRO-MAGNON

COMBE-CAPELLE

MIDDLE AND UPPER PLEISTOCENE
500,000 YEARS

MOUNT CARMEL

SHANIDAR

DJEBEL-KAFZEH

SOLO

EARLY NEANDERTHAL

STEINHEIM

ANCIENT MEN

JAVA

LOWER PLEISTOCENE
500,000 YEARS

LARGE MAN-APES

KROMDRAAI

SWARTKRANS

SMALL MAN-APES

STERKFONTEIN

MAKAPAN

FOSSIL SKULLS of Pleistocene epoch reflect transition from man-apes (*below black line*) to *Homo sapiens* (*top*). Relative age of intermediate specimens is indicated schematically by their posi- tion on page. Java man (*middle left*) and Solo man (*upper center*) are members of the genus *Pithecanthropus*, and are related to Peking man (*middle right*). The Shanidar skull (*upper left*) be-

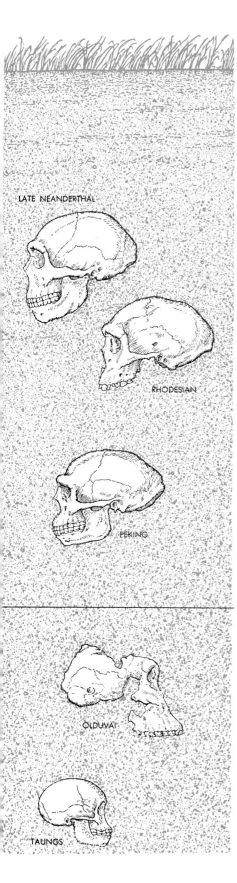

LATE NEANDERTHAL

RHODESIAN

PEKING

OLDUVAI

TAUNGS

longs to the Neanderthal family, while Mount Carmel skull shows characteristics of Neanderthal and modern man.

A man, on the other hand, can walk for many miles, and this is essential for efficient hunting. According to skeletal evidence, fully developed walkers first appeared in the ancient men who inhabited the Old World from 500,000 years ago to the middle of the last glaciation. These men were competent hunters, as is shown by the bones of the large animals they killed. But they also used fire and made complicated tools according to clearly defined traditions. Along with the change in the structure of the pelvis, the brain had doubled in size since the time of the man-apes.

The fossil record thus substantiates the suggestion, first made by Charles Darwin, that tool use is both the cause and the effect of bipedal locomotion. Some very limited bipedalism left the hands sufficiently free from locomotor functions so that stones or sticks could be carried, played with and used. The advantage that these objects gave to their users led both to more bipedalism and to more efficient tool use. English lacks any neat expression for this sort of situation, forcing us to speak of cause and effect as if they were separated, whereas in natural selection cause and effect are interrelated. Selection is based on successful behavior, and in the man-apes the beginnings of the human way of life depended on both inherited locomotor capacity and on the learned skills of tool-using. The success of the new way of life based on the use of tools changed the selection pressures on many parts of the body, notably the teeth, hands and brain, as well as on the pelvis. But it must be remembered that selection was for the whole way of life.

In all the apes and monkeys the males have large canine teeth. The long upper canine cuts against the first lower premolar, and the lower canine passes in front of the upper canine. This is an efficient fighting mechanism, backed by very large jaw muscles. I have seen male baboons drive off cheetahs and dogs, and according to reliable reports male baboons have even put leopards to flight. The females have small canines, and they hurry away with the young under the very conditions in which the males turn to fight. All the evidence from living monkeys and apes suggests that the male's large canines are of the greatest importance to the survival of the group, and that they are particularly important in ground-living forms that may not be able to climb to safety in the trees. The small, early man-apes lived in open plains country, and yet none of them had large canine teeth. It would appear that the protection of the group must have shifted from teeth to tools early in the evolution of the man-apes, and long before the appearance of the forms that have been found in association with stone tools. The tools of Sterkfontein and Olduvai represent not the beginnings of tool use, but a choice of material and knowledge in manufacture which, as is shown by the small canines of the man-apes that deposited them there, derived from a long history of tool use.

Reduction in the canine teeth is not a simple matter, but involves changes in the muscles, face, jaws and other parts of the skull. Selection builds powerful neck muscles in animals that fight with their canines, and adapts the skull to the action of these muscles. Fighting is not a matter of teeth alone, but also of seizing, shaking and hurling an enemy's body with the jaws, head and neck. Reduction in the canines is therefore accompanied by a shortening in the jaws, reduction in the ridges of bone over the eyes and a decrease in the shelf of bone in the neck area [see illustration on page 24]. The reason that the skulls of the females and young of the apes look more like man-apes than those of adult males is that, along with small canines, they have smaller muscles and all the numerous structural features that go along with them. The skull of the man-ape is that of an ape that has lost the structure for effective fighting with its teeth. Moreover, the man-ape has transferred to its hands the functions of seizing and pulling, and this has been attended by reduction of its incisors. Small canines and incisors are biological symbols of a changed way of life; their primitive functions are replaced by hand and tool.

The history of the grinding teeth— the molars—is different from that of the seizing and fighting teeth. Large size in any anatomical structure must be maintained by positive selection; the selection pressure changed first on the canine teeth and, much later, on the molars. In the man-apes the molars were very large, larger than in either ape or man. They were heavily worn, possibly because food dug from the ground with the aid of tools was very abrasive. With the men of the Middle Pleistocene, molars of human size appear along with complicated tools, hunting and fire.

The disappearance of brow ridges and the refinement of the human face may involve still another factor. One of the essential conditions for the organi-

22

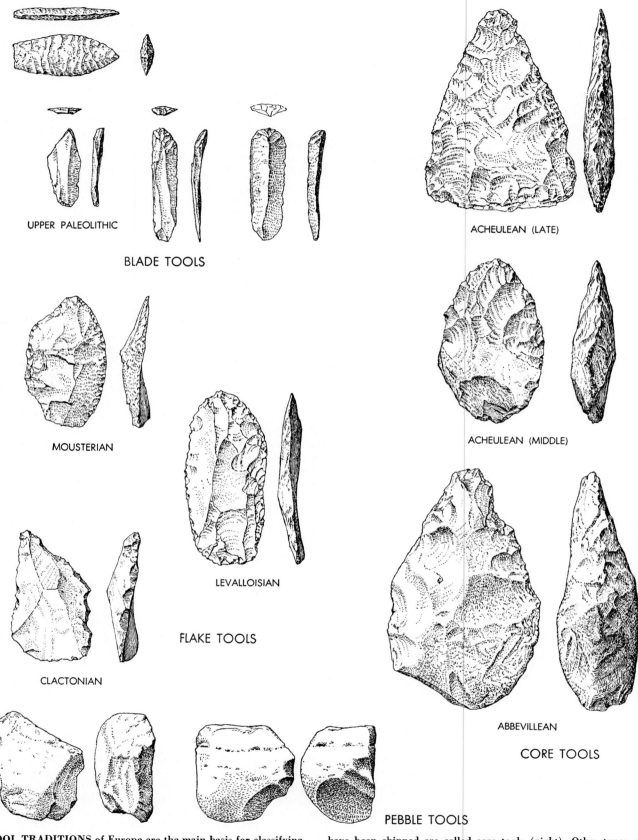

UPPER PALEOLITHIC

BLADE TOOLS

ACHEULEAN (LATE)

MOUSTERIAN

LEVALLOISIAN

FLAKE TOOLS

ACHEULEAN (MIDDLE)

CLACTONIAN

ABBEVILLEAN

CORE TOOLS

PEBBLE TOOLS

TOOL TRADITIONS of Europe are the main basis for classifying Paleolithic cultures. The earliest tools are shown at bottom of page; later ones, at top. The tools are shown from both the side and the edge, except for blade tools, which are shown in three views. Tools consisting of a piece of stone from which a few flakes have been chipped are called core tools (*right*). Other types of tool were made from flakes (*center and left*); blade tools were made from flakes with almost parallel sides. Tool traditions are named for site where tools of a given type were discovered; Acheulean tools, for example, are named for St. Acheul in France.

zation of men in co-operative societies was the suppression of rage and of the uncontrolled drive to first place in the hierarchy of dominance. Curt P. Richter of Johns Hopkins University has shown that domestic animals, chosen over the generations for willingness to adjust and for lack of rage, have relatively small adrenal glands. But the breeders who selected for this hormonal, physiological, temperamental type also picked, without realizing it, animals with small brow ridges and small faces. The skull structure of the wild rat bears the same relation to that of the tame rat as does the skull of Neanderthal man to that of *Homo sapiens*. The same is true for the cat, dog, pig, horse and cow; in each case the wild form has the larger face and muscular ridges. In the later stages of human evolution, it appears, the self-domestication of man has been exerting the same effects upon temperament, glands and skull that are seen in the domestic animals.

Of course from man-ape to man the brain-containing part of the skull has also increased greatly in size. This change is directly due to the increase in the size of the brain: as the brain grows, so grow the bones that cover it. Since there is this close correlation between brain size and bony brain-case, the brain size of the fossils can be estimated. On the scale of brain size the man-apes are scarcely distinguishable from the living apes, although their brains may have been larger with respect to body size. The brain seems to have evolved rapidly, doubling in size between man-ape and man. It then appears to have increased much more slowly; there is no substantial change in gross size during the last 100,000 years. One must remember, however, that size alone is a very crude indicator, and that brains of equal size may vary greatly in function. My belief is that although the brain of *Homo sapiens* is no larger than that of Neanderthal man, the indirect evidence strongly suggests that the first *Homo sapiens* was a much more intelligent creature.

The great increase in brain size is important because many functions of the brain seem to depend on the number of cells, and the number increases with volume. But certain parts of the brain have increased in size much more than others. As functional maps of the cortex of the brain show, the human sensory-motor cortex is not just an enlargement of that of an ape [*see illustrations on last three pages of this article*]. The areas

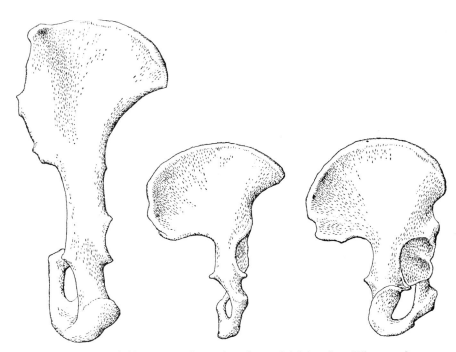

HIP BONES of ape (*left*), man-ape (*center*) and man (*right*) reflect differences between quadruped and biped. Upper part of human pelvis is wider and shorter than that of apes. Lower part of man-ape pelvis resembles that of ape; upper part resembles that of man.

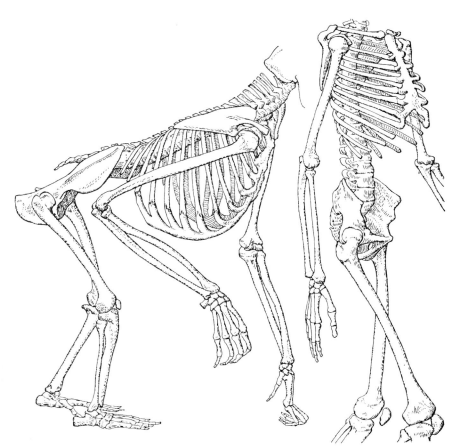

POSTURE of gorilla (*left*) and man (*right*) is related to size, shape and orientation of pelvis. Long, straight pelvis of ape provides support for quadrupedal locomotion; short, broad pelvis of man curves backward, carrying spine and torso in bipedal position.

24

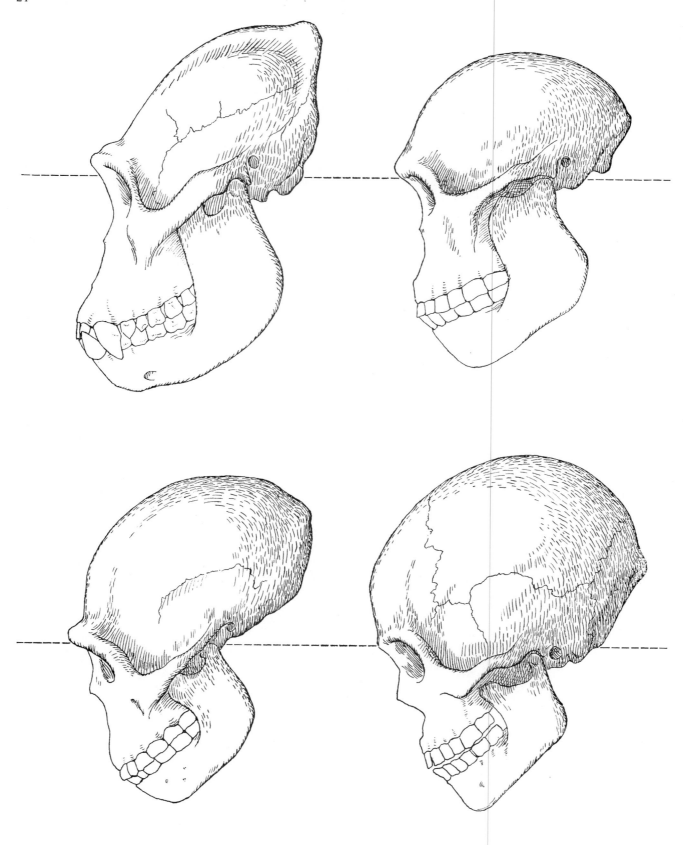

EVOLUTION OF SKULL from ape (*upper left*) to man-ape (*upper right*) to ancient man (*lower left*) to modern man (*lower right*) involves an increase in size of brain case (*part of skull above broken lines*) and a corresponding decrease in size of face (*part of skull below broken lines*). Apes also possess canine teeth that are much larger than those found in either man-apes or man.

for the hand, especially the thumb, in man are tremendously enlarged, and this is an integral part of the structural base that makes the skillful use of the hand possible. The selection pressures that favored a large thumb also favored a large cortical area to receive sensations from the thumb and to control its motor activity. Evolution favored the development of a sensitive, powerful, skillful thumb, and in all these ways —as well as in structure—a human thumb differs from that of an ape.

The same is true for other cortical areas. Much of the cortex in a monkey is still engaged in the motor and sensory functions. In man it is the areas adjacent to the primary centers that are most expanded. These areas are concerned with skills, memory, foresight and language; that is, with the mental faculties that make human social life possible. This is easiest to illustrate in the field of language. Many apes and monkeys can make a wide variety of sounds. These sounds do not, however, develop into language [see "The Origin of Speech," by Charles F. Hockett, page 415]. Some workers have devoted great efforts, with minimum results, to trying to teach chimpanzees to talk. The reason is that there is little in the brain to teach. A human child learns to speak with the greatest ease, but the storage of thousands of words takes a great deal of cortex. Even the simplest language must have given great advantage to those first men who had it. One is tempted to think that language may have appeared together with the fine tools, fire and complex hunting of the large-brained men of the Middle Pleistocene, but there is no direct proof of this.

The main point is that the kind of animal that can learn to adjust to complex, human, technical society is a very different creature from a tree-living ape, and the differences between the two are rooted in the evolutionary process. The reason that the human brain makes the human way of life possible is that it is the result of that way of life. Great masses of the tissue in the human brain are devoted to memory, planning, language and skills, because these are the abilities favored by the human way of life.

The emergence of man's large brain occasioned a profound change in the plan of human reproduction. The human mother-child relationship is unique among the primates as is the use of tools. In all the apes and monkeys the baby clings to the mother; to be able to do so,

MOTOR CORTEX OF MONKEY controls the movements of the body parts outlined by the superimposed drawing of the animal (*color*). Gray lines trace the surface features of the left half of the brain (*bottom*) and part of the right half (*top*). Colored drawing is distorted in proportion to amount of cortex associated with functions of various parts of the body. Smaller animal in right half of brain indicates location of secondary motor cortex.

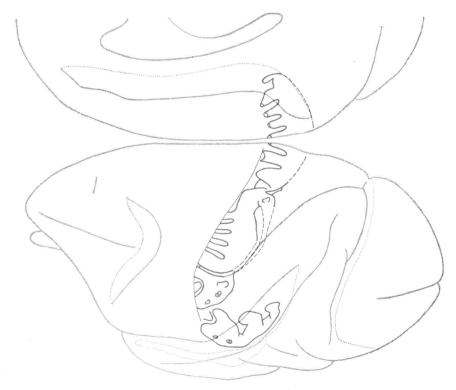

SENSORY CORTEX OF MONKEY is mapped in same way as motor cortex (*above*). As in motor cortex, a large area is associated with hands and feet. Smaller animal at bottom of left half of brain indicates location of secondary sensory cortex. Drawings are based on work of Clinton N. Woolsey and his colleagues at the University of Wisconsin Medical School.

the baby must be born with its central nervous system in an advanced state of development. But the brain of the fetus must be small enough so that birth may take place. In man adaptation to bipedal locomotion decreased the size of the bony birth-canal at the same time that the exigencies of tool use selected for larger brains. This obstetrical dilemma was solved by delivery of the fetus at a much earlier stage of development. But this was possible only because the mother, already bipedal and with hands free of locomotor necessities, could hold the helpless, immature infant. The small-brained man-ape probably developed in the uterus as much as the ape does; the human type of mother-child relation must have evolved by the time of the large-brained, fully bipedal humans of the Middle Pleistocene. Bipedalism, tool use and selection for large brains thus slowed human development and invoked far greater maternal responsibility. The slow-moving mother, carrying the baby, could not hunt, and the combination of the woman's obligation to care for slow-developing babies and the man's occupation of hunting imposed a fundamental pattern on the social organization of the human species.

As Marshall D. Sahlins suggests ["The Origin of Society," SCIENTIFIC AMERICAN Offprint 602], human society was heavily conditioned at the outset by other significant aspects of man's sexual adaptation. In monkeys and apes year-round sexual activity supplies the social bond that unites the primate horde. But sex in these species is still subject to physiological—especially glandular—controls. In man these controls are gone, and are replaced by a bewildering variety of social customs. In no other primate does

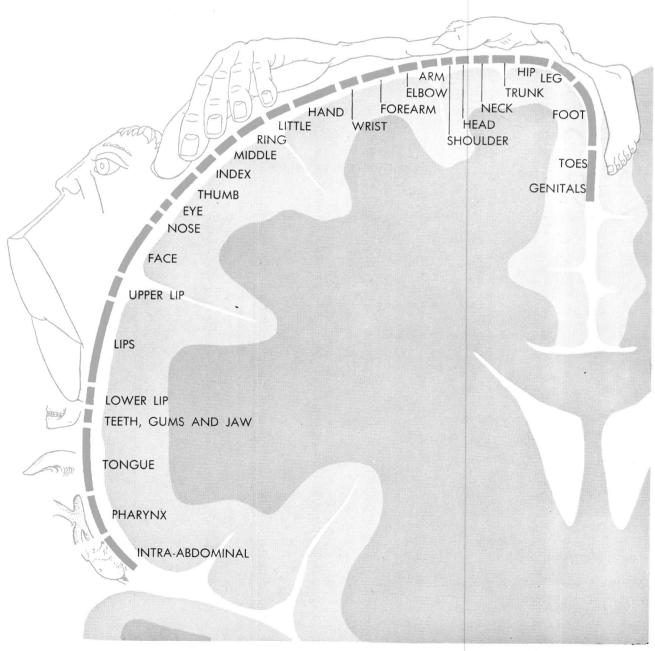

SENSORY HOMUNCULUS is a functional map of the sensory cortex of the human brain worked out by Wilder Penfield and his associates at the Montreal Neurological Institute. As in the map of the sensory cortex of the monkey that appears on the preceding page, the distorted anatomical drawing (*color*) indicates the areas of the sensory cortex associated with the various parts of the body.

a family exist that controls sexual activity by custom, that takes care of slow-growing young, and in which—as in the case of primitive human societies—the male and female provide different foods for the family members.

All these family functions are ultimately related to tools, hunting and the enlargement of the brain. Complex and technical society evolved from the sporadic tool-using of an ape, through the simple pebble tools of the man-ape and the complex toolmaking traditions of ancient men to the hugely complicated culture of modern man. Each behavioral stage was both cause and effect of biological change in bones and brain. These concomitant changes can be seen in the scanty fossil record and can be inferred from the study of the living forms.

Surely as more fossils are found these ideas will be tested. New techniques of investigation, from planned experiments in the behavior of lower primates to more refined methods of dating, will extract wholly new information from the past. It is my belief that, as these events come to pass, tool use will be found to have been a major factor, beginning with the initial differentiation of man and ape. In ourselves we see a structure, physiology and behavior that is the result of the fact that some populations of apes started to use tools a million years ago. The pebble tools constituted man's principal technical adaptation for a period at least 50 times as long as recorded history. As we contemplate man's present eminence, it is well to remember that, from the point of view of evolution, the events of the last 50,000 years occupy but a moment in time. Ancient man endured at least 10 times as long and the man-apes for an even longer time.

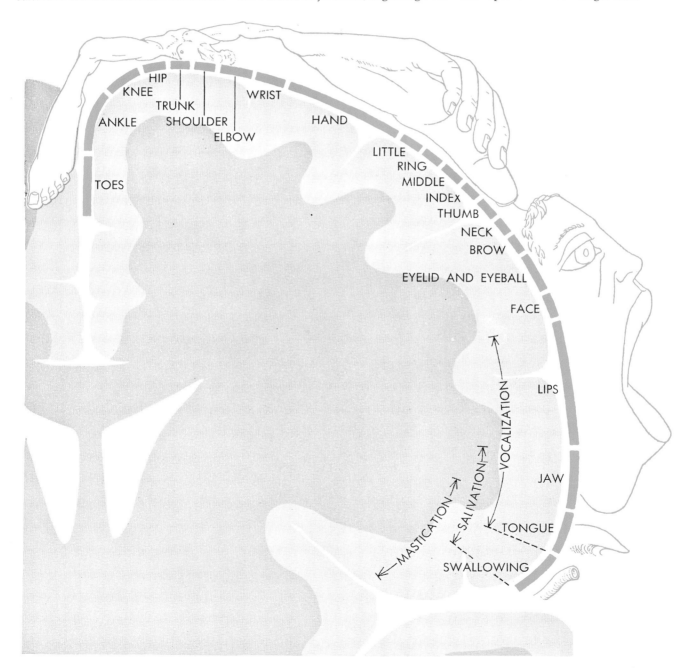

MOTOR HOMUNCULUS depicts parts of body and areas of motor cortex that control their functions. Human brain is shown here in coronal (ear-to-ear) cross section. Speech and hand areas of both motor and sensory cortex in man are proportionately much larger than corresponding areas in apes and monkeys, as can be seen by comparing homunculi with diagram of monkey cortex.

COLOR OF HUMAN SKIN is sometimes measured by physical anthropologists on the von Luschan scale. Reproduced here somewhat larger than natural size, the scale consists of numbered ceramic tiles which are compared visually to color of the underside of subject's forearm. Both sides of the scale are shown; colors range from almost pure white (*top right*) to black (*bottom left*).

3

THE DISTRIBUTION OF MAN

WILLIAM W. HOWELLS
September 1960

Men with chins, relatively small brow ridges and small facial skeletons, and with high, flat-sided skulls, probably appeared on earth in the period between the last two great continental glaciers, say from 150,000 to 50,000 years ago. If the time of their origin is blurred, the place is no less so. The new species doubtless emerged from a number of related populations distributed over a considerable part of the Old World. Thus *Homo sapiens* evolved as a species and began to differentiate into races at the same time.

In any case, our direct ancestor, like his older relatives, was at once product and master of the crude pebble tools that primitive human forms had learned to use hundreds of thousands of years earlier. His inheritance also included a social organization and some level of verbal communication.

Between these hazy beginnings and the agricultural revolution of about 10,-000 years ago *Homo sapiens* radiated over most of the earth, and differentiated into clearly distinguishable races. The processes were intimately related. Like the forces that had created man, they reflected both the workings of man's environment and of his own invention. So much can be said with reasonable confidence. The details are another matter. The when, where and how of the origin of races puzzle us not much less than they puzzled Charles Darwin.

A little over a century ago a pleasingly simple explanation of races enjoyed some popularity. The races were separate species, created by God as they are today. The Biblical account of Adam and Eve was meant to apply only to Caucasians. Heretical as the idea might be, it was argued that the Negroes appearing in Egyptian monuments, and the skulls of the ancient Indian mound-builders of Ohio, differed in no way from their living descendants, and so there could have been no important change in the only slightly longer time since the Creation itself, set by Archbishop Ussher at 4004 B.C.

With his *Origin of Species*, Darwin undid all this careful "science" at a stroke. Natural selection and the immense stretch of time provided by the geological time-scale made gradual evolution seem the obvious explanation of racial or species differences. But in his later book, *The Descent of Man*, Darwin turned his back on his own central notion of natural selection as the cause of races. He there preferred sexual selection, or the accentuation of racial features through long-established ideals of beauty in different segments of mankind. This proposition failed to impress anthropologists, and so Darwin's demolishing of the old views left something of a void that has never been satisfactorily filled.

Not for want of trying. Some students continued, until recent years, to insist that races are indeed separate species, or even separate genera, with Whites descended from chimpanzees, Negroes from gorillas and Mongoloids from orangutans. Darwin himself had already argued against such a possibility when a contemporary proposed that these same apes had in turn descended from three different monkey species. Darwin pointed out that so great a degree of convergence in evolution, producing thoroughgoing identities in detail (as opposed to, say, the superficial resemblance of whales and fishes) simply could not be expected. The same objection applies to a milder hypothesis, formulated by the late Franz Weidenreich during the 1940's. Races, he held, descended separately, not from such extremely divergent parents as the several great apes, but from the less-separated lines of fossil men. For example, Peking man led to the Mongoloids, and Rhodesian man to the "Africans." But again there are more marked distinctions between those fossil men than between living races.

Actually the most reasonable—I should say the only reasonable—pattern suggested· by animal evolution in general is that of racial divergence within a stock already possessing distinctive features of *Homo sapiens*. As I have indicated, such a stock had appeared at the latest by the beginning of the last glacial advance and almost certainly much earlier, perhaps by the end of the preceding glaciation, which is dated at some 150,000 years ago.

Even if fossil remains were more plentiful than they are, they might not in themselves decide the questions of time and place much more accurately. By the time *Homo sapiens* was common enough to provide a chance of our finding some of his fossil remains, he was probably already sufficiently widespread as to give only a general idea of his "place of origin." Moreover, bones and artifacts may concentrate in misleading places. (Consider the parallel case of the australopithecine "man-apes" known so well from the Lower Pleistocene of South Africa. This area is thought of as their home. In fact the region actually was a geographical *cul-de-sac,* and merely a good fossil trap at that time. It is now clear that such prehumans were widespread not only in Africa but also in Asia. We have no real idea of their first center of dispersion, and we should assume that our earliest knowledge of them is not from the actual dawn of their existence.)

In attempting to fix the emergence

of modern races of man somewhat more precisely we can apply something like the chronological reasoning of the pre-Darwinians. The Upper Paleolithic invaders of Europe (*e.g.,* the Cro-Magnons) mark the definite entrance of *Homo sapiens,* and these men were already stamped with a "White" racial nature at about 35,000 B.C. But a recently discovered skull from Liukiang in China, probably of the same order of age, is definitely not Caucasian, whatever else it may be. And the earliest American fossil men, perhaps 20,000 years old, are recognizable as Indians. No other remains are certainly so old; we cannot now say anything about the first Negroes. Thus racial differences are definitely older than 35,000 years. And yet—this is sheer guess—the more successful *Homo sapiens* would probably have overcome the other human types, such as Neanderthal and Rhodesian men, much earlier if he had reached his full development long before. But these types survived well into the last 50,000 years. So we might assume that *Homo sapiens,* and his earliest racial distinctions, is a product of the period between the last two glaciations, coming into his own early during the last glaciation.

When we try to envisage the causes of racial development, we think today of four factors: natural selection, genetic drift, mutation and mixture (interbreeding). With regard to basic divergence at the level of races, the first two are undoubtedly the chief determinants. If forces of any kind favor individuals of one genetic complexion over others, in the sense that they live and reproduce more successfully, the favored individuals will necessarily increase their bequest of genes to the next generation relative to the rest of the population. That is selection; a force with direction.

Genetic drift is a force without direction, an accidental change in the gene proportions of a population. Other things being equal, some parents just have more offspring than others. If such variations can build up, an originally homogeneous population may split into two different ones by chance. It is somewhat as though there were a sack containing 50 red and 50 white billiard balls, each periodically reproducing itself, say by doubling. Suppose you start a new population, drawing out 50 balls without looking. The most likely single result would be 25 of each color, but it is more likely that you would end up with some other combination, perhaps as extreme as 20 reds and 30 whites. After this population divides, you make a new drawing, and so on. Of course at each

subsequent step the departure from the then-prevailing proportion is as likely to favor red as white. Nevertheless, once the first drawing has been made with the above result, red has the better chance of vanishing. So it is with genes for hereditary traits.

Both drift and selection should have stronger effects the smaller and more isolated the population. It is easy to imagine them in action among bands of ancient men, living close to nature. (It would be a great mistake, however, to imagine that selection is not also effective in modern populations.) Hence we can look upon racial beginnings as part accident, part design, design meaning any pattern of minor change obedient to natural selection.

Darwin was probably right the first time, then, and natural selection is more important in racial adaptation than he himself later came to think. Curiously, however, it is extremely difficult to find demonstrable, or even logically appealing, adaptive advantages in racial features. The two leading examples of adaptation in human physique are not usually considered racial at all. One is the tendency among warm-blooded animals of the same species to be larger in colder parts of their territory. As an animal of a given shape gets larger, its inner bulk increases faster than its outer surface,

DISTRIBUTION OF MAN and his races in three epochs is depicted in the maps on these and the following two pages. Key to the races appears in legend below. Solid blue areas in map at top represent glaciers. According to available evidence, it is believed that by 8000 B.C. (*map at top*) early Mongoloids had already spread from the Old World to the New World, while late Mongoloids inhabited a large part of northern Asia. Distribution in A.D. 1000 (*map at bottom*) has late Mongoloids dominating Asia, northern Canada and southern Greenland, and early Mongoloids dominating the Americas. The Pygmies and Bushmen of Africa began a decline that has continued up to the present (*see map on next two pages*).

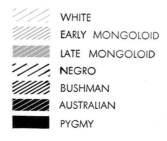

WHITE
EARLY MONGOLOID
LATE MONGOLOID
NEGRO
BUSHMAN
AUSTRALIAN
PYGMY

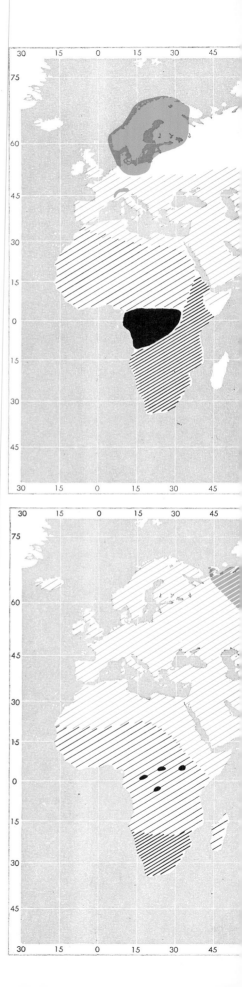

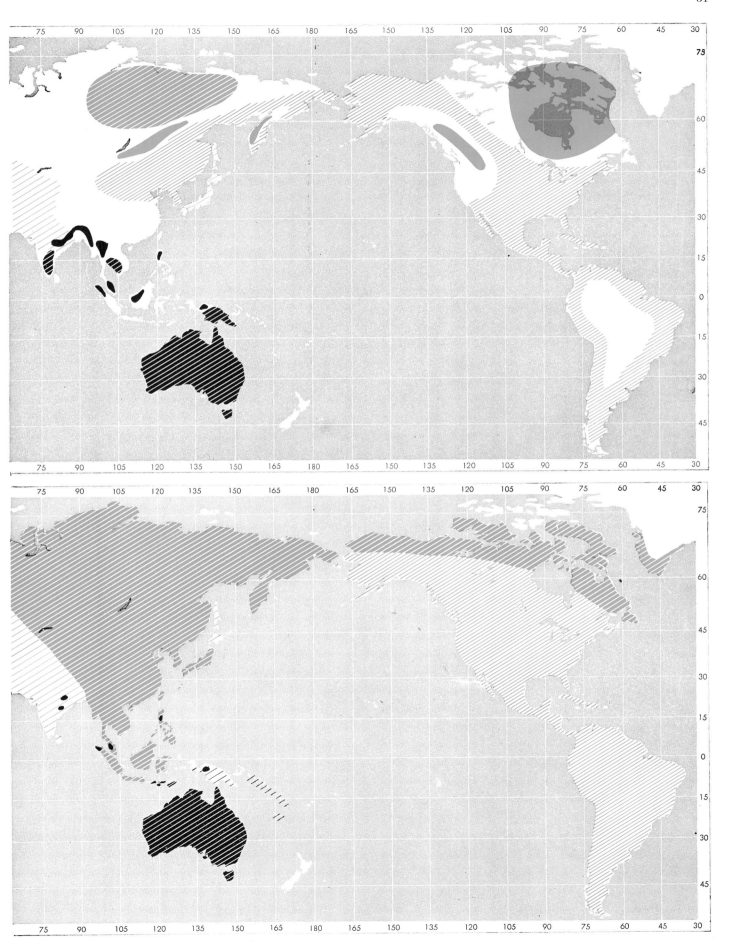

so the ratio of heat produced to heat dissipated is higher in larger individuals. It has, indeed, been shown that the average body weight of man goes up as annual mean temperature goes down, speaking very broadly, and considering those populations that have remained where they are a long time. The second example concerns the size of extremities (limbs, ears, muzzles). They are smaller in colder parts of the range and larger in warmer, for the same basic reason—heat conservation and dissipation. Man obeys this rule also, producing lanky, long-limbed populations in hot deserts and

dumpy, short-limbed peoples in the Arctic.

This does not carry us far with the major, historic races as we know them. Perhaps the most striking of all racial features is the dark skin of Negroes. The color of Negro skin is due to a concentration of melanin, the universal human pigment that diffuses sunlight and screens out its damaging ultraviolet component. Does it not seem obvious that in the long course of time the Negroes, living astride the Equator in Africa and in the western Pacific, developed their dark skins as a direct response to a strong sun? It makes sense. It would be folly to deny that such an adaptation is present. But a great deal of the present Negro habitat is shade forest and not bright sun, which is in fact strongest in the deserts some distance north of the Equator. The Pygmies are decidedly forest dwellers, not only in Africa but in their several habitats in southeastern Asia as well.

At any rate there is enough doubt to have called forth other suggestions. One is that forest hunters needed protective

coloration, both for stalking and for their protection from predators; dark skin would have lowest visibility in the patchy light and shade beneath the trees. Another is that densely pigmented skins may have other qualities—e.g., resistance to infection—of which we are unaware.

A more straightforward way out of the dilemma is to suppose that the Negroes are actually new to the Congo forest, and that they served their racial apprenticeship hunting and fishing in the sunny grasslands of the southern Sahara. If so, their Pygmy relatives might represent the first accommodation of the race to the forest, before agriculture but after dark skin had been acquired. Smaller size certainly makes a chase after game through the undergrowth less exhausting and faster. As for woolly hair, it is easy to see it (still without proof) as an excellent, nonmatting insulation against solar heat. Thick Negro lips? Every suggestion yet made has a zany sound. They may only be a side effect of some properties of heavily pigmented

WHITE
EARLY MONGOLOID
LATE MONGOLOID
NEGRO
BUSHMAN
AUSTRALIAN
PYGMY

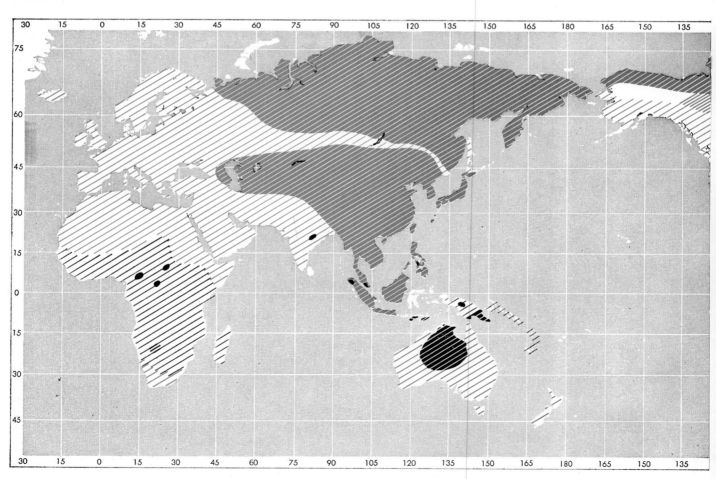

PRESENT DISTRIBUTION OF RACES OF MAN reflects dominance of White, late Mongoloid and Negro races. Diffusion of Whites has been attended by decline of early Mongoloids in America, Bushmen in Africa and indigenous population in Australia.

skin (ability to produce thick scar tissue, for example), even as blond hair is doubtless a side effect of the general depigmentation of men that has occurred in northern Europe.

At some remove racially from Negroes and Pygmies are the Bushmen and Hottentots of southern Africa. They are small, or at least lightly built, with distinctive wide, small, flat faces; they are rather infantile looking, and have a five-cornered skull outline that seems to be an ancient inheritance. Their skin is yellowish-brown, not dark. None of this has been clearly interpreted, although the small size is thought to be an accommodation to water and food economy in the arid environment. The light skin, in an open sunny country, contradicts the sun-pigment theory, and has in fact been used in favor of the protective-coloration hypothesis. Bushmen and background blend beautifully for color, at least as human beings see color.

Bushmen, and especially Hottentots, have another dramatic characteristic:

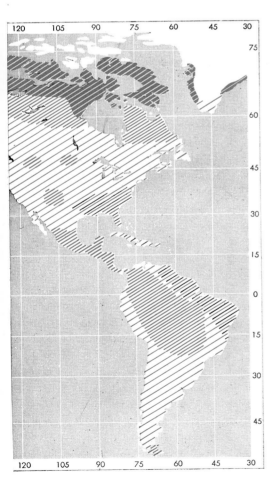

Narrow band of Whites in Asia represents Russian colonization of southern Siberia.

steatopygia. If they are well nourished, the adult women accumulate a surprising quantity of fat on their buttocks. This seems to be a simple storehouse mechanism reminiscent of the camel's hump; a storehouse that is not distributed like a blanket over the torso generally, where it would be disadvantageous in a hot climate. The characteristic nicely demonstrates adaptive selection working in a human racial population.

The Caucasians make the best argument for skin color as an ultraviolet screen. They extend from cloudy northern Europe, where the ultraviolet in the little available sunlight is not only acceptable but desirable, down to the fiercely sun-baked Sahara and peninsular India. All the way, the correspondence with skin color is good: blond around the Baltic, swarthy on the Mediterranean, brunet in Africa and Arabia, dark brown in India. Thus, given a long enough time of occupation, and doubtless some mixture to provide dark-skinned genes in the south, natural selection could well be held responsible.

On the other hand, the Caucasians' straight faces and often prominent noses lack any evident adaptive significance. It is the reverse with the Mongoloids, whose countenances form a coherent pattern that seems consistent with their racial history. From the standpoint of evolution it is Western man, not the Oriental, who is inscrutable. The "almond" eyes of the Mongoloid are deeply set in protective fat-lined lids, the nose and forehead are flattish and the cheeks are broad and fat-padded. In every way, it has been pointed out, this is an ideal mask to protect eyes, nose and sinuses against bitterly cold weather. Such a face is the pole toward which the peoples of eastern Asia point, and it reaches its most marked and uniform expression in the cold northeastern part of the continent, from Korea north.

Theoretically the Mongoloid face developed under intense natural selection some time during the last glacial advance among peoples trapped north of a ring of mountain glaciers and subjected to fierce cold, which would have weeded out the less adapted, in the most classic Darwinian fashion, through pneumonia and sinus infections. If the picture is accurate, this face type is the latest major human adaptation. It could not be very old. For one thing, the population would have had to reach a stage of advanced skill in hunting and living to survive at all in such cold, a stage probably not attained before the Upper Paleolithic (beginning about 35,000 B.C.). For an-

other, the adaptation must have occurred after the American Indians, who are Mongoloid but without the transformed face, migrated across the Bering Strait. (Only the Eskimos reflect the extension of full-fledged, recent Mongoloids into America.) All this suggests a process taking a relatively small number of generations (about 600) between 25,000 and 10,000 B. C.

The discussion so far has treated human beings as though they were any mammal under the influence of natural selection and the other forces of evolution. It says very little about why man invaded the various environments that have shaped him and how he got himself distributed in the way we find him now. For an understanding of these processes we must take into account man's own peculiar abilities. He has created culture, a milieu for action and development that must be added to the simplicities of sun, snow, forest or plain.

Let us go back to the beginning. Man started as an apelike creature, certainly vegetarian, certainly connected with wooded zones, limited like all other primates to tropical or near-tropical regions. In becoming a walker he had begun to extend his range. Tools, social rules and intelligence all progressed together; he learned to form efficient groups, armed with weapons not provided by nature. He started to eat meat, and later to cook it; the more concentrated diet widened his possibilities for using his time; the hunting of animals beckoned him still farther in various directions.

All this was probably accomplished during the small-brained australopithecine stage. It put man on a new plane, with the potential to reach all parts of the earth, and not only those in which he could find food ready to his hand, or be comfortable in his bare skin. He did not actually reach his limits until the end of the last glaciation, and in fact left large tracts empty for most of the period. By then he had become *Homo sapiens,* with a large brain. He had tools keen enough to give him clothes of animal skin. He had invented projectiles to widen the perimeter of his striking power: bolas, javelins with spear throwers, arrows with bows. He was using dogs to widen the perimeter of his senses in tracking. He had found what could be eaten from the sea and its shores. He could move only slowly, and was probably by no means adventurous. But hunting territory was precious, and the surplus of an expanding population had

34

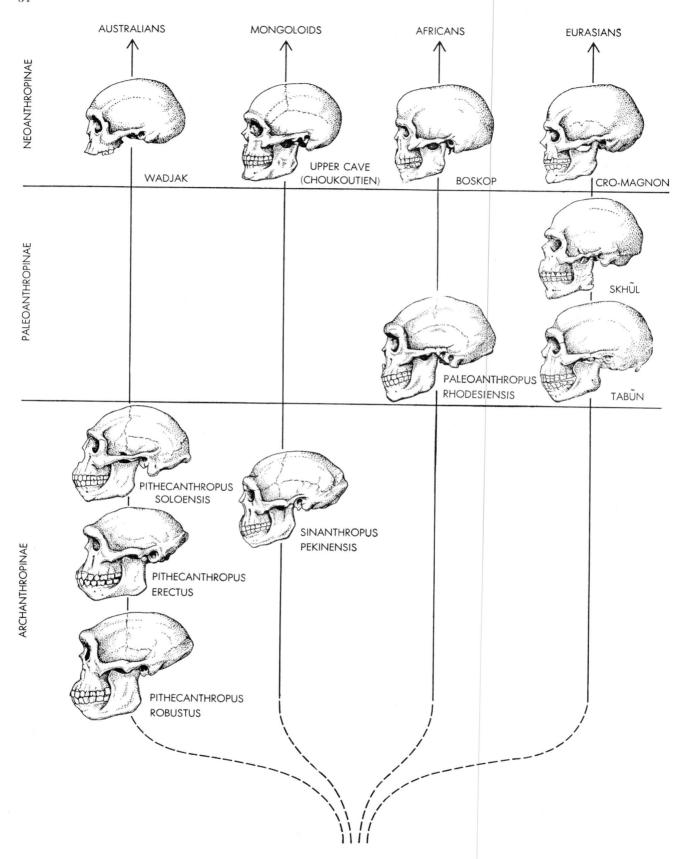

AUSTRALIANS   MONGOLOIDS   AFRICANS   EURASIANS

NEOANTHROPINAE

WADJAK   UPPER CAVE (CHOUKOUTIEN)   BOSKOP   CRO-MAGNON

PALEOANTHROPINAE

SKHŪL

PALEOANTHROPUS RHODESIENSIS   TABŪN

ARCHANTHROPINAE

PITHECANTHROPUS SOLOENSIS

SINANTHROPUS PEKINENSIS

PITHECANTHROPUS ERECTUS

PITHECANTHROPUS ROBUSTUS

POLYPHYLETIC SCHOOL of anthropology, chiefly identified with Franz Weidenreich, conceives modern races of man descending from four ancestral lines. According to this school, ancestors of **Australians** (*left*) include *Pithecanthropus soloensis* (Solo man) and *Pithecanthropus erectus* (Java man). Original ancestor of Mongoloids is *Sinanthropus pekinensis* (Peking man); of Africans, *Paleoanthropus rhodesiensis* (Rhodesian man). Four skulls at top are early *Homo sapiens*. Alternative theory is shown on next page.

to stake out new preserves wherever there was freedom ahead. So this pressure, and man's command of nature, primitive though it still was, sent the hunters of the end of the Ice Age throughout the Old World, out into Australia, up into the far north, over the Bering Strait and down the whole length of the Americas to Tierra del Fuego. At the beginning of this dispersion we have brutes barely able to shape a stone tool; at the end, the wily, self-reliant Eskimo, with his complicated traps, weapons and sledges and his clever hunting tricks.

The great racial radiation carried out by migratory hunters culminated in the world as it was about 10,000 years ago. The Whites occupied Europe, northern and eastern Africa and the Near East, and extended far to the east in Central Asia toward the Pacific shore. Negroes occupied the Sahara, better watered then, and Pygmies the African equatorial forest; south, in the open country, were Bushmen only. Other Pygmies, the Negritos, lived in the forests of much of India and southeastern Asia; while in the open country of these areas and in Australia were men like the present Australian aborigines: brown, beetle-browed and wavy-haired. Most of the Pacific was empty. People such as the American Indians stretched from China and Mongolia over Alaska to the Straits of Magellan; the more strongly Mongoloid peoples had not yet attained their domination of the Far East.

During the whole period the human population had depended on the supply of wild game for food, and the accent had been on relative isolation of peoples and groups. Still close to nature (as we think of nature), man was in a good position for rapid small-scale evolution, both through natural selection and through the operation of chance in causing differences among widely separated tribes even if selection was not strong.

Then opened the Neolithic period, the beginning of a great change. Agriculture was invented, at first inefficient and feeble, but in our day able to feed phenomenally large populations while freeing them from looking for food. The limit on local numbers of people was gradually removed, and with it the necessity for the isolation and spacing of groups and the careful observation of boundaries. Now, as there began to be surpluses available for trading, connections between communities became more useful. Later came a spreading of bonds from higher centers of trade and of authority. Isolation gave way to contact,

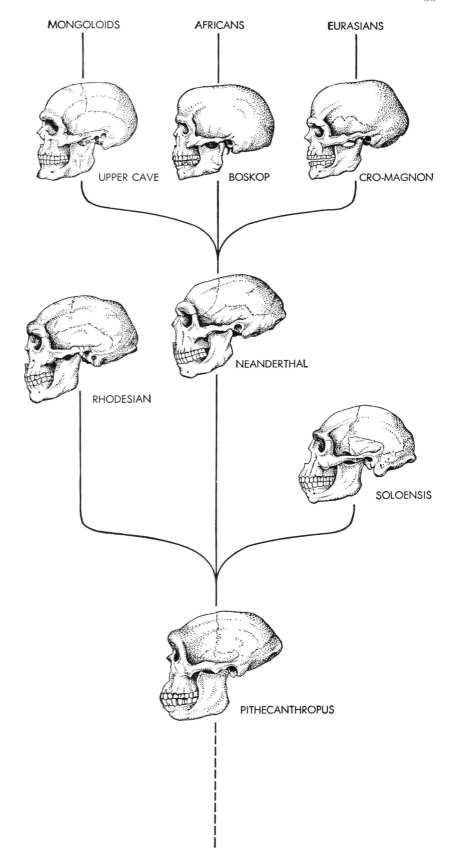

UNILINEAR OR "HAT-RACK" SCHOOL predicates three races descending from single ancestral line, as opposed to polyphyletic theory depicted at left. Rhodesian, Neanderthal and Solo man all descend from *Pithecanthropus*. Neanderthal is ancestor of early *Homo sapiens* (Upper Cave, Boskop and Cro-Magnon) from which modern races descended.

even when contact meant war.

The change was not speedy by our standards, though in comparison with the pace of the Stone Age it seems like a headlong rush. The new economy planted people much more solidly, of course. Farmers have been uprooting and displacing hunters from the time of the first planters to our own day, when Bushman survivors are still losing reservation land to agriculturalists in southwestern Africa. These Bushmen, a scattering of Australian aborigines, the Eskimos and a few other groups are the only representatives of their age still in place. On the other hand, primitive representatives of the Neolithic level of farming still live in many places after the thousands of years since they first became established there.

Nevertheless mobility increased and has increased ever since. Early woodland farmers were partly nomadic, moving every generation following exhaustion of the soil, however solidly fixed they may have been during each sojourn. The Danubians of 6,000 years ago can be traced archeologically as they made the same kind of periodic removes as central Africans, Iroquois Indians and pioneer Yankee farmers. Another side of farming—animal husbandry—gave rise to pastoral nomadism. Herders were much lighter of foot, and historically have tended to be warlike and domineering. With irrigation, villages could settle forever and evolve into the urban centers of high civilizations. Far from immobilizing man, however, these centers served

as fixed bases from which contact (and conflict) worked outward.

The rest of the story is written more clearly. New crops or new agricultural methods opened new territories, such as equatorial Africa, and the great plains of the U. S., never successfully farmed by the Indians. New materials such as copper and tin made places once hopeless for habitation desirable as sources of raw material or as way stations for trade. Thus an island like Crete rose from nothing to dominate the eastern Mediterranean for centuries. Well before the earliest historians had made records, big population shifts were taking place. Our mental picture of the aboriginal world is actually a recent one. The Bantu Negroes moved into central and

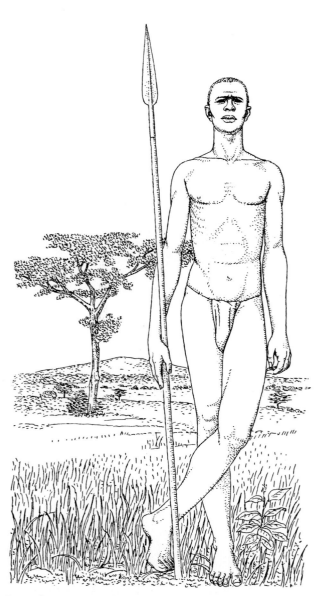

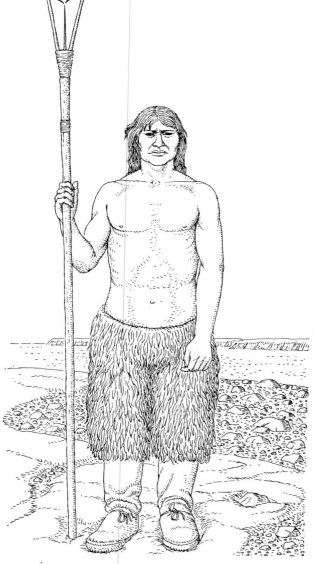

HUMAN ADAPTATION TO CLIMATE is typified by Nilotic Negro of the Sudan (*left*) and arctic Eskimo (*right*). Greater body surface of Negro facilitates dissipation of unneeded body heat; proportionately greater bulk of the Eskimo conserves body heat.

southern Africa, peoples of Mongoloid type went south through China and into Japan, and ancient folk of Negrito and Australoid racial nature were submerged by Caucasians in India. Various interesting but inconsequential trickles also ran hither and yon; for example, the migration of the Polynesians into the far Pacific.

The greatest movement came with the advent of ocean sailing in Europe. (The Polynesians had sailed the high seas earlier, of course, but they had no high culture, nor did Providence interpose a continent across their route at a feasible distance, as it did for Columbus.) The Europeans poured out on the world. From the 15th to the 19th centuries they compelled other civilized peoples to accept contact, and subjected or erased the uncivilized. So today, once again, we have a quite different distribution of mankind from that of 1492.

It seems obvious that we stand at the beginning of still another phase. Contact is immediate, borders are slamming shut and competition is fierce. Biological fitness in races is now hard to trace, and even reproduction is heavily controlled by medicine and by social values. The racial picture of the future will be determined less by natural selection and disease resistances than by success in government and in the adjustment of numbers. The end of direct European dominance in Africa and Asia seems to mean the end of any possibility of the infiltration and expansion of the European variety of man there, on the New World model. History as we know it has been largely the expansion of the European horizon and of European peoples. But the end in China of mere absorption of Occidental invention, and the passionate self-assertion of the African tribes, make it likely that racial lines and territories will again be more sharply drawn than they have been for centuries. What man will make of himself next is a question that lies in the province of prophets, not anthropologists.

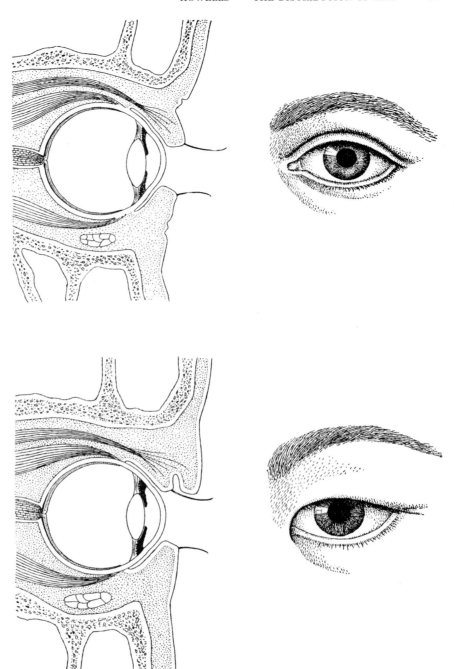

"ALMOND" EYE OF MONGOLOID RACES is among latest major human adaptations to environment. The Mongoloid fold, shown in lower drawings, protects the eye against the severe Asian winter. Drawings at top show the Caucasian eye with its single, fatty lid.

4

THE PRESENT EVOLUTION OF MAN

THEODOSIUS DOBZHANSKY
September 1960

Any discussion of the evolution of the human species deals with a natural process that has transcended itself. Only once before, when life originated out of inorganic matter, has there occurred a comparable event.

After that first momentous step, living forms evolved by adapting to their environments. Adaptation—the maintenance or advancement of conformity between an organism and its surroundings —takes place through natural selection. The raw materials with which natural selection works are supplied by mutation and sexual recombination of hereditary units: the genes.

Mutation, sexual recombination and natural selection led to the emergence of *Homo sapiens*. The creatures that preceded him had already developed the rudiments of tool-using, toolmaking and cultural transmission. But the next evolutionary step was so great as to constitute a difference in kind from those before it. There now appeared an organism whose mastery of technology and of symbolic communication enabled it to create a supraorganic culture. Other organisms adapt to their environments by changing their genes in accordance with the demands of the surroundings. Man and man alone can also adapt by changing his environments to fit his genes. His genes enable him to invent new tools, to alter his opinions, his aims and his conduct, to acquire new knowledge and new wisdom.

Numerous authors of numerous studies have shown how the possession of these faculties brought the human species to its present biological eminence. Man has spread to every section of the earth, bringing high culture to much of it. He is now the most numerous of the mammals. By these or any other reasonable standards, he is by far the most successful product of biological evolution.

For better or worse, biological evolution did not stop when culture appeared. In this short article we address ourselves to the question of where evolution is now taking man. The literature of this subject has not lacked for prophets who wish to divine man's eventual fate. In our age of anxiety, prediction of final extinction has become the fashionable view, replacing the hopes for emergence of a race of demigods that more optimistic authorities used to foresee. Our purpose is less ambitious. What biological evolutionary processes are now at work is a problem both serious and complex enough to occupy us here.

The impact of human works on the environment is so strong that it has become very hard to make out the forces to which the human species is now adjusting. It has even been argued that *Homo sapiens* has already emancipated himself from the operation of natural selection. At the other extreme are those who still assume that man is nothing but an animal. The second fallacy is the more pernicious, leading as it does to theories of biological racism and the justification of race and class prejudice which are bringing suffering to millions of people from South Africa to Arkansas. Assuming that man's genetic endowment can be ignored is the converse falsehood, perhaps less disastrous in its immediate effects, but more insidious in the long run.

Like all other animals, man remains the product of his biological inheritance. The first, and basic, feature of his present evolution is that his genes continue to mutate, as they have since he first appeared. Every one of the tens of thousands of genes inherited by an individual has a tiny probability of changing in some way during his generation. Among the small, and probably atypical, sample of human genes for which very rough estimates of the mutation frequencies are available, the rates of mutation vary from one in 10,000 to one in about 250,000. For example, it has been calculated that approximately one sex cell in every 50,000 produced by a normal person carries a new mutant gene causing retinoblastoma, a cancer of the eye affecting children.

These figures are "spontaneous" frequencies in people not exposed to any special agents that can induce mutation. As is now widely known, the existence of such agents, including ionizing radiation and certain chemicals, has been demonstrated with organisms other than man. New mutagens are constantly being discovered. It can hardly be doubted that at least some of them affect human genes. As a consequence the members of an industrial civilization have increased genetic variability through rising mutation rates.

There is no question that many mutations produce hereditary diseases, malformations and constitutional weaknesses of various kinds. Some few must also be useful, at least in certain environments; otherwise there would be no evolution. (Useful mutants have actually been observed in experiments on lower organisms.) But what about minor variations that produce a little more or a little less hair, a slightly longer or a slightly shorter nose, blood of type O or type A? These traits seem neither useful nor harmful. Here, however, we must proceed with the greatest caution. Beneficial or damaging effects of ostensibly neutral traits may eventually be discovered. For example, recent evidence indicates that people with blood of type O have a slightly higher rate of duodenal ulcer than does the general population. Does it follow that O blood is bad? Not necessarily; it is the most frequent type in many populations, and it may conceivably confer some advantages yet undiscovered.

Still other mutants that are detrimental when present in double dose (the so-called homozygous condition, where the same type of gene has been inherited from both parents) lead to hybrid vigor in single dose (the heterozygous condition). How frequently this happens is uncertain. The effect surely operates in the breeding of domestic animals and plants, and it has been detected among X-ray-induced mutations in fruit flies. Only one case is thus far known in man. Anthony C. Allison of the University of Oxford has found that the gene causing sickle-cell anemia in the homozygous condition makes its heterozygous carriers relatively resistant to certain forms of malaria. This gene is very frequent in the native population of the central African lowlands, where malaria has long been endemic, and relatively rare in the inhabitants of the more salubrious

highlands. Certainly there are other such adaptively ambivalent genes in human populations, but we do not know how many.

Despite these uncertainties, which cannot be glossed over, it is generally agreed among geneticists that the effects of mutation are on the average detrimental. Any increase of mutation rate, no matter how small, can only augment the mass of human misery due to defective heredity. The matter has rightly attracted wide attention in connection with ionizing radiation from military and industrial operations and medical X-rays. Yet these form only a part of a larger and more portentous issue.

Of the almost countless mutant genes that have arisen since life on earth began, only a minute fraction were preserved. They were preserved because they were useful, or at least not very harmful, to their possessors. A great majority of gene changes were elimi-

nated. The agency that preserved useful mutants and eliminated injurious ones was natural selection. Is natural selection still operating in mankind, and can it be trusted to keep man fit to live in environments created by his civilization?

One must beware of words taken from everyday language to construct scientific terminology. "Natural" in "natural selection" does not mean the state of affairs preceding or excluding man-made changes. Artificially or not, man's environment has altered. Would it now be natural to try to make your living as a Stone Age hunter?

Then there are phrases like "the struggle for life" and "survival of the fittest." Now "struggle" was to Darwin a metaphor. Animals struggle against cold by growing warm fur, and plants against dryness by reducing the evaporating leaf surface. It was the school of so-called social Darwinists (to which Darwin did not belong) who equated "struggle" with violence, warfare and competition

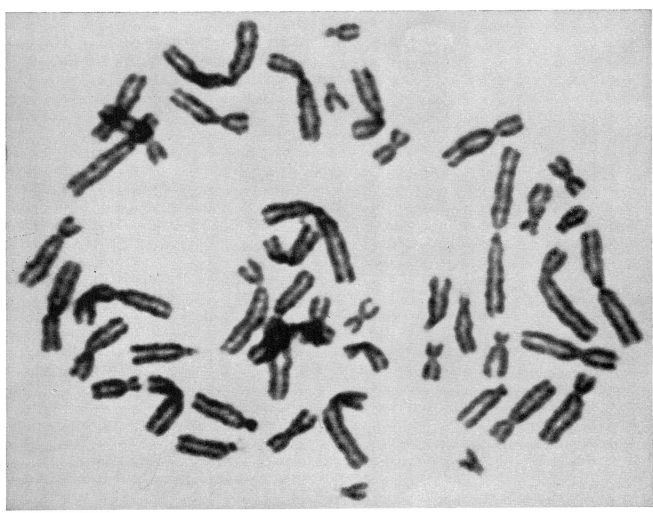

HUMAN CHROMOSOMES are enlarged some 5,000 times in this photomicrograph made by J. H. Tjio and Theodore T. Puck at the University of Colorado Medical Center. The photomicrograph shows all of the 23 pairs of chromosomes in a dividing body cell.

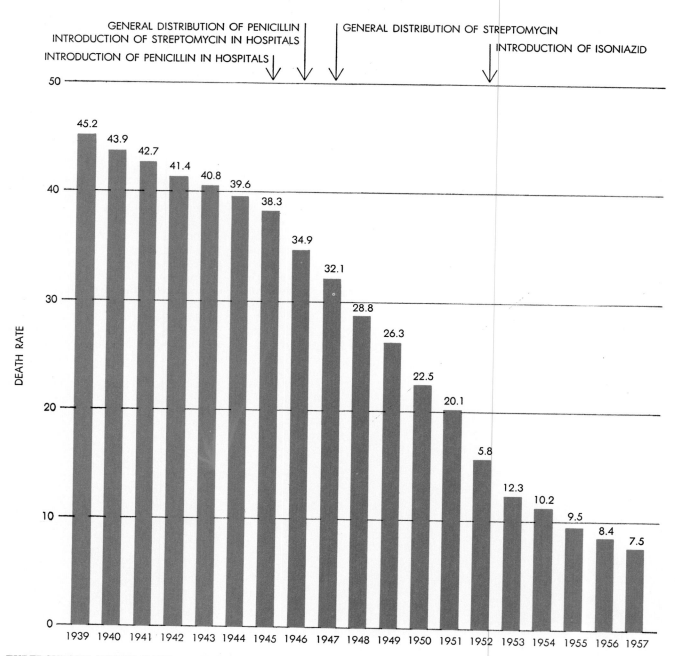

GENERAL DISTRIBUTION OF PENICILLIN
INTRODUCTION OF STREPTOMYCIN IN HOSPITALS

GENERAL DISTRIBUTION OF STREPTOMYCIN

INTRODUCTION OF PENICILLIN IN HOSPITALS

INTRODUCTION OF ISONIAZID

DEATH RATE

1939 1940 1941 1942 1943 1944 1945 1946 1947 1948 1949 1950 1951 1952 1953 1954 1955 1956 1957

TUBERCULOSIS DEATH RATE per 100,000 people showed a dramatic decline with the introduction of antibiotics and later of the antituberculosis drug isoniazid. As tuberculosis becomes less prevalent, so does its threat to genetically susceptible individuals, who are enabled to survive and reproduce. The chart is based upon information from the U. S. National Office of Vital Statistics.

without quarter. The idea has long been discredited.

We do not deny the reality of competition and combat in nature, but suggest that they do not tell the whole story. Struggle for existence may be won not only by strife but also by mutual help. The surviving fit in human societies may in some circumstances be those with the strongest fists and the greatest readiness to use them. In others they may be those who live in peace with their neighbors and assist them in hour of need. Indeed, co-operation has a long and honorable record. The first human societies, the hunters of the Old Stone Age, depended on co-operation to kill big game.

Moreover, modern genetics shows that "fitness" has a quite special meaning in connection with evolution. Biologists now speak of Darwinian fitness, or adaptive value, or selective value in a reproductive sense. Consider the condition known as achondroplastic dwarfism, caused by a gene mutation that produces people with normal heads and trunks, but short arms and legs. As adults they may enjoy good health. Nevertheless, E. T. Mørch in Denmark has discovered that achondroplastic dwarfs produce, on the average, only some 20 surviving children for every 100 children produced by their normal brothers and sisters. In technical terms we say that the Darwinian fitness of achondroplasts is .2 or, alternatively that achondroplastic dwarfism is opposed by a selection-coefficient of .8.

This is a very strong selection, and the reasons for it are only partly understood. What matters from an evolutionary point of view is that achondroplasts are much less efficient in transmitting their genes to the following generations than are nondwarfs. Darwinian fitness is reproductive fitness. Genetically the surviving fittest is neither superman nor conquering hero; he is merely the parent of the largest surviving progeny.

With these definitions in mind, we can answer the question whether natural selection is still active in mankind by considering how such selection might be set aside. If all adults married, and each couple produced exactly the same number of children, all of whom survived to get married in turn and so on, there would be no selection at all. Alternatively, the number of children, if any, that each person produced might be determined by himself or some outside authority on the basis of the desirability of his hereditary endowment. This would be replacing natural selection by artificial selection. Some day it may come to pass. Meantime natural selection is going on.

It goes on, however, always within the context of environment. As that changes, the Darwinian fitness of various traits changes with it. Thus by his own efforts man is continually altering the selective pressure for or against certain genes.

The most obvious example, and one with disturbing overtones, is to be found in the advance of medicine and public health. Retinoblastoma, the eye cancer of children, is almost always fatal if it is not treated. Here is "natural" selection at its most rigorous, weeding out virtually all of the harmful mutant genes

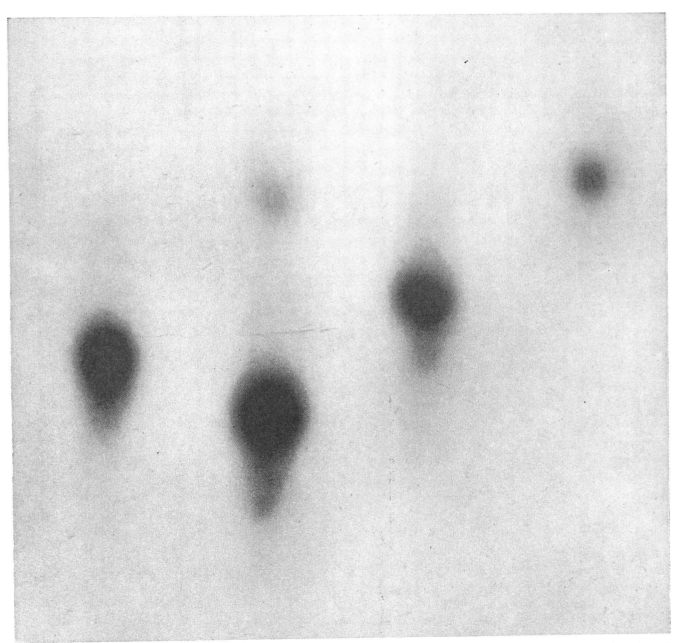

CHEMICAL STRUCTURE OF HEMOGLOBIN in an individual's blood is determined by his genes. Normal and abnormal hemoglobins move at different speeds in an electric field. This photograph, made by Henry G. Kunkel of the Rockefeller Institute, shows surface of a slab of moist starch on which samples of four kinds of human hemoglobin were lined up at top, between a negative electrode at top and a positive electrode at bottom (electrodes are not shown). When current was turned on, the samples migrated toward positive electrode. At right hemoglobin C, the cause of a rare hereditary anemia, has moved down only a short way. Second from right is hemoglobin S, the cause of sickle-cell anemia, which has moved farther in same length of time. Normal hemoglobin, third from right, has separated into its A and A_2 constituents. At left is normal fetal hemoglobin F, obtained from an umbilical cord.

before they can be passed on even once. With proper treatment, however, almost 70 per cent of the carriers of the gene for retinoblastoma survive, become able to reproduce and therefore to transmit the defect to half their children.

More dramatic, if genetically less clear-cut, instances are afforded by advances in the control of tuberculosis and malaria. A century ago the annual death rate from tuberculosis in industrially advanced countries was close to 500 per 100,000. Improvement in living conditions and, more recently, the advent of antibiotic drugs have reduced the death rate to 7.5 per 100,000 in the U. S. today. A similarly steep decline is under way in the mortality from malaria, which used to afflict a seventh of the earth's population.

Being infectious, tuberculosis and malaria are hazards of the environment. There is good evidence, however, that individual susceptibility, both as to contracting the infection and as to the severity of the disease, is genetically conditioned. (We have already mentioned the protective effect of the gene for sickle-cell anemia. This is probably only one of several forms of genetic resistance to malaria.) As the prevalence of these diseases decreases, so does the threat to susceptible individuals. In other words, the Darwinian fitness of such individuals has increased.

It was pointed out earlier that one effect of civilization is to increase mutation rates and hence the supply of harmful genes. A second effect is to decrease the rate of discrimination against such genes, and consequently the rate of their elimination from human populations by natural selection. In thus disturbing the former genetic equilibrium of inflow and outflow, is man not frustrating natural selection and polluting his genetic pool?

The danger exists and cannot be ignored. But in the present state of knowledge the problem is tremendously complex. If our culture has an ideal, it is the sacredness of human life. A society that refused, on eugenic grounds, to cure children of retinoblastoma would, in our eyes, lose more by moral degradation than it gained genetically. Not so easy, however, is the question whether a person who knows he carries the gene for retinoblastoma, or a similarly deleterious gene, has a right to have children.

Even here the genetic issue is clear, although the moral issue may not be. This is no longer true when we come to genes that are harmful in double dose,

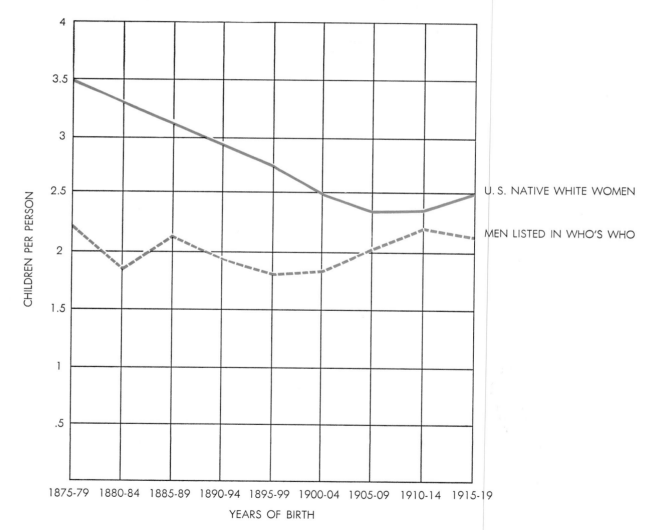

FERTILITY RATE among relatively intelligent people, as represented by a random sample of men listed in *Who's Who in America* for 1956 and 1957, is lower than fertility rate of the U. S. population as a whole, as represented by all native white women. The two fertility rates have recently been moving toward each other. Vertical scale shows average number of children per person; horizontal scale shows approximate birth date of parents. Chart is based upon information collected by Dudley Kirk of the Population Council.

but beneficial in single. If the central African peoples had decided some time ago to breed out the sickle-cell gene, they might have succumbed in much larger numbers to malaria. Fortunately this particular dilemma has been resolved by successful methods of mosquito control. How many other hereditary diseases and malformations are maintained by the advantages their genes confer in heterozygous carriers, we simply do not know.

Conversely, we cannot yet predict the genetic effect of relaxing selection pressure. If, for example, susceptibility to tuberculosis is maintained by recurrent mutations, then the conquest of the disease should increase the concentration of mutant genes as time goes on. On the other hand, if resistance arises from a single dose of genes that make for susceptibility in the double dose, the effects of eradication become much less clear. Other selective forces might then determine the fate of these genes in the population.

In any case, although we cannot see all the consequences, we can be sure that ancient genetic patterns will continue to shift under the shelter of modern medicine. We would not wish it otherwise. It may well be, however, that the social cost of maintaining some genetic variants will be so great that artificial selection against them is ethically, as well as economically, the most acceptable and wisest solution.

If the evolutionary impact of such biological tools as antibiotics and vaccines is still unclear, then computers and rockets, to say nothing of social organizations as a whole, present an even deeper puzzle. There is no doubt that human survival will continue to depend more and more on human intellect and technology. It is idle to argue whether this is good or bad. The point of no return was passed long ago, before anyone knew it was happening.

But to grant that the situation is inevitable is not to ignore the problems it raises. Selection in modern societies does not always encourage characteristics that we regard as desirable. Let us consider one example. Much has been written about the differential fertility that in advanced human societies favors less intelligent over more intelligent people. Studies in several countries have shown that school children from large families tend to score lower on so-called intelligence tests than their classmates with few or no brothers and sisters. Moreover, parents who score lower on these tests have more children on the average

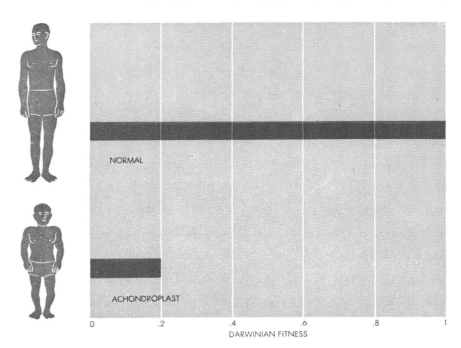

DARWINIAN FITNESS of achondroplastic dwarfs is low. Dwarfs may be healthy, but they have only 20 surviving children to every 100 surviving children of normal parents.

than those who get higher marks.

We cannot put our finger on the forces responsible for this presumed selection against intelligence. As a matter of fact, there is some evidence that matters are changing, in the U. S. at least. People included in *Who's Who in America* (assuming that people listed in this directory are on the average more intelligent than people not listed there) had fewer children than the general population during the period from 1875 to 1904. In the next two decades, however, the difference seemed to be disappearing. L. S. Penrose of University College London, one of the outstanding human geneticists, has pointed out that a negative correlation between intelligence and family size may in part be corrected by the relative infertility of low-grade mental defectives. He suggests that selection may thus be working toward maintaining a constant level of genetic conditioning for intelligence in human populations. The evidence presently available is insufficient either to prove or to contradict this hypothesis.

It must also be recognized that in man and other social animals qualities making for successful individuals are not necessarily those most useful to the society as a whole. If there were a gene for altruism, natural selection might well discriminate against it on the individual level, but favor it on the population level. In that case the fate of the gene would be hard to predict.

If this article has asked many more questions than it has answered, the purpose is to suggest that answers be sought with all possible speed. Natural selection is a very remarkable phenomenon. But it does not even guarantee the survival of a species. Most living forms have become extinct without the "softening" influence of civilization, simply by becoming too narrowly specialized. Natural selection is opportunistic; in shaping an organism to fit its surroundings it may leave the organism unable to cope with a change in environment. In this light, man's explosive ability to change his environment may offer as much threat as promise. Technological evolution may have outstripped biological evolution.

Yet man is the only product of biological evolution who knows that he has evolved and is evolving further. He should be able to replace the blind force of natural selection by conscious direction, based on his knowledge of nature and on his values. It is as certain that such direction will be needed as it is questionable whether man is ready to provide it. He is unready because his knowledge of his own nature and its evolution is insufficient; because a vast majority of people are unaware of the necessity of facing the problem; and because there is so wide a gap between the way people actually live and the values and ideals to which they pay lip service.

II

THE EVOLUTION AND DEVELOPMENT OF BEHAVIOR: INSTINCT AND EXPERIENCE

II

THE EVOLUTION AND DEVELOPMENT OF BEHAVIOR: INSTINCT AND EXPERIENCE

INTRODUCTION

The concept of "instinct" has been at the center of marked and sometimes violent controversies. In modern terms, instinctive behavior refers simply to behavior patterns that are strongly controlled by innate or genetic mechanisms. It is a truism today that all patterns of behavior are influenced both by genetic and by environmental factors. More interest is focused now on the actual mechanisms that underlie behavior than on the "nature–nuture" controversy. There is no question, however, that many forms of behavior, particularly in lower animals, are dominated by innate mechanisms. The more stereotyped behavior patterns, often called "fixed action patterns," are a favorite topic of ethologists, those biologists who study animal behavior as it occurs in the natural habitat. It is no accident that much of the literature of ethology deals with birds: they exhibit clear, stereotyped behaviors. Higher mammals seem to have developed more flexible learning mechanisms for adaptive behavior. This plasticity is particularly evident in the development of young animals. However, innate behavior patterns probably exist even in adult *Homo sapiens* — in whom they are much more difficult to identify.

The field of modern ethology owes much to the work of Konrad Z. Lorenz and N. Tinbergen. In the first article in this section, "The Evolution of Behavior," Lorenz provides many striking examples of behavior sequences and traits that are species-specific — that is, that characterize a species as much as bodily structure and form. Although clearly programmed by innate factors, these behaviors must be elicited by appropriate environmental stimuli and conditions. The work by Daniel S. Lehrman ("The Reproductive Behavior of Ring Doves") is a brilliant analysis both of the innate and the experimental factors that interact to produce a relatively stereotyped, although very complex, behavior sequence. External stimuli and hormonal factors are involved in courtship, which, in turn, establishes hormone and brain changes that lead to nest building, which provides stimuli for further internal changes associated with egg laying and incubation. This complex sequence of behaviors depends on the existence of appropriate external stimuli and internal hormonal events and brain mechanisms at every step. The total sequence begins with external stimuli, which lead through hormone secretions and brain changes to changes in behavior that provide further external stimuli, which, in turn, lead back to the brain and hormones.

Growth and development are perhaps the most pervasive facts of life. Higher organisms are born small, relatively helpless, and undeveloped. Indeed, man is born particularly so; he is well described as "a fetal ape." One of the fundamental issues in the biology of human behavior is the mechanism of the development of behavior. Do we learn most aspects of our behavior and our perception of the world through experience as we grow, or are many aspects of behavior and perception built into our brains, to unfold like the fixed action patterns of lower animals? Although we know far too little about human development, it appears certain that neither of these extremes is entirely true.

The role of early experience in the development of normal behavior is examined by William R. Thompson and Ronald Melzack in their studies of Scottish terriers raised in restricted environments ("Early Environment"). Upon weaning, half of each litter of puppies was raised in a small, opaque cage for several months. When freed and tested in the normal environment, these restricted animals showed a striking variety of abnormal behaviors. Robert L. Fantz, in his article "The Origin of Form Perception," discusses several species ranging from chicken to man. Although it seems clear that many lower organisms are born equipped to perceive the world, or at least those features of their world necessary for survival, little is known about the perceptions of human infants. Are they born as a "blank slate" upon which experience writes perception, or are some aspects of perception wired into the brain? Thanks in part to Fantz's work, the latter view appears to be gaining ground. Very young human infants look longer at a proper drawing of a human face than a scrambled version.

The development of love and affection is one of the more important and less understood aspects of human growth. The fundamental and far-reaching studies of Harry F. Harlow (see his article "Love in Infant Monkeys") have provided most of our information in this area. As Harlow demonstrates, bodily contact is far more important in the development of love than the reduction of hunger and thirst associated with feeding. Harlow's work is the first to identify the physical and physiological variables that are critical to the development of affection and love in primates.

5

THE EVOLUTION OF BEHAVIOR

KONRAD Z. LORENZ
December 1958

A whale's flipper, a bat's wing and a man's arm are as different from one another in outward appearance as they are in the functions they serve. But the bones of these structures reveal an essential similarity of design. The zoologist concludes that whale, bat and man evolved from a common ancestor. Even if there were no other evidence, the comparison of the skeletons of these creatures would suffice to establish that conclusion. The similarity of skeletons shows that a basic structure may persist over geologic periods in spite of a wide divergence of function.

Following the example of zoologists, who have long exploited the comparative method, students of animal behavior have now begun to ask a penetrating question. We all know how greatly the behavior of animals can vary, especially under the influence of the learning process. Psychologists have mostly observed and experimented with the behavior of individual animals; few have considered the behavior of species. But is it not possible that beneath all the variations of individual behavior there lies an inner structure of inherited behavior which characterizes all the members of a given species, genus or larger taxonomic group —just as the skeleton of a primordial ancestor characterizes the form and structure of all mammals today?

Yes, it is possible! Let me give an example which, while seemingly trivial, has a bearing on this question. Anyone who has watched a dog scratch its jaw or a bird preen its head feathers can attest to the fact that they do so in the same way. The dog props itself on the tripod formed by its haunches and two forelegs and reaches a hindleg forward in front of its shoulder. Now the odd fact is that most birds (as well as virtu-

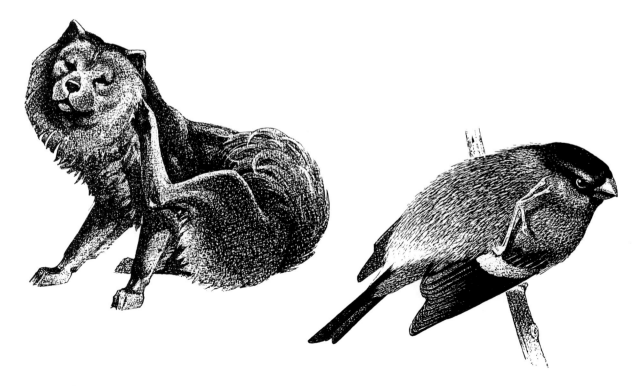

SCRATCHING BEHAVIOR of a dog and a European bullfinch is part of their genetic heritage and is not changed by training. The widespread habit of scratching with a hindlimb crossed over a forelimb is common to most Amniota (birds, reptiles and mammals).

DISPLAY BEHAVIOR of seagulls shows how behavior traits inherent in all gulls have adapted to the needs of an aberrant species. At top is a typical gull, the herring gull, which breeds on the shore. It is shown in the "choking" posture which advertises its nest site. In middle the herring gull is shown in the "oblique" and "long call" postures, used to defend its territory. At bottom is the aberrant kittiwake, which unlike other gulls breeds on narrow ledges and has no territory other than its nest site. The kittiwake does not use the "oblique" or "long call" postures, but employs the "choking" stance for both advertisement and defense.

ally all mammals and reptiles) scratch with precisely the same motion! A bird also scratches with a hindlimb (that is, its claw), and in doing so it lowers its wing and reaches its claw forward in front of its shoulder. One might think that it would be simpler for the bird to move its claw directly to its head without moving its wing, which lies folded out of the way on its back. I do not see how to explain this clumsy action unless we admit that it is inborn. Before the bird can scratch, it must reconstruct the old spatial relationship of the limbs of the four-legged common ancestor which it shares with mammals.

In retrospect it seems peculiar that psychologists have been so slow to pursue such clues to hereditary behavior. It is nearly 100 years since T. H. Huxley, upon making his first acquaintance with Charles Darwin's concept of natural selection, exclaimed: "How stupid of me, not to have thought of that!" Darwinian evolution quickly fired the imagination of biologists. Indeed, it swept through the scientific world with the speed characteristic of all long-overdue ideas. But somehow the new approach stopped short at the borders of psychology. The psychologists did not draw on Darwin's comparative method, or on his sense of the species as the protagonist of the evolutionary process.

Perhaps, with their heritage from philosophy, they were too engrossed in purely doctrinal dissension. For exactly opposite reasons the "behaviorists" and the "purposivists" were convinced that behavior was much too variable to permit its reduction to a set of traits characteristic of a species. The purposivist school of psychology argued for the existence of instincts; the behaviorists argued against them. The purposivists believed that instincts set the goals of animal behavior, but left to the individual animal a boundless variety of means to reach these goals. The behaviorists held that the capacity to learn endowed the individual with unlimited plasticity of behavior. The debate over instinct versus learning kept both schools from perceiving consistent, inherited patterns in behavior, and led each to preoccupation with external influences on behavior.

If any psychologist stood apart from the sterile contention of the two schools, it was Jakob von Uexküll. He sought tirelessly for the causes of animal behavior, and was not blind to structure. But he too was caught in a philosophical trap. Uexküll was a vitalist, and he denounced Darwinism as gross materialism. He believed that the regularities he observed in the behavior of species were manifestations of nature's unchanging and unchangeable "ground plan," a notion akin to the mystical "idea" of Plato.

The Phylogeny of Behavior

But even as the psychologists debated, evolutionary thought was entering the realm of behavior studies by two back doors. At Woods Hole, Mass., Charles Otis Whitman, a founder of the Marine Biological Laboratory, was working out the family tree of pigeons, which he had bred as a hobby since early childhood. Simultaneously, but unknown to Whitman, Oskar Heinroth of the Berlin Aquarium was studying the phylogeny of waterfowl. Heinroth, too, was an amateur aviculturist who had spent a lifetime observing his own pet ducks. What a queer misnomer is the word "amateur"! How unjust that a term which means the "lover" of a subject should come to connote a superficial dabbler! As a result of their "dabbling," Whitman and Heinroth acquired an incomparably detailed knowledge of pigeon and duck behavior.

As phylogenists, Whitman and Heinroth both sought to develop in detail the relationship between families and species of birds. To define a given group they had to find its "homologous" traits: the resemblances between species which bespeak a common origin. The success or failure of their detective work hinged on the number of homologous traits they could find. As practical bird-fanciers, Whitman and Heinroth came to know bird behavior as well as bird morphology, and each independently reached an important discovery: Behavior, as well as body form and structure, displays homologous traits. As Whitman phrased it just 60 years ago: "Instincts and organs are to be studied from the common viewpoint of phyletic descent."

Sometimes these traits of behavior are common to groups larger than ducks or pigeons. The scratching habit, which I have already mentioned, is an example of a behavior pattern that is shared by a very large taxonomic group, in this case the Amniota: the reptiles, birds and mammals (all of whose embryos grow within the thin membrane of the amniotic sac). This widespread motor pattern was discovered by Heinroth, who described it in a brief essay in 1930. It is noteworthy that Heinroth observed the extreme resistance of such inborn habits to changes wrought by learning. He noticed that while most bird species maintain their incongruous over-the-shoulder

"HEAD-FLAGGING" is another form of display in which the kittiwake has adapted its behavioral birthright to meet unusual needs. Most gulls—like this pair of black-faced gulls—use this stance in courtship (by averting its menacing facial and bill coloration, the bird "appeases" the aggressive instinct of its mate). Kittiwakes alone evince this posture not only in mating adults but in ledge-bound nestlings, which use it to "appease" invaders.

scratching technique, some have lost this behavior trait. Among these are the larger parrots, which feed with their claws and use the same motion—under the wing—for scratching. Parakeets, however, scratch in the unreconstructed style, reaching around the lowered wing, and do not pick up food in their claws. There are a few exceptions to this rule. The Australian broadtailed parakeet has learned to eat with its claw. When eating, it raises its claw directly to its bill. But when scratching, it still reaches its claw around its lowered wing! This oddity is evidence in itself of the obstinacy of the old scratching habit. So far no one has been able to teach a parakeet to scratch without lowering its wing or to train a parrot to scratch around a lowered wing.

Today a growing school of investigators is working in the field opened up by Whitman and Heinroth. They have set themselves the task of discovering inherited patterns of behavior and tracing them from species to species. Many of these patterns have proved to be reliable clues to the origin and relationship of large groups of animals. There is no longer any doubt that animals in general do inherit certain deep-seated behavioral traits. In the higher animals such traits tend to be masked by learned behavior, but in such creatures as fishes and birds they reveal themselves with great clarity. These patterns of behavior must somehow be rooted in the common physiological inheritance of the species that display them. Whatever their physiological cause, they undoubtedly form a natural unit of heredity. The majority of them change but slowly with evolution in the species and stubbornly resist learning in the individual; they have a peculiar spontaneity and a considerable independence of immediate sensory stimuli. Because of their stability, they rank with the more slowly evolving skeletal structure of animals as ideal subjects for the comparative studies which aim to unravel the history of species.

I am quite aware that biologists today (especially young ones) tend to think of the comparative method as stuffy and old-fashioned—at best a branch of research that has already yielded its treasures, and like a spent gold mine no longer pays the working. I believe that this is untrue, and so I shall pause to say a few words in behalf of comparative morphology as such. Every time a biologist seeks to know *why* an organism looks and acts as it does, he must resort to the comparative method. Why does the ear have its peculiar conformation? Why is it mounted behind the jaw? To know the answer the investigator must compare the mammalian frame with that of other vertebrates. Then he will discover that the ear was once a gill slit. When the first air-breathing, four-legged vertebrates came out of the sea, they lost all but one pair of gill slits, each of which happened to lie conveniently near the

"INCITING" is a threatening movement used by the female duck to signal her mate to attack invaders of their territory. At left a female of the European sheldrake (*with head lowered*) incites her mate against an enemy that she sees directly before her. The female at right (*with head turned*) has seen an enemy to one side. Each female watches her enemy regardless of her own body orientation.

labyrinth of the inner ear. The water canal which opened into it became filled with air and adapted itself to conducting sound waves. Thus was born the ear.

This kind of thinking is 100 years old in zoology, but in the study of behavior it is only now coming into its own. The first studies leading to a true morphology of behavior have concentrated largely on those innate motor patterns that have the function of expression or communication within a species. It is easy to see why this should be so. Whether the mode of communication is aural, as in the case of bird songs, or visual, as in the "dis-play" movements of courtship, many of these motor patterns have evolved under the pressure of natural selection to serve as sharply defined stimuli influencing the social behavior of fellow-members of a species. The patterns are usually striking and unambiguous. These qualities, so essential to the natural function of the behavior patterns, also catch the eye of the human observer.

Gulls, Terns and Kittiwakes

For some years N. Tinbergen of the University of Oxford has intensively studied the innate behavior of gulls and terns: the genus *Laridae*. He has organized an international group of his students and co-workers to conduct a world-wide study of the behavior traits of gulls and terns. They are careful to observe the behavior of their subjects in the larger context of their diverse life histories and in relationship to their different environments. It is gratifying that this ambitious project has begun to meet with the success which the enthusiasm of its participants so richly deserves.

Esther Cullen, one of Tinbergen's students, has been studying an eccentric

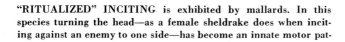

a   *b*

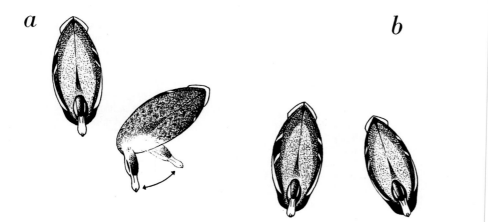
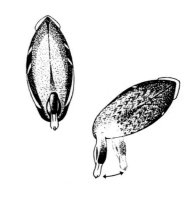

"RITUALIZED" INCITING is exhibited by mallards. In this species turning the head—as a female sheldrake does when inciting against an enemy to one side—has become an innate motor pat-tern. In situation *a* the female mallard turns her head toward the enemy. In *b*, with the enemy in front of her, she still turns her head even though this results in her turning it away from the enemy.

among the seagulls—the kittiwake. Most gulls are beachcombers and nest on the ground, and it is safe to assume that this was the original mode of life of the gull family. The kittiwake, however, is different. Except when it is breeding, it lives over the open sea. Its breeding ground is not a flat shore but the steepest of cliffs, where it nests on tiny ledges.

Mrs. Cullen has listed 33 points, both behavioral and anatomical, in which the kittiwake has come to differ from its sister species as a result of its atypical style of life. Just as the whale's flipper is a recognizable mammalian forelimb, so many of the kittiwake's habits are recognizably gull-like. But the kittiwake, like the whale, is a specialist; it has given its own twist to many of the behavior patterns that are the heritage of the *Laridae*.

For example, the male of most gull species stakes its claim to nesting territory by uttering the "long call" and striking the "oblique posture," its tail up and head down. To advertise its actual nesting site, it performs the "choking" movement. In the kittiwake the inherited patterns of behavior have been modified in accord with the habitat. On the kittiwake's tiny ledge, territory and nest sites are identical. So the kittiwake has lost the oblique posture and long call, and uses choking alone for display purposes.

Another example is the kittiwake gesture which Tinbergen calls "head-flagging." In other gull species a young gull which is not fully able to fly will run for cover when it is frightened by an adult bird. But its cliffside perch provides no cover for the young kittiwake. When it is frightened, the little kittiwake averts its head as a sign of appeasement. Such head-flagging does not occur in the young of other gulls, although it appears in the behavior of many adult gulls as the appeasement posture in a fight and in the rite of courtship. The kittiwake species has thus met an environmental demand by accelerating, in its young, the development of a standard motor habit of adult gulls.

Recently Wolfgang Wickler, one of my associates at the Max Planck Institute for Comparative Ethology, has found a similar case of adaptation by acceleration among the river-dwelling cichlid fishes. Most cichlids dig into the river bottom only at spawning time, when they excavate their nest pits. But there is an eccentric species (*Steatocranus*), a resident of the rapids of the Congo River, which lives from infancy in river-bottom burrows. In this cichlid the maturation of the digging urge of the mating fish is accelerated, appearing in

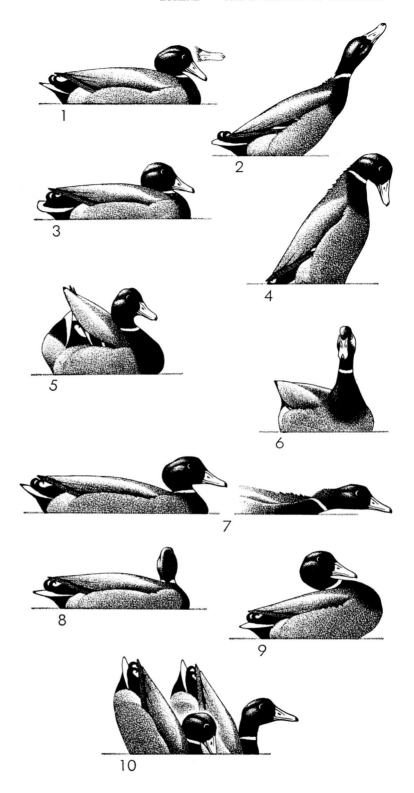

TEN COURTSHIP POSES which belong to the common genetic heritage of surface-feeding ducks are here shown as exemplified in the mallard: (1) initial bill-shake, (2) head-flick, (3) tail-shake, (4) grunt-whistle, (5) head-up tail-up, (6) turn toward the female, (7) nod-swimming, (8) turning the back of the head, (9) bridling, (10) down-up. How the mallard and two other species form sequences of these poses is illustrated on pages 54 through 57.

the infant of the species. It is not hard to conceive how selection pressure could have led to this result.

The work of the Tinbergen school has had the important result of placing innate motor habits in their proper setting. He and his co-workers have shown that these traits are highly resistant to evolutionary change, and that they often retain their original form even when their function has diverged considerably. These findings amply justify the metaphor that describes innate patterns as the skeleton of behavior. More work of the Tinbergen kind is badly needed. There

is great value in his synthetic approach, uniting the study of the physical nature and environment of animals with study of their behavior. Any such project is of course a tall order. It requires concerted field work by investigators at widely separated points on the globe.

Behavior in the Laboratory

Fortunately it is quite feasible to approach the innate motor patterns as an isolated topic for examination in the laboratory. Thanks to their stability they are not masked in the behavior of the

captive animal. If only we do not forget the existence of the many other physiological mechanisms that affect behavior, including that of learning, it is legitimate for us to begin with these innate behavior traits. The least variable part of a system is always the best one to examine first; in the complex interaction of all parts, it must appear most frequently as a cause and least frequently as an effect.

Comparative study of innate motor patterns represents an important part of the research program at the Max Planck Institute for Comparative Ethology. Our

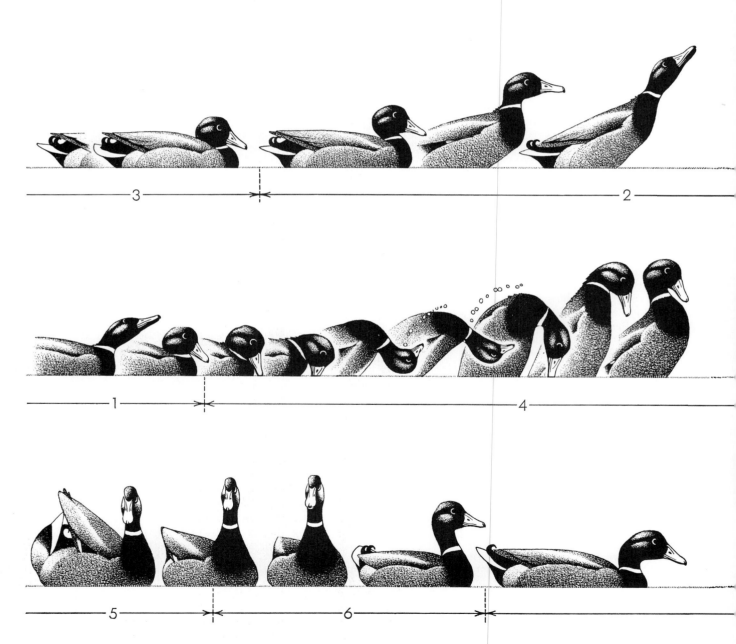

COURTSHIP SEQUENCES OF MALLARD are shown in this series of drawings, based on motion pictures made by the author at his laboratory in Seewiesen, Germany. Each sequence combines in fixed order several of the 10 innate courtship poses illustrated on

subjects are the various species of dabbling, or surface-feeding, ducks. By observing minute variations of behavior traits between species on the one hand and their hybrids on the other we hope to arrive at a phylogenetics of behavior.

Our comparative studies have developed sufficient information about the behavior traits of existing species to permit us to observe the transmission, suppression and combination of these traits in hybrid offspring. Ordinarily it is difficult to find species which differ markedly with respect to a particular characteristic and which yet will produce fertile hybrids. This is true especially with respect to behavioral traits, because these tend to be highly conservative. Species which differ sufficiently in behavior seldom produce offspring of unlimited fertility. However, closely related species which differ markedly in their patterns of sexual display are often capable of producing fertile hybrids. These motor patterns serve not only to bring about mating within a species but to prevent mating between closely allied species. Selection pressure sets in to make these patterns as different as possible as quickly as possible. As a result species will diverge markedly in sexual display behavior and yet retain the capacity to interbreed. This has turned out to be the case with dabbling ducks.

The first thing we wanted to know was how the courtship patterns of ducks become fixed. Credit is due to Sir Julian Huxley, who as long ago as 1914 had observed this process, which he called "ritualization." We see it clearly in the so-called "inciting" movement of female dabbling ducks, diving ducks, perching ducks and sheldrakes.

To see "inciting" in its original un-ritualized form, let us watch the female

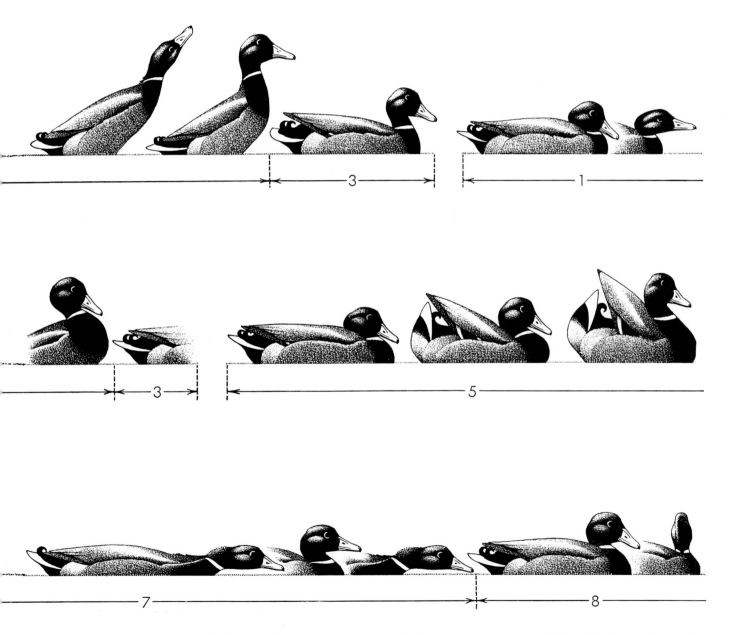

page 53. The numbers under the ducks refer to these poses. Shown here are the following obligatory sequences: tail-shake, head flick, tail-shake; bill-shake, grunt whistle, tail-shake; head-up tail-up, turn toward female, nod-swimming, turning back of the head.

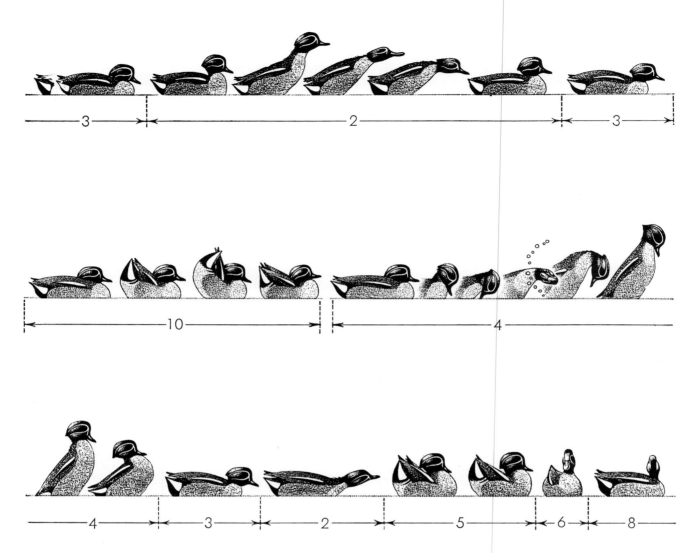

COURTSHIP OF EUROPEAN TEAL—another species of surface-feeding duck—includes tail-shake, head-flick, tail-shake (as in the mallard); down-up; grunt-whistle, tail-shake, head-flick, head-up–tail-up, turned toward the female, turning back of the head.

of the common sheldrake as she and her mate encounter another pair of sheldrakes at close quarters. Being far more excitable than her placid companion, the female attacks the "enemy" couple, that is, she adopts a threatening attitude and runs toward them at full tilt. It happens, however, that her escape reaction is quite as strong as her aggressive one. She has only to come within a certain distance of the enemy for the escape stimulus to overpower her, whereupon she turns tail and flees to the protection of her mate. When she has run a safe distance, she experiences a renewal of the aggressive impulse. Perhaps by this time she has retreated behind her mate. In that case she struts up beside him, and, as they both face the enemy, she makes threatening gestures toward them. But more likely she has not yet reached her mate when the aggressive impulse re-

turns. In that case she may stop in her tracks. With her body still oriented toward her mate, she will turn her head and threaten the enemy over her shoulder. In this stance she is said to "incite" an aggressive attitude in her partner.

Now the incitement posture of the female sheldrake does not constitute an innate behavior trait. It is the entirely plastic resultant of the pressure of two independent variables: her impulse to attack and her impulse to flee. The orientation of her head and body reflects the geometry of her position with respect to her mate and the enemy.

The same incitement posture in mallards, on the other hand, is distinctly ritualized. In striking her pose the female mallard is governed by an inherited motor pattern. She cannot help thrusting her head backward over her shoulder. She does this even if it means she must

point her bill away from the enemy! In the sheldrake this posture is the resultant of the creature's display of two conflicting impulses. In the mallard it has become a fixed motor pattern.

No doubt this motor pattern evolved fairly recently. It is interesting to note that while the female mallard is impelled to look over her shoulder when inciting, the older urge to look at the enemy is still there. Her head travels much farther backward when the enemy is behind her. If you observe closely, it is plain that her eyes are fixed on the enemy, no matter which way her head is turned.

Occasionally a female, impelled by the awkwardness of watching the enemy from the ritualized posture, will swing about and face them directly. In that case one may say that her old and new motor patterns are simultaneously active. Like the sheldrake, the mallard must once have faced the enemy during incitement. Overlying this instinct is a new one—to move her head backward over her shoulder regardless of the location of the enemy. The old orienting response survives in part. It usually displays itself at low levels of excitement. Especially at the beginning of a response, the female

mallard may stretch her neck straight forward. As her excitement mounts, however, the new motor pattern irresistibly draws her head around. This is one of many instances in which the mounting intensity of a stimulus increases the fixity of the motor coordination.

What has happened is that two inde-

pendent movements have been welded together to form a new and fixed motor pattern. It is possible that all new patterns are formed by such a welding process. Sometimes two patterns remain rigidly welded. Sometimes they weld only under great excitement.

Recently we have been studying be-

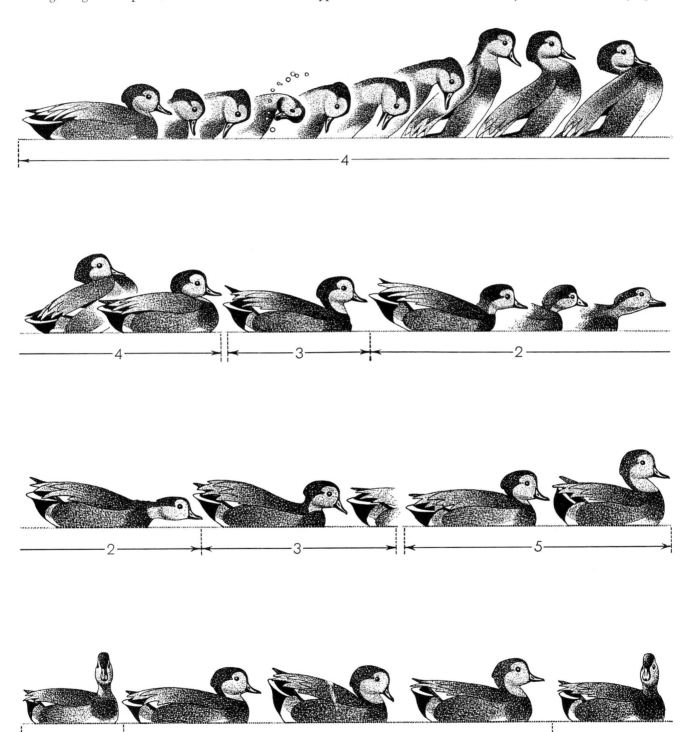

GADWALL COURTSHIP includes the grunt-whistle, always followed by the tail-shake, head-flick, tail-shake sequence also found in the other species illustrated. The head-up–tail-up (5) and the down-up (10) are always followed by a turn toward the female (6). During the most intense excitement of the courtship display, these pairs themselves become welded into the invariable sequence 5-6-10-6

havior complexes in which more than two patterns are welded. In their courtship behavior our surface-feeding ducks display some 20 elementary innate motor patterns. We have made a special study of three species which have 10 motor patterns in common but display them welded into different combinations. As shown in the illustration on page 53, these patterns are (1) initial bill-shake, (2) head-flick, (3) tail-shake, (4) grunt-whistle, (5) head-up—tail-up, (6) turn toward the female, (7) nod-swimming, (8) turning the back of the head, (9) bridling, (10) down-up movement. Some of the combinations in which these motor patterns are displayed are shown on pages 54 through 57. In some species certain of the patterns occur independently (*e.g.*, 1 and 10 in the mallard). Some simple combinations have wide distribution in other species as well (*e.g.*,

4, 3 and 5, 6 in all the species). Many combinations are more complicated, as the illustrations show.

What happens when these ducks are crossbred? By deliberate breeding we have produced new combinations of motor patterns, often combining traits of both parents, sometimes suppressing the traits of one or the other parent and sometimes exhibiting traits not apparent in either. We have even reproduced some of the behavior-pattern combinations which occur in natural species other than the parents of the hybrid. Study of our first-generation hybrids indicates that many differences in courtship patterns among our duck species may also be due to secondary loss, that is, to suppression of an inherited trait. Crosses between the Chiloe teal and the Bahama pintail regularly perform the head-up—tail-up, although neither parent is ca-

pable of this. The only possible conclusion is that one parent species is latently in possession of this behavioral trait, and that its expression in a given species is prevented by some inhibiting factor. So far our only second-generation hybrids are crosses between the Chiloe pintail and the Bahama pintail. The results look promising. The drakes of this generation differ greatly from each other and display hitherto unheard-of combinations of courtship patterns. One has even fused the down-up movement with the grunt-whistle!

Thus we have shown that the differences in innate motor patterns which distinguish species from one another can be duplicated by hybridization. This suggests that motor patterns are dependent on comparatively simple constellations of genetic factors.

6

EARLY ENVIRONMENT

WILLIAM R. THOMPSON AND RONALD MELZACK

January 1956

The child, as the poets say, "is father of the man," but we still know all too little about how the child is molded. It is a controversial as well as an interesting subject. Is intelligence, for instance, determined solely by heredity or can it be modified by the child's early environment? Although this question has been much studied, the evidence is ambiguous. And our understanding of the formation of the child's personality and emotional pattern is even more uncertain.

We do have some clear and definite information about the development of lower animals. While animals do not necessarily behave like human beings, experimental studies of them can shed light on basic reactions of organisms to their environment. From them a psychologist hopes to derive ideas which will help in studies of human beings.

The study we shall describe represents an attempt to find out how an animal is affected by severe restriction of its opportunities for development and learning during its first few months of life. Our subjects were Scottish terriers. We were interested in learning whether early upbringing in a barren environment would have permanent effects upon the dogs' intelligence, activity, emotional reactions and social behavior. The research was carried out over a period of five years in the psychological laboratory of McGill University with the help of a Rockefeller Foundation grant.

As soon as each litter of Scotties was weaned (at the age of four weeks), it was divided into two groups. One group was then raised normally as controls: the dogs were either farmed out to Montreal families or, in a few cases, reared as free pups in the laboratory. The members of the other group, who served as the experimental subjects, were all confined in cages—one dog to a cage. The cage was closed in with opaque sides and in some cases an opaque top, so that the dog could not see outside. Each day its food was placed in a small adjoining box with a sliding door. The door was opened from outside to let the dog into its "dining" room; then it was closed and the cage was cleaned. Thus the dog never saw its keepers.

The experimental animals lived in this blank, isolated environment until they were between seven and 10 months old. At the end of that time they were let out and given the same handling and daily exercise as the controls, which were brought back from their homes to the laboratory. The two groups were then observed and given various psychological tests.

It was immediately obvious even to a casual observer that restriction had had a profound and surprising effect on the experimental Scotties. After their release these dogs were exceptionally active and playful, showing a puppylike exuberance that belied their physical maturity. This behavior was almost opposite to what one might have expected, because it is commonly supposed that early separation from contacts with others has a depressing effect. Visitors to the laboratory, on being asked to pick out the restricted dogs from those raised normally, almost invariably chose the more sedate and subdued normal dogs.

We designed several tests to measure the Scotties' activity level systematically. In the first, each animal was put into a small room and observed for 30 minutes to see how much time it spent exploring the room, as opposed to merely sitting or lying down. This test was given four times, on four consecutive days, to seven normal and 11 restricted dogs. The normal dogs soon became bored with the monotony of the room and quietly relaxed, but those that had had a restricted upbringing went on exploring for a considerably longer time.

The amount of activity also varied inversely with age. Older dogs became bored much more readily than younger animals. This supports the idea that the behavior of the experimentals was a sign of immaturity.

In a second activity test, the experimental and the normal Scotties were invited to explore a maze. They were observed for four 10-minute sessions. At first both groups were equally curious. But the novelty of the situation wore off much more quickly for the normal animals, and their exploratory inspection of the maze rapidly declined, whereas the dogs that had been starved of experience in their early lives continued to run about in it more actively. Even several years after they had left their early cages, experimental Scotties still showed more activity in the tests than normally raised dogs of the same age—an indication that the effects of their early restriction were enduring.

These findings should not be interpreted to mean that maturity or a rich early life dulls curiosity. Rather they decrease over-curiosity. They produce an animal which is just as curious about any new situation, but which has the means to satisfy its curiosity quickly. In other words, the experienced animal exhibits more intelligence. There may be something delightful about a child who can spend an hour completely absorbed in a clothespin, but this is not intelligent, adult behavior.

We next examined the Scotties' emotional behavior. The severely limited early upbringing of the experimental dogs gave us a good opportunity to investigate the origin of so-called "irrational" or "spontaneous" fears, which have recently attracted much attention from psychologists.

It used to be thought that all fears of objects or stimuli were "conditioned"—an idea espoused by the behaviorist John B. Watson. The association of pain, a fall or a loud noise with an object may cause a child to fear it thereafter, even if the object is harmless. But many psychologists now are convinced that there is a type of fear which cannot be explained in terms of conditioning. Fear may be evoked simply by the unusual or the unexpected—a leaf suddenly swirling past one's face on a dark country road, a knock on a window at night, any mysterious happening or behavior. There is a classic case of a three-year-old girl who was severely frightened by her father when he dressed up as an elephant, even though she knew it was her father. D. O. Hebb of McGill University, investigating this type of fear systematically in chimpanzees, has found that they often show violent fear at the first sight of a strange person, a skull, a snake or a death mask of another chim-

panzee. Charles Darwin long ago noticed the same phenomenon in dogs: in *The Descent of Man* he described how he had watched his dog avoid an open parasol being blown along the lawn by a breeze and had speculated on the dog's behavior. Darwin thought the dog must have reasoned unconsciously to itself "that movement without apparent cause indicated the presence of some strange living agent." It is doubtful that Darwin's dog, even after long association with a genius, could have reasoned in this way. Nonetheless, the significant fact Darwin recognized was that an animal with a highly developed brain may fear the mysterious.

Are such fears "innate" or developed? Helen Mahut of McGill University tested the reactions of various breeds of dogs, all reared normally, to certain harmless but emotion-evoking objects, and she discovered that each breed responded to these objects in a characteristic way. Thus the emotional behavior clearly must have some hereditary basis. Yet we can hardly assume that an animal

is born with innate fears of specific objects or people. Obviously the animal's experiences determine to a large degree what is unusual and what is not. With our experimental Scotties, whose early experience had been extremely meager, we had an excellent opportunity to study the interaction of heredity and learning in determining emotional behavior.

About three weeks after the restricted dogs had been released from their cages, we exposed them to various strange phenomena, such as a human skull, a slowly swelling balloon, an opening umbrella and so on. Normally-reared young Scotties usually run away from such objects, without showing much excitement. But the restricted Scotties behaved very differently. They became highly agitated, jumped back and forth near the object, whirled around it, "stalked" it and generally displayed much excitement but little purposeful activity. Their behavior may be called "diffuse" or "undifferentiated"—they appeared not to know what to do about the object.

A year later the restricted and normal

EXPERIMENTAL SCOTTIES were placed after weaning in a closed cage, the front of which is cut away in this drawing. They remained in the cage until they had reached an age of seven to 10 months. The cage has two compartments for feeding and cleaning.

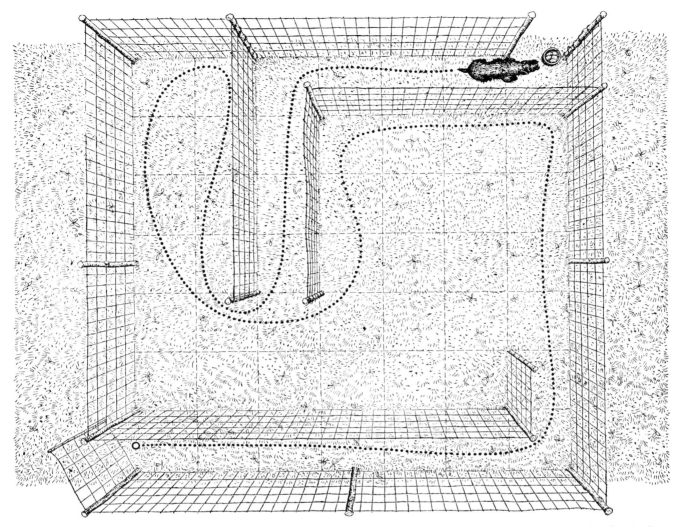

MAZE was used to compare the curiosity of normal and restricted Scotties. The dogs were released at lower left and encouraged to find the food at upper right. The performance of each animal was scored by tabulating the number of times it entered an "error zone."

dogs were again tested with the same objects. The normal dogs now added a new response to their earlier avoidance: they attacked the object with a playful aggression—growling, barking, snapping and sometimes biting. The restricted dogs still showed considerable excitement of a diffuse kind, but they had also developed a purposeful pattern of avoidance. That is to say, they had reached a stage of response somewhat like that which the normal dogs had achieved a year earlier.

The experiment indicated that the hereditary pattern of adaptive emotional behavior, such as avoidance and aggression, emerges only after an animal has had considerable experience with a stimulating environment, acquired over a long period. Without such experience, the animal expends a great deal of undirected and ineffectual energy.

This experiment led to an even more interesting question: How will an animal deprived of experience respond to a stimulus which is painful rather than harmless? Is avoidance of pain a simple reflex reaction that comes naturally to any animal, as many psychologists have long assumed? Further experiments showed in the clearest possible fashion that it is not.

In one of these experiments the dogs were pursued by a toy car which gave them an electric shock when it hit them. Normal dogs quickly learned to avoid being hit. After six shocks, on the average, the experimenter no longer was able to touch them with the car. Moreover, they reacted to the threat calmly and deliberately: they sat watching the car, flicked aside a leg or the tail to avoid it, and jumped up to run away only at the last moment when the car came directly at them.

In contrast, the restricted dogs behaved wildly and aimlessly. They jumped about, galloped in circles and actually ran into the car when it was held still in their path. It took these dogs an average of 25 shocks each to learn to avoid the car, and even then they became excited whenever they saw it. Two of the experimental dogs were subjected to the test again two years after they had been released from restriction. They still reacted to the electric shock with the same wild agitation, and one of them learned to avoid the car only after 23 shocks.

In this and other tests of their responses to painful stimuli, some of which could have injured them seriously, most of the restricted dogs behaved as if they were unaware that the source of the pain was in the environment; they might have reacted in the same way to a bellyache. Whereas normal dogs usually dashed away from the pain-causing object, the restricted dogs spent considerably more time around it after they had been hurt than before. To the astonishment of the experimenters, these dogs often toyed with a painful stimulus and frequently walked into it. For example, they repeatedly struck their heads against some water pipes along the walls in one of the testing rooms: one dog banged his head against these pipes more than 30 times, by actual count, in a single hour. The dogs gave no sign of pain when they ran into the pipes.

These experiments support a great deal of other recent evidence that pain-avoidance is by no means the simple protective "instinct" it was long thought to be. It is not a mere matter of nerve stimulation and response. Both the perception of pain and the response to it are complex processes, in which the brain plays an important part. The appropriate response to pain is acquired, at least in part, by learning. And if an animal does not learn it in infancy, apparently it is unlikely ever to achieve the calm, precise response of a normal adult.

We made a number of direct tests of the restricted dogs' intelligence, or problem-solving ability. In one simple test the dogs were first trained to get food by running along a wall of a room from one corner to the next. Then the experimenter placed the food in some other corner of the room. This was done in full sight of the dog, and the experimenter called emphatic attention to the new position by banging the food pan on the floor. A normal dog usually ran straight to the new position. But the restricted dogs almost invariably ran pell-mell toward the old corner; at best they might veer off before they reached it and get to the correct goal by a roundabout route. In a variation of this test, a chicken-wire barrier was placed in front of the food to see whether the dog would be intelligent enough to go around the barrier. Again the restricted animals showed strikingly unintelligent behavior. Normal dogs usually learned to go around after one or two trials, but the puppylike restricteds repeatedly dashed up to the barrier, pawed at it and tried to push their muzzles through the mesh in a vain and frantic attempt to get at the food.

A more difficult delayed-response test measured the Scotties' ability to note and remember the location of food. Each dog was allowed to watch the experimenter put some food in one of a pair of boxes and to sniff the food. The dog was taken away and then released after a short time to test whether he would remember the correct box. Normal dogs, on the average, were able to choose the food box consistently after delays of up to four minutes. But the restricted dogs, as a rule, could not select the correct box

TOY AUTOMOBILE which could be controlled remotely by the experimenter was fitted with prongs through which the Scotties would receive a mild electric shock. The normal dog (*top*) quickly learned to avoid the automobile without excitement. The restricted dog (*bottom*) took much longer to learn this lesson, and was excited when it saw the automobile.

reliably even when they were released without any delay at all.

The final test was a set of 18 different maze problems. The Scotties were scored on the number of errors they made and the time it took them to solve each maze and reach the food at the end of it. Two features of this series of tests seem to us especially noteworthy. In the first place, the 18 different mazes tested a wide range of abilities. And secondly, all the dogs were trained beforehand on simpler mazes so that they had practice and were proficient in solving the maze type of problem. This meant that the conditions were analogous to those obtaining in human intelligence tests, for the persons taking them have had previous training in answering questions of the sort asked in the test. Just as in testing human intelligence, one can hardly expect to appraise an animal's intelligence properly by presenting it with a single problem of a kind it has never encountered before, as is often done in laboratory maze tests.

As we expected, the restricted Scotties' performance on the 18 maze problems was substantially inferior to that of their normally reared littermates. They made about 50 per cent more errors on

the series of problems. Even dogs which had been out of restriction for several years scored lower than their contemporaries, which seems to indicate that the retardation imposed by their early restriction was more or less permanent.

Having examined the effects of a barren early upbringing on the dogs' activity, emotionality and intelligence, we were curious to know how it would shape their social behavior. The social life of dogs is rather elementary compared with that of human beings. As any dog-owner can testify, the domestic dog is not a particularly social animal, as far as association with others of its own kind is concerned. Yet dogs certainy do interact socially when they have the opportunity. Their social behavior is determined partly by heredity (some breeds are notoriously more aggressive than others) and partly by upbringing.

We first studied the effect of a restricted upbringing on the trait of dominance (or submissiveness). The test situation was simple: a restricted dog and a normally raised dog were allowed to compete for a bone. Almost without exception the normal dogs dominated the restricted animals in this competi-

tion. Upbringing even overcame the powerful factor of seniority, for normal animals dominated the restricted ones that were considerably older.

The dogs were also compared on a test designed to measure "sociability." Each subject was released in a large room containing two other dogs, enclosed in separate chicken-wire pens in opposite corners of the room. The subject's interest in socializing was not difficult to measure. A sociable subject typically would approach one of the pens, stare at the animal inside, wag its tail and bark. Others ignored the occupants of the pens and sometimes even urinated on a pen as if there were no one inside. Our measure of sociability was the amount of time spent by the subject in taking social notice of the penned dogs during a 10-minute session.

In this test the normal Scotties proved to be much more sociable than those with a restricted upbringing. The latter paid little attention to the dogs in the pens, especially during the first session, and spent most of their time exploring the room itself. They were apparently a great deal more interested in the inanimate physical aspects of the room than in its live occupants. This lack of interest in companionship persisted years after the experimental dogs had been released from their early restriction.

The experiments we have described clearly indicate that a rich and stimulating environment in early life is an important condition for normal development. Restriction of experience during this crucial period can result in enduring retardation of an animal in various psychological traits. It must be emphasized that our studies of Scotties have little specific bearing on human beings, for the environmental situations are drastically different. But the experiments bring out clearly that any animal needs varied sensory stimulation in order to develop normally, just as it needs food and drink. This is a fact that has frequently been neglected by psychologists. It has long been assumed, either explicitly or implicitly, that all behavior is governed by a basic need to minimize tensions and disturbances in order to preserve the stability of the organism. This is evidently not so. Organisms like to be disturbed (as by an exciting novel, climbing a mountain and so on). And indeed they cannot live normally and fully if they are not. Especially during the early, plastic period of life, they must have a good deal of stimulation in their environment. If they do not, they may remain forever immature.

IRRATIONAL FEARS of normal and restricted dogs were compared by exposing them to an emotion-evoking object such as an opening umbrella. Here again the normal dog (*background*) soon accepted the object, while the restricted dog continued to be frightened by it.

7

THE REPRODUCTIVE BEHAVIOR OF RING DOVES

DANIEL S. LEHRMAN
November 1964

In recent years the study of animal behavior has proceeded along two different lines, with two groups of investigators formulating problems in different ways and indeed approaching the problems from different points of view. The comparative psychologist traditionally tends first to ask a question and then to attack it by way of animal experimentation. The ethologist, on the other hand, usually begins by observing the normal activity of an animal and then seeks to identify and analyze specific behavior patterns characteristic of the species.

The two attitudes can be combined. The psychologist can begin, like the ethologist, by watching an animal do what it does naturally, and only then ask questions that flow from his observations. He can go on to manipulate experimental conditions in an effort to discover the psychological and biological events that give rise to the behavior under study and perhaps to that of other animals as well. At the Institute of Animal Behavior at Rutgers University we have taken this approach to study in detail the reproductive-behavior cycle of the ring dove (*Streptopelia risoria*). The highly specific changes in behavior that occur in the course of the cycle, we find, are governed by complex psycho-

REPRODUCTIVE-BEHAVIOR CYCLE begins soon after a male and a female ring dove are introduced into a cage containing nest- ing material (hay in this case) and an empty glass nest bowl (*1*). Courtship activity, on the first day, is characterized by the "bowing

  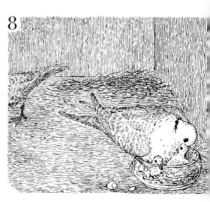

CYCLE CONTINUES as the adult birds take turns incubating the eggs (*6*), which hatch after about 14 days (*7*). The newly hatched squabs are fed "crop-milk," a liquid secreted in the gullets of the adults (*8*). The parents continue to feed them, albeit reluctantly,

biological interactions of the birds' inner and outer environments.

The ring dove, a small relative of the domestic pigeon, has a light gray back, creamy underparts and a black semicircle (the "ring") around the back of its neck. The male and female look alike and can only be distinguished by surgical exploration. If we place a male and a female ring dove with previous breeding experience in a cage containing an empty glass bowl and a supply of nesting material, the birds invariably enter on their normal behavioral cycle, which follows a predictable course and a fairly regular time schedule. During the first day the principal activity is courtship: the male struts around, bowing and cooing at the female. After several hours the birds announce their selection of a nest site (which in nature would be a concave place and in our cages is the glass bowl) by crouching in it and uttering a distinctive coo. Both birds participate in building the nest, the male usually gathering material and carrying it to the female, who stands in the bowl and constructs the nest. After a week or more of nest-building, in the course of which the birds copulate, the female becomes noticeably more attached to the nest and difficult to dislodge; if one attempts to lift her off the nest, she may grasp it with her claws and take it along. This behavior usually indicates that the female is about to lay her eggs. Between seven and 11 days after the beginning of the courtship she produces her first egg, usually at about five o'clock in the afternoon. The female dove sits on the egg and then lays a second one, usually at about nine o'clock in the morning two days later. Sometime that day the male takes a turn sitting; thereafter the two birds alternate, the male sitting for about six hours in the middle of each day, the female for the remaining 18 hours a day.

In about 14 days the eggs hatch and the parents begin to feed their young "crop-milk," a liquid secreted at this stage of the cycle by the lining of the adult dove's crop, a pouch in the bird's gullet. When they are 10 or 12 days old, the squabs leave the cage, but they continue to beg for and to receive food from the parents. This continues until the squabs are about two weeks old, when the parents become less and less willing to feed them as the young birds gradually develop the ability to peck for grain on the floor of the cage. When the young are about 15 to 25 days old, the adult male begins once again to bow and coo; nest-building is resumed, a new clutch of eggs is laid and the cycle is repeated. The entire cycle lasts about six or seven weeks and—at least in our laboratory, where it is always spring because of controlled light and temperature conditions—it can continue throughout the year.

The variations in behavior that constitute the cycle are not merely casual or superficial changes in the birds' preoccupations; they represent striking changes in the overall pattern of activity and in the atmosphere of the breeding cage. At its appropriate stage each of the kinds of behavior I have described represents the predominant activity of the animals at the time. Furthermore, these changes in behavior are not just responses to changes in the external situation. The birds do not build the nest merely because the nesting material is available; even if nesting material is in the cage throughout the cycle, nest-building behavior is concentrated,

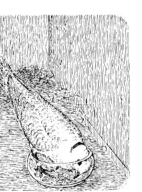

coo" of the male (2). The male and then the female utter a distinctive "nest call" to indicate their selection of a nesting site (3).

There follows a week or more of cooperation in nest-building (4), culminating in the laying of two eggs at precise times of day (5).

as the young birds learn to peck for grain themselves (9). When the squabs are between two and three weeks old, the adults ignore

them and start to court once again, and a new cycle begins (10). Physical changes during the cycle are shown on the next page.

as described, at one stage. Similarly, the birds react to the eggs and to the young only at appropriate stages in the cycle.

These cyclic changes in behavior therefore represent, at least in part, changes in the internal condition of the animals rather than merely changes in their external situation. Furthermore, the changes in behavior are associated with equally striking and equally pervasive changes in the anatomy and the physiological state of the birds. For example, when the female dove is first introduced into the cage, her oviduct weighs some 800 milligrams. Eight or nine days later, when she lays her first egg, the oviduct may weigh 4,000 milligrams. The crops of both the male and the female weigh some 900 milligrams when the birds are placed in the cage, and when they start to sit on the eggs some 10 days later they still weigh about the same. But two weeks afterward, when the eggs hatch, the parents' crops may weigh as much as 3,000 milligrams. Equally striking changes in the condition of the ovary, the weight of the testes, the length of the gut, the weight of the liver, the microscopic structure of the pituitary gland and other physiological indices are correlated with the behavioral cycle.

Now, if a male or a female dove is placed alone in a cage with nesting material, no such cycle of behavioral or anatomical changes takes place. Far from producing two eggs every six or seven weeks, a female alone in a cage lays no eggs at all. A male alone shows no interest when we offer it nesting material, eggs or young. The cycle of psychobiological changes I have described is, then, one that occurs more or less synchronously in each member of a pair of doves living together but that will not occur independently in either of the pair living alone.

In a normal breeding cycle both the male and the female sit on the eggs almost immediately after they are laid. The first question we asked ourselves was whether this is because the birds are always ready to sit on eggs or because they come into some special condition of readiness to incubate at about the time the eggs are produced.

We kept male and female doves in isolation for several weeks and then placed male-female pairs in test cages, each supplied with a nest bowl containing a normal dove nest with two eggs. The birds did not sit; they acted almost as if the eggs were not there. They courted, then built their own nest (usually on top of the planted nest and its eggs, which we had to keep fishing out to keep the stimulus situation constant!), then finally sat on the eggs—five to seven days after they had first encountered each other.

This clearly indicated that the doves are not always ready to sit on eggs; under the experimental conditions they changed from birds that did not want to incubate to birds that did want to incubate in five to seven days. What had induced this change? It could not have been merely the passage of time since their last breeding experience, because this had varied from four to six or more weeks in different pairs, whereas the variation in time spent in the test cage before sitting was only a couple of days.

Could the delay of five to seven days represent the time required for the birds to get over the stress of being handled and become accustomed to the strange cage? To test this possibility we placed pairs of doves in cages without any nest bowls or nesting material and separated each male and female by an opaque partition. After seven days we removed the partition and introduced nesting material and a formed nest with eggs. If the birds had merely needed time to recover from being handled and become acclimated to the cage, they should now have sat on the eggs immediately. They did not do so; they sat only after five to seven days, just as if they had been introduced into the cage only when the opaque partition was removed.

The next possibility we considered was that in this artificial situation stimulation from the eggs might induce the change from a nonsitting to a sitting "mood" but that this effect required five to seven days to reach a threshold value at which the behavior would change.

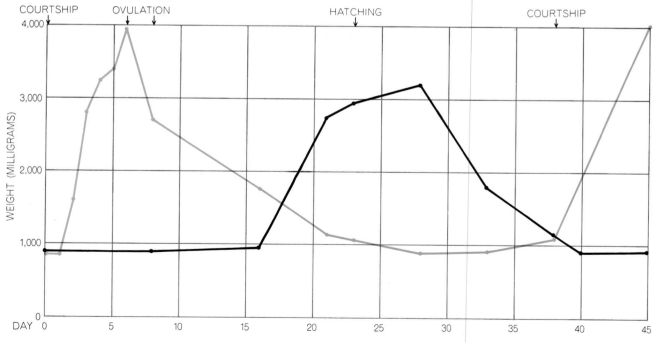

ANATOMICAL AND PHYSIOLOGICAL changes are associated with the behavioral changes of the cycle. The chart gives average weights of the crop (*black curve*) and the female oviduct (*color*) at various stages measured in days after the beginning of courtship.

We therefore placed pairs of birds in test cages with empty nest bowls and a supply of nesting material but no eggs. The birds courted and built nests. After seven days we removed the nest bowl and its nest and replaced it with a fresh bowl containing a nest and eggs. All these birds sat within two hours.

It was now apparent that some combination of influences arising from the presence of the mate and the availability of the nest bowl and nesting material induced the change from nonreadiness to incubate to readiness. In order to distinguish between these influences we put a new group of pairs of doves in test cages without any nest bowl or nesting material. When, seven days later, we offered these birds nesting material and nests with eggs, most of them did not sit immediately. Nor did they wait the full five to seven days to do so; they sat after one day, during which they engaged in intensive nest-building. A final group, placed singly in cages with nests and eggs, failed to incubate at all, even after weeks in the cages.

In summary, the doves do not build nests as soon as they are introduced into a cage containing nesting material, but they will do so immediately if the nesting material is introduced for the first time after they have spent a while together; they will not sit immediately on eggs offered after the birds have been in a bare cage together for some days, but they will do so if they were able to do some nest-building during the end of their period together. From these experiments it is apparent that there are two kinds of change induced in these birds: first, they are changed from birds primarily interested in courtship to birds primarily interested in nest-building, and this change is brought about by stimulation arising from association with a mate; second, under these conditions they are further changed from birds primarily interested in nest-building to birds interested in sitting on eggs, and this change is encouraged by participation in nest-building.

The course of development of readiness to incubate is shown graphically by the results of another experiment, which Philip N. Brody, Rochelle Wortis and I undertook shortly after the ones just described. We placed pairs of birds in test cages for varying numbers of days, in some cases with and in others without a nest bowl and nesting material. Then we introduced a nest and eggs into the cage. If neither bird sat within three hours, the test was scored as nega-

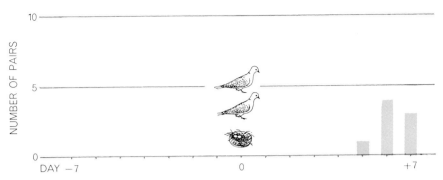

READINESS TO INCUBATE was tested with four groups of eight pairs of doves. Birds of the first group were placed in a cage containing a nest and eggs. They went through courtship and nest-building behavior before finally sitting after between five and seven days.

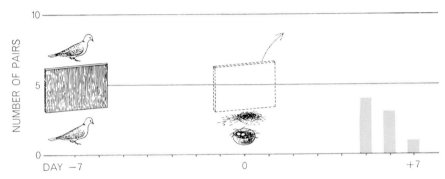

EFFECT OF HABITUATION was tested by keeping two birds separated for seven days in the cage before introducing nest and eggs. They still sat only after five to seven days.

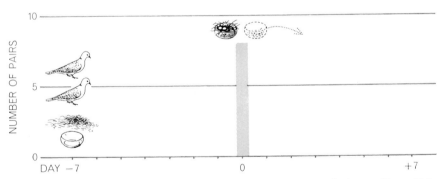

MATE AND NESTING MATERIAL had a dramatic effect on incubation-readiness. Pairs that had spent seven days in courtship and nest-building sat as soon as eggs were offered.

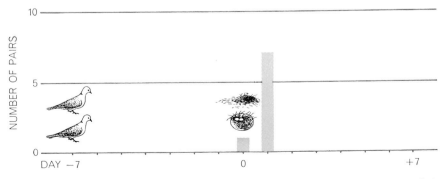

PRESENCE OF MATE without nesting activity had less effect. Birds that spent a week in cages with no nest bowls or hay took a day to sit after nests with eggs were introduced.

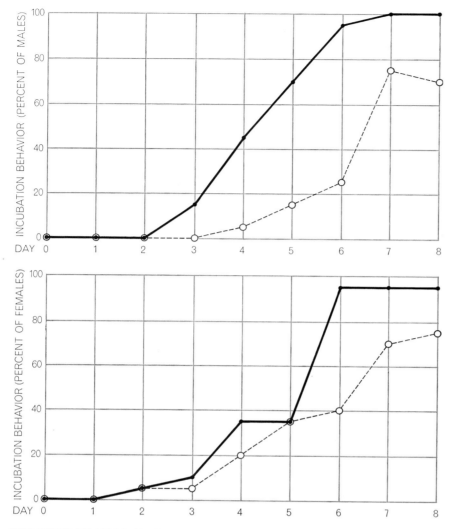

DURATION OF ASSOCIATION with mate and nesting material affects incubation behavior. The abscissas give the length of the association for different groups of birds. The plotted points show what percentage of each group sat within three hours of being offered eggs. The percentage increases for males (*top*) and females (*bottom*) as a function of time previously spent with mate (*open circles*) or with mate and nesting material (*solid dots*).

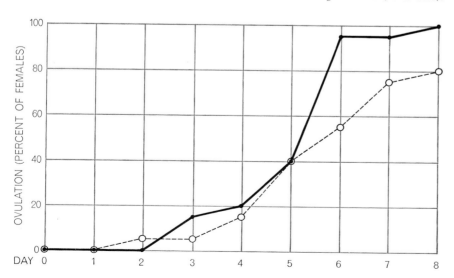

OVULATION is similarly affected. These curves, coinciding closely with those of the bottom chart above, show the occurrence of ovulation in the same birds represented there.

tive and both birds were removed for autopsy. If either bird sat within three hours, that bird was removed and the other bird was given an additional three hours to sit. The experiment therefore tested—independently for the male and the female—the development of readiness to incubate as a function of the number of days spent with the mate, with or without the opportunity to build a nest.

It is apparent [*see top illustration at left*] that association with the mate gradually brings the birds into a condition of readiness to incubate and that this effect is greatly enhanced by the presence of nesting material. Exposure to the nesting situation does not stimulate the onset of readiness to incubate in an all-or-nothing way; rather, its effect is additive with the effect of stimulation provided by the mate. Other experiments show, moreover, that the stimulation from the mate and nesting material is sustained. If either is removed, the incidence of incubation behavior decreases.

The experiments described so far made it clear that external stimuli normally associated with the breeding situation play an important role in inducing a state of readiness to incubate. We next asked what this state consists of physiologically. As a first approach to this problem we attempted to induce incubation behavior by injecting hormones into the birds instead of by manipulating the external stimulation. We treated birds just as we had in the first experiment but injected some of the birds with hormones while they were in isolation, starting one week before they were due to be placed in pairs in the test cages. When both members of the pair had been injected with the ovarian hormone progesterone, more than 90 percent of the eggs were covered by one of the birds within three hours after their introduction into the cage instead of five to seven days later. When the injected substance was another ovarian hormone—estrogen—the effect on most birds was to make them incubate after a latent period of one to three days, during which they engaged in nest-building behavior. The male hormone testosterone had no effect on incubation behavior.

During the 14 days when the doves are sitting on the eggs, their crops increase enormously in weight. Crop growth is a reliable indicator of the secretion of the hormone prolactin by the birds' pituitary glands. Since this growth coincides with the development of incubation behavior and culminates in the secretion of the crop-milk the birds feed to their young after the eggs hatch, Brody and I have recently examined the effect of injected prolactin on incubation behavior. We find that prolactin is not so effective as progesterone in inducing incubation behavior, even at dosage levels that induce full development of the crop. For example, a total prolactin dose of 400 international units induced only 40 percent of the birds to sit on eggs early, even though their average crop weight was about 3,000 milligrams, or more than three times the normal weight. Injection of 10 units of the hormone induced significant increases in crop weight (to 1,200 milligrams) but no increase in the frequency of incubation behavior. These results, together with the fact that in a normal breeding cycle the crop begins to increase in weight only after incubation begins, make it unlikely that prolactin plays an important role in the initiation of normal incubation behavior in this species. It does, however, seem to help to maintain such behavior until the eggs hatch.

Prolactin is much more effective in inducing ring doves to show regurgitation-feeding responses to squabs. When 12 adult doves with previous breeding experience were each injected with 450 units of prolactin over a seven-day period and placed, one bird at a time, in cages with squabs, 10 of the 12 fed the squabs from their engorged crops, whereas none of 12 uninjected controls did so or even made any parental approaches to the squabs.

This experiment showed that prolactin, which is normally present in considerable quantities in the parents when the eggs hatch, does contribute to the doves' ability to show parental feeding behavior. I originally interpreted it to mean that the prolactin-induced engorgement of the crop was necessary in order for any regurgitation feeding to take place, but E. Klinghammer and E. H. Hess of the University of Chicago have correctly pointed out that this was an error, that ring doves are capable of feeding young if presented with them rather early in the incubation period. They do so even though they have no crop-milk, feeding a mixture of regurgitated seeds and a liquid. We are now studying the question of how early the birds can do this and how this ability is related to the onset of prolactin secretion.

The work with gonad-stimulating hormones and prolactin demonstrates that the various hormones successively produced by the birds' glands during their reproductive cycle are capable of inducing the successive behavioral changes that characterize the cycle.

Up to this point I have described two main groups of experiments. One group demonstrates that external stimuli induce changes in behavioral status of a kind normally associated with the progress of the reproductive cycle; the second shows that these behavioral changes can also be induced by hormone administration, provided that the choice of hormones is guided by knowledge of the succession of hormone secretions during a normal reproductive cycle. An obvious—and challenging—implication of these results is that external stimuli may induce changes in hormone secretion, and that environment-induced hormone secretion may constitute an integral part of the mechanism of the reproductive behavior cycle. We have attacked the problem of the environmental stimulation of hormone secretion in a series of experiments in which, in addition to examining the effects of external stimuli on the birds' behavioral status, we have examined their effects on well-established anatomical indicators of the presence of various hormones.

Background for this work was provided by two classic experiments with the domestic pigeon, published during the 1930's, which we have verified in the ring dove. At the London Zoo, L. H. Matthews found that a female pigeon would lay eggs as a result of being placed in a cage with a male from whom she was separated by a glass plate. This was an unequivocal demonstration that visual and/or auditory stimulation provided by the male induces ovarian development in the female. (Birds are quite insensitive to olfactory stimulation.) And M. D. Patel of the University of Wisconsin found that the crops of breeding pigeons, which develop strikingly during the incubation period, would regress to their resting state if the incubating birds were removed from their nests and would fail to develop at all if the birds were removed before crop growth had begun. If, however, a male pigeon, after being removed from his nest, was placed in an adjacent cage from which he could see his mate still sitting on the eggs, his crop would develop just as if he were himself incubating! Clearly stimuli arising from participation in incubation, including visual stimuli, cause the doves' pituitary glands to secrete prolactin.

Our autopsies showed that the incidence of ovulation in females that had associated with males for various periods coincided closely with the incidence of incubation behavior [see bottom illustration on opposite page]; statistical analysis reveals a very high degree of association. The process by which the dove's ovary develops to the point of ovulation includes a period of estrogen secretion followed by one of progesterone secretion, both induced by appropriate ovary-stimulating hormones from the pituitary gland. We therefore conclude that stimuli provided by the male, augmented by the presence of the nest bowl and nesting material, induce the secretion of gonad-stimulating hormones by the female's pituitary, and that the onset of readiness to incubate is a result of this process.

As I have indicated, ovarian development, culminating in ovulation and egg-laying, can be induced in a female dove merely as a result of her seeing a male through a glass plate. Is this the result of the mere presence of another bird or of something the male does because he is a male? Carl Erickson and I have begun to deal with this question. We placed 40 female doves in separate cages, each separated from a male by a glass plate. Twenty of the stimulus animals were normal, intact males, whereas the remaining 20 had been castrated several weeks before. The intact males all exhibited vigorous bow-cooing immediately on being placed in the cage, whereas none of the castrates did so. Thirteen of the 20 females with intact males ovulated during the next seven days, whereas only two of those with the castrates did so. Clearly ovarian development in the female is not induced merely by seeing another bird but by seeing or hearing it act like a male as the result of the effects of its own male hormone on its nervous system.

Although crop growth, which begins early in the incubation period, is apparently stimulated by participation in incubation, the crop continues to be large and actively secreting for quite some time after the hatching of the eggs. This suggests that stimuli provided by the squabs may also stimulate prolactin secretion. In our laboratory Ernst Hansen substituted three-day-old squabs for eggs in various stages of incubation and after four days compared the adults' crop weights with those of birds that had continued to sit on their eggs dur-

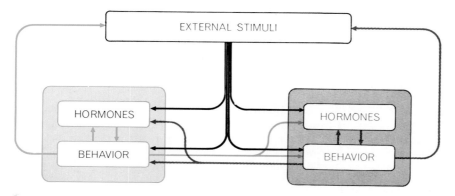

INTERACTIONS that appear to govern the reproductive-behavior cycle are suggested here. Hormones regulate behavior and are themselves affected by behavioral and other stimuli. And the behavior of each bird affects the hormones and the behavior of its mate.

ing the four days. He found that the crops grow even faster when squabs are in the nest than when the adults are under the influence of the eggs; the presence of squabs can stimulate a dove's pituitary glands to secrete more prolactin even before the stage in the cycle when the squabs normally appear.

This does not mean, however, that any of the stimuli we have used can induce hormone secretion at *any* time, regardless of the bird's physiological condition. If we place a pair of ring doves in a cage and allow them to go through the normal cycle until they have been sitting on eggs for, say, six days and we then place a glass partition in the cage to separate the male from the female and the nest, the female will continue to sit on the eggs and the male's crop will continue to develop just as if he were himself incubating. This is a simple replication of one of Patel's experiments. Miriam Friedman and I have found, however, that if the male and female are separated from the beginning, so that the female must build the nest by herself and sit alone from the beginning, the crop of the male does

not grow. By inserting the glass plate at various times during the cycle in different groups of birds, we have found that the crop of the male develops fully only if he is not separated from the female until 72 hours or more after the second egg is laid. This means that the sight of the female incubating induces prolactin secretion in the male only if he is in the physiological condition to which participation in nest-building brings him. External stimuli associated with the breeding situation do indeed induce changes in hormone secretion.

The experiments summarized here point to the conclusion that changes in the activity of the endocrine system are induced or facilitated by stimuli coming from various aspects of the environment at different stages of the breeding cycle, and that these changes in hormone secretion induce changes in behavior that may themselves be a source of further stimulation.

The regulation of the reproductive cycle of the ring dove appears to depend, at least in part, on a double set of reciprocal interrelations. First, there

is an interaction of the effects of hormones on behavior and the effects of external stimuli—including those that arise from the behavior of the animal and its mate—on the secretion of hormones. Second, there is a complicated reciprocal relation between the effects of the presence and behavior of one mate on the endocrine system of the other and the effects of the presence and behavior of the second bird (including those aspects of its behavior induced by these endocrine effects) back on the endocrine system of the first. The occurrence in each member of the pair of a cycle found in neither bird in isolation, and the synchronization of the cycles in the two mates, can now readily be understood as consequences of this interaction of the inner and outer environments.

The physiological explanation of these phenomena lies partly in the fact that the activity of the pituitary gland, which secretes prolactin and the gonad-stimulating hormones, is largely controlled by the nervous system through the hypothalamus. The precise neural mechanisms for any complex response are still deeply mysterious, but physiological knowledge of the brain-pituitary link is sufficiently detailed and definite so that the occurrence of a specific hormonal response to a specific external stimulus is at least no more mysterious than any other stimulus-response relation. We are currently exploring these responses in more detail, seeking to learn, among other things, the precise sites at which the various hormones act. And we have begun to investigate another aspect of the problem: the effect of previous experience on a bird's reproductive behavior and the interactions between these experiential influences and the hormonal effects.

8

THE ORIGIN OF FORM PERCEPTION

ROBERT L. FANTZ
May 1961

Long before an infant can explore his surroundings with hands and feet he is busy exploring it with his eyes. What goes on in the infant's mind as he stares, blinks, looks this way and that? Does he sense only a chaotic patchwork of color and brightness or does he perceive and differentiate among distinctive forms? The question has always fascinated philosophers and scientists, for it bears on the nature and origin of knowledge. At issue is the perennial question of nature v. nurture. On one side is the nativist, who believes that the infant has a wide range of innate visual capacities and predilections, which have evolved in animals over millions of years, and that these give a primitive order and meaning to the world from the "first look." On the other side is the extreme empiricist, who holds that the infant learns to see and to use what he sees only by trial and error or association, starting, as John Locke put it, with a mind like a blank slate.

It has long been known that very young infants can see light, color and movement. But it is often argued that they cannot respond to such stimuli as shape, pattern, size or solidity; in short, that they cannot perceive form. This position is the last stronghold of the empiricist, and it has been a hard one to attack. How is one to know what an infant sees? My colleagues and I have recently developed an experimental method of finding out. We have already disposed of the basic question, that of whether babies can perceive form at all. They can, at least to some degree, although it appears that neither the view of the simple nativist nor that of the simple empiricist tells the whole story. Now we are investigating the further question of how and when infants use their capacity to perceive form to confer order and meaning on their environment.

The technique grew out of studies with lower animals, which are of importance in themselves. They were undertaken in 1951 at the University of Chicago with newly hatched chicks. Paradoxically, chicks can "tell" more directly what they see than higher animals can. Soon after they break out of the shell they go about the business of finding things to peck at and eat. Their purposeful, visually dominated behavior is ideally suited for observation and experiment.

We presented the chicks with a number of small objects of different shapes.

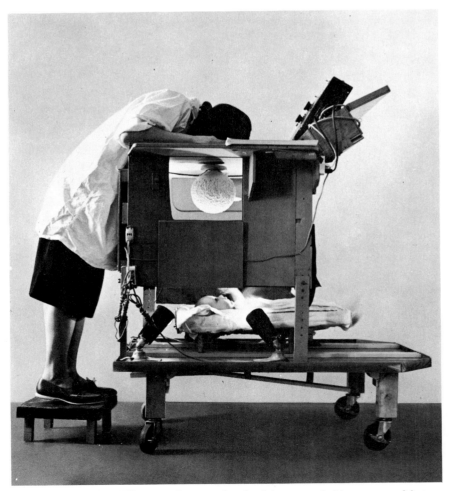

"LOOKING CHAMBER" was used to test the visual interests of chimpanzee and human infants. Here a human infant lies on a crib in the chamber, looking at objects hung from the ceiling. The observer, watching through a peephole, records the attention given each object.

Each object was enclosed in a clear plastic container to eliminate the possible influence of touch, smell or taste, but this did not prevent the chicks from pecking at preferred forms for hours on end. An electrical circuit attached to each container recorded the number of pecks at it.

More than 1,000 chicks were tested on some 100 objects. To exclude any opportunity for learning, the chicks were hatched in darkness and tested on their first exposure to light, before they had had any experience with real food. Presented with eight objects of graded angularity, from a sphere to a pyramid, the subjects pecked 10 times oftener at the sphere than they did at the pyramid. Among the flat forms, circles were preferred to triangles regardless of comparative size; among circles, those of ⅛-inch diameter drew the most attention. In a test of the effect of three-dimensionality the chicks consistently selected a sphere over a flat disk.

The results provided conclusive evidence that the chick has an innate ability to perceive shape, three-dimensionality and size. Furthermore, the chick uses the ability in a "meaningful" way by selecting, without learning, those objects most likely to be edible: round, three-dimensional shapes about the size of grain or seeds. Other birds exhibit similar visual capacity. For example, N. Tinbergen of the University of Oxford found selective pecking by newly hatched herring gulls. These chicks prefer shapes resembling that of the bill of the parent bird, from which they are fed [see "The Evolution of Behavior in Gulls," by N. Tinbergen; SCIENTIFIC AMERICAN Offprint 456].

Of course, what holds true for birds does not necessarily apply to human beings. The inherent capacity for form perception that has developed in birds may have been lost somewhere along the evolutionary branch leading to the primates, unlikely as it seems. Or, more plausibly, the primate infant may require a period of postnatal development to reach the level of function of the comparatively precocious chick.

When we set out to determine the visual abilities of helpless infants, the only indicator we could find was the activity of the eyes themselves. If an infant consistently turns its gaze toward some forms more often than toward others, it must be able to perceive form. Working on this premise, we developed a visual-interest test, using as our first subjects infant chimpanzees at the Yerkes Laboratories of Primate Biology in Orange Park, Fla.

A young chimpanzee lay on its back in a comfortable crib inside a "looking chamber" of uniform color and illumination. We attached to the ceiling of the chamber pairs of test objects, slightly separated from each other. They were exposed to view, alternately at right and left, in a series of short periods. Through a peephole in the ceiling we could see tiny images of the objects mirrored in the subjects' eyes. When the image of

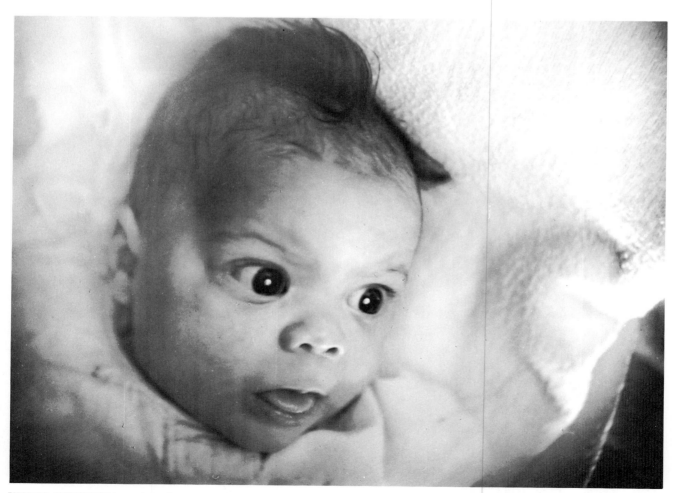

VISUAL INTEREST in various shapes was determined by noting reflections in the subject's eyes. In this case, with the reflection over the center of the infant's eye, the reflected object is being fixated, or looked at directly. (Because this young infant's binocular coordination is poor, only the right eye is fixating the object.) The length of each such fixation was recorded electrically.

one of the objects was at the center of the eye, over the pupil, we knew the chimpanzee was looking directly at it. The experimenter recorded on an electric timer the amount of attention given each target. The results were then analyzed to determine their statistical significance. Our first subject was a five-month-old chimpanzee. Later we followed a chimpanzee from birth, keeping it in darkness except during the tests. In both cases we found a definite preference for certain objects, indicating an inborn ability to distinguish among them.

Turning to human infants, we made no major change in our procedure except that we did not tamper with their everyday environment. The experiments did not disturb the infants but they did demand great patience of the investigators. Human infants are more rapidly bored than chimpanzees and they tend to go to sleep.

In the first experiment we tested 30 infants, aged one to 15 weeks, at weekly intervals. Four pairs of test patterns were presented in random sequence. In decreasing order of complexity they were: horizontal stripes and a bull's-eye design, a checkerboard and two sizes of plain square, a cross and a circle, and two identical triangles. The total time spent looking at the various pairs differed sharply, the more complex pairs drawing the greater attention. Moreover, the relative attractiveness of the two members of a pair depended on the presence of a pattern difference. There were strong preferences between stripes and bull's-eye and between checkerboard and square. Neither the cross and circle nor the two triangles aroused a significant differential interest. The differential response to pattern was shown at all ages tested, indicating that it was not the result of a learning process. The direction of preference between stripes and bull's-eye, on the other hand, changed at two months of age, due either to learning or to maturation.

Later we learned that a Swiss pediatrician, F. Stirnimann, had obtained similar results with still younger infants. He held cards up to the eyes of infants one to 14 days old and found that patterned cards were of more interest than those with plain colors.

Clearly some degree of form perception is innate. This, however, does not dispose of the role of physiological growth or of learning in the further development of visual behavior. Accordingly we turned our attention to the influence of these factors.

PATTERN PREFERENCE of newly hatched chicks is studied by recording their pecks at each of a number of different shapes in plastic containers set into the wall of a test box.

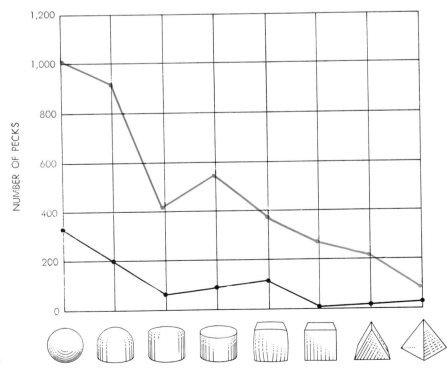

PREFERENCE FOR ROUNDNESS is shown by this record of total pecks by 112 chicks at the eight test objects shown across the bottom of the chart. The results are for the chicks' first 10 minutes (*black line*) and first 40 minutes (*colored line*) of visual experience.

By demonstrating the existence of form perception in very young infants we had already disproved the widely held notion that they are anatomically incapable of seeing anything but blobs of light and dark. Nevertheless, it seems to be true that the eye, the visual nerve-pathways and the visual part of the brain are poorly developed at birth. If this is so, then the acuteness of vision—the ability to distinguish detail in patterns—should increase as the infant matures.

To measure the change in visual acuity we presented infants in the looking chamber with a series of patterns composed of black and white stripes, each pattern paired with a gray square of equal brightness. The width of the stripes was decreased in graded steps from one pattern to the next. Since we already knew that infants tend to look longer and more frequently at a patterned object than at a plain one, the width of the stripes of the finest pattern that was preferred to gray would provide an index to visual acuity. In this modified version the visual-interest test again solved the difficulties involved in getting infants to reveal what they see.

The width of the finest stripes that could be distinguished turned out to decrease steadily with increasing age during the first half-year of life. By six months babies could see stripes 1/64 inch wide at a distance of 10 inches—a visual angle of five minutes of arc, or 1/12 degree. (The adult standard is one minute of arc.) Even when still less than a month old, infants were able to perceive ⅛-inch stripes at 10 inches, corresponding to a visual angle of a little less than one degree. This is poor performance compared to that of an adult, but it is a far cry from a complete lack of ability to perceive pattern.

The effects of maturation on visual acuity are relatively clear and not too hard to measure. The problem of learning is more subtle. Other investigators have shown that depriving animals of patterned visual stimuli for a period after birth impairs their later visual performance, especially in form perception [see "Arrested Vision," by Austin H. Riesen; SCIENTIFIC AMERICAN Offprint 408]. Learned behavior is particularly vulnerable, but even innate responses are affected. For example, chicks kept in darkness for several weeks after hatching lose the ability to peck at food.

Research is now under way at Western Reserve University on this perplexing problem. We have raised monkeys in darkness for periods varying from one to 11 weeks. In general, the longer the period of deprivation, the poorer the performance when the animals were finally exposed to light and the more time they required to achieve normal responses. When first brought into the light, the older infant monkeys bumped into things, fell off tables, could not locate objects visually—for all practical purposes they were blind. It sometimes took weeks for them to "learn to see."

Monkeys kept a shorter time in the dark usually showed good spatial orientation in a few hours or days. Moreover, they showed normal interest in patterned objects, whereas the animals deprived of light for longer periods seemed more interested in color, brightness and size.

These results cannot be explained by innate capacity, maturation or learning alone. If form perception were wholly innate, it would be evident without experience at any age, and visual deprivation would have no effect. If maturation were the controlling factor, younger infant animals would be inferior rather than superior to older ones with or without visual experience. If form perception were entirely learned, the same period of experience would be required regardless of age and length of deprivation.

Instead there appears to be a complex interplay of innate ability, maturation

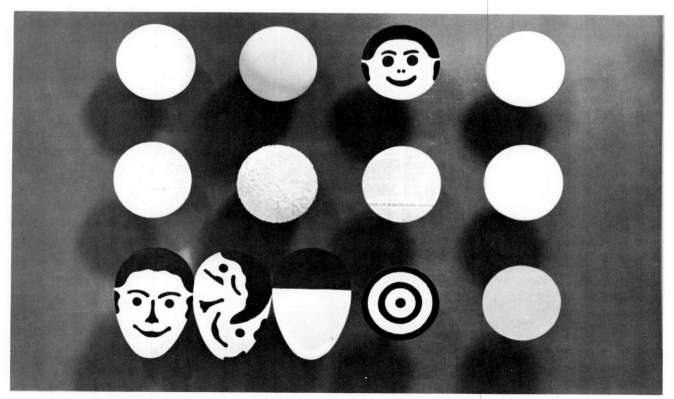

TEST OBJECTS included smooth and textured disks and spheres (*upper left*) to check interest in solidity. Attention to faces was tested with three patterns at lower left. The six round patterns at the right included (*top to bottom, left to right*) a face, a piece of printed matter, a bull's-eye, yellow, white and red disks. Round objects are six inches in diameter; "faces," nine inches long.

and learning in the molding of visual behavior, operating in this manner: there is a critical age for the development of a given visual response when the visual, mental and motor capacities are ready to be used and under normal circumstances will be used together. At that time the animal will either show the response without experience or will learn it readily. If the response is not "imprinted" at the critical age for want of visual stimulus, development proceeds abnormally, without the visual component. Presented with the stimulus later on, the animal learns to respond, if it responds at all, only with extensive experience and training. This explanation, if verified by further studies, would help to reconcile the conflicting claims of the nativist and the empiricist on the origin of visual perception.

To return to human infants, the work described so far does not answer the second question posed earlier in this article: whether or not the infant's innate capacity for form perception introduces a measure of order and meaning into what would otherwise be a chaotic jumble of sensations. An active selection process is necessary to sort out these sensations and make use of them in behavior. In the case of chicks such a process is apparent in the selection of forms likely to be edible.

In the world of the infant, people have an importance that is perhaps comparable to the importance of grain in the chick's world. Facial pattern is the most distinctive aspect of a person, the most reliable for distinguishing a human being from other objects and for identifying him. So a facelike pattern might be expected to bring out selective perception in an infant if anything could.

We tested infants with three flat objects the size and shape of a head. On one we painted a stylized face in black on a pink background, on the second we rearranged the features in a scrambled pattern, and on the third we painted a solid patch of black at one end with an area equal to that covered by all the features. We made the features large enough to be perceived by the youngest baby, so acuity of vision was not a factor. The three objects, paired in all possible combinations, were shown to 49 infants from four days to six months old.

The results were about the same for all age levels: the infants looked mostly at the "real" face, somewhat less often at the scrambled face, and largely ignored the control pattern. The degree of preference for the "real" face to the other one was not large, but it was

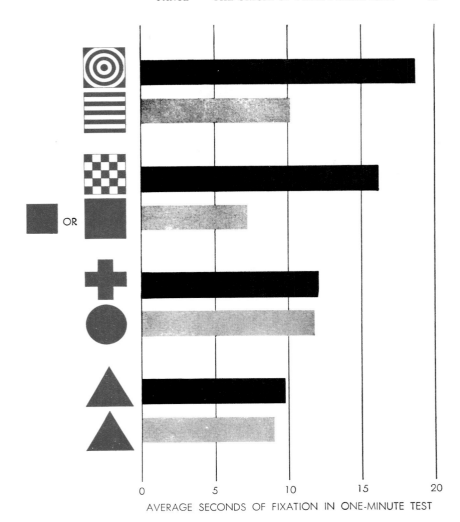

AVERAGE SECONDS OF FIXATION IN ONE-MINUTE TEST

INTEREST IN FORM was proved by infants' reactions to various pairs of patterns (*left*) presented together. (The small and large plain squares were used alternately.) The more complex pairs received the most attention, and within each of these pairs differential interest was based on pattern differences. These results are for 22 infants in 10 weekly tests.

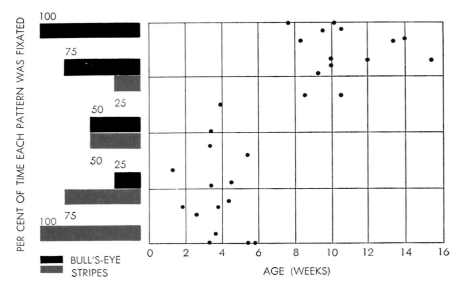

BULL'S-EYE
STRIPES

PER CENT OF TIME EACH PATTERN WAS FIXATED

AGE (WEEKS)

REVERSAL OF INTEREST from the striped pattern to the bull's-eye was apparent at two months of age. Each dot is for a single infant's first test session. It shows the time spent looking at the bull's-eye and at the stripes as a per cent of the time spent looking at both.

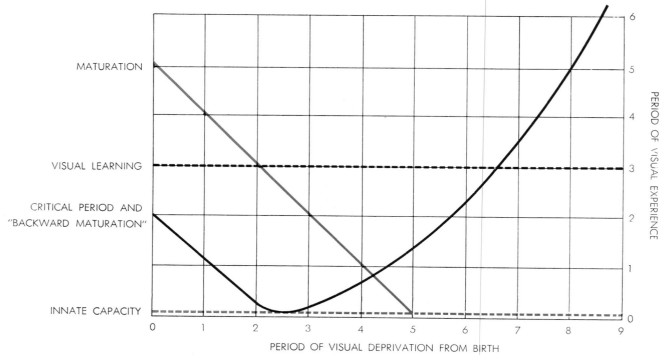

PERIOD OF VISUAL EXPERIENCE

PERIOD OF VISUAL DEPRIVATION FROM BIRTH

HYPOTHETICAL RESULTS that might be expected if any one developmental factor operated alone are plotted. The horizontal axis shows the period of rearing without visual experience; the vertical axis, the time subsequently required in the light until a given response is shown. Units of time are arbitrary. If innate capacity alone were effective, the response would always come without any experience (*broken colored line*). If maturation were necessary, the response would not be shown before a certain age, in this case five units, regardless of deprivation (*solid colored line*). If learning alone were operative, the required amount of experience would be constant (*broken black line*). Actually tests with chicks and monkey infants suggest the result shown by the solid black curve: after a short period of maturation, a "critical period" is reached when innate capacity can be manifested; more deprivation brings on "backward maturation," in which more and more experience is required before a response is shown.

consistent among individual infants, especially the younger ones. The experiment suggested that there is an unlearned, primitive meaning in the form perception of infants as well as of chicks.

Further support for the idea was obtained when we offered our infant subjects a choice between a solid sphere and a flat circle of the same diameter. When the texture and shading clearly differentiated the sphere from the circle —in other words, when there was a noticeable difference in pattern—the solid form was the more interesting to infants from one to six months old. This unlearned selection of a pattern associated with a solid object gives the infant a basis for perceiving depth.

The last experiment to be considered is a dramatic demonstration of the interest in pattern in comparison to color and brightness. This time there were six test objects: flat disks six inches in diameter. Three were patterned—a face, a bull's-eye and a patch of printed matter. Three were plain—red, fluorescent yellow and white. We presented them, against a blue background, one at a time in varied sequence and timed the length of the first glance at each.

The face pattern was overwhelmingly the most interesting, followed by the printing and the bull's-eye. The three brightly colored plain circles trailed far behind and received no first choices. There was no indication that the interest in pattern was secondary or acquired.

What makes pattern so intrinsically interesting to young infants? It seems to me that the answer must lie in the uses of vision for the child and adult.

One of these functions is the recognition of objects under various conditions. The color and brightness of objects

VISUAL ACUITY was tested with these stripes: 1/8, 1/16, 1/32 and 1/64 inch wide. Each pattern was displayed with a gray square of equal brightness 10 inches from the infants' eyes. The finest pattern consistently preferred to gray showed how narrow a stripe the infant could perceive. Infants under a month old could see the 1/8-inch stripes and the six-month-olds could see 1/64-inch stripes.

change with illumination; apparent size changes with distance; outline changes with point of view; binocular depth perception is helpful only at short range. But the pattern of an object—the texture, the arrangement of details, the complexity of contours—can be relied on for identification under diverse conditions.

A good example is social perception. As noted earlier, the general configuration of a face identifies a human being to an infant. At a later age a specific person is recognized primarily by more precise perception of facial pattern. Still later, subtle details of facial expression tell the child whether a person is happy or sad, pleased or displeased, friendly or unfriendly.

Another important function of vision is to provide orientation in space. For this purpose James J. Gibson of Cornell University has shown clearly the importance of a specific type of pattern: surface texture. For example, texture indicates a solid surface, whereas untextured light usually indicates air or water. Gradual changes in texture show whether a surface is vertical or horizontal or oblique, flat or curved or angular—and therefore indicate whether it can be walked on, walked around or climbed over. Discontinuities in texture mark the edges of objects and abrupt changes in surfaces.

From these few examples there can be no question of the importance of visual pattern in everyday life. It is therefore reasonable to suppose that the early interest of infants in form and pattern in general, as well as in particular kinds of pattern, play an important role in the development of behavior by focusing attention on stimuli that will later have adaptive significance.

Further research is necessary to pin down this and other implications more concretely, but the results to date do require the rejection of the view that the newborn infant or animal must start from scratch to learn to see and to organize patterned stimulation. Lowly chicks as well as lofty primates perceive and respond to form without experience if given the opportunity at the appropriate stage of development. Innate knowledge of the environment is demonstrated by the preference of newly hatched chicks for forms likely to be edible and by the interest of young infants in kinds of form that will later aid in object recognition, social responsiveness and spatial orientation. This primitive knowledge provides a foundation for the vast accumulation of knowledge through experience.

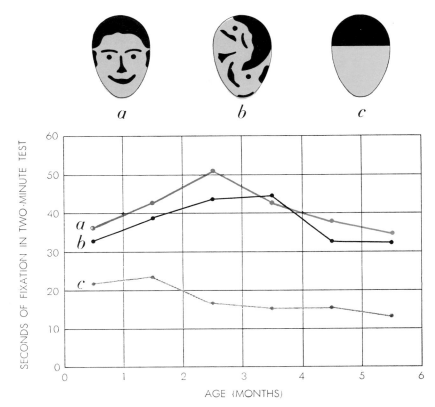

ADAPTIVE SIGNIFICANCE of form perception was indicated by the preference that infants showed for a "real" face (*a*) over a scrambled face (*b*), and for both over a control (*c*). The results charted here show the average time scores for infants at various ages when presented with the three face-shaped objects paired in all the possible combinations.

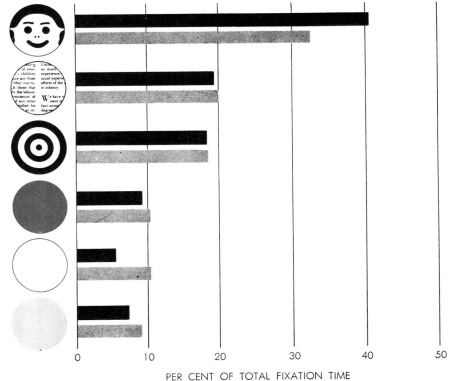

IMPORTANCE OF PATTERN rather than color or brightness was illustrated by the response of infants to a face, a piece of printed matter, a bull's-eye and plain red, white and yellow disks. Even the youngest infants preferred patterns. Black bars show the results for infants from two to three months old; gray bars, for infants more than three months old.

9

LOVE IN INFANT MONKEYS

HARRY F. HARLOW
June 1959

The first love of the human infant is for his mother. The tender intimacy of this attachment is such that it is sometimes regarded as a sacred or mystical force, an instinct incapable of analysis. No doubt such compunctions, along with the obvious obstacles in the way of objective study, have hampered experimental observation of the bonds between child and mother.

Though the data are thin, the theoretical literature on the subject is rich. Psychologists, sociologists and anthropologists commonly hold that the infant's love is learned through the association of the mother's face, body and other physical characteristics with the alleviation of internal biological tensions, particularly hunger and thirst. Traditional psychoanalysts have tended to emphasize the role of attaining and sucking at the breast as the basis for affectional development. Recently a number of child psychiatrists have questioned such simple explanations. Some argue that affectionate handling in the act of nursing is a variable of importance, whereas a few workers suggest that the composite activities of nursing, contact, clinging and even seeing and hearing work together to elicit the infant's love for his mother.

Now it is difficult, if not impossible, to use human infants as subjects for the studies necessary to break through the present speculative impasse. At birth the infant is so immature that he has little or no control over any motor system other than that involved in sucking. Furthermore, his physical maturation is so slow that by the time he can achieve precise, coordinated, measurable responses of his head, hands, feet and body, the nature and sequence of development have been hopelessly confounded and obscured. Clearly research into

the infant-mother relationship has need of a more suitable laboratory animal. We believe we have found it in the infant monkey. For the past several years our group at the Primate Laboratory of the University of Wisconsin has been employing baby rhesus monkeys in a study that we believe has begun to yield significant insights into the origin of the infant's love for his mother.

Baby monkeys are far better coordinated at birth than human infants. Their responses can be observed and evaluated with confidence at an age of 10 days or even earlier. Though they mature much more rapidly than their human contemporaries, infants of both species follow much the same general pattern of development.

Our interest in infant-monkey love grew out of a research program that involved the separation of monkeys from their mothers a few hours after birth. Employing techniques developed by Gertrude van Wagenen of Yale University, we had been rearing infant monkeys on the bottle with a mortality far less than that among monkeys nursed by their mothers. We were particularly careful to provide the infant monkeys with a folded gauze diaper on the floor of their cages, in accord with Dr. van Wagenen's observation that they would tend to maintain intimate contact with such soft, pliant surfaces, especially during nursing. We were impressed by the deep personal attachments that the monkeys formed for these diaper pads, and by the distress that they exhibited when the pads were briefly removed once a day for purposes of sanitation. The behavior of the infant monkeys was reminiscent of the human infant's attachment to its blankets, pillows, rag dolls or cuddly teddy bears.

These observations suggested the series of experiments in which we have sought to compare the importance of nursing and all associated activities with that of simple bodily contact in engendering the infant monkey's attachment to its mother. For this purpose we contrived two surrogate mother monkeys. One is a bare welded-wire cylindrical form surmounted by a wooden head with a crude face. In the other the welded wire is cushioned by a sheathing of terry cloth. We placed eight newborn monkeys in individual cages, each with equal access to a cloth and a wire mother [*see illustration on opposite page*]. Four of the infants received their milk from one mother and four from the other, the milk being furnished in each case by a nursing bottle, with its nipple protruding from the mother's "breast."

The two mothers quickly proved to be physiologically equivalent. The monkeys in the two groups drank the same amount of milk and gained weight at the same rate. But the two mothers proved to be by no means psychologically equivalent. Records made automatically showed that both groups of infants spent far more time climbing and clinging on their cloth-covered mothers than they did on their wire mothers. During the infants' first 14 days of life the floors of the cages were warmed by an electric heating pad, but most of the infants left the pad as soon as they could climb on the unheated cloth mother. Moreover, as the monkeys grew older, they tended to spend an increasing amount of time clinging and cuddling on her pliant terry-cloth surface. Those that secured their nourishment from the wire mother showed no tendency to spend more time on her than feeding required, contradicting the idea that affection is a response that is learned or derived in asso-

CLOTH AND WIRE MOTHER-SURROGATES were used to test the preferences of infant monkeys. The infants spent most of their time clinging to the soft cloth "mother," (*foreground*) even when nursing bottles were attached to the wire mother (*background*).

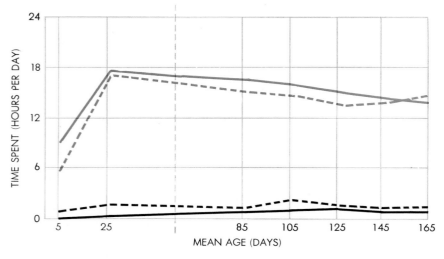

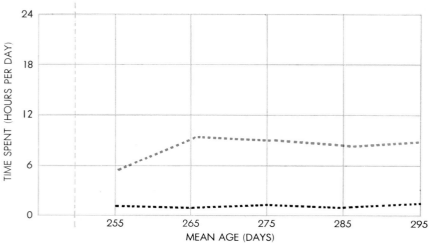

STRONG PREFERENCE FOR CLOTH MOTHER was shown by all infant monkeys. Infants reared with access to both mothers from birth (*top chart*) spent far more time on the cloth mother (*colored curves*) than on the wire mother (*black curves*). This was true regardless of whether they had been fed on the cloth (*solid lines*) or on the wire mother (*broken lines*). Infants that had known no mother during their first eight months (*bottom chart*) soon came to prefer cloth mother, but spent less time on her than the other infants.

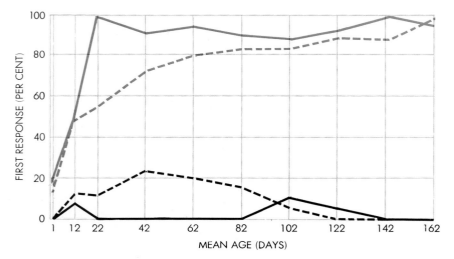

RESULTS OF "FEAR TEST" (*see photographs on opposite page*) showed that infants confronted by a strange object quickly learned to seek reassurance from the cloth mother (*colored curves*) rather than from the wire mother (*black curves*). Again infants fed on the wire mother (*broken lines*) behaved much like those fed on cloth mother (*solid lines*)

ciation with the reduction of hunger or thirst.

These results attest the importance—possibly the overwhelming importance—of bodily contact and the immediate comfort it supplies in forming the infant's attachment for its mother. All our experience, in fact, indicates that our cloth-covered mother surrogate is an eminently satisfactory mother. She is available 24 hours a day to satisfy her infant's overwhelming compulsion to seek bodily contact; she possesses infinite patience, never scolding her baby or biting it in anger. In these respects we regard her as superior to a living monkey mother, though monkey fathers would probably not endorse this opinion.

Of course this does not mean that nursing has no psychological importance. No act so effectively guarantees intimate bodily contact between mother and child. Furthermore, the mother who finds nursing a pleasant experience will probably be temperamentally inclined to give her infant plenty of handling and fondling. The real-life attachment of the infant to its mother is doubtless influenced by subtle multiple variables, contributed in part by the mother and in part by the child. We make no claim to having unraveled these in only two years of investigation. But no matter what evidence the future may disclose, our first experiments have shown that contact comfort is a decisive variable in this relationship.

Such generalization is powerfully supported by the results of the next phase of our investigation. The time that the infant monkeys spent cuddling on their surrogate mothers was a strong but perhaps not conclusive index of emotional attachment. Would they also seek the inanimate mother for comfort and security when they were subjected to emotional stress? With this question in mind we exposed our monkey infants to the stress of fear by presenting them with strange objects, for example a mechanical teddy bear which moved forward, beating a drum. Whether the infants had nursed from the wire or the cloth mother, they overwhelmingly sought succor from the cloth one; this differential in behavior was enhanced with the passage of time and the accrual of experience. Early in this series of experiments the terrified infant might rush blindly to the wire mother, but even if it did so it would soon abandon her for the cloth mother. The infant would cling to its cloth mother, rubbing its body against hers. Then, with its fears assuaged through intimate contact with the moth-

FRIGHTENING OBJECTS such as a mechanical teddy bear caused almost all infant monkeys to flee blindly to the cloth mother, as in the top photograph. Once reassured by pressing and rubbing against her, they would then look at the strange object (*bottom*).

"OPEN FIELD TEST" involved placing a monkey in a room far larger than its accustomed cage; unfamiliar objects added an additional disturbing element. If no mother was present, the infant would typically huddle in a corner (*left*). The wire mother did

er, it would turn to look at the previously terrifying bear without the slightest sign of alarm. Indeed, the infant would sometimes even leave the protection of the mother and approach the object that a few minutes before had reduced it to abject terror.

The analogy with the behavior of human infants requires no elaboration. We found that the analogy extends even to less obviously stressful situations. When a child is taken to a strange place, he usually remains composed and happy so long as his mother is nearby. If the mother gets out of sight, however, the child is often seized with fear and distress. We developed the same response in our infant monkeys when we exposed them to a room that was far larger than the cages to which they were accustomed. In the room we had placed a number of unfamiliar objects such as a small artificial tree, a crumpled piece of paper, a folded gauze diaper, a wooden block and a doorknob [*a similar experiment is depicted in the illustrations on these two pages*]. If the cloth mother was in the room, the infant would rush wildly to her, climb upon her, rub against her and cling to her tightly. As in the previous experiment, its fear then sharply diminished or vanished. The infant would begin to climb over the mother's body and to explore and manipulate her face. Soon it would leave the mother to investigate the new world, and the unfamiliar objects would become playthings. In a typical behavior sequence, the infant might manipulate the tree, return to the mother, crumple the wad of paper, bring it to the mother, explore the block, ex-

plore the doorknob, play with the paper and return to the mother. So long as the mother provided a psychological "base of operations" the infants were unafraid and their behavior remained positive, exploratory and playful.

If the cloth mother was absent, however, the infants would rush across the test room and throw themselves face-down on the floor, clutching their heads and bodies and screaming their distress. Records kept by two independent observers—scoring for such "fear indices" as crying, crouching, rocking and thumb- and toe-sucking—showed that the emotionality scores of the infants nearly tripled. But no quantitative measurement can convey the contrast between the positive, outgoing activities in the presence of the cloth mother and the stereotyped withdrawn and disturbed behavior in the motherless situation.

The bare wire mother provided no more reassurance in this "open field" test than no mother at all. Control tests on monkeys that from birth had known only the wire mother revealed that even these infants showed no affection for her and obtained no comfort from her presence. Indeed, this group of animals exhibited the highest emotionality scores of all. Typically they would run to some wall or corner of the room, clasp their heads and bodies and rock convulsively back and forth. Such activities closely resemble the autistic behavior seen frequently among neglected children in and out of institutions.

In a final comparison of the cloth and wire mothers, we adapted an experiment originally devised by Robert A. Butler

at the Primate Laboratory. Butler had found that monkeys enclosed in a dimly lighted box would press a lever to open and reopen a window for hours on end for no reward other than the chance to look out. The rate of lever-pressing depended on what the monkeys saw through the opened window; the sight of another monkey elicited far more activity than that of a bowl of fruit or an empty room [see the article "Curiosity in Monkeys," by Robert A. Butler, beginning on page 301]. We now know that this "curiosity response" is innate. Three-day-old monkeys, barely able to walk, will crawl across the floor of the box to reach a lever which briefly opens the window; some press the lever hundreds of times within a few hours.

When we tested our monkey infants in the "Butler box," we found that those reared with both cloth and wire mothers showed as high a response to the cloth mother as to another monkey, but displayed no more interest in the wire mother than in an empty room. In this test, as in all the others, the monkeys fed on the wire mother behaved the same as those fed on the cloth mother. A control group raised with no mothers at all found the cloth mother no more interesting than the wire mother and neither as interesting as another monkey.

Thus all the objective tests we have been able to devise agree in showing that the infant monkey's relationship to its surrogate mother is a full one. Comparison with the behavior of infant monkeys raised by their real mothers confirms this view. Like our experimental monkeys, these infants spend many

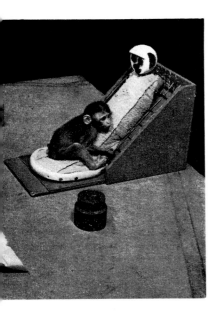 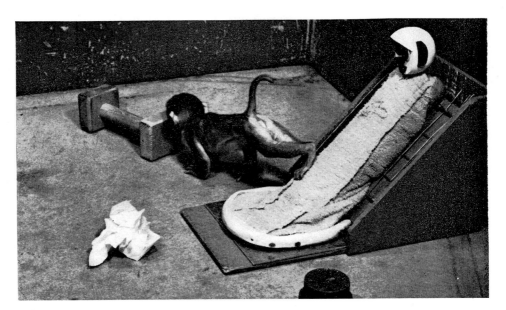

not alter this pattern of fearful behavior, but the cloth mother provided quick reassurance. The infant would first cling to her *(center)* and then set out to explore the room and play with the objects *(right)*, returning from time to time for more reassurance.

hours a day clinging to their mothers, and run to them for comfort or reassurance when they are frightened. The deep and abiding bond between mother and child appears to be essentially the same, whether the mother is real or a cloth surrogate.

While bodily contact clearly plays the prime role in developing infantile affection, other types of stimulation presumably supplement its effects. We have therefore embarked on a search for these other factors. The activity of a live monkey mother, for example, provides her infant with frequent motion stimulation. In many human cultures mothers bind their babies to them when they go about their daily chores; in our own culture parents know very well that rocking a baby or walking with him somehow promotes his psychological and physiological well-being. Accordingly we compared the responsiveness of infant monkeys to two cloth mothers, one stationary and one rocking. All of them preferred the rocking mother, though the degree of preference varied considerably from day to day and from monkey to monkey. An experiment with a rocking crib and a stationary one gave similar results. Motion does appear to enhance affection, albeit far less significantly than simple contact.

The act of clinging, in itself, also seems to have a role in promoting psychological and physiological well-being. Even before we began our studies of affection, we noticed that a newborn monkey raised in a bare wire cage survived with difficulty unless we provided it with a cone to which it could cling. Recently we have raised two groups of monkeys, one with a padded crib instead of a mother and the other with a cloth mother as well as a crib. Infants in the latter group actually spend more time on the crib than on the mother, probably because the steep incline of the mother's cloth surface makes her a less satisfactory sleeping platform. In the open-field test, the infants raised with a crib but no mother clearly derived some emotional support from the presence of the crib. But those raised with both showed an unequivocal preference for the mother they could cling to, and they evidenced the benefit of the superior emotional succor they gained from her.

Still other elements in the relationship remain to be investigated systematically. Common sense would suggest that the warmth of the mother's body plays its part in strengthening the infant's ties to her. Our own observations have not yet confirmed this hypothesis. Heating a cloth mother does not seem to increase her attractiveness to the infant monkey, and infants readily abandon a heating pad for an unheated mother surrogate. However, our laboratory is kept comfortably warm at all times; experiments in a chilly environment might well yield quite different results.

Visual stimulation may forge an additional link. When they are about three months old, the monkeys begin to observe and manipulate the head, face and eyes of their mother surrogates; human infants show the same sort of delayed responsiveness to visual stimuli. Such stimuli are known to have marked effects on the behavior of many young animals. The Austrian zoologist Konrad Lorenz has demonstrated a process called "imprinting"; he has shown that the young of some species of birds become attached to the first moving object they perceive, normally their mothers [see " 'Imprinting' in Animals," by Eckhard H. Hess; SCIENTIFIC AMERICAN, March, 1958]. It is also possible that particular sounds and even odors may play some role in the normal development of responses or attention.

The depth and persistence of attachment to the mother depend not only on the kind of stimuli that the young animal receives but also on when it receives them. Experiments with ducks show that imprinting is most effective during a critical period soon after hatching; beyond a certain age it cannot take place at all. Clinical experience with human beings indicates that people who have been deprived of affection in infancy may have difficulty forming affectional ties in later life. From preliminary experiments with our monkeys we have found that their affectional responses develop, or fail to develop, according to a similar pattern.

Early in our investigation we had segregated four infant monkeys as a general control group, denying them physical contact either with a mother surrogate or with other monkeys. After about eight months we placed them in cages with access to both cloth and wire mothers. At first they were afraid of both surrogates, but within a few days they began to respond in much the same way as the other infants. Soon they were

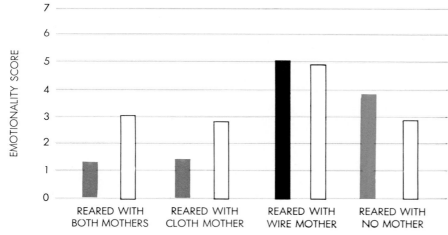

SCORES IN OPEN FIELD TEST show that all infant monkeys familiar with the cloth mother were much less disturbed when she was present (*color*) than when no mother was present (*white*); scores under 2 indicate unfrightened behavior. Infants that had known only the wire mother were greatly disturbed whether she was present (*black*) or not (*white*).

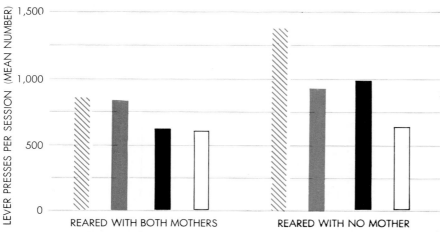

"CURIOSITY TEST" SHOWED THAT monkeys reared with both mothers displayed as much interest in the cloth mother (*solid color*) as in another monkey (*hatched color*); the wire mother (*black*) was no more interesting than an empty chamber (*white*). Monkeys reared with no mother found cloth and wire mother less interesting than another monkey.

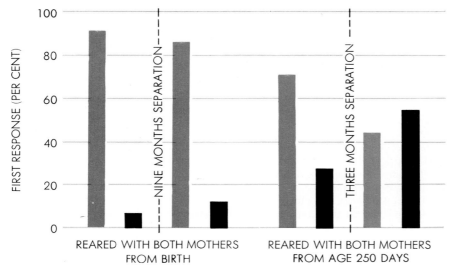

EARLY "MOTHERING" produced a strong and unchanging preference for the cloth mother (*color*) over the wire mother (*black*). Monkeys deprived of early mothering showed less marked preferences before separation and no significant preference subsequently.

spending less than an hour a day with the wire mother and eight to 10 hours with the cloth mother. Significantly, however, they spent little more than half as much time with the cloth mother as did infants raised with her from birth.

In the open-field test these "orphan" monkeys derived far less reassurance from the cloth mothers than did the other infants. The deprivation of physical contact during their first eight months had plainly affected the capacity of these infants to develop the full and normal pattern of affection. We found a further indication of the psychological damage wrought by early lack of mothering when we tested the degree to which infant monkeys retained their attachments to their mothers. Infants raised with a cloth mother from birth and separated from her at about five and a half months showed little or no loss of responsiveness even after 18 months of separation. In some cases it seemed that absence had made the heart grow fonder. The monkeys that had known a mother surrogate only after the age of eight months, however, rapidly lost whatever responsiveness they had acquired. The long period of maternal deprivation had evidently left them incapable of forming a lasting affectional tie.

The effects of maternal separation and deprivation in the human infant have scarcely been investigated, in spite of their implications concerning child-rearing practices. The long period of infant-maternal dependency in the monkey provides a real opportunity for investigating persisting disturbances produced by inconsistent or punishing mother surrogates.

Above and beyond demonstration of the surprising importance of contact comfort as a prime requisite in the formation of an infant's love for its mother —and the discovery of the unimportant or nonexistent role of the breast and act of nursing—our investigations have established a secure experimental approach to this realm of dramatic and subtle emotional relationships. The further exploitation of the broad field of research that now opens up depends merely upon the availability of infant monkeys. We expect to extend our researches by undertaking the study of the mother's (and even the father's!) love for the infant, using real monkey infants or infant surrogates. Finally, with such techniques established, there appears to be no reason why we cannot at some future time investigate the fundamental neurophysiological and biochemical variables underlying affection and love.

III

BRAIN AND CONSCIOUSNESS

III

BRAIN AND CONSCIOUSNESS

INTRODUCTION

This section discusses the human brain, the physical basis of all human behavior and experience. Although the human brain is the most complex organ known, certain principles of organization permit a relatively simple general overview of how it functions. It may ultimately be impossible for the brain to understand itself completely. At present, however, we are making enormous advances in our understanding of how the brain works to control at least the simpler aspects of behavior. The study of the brain is perhaps the most challenging and exciting field of human endeavor.

In the first article, "'The Great Ravelled Knot,'" George W. Gray presents an interesting overview of the human brain, particularly the cerebral cortex, "the supremely distinctive organ of the human species." J. D. French, in his article "The Reticular Formation," describes that network of cells in the lower region of the brain, a structure that appears to play a critical role in the control of sleep, waking, and consciousness. The alpha rhythm, currently a topic of great popular interest, is one of several types of brain waves characteristic of man and higher mammals. Mary A. B. Brazier presents a comprehensive account of brain waves, their characteristics and meaning, in her article "The Analysis of Brain Waves." The alpha rhythm, incidentally, was described and named by Hans Berger, the German psychiatrist who first discovered human brain waves in 1924. Dr. Brazier describes modern techniques used to analyze brain waves and discusses the possible meanings of various brain-wave patterns.

An intriguing fact about brains is that there are two in every head. From such primitive animals as flatworms to such complex ones as men, the brain is bilaterally symmetrical: it exists as two separate hemispheres connected by massive bands of fibers. Surgical separation of the two hemispheres in animals and man has led to important advances in our understanding of awareness and consciousness. Among the most striking and important work on human consciousness are the studies by R. W. Sperry, Michael S. Gazzaniga, and their associates at the California Institute of Technology. These studies are described by Gazzaniga in his article "The Split Brain in Man." The interconnecting fibers between the hemispheres were severed in several patients with uncontrollable epilepsy to prevent the spread of unilateral seizures from one hemisphere to the other. The treatment appears to have been successful. Of more interest in this context, however, is the fact that the patients seem to have two independently functioning brain hemispheres and two independent "consciousnesses."

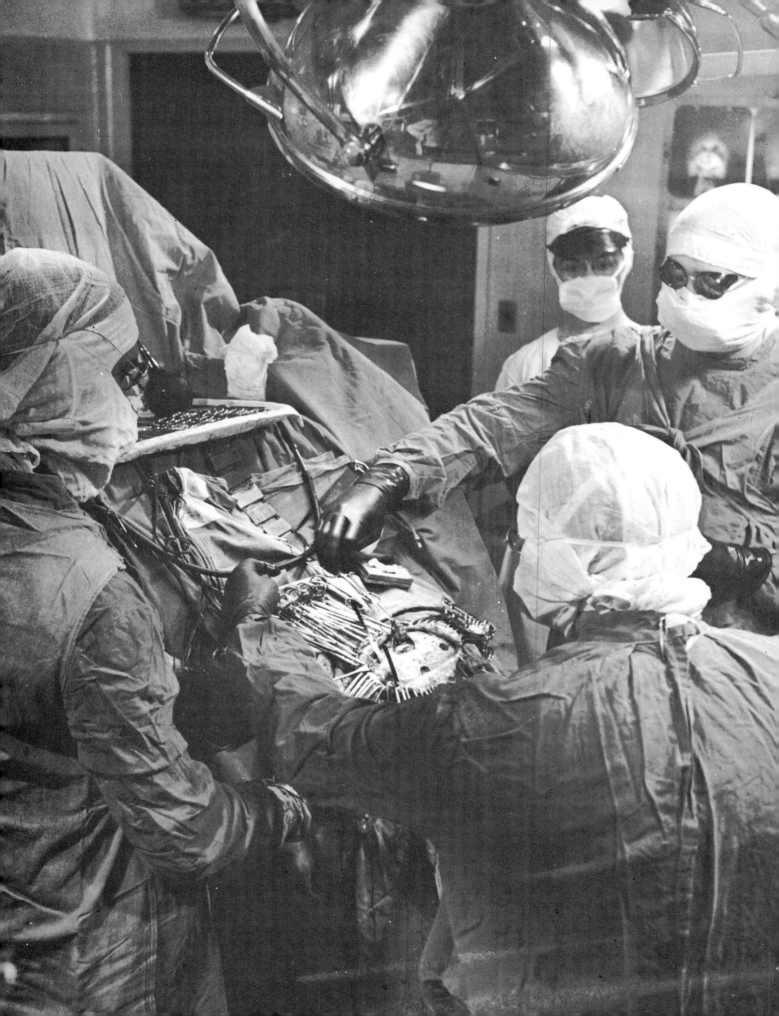

10

"THE GREAT RAVELLED KNOT"

GEORGE W. GRAY
October 1948

THOUSANDS of millions of nerve cells are woven into the texture of the human brain, and each can communicate with near or distant neighbors. Judson Herrick, the University of Chicago neurologist, has calculated that if only a million of these nerve cells were joined two by two in every possible way, the number of combinations would total $10^{2,783,000}$. This is a figure so tremendous that if it were written out and set up in the type you are reading, more than 350 pages of SCIENTIFIC AMERICAN would be required to print it. And we may be sure that the brain has many times a million nerve cells, each capable of groupings of far more than two cells per hookup.

Life has created innumerable patterns in its long climb from the Archeozoic ooze, but none can compare in intricacy of design and virtuosity of function with "The great ravelled knot," as the famous English physiologist Sir Charles Sherrington described it, by which we feel, see, hear, think and decide. This "master tissue of the human body" is perhaps the most challenging of all biological researches.

One can trace the evolution of the master tissue from fish to man, and observe brain part after brain part originate as each succeeding species becomes better adapted to the complex conditions of life on land, more versatile in its capacity for survival—and more intelligent. Similarly, in the developing human embryo the brain forms by the dual process of multiplying the number of cells and increasing their specialization. In the beginning, a few days after conception, certain skin cells are selected as tissue for nerve function. From this microscopic neural tube the spinal cord forms, and simultaneously the hindbrain, midbrain and forebrain develop from the same germinal structure.

It is the forebrain that attains the crowning organization and integration of the nervous system—the cerebral cortex.

SURGEONS at Montreal Neurological Institute operate on patient for brain disorder. Localization experiments are performed at same time.

Beginning as an insignificant segment of the embryonic brain, this gray mantle eventually grows so large that it must fold in on itself in wrinkles to accommodate its expanding surface to the walls of the skull. When fully grown, the cerebral cortex completely covers the brain structures from which it developed. It overshadows and dominates them, taking control of many of their functions. From every nerve cell, or neurone, fibers pass to other neurones, both of the cortex and of the other brain parts. Millions of lines of communication connect one region of gray matter with another, and these in turn with distant organs. By such means the brain is in communication with the lungs, the heart and other organs; with the specialized cells which serve as the receptors of touch, taste, smell, vision, hearing and other sensations; and with the muscles which produce action.

The cortex may be compared to a holding corporation formed to integrate and extend the services of a number of older companies which are housed in the stem of the brain. Under the consolidation the older companies are not abolished. They are continued as useful adjuncts of the more modern organization: to take care of routine activities such as breathing and digestion, to serve as channels of communication, perhaps to be held in reserve as stand-by agencies capable of resuming their former higher functions in emergencies. But the offices of inquiry and foresight, of planning, initiative, the creating of new ideas, the venturing into new projects, are executed by the holding corporation upstairs, and control of the consolidated system is administered there.

This roof brain is the supremely distinctive organ of the human species. What goes on within its network of cells makes the fundamental difference between man and brute. The functioning of the cerebral cortex not only distinguishes man from the animals, but more than any other faculty it distinguishes man from man. It marks the fateful difference between the meek follower and the dynamic leader, between the scholar and the artist, between the genius and the moron.

If the proper study of mankind is man, surely the supreme biological interest of man is his brain, particularly the gray cortex of two billion cells without the orchestration of which "there can be no thought, no sweet sonnets of Shakespeare, no joy and no sorrow."

The Cortex

No cortex is an exact duplicate of another, either in the number or size of its convolutions. Indeed, it seems likely that each roof brain is as individual to its possessor as his face, but certain surface landmarks are characteristic of all. The most conspicuous is the longitudinal division into two approximately equal hemispheres (*see drawing on page 90*). Then there is the large fissure that cuts laterally across each hemisphere, originating in the longitudinal division, traveling over the cerebral crest, and continuing down the side of the brain in a direction which if continued would bring it about opposite the ear. This great central fissure (also called the Rolandic fissure) is found in the brains of men, apes and monkeys. Another standard feature which appears also in the primates is the Sylvian fissure. It is the cerebral Grand Canyon, a deep

---

ACKNOWLEDGEMENT

The author acknowledges with thanks the help of the following scientists who were consulted in the preparation of this article: Drs. Philip Bard and Clinton N. Woolsey of Johns Hopkins University; John F. Fulton of Yale; Marion Hines of Emory University; Robert S. Morison of the Rockefeller Foundation; J. M. Nielsen of the University of Southern California; Wilder Penfield and Herbert Jasper of the Montreal Neurological Institute; George L. Streeter of the Carnegie Institution of Washington; and H. A. Teitelbaum of Baltimore.

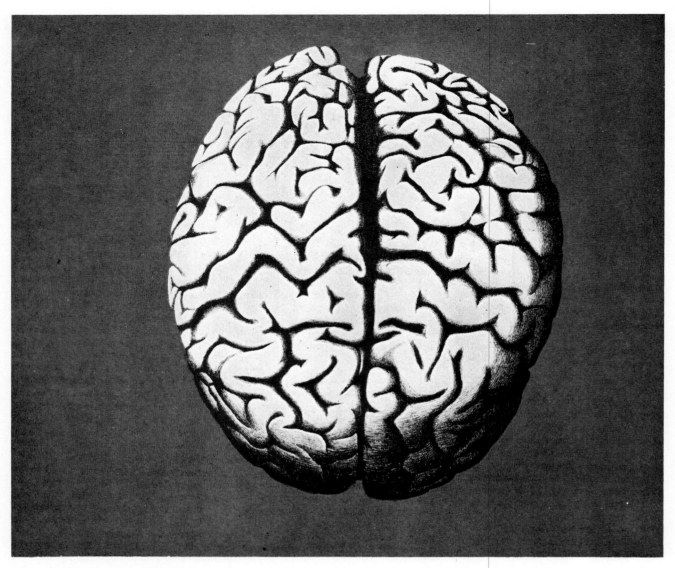

TOP VIEW OF THE BRAIN shows its principal division into two almost equal hemispheres. The surface is folded into convolutions, probably the product of evolutionary overcrowding of nerve cells within the skull.

gorge which emerges from the bottom of each hemisphere and curves upward and back along the side. The Sylvian fissure perpetuates the name of the 17th-century French anatomist, Franciscus de le Boe Sylvius.

These two prominent depressions provide natural boundaries for subdividing the hemispheres into regions, and almost the first efforts of brain anatomists were directed toward mapping these sections. All that part of each hemisphere which lies in front of the central and Sylvian fissures was designated the frontal lobe. The bulbous rear, which lies under the occipital bone of the skull, was named the occipital lobe. And between these front and rear lobes two others were early laid out: an upper intermediate zone (the parietal lobe, so-called because it lies under the parietal bone of the skull) and a lower intermediate zone (the temporal lobe, below the Sylvian fissure). There is also a limbic lobe, mapped in the cleft

between the hemispheres, around the root of the cerebral cortex, where the gray convolutions face one another.

In subdividing the cerebrum into these lobes, the early anatomists apparently had no thought of identifying special functions with each. The accepted idea was that the brain acted as a unit; if by accident or disease one part of the cortex became incapacitated, its faculties were taken over by other parts. This was the almost undisputed view up to the early years of the 19th century.

Then, in about 1805, the Viennese physician Franz Joseph Gall began to teach that the faculty of speech was localized in the frontal lobe, just above the eyes. He had observed that certain fluent speakers had prominent eyes, and decided that this was because their frontal lobes were extraordinarily developed and pressed the eyes forward and downward, with the effect of making the lower lids bulge out.

Others pointed out that there were

quite a few orators who did not have prominent eyes and baggy lower lids, but Gall's teaching won many followers. Presently he expanded his idea of localization to include 24 areas of the cortex which he claimed were the control centers for as many faculties, including such traits as cruelty, acquisitiveness, the love of food, mathematical aptitude, the sense of melody, the sense of order and even the sense of time.

Gall gave no attention to such faculties as vision, hearing and other sensory abilities which we regard today as the primary functions of the brain, but was concerned with localizing the moral qualities. Phrenology thus was launched as a "science" by which an individual's character and mental faculties were appraised by measuring the bumps on his head, and for many decades it ran a prosperous course as one of the leading superstitions.

While this preposterous notion was sweeping the world, a few pioneering phy-

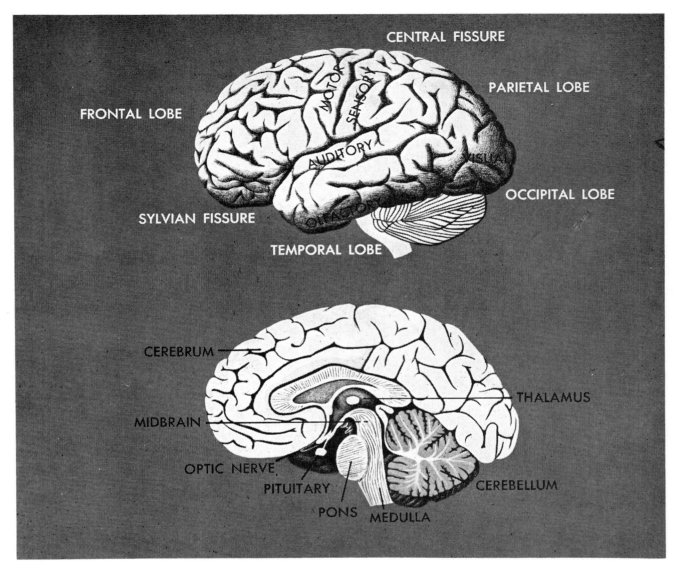

CENTRAL FISSURE

FRONTAL LOBE

PARIETAL LOBE

MOTOR

SENSORY

AUDITORY

VISUAL

OCCIPITAL LOBE

SYLVIAN FISSURE

OLFACTORY

TEMPORAL LOBE

CEREBRUM

THALAMUS

MIDBRAIN

OPTIC NERVE

PITUITARY

PONS MEDULLA

CEREBELLUM

ANATOMICAL FEATURES of the brain, described in detail in the text of this article, are indicated in a side view and cross section. Several of the basic functional areas are also lettered on the upper drawing.

sicians were making some real progress in exploring the functions of the brain. It was slow business, for both anesthesia and antisepsis were still in the future, and opening the skull was regarded as equivalent to a death sentence. But there were certain conditions that provided indirect evidence, and one of these was the paralytic stroke affecting only one side of the body.

Early Localization

Marc Dax of Paris noticed that whenever a stroke paralyzed the right side of a right-handed person, the patient usually suffered some loss in his faculty of speech. It was known from anatomical dissection that the nervous pathways of the left hemisphere cross over in the brain stem and pass on to the muscles in the right side of the body. From this Dax reasoned that the speech center must lie in the left hemisphere, and that the same injury which paralyzed the control of the mus-

cles also damaged the speech center.

Localization was carried a step further in 1861 when another French doctor, Paul Broca, reported on the post-mortem examination of two paralytics. In each case the patient had been paralyzed only on the right side, and had suffered a serious aphasia which had rendered him speechless. In the autopsies Broca found a serious deterioration of tissue in part of the left frontal lobe. On this evidence he asserted that the brain's control of the vocal cords was not only confined to the left frontal lobe, but that it was localized in a small area at the base of the third frontal convolution.

Broca's fissure and Broca's area have been recognized landmarks of the frontal lobe ever since. Later explorers of the brain, using new tools and improved techniques, have more precisely located the center for the control of speech organs. But it remains in the neighborhood that Broca identified from the scant evidence

of his autopsies, and he is appropriately commemorated as the great trail blazer of cerebral localization.

Closely following Broca came the English neurologist Hughlings Jackson, who began to apply the idea of localization to his study of epilepsy, chorea and other brain diseases. By 1869 Jackson had arrived at a clarifying generalization, the astuteness of which is especially impressive because he had no means of checking his speculation by surgery or animal experimentation. Guided entirely by what he observed in patients and found in post-mortem examinations of brains, Jackson announced that there was a primary functional division of the cerebral cortex which cut across both hemispheres. All the *sensory* functions of the brain—its reception of sights, sounds, touches and other signals from sensory organs—were confined to the lobes back of the central fissures, he suggested, while all of its *motor* functions were located in front of them.

The first verification of this bold hypothesis came a year later in Berlin when G. Fritsch and E. Hitzig began experimenting with the brains of dogs. By applying weak electrical currents to the frontal region of a dog's right hemisphere, they obtained movements of the left legs. Similarly, by stimulating frontal areas of

tion is confined to the back lobes of the brain and motor control to the frontal lobe, should there not be some difference in the cellular structure of the contrasting regions? This led to a large-scale search of brain tissue. It was not until methods of staining tissues for microscopic study were devised that real progress could be

packed section of granular cells; 5) a layer of more numerous and larger pyramidal cells; 6) a bottom layer of smaller, spindlelike cells.

This six-layer pattern is typical, but in examining segments taken from different cortical regions the investigators found departures from it. The most striking contrast appeared when the area immediately in front of the central fissure was compared with areas to the rear, notably those which have been identified with seeing, hearing and other sensory functions. Microscopic surveys of these sensory areas show that the pyramidal cells of the third and fifth layers are much reduced in size, while the two granular layers are thickly populated with their characteristic small globular cells. By contrast, just the reverse was found in the motor area. Thus not only brain areas but brain cells appear to be consecrated to specific functions. Granular cells function in the reception of sensory messages while pyramidal cells play a corresponding role in transmitting motor signals.

Can we go further? We yearn to know the nature of the nerve impulses that can bring about such an exquisite orchestration of activity. Where and how do they operate so that one impulse is interpreted as a touch, another as a sound, a third as a sight? And where does memory dwell, where are judgment, the imagination, all those higher faculties that we call intellectual, artistic, moral?

No one would claim that more than a beginning has been made toward answering these questions. Some of the answers are more fragmentary than others, but efforts at completing them never slacken, for the incentives to the search are compelling. Fundamentally the incentives are two: intellectual curiosity and the desire to alleviate disease. Not only laboratory investigators but clinicians, following in the train of Broca and Jackson, have been prolific contributors of new knowledge. It has taken many minds, many stratagems, the use of many tools and techniques to chart our present map of the brain.

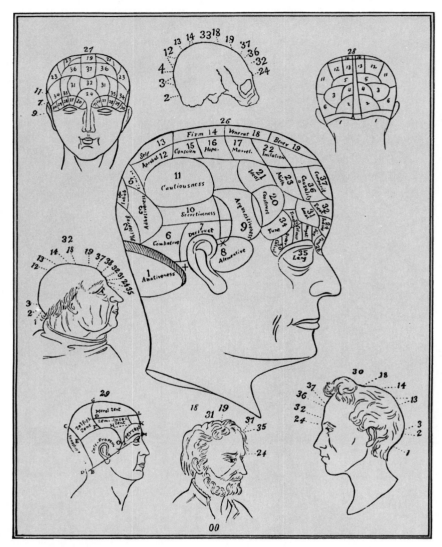

PHRENOLOGY, the persistent nonsense that was introduced early in the 19th century by a Viennese named Franz Joseph Gall, ironically was one of the first suggestions of the localization of brain function. Gall, however, did not try to locate real functions of the brain. He localized "moral" qualities.

the left hemisphere, they obtained muscular responses from the right side of the animal. But when the same electrical currents were applied to the back of the brain, no muscle gave the slightest response although the stimulus was many times repeated.

Jackson was jubilant at this experimental confirmation of his idea, and many other neurologists also rejoiced. At last, it seemed, a clue had been found to the general organization of the cortex.

But, it was reasoned, if sensory recep-

made. In particular, three staining techniques were perfected: one by Camillo Golgi in Italy, one by Franz Nissl in Germany, and the third by Karl Weigert, also of Germany. Each stain brought out different details of the tissue, and histologists were enabled to see that the gray matter of the cerebral cortex is built of several kinds of cells arranged in six layers: 1) the surface or molecular layer, a paving of small structures called horizontal cells; 2) a layer of granular cells, small and roundish; 3) pyramidal cells; 4) a closely

Electrical Exploration

Today the principal tools for prospecting the brain are electrical. This is only natural, for the gray matter itself is a generator of electric impulses, and the messages that it receives from the sense organs and the directives that it issues to the muscles are all electrical in nature. Electric currents can therefore be used to stimulate the brain in a way that is entirely normal to its function. Conversely, electric impulses generated by the brain and its tributary system of nerves can be picked up and measured to determine the degree of activity in any selected area.

Of the two general kinds of electrical prospecting techniques, one works from the brain outward to the body responses, and the other from the sense organs inward to the brain. In the first method a delicate electrode carrying an alternating current at low voltage is applied to a selected area of the exposed brain. This technique has been most successful in exploring the motor areas of the cortex. The body-to-brain method, on the other hand, introduces no electric current, but merely picks up the currents that the brain itself generates. In this kind of research the investigator applies an appropriate stimulus to a sense organ, and electrodes moved over the brain determine the destination at which the sensory message arrives. The stimulus may be a slight touch on the bottom of the foot, a flashing light or a sound. The skin, eye or ear then starts a nerve impulse which moves to the cortex, and the area which receives the message announces the arrival by increasing its electrical output. These discharges are so delicate that it was not until the development of the vacuum-tube amplifier that researchers were able to build receivers sufficiently sensitive to measure them.

The vacuum-tube amplifier has been harnessed to this task in two ways: by the cathode-ray oscillograph and by the electroencephalograph. In the electroencephalograph, the feeble electrical discharges picked up from the brain may be amplified millions of times to produce voltages which when relayed through an electromagnet cause a pen to write the pattern of electrical pulsations on a moving paper tape. These brain waves provide an exact record of the fluctuating electrical activity of the brain area upon which the electrode rests.

The principle of the cathode-ray oscillograph is the same, but the manner of applying it is somewhat different. Here the brain currents picked up by the electrodes are similarly amplified, but instead of writing a record on a tape, they deflect a beam of electrons moving in a cathode-ray tube. The moving beam is projected on a fluorescent screen and appears as a quivering luminous line. Whenever the brain area under investigation flares with increased electrical activity, the line pulses in unison with the accelerated discharge. The frequency and amplitude of peaks and valleys in line are measures of the electrical output of the discharging brain cells.

The cathode-ray beam is a more sensitive and precise instrument than the electroencephalograph. It is particularly convenient for surveys of the kind carried on by Clinton N. Woolsey, Philip Bard, W. H. Marshall and their associates at the Johns Hopkins Medical School: exhaustive studies in which a single experiment may last as long as 90 hours. In these surveys, which are made on animals under deep anesthesia, a vibrator may be set to touch the hair of a paw and then, while this repetitive touching stimulus continues, an electrode will be shifted from

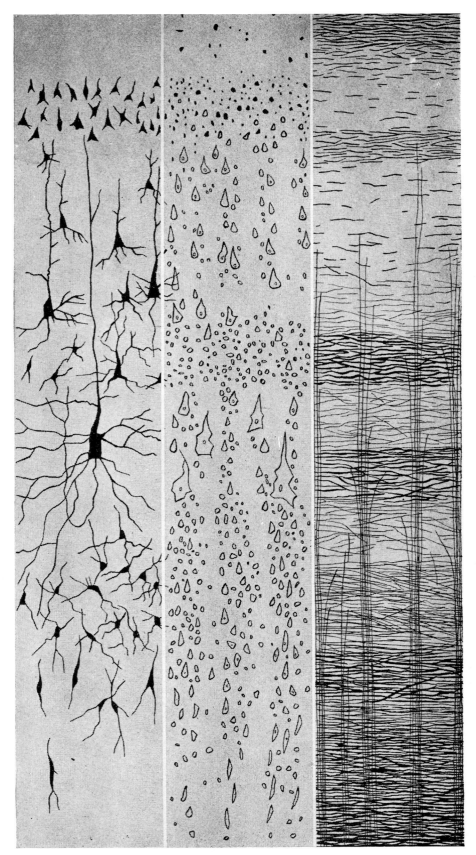

ORGANIZATION OF CELLS in the cortex is brought out differently by three staining techniques. The basic six-layer pattern, however, is visible. From top, layers are: 1) small cells, 2) granular cells, 3) pyramidal cells, 4) more granular cells, 5) larger pyramidal cells and 6) spindle-shaped cells.

point to point on the brain. At the same time the researcher or his assistant keeps watch over the quivering line of the oscillograph beam. Sometimes several point positions must be tested before the sudden sharp deflection of the beam announces that here at last is the group of cells where the brain responds to the touch on the paw. After that, the area can be surveyed half-millimeter by half-millimeter, and its boundaries staked out.

In certain studies the electroencephalograph is the preferred tool. It is indispensable when there is need for an appraisal of the background activity of the brain, with its continuously fluctuating pattern of waves. It is also possible to measure the electrical discharges from a number of different areas simultaneously, and electroencephalographs now in use will pick up and record six or more wave tracks, writing them side by side on the same tape for comparison (*see page 100*). Of course the same can be done by a battery of cathode-ray oscillographs working simultaneously, using photography to record the waves.

Surgery has also contributed prodigiously to the localization of brain function. Certain parts of the brain have been removed from animals, and the subsequent behavior of the animals has provided direct evidence of the functions that were related to the lost areas. Performing surgery on human beings is another fruitful source of information. Of course human brains are not deliberately exposed for experimental studies, but when the skull must be opened to remove a tumor, to excise a portion of diseased cerebral tissue or for any other clinical reason, it is often possible to make experimental observations of localization, sometimes to confirm in the human brain what has been discovered in lower animals.

Projection

The meaning that a nerve message conveys does not depend on its source. Whether it is sent by eye, ear, nose, taste buds or organs of touch will make no difference unless the message reaches the appropriate nerve endings in the brain.

"HOMUNCULI" are an actual map of the brain's somatic sensory area and motor area. Here they are projected on facing cross sections of the same hemisphere. Each of the areas outlined by these grotesque manikins

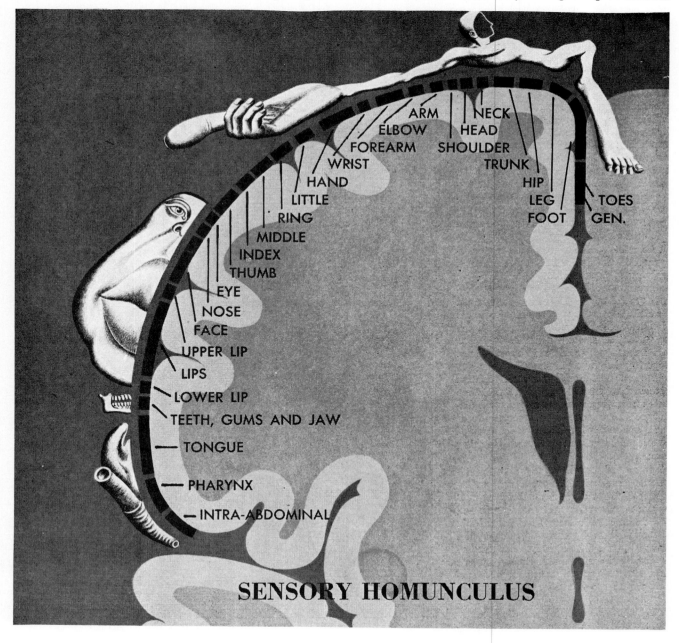

SENSORY HOMUNCULUS

Any nerve impulse arriving at the auditory area and carrying sufficient voltage to discharge its neurones is received and interpreted as a sound, no matter what its origin. Presumably one might hear a smell, if an impulse starting from the olfactory organs should get switched in transit and arrive at the brain's center for hearing.

Certain varieties of focal epilepsy provide dramatic evidence that the brain can generate its own sensations. One victim of this disease reported that just before he was seized with convulsions he always saw rings of light. Another patient's preliminary sensation was sound; he heard discordant noises. There have been cases in which the first sign of an epileptic seizure

was a foul smell or a curious taste. These abnormal sensations are produced within the brain by the spontaneous discharge of certain hyperactive cells, and it happened that in one patient the hyperactive cells were connected with the visual area, in another with the auditory area, and so on.

The parts of the cortex that have become specialized for the reception of sensory messages and for the dispatch of motor directives are known as projection areas. For all the motor functions, the projection area is where Fritsch and Hitzig found it by electrical stimulation 78 years ago. In man this means the frontal lobe, just forward of the central fissure.

Facing this motor region, stretching along the rear slope of the central fissure

and occupying the adjacent plateau of the parietal lobe, is the somatic sensory projection area, the region where sensations of touch are received from all parts of the body. Far back in the brain, at the very rear of the occipital lobe, is a whitish patch known as the striate cortex, the visual projection area. The upper rear of the temporal lobe, on the lower bank of the Sylvian fissure, is the auditory projection area. Impulses generated by odors pass from the nerve endings in the nose to the olfactory bulb, on the underside of the cortex, and from this diminutive area are distributed to a number of ill-defined areas. Actually the neurologists know very little of the topography and physiology of smell. They know even less of the

is devoted to receiving impulses from the corresponding part of the body (sensory homunculus) or sending them **(motor). Parts of homunculi are enlarged or diminished in proportion to how much related part of body is used.**

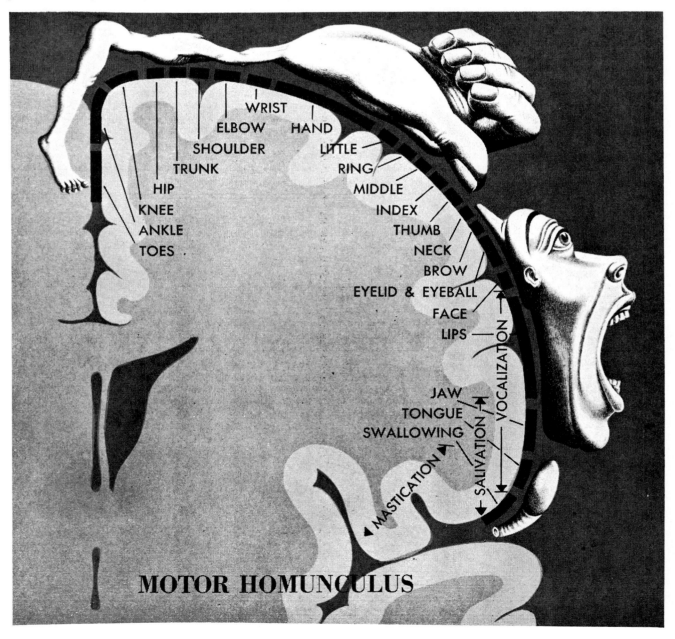

MOTOR HOMUNCULUS

projection area for taste. There is some evidence, according to T. Ruch and H. D. Patton, that this gustatory headquarters may be on the underside of the parietal lobe, in the part known as the parietal operculum.

The sense organs that send messages literally project images of themselves upon the brain. The cochlea, that spiral harp of the inner ear with its coiled membrane of nerve tissue attuned to vibrate over the entire scale of audible frequencies, is the critical organ of hearing—and an image of the cochlea is projected on the auditory area of the temporal lobe. The part of the eye upon which the lens focuses an image of what we see is a tiny section in the center of the retina. This microscopic patch is projected precisely on the visual area of the striate cortex in the occipital lobe, though in an enlarged replica. The brain actually magnifies the picture which illuminates the rods and cones of the retina by several thousand times. Just what sort of images the taste buds and smell organs project would be difficult to imagine. But when one reaches the somatic sensory area and the motor area, there remains no serious doubt or speculation. The image projected here is that of a little man—a grotesque and somewhat dismembered miniature of the human body.

A number of distinguished neurologists, most of them surgeons, have explored the motor and somatic functions of the human brain, and in terms of localization we know more of these two areas than of any other parts of the cerebrum. Horsley, Bidwell and Sherrington in Britain, Keen, Cushing and Ransom in the United States, Foerster in Germany, and others pioneered this field. The most extensive studies have been made by Wilder Penfield and his associates at the Montreal Neurological Institute. With the assent of patients upon whom he performed surgery, Dr. Penfield used electrical prospecting methods to survey the cerebral cortex. Now he has data from several hundred persons.

These accumulated results show that the amount of brain surface related to a specific part of the body is not proportional to the size of the part but to the extent of its use. The area concerned with the hands and fingers looms larger than those related to the feet and toes because we make more use of our hands. The projection of the lips occupies more of the somatic sensory area than all the rest of the head. The brain represents the somatic and motor functions as a kind of dismemberment of the body, with arms and legs joined, torso almost nonexistent, head separated from body, and tongue separated from head. On pages 94 and 95 are drawings of two such "homunculi" from Dr. Penfield's forthcoming monograph *The Cerebral Cortex of Man*. They are used with his kind permission.

This distortion of the body as the brain projects it becomes less exaggerated in animals farther down the scale of evolution. The research group in neurophysiology at Johns Hopkins has studied somatic representation in a succession of animals—monkeys, dogs, cats, sheep, pigs, rabbits and rats. Dr. Woolsey says that it was not until the group studied the rat that it found a brain whose projection gave a reasonable facsimile of the animal's body. The projection on the brain of the monkey is more in one piece than Dr. Penfield's homunculus, but it would be difficult to recognize in the image the animal it is supposed to represent. The cat's image is better assembled, but still is a mutilated edition of its body. The rat, though grotesque, with enormous head and exaggerated lips, is approximately ratlike.

These distortions tell us that each cortex reflects the pattern of the body's daily life. In a pig's brain most of the somatic projection area is devoted to snout; in a spider monkey, with its prehensile tail, there is an enormous tail area; in some dogs it is the olfactory area that holds a position of prime importance. E. D. Adrian of England's Cambridge University reports experiments with a hedgehog in which a current of air was passed through the animal's nostrils. Although the air carried no odor that the investigator could smell, electrical activity flared up over two thirds of the surface of the hedgehog's brain.

Several years ago Adrian was making an electrical survey of a cat's cortex and discovered a second somatic projection area separate from the known area. Shortly thereafter Samuel A. Talbot at Johns Hopkins found that in the cat brain the visual function also had a second projection area. Another series of studies at Johns Hopkins, by Dr. Woolsey and Edward M. Walzl, disclosed that, in addition, the cat has a second auditory area. Since then two-area projection has been demonstrated in several other animals, but in no instance has it been detected for either smell or taste.

Recently Montreal's Dr. Penfield found that man, too, has an extra somatic area. This second projection center is in the parietal lobe, but separate from the better-known area adjoining the central fissure.

Association

Whether man, like the animals, has two projection areas for vision and two for hearing is unknown. Nor have we any inkling of the working of the new-found somatic area, whether it operates subordinate to or coequal with the primary area. Certain experiments with dogs suggest that in the auditory function the second projection area comes into action only when loud sounds are heard; they also indicate that this area gives a less detailed image of the sound pattern than that projected on the primary hearing centers.

The sights, sounds, touches and other signals that the projection areas receive are a miscellany of random information, every item of which would be endlessly new, bewildering and useless were it not for the functioning of other areas of the roof brain. The burned child avoids the fire, but not because of the sharp signal of pain received in the somatic sensory area. It is the association that teaches the lesson—the association of pain with the sight of fire, perhaps with the sound of a warning scream, with the muscular action of drawing away, and so on.

The brain must have memory in order to relate the information of the moment with that of the past and to recognize its significance. This means millions of functional correlations, countless hookups of sensory centers with one another and with motor centers, repeated exchanges of data for analysis, comparison and synthesis. These elaborative functions of the cortex are performed by the association areas.

It would be meaningless to say that association areas are more important than projection areas, for without the latter, if we can imagine such a thing, the cortex would have no information about the outside world and no means of voluntarily controlling the body's muscular action. But even though it be indispensable, projection is the lowest level of cortical activity. As we go down the scale of animal intelligence we find the proportion of brain devoted to projection areas growing greater, and that occupied by association declining. In the rat almost the entire cortex is given over to projection, says Dr. Woolsey, "and it is difficult to see where there is any room for association areas."

In man more than three fourths of the roof brain is occupied by association areas. For example, that patch of striate cortex at the rear of the occipital lobe, the sensory area upon which the retina projects its images, is surrounded by an association area known as the parastriate cortex. Encircling this, and so closely interwoven that the boundary is obscure, lies a second visual association area, the peristriate cortex. It is possible to trace fibers connecting these three. In addition, fibers from the peristriate area run beneath the central fissure to connect with parts of the frontal lobe. Thus the seeing department of the brain, though housed in a small area in the back of the occipital lobe, has connections which link it with much of the roof brain. Even if we consider only the parastriate and peristriate surfaces, they have many times the area of the visual projection center.

An injury that destroys the visual projection area in both hemispheres causes total organic blindness—cortical blindness, the neurologists call it. If the injury is confined to the parastriate (first association) area, the victim can see but is unable to recognize or identify what he sees. This is mind blindness, a form of agnosia (loss of recognition). If it is the peristriate (second association) area that suffers the injury, the mind may have no difficulty recognizing objects but cannot recall their appearance when they are not in view. This kind of disability was early recognized in disturbances of the use of language, when the patient was unable to associate the printed or written word with any meaning. So the loss of function of the second visual association area is commonly called word blindness, one of the so-called sensory aphasias (loss of speech).

During a poliomyelitis epidemic in Los Angeles, a hospital nurse fell victim to the infection. She escaped paralysis, but in about three weeks it became manifest that her visual faculty had been damaged. "Why are the nurses wearing black uniforms?" she suddenly asked an attendant one day. Tests showed there were other things besides the starched white uniforms that she failed to recognize.

"When we asked her to read," relates J. M. Nielsen, who reports the case in his book *Agnosia, Apraxia, Aphasia*, "she claimed she could not see. When an O about ten centimeters in height was written for her, she peered at it and said we were holding it too close. The position was corrected, after which she said we were holding it too far away. She kept turning the paper about and peering in various directions, but was unable to read it. She then traced it with her finger (proof that she could see) and immediately read it correctly. Other letters were then tried, and it was found that she could see even small letters and could read complete sentences if she was allowed to trace the letters with her fingers. She even began to complete words before she had quite finished tracing them. Here it should be noted that she traced them by arm, not finger, movements. On certain days she did not recognize colors at all; on other days she recognized some of them."

Keys on a ring were exhibited to the nurse; she shook her head, but as soon as the keys were rattled she said, "Keys." When a saucepan was exhibited, her mind was again a complete blank, but when the pan was tapped with a spoon her face lighted up with recognition. A watch was seen only as "something bright," but when the ticking object was placed to her ear she murmured, "Watch." It was not until a piece of paper was crumpled, producing a crackling sound, that she was able to identify it. Looking at an orange meant nothing, but when the nurse smelled it, recognition was immediate.

The agnosia here was of the first order, mind blindness, caused by a disturbance of the functioning of the parastriate cortex. There was no disability of hearing, smell or touch, no disorder of the motor faculties, so the case was relatively simple compared with some complications in which mind blindness is combined, for example, with mind deafness, or, as sometimes happens, when an agnosia of one

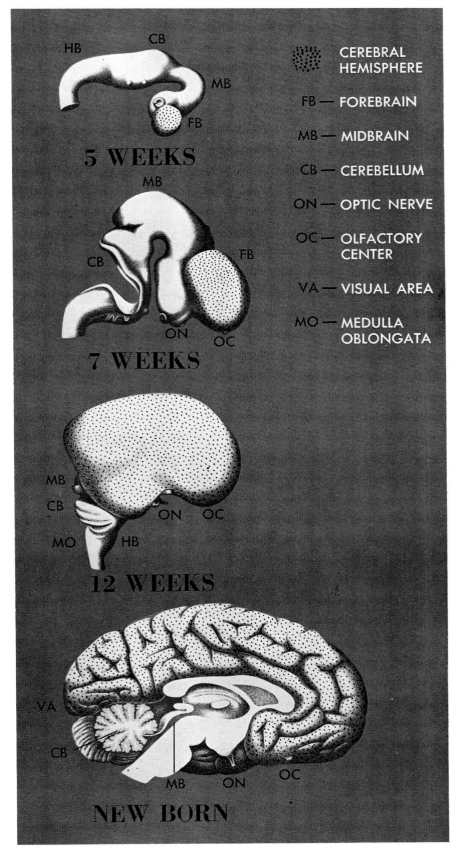

DEVELOPMENT OF THE BRAIN in the embryo of man is a history of the organ's evolution. At top the forebrain is an insignificant part of the whole. At the bottom it comes to dominate the more primitive parts. A few anatomical and functional features are repeated as points of reference.

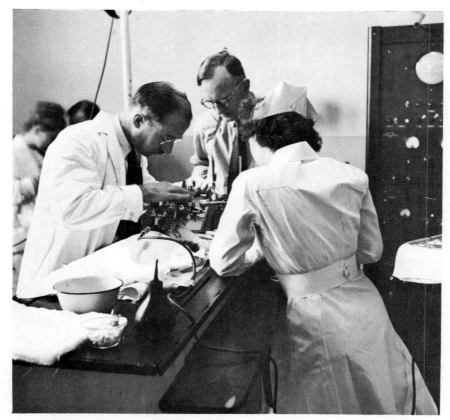

CAT BRAIN IS EXPLORED with probes that pick up electrical activity deep in the cortex. Activity is recorded on the face of the cathode-ray tube at the upper right. Animal is deeply anesthetized before experiment.

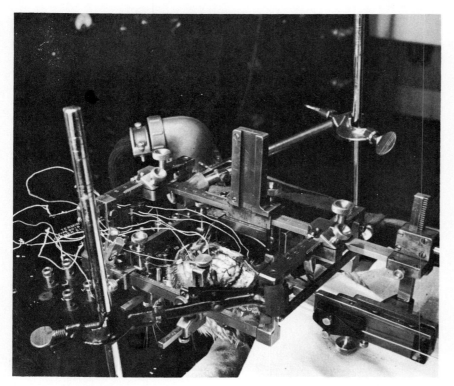

AID TO EXPLORING the cat's brain is the stereotaxic apparatus. This makes it possible to insert probe and determine its position with great accuracy. Experiment was performed at Montreal Neurological Institute.

order of association is combined with an aphasia of another order.

Various brain injuries have disabled the other senses in a manner corresponding to the cortical blindness, mind blindness and word blindness of the visual area. From this we infer that each sense has its successive areas of association, although the actual topography of the areas is not completely known for the visual faculty and is even less definitely mapped for the others.

Sometimes the effect of injury is an amnesia, the disability of forgetting. Dr. Nielsen tells of a man who periodically forgot the left side of his body. He washed his face only on the right side and bathed only his right arm and leg. When his wife called attention to this curious favoritism he was highly amused, admitted that he did have limbs over there on the left, and dutifully bathed them. But when he came to dress, again he forgot his left side and tried to put clothes only on the right. This amnesia became progressively worse until a brain operation was performed and a tumor in an area of the parietal lobe, near the somatic sensory region, was disclosed.

The motor side of the cortex, in the frontal lobe, also has its association areas. Broca's area, mentioned earlier in this article, is one of these. This association area for the elaboration of speech function is found normally only on one side of the brain: in the left hemisphere of right-handed persons, in the right hemisphere of the left-handed. Nearby is the association area for certain motor functions controlling manual dexterity. Anthropology teaches that the complicated business of developing and using language is closely related to using tools and developing other skills of the master hand. Some suggest that the earliest language may have been a system of signaling with the hands. Broca's area is closely connected with other association areas of the motor side of the cortex and also with areas on the sensory side, e.g., with the visual area (for reading language), the auditory area (for hearing language) and possibly with the somatic area as well (for correlations essential to writing).

Damage to the motor association areas or their connecting fibers may bring two kinds of result: 1) apraxia; 2) motor aphasia. In the first instance the individual is unable to perform purposeful movements—he suddenly finds he cannot tie a shoelace or thread a needle or guide a pen. Told to sign a letter, he cannot do it, although he wrote the letter without difficulty. Apraxia is the motor equivalent of sensory agnosia—a disability of the first order of motor elaboration. In motor aphasia the ability to speak is affected, just as in sensory aphasia the subject no longer understands the significance of what he sees, hears, or touches. In other words, when motor association areas of the first order are damaged, purposeful movement is impaired; when those of the second order are damaged, speech is impaired. Broca's area appears to be an elaborative zone of the second order.

Loss of speech is the most frequently encountered symptom of higher functional impairment, and it may take many forms. Sometimes the disability seems a mere eccentricity, like that of the patient reported by H. A. Teitelbaum of Johns Hopkins who could read the digits 5 and 7 but not 57. Complete speechlessness is the extreme form, though usually the victim can say a few simple words like yes or no. Sometimes the speech is meaningless jargon. It is quite common for aphasic patients to say the same word over and over again, and often it is a word they don't want to say, while at the same

ledge of stone, and, after laying in the gunpowder, was tamping it with a crowbar, when suddenly the charge ignited. The crowbar shot upward into the man's cheek, passed into his skull, and tore an ugly wound in both frontal lobes. Someone rushed to his assistance, pulled the steel out, and by a miracle the wound healed. Months later the quarryman returned to work. Although he was not able to take on his former job as a foreman, he proved to be entirely capable as a worker. His memory was good, his skill as a stoneworker seemed about the same as before the accident, but everyone associated with him noticed a marked change in his behavior. He was profane in speech, indifferent to the interests of others, care-

London in 1935. At the close of Fulton's address Egaz Moniz, a neurologist from Lisbon, proposed: "Why wouldn't it be feasible to relieve anxiety states in men by surgical means?" Dr. Fulton admits that the suggestion of so immediately applying the result of an animal experiment to the treatment of human illness rather startled him. But within a year Moniz had enlisted the cooperation of a surgeon, Almeida Lima, and together they had operated on 50 hopeless mental patients in Portugal. Dr. Lima did not remove any part of the cortex, but severed the pathways between the prefrontal region and the thalamic center in the brain stem. Because it was the fibrous white tissue that was cut, he called the operation leucotomy (from the Greek *leukos*, meaning white). The following year, the first leucotomy in the U. S. was performed by Walter Freeman and James W. Watts in Washington. The method has since been taken up by other surgeons and close to 2,000 persons in North America have been operated on by leucotomy or related techniques.

This severing of the connecting fibers apparently releases the "new" brain of the prefrontal region from the emotional dominance of the "old" brain of the cerebral stem—though we have no knowledge of the nature of this emotional dominance. Whatever the mechanism, there have been amazing transformations of violently insane persons into seemingly normal ones. Sufferers from involutional melancholia and other dementias associated with middle age, and even schizophrenics, have benefited. Some leucotomies are unsuccessful, but it is claimed that better than 60 per cent of the subjects have shown improvement following the operation. Adverse personality changes also result, however, and efforts are now being made to determine the total effect of leucotomy, weighing the good—the relief of psychotic symptoms—against the bad—the deterioration in personality. Among these personality changes are intensified selfishness, indifference to moral obligations, failure to foresee the consequences of acts, gauche manners and emotional instability.

		SENSORY		MOTOR	
		NORMAL	DEFECTIVE	NORMAL	DEFECTIVE
PROJECTION	Integrations of little complexity	Primary Sensation	Anesthesia	Voluntary contraction	Paralysis
ASSOCIATION	Integrations of greater complexity	Recognition	Agnosia	Purposeful Movement	Apraxia
	Integrations of greatest complexity	Understanding	Sensory aphasia	Meaningful speech	Motor aphasia

NORMAL AND DEFECTIVE behavior of brain areas are related in chart. Both projection areas (like those shown on pages 94 and 95) and association areas are listed. Exact location of many of the latter is still unknown.

time they can't form the word they do want to say. The writer knew one man who could recite poems, quote Shakespeare and sing songs without skipping a syllable, and yet was unable to use the same words in conversation.

These disorders of association rarely occur as uncomplicated conditions, the effects of which point unerringly to specific areas of disturbance. Often there is a mixture of symptoms that confounds all our efforts to portray the great ravelled knot as a compartmented organization. The roof brain is not that simple.

The Silent Areas

The frontal lobes are the largest segments of the brain. After mapping the extensive motor areas in front of the central fissure and other motor association areas even farther forward, the neurologists are left with considerable territory still to explain. This prefrontal region, the prow of the brain, overhanging the eyes like a gray canopy, does not respond to electrical stimulation. For that reason it has been called the silent area. From classical times it was regarded as the dwelling place of memory and of the higher intellectual faculties—the seat of intelligence.

But a hundred years ago a quarryman in Vermont sustained a violent injury to his frontal lobes and did not seem to suffer a serious impairment of intelligence. The quarryman had drilled a hole in a

less of his obligations—traits which the neighbors were disposed to overlook, remembering that he had passed through a nerve-racking experience.

Numerous frontal-lobe experiments have been attempted with animals, and one that will go down in history was begun at the Yale Medical School in 1933. In the physiological laboratory there, John F. Fulton and Carlyle Jacobsen were curious to see what effect removal of the prefrontal region would have upon two chimpanzees. From October to the following March the two apes Becky and Lucy were put through intensive training. Then a surgical operation was performed removing the prefrontal region of one hemisphere in each animal. The operation did not change their behavior appreciably. After the wounds healed the chimpanzees were subjected to intelligence tests again and their responses continued as before. In June another operation was performed, removing the remaining prefrontal region from each. When Becky and Lucy were given the tests this time, Fulton and Jacobsen found that a radical change had taken place. The tantrums that used to flare up after the chimpanzees had made the wrong choice and had been denied food or other rewards no longer appeared. "If a wrong choice were made now," said Dr. Fulton, "the animal merely shrugged its shoulders and went on doing something else."

Fulton and Jacobsen reported the experiment to a meeting of medical men in

Wars and accidents have provided thousands of cases of men with brain injuries, as have surgical operations for removal of tumors and other diseased frontal tissue. While examining battle-wounded men, Kurt Goldstein of Montefiore Hospital in New York was impressed by the lack of imagination and by the defective judgment found in many with frontal-lobe injuries. Dr. Goldstein observed that such a man, so long as he was confronted with concrete situations with which he had had experience, seemed perfectly normal, but when the situation was new and a method of meeting it had to be improvised, the patient's deficiency was strikingly apparent; he was unable to assume an attitude toward the abstract.

This failure to draw inferences from

abstractions was brought out by a test used by Gösta Rylander of Stockholm in a follow-up study of 32 Swedish cases. The test (only one of many used) quoted a series of proverbs and asked what each meant. For example, "The pitcher which goes oft to the well gets broken at last" is universally familiar, but many of these men and women who had lost part of their prefrontal cortex interpreted the parable quite literally and found it incongruous. The response of a clergyman, the most highly educated member of the group, was, "But a pitcher can't possibly walk." After reading "A blind hen may also find a seed," he laughed hilariously and retorted, "Not if she can't see."

Perhaps this Swedish clergyman's case gives as striking an example as may be found of the characteristic effects of prefrontal injury. The patient was 53 years old, graduate of a prominent theological college, minister of an important parish. A recognized leader, he possessed marked organizing talent, and as a preacher was known for the thoughtful content of his sermons and their wealth of figurative expression. He was an omnivorous reader, modest of manner, of heart-warming friendliness, but extremely conservative

in theology. In mid-life, the man suddenly began to fail mentally; his memory became defective; he had occasional lapses of consciousness, even mild epileptic attacks. A surgical operation showed a large tumor, the removal of which necessitated cutting out a sizable prefrontal section. Two and a half years after the operation, Dr. Rylander examined the clergyman. He was still good-tempered as a rule, but sometimes he flew into a sudden rage or broke into tears over trifles. He was given to making facetious, shallow and often tactless remarks. He never opened a book now, but he read newspapers and was interested only in current events. He found conversation in a group difficult to follow, but he spoke readily with one individual. He avoided tasks involving concentrated attention, ignored responsibility, left all planning and execution of plans to his wife. When invited to preach he pieced together an old sermon. His bishop did not dare return him to his former charge, but waiting for a new assignment did not seem to bother the minister any more than the fact that his allowance for leave of absence would soon be reduced. "The patient could by no means be called mentally deteriorated in the ordinary sense,"

reported Dr. Rylander. "He seemed still to have a good command of his own sphere. He could converse well on religious subjects, showing good judgment and an ability to throw light on different problems." But in intelligence tests, he attained an I.Q. of only 72, as compared with 110 for another clergyman used by the neurologist as a control.

Summing up his observations of the 32 individuals, Dr. Rylander finds that emotional changes occurred in 30, changes in volitional and psychomotor activity in 22, and intellectual changes (mainly involving the higher faculties) in 21. He concludes that while the changes usually do not destroy the subject's ability to lead a normal social existence, they can be disastrous "to persons doing qualified intellectual work."

A more extensive and prolonged study of effects of prefrontal loss is reported in the recently published *Brain and Intelligence* by the psychologist Ward C. Halstead. Halstead has been directing a laboratory for the investigation of neurological patients at the University of Chicago Clinics since 1935. He has examined 237 persons, including brain-injured patients, psychiatric patients and normal individuals used as a control group. Defining biological intelligence in operational terms of four basic factors, the psychologist has carried each of his subjects through an extensive series of tests to measure individual ability in each factor. The findings of his 12-year inquiry may be briefly summarized as follows: that biological intelligence is represented throughout the cerebral cortex; that its representation is not equal throughout; that it reaches its maximum in the cortex of the frontal lobes. Dr. Halstead concludes that "the frontal lobes, long regarded as silent areas, are the portion of the brain most essential to biological intelligence."

But we are still in a realm of speculation so far as a completely consistent picture of brain organization is concerned. Some authorities cling to the idea that learning, intelligence, imagination and the other intellectual faculties are a function of the brain-as-a-whole—and certainly there is evidence for such a view, along with the evidence for localization. Despite the substantial progress that has been made in identifying certain unmistakable areas (of which this article is a brief review), the cortex remains a vast entanglement of interconnecting lines and nodes. It is these interconnections that present the supreme enigma of neural organization. Whether the brain of man is capable of unraveling and comprehending its own complexity is, of course, a question. The very existence of that unresolved complexity constitutes a challenge. Physics, chemistry and mathematics, of which only limited use has been made by neurology up to now, will undoubtedly become major partners in the grand-scale teamwork of research that is ahead.

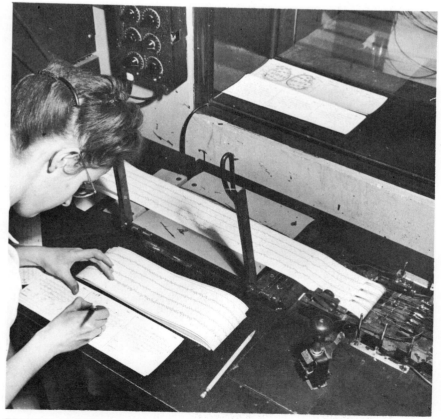

ELECTROENCEPHALOGRAPH curve is compared with standard chart by technician at the Montreal Neurological Institute. Longer strip above is inscribed by four pens connected by wires to contacts on patient's scalp.

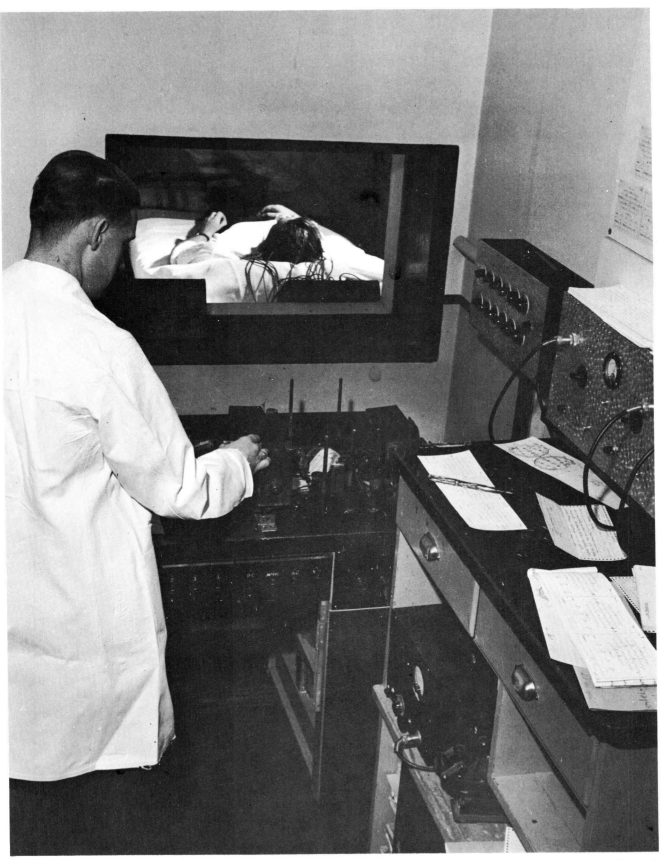

ELECTROENCEPHALOGRAM IS MADE with patient inside a shielded room. Electroencephalograph apparatus is in foreground. This method of recording brain activity is somewhat less sensitive than the cathode-ray tube shown on page 98. It is standard, however, for diagnosing epilepsy and locating brain damage.

11

THE RETICULAR FORMATION

J. D. FRENCH
May 1957

The title "reticular formation" might suggest various things—a football line-up, a chess gambit, a geological structure or whatnot—but as readers of SCIENTIFIC AMERICAN well know, it is actually a part of the brain, a once mysterious part which has re-cently come in for a great deal of attention from biologists. The reticular formation is a tiny nerve network in the central part of the brain stem. Investigators have discovered that this bit of nerve tissue, no bigger than your little finger, is a far more important structure than anyone had dreamed. It underlies our awareness of the world and our ability to think, to learn and to act. Without it, an individual is reduced to a helpless, senseless, paralyzed blob of protoplasm.

The actual seat of the power to think,

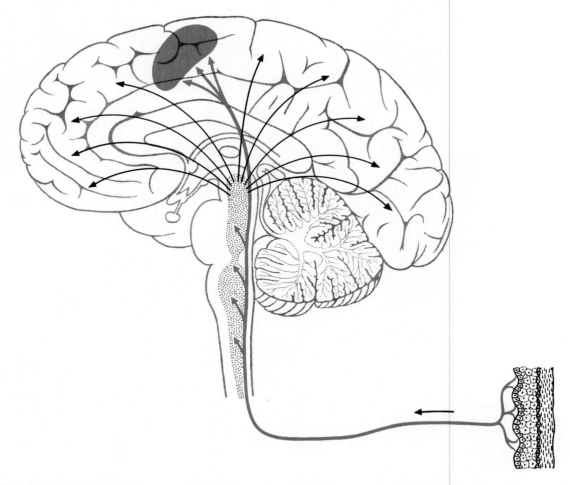

THE RETICULAR FORMATION is the area stippled with red in this cross section of the brain. A sense organ (*lower right*) is connected to a sensory area in the brain (*upper left*) by a path-way extending up the spinal cord. This pathway branches into the reticular formation. When a stimulus travels along the pathway, the reticular formation may "awaken" the entire brain (*black arrows*)

to perceive, indeed to respond to a stimulus with anything more than a reflex reaction, lies in the cortex of the brain. But the cortex cannot perceive or think unless it is "awake." Consider the alarm ring that awakens you in the morning: several seconds pass before you recognize the disturbance and can respond to stop the painful jangle. A sensory signal arriving at the cortex while it is asleep goes unrecognized. Experiments on anesthetized individuals have shown further that stimulation of the cortex alone is not sufficient to awaken the brain. Something else must arouse the cortex: that something is the reticular formation.

It was only about eight years ago that two eminent physiologists, H. W. Magoun of the U. S. and Giuseppe Moruzzi of Italy, working together at Northwestern University, discovered this fact. They were exploring the mystery of the reticular formation's functions by means of an electrode planted in this area in the brain of a cat. They found that stimulation of the area with a small electric current would awaken a drowsing cat as peacefully as a scratch on the head. The animal's behavior, and recordings of changes in its brain waves with the electroencephalograph, showed all the signs of a normal arousal from sleep. Magoun and Moruzzi decided that the reticular formation acted as a kind of sentinel which aroused the cortex, and they named it the RAS (reticular activating system).

Now mysteries began to clear—not only with regard to the function of the reticular formation but also as to some previously puzzling features of the nervous system's anatomy. All the great sensory nerve trunks in the body have brush-like branches which stream into the reticular formation. Sensory signals from all parts of the body go to the cortex by direct pathways, but on the way through the brain stem they also feed into the reticular formation. Evidently the reticular formation, when so stimulated, sends arousing signals to the cortex. The awakened cortex can then interpret the sensory signals it is receiving directly.

The RAS is a kind of general alarm: that is to say, it responds in the same way to any sensory stimulus, whether from the organs of hearing, seeing, touch or whatever. Its response is simply to arouse the brain, not to relay any specific message. Its signals spray the entire cortex rather than any one center of sensation. A noise, a flash of light, a pinch on the hand, the smell of burning wood, a

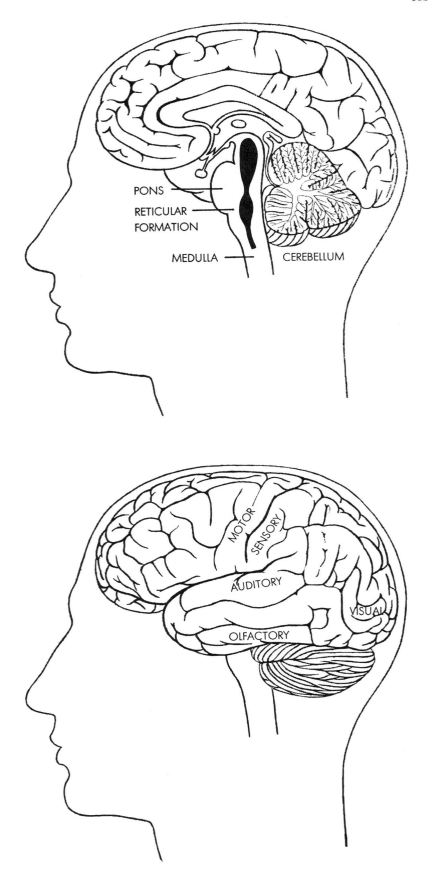

RELATIONSHIP OF THE RETICULAR FORMATION (*black area*) **to various parts of the brain is indicated at the top. The functional areas of the brain are outlined at bottom.**

pain in the stomach—any of these excites the reticular formation to alert the cortex to a state of wakefulness, so that when the specific stimulus arrives at the appropriate center in the cortex, the brain can identify it.

Apparently the RAS learns to be selective in its sensitivity to particular stimuli. A mother may be instantly awakened by the faintest whimper of her baby. Father, on the other hand, may sleep through baby's fiercest bellowings but be aroused by a faint smell of smoke. A city dweller may sleep peacefully in the midst of the riotous din of traffic while his visitor from the country spends a sleepless night wishing he were elsewhere. It is as if the RAS becomes endowed by experience with the ability to discriminate among stimuli, disregarding those it has found unimportant and responding to those that are helpful. Happily so. Imagine how unbearable life would be if you could not shut out most of the environment from consciousness and were at the mercy of the thousands of sights and sounds simultaneously clamoring for attention.

The RAS, like the starter in an automobile, starts the brain engine running, but this is by no means the end of its job. It goes on functioning to keep the individual in a conscious state. ("Consciousness" is a controversial word among psychologists, but for our purposes its meaning is clear enough.) If the RAS cannot function normally, consciousness is impossible. A person whose reticular formation has been permanently injured or destroyed falls into a coma from which he can never recover. He may live on for a year or more, but he remains as helpless and shut off from communication as a vegetable.

If uninjured, the RAS can maintain a wakeful state (but not consciousness) even in the absence of the cortex. In a newborn baby the cortex has not yet begun to function, but the infant nevertheless has short periods of wakefulness throughout the day. The same is true of the tragic creatures born without any cortex at all (called anencephalic monsters). Such a child (sometimes kept alive for three or four years) never achieves any understanding or real contact with its surroundings, but it has periods of wakefulness during which it swallows and digests food, smiles and coos when fondled and cries when treated roughly. We must conclude, therefore, that wakefulness of a very crude sort is possible without the cortex, so long as the RAS can function.

For sustained wakefulness, however,

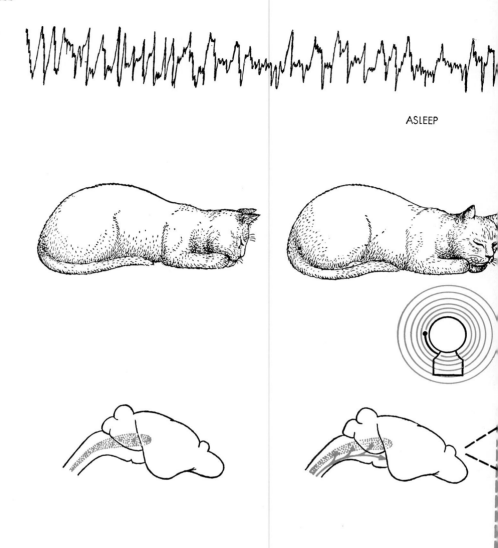

ASLEEP

CAT IS AWAKENED by the sound of a bell. The sound stimuli (*incoming red arrows*) reach the reticular activating system, or RAS, and the auditory area of the brain. The RAS acts (*black arrows*) to awaken the cortex so that it can "hear" signals arriving in the auditory

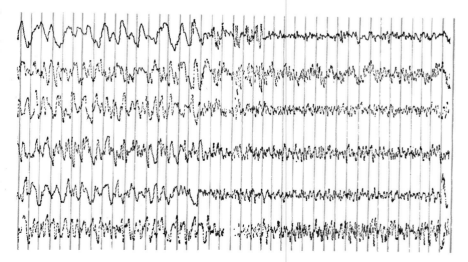

CORTEX IS STIMULATED by passing an electric current to the brain surface of a sleeping monkey. Six recording electrodes show the RAS has been activated to awaken the brain.

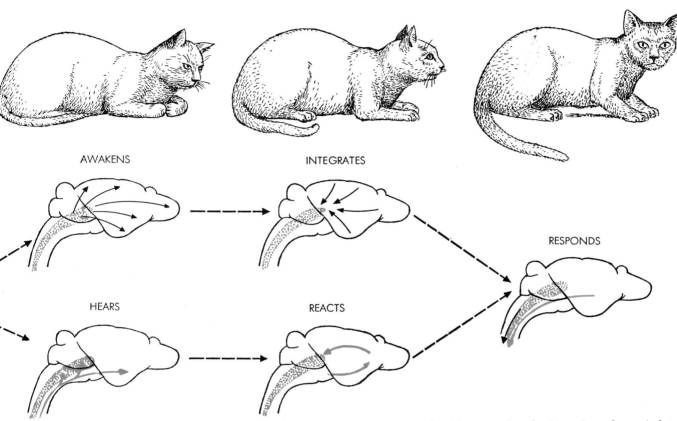

AWAKE

AWAKENS   INTEGRATES

                                                          RESPONDS

HEARS   REACTS

area. The brain waves at the top change from a pattern of sleep to one of wakefulness. The RAS then integrates the brain's activity so that the brain can react as a whole. The cat finally responds with a motor impulse (*outgoing red arrow*) that is regulated by the RAS. The cat then jumps to its feet and runs away. The entire process takes place in a matter of a few seconds.

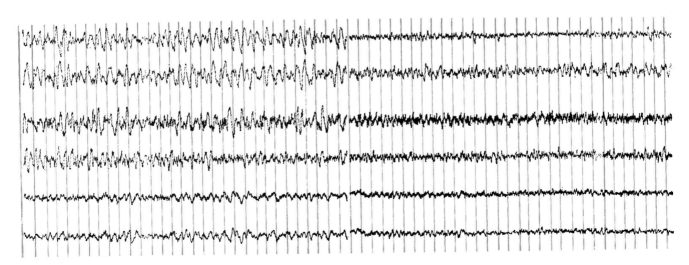

RAS IS STIMULATED by passing an electric current into the brain stem of a sleeping monkey. Recording electrodes show a more abrupt transition from sleep to wakefulness. The waves become sharp, short and more frequent. This is a typical waking pattern.

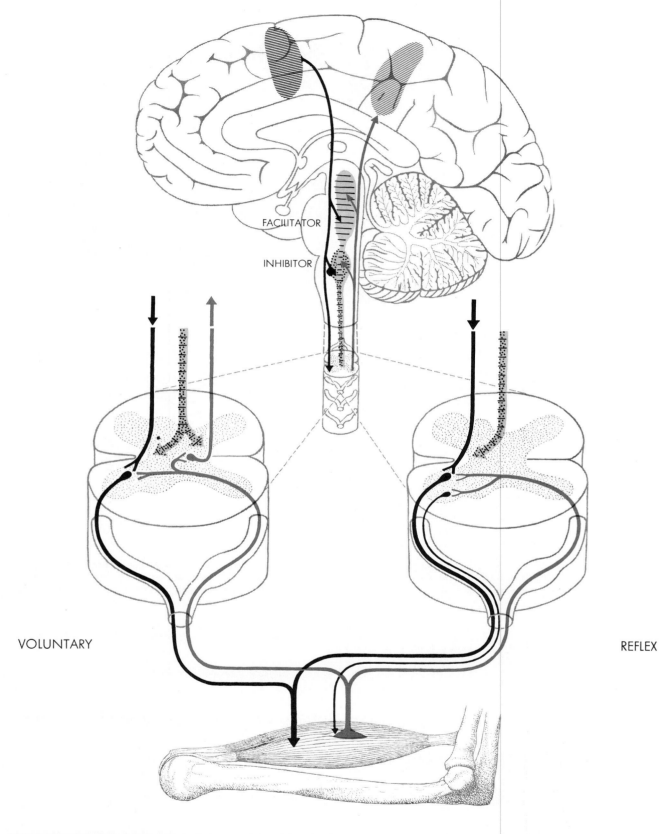

FACILITATOR

INHIBITOR

VOLUNTARY

REFLEX

MOVEMENTS ARE MODIFIED by the RAS. In voluntary movement sensory nerves (*red*) conduct impulses from the muscle spindle (*bottom*) to a sensory area in the brain (*red hatching*). Motor nerves (*black*) conduct impulses from the motor area (*black hatching*) to the muscle. Both nerve systems branch into the RAS.

The RAS sends down impulses (*heavy red arrows*) that facilitate or inhibit the response. In reflex movement sensory impulses are passed on immediately to motor nerves in the spinal cord. One nerve activates the muscle and maintains its "tone." The other (*thin black line*) sensitizes the spindle. The RAS controls both.

the cortex certainly is essential. The alert state seems to depend upon an interplay between the cortex and the RAS. The reticular formation is stimulated not only by the sensory nerves but also by impulses from some parts of the cortex. This has been demonstrated by electrical stimulation of certain areas of the cortex in monkeys: such stimulation will awaken a sleeping monkey. When the experiment is tried on a monkey that is awake, it evokes a dramatic response. The monkey instantly stops whatever it is doing and looks about intently and slightly puzzled, as if to say: "What was that?" It does not seem distressed or agitated—only warily alert. So it would seem that in the waking state the RAS plays a part, in combination with the cortex, in focusing attention and probably in many other mental processes.

All this raises the possibility that the RAS may be importantly involved in mental disorders. Investigations of this possibility have already begun by means of experiments with drugs. It is natural to start with anesthetic and sleep-inducing drugs, to see how they affect the RAS. The results of these experiments are illuminating but not surprising. They show that the drug blocks the flow of nerve impulses in the reticular formation but has little effect on the flow along the direct pathways from sense organs to the cortex. As the anesthesia wears off, the flow in the RAS returns to normal. A stimulating drug, on the other hand, has the opposite effect: it enhances the conduction of impulses in the RAS. It will be interesting to extend these experiments to the new tranquilizing drugs and the substances that produce experimental psychoses. Already there is evidence that these drugs do affect the functioning of the RAS.

Still another domain is under the control of this amazingly cogent bit of tissue in the brain. The RAS apparently has a hand in regulating all the motor activities of the body. It can modify muscle movements of both the voluntary type (controlled by the brain) and the reflex type (controlled in the spinal cord).

Just as the brain cortex has specific centers of sensation, it also has specific motor centers which generate muscle contractions. If one stimulates a motor center with an electric current, the appropriate muscles will respond, but the resulting body movements are jerky and uncontrolled. These powerful movements are normally controlled and polished by other motor centers of the

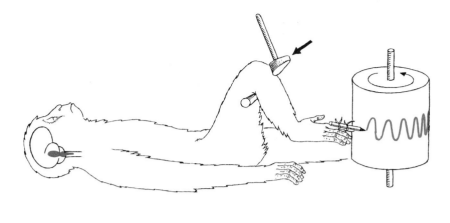

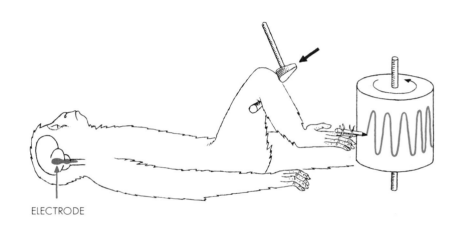

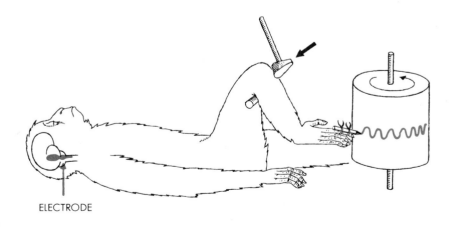

CONTROL OF REFLEX MOTOR REACTIONS by the reticular formation was demonstrated by this experiment on an anesthetized monkey. When the monkey's knee is tapped regularly, its knee jerks record a series of regular curves on a rotating drum (*top*). When the upper part of the monkey's reticular formation is stimulated, the jerks are larger (*middle*). When the lower part of the formation is stimulated, the jerks are smaller (*bottom*).

cortex, acting through the reticular formation. If the RAS is not stimulated or does not function properly, the movements will be jerky.

More surprising is the fact that the RAS can also act on the reflexes, centered in the spinal cord. The reflex apparatus has two functions. First, it generates automatic muscle movements. When signals from a sudden and alarming sensory stimulus (*e.g.*, touching something hot) arrive at the spinal cord, they are passed on immediately to an adjacent motor nerve and travel right back to the affected part of the body to jerk it away. In general, the automatic, reflex activities are protective—responses to danger or sudden challenges in the surroundings. But some of them can be tricked into action by suddenly stretching a muscle: for example, a tap on the knee elicits the well-known knee jerk.

The second function of the reflex system is to keep the muscles ready for action by maintaining "tone"—that is, a state of partial contraction. Just as a violin string must be stretched to a certain tension before it can emit music, so a muscle must be maintained at a certain tension to respond efficiently to a stimulus. The mechanism that regulates its resting tension, or "tone," is a small structure within the muscle called a "spindle." When a muscle contracts, it squeezes the spindle; when it relaxes, the pressure on the spindle loosens. Either departure from normal tone causes

the spindle to send signals by way of a sensory nerve to the spinal cord; there they excite a motor nerve to correct the contraction or relaxation of the muscle. This feedback system automatically keeps each muscle at precisely the right tone. And the appropriate tone itself is adjusted to suit the needs of the moment by nerve impulses which regulate the sensitivity of the spindle.

Now experiments have clearly demonstrated that the RAS exerts some control over voluntary and reflex motor reactions. Let us take for illustration an experiment on the reflex knee jerk, which is easy and convenient to perform. A monkey is anesthetized and a pen is tied to its toe to record the size of its knee kicks on a rotating drum. We keep tapping its knee and we get a uniform response, recorded as a nice series of regular curves on the drum. Then we suddenly stimulate the reticular formation electrically. The knee jerks immediately become larger: the RAS has enhanced them. When we stop stimulating it, the kicks return to normal size. Now in the course of exploratory experiments along the reticular formation a new fact emerges. If we stimulate the formation at a point toward its lower end in the brain stem, the kicks are not enhanced but instead are inhibited!

Following up this finding, we discover that these centers can enhance or inhibit sensory as well as motor impulses. In short, the RAS acts as a kind

of traffic control center, facilitating or inhibiting the flow of signals in the nervous system.

The astonishing generality of the RAS gives us a new outlook on the nervous system. Neurologists have tended to think of the nervous system as a collection of more or less separate circuits, each doing a particular job. It now appears that the system is much more closely integrated than had been thought. This should hardly surprise us. A simple organism such as the amoeba reacts with totality toward stimuli: the whole cell is occupied in the act of finding, engulfing and digesting food. Man, even with his 10 billion nerve cells, is not radically different. He must focus his sensory and motor systems on the problem in hand, and for this he obviously must be equipped with some integrating machine.

The RAS seems to be such a machine. It awakens the brain to consciousness and keeps it alert; it directs the traffic of messages in the nervous system; it monitors the myriads of stimuli that beat upon our senses, accepting what we need to perceive and rejecting what is irrelevant; it tempers and refines our muscular activity and bodily movements. We can go even further and say that it contributes in an important way to the highest mental processes– the focusing of attention, introspection and doubtless all forms of reasoning.

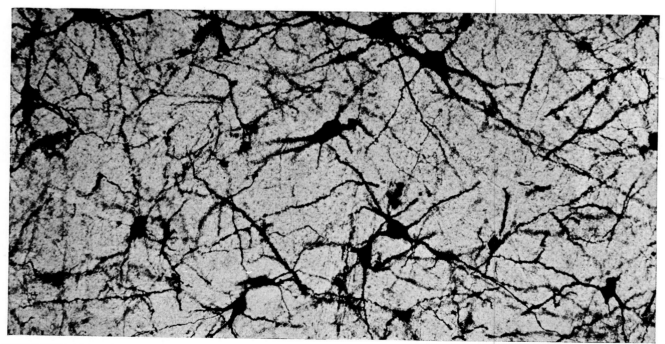

EXTENSIVE BRANCHING OF CELLS in the reticular formation is depicted by this photomicrograph of a section of the reticular formation in the brain of a dog. The dark areas in the photo-micrograph are cells of the formation which have been stained with silver. The section was lent by Drs. M. and A. Scheibel of the Medical School of the University of California at Los Angeles.

12

THE ANALYSIS OF BRAIN WAVES

MARY A. B. BRAZIER
June 1962

The electrical activity that can be recorded from the surface of the human head is probably the most baffling cryptogram to be found in nature. It is therefore not surprising that electrophysiologists have turned to electronic computers for help. First observed in animals by the English physiologist Richard Caton in 1875, the surface waves reflect the rich and constantly changing electrical activity of the brain. The first recordings from the human brain were made in 1924 by Hans Berger, a German psychiatrist who, because of his oddly secretive nature, withheld publication of his "electroencephalograms" until 1929. The reception was at first skeptical, but the electroencephalogram, or EEG, soon demonstrated its value in the diagnosis of epilepsy and other brain damage. Now, within the past 20 years, physiologists have made a start at decoding the EEG and have begun to show how it is related to the functioning of the nervous system.

For analyzing the electrical activity of the brain the electronic computer has emerged as an instrument of great power and versatility. One of the principal uses of the computer is to extract meaningful signals from the background electrical noise generated by the brain, which normally makes any single recording undecipherable. Although analyses of this sort are usually performed with magnetic-tape records of the brain's activity, the computer becomes even more useful when it is designed to make its analyses in "real" time, while the subject is still connected to the recording apparatus and while the investigator is still able to manipulate the experimental variables. Employed in this way, the computer becomes a subtle new tool for the studies of neurophysiology.

In man the fluctuating potential difference between leads on the unshaved scalp is commonly between 50 and 100 millionths of a volt, or about a tenth the magnitude of electrocardiographic potentials. These waves are most prominent at the back of the head over the visual-association areas of the brain; waves recorded there are called alpha waves. The alpha rhythm, which has a frequency of between eight and 13 per second in adult subjects, is most conspicuous when the eyes are closed. The alpha waves disappear momentarily when the eyes are opened.

Because of the regularity of the alpha rhythm, its frequency characteristics received most of the attention in the early days of electroencephalography. Physi-

ELECTRODES ON SCALP detect brain waves. This subject, in an isolated room, is viewing brief flashes of light at regular intervals. A special computer simultaneously analyzes the brain waves from the visual region in back of head, producing the record seen in illustration on page 10. The photograph was made at the Massachusetts Institute of Technology.

FIRST PUBLISHED ELECTROENCEPHALOGRAM (EEG) of man appeared in 1929. The recording was made by the German psychiatrist Hans Berger from the scalp of his young son. Upper channel is the EEG, lower one an artificial sine wave used as a marker.

ologists reasoned that if these waves were analyzed mathematically, using the technique known as Fourier analysis, components might be uncovered that were hidden to the unaided eye. The principle behind Fourier analysis is that any periodic wave form, however complex, can be resolved into elementary sine-wave components. Unfortunately the brain emits so many irregular and nonperiodic potential changes that the usefulness of this well-known principle is open to challenge.

During World War II W. Grey Walter of the Burden Neurological Institute in England spearheaded the development of the first practical instrument for making an automatic frequency analysis of consecutive short segments—each arbitrarily limited to 10 seconds—of an EEG trace. The Walter analyzer reports the mean relative amplitude at each frequency over the whole period being integrated but cannot indicate the time sequence in which the frequencies occur. A short wave train of high amplitude has the same effect on the integrating device as a long train of low amplitude. Also lost is all information about phase relations between trains of waves.

This type of analysis proved especially valuable when coupled with the finding that the frequency characteristics of the human EEG can often be controlled by having the subject look at a flashing light; the technique, called photic driving, was discovered in the early 1940's. Subsequently it was found that flashes of specific frequency will induce epileptic seizures in some epileptic patients. This is an example of a physiological finding reaching over into medicine to become a clinical diagnostic test. The Walter analyzer, which can be regarded as an early form of computer, still provides the simplest and most practical method for obtaining the average frequency spectrum of an EEG trace.

The rapid development of high-speed general-purpose and special-purpose computers in the past decade has opened up many new ways of analyzing the brain's electrical activity. At the same time techniques have been perfected for recording from electrodes implanted within the unanesthetized brain and left in place for weeks or months. Although used primarily with animals, the technique has been extended to man for diagnostic and therapeutic purposes.

It is therefore now possible to study the relation of the brain's electrical activity to behavioral performance and, in the case of man, to subjective experience. After a long period of concentrating on the rhythm observable when the subject was at rest with the eyes closed, electroencephalographers began to divert their attention from "the engine when idling" to the "engine at work," thereby examining how the brain responds to various stimuli.

Many types of stimulation can be used —sounds, odors, flashes of light, touch and so on—and their effect can be traced in brain recordings made both at the surface and deep within the brain. When such studies were first attempted in unanesthetized animals and man, it was soon discovered that the specific responses were largely masked, in the unanalyzed trace, by the ongoing EEG activity of the normal brain, activity that had been conveniently depressed by the anesthetic agents in the earlier studies. Since the electrodes used must be small enough to discriminate between neuronal structures less than a millimeter apart, appropriate computer techniques are essential for detecting the faint signals that are all but lost in the roar of biological noise that is the normal milieu of the active brain.

The principal means for increasing the signal-to-noise ratio is simply to have the computer add up a large number of responses—anywhere from a few dozen to a few hundred—and calculate an average response. One can then regard this average response, or certain features of it, as the characteristic "signal" elicited by a given stimulus. In applying this technique the neurophysiologist must necessarily make certain assumptions about the character of the biological phenomena he regards as signal and that which he chooses to call noise.

In the usual averaging procedure the brain's potential changes, as picked up by several electrodes, are recorded on multichannel magnetic tape, in which one channel carries a pulse coincident with delivery of the stimulus. Since the stimulus may be presented at irregular intervals, a pulse is needed as a time marker from which the responses are "lined up" for averaging. In the averaging process only those potential changes that occur with a constant time relation to the pulse are preserved and emphasized. Those unrelated in time cancel out in the averaging process, even though in any single record they may be of higher amplitude. In this way responses never before detectable at the surface of the human skull not only can be found but also can be correlated with the subject's report of his sensations.

For example, the lightest of taps on the back of the hand is found to evoke a clear-cut response in one special area on the opposite side of the head [see illustrations on page 115]. Other computer analyses show that a click in the ear gives a decipherable response in another location on the scalp. A flash of light not only evokes an immediate sharp response in the visual area at the back of the head but also gives rise to a long-lasting train of waves, all time-locked to the flash [see illustration on page 117]. It has been shown, moreover, that clinical patients who report a disturbance in their subjective sensation of touch, hearing or sight produce EEG traces that reveal distortions when analyzed by computer.

The long-lasting train of waves evoked by a flash of light raises a number of

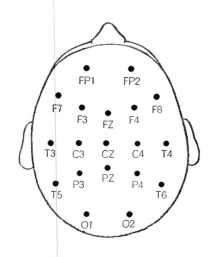

TYPICAL MODERN EEG shows that different regions of cortex give rhythms that differ widely. Berger thought the whole brain

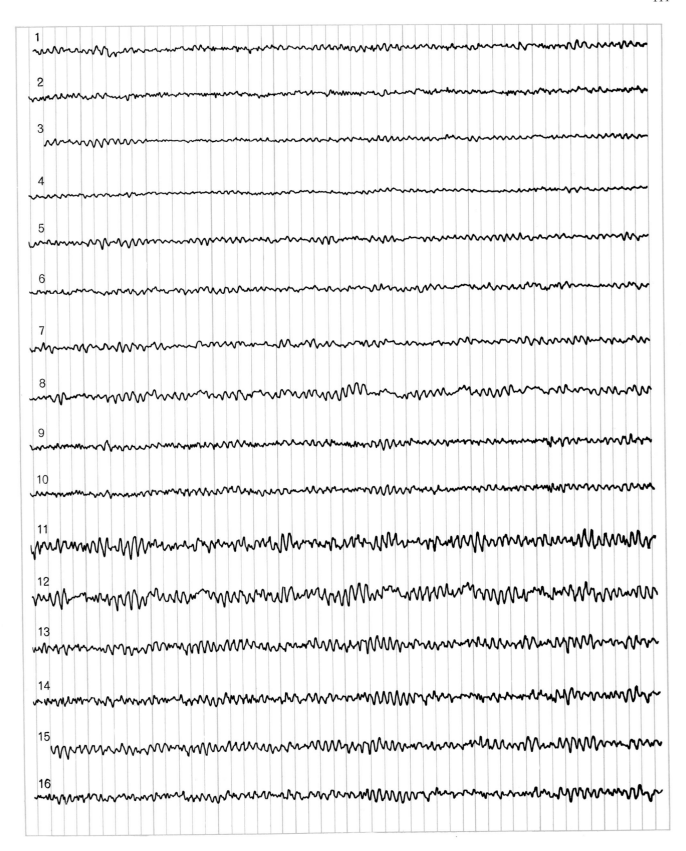

emitted only one rhythm. Today as many as 16, 24 and even 32 channels can be used. The great complexity obviously makes computer analysis desirable. Each EEG trace records changes in electric potential between two electrodes. Thus line 1 came from electrodes FP1 and F7 on head as diagramed at left, while line 10 came from FP2 and C4. This data has not been processed by a computer.

questions. Is this the electrical sign of further processing of the initial message received by the eye? Is it the sign that the experience is being passed into storage, initiating in its passage the cellular changes that underlie memory? There is already evidence that under conditions that retain the initial sharp response but obliterate the subsequent wave train all memory of the experience is expunged. Two such conditions, which support this suggestion in human experiments, are anesthesia and hypnotically induced blindness.

Valuable though computers can be for averaging taped EEG records, they still leave the investigator feeling somewhat frustrated. Hours, and sometimes days, may elapse between the experiment and the completed analysis of the recordings. When he sees the results, the investigator often wishes he could have changed the experimental conditions slightly, perhaps to accentuate a trend of some sort that seemed to be developing, but it is too late. The experimental material of the biologist, and

particularly of the electrophysiologist studying the brain, is living, changing material from which he must seize the opportunity to extract all possible information before the passage of time introduces new variables. The computers familiar to business and industry have not been designed with this problem in mind.

To meet the needs of the neurophysiologist a few computers have now been built that process brain recordings virtually as fast as data is fed in from the electrodes. The investigator can observe the results of his manipulations on the face of a cathode-ray tube or other display device and can modify his experiment at will. One of the first machines built to operate in this way is the Average Response Computer (ARC), designed by W. A. Clark, Jr., of the Lincoln Laboratory of the Massachusetts Institute of Technology [see illustration on this page]. ARC is a simple-to-operate, special-purpose digital computer that requires no programmer as a middleman between the biologist and the machine.

When searching for an evoked response, Clark's computer samples the EEG at a prescribed interval after the stimulus, converts it into a seven-digit binary number proportional to the amplitude and sends the number into one of the many memory registers. This particular register receives and adds all further numbers obtained at the same interval after each stimulus. ARC is equipped to sample the EEG at 254 different time intervals and to store thousands of samples at each interval. Only rarely, however, is the full capacity of the register required. The cumulative sums in each register are displayed on an oscilloscope after each stimulus [see illustration on page 113]. The investigator watches the cumulative display and stops the stimulation when he sees that he has enough signal-to-noise discrimination to satisfy the needs of the experiment. He can then photograph the face of the oscilloscope or have the cumulative wave form printed out graphically by a plotter.

What might one see if one were to watch the build-up of summed re-

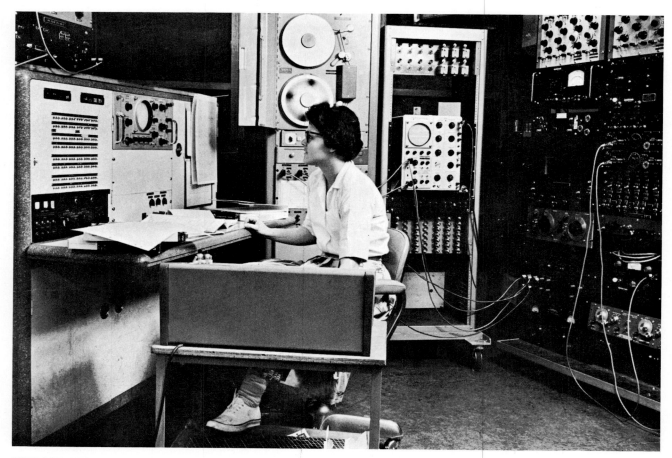

AVERAGE RESPONSE COMPUTER (ARC) was designed by W. A. Clark, Jr., of the Lincoln Laboratory of M.I.T. It samples the brain waves for a prescribed interval after each stimulus, adding and averaging the samples. Oscilloscope face on computer (left) displays trace of average as the experiment proceeds. Reels of magnetic tape (center, rear) permanently record all the raw data. In the foreground, beside the laboratory technician, is an "X-Y plotter," which makes pen tracings of the averaged data.

sponses? If the man or animal being studied were anesthetized, the response would be markedly stereotyped; the averaged sum of 100 responses would look very much like the average of 50 responses. This is not so if the subject is unanesthetized. Responses to a series of clicks or flashes of light may show great variation, both in wave shape and in amplitude, and may require many samples before the characteristic signal emerges clearly from the background noise.

Operating in another of its modes, ARC can give an amplitude histogram, or profile, at any chosen interval after the stimulus. Such histograms indicate the degree of fluctuation of the response and its complexity. They supply the investigator with important clues to the behavioral state of the subject, to his level of wakefulness, to the degree of attention he is paying to the stimulus and to the feelings the stimulus arouses.

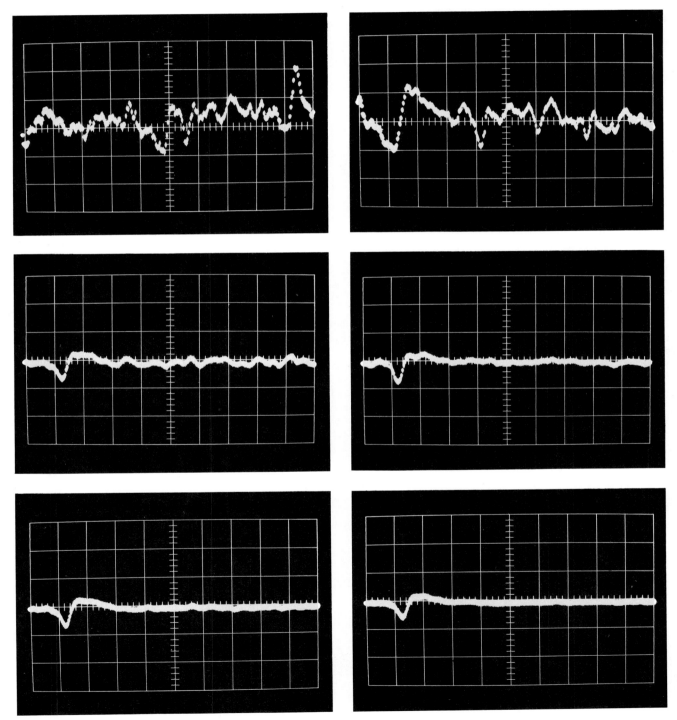

OSCILLOSCOPE TRACES of responses as averaged by computer appear while experiment is in progress, enabling experimenter to observe in "real time." As a result he can change conditions and stop when he has enough data. The traces (*left to right, top to bottom*) are averages of 1, 2, 32, 64, 128 and 512 responses. These traces appeared during an experiment by Nelson Kiang of the Eaton-Peabody Laboratory of the Massachusetts Eye and Ear Infirmary in Boston. The subject was responding to a long series of clicks.

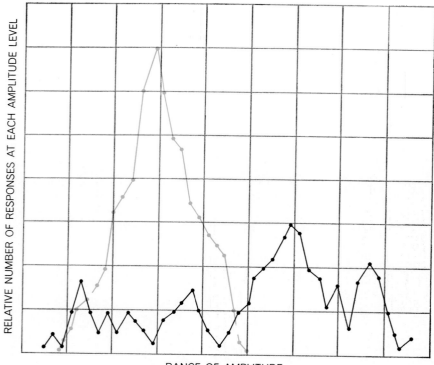

RANGE OF AMPLITUDE

(vertical axis label) RELATIVE NUMBER OF RESPONSES AT EACH AMPLITUDE LEVEL

STEREOTYPED RESPONSE of brain of anesthetized animal to flash of light (*colored curve*) shows plainly when computer is programed to give information on amplitude variation. Unanesthetized animal gives widely fluctuating response (*black curve*). In each case the computer analyzed point in time at which response reached its maximum amplitude.

When ARC is operated in the histogram mode, the memory registers are set to count the number of times the amplitude, or voltage, of the EEG falls within a certain preset range. Each register is set for a different range and the results are finally written out as a histogram for the chosen interval [*see top illustration on this page*]. By analyzing other intervals similarly one can put together a composite survey.

The study of such records may reveal little dispersion of amplitude at some particular interval after the stimulus and a much greater dispersion at some other interval. This may be a clue that the neuronal message in the first case has traveled over a nerve pathway containing few synapses, or relays, and thus has been subject to little dispersion, whereas in the second case the message has reached the recording site after traveling through multiple paths that finally converge. The complex wave train evoked by a single flash of light is susceptible to this interpretation. The initial deflection is caused by impulses that have traveled through a few synapses only and by means of the large, rapidly conducting fibers of the specific visual system. The subsequent shallower waves—so clearly revealed by the computer—reach the cortex through the more slowly conducting, indirect, nonspecific system with its many relay stations. The histogram of the earlier event, being more stereotyped, shows less dispersion around the median than does the histogram of the later events. Still more elaborate processing of histograms can show whether the amplitudes follow a normal, bell-shaped distribution pattern or are skewed in some manner.

If a physicist were to analyze the results of a series of complex experiments in his field, he would normally expect to find the results to be invariant. The biologist, working with an unanesthetized animal or man, can search in vain for an invariant response. It is precisely this subtlety of variation that electrophysiologists have recently identified as the concomitant of behavioral change. One such change is known as habituation. Early workers in electrophysiology could perceive, in their unanalyzed records, subtle changes in the shape of an EEG trace when the subject had been repeatedly exposed to the same stimulus. Computer analyses have now revealed clearly that under such conditions significant changes take place not only in the EEG as recorded outside the skull but even more markedly in recordings made deep within the brain.

For example, the Average Response Computer has been used to analyze the electrical activity recorded from a particular relay station in a nucleus located deep in the mid-line region of an animal's brain. The nucleus, in turn, lies within the portion of the brain called the thalamus. Until a dozen years ago little except its anatomy was known about this mid-line region of the thalamus and its inflow from the portion of the brain stem called the reticular formation. The thalamic region and the reticular formation together constitute the nonspecific sensory system mentioned earlier.

In 1949 H. W. Magoun (now at the

0   10   20   30   40
TIME (SECONDS)

0   .25   .5   .75   1   0   .25   .5   .75   1
TIME (SECONDS)

HISTOGRAMS showing distribution of cell discharges relative to stimulus were made by George L. Gerstein at M.I.T. Upper line shows a short section of raw data consisting of cell discharges in the auditory part of a cat's brain in response to one-per-second clicks. The histogram at left shows number of cell discharges at fractional-second intervals after clicks. The histogram at right shows same analysis of cell discharges when no click occurred.

University of California in Los Angeles) and G. Moruzzi (now at the University of Pisa) jointly discovered that the reticular system is crucially concerned with the organism's state of alertness and with the behavioral nuances that lie in the continuum between vigi-

lant attention and the oblivion of sleep. Later work has revealed further nuances that can be discerned in the electrical record only with the fine-grained analyses that a computer can provide.

Computer analyses of records from one of the mid-line nuclei of this non-

specific sensory system in an unanesthetized animal have detected many unsuspected details. For example, when a light, flashing at a constant rate, is directed into the animal's eye, the ARC oscilloscope reveals that the averaged response is not at all simple but contains

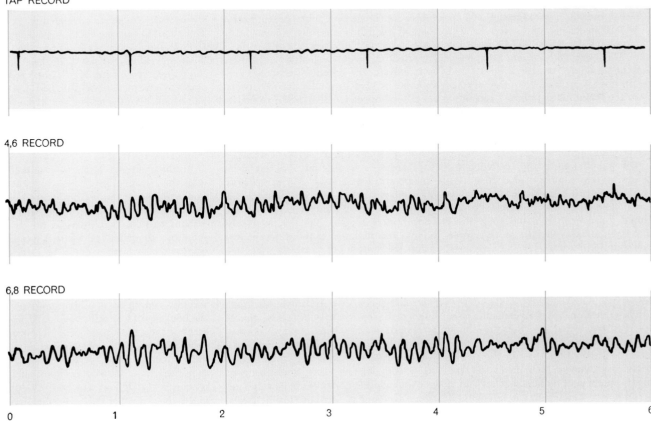

TAP RECORD

4,6 RECORD

6,8 RECORD

0   1   2   3   4   5   6

TIME (SECONDS)

REGULAR TAPS ON LEFT HAND, indicated by top trace, do not show up in standard EEG *(next two traces)*. Ongoing activity of brain drowns signal even though electrode 4 *(see diagram of head on next page)* is over area that receives nerve inflow from hand.

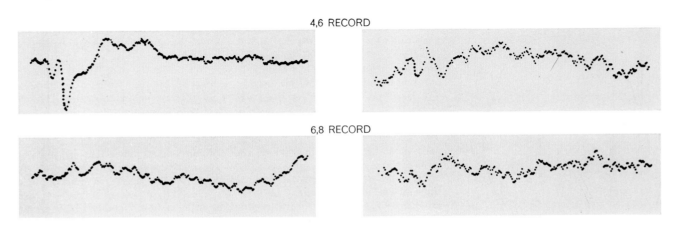

4,6 RECORD

6,8 RECORD

AVERAGED RESPONSE after 90 taps, however, tells a different story. Upper trace at left, from electrodes 4 and 6, shows that the brain definitely reacts to the taps. The computer also detects a faint response when the right hand, which is on the same side of the body as the electrodes, is tapped. (Nerves on the left side of the body are connected with the right side of the brain and vice versa.)

three distinct components and that, as time passes, one of these components gradually fades out. If the computer's mode of operation is then changed so as to produce amplitude histograms, the third component is found to have a greater dispersion than the other two and a skewed distribution.

A hypothesis suggests itself. One of the relatively constant components may pass on to the visual cortex, thereby signifying to the animal that the stimulus is visual and not, say, olfactory or auditory. Perhaps the second component indicates that the stimulus is a recurrent one. The third and waning component may be signaling "unexpectedness" and, by dropping out, may carry the message that the stimulus is simply repeating over and over without change. It may be saying, in effect, that the stimulus is devoid of novelty (or information) and can be safely ignored.

The experimenter, still watching the computer's oscilloscope, can then proceed to test this hypothesis by introducing novelty into the stimulus. For example, he can change the strength of the flash, its wavelength or its repetition rate, and watch for the reappearance of the third component. In this way the three-way interlocution between investigator, subject and machine proceeds.

The questions the investigator asks are not exhausted by those outlined above. He may want to know what the individual cells of the brain are doing. It has been known for many years that the frequency of action "spikes" in a nerve fiber is related to the intensity of the stimulus. As a rule the more intense the stimulus, the higher the firing rate. But how wasteful of "channel capacity"

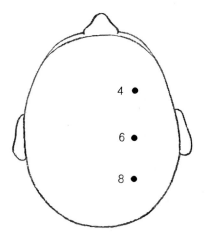

The averaged record from electrodes 6 and 8, which are not over the "hand area" of the brain, shows no response to the taps.

(to use the language of information theory) it would be if the only information conveyed by the action spikes were limited to stimulus intensity.

This has led investigators to consider the fluctuations in the groupings of these unit discharges. The unanalyzed record is bewildering, because different kinds of cell give different patterns of response to a given stimulus. Some that were busily active stop firing when the stimulus is given; others wake from idleness and burst into activity; still others signal their response by a change in the pattern of discharge.

Computers are invaluable for this type of analysis. The Average Response Computer, as one example, has a special mode of operation that helps to clarify this patterning of activity in individual brain cells. It does this by giving a histogram of the time intervals between successive cell discharges. Each of its memory registers is allotted a different interspike interval. Whenever a cell fires, the interval since the last firing is established and a digit is added to the appropriate register. On command, the digits accumulated in the different registers are written out as a histogram [*see bottom illustration on page 114*]. Analyses of this kind, pioneered by George L. Gerstein with the TX-O computer at the Massachusetts Institute of Technology, have revealed a differentiation of response mechanisms among cortical cells that indicates a far greater degree of discriminatory capability than the old frequency-intensity rule would suggest.

Among other computer techniques under development are those for identification of temporal patterns in the EEG. These techniques should relieve the electroencephalographer of the tedium of searching many yards of records for meaningful changes. For example, Belmont Farley of the Lincoln Laboratory of M.I.T. has worked out programs for analyzing the trains of alpha rhythm that come and go in the EEG of man and provide clues to his level of consciousness and to the normality of his brain.

Farley's program specifies the range of amplitude, frequency and duration of the pattern known as an alpha burst. The program allows the investigator to make a statistical examination of the EEG of the same individual, as recorded under different experimental circumstances. The investigator may be interested in the effect of drugs or the changes brought about by conditioning of behavior. The degree of variation in the EEG can be accurately and objectively assessed, removing the hazards of subjective judgment. It is obvious that

such objective methods of appraisal can be of great value in the clinical use of the EEG.

The rhythmicity of the EEG, as exemplified in the alpha rhythm, continues to be a mystery. It was first thought that brain waves were merely the envelopes of the spike discharges of the underlying neurons. But this view had to be abandoned when microelectrodes, reporting from inside the brain, showed the hypothesis untenable. It is now thought that the EEG waves reflect the waxing and waning of excitability in what are called the dendritic layers of the cortex. (Dendrites are hairlike processes that extend from the body of a nerve cell.) Quite unlike the explosive discharge of the nerve cell itself, the finely graded changes in dendritic activity seem to modulate cortical excitability.

In the common laboratory animals, with their comparatively small association cortexes, the simple, almost sinusoidal oscillation of the alpha rhythm is hard to find, if it exists at all. It is therefore tempting to relate rhythmic waves to the large volume of association cortex possessed by man. These rhythmic waves usually signify that the brain is not under bombardment by stimuli, and their stability may reflect the homeostatic, or self-stabilizing, processes of the association cortex when undisturbed by the processing of transmitted messages.

In the course of evolution homeostatic processes throughout the body, largely under the control of the brain stem, have provided the higher animals with a remarkably constant internal environment. The constancy of this *milieu intérieur*, as the French physiologist Claude Bernard pointed out, is "la condition de la vie libre." Conceivably it is the stabilizing effect of the brain stem that frees the cortex of man for its highest achievements.

Whatever the case, it has been discovered by the statistical method of autocorrelation analysis that EEG recordings from man often show a long-persisting phase constancy that has not been found in lower animals. There are also individual differences. In some people phase-locking of oscillations is, for long periods, nearly as predictable as a clock. In others (a minority) there is little, if any, stability of phase. Are the people who lack a stable phase-locked oscillation unable to clear their association cortex of interfering activity? Have they not yet attained the "free life" of Claude Bernard?

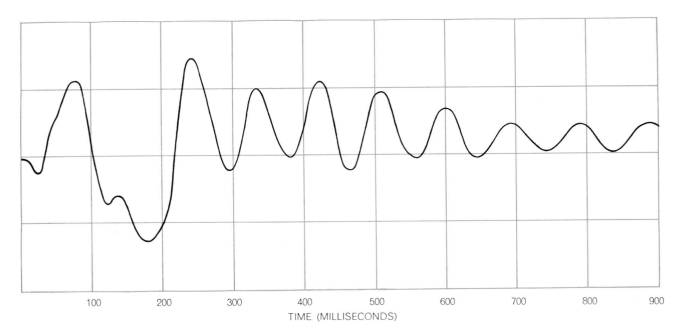

TIME (MILLISECONDS)

LONG-LASTING TRAIN OF WAVES can be recorded from scalp following flash of light. This, of course, is an averaged record of many responses to many flashes. It emphasizes only the changes in electric potential time-locked to the flash and washes out the "noisy" background activity, which is actually of much higher amplitude. The flashes were all synchronized with beginning of trace.

One of the earliest workers to encourage electroencephalographers to explore this approach was the M.I.T. mathematician Norbert Wiener. His strong influence lies behind much of the computer work in this area, and especially that which has come from the laboratory of Walter A. Rosenblith of M.I.T.'s Research Laboratory for Electronics.

No account of the electroencephalographer's use of computers should omit their recent use in seeking information about the correlations between deep and superficial activity in various parts of the brain. What is the correlation between the waves recorded from the outside of man's skull and activity in the depths? With what confidence can one say that an EEG is "normal" when only scalp recordings can be made?

The first answers to these and many other questions are just emerging as computer analyses of electrical potentials from inside man's head are being correlated with those simultaneously recorded from his scalp. As more and more clinical investigators adopt computer techniques it should be possible to build up for the electroencephalographer, who can record only from the surface of the unopened scalp, a reference library of correlations to use in assessing the probability of events in the hidden depths of the brain.

Nearly all the applications of the computer described here have involved averaging. This is not only because the average is an empirically useful statistic but also because many brain investigators suspect that the brain may work on a probabilistic basis rather than a deterministic one. To analyze the myriad complexities of the brain's function by nonstatistical description is too gigantic a task to be conceived, but exploration in terms of probability theory is both practical and rational. In characterizing nervous activity one would not therefore attempt the precise definition that arithmetic demands but would seek the statistical characteristics of the phenomena that appear to be relevant.

The margin of safety that the brain has for acting appropriately on a probabilistic basis would be much greater than that which would be imposed by a deterministic arithmetically precise operation. Chaos would result from the least slip-up of the latter, whereas only a major divergence from the mean would disturb a system working on a probability basis. The rigidity of arithmetic is not for the brain, and a search for a deterministic code based on arithmetical precision is surely doomed to disappointment.

One can speculate how a brain might work on statistical principles. Incoming sensory messages would be compared with the statistical distribution of nerve cell characteristics that have developed as functions of the past activities of these cells. Significance of the message would then be evaluated and, according to the odds, its message could be appropriately acted on or ignored. The brain, with its wealth of interconnections, has an enormous capacity for storage, and one can observe the development of appropriate responses by watching the limited capacity of the child grow to the superior capacity of the man.

One might ask why it is the brain investigator, among biological scientists, who has reached out most eagerly to the computer for help. A likely answer is that within man's skull—a not very large, rigidly limited space—a greater number of transactions are taking place simultaneously than in any other known system of its size. The multiplicity of signals that these transactions emit and the truly formidable complexity of codes that they may use have proved beyond the capabilities of analysis by the methods of an earlier age.

The neurophysiologist cannot hope to study a single variable in isolation. The living brain will not still its busy activity so that the investigator can control whatever he wishes; neither will it forget its past. Every stimulus, however "constant" the experimenter may succeed in making it, enters a nervous system that is in an ever changing state. The "stimulus-response" experiment of an earlier day is no longer adequate. Experiment has to enter a phase of greater sophistication that may well prove out of reach without the help of the computer.

13

THE SPLIT BRAIN IN MAN

MICHAEL S. GAZZANIGA
August 1967

The brain of the higher animals, including man, is a double organ, consisting of right and left hemispheres connected by an isthmus of nerve tissue called the corpus callosum. Some 15 years ago Ronald E. Myers and R. W. Sperry, then at the University of Chicago, made a surprising discovery: When this connection between the two halves of the cerebrum was cut, each hemisphere functioned independently as if it were a complete brain. The phenomenon was first investigated in a cat in which not only the brain but also the optic chiasm, the crossover of the optic nerves, was divided, so that visual information from the left eye was dispatched only to the left brain and information from the right eye only to the right brain. Working on a problem with one eye, the animal could respond normally and learn to perform a task; when that eye was covered and the same problem was presented to the other eye, the animal evinced no recognition of the problem and had to learn it again from the beginning with the other half of the brain.

The finding introduced entirely new questions in the study of brain mechanisms. Was the corpus callosum responsible for integration of the operations of the two cerebral hemispheres in the intact brain? Did it serve to keep each hemisphere informed about what was going on in the other? To put the question another way, would cutting the corpus callosum literally result in the right hand not knowing what the left was doing? To what extent were the two half-brains actually independent when they were separated? Could they have separate thoughts, even separate emotions?

Such questions have been pursued by Sperry and his co-workers in a wide-ranging series of animal studies at the California Institute of Technology over the past decade [see "The Great Cerebral Commissure," by R. W. Sperry; SCIENTIFIC AMERICAN Offprint 174]. Recently these questions have been investigated in human patients who underwent the brain-splitting operation for medical reasons. The demonstration in experimental animals that sectioning of the corpus callosum did not seriously impair mental faculties had encouraged surgeons to resort to this operation for people afflicted with uncontrollable epilepsy. The hope was to confine a seizure to one hemisphere. The operation proved to be remarkably successful; curiously there is an almost total elimination of all attacks, including unilateral ones. It is as if the intact callosum had served in these patients to facilitate seizure activity.

This article is a brief survey of investigations Sperry and I have carried out at Cal Tech over the past five years with some of these patients. The operations were performed by P. J. Vogel and J. E. Bogen of the California College of Medicine. Our studies date back to 1961, when the first patient, a 48-year-old war veteran, underwent the operation: cutting of the corpus callosum and other commissure structures connecting the two halves of the cerebral cortex [*see illustration on page 120*]. As of today 10 patients have had the operation, and we have examined four thoroughly over a long period with many tests.

From the beginning one of the most striking observations was that the operation produced no noticeable change in the patients' temperament, personality or general intelligence. In the first case the patient could not speak for 30 days after the operation, but he then recovered his speech. More typical was the third case: on awaking from the surgery the patient quipped that he had a "splitting headache," and in his still drowsy state he was able to repeat the tongue twister "Peter Piper picked a peck of pickled peppers."

Close observation, however, soon revealed some changes in the patients' everyday behavior. For example, it could be seen that in moving about and responding to sensory stimuli the patients favored the right side of the body, which is controlled by the dominant left half of the brain. For a considerable period after the operation the left side of the body rarely showed spontaneous activity, and the patient generally did not respond to stimulation of that side: when he brushed against something with his left side he did not notice that he had done so, and when an object was placed in his left hand he generally denied its presence.

More specific tests identified the main features of the bisected-brain syndrome. One of these tests examined responses to visual stimulation. While the patient fixed his gaze on a central point on a board, spots of light were flashed (for a tenth of a second) in a row across the board that spanned both the left and the right half of his visual field. The patient was asked to tell what he had seen. Each patient reported that lights had been flashed in the right half of the visual field. When lights were flashed only in the left half of the field, however, the patients generally denied having seen any lights. Since the right side of the visual field is normally projected to the left hemisphere of the brain and the left field to the right hemisphere, one might have concluded that in these patients with divided brains the right hemisphere was in effect blind. We found, however, that this was not the case when the patients were directed to point to the lights that had flashed instead of giving a verbal report. With this manual response they were able to indicate when lights had been flashed in the left visual field, and perception with the brain's right hemisphere proved to be almost equal to perception with the left. Clearly, then, the patients' failure to report the right hemisphere's perception verbally was due to the fact that the speech centers of the brain are located in the left hemisphere.

Our tests of the patients' ability to recognize objects by touch at first resulted in the same general finding. When the object was held in the right hand, from which sensory information is sent to the left hemisphere, the patient was able to name and describe the object. When it was held in the left hand (from which information goes primarily to the right hemisphere), the patient could not describe the object verbally but was able to identify it in a nonverbal test—matching it, for example, to the same object in a varied collection of things. We soon realized, however, that each hemisphere receives, in addition to the main input from the opposite side of the body, some input from the same side. This "ipsilateral" input is crude; it is apparently good mainly for "cuing in" the hemisphere as to the presence or absence of stimulation and relaying fairly gross information about the location of a stimulus on the surface of the body. It is unable, as a rule, to relay information concerning the qualitative nature of an object.

Tests of motor control in these split-brain patients revealed that the left hemisphere of the brain exercised normal control over the right hand but had less than full control of the left hand (for instance, it was poor at directing individual movements of the fingers). Similarly, the right hemisphere had full control of the left hand but not of the right hand. When the two hemispheres were in conflict, dictating different movements for the same hand, the hemisphere on the side opposite the hand generally took charge and overruled the orders of the side of the brain with the weaker control. In general the motor findings in the human patients were much the same as those in split-brain monkeys.

We come now to the main question on which we centered our studies, namely how the separation of the hemispheres affects the mental capacities of the human brain. For these psychological tests we used two different devices. One was visual: a picture or written information was flashed (for a tenth of a second) in either the right or the left visual field, so that the information was transmitted only to the left or to the right brain hemisphere [see illustration on page 121]. The other type of test was

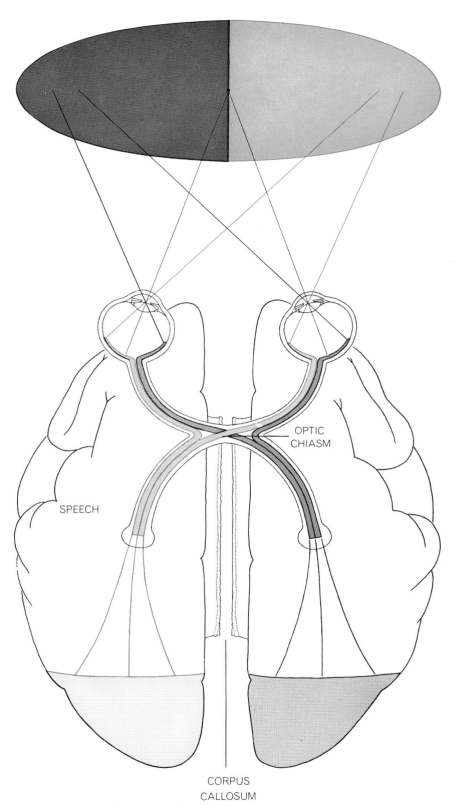

VISUAL INPUT to bisected brain was limited to one hemisphere by presenting information only in one visual field. The right and left fields of view are projected, via the optic chiasm, to the left and right hemispheres of the brain respectively. If a person fixes his gaze on a point, therefore, information to the left of the point goes only to the right hemisphere and information to the right of the point goes to the left hemisphere. Stimuli in the left visual field cannot be described by a split-brain patient because of the disconnection between the right hemisphere and the speech center, which is in the left hemisphere.

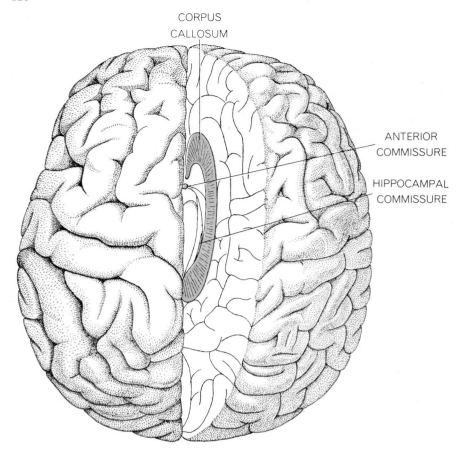

CORPUS
CALLOSUM

ANTERIOR
COMMISSURE

HIPPOCAMPAL
COMMISSURE

TWO HEMISPHERES of the human brain are divided by neurosurgeons to control epileptic seizures. In this top view of the brain the right hemisphere is retracted and the corpus callosum and other commissures, or connectors, that are generally cut are shown in color.

tactile: an object was placed out of view in the patient's right or left hand, again for the purpose of conveying the information to just one hemisphere—the hemisphere on the side opposite the hand.

When the information (visual or tactile) was presented to the dominant left hemisphere, the patients were able to deal with and describe it quite normally, both orally and in writing. For example, when a picture of a spoon was shown in the right visual field or a spoon was placed in the right hand, all the patients readily identified and described it. They were able to read out written messages and to perform problems in calculation that were presented to the left hemisphere.

In contrast, when the same information was presented to the right hemisphere, it failed to elicit such spoken or written responses. A picture transmitted to the right hemisphere evoked either a haphazard guess or no verbal response at all. Similarly, a pencil placed in the left hand (behind a screen that cut off vision) might be called a can opener or a cigarette lighter, or the patient might not even attempt to describe it. The verbal guesses presumably came not from the right hemisphere but from the left, which had no perception of the object but might attempt to identify it from indirect clues.

Did this impotence of the right hemisphere mean that its surgical separation from the left had reduced its mental powers to an imbecilic level? The earlier tests of its nonverbal capacities suggested that this was almost certainly not so. Indeed, when we switched to asking for nonverbal answers to the visual and tactile information presented in our new psychological tests, the right hemisphere in several patients showed considerable capacity for accurate performance. For example, when a picture of a spoon was presented to the right hemisphere, the patients were able to feel around with the left hand among a varied group of objects (screened from sight) and select a spoon as a match for the picture. Furthermore, when they were shown a picture of a cigarette they succeeded in selecting an ashtray, from a group of 10 objects that did not include a cigarette, as the article most closely related to the picture. Oddly enough, however, even after their correct response, and while they were holding the spoon or the ashtray in their left hand, they were unable to name or describe the object or the picture. Evidently the left hemisphere was completely divorced, in perception and knowledge, from the right.

Other tests showed that the right hemisphere did possess a certain amount of language comprehension. For example, when the word "pencil" was flashed to the right hemisphere, the patients were able to pick out a pencil from a group of unseen objects with the left hand. And when a patient held an object in the left hand (out of view), although he could not say its name or describe it, he was later able to point to a card on which the name of the object was written.

In one particularly interesting test the word "heart" was flashed across the center of the visual field, with the "he" portion to the left of the center and "art" to the right. Asked to tell what the word was, the patients would say they had seen "art"—the portion projected to the left brain hemisphere (which is responsible for speech). Curiously when, after "heart" had been flashed in the same way, the patients were asked to point with the left hand to one of two cards— "art" or "he"—to identify the word they had seen, they invariably pointed to "he." The experiment showed clearly that both hemispheres had simultaneously observed the portions of the word available to them and that in this particular case the right hemisphere, when it had had the opportunity to express itself, had prevailed over the left.

Because an auditory input to one ear goes to both sides of the brain, we conducted tests for the comprehension of words presented audibly to the right hemisphere not by trying to limit the original input but by limiting the ability to answer to the right hemisphere. This was done most easily by having a patient use his left hand to retrieve, from a grab bag held out of view, an object named by the examiner. We found that the patients could easily retrieve such objects as a watch, comb, marble or coin. The object to be retrieved did not even have to be named; it might simply be described or alluded to. For example, the command "Retrieve the fruit monkeys like best" results in the patients' pulling out a banana from a grab bag full of plastic fruit; at the command "Sunkist sells a lot of them" the patients retrieve an orange. We knew that touch information from the left hand was going exclusively to the right hemisphere because moments later, when the patients were asked to name various pieces of fruit placed in the left hand, they were unable to score above a chance level.

The upper limit of linguistic abilities in each hemisphere varies from subject to subject. In one case there was little or no evidence for language abilities in the right hemisphere, whereas in the other three the amount and extent of the capacities varied. The most adept patient showed some evidence of even being able to spell simple words by placing plastic letters on a table with his left hand. The subject was told to spell a word such as "pie," and the examiner then placed the three appropriate letters, one at a time in a random order, in his left hand to be arranged on the table. The patient was able to spell even more abstract words such as "how," "what" and "the." In another test three or four letters were placed in a pile, again out of view, to be felt with the left hand. The letters available in each trial would spell only one word, and the instructions to the subject were "Spell a word." The patient was able to spell such words as "cup" and "love." Yet after he had completed this task, the patient was unable to name the word he had just spelled!

The possibility that the right hemisphere has not only some language but even some speech capabilities cannot be ruled out, although at present there is no firm evidence for this. It would not be surprising to discover that the patients are capable of a few simple exclamatory remarks, particularly when under emotional stress. The possibility also remains, of course, that speech of some type could be trained into the right hemisphere. Tests aimed at this question, however, would have to be closely scrutinized and controlled.

The reason is that here, as in many of the tests, "cross-cuing" from one hemisphere to the other could be held responsible for any positive findings. We had a case of such cross-cuing during a series of tests of whether the right hemisphere could respond verbally to simple red or green stimuli. At first, after either a red or a green light was flashed to the right hemisphere, the patient would guess the color at a chance level, as might be expected if the speech mechanism is solely represented in the left hemisphere. After a few trials, however, the score improved whenever the examiner allowed a second guess.

We soon caught on to the strategy the patient used. If a red light was flashed and the patient by chance guessed red, he would stick with that answer. If the flashed light was red and the patient by chance guessed green, he would frown,

shake his head and then say, "Oh no, I meant red." What was happening was that the right hemisphere saw the red light and heard the left hemisphere make the guess "green." Knowing that the answer was wrong, the right hemisphere precipitated a frown and a shake of the head, which in turn cued in the left hemisphere to the fact that the answer was wrong and that it had better correct itself! We have learned that this cross-cuing mechanism can become extremely refined. The realization that the neurological patient has various strategies at his command emphasizes how difficult it is to obtain a clear neurological description of a human being with brain damage.

Is the language comprehension by the right hemisphere that the patients exhibited in these tests a normal capability of that hemisphere or was it acquired by learning after their operation, perhaps during the course of the experiments themselves? The issue is difficult to decide. We must remember that we are examining a half of the human brain, a system easily capable of learning from a single trial in a test. We do know that the right hemisphere is decidedly inferior to the left in its overall command of language. We have established, for instance, that although the right hemisphere can respond to a concrete noun such as "pencil," it cannot do as well with verbs; patients are unable to re-

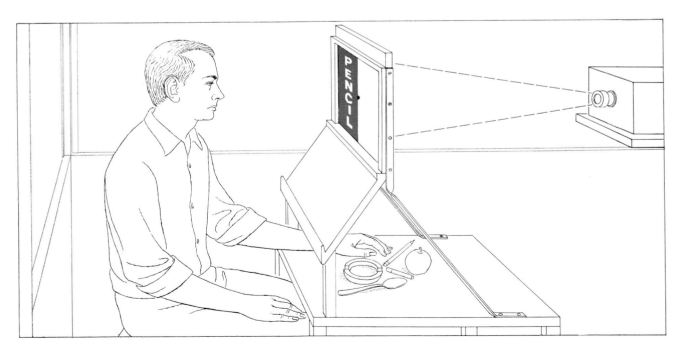

RESPONSE TO VISUAL STIMULUS is tested by flashing a word or a picture of an object on a translucent screen. The examiner first checks the subject's gaze to be sure it is fixed on a dot that marks the center of the visual field. The examiner may call for a verbal response—reading the flashed word, for example—or for a nonverbal one, such as picking up the object that is named from among a number of things spread on the table. The objects are hidden from the subject's view so that they can be identified only by touch.

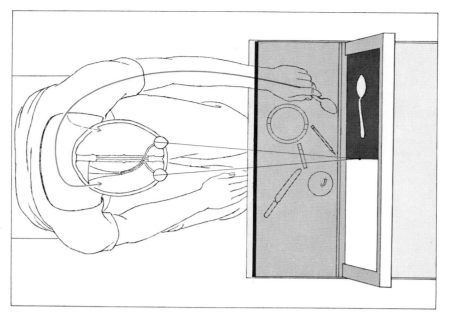

VISUAL-TACTILE ASSOCIATION is performed by a split-brain patient. A picture of a spoon is flashed to the right hemisphere; with the left hand he retrieves a spoon from behind the screen. The touch information from the left hand projects (*color*) mainly to the right hemisphere, but a weak "ipsilateral" component goes to the left hemisphere. This is usually not enough to enable him to say (using the left hemisphere) what he has picked up.

EXAMPLE	LEFT HAND	RIGHT HAND

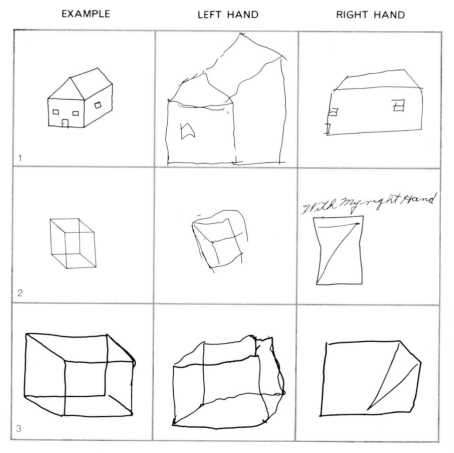

"VISUAL-CONSTRUCTIONAL" tasks are handled better by the right hemisphere. This was seen most clearly in the first patient, who had poor ipsilateral control of his right hand. Although right-handed, he could copy the examples only with his left hand.

spond appropriately to simple printed instructions, such as "smile" or "frown," when these words are flashed to the right hemisphere, nor can they point to a picture that corresponds to a flashed verb. Some of our recent studies at the University of California at Santa Barbara also indicate that the right hemisphere has a very poorly developed grammar; it seems to be incapable of forming the plural of a given word, for example.

In general, then, the extent of language present in the adult right hemisphere in no way compares with that present in the left hemisphere or, for that matter, with the extent of language present in the child's right hemisphere. Up to the age of four or so, it would appear from a variety of neurological observations, the right hemisphere is about as proficient in handling language as the left. Moreover, studies of the child's development of language, particularly with respect to grammar, strongly suggest that the foundations of grammar—a ground plan for language, so to speak—are somehow inherent in the human organism and are fully realized between the ages of two and three. In other words, in the young child each hemisphere is about equally developed with respect to language and speech function. We are thus faced with the interesting question of why the right hemisphere at an early age and stage of development possesses substantial language capacity whereas at a more adult stage it possesses a rather poor capacity. It is difficult indeed to conceive of the underlying neurological mechanism that would allow for the establishment of a capacity of a high order in a particular hemisphere on a temporary basis. The implication is that during maturation the processes and systems active in making this capacity manifest are somehow inhibited and dismantled in the right hemisphere and allowed to reside only in the dominant left hemisphere.

Yet the right hemisphere is not in all respects inferior or subordinate to the left. Tests have demonstrated that it excels the left in some specialized functions. As an example, tests by us and by Bogen have shown that in these patients the left hand is capable of arranging blocks to match a pictured design and of drawing a cube in three dimensions, whereas the right hand, deprived of instructions from the right hemisphere, could not perform either of these tasks.

It is of interest to note, however, that although the patients (our first subject in particular) could not execute such tasks with the right hand, they were capable of matching a test stimulus to the correct design when it appeared among five related patterns presented in their right visual field. This showed that the dominant left hemisphere is capable of discriminating between correct and incorrect stimuli. Since it is also true that the patients have no motor problems with their right hand, the patients' inability to perform these tasks must reflect a breakdown of an integrative process somewhere between the sensory system and the motor system.

We found that in certain other mental processes the right hemisphere is on a par with the left. In particular, it can independently generate an emotional reaction. In one of our experiments exploring the matter we would present a series of ordinary objects and then suddenly flash a picture of a nude woman. This evoked an amused reaction regardless of whether the picture was presented to the left hemisphere or to the right. When the picture was flashed to the left hemisphere of a female patient, she laughed and verbally identified the picture as a nude. When it was later presented to the right hemisphere, she said in reply to a question that she saw nothing, but almost immediately a sly smile spread over her face and she began to chuckle. Asked what she was laughing at, she said: "I don't know...nothing...oh—that funny machine." Although the right hemisphere could not describe what it had seen, the sight nevertheless elicited an emotional response like the one evoked from the left hemisphere.

Taken together, our studies seem to demonstrate conclusively that in a split-brain situation we are really dealing with two brains, each separately capable of mental functions of a high order. This implies that the two brains should have twice as large a span of attention—that is, should be able to handle twice as much information—as a normal whole brain. We have not yet tested this precisely in human patients, but E. D. Young and I have found that a split-brain monkey can indeed deal with nearly twice as much information as a normal animal [see illustration below]. We have so far determined also that brain-bisected patients can carry out two tasks as fast as a normal person can do one.

Just how does the corpus callosum of the intact brain combine and integrate the perceptions and knowledge of the two cerebral hemispheres? This has been investigated recently by Giovanni Berlucchi, Giacomo Rizzolati and me at the Istituto di Fisiologia Umana in Pisa. We made recordings of neural activity in the posterior part of the callosum of the cat with the hope of relating the responses of that structure to stimulation of the animal's visual fields. The kinds of responses recorded turned out to be similar to those observed in the visual cortex of the cat. In other words, the results suggest that visual pattern information can be transmitted through the callosum. This finding militates against the notion that learning and memory are transferred across the callosum, as has usually been suggested. Instead, it looks as though in animals with an intact callosum a copy of the visual world as seen in one hemisphere is sent over to the other, with the result that both hemispheres can learn together a discrimination presented to just one hemisphere. In the split-brain animal this extension of the visual pathway is cut off; this would explain rather simply why no learning proceeds in the visually isolated hemisphere and why it has to learn the discrimination from scratch.

Curiously, however, the neural activity in the callosum came only in response to stimuli at the midline of the visual field. This finding raises difficult questions. How can it be reconciled with the well-established observation that the left hemisphere of a normal person can give a running description of all the visual information presented throughout the entire half-field projected to the right hemisphere? For this reason alone one is wearily driven back to the conclusion that somewhere and somehow all or part of the callosum transmits not only a visual scene but also a complicated neural code of a higher order.

All the evidence indicates that separation of the hemispheres creates two independent spheres of consciousness within a single cranium, that is to say, within a single organism. This conclusion is disturbing to some people who view consciousness as an indivisible property of the human brain. It seems premature to others, who insist that the capacities revealed thus far for the right hemisphere are at the level of an automaton. There is, to be sure, hemispheric inequality in the present cases, but it may well be a characteristic of the individuals we have studied. It is entirely possible that if a human brain were divided in a very young person, both hemispheres could as a result separately and independently develop mental functions of a high order at the level attained only in the left hemisphere of normal individuals.

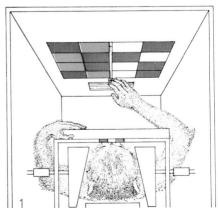 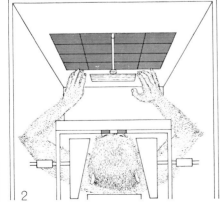 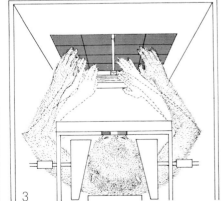

SPLIT-BRAIN MONKEYS can handle more visual information than normal animals. When the monkey pulls a knob (1), eight of the 16 panels light momentarily. The monkey must then start at the bottom and punch the lights that were lit and no others (2). With the panels lit for 600 milliseconds normal monkeys get up to the third row from the bottom before forgetting which panels were lit (3). Split-brain monkeys complete the entire task with the panels lit only 200 milliseconds. The monkeys look at the panels through filters; since the optic chiasm is cut in these animals, the filters allow each hemisphere to see the colored panels on one side only.

IV

NEURON AND SYNAPSE:
THE BASIS OF INTEGRATION
AND PLASTICITY IN THE BRAIN

IV

NEURON AND SYNAPSE: THE BASIS OF INTEGRATION AND PLASTICITY IN THE BRAIN

INTRODUCTION

The conduction of information along the fiber of a nerve cell and the transmission of information from one nerve cell to another at a synapse are the fundamental processes of communication in the nervous system. The brain, after all, is nothing more than a series of interconnections among neurons. Although the patterns of those interconnections are complex, the basic mechanisms of fiber conduction and synaptic transmission appear to be fundamentally similar throughout the brain. There are two aspects to understanding how the brain works. One concerns the mechanisms of communication among nerve cells (synaptic transmission, for example), and the other has to do with the ways in which neurons are organized in complex pathways and circuits. Both topics are treated here.

The mechanisms of nerve conduction along the axon are treated by Richard D. Keynes, who describes the work that he, A. L. Hodgkin, and A. F. Huxley have done on giant nerve fibers in the squid ("The Nerve Impulse and the Squid"). In the squid, nature has provided us with a convenient model for study of the nerve impulse—it has a specialized, single, long axon nearly a millimeter in diameter, which is many times larger than any nerve fiber in the human nervous system. The basic mechanism of nerve-impulse conduction appears to be the same in the giant axon of the squid and in the axons of the human brain. As Keynes explains, when the resting axon's barrier to sodium ions breaks down, sodium rushes into the cell and potassium then moves out, these processes generating the electrical current that travels down the axon.

The functional interconnections between nerve cells are described by Sir John Eccles, who won the Nobel prize for this work, in his article "The Synapse." When the electrical current arrives at the end of the axon it meets the synapse, a space between the axon terminal and the next nerve-cell body. Instead of simply inducing electrical activity across the synaptic space, as was thought earlier, the axon terminal releases a small amount of a chemical "transmitter" substance that activates the adjacent nerve cell. Excitation and inhibition of nerve-cell activity are both accomplished in this way. In the next article, "Nerve Cells and Behavior," Eric R. Kandel illustrates how we can understand the functioning of simple circuits of neurons in terms of the basic properties of synaptic transmission. He uses portions of the nervous system of the sea slug *Aplysia*, which has relatively few giant neurons that can be studied individually, and shows that processes as complex and important for behavior as habituation can be studied by his simple but elegant method.

The last article of this section is Lennart Heimer's "Pathways in the Brain." Heimer discusses methods of studying such pathways. His techniques utilize the fact that certain nerve cells, and particular elements within nerve cells, turn color or are stained differently by certain chemicals. The electron microscope has been a powerful new tool in this work. Some of the new methods of tracing pathways depend on the fact that different nerve circuits in the brain appear to use different chemical transmitter substances at their synapses; consequently, various functional pathways can be identified and traced. An understanding of the basic mechanisms of information transmission and the organization of synapses and pathways into functional circuits in the brain are a necessary foundation for the study of more complex phenomena of brain function and experience.

14

THE NERVE IMPULSE AND THE SQUID

RICHARD D. KEYNES
December 1958

An invention of nature, once we have learned to appreciate it, may facilitate the progress of knowledge more significantly than a new instrument devised by human ingenuity. Such is the case with the giant axon of the squid. In the living animal the usefulness of this large-sized nerve cable is demonstrated when the creature suddenly changes course and darts away by jet propulsion. An array of giant axons activate the muscles that furnish this auxiliary mode of locomotion. In the laboratory the investigator can easily dissect a convenient length of axon from the tissues of a squid. The transparent tubelike axon, up to a millimeter in diameter, gives him a nerve fiber that he can handle and study with far greater ease than the tenuous fibers, 50 to 1,000 times thinner, available from most animals. In particular the large diameter of the giant axon makes the events that go on at the inner surface of its enclosing membrane accessible to investigation. During the past 20 years work with giant axons has opened the way to the principal advances in our understanding of the generation and propagation of the nerve impulse.

By the beginning of this century, physiologists had shown that the nerve impulse is a transient wave of electrical excitation that travels from point to point down the length of a nerve fiber. They had also established that the fiber may be likened in structure to a cable with a low-resistance core of cytoplasm surrounded by a high-resistance insulating membrane. Outside the membrane the salt-containing tissue fluids provide a low-resistance medium which itself plays an important role in the propagation of the nerve impulse. With the comparatively insensitive instruments of the day, workers had found that there was a steady difference in electrical potential across the membrane when the fiber was in the resting state, the inside of the membrane being charged negative with respect to the outside. They had detected the nerve impulse as a brief wave of external negativity that traveled along the outer sur-

SQUID (*Loligo*) is found in great numbers on both sides of the North Atlantic. It normally swims by moving its fins but can also dart backward or forward by expelling a jet of water. The "jet propulsion" mechanism is controlled by two sets of giant nerve fibers.

face of the membrane with constant amplitude and velocity.

In 1902 Julius Bernstein of the University of Halle in Germany put forward what proved to be for many years the most satisfactory explanation of this phenomenon. As was by then well known, the cells of all the excitable tissues of the body, muscle as well as nerve, contain an appreciably higher concentration of potassium ions than the body fluid, while the body fluid contains a relatively higher concentration of the ions of sodium. Bernstein suggested that the membrane's selective permeability to potassium might account for the resting potential. In the dynamic equilibrium of electrochemical forces, the negative charge on the inside of the membrane opposes the tendency of the positively charged potassium ions to escape. Bernstein further proposed that during the passage of a nerve impulse the membrane momentarily lost its selective resistance to the electrochemical pressure of the ions in the external fluid. With the rush of these ions into the interior of the fiber, the potential across the membrane would collapse to zero. Electric currents generated by the movement of the ions would then spread the loss of selectivity to the next section of the membrane. Thus the impulse was made to travel by self-regeneration down the length of the fiber.

Neurophysiologists long accepted Bernstein's "membrane" hypothesis as the best guess that could be made at the truth. But they could develop little direct evidence to support it. The high speed of the reaction, the minute quantities of material involved and the tiny dimensions of most nerve fibers defied the experimental ingenuity of investigators for the next three decades.

The way around the impasse was discovered in 1933, when J. Z. Young, now at University College London, undertook an investigation of the nervous system in squids and other cephalopods. Young immediately pointed out that the big nerve fibers of these animals would provide exceptionally favorable material for research into the propagation of the nerve impulse. The soundness of this observation is reflected in the degree to which the marine biological laboratories at Plymouth, England, and Woods Hole, Mass., have since figured in the literature of the nerve impulse.

It is difficult to transport living squid any distance from the coastal waters in which they are taken by trapping or trawling; the creatures are most numerous in late summer and early autumn. As a result nerve physiologists are to be found spending their vacations busily dissecting squid by the seaside.

The process of freeing the giant axon from the mantle of the squid and then cleaning away the small nerve fibers that run with it requires an hour or two of exacting work with fine forceps and scissors and a binocular dissecting microscope. The axon is then mounted in a bath of sea water which substitutes for the body fluids that bathe it in the living animal. In this state the axon will continue to conduct impulses in an essentially normal fashion for 12 hours or more. The cuttlefish *Sepia officinalis* has the merit of surviving better in captivity, and we have managed to keep ourselves supplied with *Sepia* at the University of Cambridge through several winters. The cuttlefish axon, with a diameter of .2 millimeter, is appreciably smaller than that of the squid, but nevertheless has proved highly satisfactory for our work with radioactive tracers.

The first six years of investigation of the giant axons established firmly the various vital facts about their physical and chemical structure. At Woods Hole in 1936 K. S. Cole and H. J. Curtis mounted single axons as one arm in a Wheatstone bridge, a standard device for determining the electrical properties of conductors. They were thus able to measure the resistance across the membrane and to determine its capacitance (its capacity to hold an electrostatic charge) as one microfarad per square centimeter of surface. Later, having perfected the technique, they provided a classical demonstration that the drop in resistance across the membrane, implied by Bernstein's postulated loss of selectivity, does indeed occur. In this connection they found that the inherent capacitance of the membrane does not change, thus confirming the indications that the drop in resistance is associated with increased permeability to the flow of ions. Cole and A. L. Hodgkin of the University of Cambridge investigated the details of the process by which a change in the potential across the membrane spreads passively down the axon, by virtue of its cable-like structure. In another series of experiments Hodgkin demonstrated that the velocity of propagation varies with the resistance of the external medium, the impulse traveling only half as fast in moist air as it does in the more natural environment of sea water, where resistance is low. All this work fitted nicely into the concepts embodied in Bernstein's hypothesis, but it did not

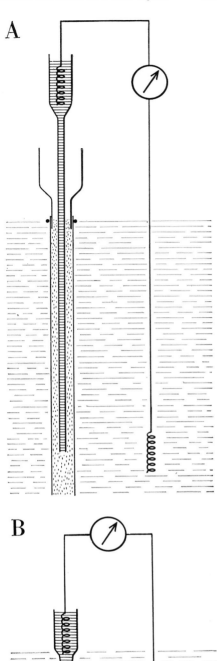

TWO METHODS of measuring the internal potential of a nerve fiber are shown here. In A a tube .1 mm. in diameter, filled with potassium chloride, is inserted down the length of a giant axon, the only nerve fiber large enough to accommodate it. In B a micropipette only .0005 mm. across at the tip is thrust through the cell membrane. This fine-drawn tool can be used on the far thinner nerve fibers more often found in animals.

yet provide a basis for much extension of the theory.

Work on the chemical composition and activity of the axon made parallel progress when investigators learned to extrude the cytoplasm from squid axons, much as one extrudes toothpaste from a tube. With several milligrams of the material thus isolated from contamination with the external medium, the intracellular concentrations of salts and other materials could be determined without ambiguity.

The first really critical test of the Bernstein hypothesis and the first important advance beyond it came in 1939, when workers took advantage of the relatively large diameter of squid axons and slipped micropipettes inside them down their length from the cut end. Up to this time all measurements of nerve potential had been made from the outside. Short-circuiting by the external fluid and the uncertainty of potentials measured at liquid junctions had made it impossible to get a reliable test of Bernstein's key hypothesis: that the potential across the membrane falls to zero at the peak of the "spike," as the recorded nerve impulse is often called. In the summer of 1939, simultaneously and independently, Cole and Curtis at Woods

Hole and Hodgkin and A. F. Huxley at Plymouth devised closely similar techniques to measure the membrane potential of the squid axon from the inside. They pushed a micropipette, .1 millimeter in outside diameter, two or three centimeters down the inside of the axon, carefully steering the tip to avoid scraping the membrane at any point. They could then measure the potential difference between the solution inside the pipette and the sea water outside the axon, this being in effect the potential across the nerve membrane at the tip of the pipette.

Their measurements yielded a surprising result. At the peak of the spike the membrane potential did not merely drop to zero, but was reversed. The charge on the inside of the membrane became momentarily positive by 40 millivolts or more. This interior reversal of charge corresponded with the exterior wave of negativity that had been observed so many years before. But it did not tally with Bernstein's ideas. It was some years, however, before further investigation resolved this discrepancy of observation with theory, since the talents of many biologists as well as physicists were temporarily diverted into other channels in the autumn of 1939.

The relevance of the giant-axon work

to excitable tissues in general was established soon after the war when Ralph W. Gerard and Gilbert Ling, then at the University of Chicago, devised another form of micropipette with a tip tapering to a point no more than .0005 millimeter across. This tool can be thrust through the membrane to reach the interior of the thin fibers that are found more commonly in nature than the giant axons. The membrane seals off fairly well around the tip of the pipette, making it possible to measure the potential difference between the interior of the fiber and the outside of the membrane. It was not long before these microelectrodes were being used to penetrate every kind of excitable cell, from the nerve cells in the spinal cord of the cat to the specially modified muscle cells which generate the electricity of the electric eel, and they have now become a standard tool in every physiological laboratory. Many, but not all, these cells produce a spike with the same reversal of membrane potential as that first seen in squid axons. The potential change occurs at different rates in different tissues; the spike lasts under one millisecond in the nerve of a mammal and more than half a second in the muscle fibers of a frog's heart. But the potentials have roughly the same magnitude from species to species. In most

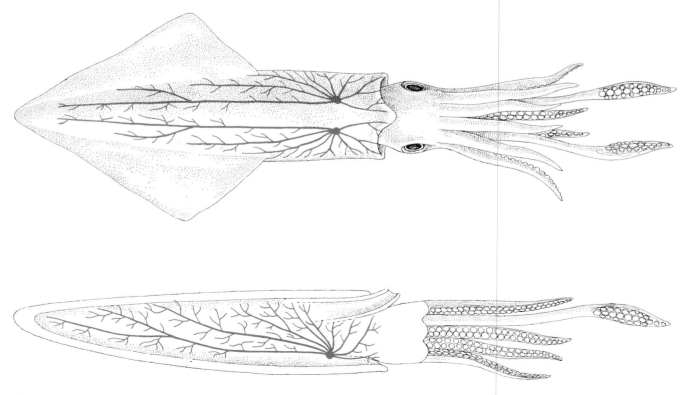

GIANT AXONS of the squid (*in color*) are shown from above in the upper drawing and in simplified cross section below. Dissected from the animal and mounted in a bath of sea water, the fibers will continue to conduct nerve impulses for 12 hours or longer.

cells the resting potential lies between 50 and 100 millivolts, while at the peak of the spike the potential is reversed by 20 to 50 millivolts.

The most satisfactory present explanation for the reversal of the membrane potential was proposed by Hodgkin and Bernhard Katz after they had spent the summer of 1947 working on squid axons at Plymouth. Their "sodium hypothesis" holds that the nerve membrane does not merely lose its selectivity during the rising phase of the spike, as Bernstein supposed, but that it becomes highly and specifically permeable to sodium ions. Since the sodium concentration outside the membrane is about 10 times greater than that inside, this could account, in an idealized case, for a reversal of potential of nearly 60 millivolts. It is further proposed that the original internal negativity of the resting nerve is restored by the subsequent exit of potassium ions from the intracellular fluid.

The sodium hypothesis suggested a whole series of fruitful experiments. An obvious first test of the idea was to find out whether a nerve impulse could be propagated when there was no sodium in the external medium. As a matter of fact, E. Overton of the University of Würzburg had shown in 1902 that frog muscle loses its excitability when immersed in a sodium-free solution; most people, however, had long since forgotten about his work. Hodgkin and Katz, working with squid axons, showed that both the size and rate of rise of the spike vary with change of sodium concentration in the external fluid in a way that fits well with theoretical prediction.

The next step was to determine whether the postulated inward transfer of sodium and outward transfer of potassium actually occur across the membrane of the nerve fiber. Here again giant axons proved invaluable. S. L. Cowan of University College London had shown in 1934 that some potassium leaked from a whole crab nerve during activity, but experiments with whole nerve trunks could not yield sufficiently accurate results to permit a critical comparison between the chemical and electrical information. Working with single giant axons, investigators found that the exchange of sodium and potassium ions is large enough to be detected after reasonably short periods of stimulation. Moreover, it is easy to count the exact number of impulses conducted and to measure the membrane area involved. Using radioactive isotopes of sodium and potassium, Harry Grundfest and David

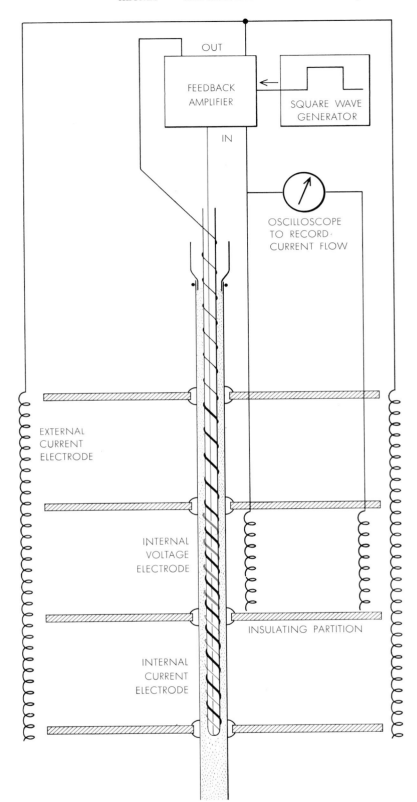

"VOLTAGE CLAMP" TECHNIQUE measures electrical changes across an isolated part of the membrane. A micropipette bearing two separate electrodes (insulated except where drawn heavily) is thrust into the fiber. A rapid change in the fiber's internal potential, produced by the square wave generator, is measured by the internal voltage electrode (*in color*) and fed back to the feedback amplifier which "clamps" the potential at the given level. The electrical current which flows across the membrane at this potential, measured by the two small electrodes at right, reflects changes in the flow of ions across the membrane.

132

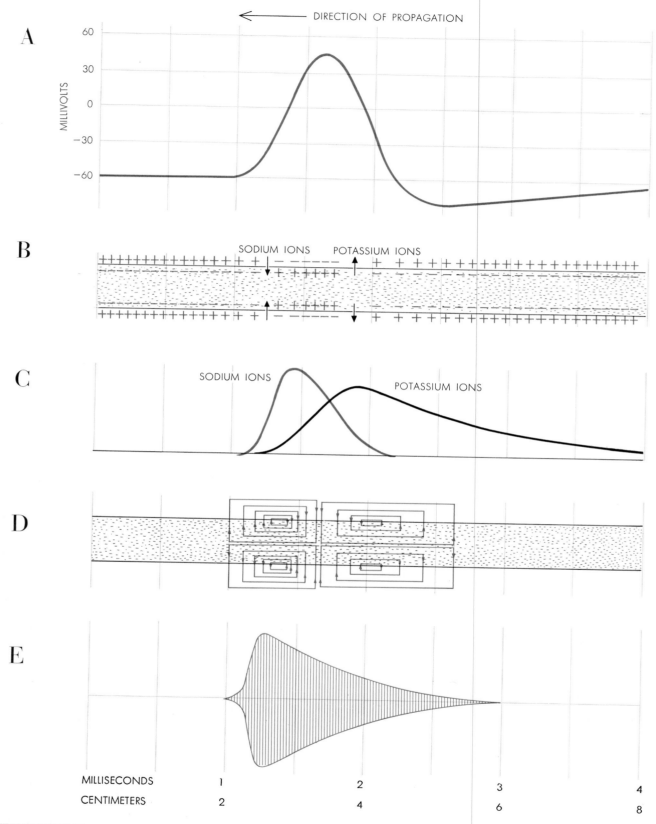

DIRECTION OF PROPAGATION

A

MILLIVOLTS

60
30
0
-30
-60

B

SODIUM IONS   POTASSIUM IONS

C

SODIUM IONS   POTASSIUM IONS

D

E

| MILLISECONDS | 1 | 2 | 3 | 4 |
| CENTIMETERS | 2 | 4 | 6 | 8 |

NERVE IMPULSE travels along a nerve fiber as a self-propagating wave of electrical activity. The potential across the outer membrane of the fiber reverses and then returns to normal again (A). These changes are caused by rises in ionic permeability (C), which permit rapid movement of sodium ions into the fiber, followed by an egress of potassium ions (B). The altered potential across the disturbed part of the membrane causes electrical currents to flow in the external medium and within the fiber (D). These depolarize the membrane ahead of the advancing impulse, triggering permeability changes and thus producing a wave of increased conductance (E).

Nachmansohn made measurements at Woods Hole on the inflow of sodium and outflow of potassium in squid axons, while I have used these isotopes in similar experiments on cuttlefish axons. P. R. Lewis and I have also employed a special microanalytical method to determine the initial concentration of the elements in the resting fiber; this involves irradiating samples with neutrons in an atomic pile and then measuring the amounts of different radioactive isotopes formed in them. By this means we have succeeded in determining the net gain of sodium and the net loss of potassium in the stimulated fiber. The upshot of all this work is that the measured movements of sodium and potassium are large enough to alter the potential across the nerve membrane to the extent observed. The close fit of the electrical and chemical observations lends strong support to the sodium hypothesis.

Although tracer experiments yield admirably unambiguous results, they represent the cumulative effect of a few thousand impulses. They do not, in consequence, reveal the sequence and the timing of the changes in the permeability of the membrane that take place in the course of a single impulse. The next step in the investigation called for a means of observing the flow of current across a measured area of nerve membrane and for deducing how much the fluxes of sodium and potassium each contributed to this current. The need was met by the so-called "voltage-clamp" technique, first developed by Cole and George Marmont at Woods Hole, and later used extensively by Hodgkin, Huxley and Katz at Plymouth. This experiment involves the insertion of two internal electrodes into the nerve [see illustration on opposite page]. One electrode records the internal potential, while the other receives just sufficient current from the output of a feed-back amplifier to "clamp" the potential at the desired level. Two other electrodes in the sea water outside measure the current that flows during the instant after the potential is established. A typical record from one of these experiments shows that, as a result of the reduction of internal potential, there is a brief phase of inward current, followed by a prolonged flow of current in the opposite direction, outward from the fiber [see illustration at right].

The disappearance of the inward current when the experiment was repeated in sodium-free solutions demonstrated that this current is carried by sodium ions. Experiments which simultaneously measured the membrane current and the

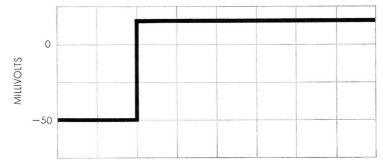

CHANGE IN INTERNAL POTENTIAL

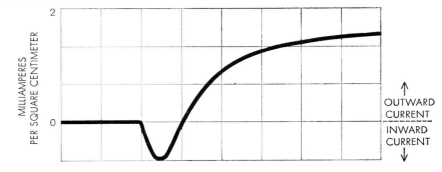

AXON IN SEA WATER

AXON IN SODIUM FREE MEDIUM

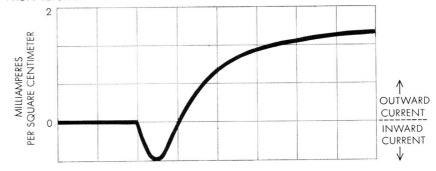

AXON RETURNED TO SEA WATER

"VOLTAGE CLAMP" RECORDS show that a change in the internal potential produces a brief inward current before the main flow of current outward. Since the inward flow does not occur in a sodium-free medium, it must be due to the movement of sodium ions into the axon.

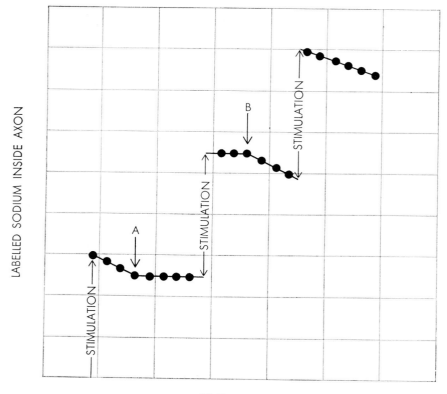

THREE SUCCESSIVE STIMULATIONS increased the concentration of radioactive sodium in a giant axon. The "sodium pump" then caused the concentration to fall slowly. (The sodium measurements are indicated by dots.) Between A and B the pump was blocked by a metabolic poison; axon could take up sodium upon stimulation, but could not eliminate it.

outward passage of potassium tracer-ions proved that almost all the outward current is carried by potassium ions. The sodium-ion current builds up quickly after the potential change, but switches off after approximately one millisecond; the potassium-ion current then rises and stays high so long as the potential is maintained. After recording the current and ion flow associated with many different sequences of potential change, Hodgkin and Huxley were able to work out the precise curves linking the changes in the permeability of the membrane to the changes in its potential over the duration of a spike [see illustration on page 132].

At present we have almost no idea what kind of molecular mechanism underlies the all-important changes in the permeability of the membrane. It is clear that a very small change in potential brings a relatively huge change in permeability; the permeability to sodium increases more than eight times in response to a potential shift of only 10 millivolts. This suggests some rearrangement of charged groups in the structure of the membrane. Nothing is known, however, about the chemical nature of

these groups. No chemical compound yet described can discriminate between sodium and potassium so effectively as a nerve membrane. It may be that the membrane mechanism exploits some physico-chemical difference between the two ions, the subtlety of which at present eludes us.

We come now to an interesting new question which is raised by what we have learned about the propagation of the nerve impulse. We have sought for the source of electrical energy that moves the impulse along the fiber. And we have found that source in the electrochemical pressure exerted by the concentration of sodium on one side of the membrane and potassium on the other. This energy is released and electric currents flow across the membrane when the changing permeability of the membrane permits the ions to penetrate it. We are now, therefore, prompted to ask how these concentration gradients are built up in the first place. We must ask also how they are maintained, despite the gain of sodium and loss of potassium that occur every time an impulse travels along the nerve. The question has gen-

eral importance, for the same concentration gradients of low internal sodium and high internal potassium exist in many other kinds of cells.

The cells must build up these concentrations by forcing the sodium and potassium ions to move uphill against their respective gradients, as contrasted with the downhill transfer that occurs during the spike. Some still-unidentified source of energy in the metabolism of the cell must pump the sodium out of the fiber into the surrounding fluid in which 10 times as much sodium is present, and must take potassium up into the intracellular medium in which potassium predominates. So far we have learned very little about this process of "active transport," but we owe much of what we have learned to work with giant axons.

Using radioactive isotopes, Hodgkin and I have obtained evidence that the outward passage of sodium is normally (but not, it seems, invariably) linked to the uptake of an equivalent quantity of potassium. The working of this coupled "sodium pump" could be interrupted, we found, by treating a squid axon with dinitrophenol, a metabolic poison. The presence of this poison brought the outward passage of labeled sodium to a standstill. It did not, however, reduce appreciably the downhill inflow of sodium during stimulation of the axon. When we washed the inhibitor away, the sodium pump started up again [see illustration on this page]. Parallel experiments which measured the movement of labeled potassium proved that metabolic inhibitors cut down the uptake of potassium and the extrusion of sodium to roughly the same extent.

It would be very interesting to know how the energy, which must be derived ultimately from the oxidation of foodstuff, is supplied to the sodium pump. Most biochemists would suspect that the fuel is the energy-rich substance adenosine triphosphate (ATP) produced by the oxidative metabolism of the cell. P. C. Caldwell, working at Plymouth, accordingly set out to analyze the amount of ATP and related phosphates in cytoplasm extruded from squid axons. He found that the rate at which ATP disappeared during treatment with metabolic inhibitors fitted fairly well with the rate at which the sodium pump slowed down and switched off. Moreover, ATP reappeared in the cytoplasm of the axon when the inhibitors were washed away. Recently I have joined forces with him to examine the role of ATP more directly. By means of a microinjection technique made possible by the large diameter of the squid axon, we introduced measured amounts of ATP into cells whose own ATP-synthesizing machinery had been poisoned. We found that injected ATP can indeed restore the rate of sodium extrusion, but only temporarily and never to the level observed in an unpoisoned axon. However, it would be premature to conclude that the sodium pump is driven by ATP alone.

The active-transport system is even more exact than the spike mechanism in distinguishing between sodium and potassium. It moves sodium outward from the intracellular medium, which is rich in potassium, and draws potassium inward from an environment containing 50 times as much sodium. Lithium can be substituted for sodium in the external medium without causing any perceptible change in the spike. On the other hand, lithium that has entered the cell is extruded very slowly; the sodium pump, unlike the spike mechanism, does discriminate between sodium and lithium.

Several theoretical schemes have been proposed for the sodium pump. Mostly they postulate carrier molecules which move the sodium from inside to outside, there releasing the sodium, and then change their affinity to move back to the inner surface of the membrane carrying potassium. But so far not even a plausible guess has been made at the identity of these carriers. We should not be surprised if it turns out eventually that the sodium pump works on some other principle entirely.

The reader may reasonably ask how much of the work on giant axons is relevant to the properties of other types of nerve fibers. It is always dangerous to extrapolate too slavishly from one species to another. Size is not the only important difference between squid axons and vertebrate nerves. Many of the latter are sheathed in myelin, a fatty material which insulates the membrane except at interruptions (called the nodes of Ranvier) which occur at intervals of about a millimeter. Study of frog nerves, however, indicates that the membrane at the nodes undergoes permeability changes basically similar to those which occur over the whole surface of a squid axon. It is now agreed that the function of the myelin sheath is to force the impulse to skip from node to node in a "saltatory" manner. This confers an important advantage on vertebrates; it provides them at strategic points with nerves able to conduct impulses much faster than nonmyelinated fibers of equal bulk. The conduction mechanisms in vertebrate and invertebrate nerves thus seem to be fundamentally the same.

15

THE SYNAPSE

SIR JOHN ECCLES
January 1965

The human brain is the most highly organized form of matter known, and in complexity the brains of the other higher animals are not greatly inferior. For certain purposes it is expedient to regard the brain as being analogous to a machine. Even if it is so regarded, however, it is a machine of a totally different kind from those made by man. In trying to understand the workings of his own brain man meets his highest challenge. Nothing is given; there are no operating diagrams, no maker's instructions.

The first step in trying to understand the brain is to examine its structure in order to discover the components from which it is built and how they are related to one another. After that one can attempt to understand the mode of operation of the simplest components. These two modes of investigation—the morphological and the physiological—have now become complementary. In studying the nervous system with today's sensitive electrical devices, however, it is all too easy to find physiological events that cannot be correlated with any known anatomical structure. Con-

versely, the electron microscope reveals many structural details whose physiological significance is obscure or unknown.

At the close of the past century the Spanish anatomist Santiago Ramón y Cajal showed how all parts of the nervous system are built up of individual nerve cells of many different shapes and sizes. Like other cells, each nerve cell has a nucleus and a surrounding cytoplasm. Its outer surface consists of numerous fine branches—the dendrites—that receive nerve impulses from other nerve cells, and one relatively long branch—the axon—that transmits nerve impulses. Near its end the axon divides into branches that terminate at the dendrites or bodies of other nerve cells. The axon can be as short as a fraction of a millimeter or as long as a meter, depending on its place and function. It has many of the properties of an electric cable and is uniquely specialized to conduct the brief electrical waves called nerve impulses [see "How Cells Communicate," by Bernhard Katz; SCIENTIFIC AMERICAN Offprint 98]. In very thin axons these impulses travel at less than

one meter per second; in others, for example in the large axons of the nerve cells that activate muscles, they travel as fast as 100 meters per second.

The electrical impulse that travels along the axon ceases abruptly when it comes to the point where the axon's terminal fibers make contact with another nerve cell. These junction points were given the name "synapses" by Sir Charles Sherrington, who laid the foundations of what is sometimes called synaptology. If the nerve impulse is to continue beyond the synapse, it must be regenerated afresh on the other side. As recently as 15 years ago some physiologists held that transmission at the synapse was predominantly, if not exclusively, an electrical phenomenon. Now, however, there is abundant evidence that transmission is effectuated by the release of specific chemical substances that trigger a regeneration of the impulse. In fact, the first strong evidence showing that a transmitter substance acts across the synapse was provided more than 40 years ago by Sir Henry Dale and Otto Loewi.

It has been estimated that the hu-

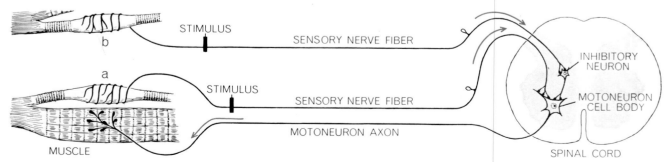

REFLEX ARCS provide simple pathways for studying the transmission of nerve impulses from one nerve cell to another. This transmission is effectuated at the junction points called synapses. In the illustration the sensory fiber from one muscle stretch receptor (*a*) makes direct synaptic contact with a motoneuron in the spinal cord. Nerve impulses generated by the moto-neuron activate the muscle to which the stretch receptor is attached. Stretch receptor *b* responds to the tension in a neighboring antagonistic muscle and sends impulses to a nerve cell that can inhibit the firing of the motoneuron. By electrically stimulating the appropriate stretch-receptor fibers one can study the effect of excitatory and inhibitory impulses on motoneurons.

man central nervous system, which of course includes the spinal cord as well as the brain itself, consists of about 10 billion (10^{10}) nerve cells. With rare exceptions each nerve cell receives information directly in the form of impulses from many other nerve cells—often hundreds—and transmits information to a like number. Depending on its threshold of response, a given nerve cell may fire an impulse when stimulated by only a few incoming fibers or it may not fire until stimulated by many incoming fibers. It has long been known that this threshold can be raised or lowered by various factors. Moreover, it was conjectured some 60 years ago that some of the incoming fibers must inhibit the firing of the receiving cell rather than excite it [*see illustration at right*]. The conjecture was subsequently confirmed, and the mechanism of the inhibitory effect has now been clarified. This mechanism and its equally fundamental counterpart—nerve-cell excitation—are the subject of this article.

Probing the Nerve Cell

At the level of anatomy there are some clues to indicate how the fine axon terminals impinging on a nerve cell can make the cell regenerate a nerve impulse of its own. The top illustration on the next page shows how a nerve cell and its dendrites are covered by fine branches of nerve fibers that terminate in knoblike structures. These structures are the synapses.

The electron microscope has revealed structural details of synapses that fit in nicely with the view that a chemical transmitter is involved in nerve transmission [*see lower two illustrations on next page*]. Enclosed in the synaptic knob are many vesicles, or tiny sacs, which appear to contain the transmitter substances that induce synaptic transmission. Between the synaptic knob and the synaptic membrane of the adjoining nerve cell is a remarkably uniform space of about 20 millimicrons that is termed the synaptic cleft. Many of the synaptic vesicles are concentrated adjacent to this cleft; it seems plausible that the transmitter substance is discharged from the nearest vesicles into the cleft, where it can act on the adjacent cell membrane. This hypothesis is supported by the discovery that the transmitter is released in packets of a few thousand molecules.

The study of synaptic transmission was revolutionized in 1951 by the introduction of delicate techniques for recording electrically from the interior

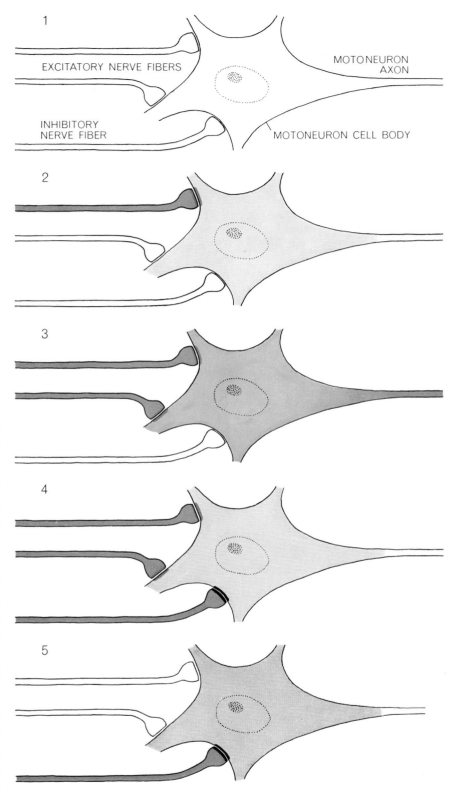

EXCITATION AND INHIBITION of a nerve cell are accomplished by the nerve fibers that form synapses on its surface. Diagram *1* shows a motoneuron in the resting state. In *2* impulses received from one excitatory fiber are inadequate to cause the motoneuron to fire. In *3* impulses from a second excitatory fiber raise the motoneuron to firing threshold. In *4* impulses carried by an inhibitory fiber restore the subthreshold condition. In *5* the inhibitory fiber alone is carrying impulses. There is no difference in the electrical impulses carried by excitatory and inhibitory nerve fibers. They achieve opposite effects because they release different chemical transmitter substances at their synaptic endings.

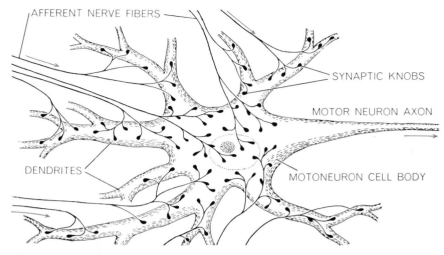

MOTONEURON CELL BODY and branches called dendrites are covered with synaptic knobs, which represent the terminals of axons, or impulse-carrying fibers, from other nerve cells. The axon of each motoneuron, in turn, terminates at a muscle fiber.

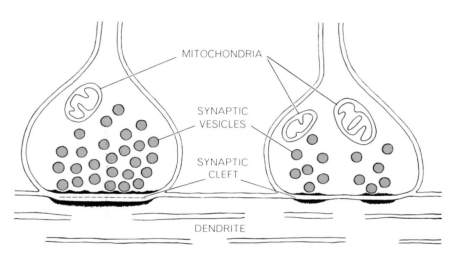

SYNAPTIC KNOBS are designed to deliver short bursts of a chemical transmitter substance into the synaptic cleft, where it can act on the surface of the nerve-cell membrane below. Before release, molecules of the chemical transmitter are stored in numerous vesicles, or sacs. Mitochondria are specialized structures that help to supply the cell with energy.

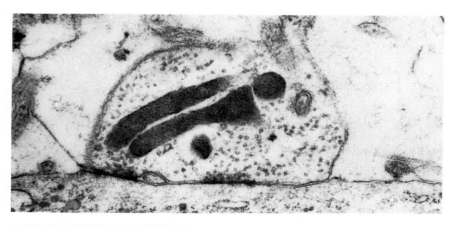

ASSUMED INHIBITORY SYNAPSE on a nerve cell is magnified 28,000 diameters in this electron micrograph by the late L. H. Hamlyn of University College London. Synaptic vesicles, believed to contain the transmitter substance, are bunched in two regions along the synaptic cleft. The darkening of the cleft in these regions is so far unexplained.

of single nerve cells. This is done by inserting into the nerve cell an extremely fine glass pipette with a diameter of .5 micron—about a fifty-thousandth of an inch. The pipette is filled with an electrically conducting salt solution such as concentrated potassium chloride. If the pipette is carefully inserted and held rigidly in place, the cell membrane appears to seal quickly around the glass, thus preventing the flow of a short-circuiting current through the puncture in the cell membrane. Impaled in this fashion, nerve cells can function normally for hours. Although there is no way of observing the cells during the insertion of the pipette, the insertion can be guided by using as clues the electric signals that the pipette picks up when close to active nerve cells.

When my colleagues and I in New Zealand and later at the John Curtin School of Medical Research in Canberra first employed this technique, we chose to study the large nerve cells called motoneurons, which lie in the spinal cord and whose function is to activate muscles. This was a fortunate choice: intracellular investigations with motoneurons have proved to be easier and more rewarding than those with any other kind of mammalian nerve cell.

We soon found that when the nerve cell responds to the chemical synaptic transmitter, the response depends in part on characteristic features of ionic composition that are also concerned with the transmission of impulses in the cell and along its axon. When the nerve cell is at rest, its physiological makeup resembles that of most other cells in that the water solution inside the cell is quite different in composition from the solution in which the cell is bathed. The nerve cell is able to exploit this difference between external and internal composition and use it in quite different ways for generating an electrical impulse and for synaptic transmission.

The composition of the external solution is well established because the solution is essentially the same as blood from which cells and proteins have been removed. The composition of the internal solution is known only approximately. Indirect evidence indicates that the concentrations of sodium and chloride ions outside the cell are respectively some 10 and 14 times higher than the concentrations inside the cell. In contrast, the concentration of potassium ions inside the cell is about 30 times higher than the concentration outside.

How can one account for this remarkable state of affairs? Part of the explanation is that the inside of the cell is negatively charged with respect to the outside of the cell by about 70 millivolts. Since like charges repel each other, this internal negative charge tends to drive chloride ions (Cl⁻) outward through the cell membrane and, at the same time, to impede their inward movement. In fact, a potential difference of 70 millivolts is just sufficient to maintain the observed disparity in the concentration of chloride ions inside the cell and outside it; chloride ions diffuse inward and outward at equal rates. A drop of 70 millivolts across the membrane therefore defines the "equilibrium potential" for chloride ions.

To obtain a concentration of potassium ions (K^+) that is 30 times higher inside the cell than outside would require that the interior of the cell membrane be about 90 millivolts negative with respect to the exterior. Since the

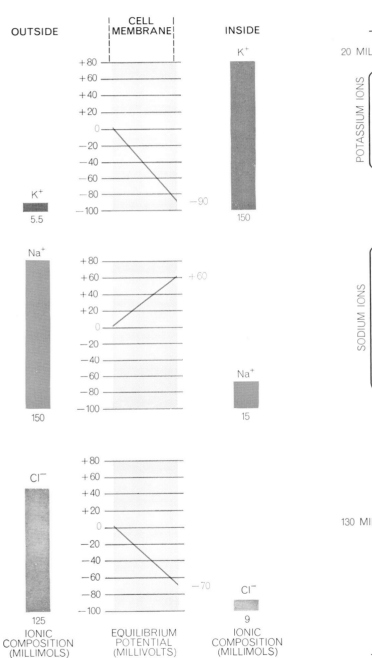

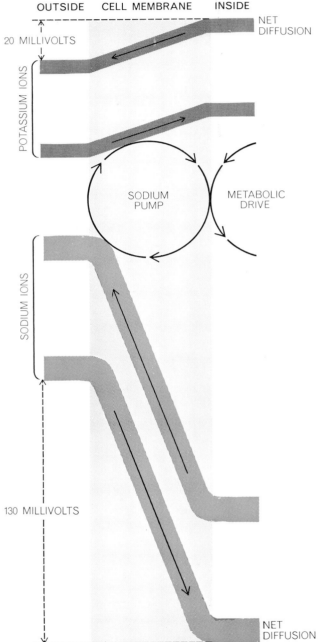

IONIC COMPOSITION outside and inside the nerve cell is markedly different. The "equilibrium potential" is the voltage drop that would have to exist across the membrane of the nerve cell to produce the observed difference in concentration for each type of ion. The actual voltage drop is about 70 millivolts, with the inside being negative. Given this drop, chloride ions diffuse inward and outward at equal rates, but the concentration of sodium and potassium must be maintained by some auxiliary mechanism (*right*).

METABOLIC PUMP must be postulated to account for the observed concentrations of potassium and sodium ions on opposite sides of the nerve-cell membrane. The negative potential inside is 20 millivolts short of the equilibrium potential for potassium ions. Thus there is a net outward diffusion of potassium ions that must be balanced by the pump. For sodium ions the potential across the membrane is 130 millivolts in the wrong direction, so very energetic pumping is needed. Chloride ions are in equilibrium.

actual interior is only 70 millivolts negative, it falls short of the equilibrium potential for potassium ions by 20 millivolts. Evidently the thirtyfold concentration can be achieved and maintained only if there is some auxiliary mechanism for "pumping" potassium ions into the cell at a rate equal to their spontaneous net outward diffusion.

The pumping mechanism has the still more difficult task of pumping sodium ions (Na^+) out of the cell against a potential gradient of 130 millivolts. This figure is obtained by adding the 70 millivolts of internal negative charge to the equilibrium potential for sodium ions, which is 60 millivolts of internal *positive* charge [*see illustrations on preceding page*]. If it were not for this postulated pump, the concentration of sodium ions inside and outside the cell would be almost the reverse of what is observed.

In their classic studies of nerve-impulse transmission in the giant axon of the squid, A. L. Hodgkin, A. F. Huxley and Bernhard Katz of Britain demonstrated that the propagation of the impulse coincides with abrupt changes in the permeability of the axon membrane. When a nerve impulse has been triggered in some way, what can be described as a gate opens and lets sodium ions pour into the axon during the advance of the impulse, making the interior of the axon locally positive. The process is self-reinforcing in that the flow of some sodium ions through the membrane opens the gate further and makes it easier for others to follow. The sharp reversal of the internal polarity of the membrane constitutes the nerve impulse, which moves like a wave until it has traveled the length of the axon. In the wake of the impulse the sodium gate closes and a potassium gate opens, thereby restoring the normal polarity of the membrane within a millisecond or less.

With this understanding of the nerve impulse in hand, one is ready to follow the electrical events at the excitatory synapse. One might guess that if the nerve impulse results from an abrupt inflow of sodium ions and a rapid change in the electrical polarity of the axon's interior, something similar must happen at the body and dendrites of the nerve cell in order to generate the impulse in the first place. Indeed, the function of the excitatory synaptic terminals on the cell body and its dendrites is to depolarize the interior of the cell membrane essentially by permitting an inflow of sodium ions. When the depolarization reaches a threshold value, a nerve impulse is triggered.

As a simple instance of this phenomenon we have recorded the depolarization that occurs in a single motoneuron activated directly by the large nerve fibers that enter the spinal cord from special stretch-receptors known as annulospiral endings. These receptors in turn are located in the same muscle that

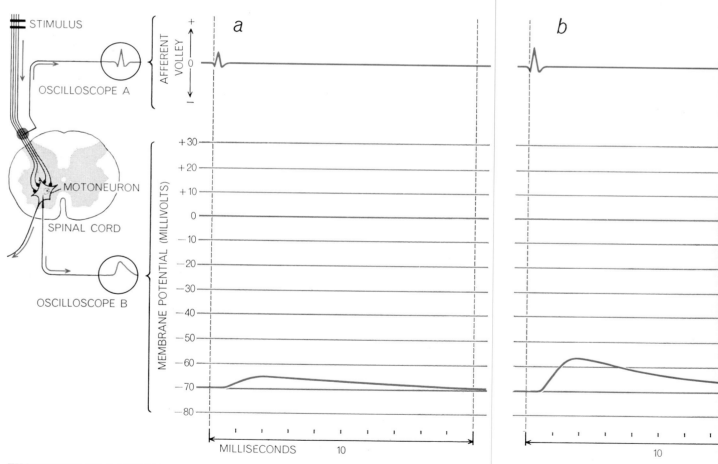

EXCITATION OF A MOTONEURON is studied by stimulating the sensory fibers that send impulses to it. The size of the "afferent volleys" reaching the motoneuron is displayed on oscilloscope *A*. A microelectrode implanted in the motoneuron measures the changes in the cell's internal electric potential. These changes, called excitatory postsynaptic potentials (EPSP's), appear on os-cilloscope *B*. The size of the afferent volley is proportional to the number of fibers stimulated to fire. It is assumed here that one to four fibers can be activated. When only one fiber is activated (*a*), the potential inside the motoneuron shifts only slightly. When two fibers are activated (*b*), the shift is somewhat greater. When three fibers are activated (*c*), the potential reaches the threshold

is activated by the motoneuron under study. Thus the whole system forms a typical reflex arc, such as the arc responsible for the patellar reflex, or "knee jerk" [*see illustration on page 136*].

To conduct the experiment we anesthetize an animal (most often a cat) and free by dissection a muscle nerve that contains these large nerve fibers. By applying a mild electric shock to the exposed nerve one can produce a single impulse in each of the fibers; since the impulses travel to the spinal cord almost synchronously they are referred to collectively as a volley. The number of impulses contained in the volley can be reduced by reducing the stimulation applied to the nerve. The volley strength is measured at a point just outside the spinal cord and is displayed on an oscilloscope. About half a millisecond after detection of a volley there is a wavelike change in the voltage inside the motoneuron that has received the volley. The change is detected by a microelectrode

inserted in the motoneuron and is displayed on another oscilloscope.

What we find is that the negative voltage inside the cell becomes progressively less negative as more of the fibers impinging on the cell are stimulated to fire. This observed depolarization is in fact a simple summation of the depolarizations produced by each individual synapse. When the depolarization of the interior of the motoneuron reaches a critical point, a "spike" suddenly appears on the second oscilloscope, showing that a nerve impulse has been generated. During the spike the voltage inside the cell changes from about 70 millivolts negative to as much as 30 millivolts positive. The spike regularly appears when the depolarization, or reduction of membrane potential, reaches a critical level, which is usually between 10 and 18 millivolts. The only effect of a further strengthening of the synaptic stimulus is to shorten the time needed for the motoneuron to reach the firing threshold [*see illustration at left*]. The depolarizing potentials produced in the cell membrane by excitatory synapses are called excitatory postsynaptic potentials, or EPSP's.

Through one barrel of a double-barreled microelectrode one can apply a background current to change the resting potential of the interior of the cell membrane, either increasing it or decreasing it. When the potential is made more negative, the EPSP rises more steeply to an earlier peak. When the potential is made less negative, the EPSP rises more slowly to a lower peak. Finally, when the charge inside the cell is reversed so as to be positive with respect to the exterior, the excitatory synapses give rise to an EPSP that is actually the reverse of the normal one [*see illustration at right*].

These observations support the hypothesis that excitatory synapses produce what amounts virtually to a short circuit in the synaptic membrane potential. When this occurs, the membrane no longer acts as a barrier to the passage of ions but lets them flow through in response to the differing electric potential on the two sides of the membrane. In other words, the ions are momentarily allowed to travel freely down their electrochemical gradients, which means that sodium ions flow into the cell and, to a lesser degree, potassium ions flow out. It is this net flow of positive ions that creates the excitatory postsynaptic potential. The flow of negative ions, such as the chloride ion, is apparently not involved. By artificially

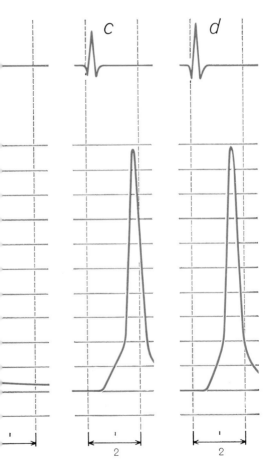

at which depolarization proceeds swiftly and a spike appears on oscilloscope *B*. The spike signifies that the motoneuron has generated a nerve impulse of its own. When four or more fibers are activated (*d*), the motoneuron reaches the threshold more quickly.

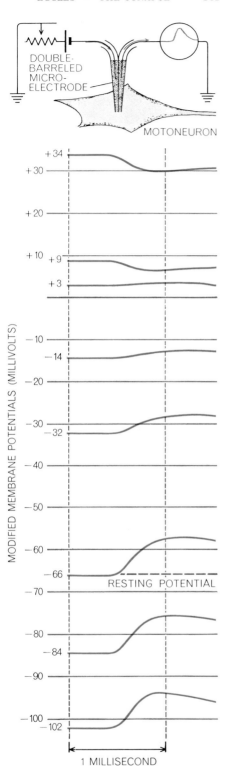

MANIPULATION of the resting potential of a motoneuron clarifies the nature of the EPSP. A steady background current applied through the left barrel of a microelectrode (*top*) shifts the membrane potential away from its normal resting level (minus 66 millivolts in this particular cell). The other barrel records the EPSP. The equilibrium potential, the potential at which the EPSP reverses direction, is about zero millivolts.

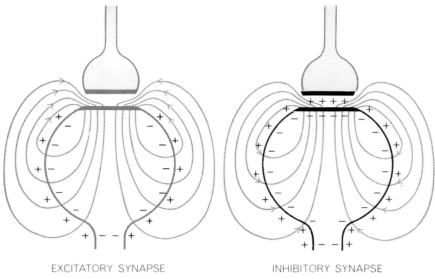

EXCITATORY SYNAPSE   INHIBITORY SYNAPSE

CURRENT FLOWS induced by excitatory and inhibitory synapses are respectively shown
at left and right. When the nerve cell is at rest, the interior of the cell membrane is uni-
formly negative with respect to the exterior. The excitatory synapse releases a chemical
substance that depolarizes the cell membrane below the synaptic cleft, thus letting current flow into the cell at that point. At an inhibitory synapse the current flow is reversed.

altering the potential inside the cell one
can establish that there is no flow of
ions, and therefore no EPSP, when the
voltage drop across the membrane is
zero.

How is the synaptic membrane converted from a strong ionic barrier into
an ion-permeable state? It is currently
accepted that the agency of conversion
is the chemical transmitter substance
contained in the vesicles inside the synaptic knob. When a nerve impulse
reaches the synaptic knob, some of the
vesicles are caused to eject the transmitter substance into the synaptic cleft
[*see illustration below*]. The molecules
of the substance would take only a few
microseconds to diffuse across the cleft
and become attached to specific receptor sites on the surface membrane of the
adjacent nerve cell.

Presumably the receptor sites are as-

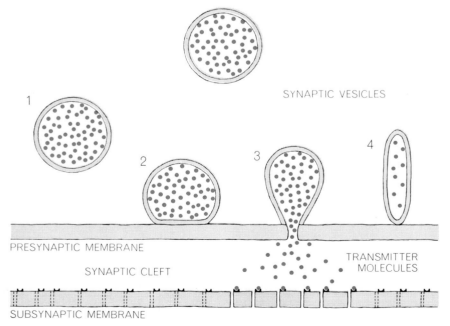

SYNAPTIC VESICLES

1

2

3

4

TRANSMITTER
MOLECULES

PRESYNAPTIC MEMBRANE

SYNAPTIC CLEFT

SUBSYNAPTIC MEMBRANE

SYNAPTIC VESICLES containing a chemical transmitter are distributed throughout the
synaptic knob. They are arranged here in a probable sequence, showing how they move
up to the synaptic cleft, discharge their contents and return to the interior for recharging.

sociated with fine channels in the membrane that are opened in some way by
the attachment of the transmitter-sub-
stance molecules to the receptor sites.
With the channels thus opened, sodium
and potassium ions flow through the
membrane thousands of times more
readily than they normally do, thereby
producing the intense ionic flux that depolarizes the cell membrane and produces the EPSP. In many synapses the
current flows strongly for only about a
millisecond before the transmitter substance is eliminated from the synaptic
cleft, either by diffusion into the surrounding regions or as a result of being
destroyed by enzymes. The latter process is known to occur when the transmitter substance is acetylcholine, which
is destroyed by the enzyme acetylcho-
linesterase.

The substantiation of this general picture of synaptic transmission requires
the solution of many fundamental problems. Since we do not know the specific
transmitter substance for the vast majority of synapses in the nervous system
we do not know if there are many different substances or only a few. The
only one identified with reasonable certainty in the mammalian central nervous
system is acetylcholine. We know practically nothing about the mechanism
by which a presynaptic nerve impulse
causes the transmitter substance to be
injected into the synaptic cleft. Nor do
we know how the synaptic vesicles not
immediately adjacent to the synaptic
cleft are moved up to the firing line to
replace the emptied vesicles. It is conjectured that the vesicles contain the
enzyme systems needed to recharge
themselves. The entire process must be
swift and efficient: the total amount of
transmitter substance in synaptic terminals is enough for only a few minutes of
synaptic activity at normal operating
rates. There are also knotty problems
to be solved on the other side of the
synaptic cleft. What, for example, is the
nature of the receptor sites? How are
the ionic channels in the membrane
opened up?

The Inhibitory Synapse

Let us turn now to the second type
of synapse that has been identified in
the nervous system. These are the synapses that can inhibit the firing of a
nerve cell even though it may be receiving a volley of excitatory impulses.
When inhibitory synapses are examined
in the electron microscope, they look
very much like excitatory synapses.

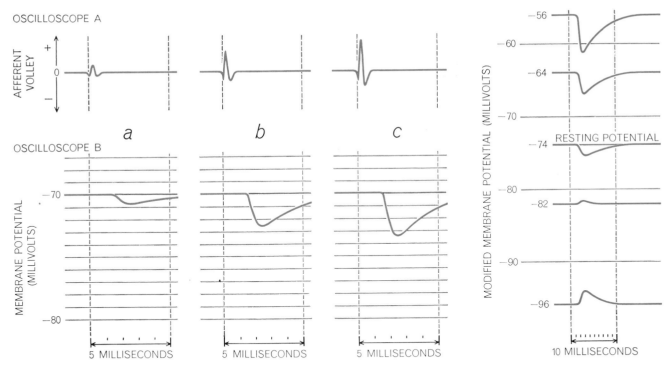

INHIBITION OF A MOTONEURON is investigated by methods like those used for studying the EPSP. The inhibitory counterpart of the EPSP is the IPSP: the inhibitory postsynaptic potential. Oscilloscope A records an afferent volley that travels to a number of inhibitory nerve cells whose axons form synapses on a nearby motoneuron (*see illustration on page 136*). A microelec-

trode in the motoneuron is connected to oscilloscope B. The sequence a, b and c shows how successively larger afferent volleys produce successively deeper IPSP's. Curves at right show how the IPSP is modified when a background current is used to change the motoneuron's resting potential. The equilibrium potential where the IPSP reverses direction is about minus 80 millivolts.

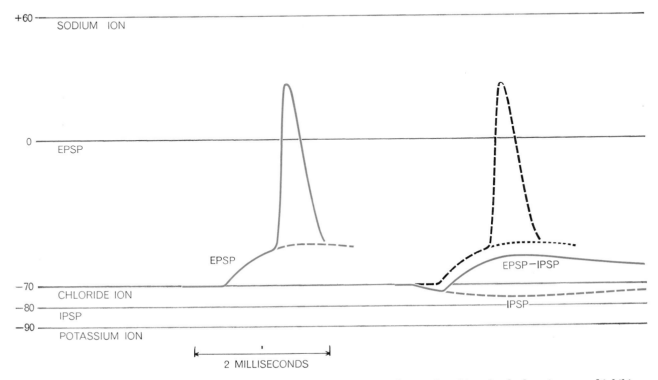

INHIBITION OF A SPIKE DISCHARGE is an electrical subtraction process. When a normal EPSP reaches a threshold (*left*), it will ordinarily produce a spike. An IPSP widens the gap between the cell's internal potential and the firing threshold. Thus if

a cell is simultaneously subjected to both excitatory and inhibitory stimulation, the IPSP is subtracted from the EPSP (*right*) and no spike occurs. The five horizontal lines show equilibrium potentials for the three principal ions as well as for the EPSP and IPSP.

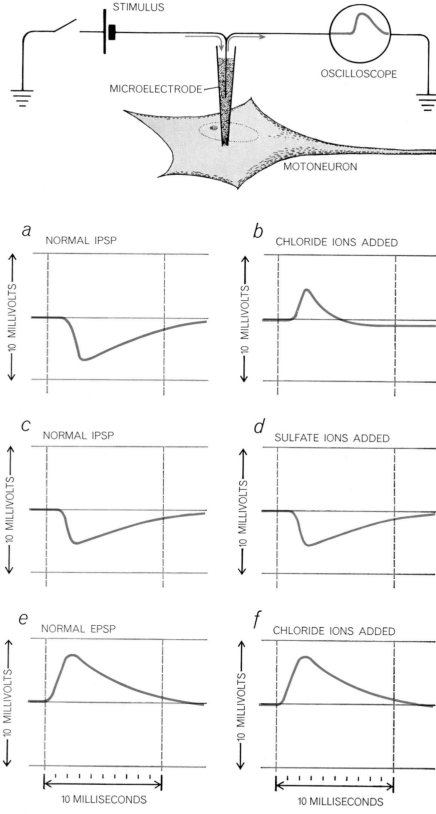

STIMULUS

OSCILLOSCOPE

MICROELECTRODE

MOTONEURON

a NORMAL IPSP

10 MILLIVOLTS

b CHLORIDE IONS ADDED

10 MILLIVOLTS

c NORMAL IPSP

10 MILLIVOLTS

d SULFATE IONS ADDED

10 MILLIVOLTS

e NORMAL EPSP

10 MILLIVOLTS

f CHLORIDE IONS ADDED

10 MILLIVOLTS

10 MILLISECONDS

10 MILLISECONDS

MODIFICATION OF ION CONCENTRATION within the nerve cell gives information about the permeability of the cell membrane. The internal ionic composition is altered by injecting selected ions through a microelectrode a minute or so before applying an afferent volley and recording the EPSP or IPSP. In the first experiment a normal IPSP (*a*) is changed to a pseudo-EPSP (*b*) by an injection of chloride ions. When sulfate ions are similarly injected, the IPSP is practically unchanged (*b, c*). The third experiment shows that an injection of chloride ions has no significant effect on the EPSP (*e, f*).

(There are probably some subtle differences, but they need not concern us here.) Microelectrode recordings of the activity of single motoneurons and other nerve cells have now shown that the inhibitory postsynaptic potential (IPSP) is virtually a mirror image of the EPSP [*see top illustration on preceding page*]. Moreover, individual inhibitory synapses, like excitatory synapses, have a cumulative effect. The chief difference is simply that the IPSP makes the cell's internal voltage more negative than it is normally, which is in a direction opposite to that needed for generating a spike discharge.

By driving the internal voltage of a nerve cell in the negative direction inhibitory synapses oppose the action of excitatory synapses, which of course drive it in the positive direction. Hence if the potential inside a resting cell is 70 millivolts negative, a strong volley of inhibitory impulses can drive the potential to 75 or 80 millivolts negative. One can easily see that if the potential is made more negative in this way the excitatory synapses find it more difficult to raise the internal voltage to the threshold point for the generation of a spike. Thus the nerve cell responds to the algebraic sum of the internal voltage changes produced by excitatory and inhibitory synapses [*see bottom illustration on preceding page*].

If, as in the experiment described earlier, the internal membrane potential is altered by the flow of an electric current through one barrel of a double-barreled microelectrode, one can observe the effect of such changes on the inhibitory postsynaptic potential. When the internal potential is made less negative, the inhibitory postsynaptic potential is deepened. Conversely, when the potential is made more negative, the IPSP diminishes; it finally reverses when the internal potential is driven below minus 80 millivolts.

One can therefore conclude that inhibitory synapses share with excitatory synapses the ability to change the ionic permeability of the synaptic membrane. The difference is that inhibitory synapses enable ions to flow freely down an electrochemical gradient that has an equilibrium point at minus 80 millivolts rather than at zero, as is the case for excitatory synapses. This effect could be achieved by the outward flow of positively charged ions such as potassium or the inward flow of negatively charged ions such as chloride, or by a combination of negative and positive ionic flows such that the interior reaches equilibrium at minus 80 millivolts.

In an effort to discover the permeability changes associated with the inhibitory potential my colleagues and I have altered the concentration of ions normally found in motoneurons and have introduced a variety of other ions that are not normally present. This can be done by impaling nerve cells with micropipettes that are filled with a salt solution containing the ion to be injected. The actual injection is achieved by passing a brief current through the micropipette.

If the concentration of chloride ions within the cell is in this way increased as much as three times, the inhibitory postsynaptic potential reverses and acts as a depolarizing current; that is, it resembles an excitatory potential. On the other hand, if the cell is heavily injected with sulfate ions, which are also negatively charged, there is no such reversal [see illustration on opposite page]. This simple test shows that under the influence of the inhibitory transmitter substance, which is still unidentified, the subsynaptic membrane becomes permeable momentarily to chloride ions but not to sulfate ions. During the generation of the IPSP the outflow of chloride ions is so rapid that it more than outweighs the flow of other ions that generate the normal inhibitory potential.

My colleagues have now tested the effect of injecting motoneurons with more than 30 kinds of negatively charged ion. With one exception the hydrated ions (ions bound to water) to which the cell membrane is permeable under the influence of the inhibitory transmitter substance are smaller than the hydrated ions to which the membrane is impermeable. The exception is the formate ion (HCO_2^-), which may have an ellipsoidal shape and so be able to pass through membrane pores that block smaller spherical ions.

Apart from the formate ion all the ions to which the membrane is permeable have a diameter not greater than 1.14 times the diameter of the potassium ion; that is, they are less than 2.9 angstrom units in diameter. Comparable investigations in other laboratories have found the same permeability effects, including the exceptional behavior of the formate ion, in fishes, toads and snails. It may well be that the ionic mechanism responsible for synaptic inhibition is the same throughout the animal kingdom.

The significance of these and other studies is that they strongly indicate that the inhibitory transmitter substance opens the membrane to the flow of potassium ions but not to sodium ions. It

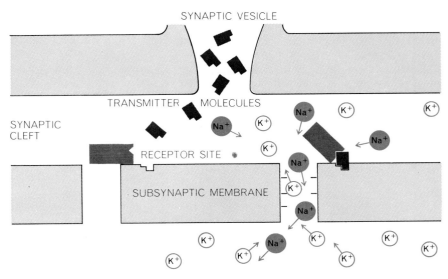

EXCITATORY SYNAPSE may employ transmitter molecules that open large channels in the nerve-cell membrane. This would permit sodium ions, which are plentiful outside the cell, to pour through the membrane freely. The outward flow of potassium ions, driven by a smaller potential gradient, would be at a much slower rate. Chloride ions (not shown) may be prevented from flowing by negative charges on the channel walls.

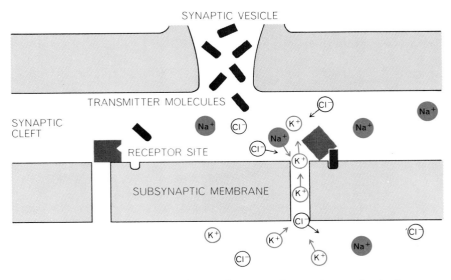

INHIBITORY SYNAPSE may employ another type of transmitter molecule that opens channels too small to pass sodium ions. The net outflow of potassium ions and inflow of chloride ions would account for the hyperpolarization that is observed as an IPSP.

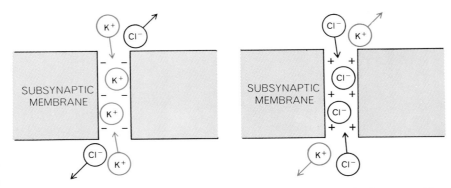

MODIFICATIONS OF INHIBITORY SYNAPSE may involve channels that carry either negative or positive charges on their walls. Negative charges (left) would permit only potassium ions to pass. Positive charges (right) would permit only chloride ions to pass.

is known that the sodium ion is somewhat larger than any of the negatively charged ions, including the formate ion, that are able to pass through the membrane during synaptic inhibition. It is not possible, however, to test the effectiveness of potassium ions by injecting excess amounts into the cell because the excess is immediately diluted by an osmotic flow of water into the cell.

As I have indicated, the concentration of potassium ions inside the nerve cell is about 30 times greater than the concentration outside, and to maintain this large difference in concentration without the help of a metabolic pump the inside of the membrane would have to be charged 90 millivolts negative with respect to the exterior. This implies that if the membrane were suddenly made porous to potassium ions, the resulting outflow of ions would make the inside potential of the membrane even more negative than it is in the resting state, and that is just what happens during synaptic inhibition. The membrane must not simultaneously become porous to sodium ions, because they exist in much higher concentration outside the cell than inside and their rapid inflow would more than compensate for the potassium outflow. In fact, the fundamental difference between synaptic excitation and synaptic inhibition is that the membrane freely passes sodium ions in response to the former and largely excludes the passage of sodium ions in response to the latter.

Channels in the Membrane

This fine discrimination between ions that are not very different in size must be explained by any hypothesis of synaptic action. It is most unlikely that the channels through the membrane are created afresh and accurately maintained for a thousandth of a second every time a burst of transmitter substance is released into the synaptic cleft. It is more likely that channels of at least two different sizes are built directly into the membrane structure. In some way the excitatory transmitter substance would selectively unplug the larger channels and permit the free inflow of sodium ions. Potassium ions would simultaneously flow out and thus would tend to counteract the large potential change that would be produced by the massive sodium inflow. The inhibitory transmitter substance would selectively unplug the smaller channels that are large enough to pass potassium and chloride ions but not sodium ions [*see upper two illustrations on previous page*].

To explain certain types of inhibition other features must be added to this hypothesis of synaptic transmission. In the simple hypothesis chloride and potassium ions can flow freely through pores of all inhibitory synapses. It has been shown, however, that the inhibition of the contraction of heart muscle by the vagus nerve is due almost exclusively to potassium-ion flow. On the other hand, in the muscles of crustaceans and in nerve cells in the snail's brain synaptic inhibition is due largely to the flow of chloride ions. This selective permeability could be explained if there were fixed charges along the walls of the channels. If such charges were negative, they would repel negatively charged ions and prevent their passage; if they were positive, they would similarly prevent the passage of positively charged ions. One can now suggest that the channels opened by the excitatory transmitter are negatively charged and so do not permit the passage of the negatively charged chloride ion, even though it is small enough to move through the channel freely.

One might wonder if a given nerve cell can have excitatory synaptic action at some of its axon terminals and inhibitory action at others. The answer is no. Two different kinds of nerve cell are needed, one for each type of transmission and synaptic transmitter substance. This can readily be demonstrated by the effect of strychnine and tetanus toxin in the spinal cord; they specifically prevent inhibitory synaptic action and leave excitatory action unaltered. As a result the synaptic excitation of nerve cells is uncontrolled and convulsions result. The special types of cell responsible for inhibitory synaptic action are now being recognized in many parts of the central nervous system.

This account of communication between nerve cells is necessarily oversimplified, yet it shows that some significant advances are being made at the level of individual components of the nervous system. By selecting the most favorable situations we have been able to throw light on some details of nerve-cell behavior. We can be encouraged by these limited successes. But the task of understanding in a comprehensive way how the human brain operates staggers its own imagination.

16

NERVE CELLS AND BEHAVIOR

ERIC R. KANDEL
July 1970

The application of biological techniques to behavior has its roots in the writings of Charles Darwin, who argued that since man had evolved from lower animals, human behaviors must have parallels in the behaviors of lower forms. Darwin's radical insights stimulated studies of animal behavior, opening the way to experimentation that was not feasible in man. The studies dealt both with the comparative aspects of behavior in different species and with the analysis of brain mechanisms, two lines of investigation that for a while developed independently.

The comparative studies of behavior proved almost immediately rewarding. It soon became evident that in spite of great variations in the behavioral capabilities of different animals, certain basic response patterns essential for survival—such as feeding, escape and sexual behaviors—were almost universal. Surprising parallels in the details of these behaviors were found in higher and lower animals. Even simple forms of learning seemed to be governed by principles applicable to widely different species.

The analysis of brain mechanisms progressed more slowly at first, but after World War II the development of techniques for studying individual nerve cells revolutionized the neural sciences and made it possible to analyze progressively more complex neuronal processes. As a result a very good understanding has been achieved of the biophysical functioning of the nerve cell and of synaptic transmission, the mechanism whereby one nerve cell communicates with another [see the article "The Synapse," by Sir John Eccles, beginning on page 136]. In addition insights have been gained into the organization of interconnected groups of neurons from cellular studies of sensory and motor systems [see the article "The Visual Cortex of the Brain," by David H. Hubel, beginning on page 253].

In recent years the investigative tradition of comparative behavior and the tradition of brain mechanisms have begun to converge. Advances in the concepts and techniques for studying individual nerve cells and interconnected groups of cells have encouraged neural scientists to apply these methods to studying complete behavioral acts and modifications of behaviors produced by learning. Guided by the lessons of the comparative behaviorists, investigators have sought to study very general behaviors, characteristic of those found in most animals, in species whose nervous systems are amenable to detailed cellular analyses. This led to an interest in certain invertebrates, such as crayfish, leeches, various insects and snails, that have the great advantage that their nervous system is made up of relatively few nerve cells (perhaps 10,000 or 100,000 compared with the trillion or so in higher animals). In these animals one can begin to trace, at the level of individual cells, not only the sensory information coming into the nervous system and the motor actions coming out of it but also the total sequence of events that underlies a behavioral response. By combining psychological techniques for demonstrating the behavioral capabilities of simple animals with cellular techniques for analyzing neural mechanisms, it is now becoming possible to clarify some relations between neural mechanisms and learning. Although cellular concepts and techniques are still far from explaining behavior and learning in higher animals, they are beginning to be useful in understanding elementary forms of behavioral modification in simple animals.

In this article I shall first outline some of the theoretical issues that have influenced modern studies of the mechanism of learning and describe how cellular neurophysiological techniques helped to clarify these issues by revealing that the synapses of nerve cells are functionally modifiable. I shall then try to illustrate how the combined use of cellular and behavioral techniques makes it possible to relate synaptic modifications in certain nerve cells to short-term modification of behavior in an invertebrate.

Cellular-Connection Approach

When investigators first began applying biological techniques to the study of the neural mechanisms of learning, several quite different strategies evolved, but only one of them—the cellular-connection approach—has proved consistently useful. The cellular-connection approach assumes that both the transformation of neural information and its storage as memory involve only nerve cells and their interconnections. This approach derives from morphological studies of the nervous system by the Spanish anatomist Santiago Ramón y Cajal, who held that the nervous system was constructed from discrete cellular units, the neurons, and that the way to understand the brain was to analyze its functional architecture—its wiring diagram. Proponents of this view have therefore focused on the properties of individual neurons, paying particular attention to the synapse, the connection between the nerve cells.

The importance of specific neuronal interconnections in behavior was first demonstrated impressively by R. W. Sperry at the University of Chicago in the 1940's. In a series of studies on the regeneration of neural connections in lower vertebrates, Sperry showed that visual perception and motor coordination could best be explained in terms of highly specific cellular interconnections.

Moreover, these connections seemed invariant and appeared not to be affected by experience [see "The Growth of Nerve Circuits," by R. W. Sperry; SCIENTIFIC AMERICAN Offprint 72].

These studies presented an interesting paradox. If the development of connections between most neurons in the nervous system is rigidly determined, how then is behavior modified? How does one reconcile the known malleability of behavior with a preprogrammed and rigidly "wired" nervous system? One of the characteristic features of learning and other behavioral modifications is their long time course; even a simple behavioral modification lasts for several minutes and certain types of learning may endure for many years. How is the modified neural activity sustained in a set of prewired connections? Do memory and learning require some further additions to the wiring diagram?

Plastic and Dynamic Change

A number of solutions for this dilemma have been proposed. The two that have proved most interesting experimentally are based on notions of the plastic and the dynamic capabilities of neurons. The plasticity hypothesis was first put forward by Cajal and several other neuroanatomists and then in more modern form by two psychologists, Jerzy Kornorski in Poland and Donald O. Hebb in Canada. A current version of this hypothesis states that even though the anatomical connections between neurons may develop according to a rigid plan, the strength or effectiveness of the connections is not entirely predetermined and the effectiveness of synapses and other properties of neurons can be altered by experience. This hypothesis predicted that neurons, and in particular their synapses, should be able to change their functional properties as a result of altered activity.

The dynamic hypothesis derived from the anatomical studies of Rafael Lorente de Nó of Rockefeller University, who showed that neurons are often interconnected in the form of closed chains. Neural activity could therefore be sustained by the circulation or reverberation of impulses within a closed chain of interconnected, self-reexciting neurons. This again would not require anatomical change; in fact, the hypothesis does not even require a functional change in the properties of neurons.

The possibility that dynamic changes could account for persistent neural activity was initially very attractive to neurophysiologists because there were many examples in the nervous system of neurons connected to one another in circular paths. As studies of the physiological functions of neural networks advanced, however, it became clear that neurons can mediate inhibition as well as excitation—can tend to quench as well as to fire a nerve impulse. What appeared anatomically to be a self-reexciting loop might therefore contain one or more inhibitory connections that could prevent reexcitation. In addition, memory was shown to survive a number of drastic experimental manipulations, such as cooling of the brain and epileptic convulsions, that would be likely to interrupt the circulation of impulses in closed chains of neurons. As a result of these findings the possibility that dynamic activity provides the neural basis of even short-term memory now seems less likely, although it has not been excluded. Studies of the plastic capabilities of neurons, on the other hand, have turned out to be surprisingly rewarding, since experiments have shown that a remarkable capacity for short-term functional modifications is built into the structure of many synapses.

The first demonstration of the plastic capability of a synapse was provided in 1947 by Martin G. Larrabee and Detlev W. Bronk, then at Johns Hopkins University. They studied a simple "monosynaptic" pathway, that is, one consisting of a single class of neurons directly connected to another class of neurons through a single set of synapses. They tetanized (repetitively stimulated at a high frequency) certain fibers leading to the stellate ganglion in the autonomic nervous system of the cat and found that the responsiveness of the stimulated monosynaptic pathway was greatly facilitated, or enhanced, for a few minutes whereas neighboring, unstimulated pathways were unaffected [see illustration on this page]. They called this phenomenon posttetanic potentiation.

A few minutes is clearly not very long compared with the duration of most learning processes, but it is long compared with the millisecond events that had characterized nerve actions known up to that time. Some behavioral modifications are indeed relatively short-lived, and a plastic mechanism such as posttetanic potentiation might underlie them. Moreover, Larrabee and Bronk showed that the duration of posttetanic potentiation could be extended by longer periods of stimulation. Recently W. Alden Spencer and Reuben Wigdor of the New York University School of Medicine and F. B. Beswick and R. T. W. L. Conroy in Britain have found that posttetanic potentiation can last for as long as two hours after a period of tetanization lasting for from 15 to 30 minutes.

After the discovery of posttetanic potentiation, a number of investigators examined other monosynaptic pathways and encountered an opposite phenomenon, a posttetanic depression, whereby

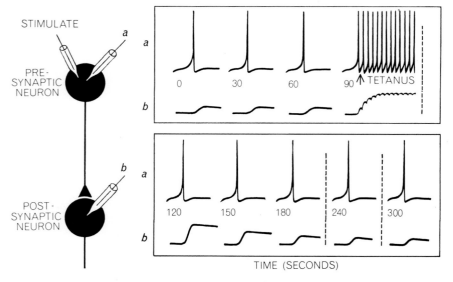

POSTTETANIC POTENTIATION is a form of plastic change in neural activity. It can be studied in some monosynaptic pathways in which both presynaptic and postsynaptic cells can be impaled with microelectrodes. Stimulation of a presynaptic neuron produces an action potential in it (a) that propagates to the nerve terminal and leads to generation of a synaptic potential in the postsynaptic cell (b). Repetitive high-frequency stimulation greatly increases the effectiveness of the stimulated pathway, as indicated by the increase in the amplitude of the postsynaptic potential. The increase persists several minutes after tetanus.

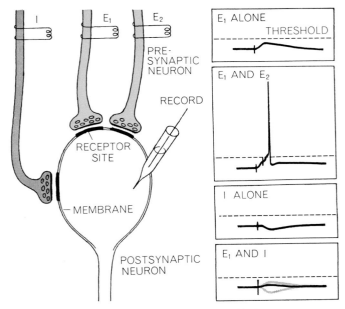

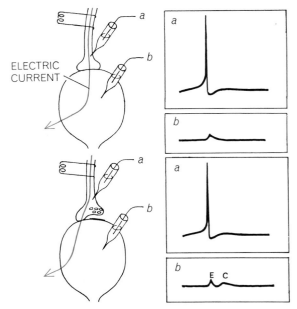

SYNAPSE is the junction between two nerve cells. Most synapses are chemical (*left*), but some are electrical (*top right*) or conjoint (*lower right*). A chemical synapse may be excitatory (*light color*) or inhibitory (*gray*). After a characteristic delay an arriving nerve impulse releases transmitter molecules, thought to be stored in vesicles in the synaptic knob of the presynaptic fiber, that diffuse across the synaptic gap to receptor sites on the postsynaptic cell membrane, increasing its permeability to certain ions and thus changing the electrical potentials of the postsynaptic cell. An impulse in one excitatory fiber (E_1) may produce only a small excitatory postsynaptic potential (EPSP) in the postsynaptic cell. Sequential impulses from two excitatory endings (E_1 *and* E_2) may combine to depolarize the membrane enough to reach threshold, firing the cell. An inhibitory fiber (*I*) changes the membrane potential in the opposite direction, counteracting any excitatory action arriving at the same time (E_1 *and* I). At an electrical synapse the gap between the presynaptic and postsynaptic neuron is reduced and the current produced by the action potential in the presynaptic neuron flows directly into the postsynaptic cell and out across its membrane, depolarizing it. A presynaptic impulse (*a*) can therefore produce an immediate electrical postsynaptic potential (*b*). In a conjoint synapse, both chemical and electrical, the presynaptic impulse (*a*) produces (*b*) first an electrical synaptic potential (*E*) and then, after a delay, a chemical synaptic potential (*C*).

repetitive stimulation leads to a decrease in synaptic effectiveness that sometimes lasts for an hour or more. Other synaptic pathways were found that do not require high-frequency stimulation to undergo plastic changes; they undergo a low-frequency depression when they are stimulated at low rates. For example, Jan Bruner and Ladislav Tauc, at the Marey Institute in Paris, recently described a profound low-frequency depression in a monosynaptic system in the marine invertebrate *Aplysia*. In some synapses one stimulus frequency produces depression and another frequency leads to facilitation. Moreover, plastic changes are not limited to excitatory synapses; they can also occur at inhibitory synapses.

The Synapse

The great advantage of monosynaptic systems is that their anatomical simplicity allows them to be examined directly. It was in monosynaptic systems that Sir Bernhard Katz and his colleagues at University College London and Sir John Eccles and his collaborators at the Australian National University first worked out the general principles that underlie chemical synaptic transmission. They showed that at the synapse the action potential, or nerve impulse, in the termi-

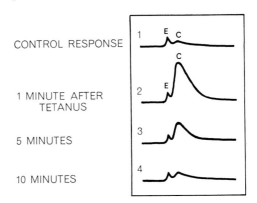

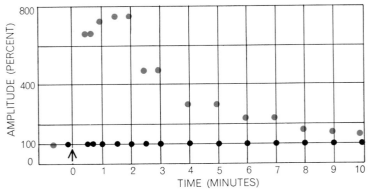

CONJOINT SYNAPSE experiment by Robert Martin and Guillermo R. J. Pilar demonstrated that the chemical synapse is subject to posttetanic potentiation but the electrical synapse is not. The electrical and chemical potential are shown in their usual relation (*1 at left*). After a brief tetanus the chemical synaptic potential is increased but not the electrical (*2*); the chemical synaptic potential remains elevated for more than 10 minutes (*3 and 4*). The chart (*right*) shows the quantitative results of the complete experiment. The arrow indicates the tetanus. The electrical EPSP (*black*) is unaffected; the chemical EPSP (*color*) rises and declines.

nal part of the neuron leading to the synapse (the presynaptic neuron) triggers the release of a "chemical messenger," or transmitter substance, such as acetylcholine [*see top illustration on preceding page*]. The chemical transmitter diffuses across the gap separating the two neurons at the synapse and interacts with a receptor site on the outer surface of the membrane of the postsynaptic cell. This interaction leads to a change in the permeability of the membrane to certain ions.

At an excitatory synapse the transmitter-receptor interaction produces an increase in the permeability of the membrane to sodium and potassium ions, resulting in a depolarizing potential change: the excitatory postsynaptic potential (EPSP). This makes the membrane potential less negative, moving it toward the threshold at which a new ac-

tion potential will be discharged in the postsynaptic cell. If the EPSP is large enough, the threshold is exceeded and an all-or-none action potential is triggered. At an inhibitory synapse the transmitter-receptor interaction increases the permeability to potassium or chloride ions, resulting in a hyperpolarizing potential change: the inhibitory postsynaptic potential (IPSP). This moves the membrane potential away from the critical threshold potential, thereby decreasing the possibility of the postsynaptic cell's discharging an action potential.

Studies of monosynaptic systems provided a basis for analyzing the cellular mechanisms of plastic change. In all instances examined plasticity of synaptic pathways has been shown to involve a change in the amplitude of the postsynaptic potential. Detailed study of mechanisms has been possible in the

case of posttetanic potentiation. O. F. Hutter of University College London found that the characteristic increase in the EPSP results from an increased amount of transmitter substance released by the presynaptic terminals with each impulse; the sensitivity of the receptor to the transmitter was unaltered. Similarly, posttetanic depression and low-frequency depression seem to be due to a decrease in the amount of transmitter released and not to a change in receptor sensitivity, but the evidence here is less complete.

In 1957 Edwin J. Furshpan and David D. Potter, then at University College London, found that the central nervous system contained not only chemical but also electrical synapses. The two classes of synapses have a number of properties in common, but the electrical synapses (which are less numerous) do not utilize a chemical transmitter; there is a direct flow of current from the presynaptic to the postsynaptic cell [*see top illustration on preceding page*]. The finding of a second class of synapses made possible further exploration of the mechanisms of plastic change. If synaptic plasticity resulted from changes in the action of transmitter substances, then electrical synapses, lacking these transmitters, should have restricted capabilities for plastic change. This hypothesis was soon tested by Robert Martin and Guillermo R. J. Pilar of the University of Utah, who compared electrical and chemical transmission in a "conjoint" synapse of the ciliary ganglion of the chick, where electrical and chemical transmission occur together. Martin and Pilar found that following repetitive stimulation only the chemically mediated EPSP changed; the electrically mediated synaptic potential was not affected. Michael V. L. Bennett of the Albert Einstein College of Medicine reached the same conclusion independently after detailed studies of more than a dozen electrical synapses.

These and other experiments suggest that the predominance of chemical over electrical transmission in the central nervous system may in part be related to the ability of many (perhaps all) chemical synapses to undergo prolonged alterations in efficacy as a result of earlier activity, and thereby to serve as elementary sites for information storage. The striking distinction between the plastic capabilities of electrical and of chemical synapses also strengthens the impression, which emerges from studies of different chemical synapses, that different synaptic pathways can vary greatly in the type and amount of the plastic change they are capable of.

PROLONGED HETEROSYNAPTIC facilitation is studied in the abdominal ganglion of the snail *Aplysia* (*top left*). A test pathway is weakly stimulated and produces a small EPSP (*1*). When a different, "priming" pathway is strongly and repetitively stimulated, it produces a larger synaptic potential, firing the cell (*2*). Priming facilitates the test pathway; it too produces a large EPSP that fires the cell (*3*). Ten seconds after priming, the test pathway alone fires the cell (*4*). It continues to produce a larger potential than control after 3.5, 10 and 20 minutes (*5, 6, 7*), reverting to control size after 30 minutes (*8*). A model postulated for this facilitation has a terminal of the priming pathway ending on the presynaptic terminal of the test pathway, controlling its transmitter release (*top right*).

The finding that the pattern of activity along a given pathway can lead to changes in synaptic efficacy at chemical synapses in that pathway was an important step toward understanding how behavior might be modified. With posttetanic potentiation or low-frequency depression, however, the changes in effectiveness are restricted to the repetitively stimulated synaptic pathway. Even simple behavioral modifications characteristically involve activity in two different pathways. Might activity in one pathway produce plastic changes in the synaptic activity of another pathway?

Heterosynaptic Facilitation

To examine this question, Tauc and I, working at the Marey Institute, investigated the effects of a more complex stimulus sequence on a number of different cells in the abdominal ganglion of *Aplysia*. In a particular cell we found that an EPSP produced by stimulation of one pathway could be greatly facilitated by activity in another pathway. We called this process heterosynaptic facilitation. Although not specific to or dependent on a precise pairing of the stimuli, the stimulus sequence used in these experiments begins to resemble the sequences used in learning experiments. The results provide a neural analogue of quasi-conditioning, or sensitization, the process whereby a strong stimulus enhances other responses.

As was the case for posttetanic potentiation, heterosynaptic facilitation did not result from a change in the threshold or in the biophysical characteristics of the postsynaptic cell membrane during facilitation. The facilitation could be produced in a pathway consisting of only a single fiber (as shown by the fact that it produced an elementary, or unitary, EPSP in the postsynaptic cell), indicating that the synaptic efficacy of the pathway was being directly controlled by the activity of another pathway. Tauc and I therefore proposed that fibers of the facilitating pathway synapse on the presynaptic terminals of the facilitated pathway, and that this presynaptic synapse acts as a governor regulating the long-term release of the chemical transmitter substance in the facilitated pathway [see *illustration on opposite page*].

The idea that activity in one pathway could control activity in another one was not new. A few years earlier Joseph Dudel and Stephen W. Kuffler of the Harvard Medical School and others had reported that some synapses undergo presynaptic inhibition, a mechanism whereby activity in one pathway de-

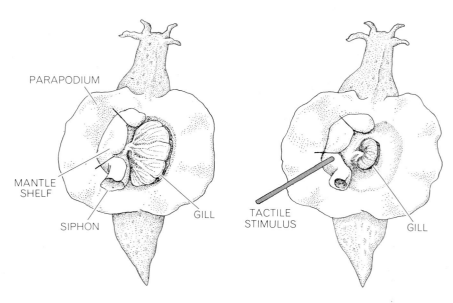

APLYSIA, a marine snail, has a vestigial shell in the mantle shelf. At rest, the gill is partially covered by the mantle shelf (*left*). When the siphon or shelf is touched, the siphon contracts and the gill retracts underneath the shelf in a typical defensive reflex (*right*).

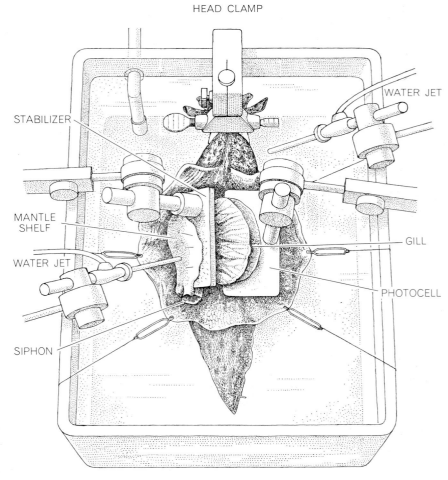

GILL-WITHDRAWAL REFLEX was studied by clamping the animal in a small aquarium and recording the extent of gill contraction with a photocell. When the siphon or shelf was stimulated by a jet of water, the gill contracted, exposing the photocell to light from above.

presses synaptic transmission in another [see "Inhibition in the Central Nervous System," by Victor J. Wilson; SCIENTIFIC AMERICAN, May, 1966]. That process generally lasts for only a few hundred milliseconds. The studies of *Aplysia* showed that certain pathways could exert a prolonged influence on the activity of others, and that this influence could be facilitatory as well as inhibitory.

To summarize, different types of plastic change lasting for many minutes and even hours occur at chemical synapses, and there is some evidence that the changes involve two types of regulatory mechanism within the presynaptic terminals that control transmitter release. One class of regulatory mechanisms underlies low-frequency depression, posttetanic depression and posttetanic facilitation and is responsive to activity limited to the stimulated (homosynaptic) pathway. The second class underlies heterosynaptic facilitation and heterosynaptic depression, and involves alterations in one synaptic pathway following activity in an adjacent pathway. The evidence for presynaptic mechanisms is incomplete, however; in several instances there remains an alternate possibility that the change in synaptic effectiveness may be due to a change in the receptor-site sensitivity of the postsynaptic cell.

The detailed study of the plastic capabilities of neurons is only beginning. It is

likely that other aspects of neuronal function—such as a cell's threshold or spontaneous firing pattern—may also prove capable of plastic change. It is clear, however, that an important prediction of the cellular-connection hypothesis has been supported: neurons and their synapses have at least some capabilities for plastic change.

Plasticity and Behavior

Given that some synapses can show plastic capabilities, how do these changes in a single nerve cell relate to behavior and its modification? In order to bridge the gap between cellular plasticity and behavior, a detailed knowledge of the anatomy and physiology of the specific neural circuit that mediates the behavior is required. This requirement is very difficult to meet in the intact brain of higher animals because these brains contain an enormous number of cells and an even larger number of interconnections. Moreover, the vertebrate brain mediates highly complex behaviors. One way around these problems is to study simple behaviors under the control of numerically reduced neural populations—either isolated portions of the vertebrate nervous system or simple invertebrate ganglia (discrete collections of cells). The most consistent progress has come from studies of habituation and dishabituation in

the spinal cord of the cat and the abdominal ganglion of *Aplysia*.

Habituation, sometimes considered the most elementary form of learning, is a decrease in a behavioral response that occurs when an initially novel stimulus is presented repeatedly. A common example is the habituation of an "orienting response" to a new stimulus. When a stimulus such as a sudden noise is presented for the first time, one's attention is immediately drawn to it, and one's heart rate and respiratory rate increase. As the same noise is repeated, one's attention and bodily responses gradually diminish (which is why one can become accustomed to working in a noisy office). In this sense habituation is learning to accommodate to stimuli that have lost novelty or meaning. Besides being important in its own right, habituation is frequently involved in more complex learning, which consists not only in acquiring new responses but also in eliminating incorrect responses. Once a response is habituated two processes can lead to its restoration. One is spontaneous recovery, which occurs as a result of withholding the stimulus to which the animal has habituated. The other is dishabituation, which occurs as a result of changing the stimulus pattern, for example by presenting a stronger stimulus to another pathway. Similar types of response decrement and restoration, last-

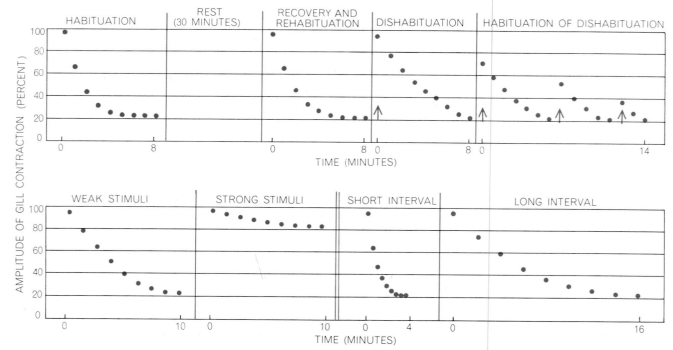

HABITUATION AND DISHABITUATION in the gill-withdrawal reflex have properties characteristic of these behavioral modifications in higher animals. The response decreased (habituation) with successive stimulations, recovered slowly after a rest period and then rehabituated when repeated stimuli were reintroduced. It could also be restored rapidly to control value (dishabituation) by the presentation of a strong new stimulus (*arrow*). The dishabituatory stimulus habituated in turn after repetition. The reflex also habituated more rapidly with weak rather than strong stimuli and with short rather than long intervals between stimuli.

ing for from several minutes to several hours, have been demonstrated for a wide variety of behaviors in all animals that have been examined, including man. The existence of such general ways of modifying behavior suggests that their neuronal mechanisms may also prove to be quite general.

The first neural analysis of habituation was undertaken in the spinal cord of the cat. The spinal cord mediates the reflex responses underlying posture and locomotion in vertebrates. In the course of analyzing the neural mechanism of spinal reflexes, Sir Charles Sherrington, the great British physiologist, found that certain reflex responses, such as the flexion withdrawal of a limb in response to stimulation of the skin, decreased with repeated stimulation and recovered only after many seconds of rest. Sherrington was greatly influenced by Cajal's work, and he tried to develop his notions of reflex action in relation to the anatomical diagrams Cajal had worked out. (In fact, it was Sherrington who coined the term "synapse" for the zone of apposition between two neurons, which Cajal had described.) Sherrington had the great insight to appreciate that neural reactions within the spinal cord differed from those in the peripheral nerves because of the numerous synaptic connections within the cord. It was therefore perhaps only natural for him to attribute the decrease in the responsiveness of the withdrawal reflex to a decrease in function at the synapses through which the motor neuron responsible for flexion was repeatedly activated. In other words, as early as 1908 Sherrington had suggested that a plastic change at central synapses could underlie response decrement. He was able to show that the decrement was not due to fatigue of either the muscles or the sensory receptors but, with the neurophysiological techniques then available, he could not fully test his intriguing synaptic hypothesis.

The problem was reinvestigated by C. Ladd Prosser and Walter Hunter of Brown University, who found that the habituated flexion withdrawal can be restored to full size (dishabituated) by the application of a strong new stimulus to another part of the skin. More recently Alden Spencer, Richard F. Thompson and Duncan R. Neilson, Jr., then at the University of Oregon, found that dishabituation is not simply a transient wiping out of habituation but an independent facilitatory process superimposed on habituation, and they established that spinal-reflex habituation resembled the habituation of more complex behavioral responses. Spencer and his colleagues

also began the cellular analysis of habituation. By recording intracellularly from a motor neuron they showed that response decrement involved a change not in the properties of the motor neurons but in the synaptic impingement on them. They could not localize the critical

changes precisely, however, because the central synaptic pathways of the flexion withdrawal reflex in the cat are complex, involving many connections between sensory and motor cells through interneurons that have not yet been worked out. Barbara Wikelgren of the Massa-

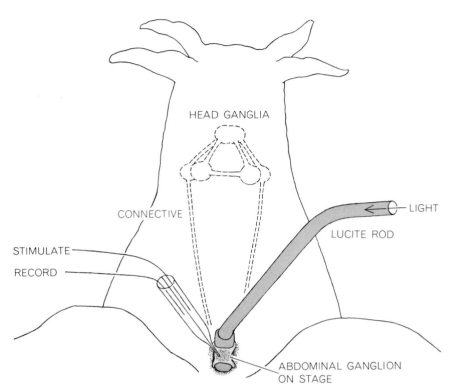

ABDOMINAL GANGLION of *Aplysia* is a group of some 1,800 cells at the forward end of the animal's abdomen, near the head. It is connected to the head ganglia by connective nerves. To study the individual cells of the abdominal ganglion, the author and his colleagues cut a slit in the skin and lift ganglion out on a stage lighted by a curved Lucite rod.

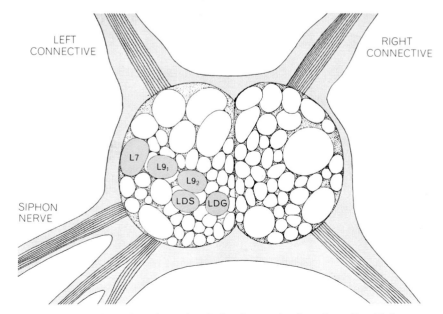

CELLS OF GANGLION have been classified and a number have been identified as recognizable individuals. By firing cells one at a time with a microelectrode, five cells (*color*) in one part of the ganglion were identified that produced movements of the withdrawal reflex.

chusetts Institute of Technology has gone on to examine several populations of interneurons and has shown that decremental changes occur only in certain classes of them, but the complexity of the pathways has still prevented her from distinguishing between plastic and dynamic changes in neuronal activity or specifying whether inhibitory or excitatory synaptic transmission is altered.

Gill Withdrawal in *Aplysia*

The further analysis of habituation required a still simpler system, one where the components of the behavioral response could be reduced to one or more monosynaptic systems. In search of such systems, a number of researchers have been attracted to the invertebrate nervous system because these systems contain relatively few cells, thus reducing the task of a behavioral analysis [see "Small Systems of Nerve Cells," by Donald Kennedy; SCIENTIFIC AMERICAN Offprint 1073]. The nervous system of marine gastropod mollusks is particularly advantageous because it contains cells that are unusually large (some reach almost one millimeter in diameter) and therefore are suitable for study with intracellular microelectrodes. For this reason my colleagues and I at the New York University School of Medicine have worked on the abdominal ganglion of *Aplysia,* a giant marine snail that grows to about a foot in size. An opisthobranch, *Aplysia* differs from the better-known pulmonate snails in having only a very small residual shell. Like some other marine mollusks, such as the octopus and the squid, *Aplysia* gives off a brilliant

purple ink when it is overly perturbed.

The abdominal ganglion of *Aplysia* has only about 1,800 cells and yet is capable of generating a number of interesting behaviors. Wesley T. Frazier, Irving Kupfermann, Rafiq Waziri and I collaborated with Richard E. Coggeshall, an anatomist at the Harvard Medical School, to classify the cells in this ganglion into different functional clusters. We also identified 30 cells as unique individuals and mapped a number of their central connections. This provided a good starting point for an attempt to examine the cellular changes in habituation and dishabituation. Our plan was to delineate a behavior that is controlled by cells in the abdominal ganglion and that undergoes habituation, to analyze the neural circuit of this behavior and then to try to specify the locus and the nature of the functional change in the neural circuit that underlies the modification of behavior. Kupfermann and I initiated this work and we were soon joined by Harold Pinsker and Vincent Castellucci.

An *Aplysia* shows a defensive withdrawal response that is in some ways analogous to the flexion withdrawal response in the cat. The snail's gill, an external respiratory organ, is partially covered by the mantle shelf, which contains the thin residual shell. When either the mantle shelf or the anal siphon, a fleshy continuation of the mantle shelf, is gently touched, the siphon contracts and the gill withdraws into the cavity underneath the mantle shelf. If the stimulus is very strong, it brings in other behavioral components, such as ink production. The defensive purpose of this reflex is clear: it protects the gill, a vital and delicate

organ, from possible damage. Gill withdrawal is therefore analogous to the withdrawal of a man's hand from a potentially damaging stimulus. As in the case of these other defensive responses, the gill-withdrawal reflex habituates when it is repeatedly elicited by a weak or harmless stimulus.

When Thompson and Spencer reviewed the literature on habituation in vertebrates, they described nine features that characterize this simple behavioral modification. We found six of these characteristic features in the gill-withdrawal reflex in *Aplysia:* (1) response decrement, typically a negative exponential function of the number of stimulus presentations; (2) recovery with rest; (3) dishabituation; (4) habituation of the dishabituatory stimulus as it is repeated; (5) greater habituation with weak rather than strong stimuli, and (6) greater habituation with short rather than long stimulus intervals.

The fit between short-term habituation in *Aplysia* and in mammals was encouraging, and we went on to analyze the neural circuit of this behavior. To this end Kupfermann and I made a small slit just forward of the snail's mantle region through which the abdominal ganglion, with its connectives and peripheral nerves attached, was lifted out on an illuminated stage [*see top illustration on preceding page*] so that various neurons could be impaled with double-barreled microelectrodes for recording and direct stimulation.

First we searched for the motor neurons of the reflex—the component leading outward from the central nervous system. We did this by firing different cells one at a time with the microelectrode and observing whether or not they produced movements of the external organs of the mantle cavity. By this means we identified five motor cells, clustered together in one part of the ganglion, that produced contractions of the gill, the siphon or the mantle shelf. Three of the five cells produced movements limited to the gill, one cell produced movement of the siphon only and one cell produced movement of the gill, the siphon and the mantle shelf [*see illustration at left*]. The motor component of this reflex, then, consists of individual elements with both restricted and overlapping distributions; it is redundant, as are other motor systems that have been described in invertebrates. Turning to the afferent component of the reflex, which leads toward the central nervous system, we next mapped the sensory receptive field of the motor cells by stimulating the surface of the animal's body with light brush-

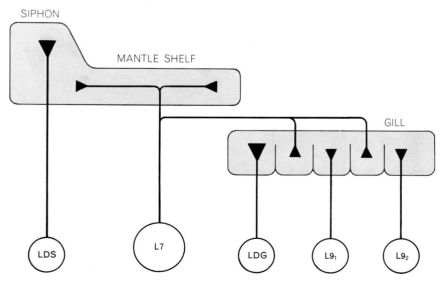

INDIVIDUAL ACTIONS of the five cells are shown. Three produce movement of the gill alone; one, movement of the siphon alone, and one, movement of gill, siphon and shelf.

strokes. We found that all five motor cells received large EPSP's, producing a brisk repetitive spike discharge, when the siphon or the mantle shelf was stimulated. The tactile receptive field of these five motor cells was identical with that of the defensive withdrawal reflex. Our analysis suggested a simple pathway for the excitatory input, in part monosynaptic and in part mediated by interneurons [*see top illustration on this page*]. At this early stage we could not exclude the possibility of an underlying inhibitory component.

The Nature of the Changes

Having analyzed at least part of the wiring diagram of the total withdrawal reflex, we next examined the changes that accompany habituation and dishabituation of the gill component of the total reflex. These changes could occur at a number of points in the circuit. The first possibility, that habituation was due to changes outside the central nervous system either in the muscle or in the sensory receptors in the skin, was quite readily excluded. Stimulation of the individual motor neurons or of the peripheral nerves innervating the gill at rates that are effective in producing habituation did not give rise to a significant decrease in gill contraction. Moreover, the size of this directly evoked gill response was the same before, during and after habituation or dishabituation of the reflex response. Finally, single sensory axons recorded in the peripheral nerves did not change their rate of firing when the sensory stimulus was repeated at rates that produced reflex habituation.

Since neither muscle fatigue nor sensory accommodation could account for the habituation of the gill reflex, habituation must result from some functional change within the central nervous system. We therefore examined the EPSP produced in the major motor neurons of the gill by tactile stimulation of the siphon or mantle shelf and found that it underwent characteristic changes that were causally related to habituation, to recovery and to dishabituation. When a tactile stimulus was repeated to produce habituation at the behavioral level, the resulting EPSP in the gill motor neuron gradually decreased in size, and the amount and frequency of the spike activity it evoked decreased correspondingly. Recovery of reflex responsiveness, produced either by rest or by a dishabituatory stimulus, was associated with an increase of the EPSP and a corresponding increase in spike activity.

We next began a more detailed ex-

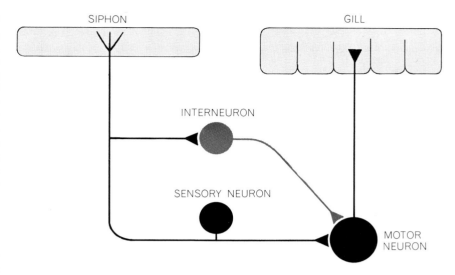

SIMPLE WIRING DIAGRAM for the gill component of the withdrawal reflex shows how the excitatory input from the sensory cells could fire the motor cells both directly and via intervening excitatory interneurons. (In *Aplysia* and other invertebrates the presynaptic neuron normally ends on the beginning of the fiber of the postsynaptic cell, as in the upper illustration on the next page. Here the synapse is indicated schematically, on the cell body.)

amination of the mechanism underlying these changes in the synaptic potential. First we examined whether the synaptic changes resulted from alteration of the synaptic impingement on the motor neuron or from a change in the biophysical properties of the motor neuron itself. The amplitude of any synaptic potential is determined by the amount of synaptic current that flows across the resistance provided by the cell membrane outside the synaptic area [*see top illustration on page 149*]. A synaptic potential can therefore be altered in two ways: (1) by a direct change in synaptic current, produced either by a change in the amount of transmitter released by presynaptic neurons or by a change in the sensitivity

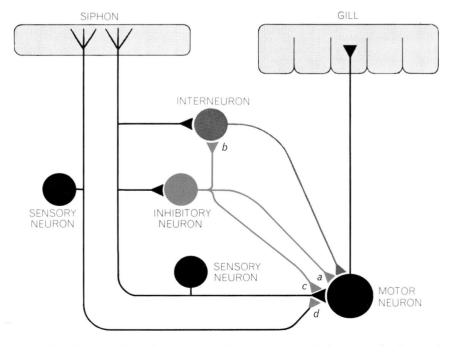

INHIBITION might reduce the excitation of motor neurons and thus cause the decreased responses of habituation. If an inhibitory interneuron were involved in the pathway, it might operate on the motor neuron itself (*a*), on an excitatory interneuron (*b*) or on the terminals of the afferent sensory fiber (*c*). Alternatively, parallel sensory fibers in a different pathway, activated by the same stimulus, might effect presynaptic inhibition (*d*).

of the postsynaptic neuron's receptor sites; (2) by a change in the resistance of the membrane of the postsynaptic cell. To distinguish between these two possibilities we measured the resistance of the postsynaptic cell and found that it was unaltered during habituation and dishabituation. The changes in the synaptic potential during habituation and dishabituation must therefore reflect changes in the synaptic current. This could have been caused by a change in receptor sensitivity or, what is more likely, by a change in the amount of transmitter that is released by the total synaptic impingement on the motor neuron.

Many elements impinge on a motor neuron and a change in synaptic impingement could therefore be caused by one of a number of factors. If for the moment we consider only habituation, then the decrease in the amplitude of the EPSP might be due to a decrease, caused by inhibition, in the number of active excitatory elements impinging on the motor neuron and thus contributing to the total synaptic potential. If the afferent fibers that excite the motor neuron also activated a side chain consisting of one or more inhibitory neurons, an inhibitory neuron could reduce the excitatory activity by acting on the motor neuron directly, on an excitatory interneuron or on the excitatory terminals of the sensory fiber [*see bottom illustration on preceding page*]. If repeated stimulation then produced a sustained increase in inhibitory action (by either dynamic or plastic means), it would result in progressive suppression of either the motor neuron or the excitatory interneuron that helps to discharge the motor neuron. Alternatively, habituation could occur without any increase of active inhibition; there might simply be a progressive decrease in the effectiveness of the individual excitatory synaptic actions.

Eliminating Inhibition

In order to distinguish between these two possibilities it was necessary to examine an individual excitatory element in isolation to see whether, in the complete absence of inhibition, the EPSP it produced would show the characteristic decrement, paralleling behavioral habituation, in the course of repeated stimulation. To this end we radically simplified the afferent component of the reflex pathway by separating a small piece of siphon skin that is part of the receptive field of the reflex together with its afferent nerve to the ganglion, and isolating the ganglion from the rest of the nervous system by removing it from the animal to an experimental chamber [*see upper illustration at left*]. In this simplified preparation we searched the skin until we found a responsive region that when stimulated produced an "elementary" EPSP in the motor neuron, that is, a unitary signal reflecting the synaptic response produced by a single sensory fiber. When this elementary EPSP was repeatedly evoked, it paralleled the gill response, decreased with repeated stimulation and recovered following rest.

This established that the change in potential was not the result of inhibition in the direct pathway from sensory to motor nerve. Inhibition was not yet ruled out, however. Since the stimulus that produced the elementary EPSP might also be activating other sensory fibers, the decrement in the synaptic potential might be due to presynaptic inhibition from parallel afferent fibers [*see bottom illustration on preceding page*]. To eliminate this last possibility we had to stimulate a single sensory neuron in isolation, thereby ensuring that it was acting alone.

This appeared at first to be a difficult experimental objective. It could best be

INDIVIDUAL EXCITATORY ELEMENT was isolated to eliminate inhibitory neurons in the pathway as sources of habituation. A piece of skin was probed to produce in the motor neuron an "elementary" EPSP, one clearly evoked by a single-cell. This EPSP showed decrement. In another experiment the cell body of an individual sensory neuron was identified and stimulated directly, and its decrement was observed. Dishabituation was also studied in this pathway, with electrical stimulation to the connective as the dishabituatory stimulus.

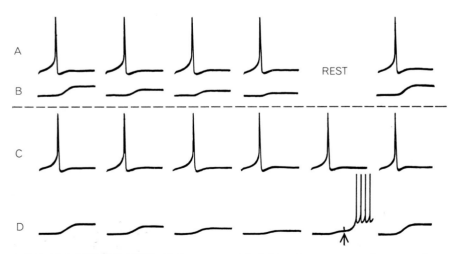

NEURAL DETERMINANTS of habituation and dishabituation are seen in these traces from an individual sensory neuron and motor neuron. Stimulation produces an action potential in the sensory neuron (*A*) that induces an elementary EPSP in the motor neuron (*B*); repeated stimulation produces a decrement of the EPSP; rest brings about recovery. Dishabituation was demonstrated by firing the sensory nerve (*C*) to produce habituation (*D*), then delivering a stronger stimulus (*arrow*) to a head connective, increasing the EPSP.

achieved by stimulating the cell body of a sensory neuron with an intracellular electrode, and the cell bodies of mechanoreceptor neurons were believed to be located in the skin, where they are difficult to isolate for recording and stimulation. Soon after we started work on this problem, however, John G. Nicholls and Denis A. Baylor of the Yale University School of Medicine reported that the cell bodies of mechanoreceptor neurons in the leech were located not in the skin but in the central ganglia; fortunately we found a similar situation in the abdominal ganglion of *Aplysia*. We identified a group of sensory cells that were excited by mechanical stimulation of small regions of the skin of the siphon and that had properties consistent with their being primary sensory neurons of the gill-withdrawal reflex. By stimulating and recording from one of these mechanosensory neurons and simultaneously recording from a gill motor neuron, we finally were able to reduce the gill reflex to its most elementary monosynaptic components and to examine the two cells in turn as well as their interaction [*see upper illustration on opposite page*].

Stimulation of one of the mechanoreceptor neurons produced a fairly large elementary EPSP in the motor neuron. Repeated stimulation produced a dramatic decrease in the amplitude of the potential; as in the case of stimulation of the skin, the potential produced by direct stimulation of the sensory neuron sometimes diminished so markedly that after a few stimuli it was barely visible. Rest led to recovery [*see lower illustration on opposite page*]. These data make it very unlikely that inhibition is involved and suggest that decrement of the EPSP is due to a plastic change in excitatory synaptic efficacy. This could result from either a decrease in the amount of transmitter released with each impulse or a decrease in the sensitivity of the postsynaptic receptor sites.

Dishabituation, the facilitation of a decreased response that occurs when a strong new stimulus is applied to another part of the receptive field, has also been studied in the isolated ganglion. We found that an EPSP that had decreased through habituation could be restored by a strong stimulus to the right or left connective nerve, which carry fibers from the head ganglia; at times the facilitated synaptic potential was even larger than it had been before habituation. In studies of the individual mechanoreceptor neurons we found that the dishabituation took place without a change in the fre-

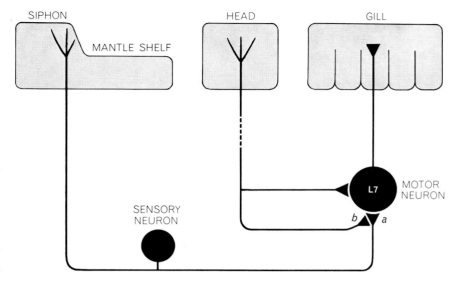

PROPOSED WIRING DIAGRAM for the elementary withdrawal reflex does not involve inhibition. The plastic change of habituation occurs at the excitatory synapse between sensory and motor neuron (*a*). Stimulation of head causes dishabituation, apparently by acting presynaptically at the synapse (*b*), increasing transmitter release from sensory terminals.

quency of firing of the sensory neuron [*see lower illustration on opposite page*]. This excludes posttetanic potentiation as a mechanism for the facilitation and suggests that dishabituation involves a heterosynaptic (presynaptic) facilitation.

As in the case of the gill-withdrawal reflex in the intact animal, the elementary monosynaptic EPSP's produced by individual sensory neurons had many of the accepted characteristics of habituation and dishabituation: (1) decrement with repeated stimulation; (2) recovery with rest; (3) facilitation following a strong stimulus to another pathway; (4) decrement of the facilitatory effect with repetition; (5) greater decrement with short rather than with long interstimulus intervals. (We have not examined the effects of the sixth variable, stimulus intensity, on the elementary EPSP.)

The Wiring Diagram

We can now propose a simplified circuit diagram to illustrate the locus and mechanism of the various plastic changes that accompany habituation and dishabituation of the gill-withdrawal reflex [*see illustration above*]. The motor neuron is *L7*, on which the work with the elementary EPSP was done. Repetitive stimulation of sensory receptors leads to habituation by producing a plastic change at the synapse between the sensory neuron and the motor neuron. The exact mechanism of the synaptic change is uncertain. We still cannot exclude a change in receptor sensitivity

but, by analogy with the brief low-frequency synaptic depression analyzed in detail in vertebrate and crayfish neuromuscular junctions, we tend to think the decrement of the elementary EPSP represents a decrease in the release of excitatory transmitter from the presynaptic terminal. Unlike the brief low-frequency depression, however, the decrement in the habituation pathway is remarkably large and prolonged. These features suggest that perhaps additional elements operate in synapses of the habituatory pathway. Stimulation of the head leads to dishabituation by producing heterosynaptic facilitation at the same synapse. This facilitation appears to operate presynaptically, perhaps by enhancing the release of transmitter substance.

We have used the monosynaptic pathway between the mechanoreceptor neurons and one of the motor neurons (*L7*) as a model for studying the total reflex. Comparable experiments with monosynaptic inputs still need to be done on other gill motor neurons and on the polysynaptic pathway in order to account quantitatively for the complete behavioral modifications. It is clear already that the unhabituated elementary EPSP's produced by a single spike in individual sensory neurons are relatively large and often trigger an action potential in the motor neuron. In addition there are at least 10 such sensory neurons that synapse on the motor neuron. It therefore seems likely that a substantial portion of the total EPSP in the gill motor neuron *L7* is due to the monosynaptic EPSP's from mechanoreceptor neurons. Furthermore, the spike activity of $L7$ contributes a substantial part of the total gill contraction. Since changes in the spike activity of the motor neuron $L7$ are directly produced by changes in EPSP amplitude, a substantial part of the habituation and dishabituation of the early component of the withdrawal reflex can be explained by alterations in the efficacy of excitatory synapses between the sensory and the motor neurons. Indeed, if similar processes occur on the other motor neurons and on the interneurons, these mechanisms could explain all the habituation and dishabituation.

Our data lead to some more general conclusions. First, habituation and dishabituation appear to involve a change in the functional effectiveness of previously existing excitatory connections. In these simple cases, at least, it therefore seems unnecessary to explain the behavioral modifications by invoking the growth of new connections or dynamic activity in a group of cells. The capability for behavioral modification seems to be built directly into the neural architecture of the behavioral reflex. Since the architecture is redundant and distributed, the capability for modification is redundant and distributed too.

Second, although a number of investigators have postulated on the basis of indirect evidence that habituation involves active inhibition, in *Aplysia,* where a major component of the synaptic mechanism of habituation can be studied directly, neither presynaptic nor postsynaptic inhibition appears to be critically involved.

Third, these experiments indicate that habituation and dishabituation are separate processes and that dishabituation is not merely an interruption of the decrease associated with habituation but an independent facilitatory process superimposed on the habituation. (Seen in this perspective, dishabituation is essentially a special case of quasi-conditioning.) Although habituation and dishabituation are independent, they do not involve different neurons with overlapping fields of action. Rather, the two processes appear to represent two independent regulatory mechanisms acting at the same synapse.

Finally, these studies strengthen the assumption that a prerequisite for studying behavioral modification is understanding the neural circuit underlying the behavior. Once the wiring diagram of the behavior is known, analysis of its modifications is simplified. The same strategy may be applicable to biochemical studies of learning that will eventually describe its mechanisms at a molecular level.

More Complex Behaviors

Studies of habituation of defensive reflexes in the cat and in *Aplysia* span six decades of research, but they represent only a small beginning; we are still far from understanding the neuronal mechanism of long-term memory and of higher learning. It would seem nevertheless that cellular approaches directed toward working out the wiring diagram of behavioral responses can now be applied to more complex learning processes. I have here considered only reflexive behaviors. Animals also display a wide variety of instinctive behaviors, or "fixed-action patterns," that are sometimes triggered by sensory stimuli but that do not require sensory information for the patterning of their behavioral sequence.

For example, in addition to its role in reflex withdrawal, the gill of *Aplysia* participates in a spontaneous withdrawal sequence that has the properties of a fixed-action pattern: it is centrally generated and highly stereotyped, and it occurs in almost identical form in the absence of sensory input in the completely isolated ganglion. Kupfermann, Waziri and I (and more recently Bertram Peretz at the University of Kentucky Medical School) have specified parts of the wiring diagram of this behavior, and it is already apparent that it is different from the reflex withdrawal and considerably more complex; it involves one or more as yet unidentified pattern-generating neurons. An even more complex fixed-action pattern, an escape response consisting of several sequential stereotypically patterned movements, occurs in *Tritonia,* a mollusk closely related to *Aplysia.* A. O. D. Willows of the University of Washington is well on the way toward providing a wiring diagram of even this higher order of instinctive behavior. It may therefore soon be possible to contrast the neural organization of several reflexive and instinctive behaviors in closely related mollusks. If the instinctive behaviors prove to be modifiable, it may then be possible to compare the mechanisms involved in the modification of reflexive and instinctive behaviors.

It would be unrealistic to expect soon a complete set of solutions to as varied and deep a set of problems as learning presents. The pace has quickened, however, and neurobiology may soon provide increasingly complete analyses of progressively more complex instances of learning.

17

PATHWAYS IN THE BRAIN

LENNART HEIMER
July 1971

The functioning of the brain plainly depends on a system of physical organization of its billions of nerve cells—a wiring plan, so to speak. The cells and the brain's various functional centers are linked together by an elaborate circuitry of pathways and interconnections forming a network of communication. In order to arrive at a detailed understanding of how the brain works we need a clear knowledge of this wiring diagram. Obviously the diagram itself could not explain the workings of the human mind, but a meaningful picture of the wiring system is a prerequisite for such understanding, and for more than a century investigators have been seeking to map the nervous pathways by studying sections of nerve tissue. Within the past few years a combination of new techniques, involving the combined use of the light microscope and the electron microscope, has made it possible to explore the circuitry of the brain in detail.

Communication in the nervous system consists in the transmission of electric signals that are relayed from cell to cell. Consider first the structural apparatus of the cell itself. It receives information through synapses (points of contact) on its cell body and on dendrites (twiglike branches) located close to the cell body. The nerve cell integrates this information and then fires impulses along its axon (a single nerve fiber), which ramifies into branches ending in boutons (synaptic bulbs) that pass the signals on **across synapses to other nerve cells [*see top illustration on page 161*]. Nerve cells are generally clustered or bundled together in groups, and the arrangement that particularly interests us here is one in which the axons are aligned side by side in a bundle that forms a pathway. Some pathways are very short, connecting only the nerve cells clustered in a group known as a nucleus. Others are

somewhat longer, connecting cell groups several millimeters apart. The pathways extending from the brain to the lower spinal cord are some two feet long, and from the spinal cord other long pathways go out to the body's sensory and motor organs.

The existence of structural pathways in the brain was recognized many years ago. Some of them, massive bundles that show up as glistening white fibers because of the myelin sheath coating the axons, are visible even without a microscope. The simple outward appearance of the pathways clothes a stupendous complexity. It is now known that the nerve cells and their interconnections constitute a mass of structures so complicated that if it were pictured in full detail it would look like a dense jungle whose components would be impossible to disentangle.

The Classic Stains

The disentanglement of this jungle began when investigators found selective stains that picked out individual features of the nerve cell for viewing under the microscope. In 1884 Franz Nissl of Germany discovered that the cytoplasm of the nerve-cell body has an affinity for methylene blue, so that this stain (and other alkaline dyes employed since) selectively shows the cell body. The Nissl method made it possible to outline and identify well-defined regions in the brain. At about the same time Camillo Golgi of Italy developed his method for the selective staining of certain nerve cells by the use of silver salts.

Golgi's staining method shows most of a nerve cell's details, including the dendrites and the axon. If the stain impregnated all the cells in a section of appreciable thickness, the details would be lost in a dense tangle of fibers. Because the

Golgi method stains only a small percentage of the cells, however, it is possible to resolve the details of these cells' structures and connections in a comparatively thick section of brain tissue, as thick as a few tenths of a millimeter. (With other staining techniques one is limited to thinner slices—a few hundredths of a millimeter—for meaningful examination of the cell processes and connections.) Thanks to the thickness of the Golgi section, a nerve cell's processes can be traced for a considerable distance, often the entire length of a short pathway connecting two clusters of nerve cells. The unique advantages of the Golgi method were soon exploited by many investigators, most notably by Santiago Ramón y Cajal of Spain. His host of drawings of nerve cells and their interconnections in various regions of the brain still provide a structural base for many of our functional concepts. Ramón y Cajal shared the 1906 Nobel prize in physiology and medicine with Golgi.

At best, a picture of a stained section in the optical microscope shows only bits and pieces of the nerve tissue. A great step forward in defining the structures that make up the pathways of the brain came when the electron microscope was brought to bear on this problem. That instrument can display, with a high degree of magnification and resolution, the details of the individual elements that constitute the complex nerve cell and the interconnections among cells. The electron microscope, limited to a slice of tissue less than a tenth of a micron thick, gives only an extremely small field of view, so small that it would be futile to try to trace even the shortest pathway by putting together a series of electron micrographs. The instrument is very effective, however, in delineating the fine structure of objects within this

160

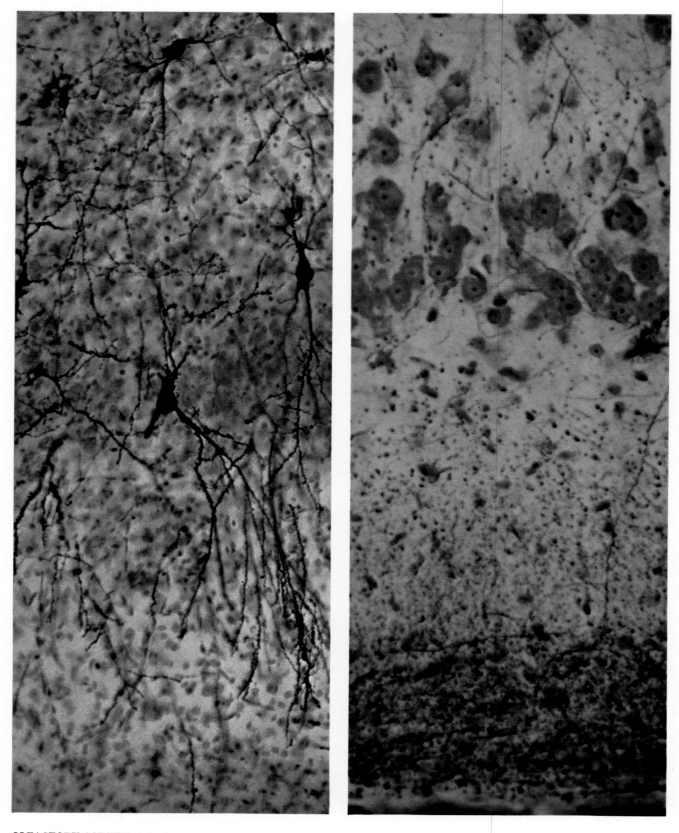

OLFACTORY CORTEX of the brain is seen in photomicrographs of sections stained by the Golgi method (*left*) and the reduced-silver method (*right*) and counterstained with cresylechtviolet. The Golgi stain (*black*) allows one to trace a few cells and their processes through a section of tissue. The Golgi section, prepared by Enrique Ramón-Moliner, shows that some of the dendrites (impulse-receiving processes) of large cortical cells (*center*) extend toward the lower surface of the brain (*bottom*). The reduced-silver method visualizes axons, or nerve fibers (*dark brown*), that have degenerated because their cell bodies were destroyed by an experimental lesion in the olfactory bulb. Five days after the lesion was made the animal was sacrificed and the brain section prepared. Degenerating axons cross near the surface (*bottom*). Above them is a zone of terminal degeneration. Large cortical cells are near top.

field of view. For example, it can be employed to analyze the elements of the synaptic contact where information flows from one cell to the next.

The synapse is a focal point for the investigation of the functioning of the brain. It is here that the interactions and modifications of nervous impulses that are responsible for determining an animal's behavior take place. Analyses of the synaptic region with the electron microscope have already cast some light on the structure of this transmission apparatus. They have shown that in the nerve cells of the brain and the spinal cord the boutons from which signals are passed across the synapse usually contain a number of clear vesicles (fluid-filled sacs) between 300 and 600 angstroms in diameter. The vesicles are believed to contain a substance that serves as a chemical transmitter of the signal. Apparently when a nerve impulse arrives at the bouton it releases a small quantity of this substance, which then crosses a cleft 200 to 300 angstroms wide to the next cell and thereby delivers a signal that excites or inhibits that cell [see the article "The Synapse," by Sir John Eccles beginning on page 136].

Tracing Pathways

Together the electron microscope and the optical microscope, with the aid of special staining techniques, now provide powerful tools for plotting the nerve pathways. Serial pictures of silver-stained bundles of nerve fibers made with the optical microscope outline the routes of pathways, and the electron microscope reveals their details. Even with these tools, however, it is seldom possible to trace an entire pathway from its beginning to its end in normal tissue. Fortunately a discovery made more than a century ago provides a means of conducting such an exploration in experimental preparations.

In 1850 Augustus Volney Waller of England noticed in experiments on nerve tissue that when a nerve cell was damaged, the fibrous structure ahead of the lesion degenerated, breaking down into fragments. Then in the 1880's Vittorio Marchi and Giovanni Algeri of Italy found a way to selectively stain fibers that are undergoing "Wallerian degeneration." Their technique stains the myelin coat of such fibers; the myelin is first treated with a solution of potassium dichromate and then stained with osmium tetroxide. This discovery made it possible to trace a pathway by following the route of fibers whose myelin is break-

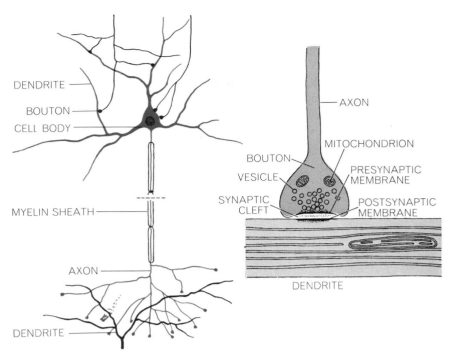

NERVE CELL and its processes (*color*) and parts of three other cells (*black*) are diagrammed at the left. A nerve impulse travels along an axon, which ramifies into a number of terminal branches that end in boutons that make contact primarily with the bodies or dendrites of other cells. Points of contact are synapses; one is diagrammed at the right.

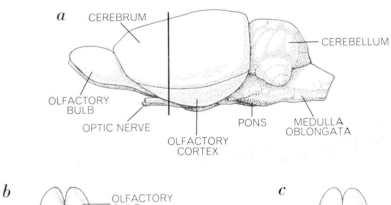

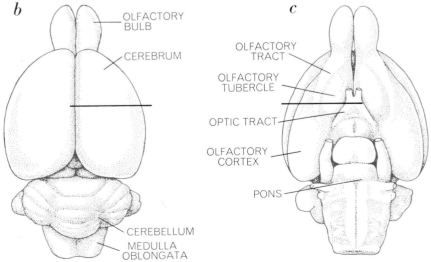

RAT BRAIN is seen from the side (*a*), the top (*b*) and the bottom (*c*). In each drawing the heavy black line shows the plane of the transverse sections in subsequent illustrations.

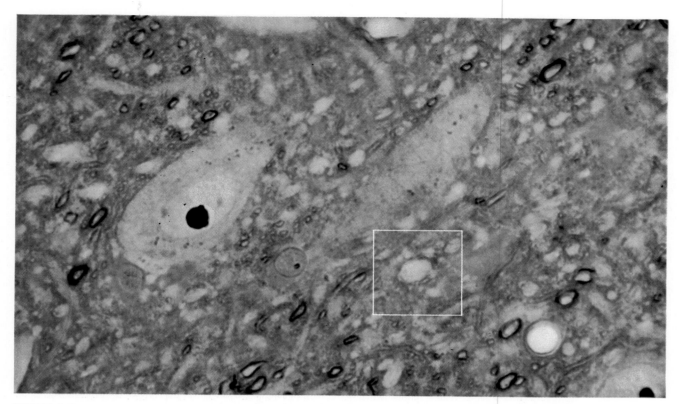

NERVE CELLS AND PROCESSES are yellow in a photomicrograph of a silver-stained section of the substantia innominata, an area where axons from the olfactory tubercle terminate. The rectangle marks a sectioned dendrite *(see illustrations on page 168)*.

SIMILAR SECTION from the substantia innominata was prepared (after a survival time of two days) following a lesion in the olfactory tubercle, part of the olfactory cortex. Large silver particles *(black)* indicate degenerating boutons *(axon terminals)* whose cell bodies were destroyed by the lesion. The electron micrograph on page 169 is from a region similar to the one in the white rectangle.

ing down. The technique still left important gaps in the picture because it failed to show those parts of the pathway that were not myelinated. This includes not only the terminal axon branches and their boutons but also many of the stem axons that are extremely thin and have no myelin sheath.

An important breakthrough came in the 1940's and 1950's, when refinements in the staining of nerve fibers with silver made it possible to mark and identify degenerating material in the interior of fibers. "Reduced silver" techniques for staining fibers had been developed at the turn of the century by Ramón y Cajal and by Max Bielschowsky in Germany, but for many years these methods were applied only to the study of normal tissues. Application of reduced-silver stains to degenerating fibers opened the way to the mapping of thinly myelinated and unmyelinated axons and boutons. The most widely employed technique was developed by Walle J. H. Nauta in collaboration with Paul A. Gygax, working first in Switzerland and later at the Walter Reed Army Institute for Research in Washington. The section is pretreated first with potassium permanganate and then with uranyl nitrate before being impregnated with a solution of silver nitrate. Thereafter it is transferred to an ammoniacal silver solution, and finally it is reduced in a dilute formalin–citric acid–alcohol solution. The technique not only highlights degenerating fibers but also suppresses the affinity of normal fibers for silver; thus it becomes easy to identify and trace fibers that are breaking down. The development of this convenient method for tracing nerve pathways through animal experiments launched a veritable boom in the exploration of the anatomy of the nervous system within the past decade, and the technique itself has been refined by a number of investigators, including the author in collaboration with Robert Fink.

Olfactory Pathways

To illustrate the tactics and the nature of the findings in these explorations, I shall describe my own work on the brain's olfactory system. In all vertebrates, including man, the olfactory system seems to be built on essentially the same basic plan. Odorous substances in the air are detected by receptor cells situated in the upper part of the nasal cavity. These cells (of which there are several million) apparently are the only peripheral sensory receptors in vertebrates that are actually nerve cells. On

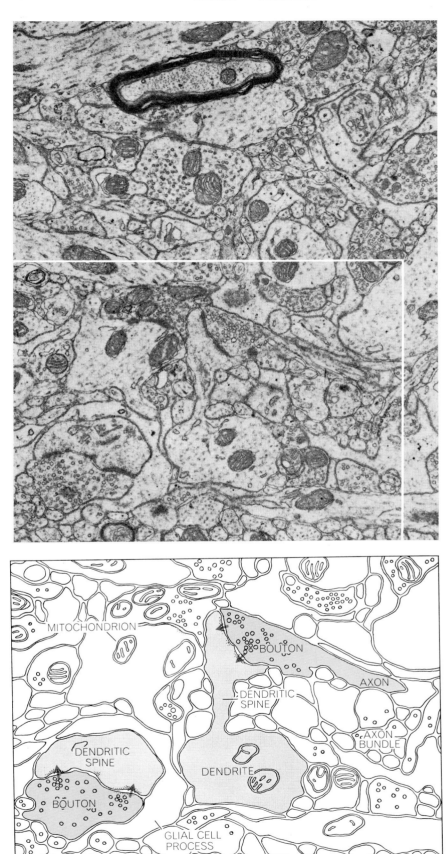

ELECTRON MICROGRAPH enlarges an olfactory cortex sample 24,000 diameters. The map identifies some components in the portion of the micrograph outlined in white. Arrows show the direction of transmission at synapses. Glial cells provide support for nerve cells.

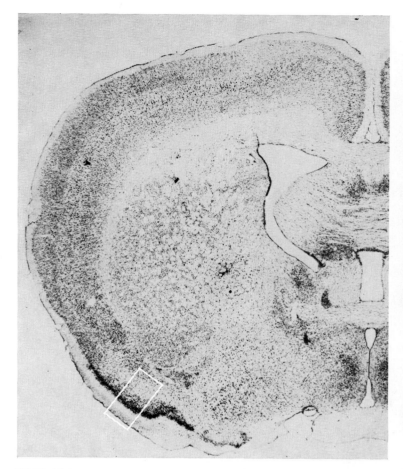

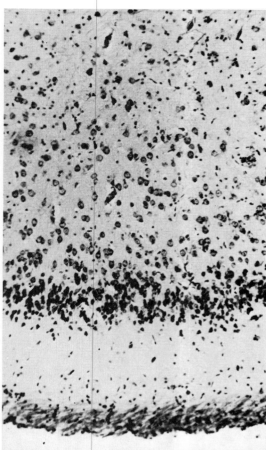

NISSL STAIN visualizes cell bodies, identifying cell "territories" in the brain. A low-power photomicrograph (*left*) of a transverse section of the rat brain, made by Walle J. H. Nauta and Harvey J. Karten, shows the layered arrangement of cells in the cortex, near the brain's surface. The packed cells in the olfactory cortex (*rectangle*) are enlarged 100 diameters in a photomicrograph (*right*).

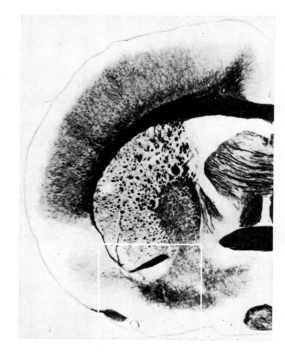

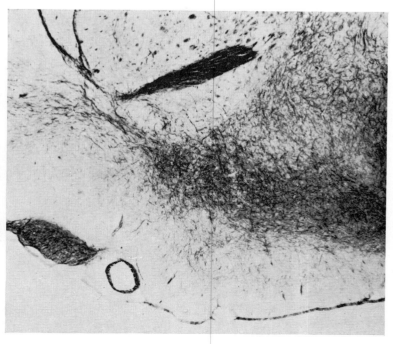

BIELSCHOWSKY STAIN is taken up mainly by large nerve fibers and is therefore effective in tracing massive pathways across a low-power micrograph (*left*). It stains all such fibers, however, so that individual fibers cannot easily be followed. When a portion of the basal part of the brain (*rectangle*) is enlarged 40 diameters, for example, complex network of fibers cannot be disentangled (*right*).

receiving the stimulus, the cells' axons convey the resulting nerve impulses to the first way station, the brain's olfactory bulb. This is a complex structure from which, on the outgoing side, several thousand mitral cells (shaped like a bishop's miter) send messages on to ol-

factory centers in other parts of the brain. Additional cell types provide for intricate circuits within the bulb, and it is conceivable that the message sensed by the olfactory receptors is greatly modified in the bulb before being transmitted to other regions of the brain.

Let us for the moment pass over the anatomical arrangements within the bulb and concentrate on the pathway stemming from the mitral cells. Our chief interest in studying the olfactory system lies in finding out where its pathways terminate. We first undertook a de-

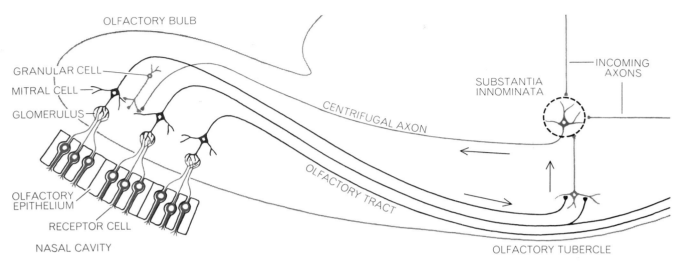

OLFACTORY SYSTEM of the rat has receptor cells in the nasal cavity that are stimulated by odorous substances and transmit messages to mitral cells in the olfactory bulb. Mitral-cell axons go to the olfactory cortex, which includes the olfactory tubercle. The author has found that olfactory tubercle cells communicate with cells in the substantia innominata. These may be the same cells

that have been found to send axons from the substantia innominata to the granular cells of the olfactory bulb; the broken circle indicates the uncertainty. The possibility of such a connection suggests the existence of a feedback loop (*arrows*) that modifies sensory inputs to the olfactory system. Other incoming pathways converging on the substantia may also modify olfactory responses.

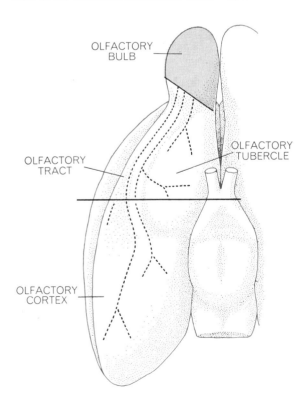

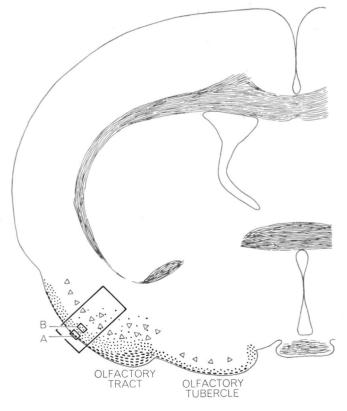

OLFACTORY PATHWAY is traced by the reduced-silver technique, which preferentially stains degenerating axons of mitral cells destroyed by a lesion in the olfactory bulb (*left*). The axons spread over the bottom surface of the cerebral hemisphere (*broken

lines*) and appear to terminate just below the surface (*right*). The large rectangle shows the approximate site of the color photomicrograph at the right on page 160; the small rectangles (**A, B**) show the sites of the two photomicrographs on the next page.

tailed study of the terminus of the mitral pathway, which has been the subject of a certain amount of controversy.

In rats we destroyed the mitral cells in the olfactory bulb by surgical intervention and, after a survival time of from three to five days, sacrificed the animal to conduct a microscopic examination of the fibers leading from these cells. Impregnated with silver by the Nauta-Gygax technique, the fibers showed a track of degeneration, marked by a line of droplike fragments connected by thin bridges, such as would be expected in a disintegrating fiber. Looking at a series of sections made consecutively through the brain, one can follow the degenerating mitral-cell axons, forming a pathway (the "olfactory tract") that is visible to the unaided eye as it curves around the olfactory tubercle. The pathway branches out and spreads its fan of disintegrating fibers over most of the cortical mantle of the basal part of the brain.

In this region, where the pathway terminates, one finds black, silver-bearing particles scattered about apparently at random [*see upper micrograph at right*]. Do they represent degenerating boutons? The particles do not show identifying features under the optical microscope. In collaboration with Alan Peters of Boston University we therefore examined silver-impregnated sections of this tissue with the electron microscope. The micrographs disclosed that many of the comparatively large, more or less spherical particles were indeed degenerating boutons. They could be identified as degenerating boutons by the density of their material, their shrunken and deformed shape and their content of vesicles or their association with a specialized membrane across a synapse. In the optical microscope the degenerating bouton shows up only as a black particle because of the microscope's lesser resolution, but in the electron microscope, where the thickness of the section is only a fifteenth of a micron, we are looking at just a small slice of the bouton—about a fifteenth to a thirtieth of its total diameter. There we can see that the degenerating bouton is only partly filled with silver, and we can make out details of its identifying structure [*see top illustration on next page*]. The electron micrographs also indicate that smaller dark particles found in the region where the mitral-cell pathway ends are fragments of the terminal branches of degenerating axons.

Let us now follow a pathway from the olfactory tubercle. Using the experimental procedure of creating superficial lesions in the tubercle with a silver plate

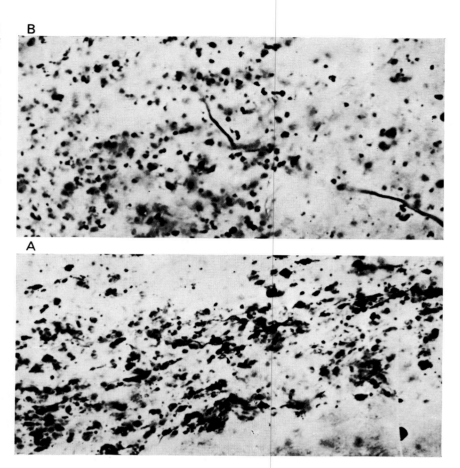

EVIDENCE for the pathway traced in the illustration at the bottom of the preceding page is in these photomicrographs of sections from the brain of an animal sacrificed five days after an olfactory-bulb lesion. Silver-stained degenerating axons are revealed as droplike fragments arranged in linear fashion (A, bottom). More spherical silver-stained particles in a deeper layer (B, top) were identified as degenerating axon branches and boutons.

heated to 70 degrees Celsius, we have traced the pathway of degenerating fibers to restricted regions in the thalamus and the hypothalamus. In addition we found that it terminates in the region called the substantia innominata, which is near (and apparently related to) the hypothalamus. A recent discovery by Joseph L. Price and Thomas P. S. Powell of the University of Oxford lends particular interest to this finding. They learned that the axons of certain large nerve cells in the substantia innominata are directed toward the olfactory bulb, where they communicate with what are called granular cells. Since the olfactory tubercle is known to be linked directly to the olfactory bulb by a pathway leading from the bulb, it seems entirely possible that return messages may be sent from the tubercle terminus to the bulb through a junction in the substantia innominata. If so, we can suppose that there is a feedback loop in which inputs originating from the bulb itself and traveling around through the tubercle and substantia innominata modify the bulb's

activity. In order to decide this question we must find out whether or not the tubercle fibers "talk to" (communicate with) the dendrites of the same substantia innominata cells that send messages to the bulb. Whatever the exact organization of these connections may be, it seems certain that the brain can modulate the transmission of olfactory information as early as the level of the first synapse of the olfactory pathway.

The substantia innominata is rich in large dendrites, which traverse the region in various directions. Analysis with the electron microscope shows that these dendrites are covered with boutons of several different types, varying in the size of their vesicles, in the character of their synaptic membranes and in other respects. Studies of cells in other regions of the brain have indicated that a given type of bouton represents a specific pathway. This suggests that the presence of more than one type of bouton on a dendrite signifies the receipt of messages from more than one source or pathway. In short, the dendrites in the substantia

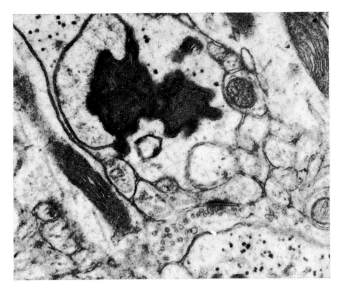

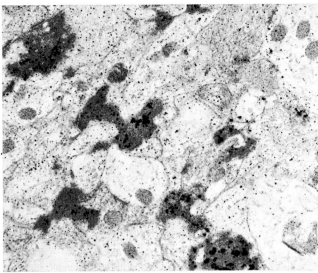

DEGENERATING BOUTON in the cortex is enlarged 25,000 diameters in an electron micrograph *(left)*. Increased density and deformation are signs of degeneration. Similar boutons in a silver-stained section (three-day survival time) contain heavy accumulations of silver *(right)*, proving that many spherical particles in photomicrographs are degenerating boutons of mitral-cell axons.

innominata may receive information not only from the olfactory tubercle but also from several other regions of the brain.

Our first step in investigating the question of the existence of a feedback loop was to try to identify the type of bouton representing the pathway from the olfactory tubercle. For this inquiry we needed a combination of information from the optical and the electron microscopes, and to avoid ambiguities the examinations had to be performed on one and the same specimen of tissue. This meant that we first had to cut a semithin section and stain it for observation in the optical microscope and then use part of the same block to cut sections thin enough for the electron microscope. The usual method of preparing thin sections of brain tissue, which is extremely soft, is to harden the tissue with a fixative

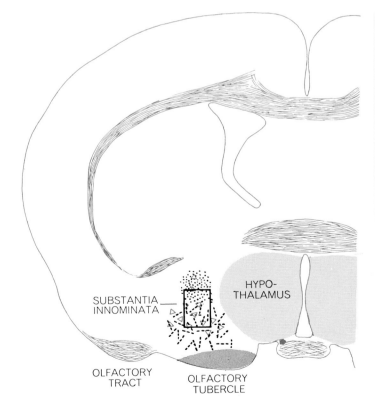

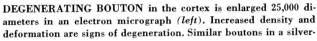

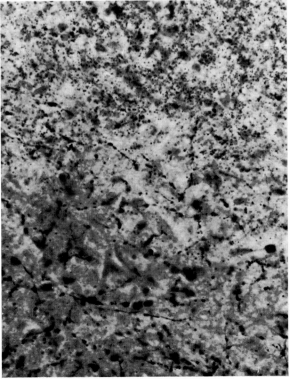

PATHWAY WAS TRACED FARTHER by making a lesion in the olfactory tubercle *(left)*, causing degeneration of the axons of cells with which the mitral-cell axons synapse. The tubercle-cell fibers could be followed to the substantia innominata, where they terminate in a localized area *(rectangle)*, as shown by boundary between region of degenerating fibers and terminal degeneration *(right)*.

such as formalin and alcohol (which pre-serves the tissue's natural structure) and then freeze it or embed it in a solid ma-terial so that thin slices can be cut with a microtome. I had found that the silver-impregnation technique for identifying degenerating fibers and boutons could be applied to tissue embedded in plastic, which is essential for cutting ultrathin sections of the tissue. After examining a semithin section about five microns thick in the optical microscope to obtain a well-defined picture of the degenerating-fiber structure we had under study, we trimmed down the block from which the section had been cut so that the block was limited to the area of interest. From this block we then cut sections about a fifteenth of a micron thick for close analysis in the electron microscope.

This analysis identified the type of bouton involved in the olfactory tubercle pathway. It indicated that the bouton probably was of a type that makes a "symmetric" synaptic contact, its mem-brane matching in appearance the mem-brane of the receiving cell structure fac-ing it across the synaptic cleft.

Identifying the Receiving Cells

We are still left with the problem of identifying the substantia innominata cells that receive the messages coming from the olfactory tubercle. Are the re-ceiving cells the ones that send their axons to the olfactory bulb, thus com-pleting a feedback loop? It is very diffi-cult to identify the cell itself, because of the electron microscope's narrow field of view. In the electron micrograph we are looking at only part of a dendrite; the picture is not broad enough to show the cell body to which the dendrite is attached. Fortunately a technique that promises to solve the problem is now be-ing developed. It is based on use of the Golgi staining method, which shows the various processes of a nerve cell, den-drites as well as the cell body and the axon. William Stell of the National In-stitutes of Health and Theodor Black-stad of the University of Aarhus in Den-mark independently found that after an entire nerve cell has been impregnated by the Golgi method to delineate its processes in silver, the block containing the cell can be trimmed down to a frag-ment showing only a part of the cell, and the fragment can then be sectioned for viewing in the electron microscope. Thus the stained material seen there (say a portion of dendrite) is known to belong to the cell that was stained and identified to begin with. There are still some diffi-

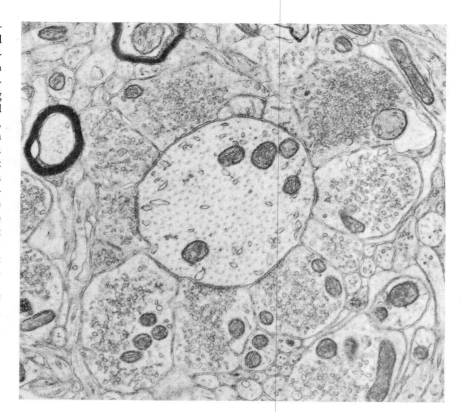

DENDRITE in substantia innominata *(see top illustration on page 162)*, enlarged 25,000 di-ameters in an electron micrograph, is surrounded by a sheath of different types of boutons.

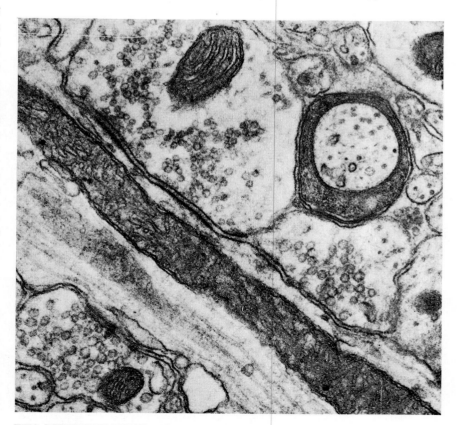

TWO DIFFERENT TYPES of boutons in the substantia innominata are enlarged 45,000 diameters in this electron micrograph. The large bouton in the upper part of the micro-graph contains small synaptic vesicles; the other two boutons have large vesicles. The question is: Does either one of the bouton types belong to olfactory-tubercle cells?

culties in applying this technique, but it will eventually help to answer the question of which cells in the substantia innominata are linked to the pathway from the olfactory tubercle.

It is a commonplace in science that, as Ramón y Cajal liked to remark, "discoveries are a function of the methods used." Certainly this truism is being demonstrated dramatically in the current

closing in on the pathways of the brain. In addition to the Golgi technique, refined silver methods and the use of the electron microscope, which continue to be the mainstay of this work, other new methods for tracing pathways are available. There are ways of making the nerve cells in certain systems fluoresce. Autoradiography also shows great promise as a tract-tracing method. And there are other chemical techniques that will have increasingly important roles in the elucidation of neuronal systems.

No one expects that it will ever be possible to map in complete detail the entire nerve plexus of the brain, with its uncountable multitude of fibers and synaptic contacts. The prospects are now good, however, for obtaining the ground plan of many of the functionally significant circuits and finding out which of these pathways converge to modify behavior. To take one specific example, it will be very interesting to identify the network of pathways, originating in various regions of the brain and converging on centrifugal systems, that feed information into the olfactory bulb. The pattern of inputs from these various sources no doubt influences the output of impulses from the bulb, with consequent effects on those behaviors that are influenced by odor—a diversity of kinds of behavior that range from eating to mating. The behavioral effect of the odor of a spicy dish of meatballs, for instance, obviously depends a great deal on whether or not one is hungry.

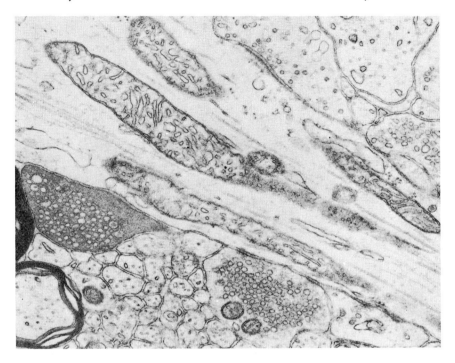

POSTLESION SECTION like the one in the photomicrograph at the bottom of page 162 was made 36 hours after a lesion in the tubercle. The electron micrograph shows a dendrite surrounded by a dark, degenerating bouton and several normal boutons. The degenerating bouton must belong to an axon coming from the damaged olfactory tubercle. Preliminary studies of this kind indicate that the olfactory-tubercle pathway is represented by large-vesicle boutons that make "symmetric" contact with dendrites of the substantia innominata cells, that is, the presynaptic and the postsynaptic membranes are of about equal density.

V

THE CHEMISTRY OF
BEHAVIOR AND EXPERIENCE:
HORMONES AND DRUGS

V

THE CHEMISTRY
OF BEHAVIOR
AND EXPERIENCE:
HORMONES
AND DRUGS

INTRODUCTION

The chemistry of the brain has become a major field of inquiry. Indeed, the use and abuse of chemicals and drugs, particularly those that influence consciousness and subjective experience, has recently become a major social issue in Western culture. In the previous section, we learned that transmission of information among nerve cells at synapses was basically a chemical process. Hormones, the circulating substances released by the endocrine glands, constitute another powerful system of chemical influences on the body and brain. These substances determine growth, the development of sexual characteristics, response to stress, and a whole host of processes that affect the brain and behavior. The actions of drugs, particularly of those that influence awareness, provide still another critically important aspect of the chemistry of behavior and experience.

In the first article in this section, "Hormones," Sir Solly Zuckerman presents a very clear and readable overview of the endocrine system. Beginning with a general discussion of the endocrine glands, he focuses on the pituitary, the master control gland in the brain that programs the actions of hormones in the body. Alan E. Fisher, in his article "Chemical Stimulation of the Brain," describes a number of intriguing observations he has made about the effects of microinjection of certain hormones and synaptic transmitter substances into the brains of rats. Certain such treatments can evoke well-organized behavior patterns that resemble those of a normally motivated animal, such as drinking and nest building. The latter behavior can be evoked in male rats, which normally never build nests, by brain injections of testosterone, the male hormone!

Very important new findings about the functions of hormones are described by Seymour Levine in his article "Stress and Behavior." Behavioral and physical stresses initiate a chain of events that mobilizes the organism for response. The mechanism appears to involve unknown brain actions in response to stress, which lead to hypotha-

18

HORMONES

SIR SOLLY ZUCKERMAN
March 1957

When a cockerel is castrated, it fails to develop into a rooster. Normal development of the secondary sexual characters that mark a male fowl depends upon a chemical substance which is secreted by the testes and transported by the bloodstream to all parts of the body, including the germ buds of the feathers and the region of the comb and wattles. The maleness and femaleness of most animals is determined in this chemical way.

The idea that something of this kind happens in the body came early in man's speculation about his physiological workings. Aristotle made observations about the effects of castration, and so did many after him. John Hunter, the distinguished 18th-century English anatomist, went a step further and experimented on transplanting the testes. When they were regrafted to another part of the abdominal cavity, the animal developed normally. This implied that the mechanism of their effects must be chemical rather than nervous, for the original nerve connections of the testes to the body were cut by the operation. But it was not until 1849 that A. A. Berthold, a young German zoologist, made a detailed study of the effects of removal and replacement of testicular tissue and so discovered the principle of what is now called endocrine action. His short paper on the subject provides the essential foundation of the modern study of hormones.

Soon afterward the observation by Claude Bernard, the famous French physiologist, that the liver "secretes" sugar into the blood led to the general understanding that there are special endocrine glands which pour their secretions directly into the bloodstream. The whole concept was given a specific meaning when, in 1904, the English physiologists Ernest Starling and William Bayliss conceived the endocrine system as a complex of chemical messengers which coordinate the functions of different tissues of the body. Starling observed that these "hormones," as he named them, "have to be carried from the organ where they are produced to the organ which they affect, by means of the bloodstream, and the continually recurring physiological needs of the organism must determine their repeated production and circulation through the body."

Modern endocrinology, in spite of all the attention it has received, remains essentially an empirical science, for we have only a vague understanding of the fundamental mechanisms of endocrine action. We observe the physiological effects of hormones, but we know little about how they act upon cells. We have nothing like a full list of the hormones themselves, or of the organs that produce them. The usual method of identifying a hormone is to remove the organ suspected of secreting a chemical messenger, analyze the effects of its removal and then try to extract the active agent. But obviously these methods are inapplicable to an organ such as the lungs, whose removal would mean immediate death. We have no present means of determining with certainty whether or not such organs secrete hormones, although they may well do so.

Of the established endocrine organs, the most important is the pituitary gland, attached to the base of the brain. It has two lobes. The posterior lobe secretes hormones which stimulate the contractions of the uterus during childbirth and also the release of milk from the mammary gland. Posterior lobe secretions also control the amount of fluid filtered by the kidneys. Hormones of the pituitary's anterior lobe control the functioning of most of the other endocrine organs of the body. They include the thyrotrophic hormone (TSH), which acts upon the thyroid gland; the adrenocorticotrophic hormone (ACTH), which stimulates the cortex (outer part) of the adrenal glands, and the gonadotrophic hormones (FSH and LH), which control the secretion of sex hormones by the ovaries and the testes, respectively. In addition, the anterior lobe produces a growth hormone, somatotrophin (STH), which acts on the whole body.

Other endocrine organs are the pancreas, which secretes insulin; the parathyroids, four beads of tissue embedded in the back of the thyroid; the adrenal medulla, the core of the adrenal glands; certain cells lining the first part of the gut; the pineal gland, attached to the brain, and the thymus gland, behind the breastplate.

Effects on Growth

We know that hormones are concerned in almost every living process, including every phase of the growth of the body. If an immature animal is deprived of the anterior lobe of its pituitary gland, it ceases to grow or mature. To grow it must be supplied with the growth hormone (STH), and for sexual maturation it requires the gonad-stimulating hormones (FSH and LH). The growth of the body as a whole is also influenced by the male sex hormones produced by the testes. This is shown by the fact that about the time of puberty

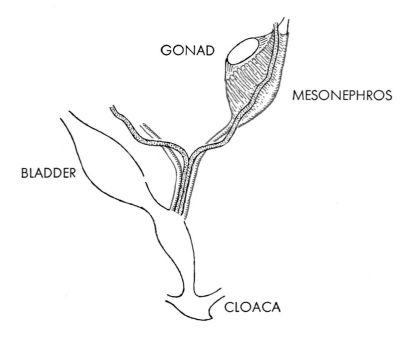

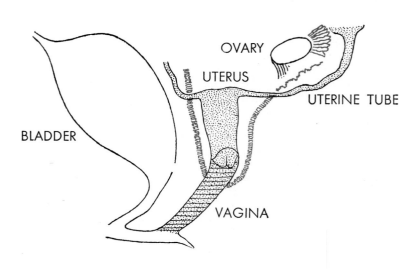

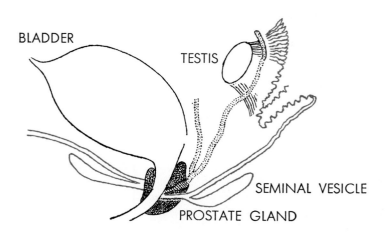

the male begins to grow bigger than the female. Indeed, it is through hormones that the animal's sex itself is determined. In the early stages the embryo is sexually neutral, possessing tissues out of which either female or male reproductive organs can be formed. If the embryo is a genetic male, its embryonic gonad produces hormone which promotes the development of masculine organs and suppresses the feminine.

The development of the body is also profoundly affected by the hormones of the thyroid gland (thyroxine and tri-iodothyronine). Removal of this gland from a young animal will inhibit growth, delay bone formation and prevent proper development of the reproductive system. These disturbances of growth combine to produce cretinism. The physical basis of the retardation of mental development in cretins has recently been clarified by experiments on rats. In an animal deprived of thyroid hormone there is a reduction in development of the network of dendrites, the tendril-like processes which act as contacts between nerve cells, and also in growth of the nerve axon, down which impulses are fired from one nerve cell to the next. As a result the animal's reflex responses are considerably slower than normal. The nerve cells of such an animal can be stimulated to resume normal growth by giving it thyroxine, if the hormone is supplied before it is too late. The treatment restores some, but not all, of its adaptive behavior.

The parathyroid glands also influence growth, by their control over calcium and phosphorus metabolism, and of course so too does the adrenal cortex; when it ceases to pour its secretions in normal fashion into the bloodstream, not only growth but life itself must stop.

Effects on Metabolism

Hormones regulate metabolism in the body in intricate and far-reaching ways. Consider the metabolism of sugar. For good health the supply or level of sugar

GONADAL SYSTEM of vertebrates is sexually neutral in the early embryo (*schematic drawing at top*). The mesonephros, an excretory organ, retains its function even after birth. If the embryo develops into a female (*center*), the outer tubes (*color*) regress while the uterine tube, uterus and vagina form from the inner ones. In the male (*bottom*), the inner tubes practically disappear while the outer ones (*color*) form the seminal vesicles and ducts from testes.

MALE HORMONE TESTOSTERONE was injected into the 18-day-old chick at left by Hans Selye of the University of Montreal.

The injection resulted in male characteristics. The normal chick at right, which is the same age, lacks precocious comb and wattles.

in the blood must be held fairly constant. Four factors enter here: (1) the rate of use of sugar for energy by the tissues; (2) the rate of absorption of sugar by the blood from the intestines and of reabsorption from the fluid filtered by the kidneys; (3) the release of sugar from the carbohydrate-storing tissues (*e.g.,* the liver and muscle), and (4) the formation of sugar from fats and proteins. In all these processes hormones play a part. Insulin, produced in the pancreas, speeds up the rate at which the tissues use sugar. If the body is deprived of this hormone, by removal or poor functioning of the pancreas (as in the disease diabetes mellitus), the level of sugar in the blood rises considerably. This can lead to death, unless insulin is given to depress the blood-sugar level. On the other hand, if the anterior lobe of the pituitary gland, as well as the pancreas, is removed from an animal, it may survive for months, in spite of the lack of insulin. Evidently the anterior pituitary normally has something to do with supplying sugar to the blood, and its removal therefore reduces the sugar level.

The pituitary apparently acts indirectly to promote both the formation of sugar and its release into the bloodstream. For example, the pituitary hormone ACTH stimulates the adrenal cortex to secrete hormones which in turn stimulate the tissues to synthesize glycogen (animal starch) from proteins. Again, the anterior pituitary causes the

thyroid to release a hormone which speeds up the oxidation of sugar by the tissues and also affects the rate at which sugar is absorbed into the bloodstream through the gut.

The metabolism of proteins likewise is considerably influenced by hormonal reactions. So too is the retention or shift of water between and within cells, which is determined mainly by the movement of sodium and potassium ions across cell membranes. One of the hormones involved in water metabolism is aldosterone, produced by the adrenal cortex: it promotes the retention of sodium and chloride in the tissues and stimulates the excretion of potassium. Other hormones that affect the body's retention of water are the hormone serotonin (found in brain tissue and in certain cells of the gut) and an antidiuretic hormone of the posterior pituitary. The sex hormones also influence water metabolism to some extent.

Controls

These examples illustrate that hormones play a vital part in the orderly development and functioning of the body, in general metabolic processes and in specific bodily adaptations such as the cyclic changes in the female reproductive organs. How are all these mechanisms organized into an orderly pattern of operation?

The pattern of control seems to be

made up of sets of reciprocal interactions between the endocrine organs. For example, the anterior pituitary and the adrenal cortex are parts of a feedback system. The pituitary hormone ACTH stimulates the adrenal cortex to secrete its steroid hormones. If one adrenal gland is removed, the ACTH stimulation causes the cortex of the remaining adrenal to increase in size. If, on the other hand, the anterior pituitary lobe is removed, the resultant lack of ACTH leads to a considerable atrophy of the cortex of both adrenal glands. If ACTH is then injected, the adrenals return to their usual size. It appears that under normal conditions the concentration of adrenal cortex hormones in the bloodstream controls the secretion of stimulating ACTH by the pituitary: when this concentration is high, less ACTH is released; when it is low, the release of ACTH increases. The same sort of "push-and-pull" mechanism is believed to operate in other cases of hormones stimulating a specific target organ. The secretion of sex hormones by the ovaries and testes is subject to a similar feedback control, and the various sex hormones in turn interact with each other. Thus the effects of estrogen, one of the two hormones produced by the ovaries, may be neutralized by an extra output of progesterone, the other ovarian hormone.

There is considerable ignorance about how all these sets of interactions are organized into a pattern. One possibility is that a chain reaction involving several endocrine organs may be called forth by a general metabolic condition or need of the body. For example, during exercise the muscles require more sugar. This single need may call a number of hormonal processes into play. Insulin stimulates the transformation of glycogen in the liver and muscle into glucose. The release and conversion of this glycogen is also promoted by adrenalin from the adrenal medulla, which is activated by nerve impulses during exercise or stress. In addition, the secretion of adrenalin apparently stimulates the anterior pituitary to secrete ACTH, which in turn causes the adrenal cortex to release hormones that promote the synthesis of glycogen from protein. Adrenalin may also stimulate the anterior pituitary to produce ACTH indirectly by way of its effects on the hypothalamus, to which the posterior part of the pituitary is connected. Finally, it has been suggested that a low level of sugar in the blood itself directly stimulates the secretion of ACTH. These various possibilities indicate the complex interplay of events that must be involved even in a single metabolic process.

The problems become still more complex in responses in which the nervous system plays a part. An example is the seasonal reproductive behavior of animals whose breeding is conditioned by the length of the day, or exposure to light. A female ferret, which is sexually dormant during the autumn and winter, can be brought into heat at that time by keeping it in artificial light for a few hours after sunset each day. But it will not respond if it is blind or if its pituitary gland or its ovaries are removed. The chain of reactions clearly follows the sequence: stimulation of the retina by light, transmission of impulses along the optic nerves to the brain, stimulation of the anterior pituitary to secrete the gonadotrophic hormone, which stimulates the ovaries to secrete estrogen which in turn produces sexual heat, marked by swelling of the genital organs. The main gap in our knowledge here is: How do the nervous impulses reaching the brain via the optic nerves trigger the secretion of gonadotrophic hormone by the anterior pituitary?

The hypothalamus, at the base of the brain, is connected to the pituitary by a stalk of nerve fibers. These are known to pass to the posterior lobe, but whether any reach the anterior lobe of the pituitary, which produces the gonadotrophic hormone, is still unsettled, in spite of considerable study. If they do, one might suppose that nerve impulses directly activate the anterior pituitary to release the hormone; if not, we might assume that the hypothalamus sends a chemical messenger to the anterior pituitary by way of the bloodstream. But unfortunately the whole problem is made completely mysterious by the experimental finding that the anterior pituitary can secrete the gonadotrophic hormone even when its nerve and blood-vessel connections to the hypothalamus are completely severed!

Hormones from Nerve Cells

There is considerable evidence, however, that the hypothalamus itself does produce hormones—hormones previously supposed to be secreted by the posterior pituitary. The hormones in question include oxytocin, which triggers labor contractions of the uterus and the release of milk by the mammary glands, and vasopressin, which raises blood pressure and reduces the excretion of urine.

Some years ago the anatomist Ernst A. Scharrer (now at the Albert Einstein College of Medicine) drew attention to the fact that certain nerve cells in the hypothalamus contained what looked like secretory granules. He therefore argued that the hypothalamus, in addition to being a primitive motor center of the brain, was also in effect a secretory organ. Similar granules were later found also within the nerve fibers of the pituitary stalk. When the stalk was tied or cut, secretory material collected in the fibers immediately above the knot, and the part of the posterior pituitary below the ligature rapidly became depleted of such material. Other experiments showed that extracts of the hypothalamus have the properties of the hormones that had been thought to be produced by the posterior pituitary. It is now believed that the hypothalamus is the source of the hormones and the posterior lobe of the pituitary is essentially a storehouse for them, although very likely it also modifies them chemically.

Action in the Cell

The concept of nerve cells secreting hormones immediately raises some provocative questions. For example, can the same cell generate a nerve impulse and secrete a hormone? However, the whole subject of the way hormonal mechanisms operate at the cell level is clouded by ignorance. It is tempting to suppose that hormones act in the cell by regulating enzyme reactions, which are involved in all metabolic transformations (e.g., the

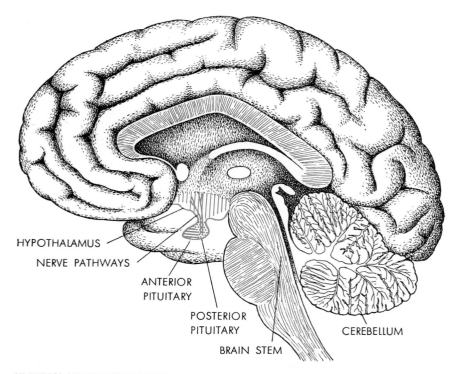

HYPOTHALAMUS

NERVE PATHWAYS

ANTERIOR PITUITARY

POSTERIOR PITUITARY

BRAIN STEM

CEREBELLUM

SECTION OF THE HUMAN BRAIN indicates the close relationship between the pituitary and the hypothalamus. The two structures are connected by a stalk of nerve fibers. It is not clear, however, whether the hypothalamus stimulates the secretions of the pituitary.

SECONDARY CHARACTERISTICS of male and female animals are brought out by hormones acting in concert with hereditary factors. Estrogen produces the plumage of the female pheasant (*top right*). Testosterone causes the development of comb and spurs in the white leghorn rooster (*right center*), the antlers of the white-tailed deer (*left center*) and probably the mane of the lion (*bottom*).

180

1

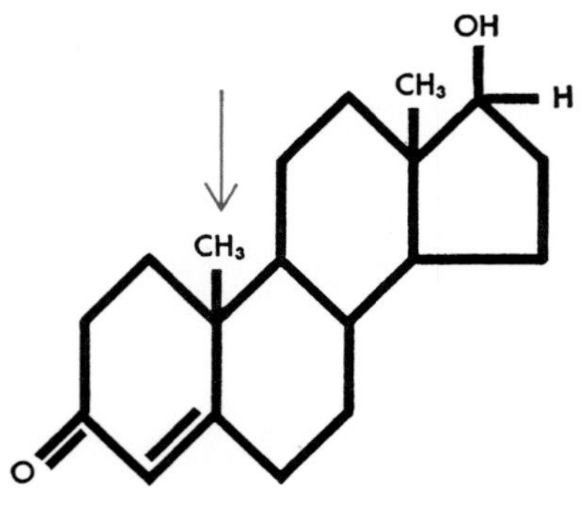

TESTOSTERONE

2

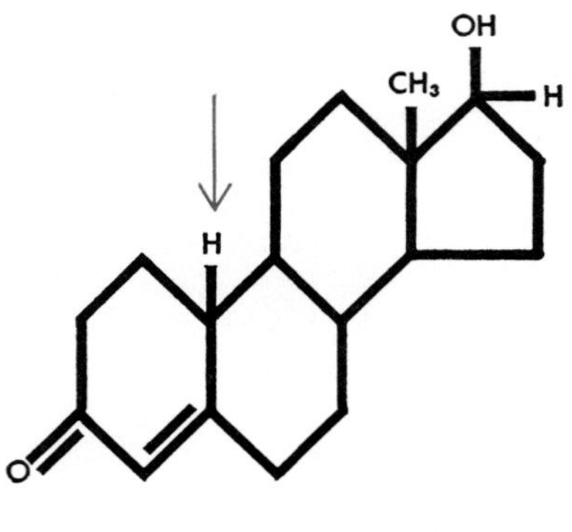

19-NOR-TESTOSTERONE

3

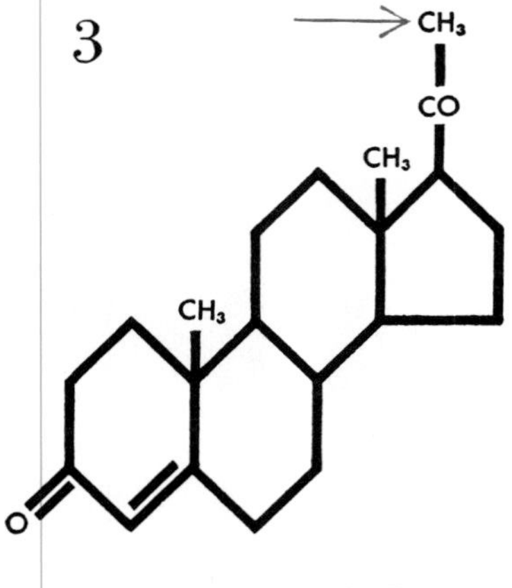

PROGESTERONE

ANDROGENS and related compounds have the molecular structures depicted in these diagrams, in which carbon rings are abbreviated. The arrows in the diagrams emphasize significant differences in structure. Male characteristics are induced by compounds 1

1

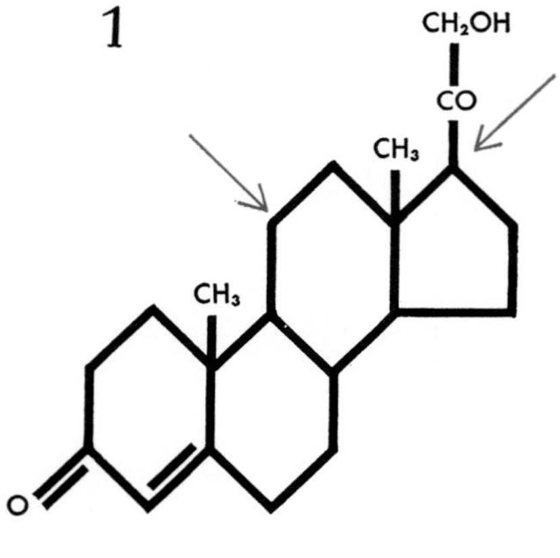

DESOXYCORTICOSTERONE

2

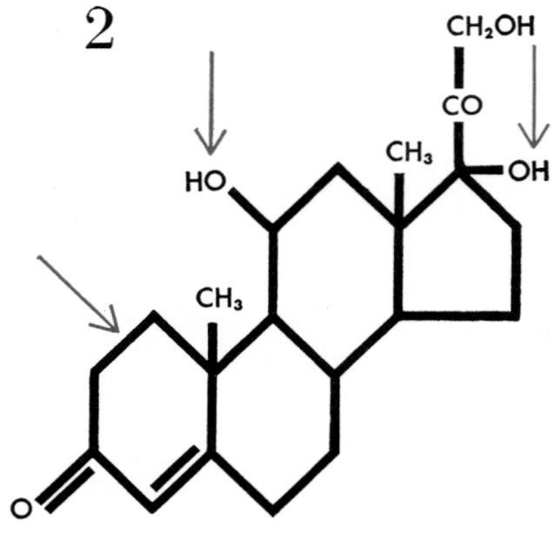

HYDROCORTISONE

3

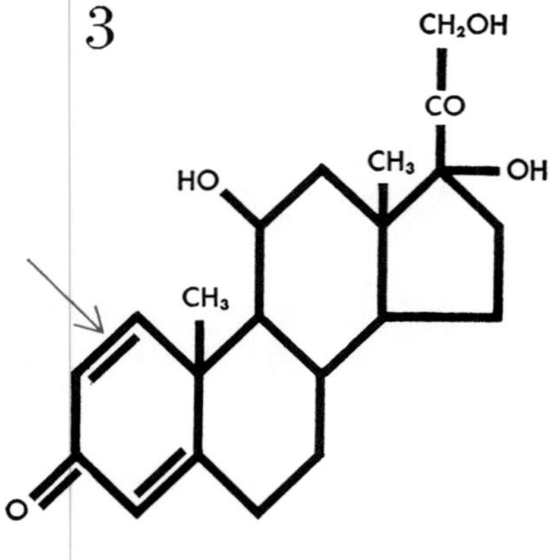

PREDNISOLONE

ADRENOCORTICAL STEROIDS and related compounds are important in the treatment of certain diseases. Compounds 1 and 4 are associated with retention of sodium and water, while 2 is associated with excretion of sodium and water and with carbohydrate-

1

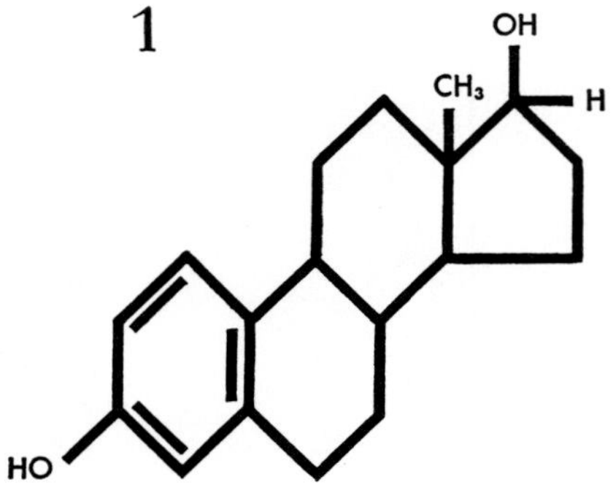

ESTRADIOL

2

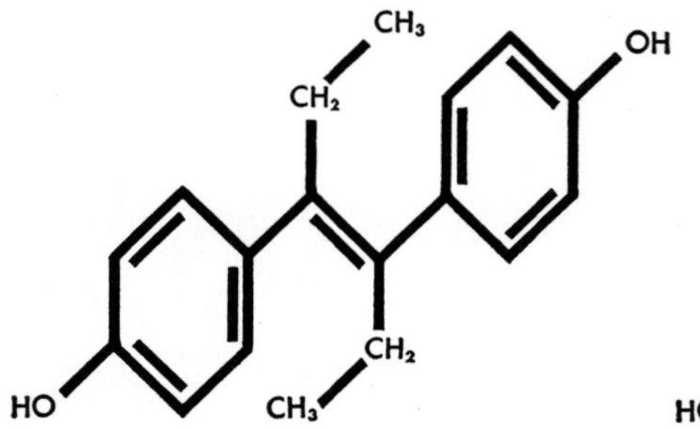

DIETHYLSTILBESTROL

3

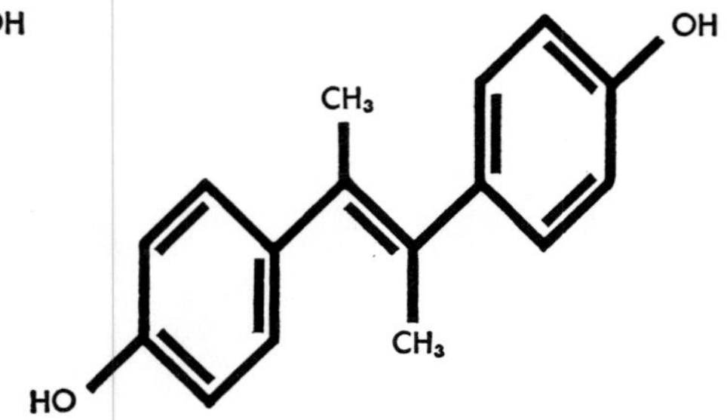

DIMETHYLSTILBESTROL

ESTROGENS and related compounds do not all have the configuration of four joined rings characteristic of the steroid hormones. Estradiol (1) is the natural female hormone. Synthetic compounds 2 and 3 are closely related but only 2 has estrogenic properties.

4 $\longrightarrow$ CH₂F

21-FLUORO-PROGESTERONE

5

AMPHENONE-B

and 2, but 1 is considerably more potent. Progesterone (3) is produced by the ovary. Compounds 4 and 5 have properties similar to 3, even though the structure of 5 is unrelated.

4

ALDOSTERONE

forming properties. Both 2 and 3 may be made synthetically; 3 is the more potent.

4

GENISTEIN

Genistein is extracted from subterranean clover, a spreading species of clover genus.

conversion of liver glycogen to glucose). If so, they must act in a great variety of ways, because the hormones are chemically very diverse: those secreted by the adrenal cortex and the gonads are steroids; insulin is a protein; the gonadotrophins are glycoproteins; the posterior pituitary hormones are polypeptides; thyroxine is an amino acid combined with iodine; adrenalin is an amine derivative. A further indication of the hormones' chemical versatility is the fact that a single hormone may act upon various enzymes: estrogen is apparently able to influence at least six enzyme reactions.

Yet all the enzyme systems with which we are acquainted appear to be able to function without the intervention of any hormone, and it has not yet been possible to trace the physiological action of hormones to their chemical action. According to some authorities, it is even possible that hormones exercise their effects not by modulating the action of particular enzymes but by influencing energy transfers. For example, it has been suggested that estrogens increase the availability of energy to the cell by altering the physical state of a part of the cell where glucose is formed. By so doing they provide energy for the synthetic processes which underlie cellular division. In addition, estrogens possibly regulate the permeability of tissues to water, partly by altering the ground substance in which the cells of the body are embedded.

Hormones which apparently differ

only slightly in molecular structure sometimes have vastly different effects. In some cases, on the other hand, compounds of very different structure produce the same effect [see formulas in bottom row at the left]. There is no obvious explanation for such facts, but in the case of the natural estrogen estradiol and the synthetic estrogen stilbestrol, the similarity of their biological effects may be due to a correspondence of interatomic distance between the two hydroxylic groups of the molecule.

Among the difficulties which prevent any real understanding of the relation of chemical structure to hormonal action is the fact that the experimentalist can rarely be certain that an isolated hormone is chemically identical with its form in the body. There is always a danger that the extracted, "chemically pure" hormone has lost some of the activities which it normally exercises in the body. It frequently turns out, too, that several pure substances are isolated from extracts of an endocrine organ and it is difficult to decide which of them is the natural hormone. For example, several clearly defined estrogens have been isolated from the ovaries. Are they all normal secretions, or are some laboratory artifacts? And in view of the chemical transformations that natural estrogens undergo in the body, can we be certain which of its natural forms is the one that acts on estrogen-sensitive tissues? Again, of some 30 different steroids isolated from the adrenal cortex, only a few are biologically active. Which of them is the important hormone? We still do not know how many active steroids the adrenal cortex produces under normal conditions, and what their respective effects are on the metabolism of carbohydrates, proteins and minerals. Studies with radioactive tracers may soon answer some of these questions, however. Such studies have already helped greatly in elucidating stages in the chemical breakdown of hormones before their excretion from the body.

One of the remarkable features of the endocrine glands is the capacity of the same cell to produce a number of different hormones. We have just seen that the cells of the adrenal cortex make several different biologically active steroids. From just a few types of cells in the anterior pituitary come diverse secretions which stimulate the thyroid, the gonads, the adrenal cortex, the mammary glands and other organs, not to speak of body growth in general. In the testes the same cells can produce male and female hormones. In fact a stallion gives forth more

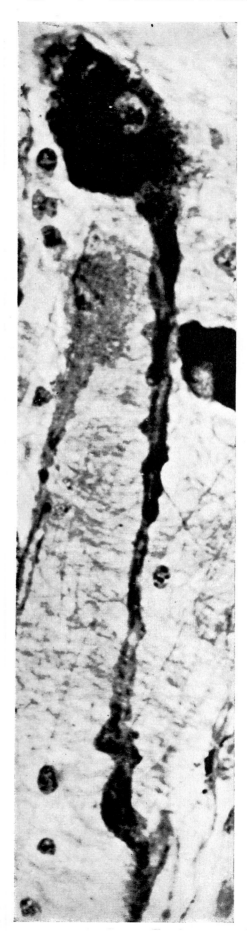

NERVE CELL of the hypothalamus secretes the dark-staining material which fills the cell body (*top*) and most of its long, thin axon. The material exudes from the end of the axon. This preparation was made from a dog's hypothalamus by Walther Hild of the University of Texas School of Medicine in Galveston. It is magnified 1,100 diameters.

estrogen than a mare does, except during a brief period of the mare's gestation!

Most hormones are produced only by a specific organ and effect a specific reaction. In some cases the target is a reaction that takes place throughout the body: for instance, the adrenal hormone aldosterone affects the water balance of all tissues. In others the target is a specific organ: the pituitary gonadotrophin acts basically on the testes or ovaries. Yet, to add to the complexity of the hormonal system, there are deviations even from this fundamental concept of specificity. The adrenal cortex can produce sex hormones; the gonads, conversely, can secrete substances with the properties of adrenocortical hormones. Some specialized reactions may be triggered by several types of stimulation: for example, menstrual bleeding, normally brought on by cessation of stimulation by ovarian hormone, can also be induced experimentally by certain adrenocortical steroids.

Hormones and Disease

In view of the complex, interlocking character of the endocrine system, it is not surprising that a derangement of the functioning of an endocrine gland produces far-reaching effects. A marked deficiency of secretion by the adrenal cortex results in Addison's disease, which manifests a variety of symptoms—extreme weakness, wasting, gastro-intestinal disturbances, a pronounced darkening of the skin—and was almost invariably fatal until the recent development of hormonal treatment. On the other hand, overactivity of the adrenal cortex may lead to various disorders: among other things, it may cause women to develop masculine characteristics, because it produces steroids with the properties of the male sex hormone. When the anterior pituitary gland functions poorly, growth of the body is impaired and puberty is delayed; development of the reproductive organs may even fail altogether. Conversely, overactivity of the pituitary leads to gigantism or, in an adult, to overgrowth of the head, hands and feet— the condition known as acromegaly. In the case of the thyroid gland, under-

functioning in childhood produces cretinism, and in adulthood it leads to a strange thickening of the skin, loss of hair, great lethargy and mental slowness. Overactivity of the thyroid (called Graves' disease) results in the familiar symptoms of a high rate of metabolism, great excitability and protruding eyes. And of course everyone knows that a deficiency of secretion of insulin by the pancreas is responsible for diabetes.

The results of derangement of the endocrine system are so pervasive that it is natural to suspect it of complicity in various systemic diseases. The estrogenic hormones are chemically related to some of the hydrocarbons that induce cancer when applied to the skin of rats and mice. These hormones stimulate the growth of cells in the reproductive organs of women, including the breast. Could they initiate malignant growth in those organs? So far all that has been proved is that estrogenic stimulation does play a part in the triggering of cancer in strains of mice genetically susceptible to the disease. Paradoxically, estrogen can be used as a treatment for certain forms of cancer—for example, cancer of the prostate.

Hans Selye of Montreal has grouped together arthritis, hypertension and kidney disease as a set of disorders resulting from derangement of the pituitary-adrenal system. The basic idea is that when the body is subjected to some general stress (such as extreme cold or shock), the adrenal cortex immediately releases and becomes temporarily depleted of its steroid hormones. If the stress continues, the anterior pituitary secretes so much ACTH as to overstimulate the adrenal cortex. This leads to pathological results, including rheumatoid arthritis. Popular interest in the idea was excited when it was found that ACTH and cortisone had an almost miraculous effect in relieving the symptoms of rheumatoid arthritis. However, the relief lasts only so long as the hormones are being administered, and if administered too long, they frequently have dangerous side effects.

The "adaptation syndrome" has been hailed as a "unified concept of disease." This seems too sweeping and overambitious a view. Nevertheless it is difficult to exaggerate the importance of the study of endocrinology. The past 10 years have seen the development of the concept of secretions by nerve cells, the synthesis of the hormones of the pituitary posterior lobe, the discovery of such potent adrenal hormones as aldosterone and hydrocortisone and the complete working out of the structure of the insulin molecule. They have also brought to light the

possible roles of hormones in immuno-
logical reactions, in the genesis of cancer
and in the control of fertility—a subject
which may have enormous importance
for the future welfare of the world. Other
vast fields of endocrine action have been
found in invertebrate animals and in
plants. Hormones are no longer regarded
merely as chemical messengers in the
bloodstream. They play a part in almost
every, if not every, living process.

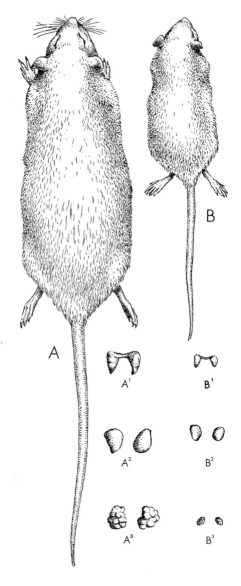

EFFECT OF PITUITARY HORMONE on
growth may be demonstrated in the rat. The
pituitary was removed from one of two littermates 36 days after birth, at which time
both rats had the same weight. After several
months the normal animal (*left*) had
tripled its weight and had matured while
the other (*right*) had gained little weight
and was maturing much more slowly. At left
are the thyroids (A1), adrenals (A2), and
ovaries (A3) of the normal rat, and at right
are glands (B1, B2, B3) of operated rat.

19

CHEMICAL STIMULATION OF THE BRAIN

ALAN E. FISHER
June 1964

It was once customary to think of the brain as an intricate switchboard and decoding system, operating by essentially electrical means. As neurophysiologists learned more about the central nervous system, however, they came to recognize that chemical mediators play an important role in brain activity. To examine this role more closely it is now possible with new techniques to apply chemical substances directly to local areas deep within the brain.

As usually happens in pioneering a new technique, there have been disappointments, puzzles, surprises and, most fruitful of all, findings that seem to contradict previous understanding. But the operation of the brain is so complex that it is only by piecing together knowledge gained in many different ways, and by reconciling conflicting data, that we can hope to penetrate its secrets.

The tracing of specific behavior to stimulation of particular areas in the brain was pioneered by Walter Rudolph Hess of the University of Zurich. In a series of illuminating experiments for which he received the Nobel prize in physiology and medicine in 1949, Hess found that by gentle electrical stimulation of certain areas in the hypothalamus of cats he could evoke fear, anger and reactions connected with digestion and other body functions. These discoveries started a train of highly fruitful experiments in electrical stimulation by many investigators, culminating in the discovery of nerve circuits that appear to control pleasure and punishment [see "Pleasure Centers in the Brain," by James Olds; SCIENTIFIC AMERICAN Offprint 30].

Nevertheless, electrical stimulation of the brain has definite limitations. The effects are often blurred or mixed, and the method has generally failed to elicit some of the basic forms of behavior, such as those prompted by the maternal and sexual drives. Two factors may account for these limitations. Electrical stimulation is not selective as far as nerve cells are concerned; it will fire any nerve cell indiscriminately. And the indications are that the neurons responsible for a particular form of behavior are not usually clumped in one place but are dispersed widely in the brain, overlapping with other functional fields or systems of neurons.

These facts prompted some neurophysiologists to search for a more specific type of stimulator: something that would selectively stimulate only the system of cells controlling a particular behavior. With the growing appreciation of the role of chemistry in brain function it seemed that carefully chosen chemical substances might exhibit the discrimination desired.

It was known, for example, that chemical messengers, or hormones, are deeply involved in the brain's activities and that other chemical substances control the basic process of transmission of nerve impulses. Acetylcholine, noradrenalin and probably other substances are released at the ends of the nerve cells and carry impulses across the synaptic gap from one neuron to the next. Other chemicals mimic or interfere with the action of these transmitters. Chemical "modulators" have also been found that alter the threshold for the cell's firing of an impulse.

The Case of the Mixed-up Rat

Was it possible that neurons or chains of neurons might be sensitive to specific substances to which they would respond selectively? Experimenters began to test this intriguing idea. The first results were not encouraging, but in 1953 Bengt Andersson in Sweden reported a significant success. Experimenting with goats, he injected a 5 per cent solution of salt into a precisely defined area in the middle of the hypothalamus, the governing center of the autonomic nervous system. The goats immediately began to drink large quantities of water. Evidently they had been induced to drink by some effect on the brain cells caused by the rise in osmotic pressure produced by the salt.

Late in 1954, while working in D. O. Hebb's laboratory at McGill University, I began to experiment with substances I hoped would produce direct chemical stimulation of specific brain cells. I started with the male sex hormone, testosterone, and injected it into specific sites in the hypothalamus of male rats. These particular regions seemed the most likely ones for action by the hormone because it was already known that they are involved in the primary drives of rats, such as courtship, care of the young, eating and drinking. I had expected, of course, that injection of the male sex hormone into the rat's brain would trigger male sex behavior.

By one of those ironic twists that are so typical of scientific research, the behavioral change produced in my first "successful" subject was a completely unexpected one. Within seconds after the male hormone was injected into his brain he began to show signs of extreme restlessness. I then put in his cage a female rat that was not in the sexually receptive state. According to the script I had in mind, the brain injection of male hormone should have driven the male to make sexual advances, although normally he would not do so with a nonreceptive female. The rat, however, followed a script of his own. He grasped the female by the tail with his teeth

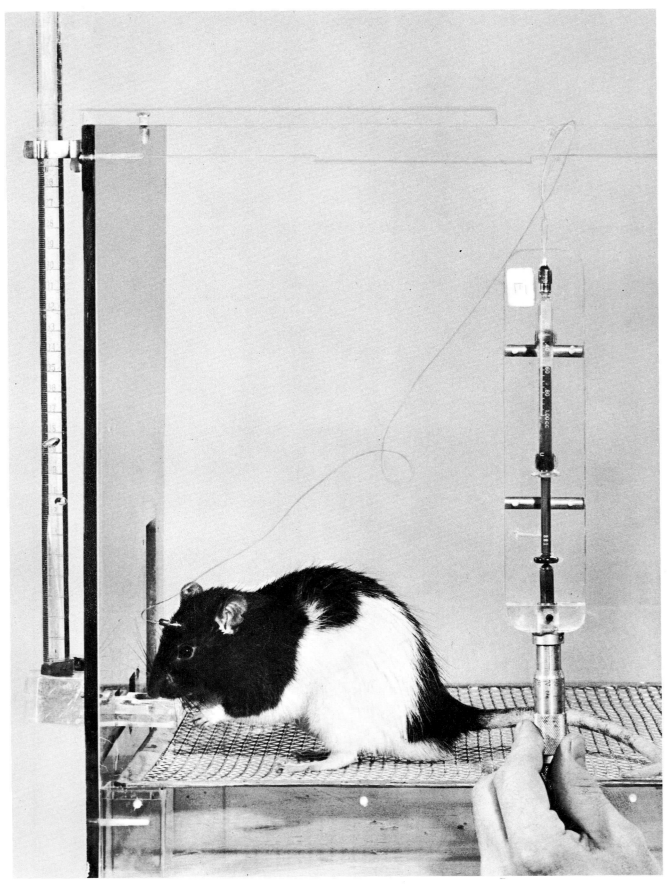

WATER-SATED RAT returns to trough to drink more within a few minutes after the brain circuit that controls the animal's thirst drive has been triggered by injection of acetylcholine. A single stimulus can make the rat drink a day's normal ration in an hour.

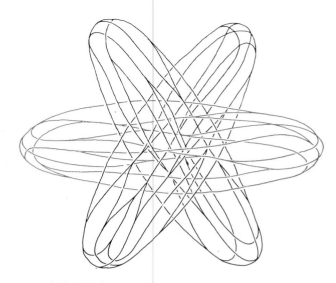

SELECTIVE STIMULATION is a primary advantage in the use of chemicals. When an electrical stimulus is applied (*left*) to a group of neurons belonging to three separate circuits, all circuits operate (*color*) and no integrated response occurs. When a chemical stimulus is applied (*right*), only one circuit, for which the chemical is specific, operates. The other two remain inactive.

and dragged her across the cage to a corner. She scurried away as soon as he let go, whereupon he dragged her back again. After several such experiences the male picked her up by the loose skin on her back, carried her to the corner and dropped her there.

I was utterly perplexed and so, no doubt, was the female rat. I finally guessed that the male was carrying on a bizarre form of maternal behavior. To test this surmise I deposited some newborn rat pups and strips of paper in the middle of the cage. The male promptly used the paper to build a nest in a corner and then carried the pups to the nest. I picked up the paper and pups and scattered them around the cage; the male responded by rebuilding the nest and retrieving the young.

After about 30 minutes the rat stopped behaving like a new mother; apparently the effect of the injected hormone had worn off. Given a new injection, he immediately returned to his adopted family. With successive lapses and reinjections, his behavior became disorganized; he engaged in all the same maternal activities, but in a haphazard, meaningless order. After an overnight rest, however, a new injection the next day elicited the well-patterned motherly behavior.

The case of the mixed-up male rat was a most auspicious one. Although the rat had not followed the experimenter's script, the result of this first experiment was highly exciting. It was an encouraging indication that the control of behavior by specific neural systems in the brain could indeed be investigated by chemical means. We proceed-

ed next to a long series of experiments to verify that the behavior in each case was actually attributable to a specific chemical implanted at a specific site in the brain rather than to some more general factor such as mechanical stimulation, general excitation of the brain cells, or changes in acidity or osmotic pressure.

We have now administered many different chemicals to the brains of hundreds of animals, mostly rats. For this work we have had to develop simple surgical techniques for implanting tiny hollow guide shafts in the animals' brains so that chemicals can be delivered to selected points. The location of each shaft is carefully established with

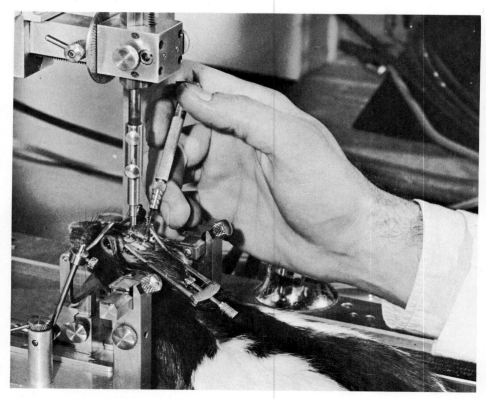

TRACING THE ROUTE OF A BRAIN CIRCUIT, one undertaking made possible by the selectivity of chemical stimuli, requires delicate techniques. At left a vernier-adjusted stereotactic machine is used in conjunction with a sectional atlas of the brain to implant

the help of a three-dimensional brain map and a stereotactic instrument, which holds the head of the anesthetized animal and guides the surgical instruments. After a tiny hole has been made in the brain the shaft is inserted and antiseptically fastened to the skull with jewelers' screws and an adhesive. Each animal can be equipped with several guide shafts at different locations. In a rat four or five shafts may be inserted; in a monkey, as many as 100. The animal recovers quickly and resumes its normal laboratory existence. Through these permanent shafts we can deliver as little as one microgram of a chemical in crystalline form or as little as a ten-thousandth of a milliliter of a solution [see illustration below].

Arousing Male Behavior

Our extended program of tests confirmed, first of all, the elicitation of maternal behavior by an injection of a testosterone solution at a specific location in the brain. When we placed the hormone in a site in the center of the brain just in front of the hypothalamus at the level of the optic tracts below it, many of the rats tested, male and female, responded with some form of maternal behavior.

An injection of the same hormone in the same general region but slightly to one side instead of in the center, brought forth a dramatically different response. Many of the animals now reacted as I had expected the original male to do—with male sexual activity. This was true even of female rats. Presented with a partner, whether male or female, the injected rat (male or female) soon tried to mount the partner. One heroic female persisted in this malelike behavior over a period of eight weeks in tests conducted every other day. The behavior was elicited only by testosterone; it did not appear when the same site was injected with other chemicals or stimulated by electricity.

When the male hormone injection was placed between the central and lateral sites in the hypothalamus, so that it impinged on both, some rats exhibited a curious combination of maternal and male behavior. They took care of the young and at the same time tried to copulate with any partner available. In several instances a male rat that had received such an injection tried to mount a nonreceptive female or male at the same time that it was carrying a rat pup in its mouth!

This was particularly puzzling because it seemed to deny the hypothesis

that functionally related brain cells are selectively sensitive to specific substances. How could the neurons that mediate two different kinds of behavior respond to one and the same hormone? The question has not yet been fully answered, but we can offer a reasonable conjecture. Testosterone is known to act not only as a male hormone but also, under appropriate circumstances, as a weak substitute for the female hormone progesterone, which is linked to pregnancy and maternal behavior. (This versatility is generally true of the family of steroid hormones; most of them can mimic one another's actions.) Therefore a concentrated injection of testosterone into the brain cells may carry enough progestational potency to stimulate the cells that are sensitive to progesterone.

This hypothesis would explain how testosterone injected into the brain of a male rat can evoke maternal behavior. The male body contains little or no progesterone, and presumably its circulating testosterone, at normal levels, has no significant progestational potency. But when a concentration of testosterone is injected directly into cells that are susceptible to progestational stimulation, the hormone's secondary activity is strong enough to stimulate them.

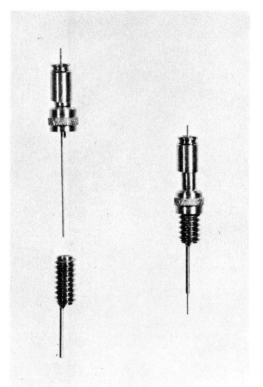

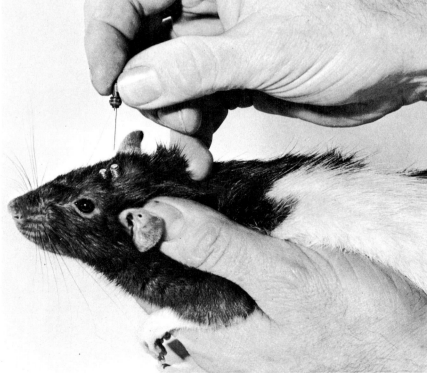

guide shafts leading to precisely calculated regions in the brain of an anesthetized rat. In the middle, unassembled and assembled, are the permanent guide shaft and the removable cannula that carries the chemical to the brain tissue. At right a rat with two guide shafts is about to receive a brain stimulus. The cannula in this instance contains the chemical agent in the form of a solid.

Whether or not this particular hypothesis is correct, the experiments in chemical stimulation seem to show that the male brain and the female brain are essentially identical in the character and organization of the neurons. In the rat, at least, both brains contain cells that can direct male behavior and other cells that can direct female behavior. Differences in sexual behavior can be attributed largely to differences in the kinds of sex hormone that enter the animal's circulatory system.

Yet even this concept is an oversimplification. Evidence obtained recently suggests that during early development sex hormones also play an organizational role, determining degrees of maleness or femaleness by permanently altering the response thresholds or growth within neural systems that will direct male and female behavior. Thus the presence or absence of a hormone during early life may determine the extent to which a nerve circuit develops the capacity for effective function. This may explain why many of our rats are unaffected by brain hormone stimulation, and why, under ordinary conditions, some males and females of every species display the behavior of the opposite sex.

The Puzzle of Steroid Action

Investigators at several other laboratories have now confirmed our finding that steroid hormones act selectively on nerve cells at specific sites in the brain. They have found, for example, that implants of estrogen in selected sites in the hypothalamus can produce sexual receptivity in a cat whose ovaries (the main natural source of estrogen) have been removed. Tracer experiments with radioactively labeled estrogen have shown further that the estrogen tends to concentrate around certain cells of the hypothalamus. A puzzling aspect of the experiment is that the radioactivity (and presumably the hormone itself) has disappeared from the brain by the time the cats become sexually receptive, which is not until five days or more after implantation.

Other puzzling findings have emerged from related studies, and there are many questions to be answered before any comprehensive or confident conclusions can be presented. One of the chief questions has to do with the speed of action of the hormones I have injected into the brain. When a steroid hormone is injected into the muscle tissue or the bloodstream of a male rat, it does not take effect until 24 to 48 hours later. Our injections into the brain, on the other hand, usually produce changes in the rat's behavior within seconds or minutes. Part of the explanation may lie in the form of the injection. Normally steroids are soluble only in oils, and it is in such a solution that they are injected into the blood or peripheral tissues. For the injections into the brain we have generally used a rare steroid that is soluble in water. Possibly an oil-soluble hormone can act rapidly only after it has been converted to a water-soluble form.

R. D. Lisk of Princeton University has recently demonstrated, however, that even an oil-soluble steroid will take effect quickly under certain conditions. He experimented with injections of progesterone to stimulate sexual receptivity in the female rat. He found that when he injected progesterone into the veins of a female that had been primed with injections of estrogen for several days, she became sexually receptive in less than 10 minutes. It takes six hours for such a female to respond fully when the progesterone is injected into muscle tissue rather than the bloodstream.

Control of Hunger and Thirst

With the chemical technique we have gone on to explore the rat brain for the location of the neural systems responsible for the control of other drives besides the sexual. Foremost among these drives, of course, are hunger and thirst. Several regions in the brain that help to control eating and the hunger drive are located in the hypothalamus and are well known. One center acts as an "appestat" (by analogy with the thermostat), and its setting can be raised or lowered. Electrical stimulation of this center will cause even a sated animal to increase its food intake sharply, whereas injury to the same center will drastically reduce an animal's appetite. The other center, in the lower middle region of the hypothalamus, acts as a satiation center, or "brake," for eating.

Some investigators have proposed that the main factor regulating the ac-

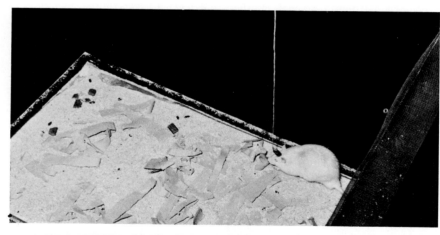

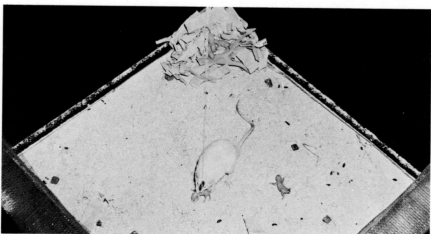

INJECTION of testosterone (*upper photograph*) induces maternal behavior in this male rat. The male gathers scattered paper strips to make a nest (*lower photograph*), ignores food pellets and carries rat pups (which males normally would eat) to shelter in the nest.

189

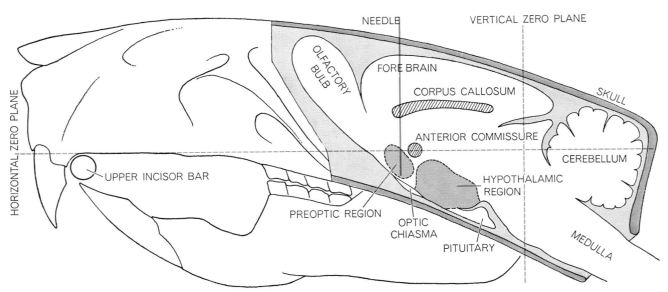

RAT'S HEAD is positioned by hooking the upper incisors over a bar on the stereotactic machine. The brain, in sagittal section (*right*), is labeled to show major anatomical features. The broken lines (*color*) show the zero coordinates for implant measurements.

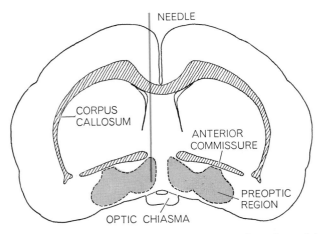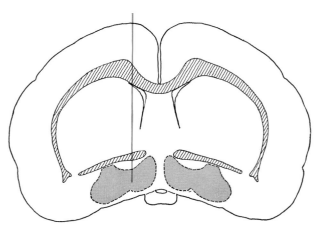

TRANSVERSE SECTIONS of rat brain were taken about eight millimeters forward of the vertical zero coordinate. The needles, or cannulas, touch points in preoptic region where testosterone induced maternal behavior (*left*) and male sexual behavior (*right*).

tivity of the appestat is the sugar level in the blood [see "Appetite and Obesity," by Jean Mayer; SCIENTIFIC AMERICAN, November, 1956]. Our first conjecture, therefore, was that the two oppositely working hormones of the pancreas that regulate the blood-sugar level—insulin and glucagon—might be the primary chemical modulators for the hunger drive, determining the settings or thresholds of the brain centers by acting directly on them. In an extensive series of attempts to stimulate these centers with the two hormones, however, we found no evidence that insulin or glucagon had any effect on them. (Indeed, it has not been conclusively proved that the blood-sugar level itself is a major factor in the regulation of appetite.)

Subsequently a Yale University graduate student, Sebastian P. Grossman,

discovered that eating and drinking could be elicited in rats by brain injections of two other chemicals. They were none other than noradrenalin and acetylcholine, the substances that have long been known as transmitters of nerve impulses. Noradrenalin, injected into a site in the brain just above the hypothalamus, would cause even a well-fed rat to start eating again. Acetylcholine, injected into the same site, would drive the rat to drink. Grossman also found that these stimulating effects could be blocked by injection of chemicals that were known to block the transmitting action of noradrenalin and acetylcholine at nerve synapses.

A Circuit Theory of Drives

I was naturally interested to learn that these two nerve-impulse transmit-

ting chemicals can do their work within the tissue of the brain itself. But even more intriguing, Grossman had shown that different chemicals released different inherent drives even though injected at exactly the same site in the brain. This immediately suggested that the neurons composing each of these major drive circuits were chemically selective and would respond only to the appropriate chemical stimulus. If such a theory were correct, a specific chemical could be released almost at random in the midst of several quite separate circuits but would selectively excite only one of them. In this way it would be possible to probe various parts of the brain with a specific chemical and actually chart the circuit responsive to that particular stimulus.

In our laboratory at the University of Pittsburgh John N. Coury and I set

190

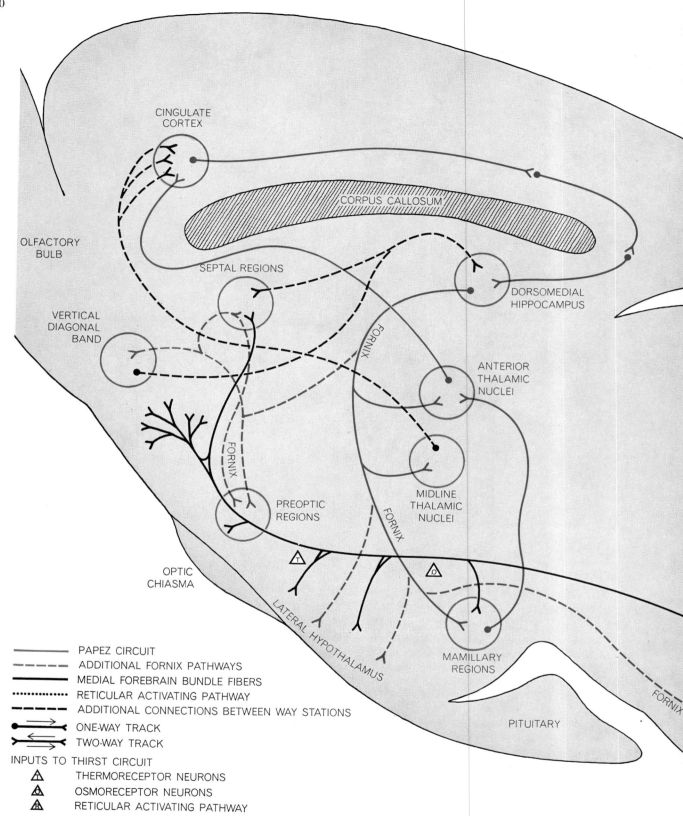

PAPEZ CIRCUIT
ADDITIONAL FORNIX PATHWAYS
MEDIAL FOREBRAIN BUNDLE FIBERS
RETICULAR ACTIVATING PATHWAY
ADDITIONAL CONNECTIONS BETWEEN WAY STATIONS
ONE-WAY TRACK
TWO-WAY TRACK

INPUTS TO THIRST CIRCUIT

⚠ THERMORECEPTOR NEURONS
⚠ OSMORECEPTOR NEURONS
⚠ RETICULAR ACTIVATING PATHWAY

SCHEMATIC CIRCUITRY of the thirst drive is superimposed on a simplified outline of a rat's brain. Although all structures appear to lie on a single plane, they are actually distributed at varying depths in each brain hemisphere. The central figure eight (*solid color*) is a limbic circuit that links the hippocampal, the hypothalamic and the thalamic regions with the cingulate cortex of the forebrain. First postulated by James W. Papez in the 1930's, this circuit proves to be part of the thirst-drive system. Chemical ex-

ploration has identified other pathways (*broken colored lines*) extending the Papez circuit; in general, all involve the brain structure called the fornix. The second major component of the thirst-drive system (*solid black*) connects many forward limbic regions with the medial midbrain; the structures involved are the descending and ascending fibers of the medial forebrain bundle. Additional circuit elements (*broken black lines*) have been found to provide alternate connections between various system

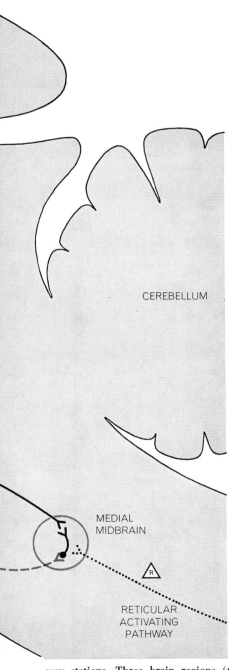

way stations. Three brain regions (*triangles*), although not sensitive to cholinergic stimuli, can trigger the thirst-drive system. These are (*left to right*) neurons that respond to an increase in blood temperature, neurons that respond to an increase in the blood's salt concentration, and the reticular activating pathway leading to the midbrain.

out to try to chart the circuit that mediates drinking. Our design was to stimulate various sites in the rat brain by injections of the thirst-inducing substance acetylcholine or a chemical that mimics its transmitter action, such as muscarine. Tests were conducted at hourly intervals. As controls for the experiment some rats received no injections and some got injections of chemicals that have no impulse-transmitting action, but which can excite or depress nerve-cell activity. All the rats were given free access to as much water and food as they wanted, and an exact record was kept of their water consumption.

Normally rats drink 25 to 35 milliliters of water a day. Some rats we stimulated with brain injections of acetylcholine or muscarine quickly developed a colossal thirst. Within 10 minutes after the injection they began to consume large quantities of water, and within an hour some rats drank as much as twice a whole day's normal intake.

We found that this behavior could be evoked by injection of the drug at any one of many sites distributed widely in the brain [*see illustration on next page*]. Almost all the sites lie within what is known as the brain's limbic system, or the primitive "smell brain." It turned out that our initial map of the thirst circuit virtually coincided with one that James W. Papez, a Cornell University Medical College neuroanatomist, had described in 1937 as a closed-loop system that seemed to be responsible for emotion-directed behavior.

Our tests have shown that all the structures Papez outlined are implicated in thirst, but there are also a few thirst-inducing regions outside his circuit [*see illustration at left*]. We are exploring the entire brain to trace the full extent of the thirst system. We are now convinced that it involves a fiber trunk in the forebrain that connects limbic structures in the front of the brain with the hypothalamus and midbrain. Presumably suitable chemical stimulation of any of these regions alerts the entire thirst-drive system. We believe that the whole circuit normally utilizes acetylcholine, or a similar cholinergic chemical, as a neurotransmitter, and that when a cholinergic chemical is injected locally into the brain it initiates the chain release of cholinergic substances at nerve-fiber terminals throughout the system. It seems significant that Olds has found the same system to be involved in the mediation of "pleasure," or reward.

Our present model of the thirst-drive circuit in the brain, based on experiments, is a highly complex affair, and its very complexity strongly supports the model's plausibility. One obvious requirement for a basic drive system is stability; that is, it should not be easily knocked out or blocked by a simple disorder or injury to the animal. The complexity of the thirst system, as traced by our experiments, provides such protection, because the circuit contains many alternate pathways that can serve to maintain its integrity if some of the pathways are blocked.

This model of the thirst-drive system has some interesting parallels to Hebb's model of the memory system in the brain. Hebb believes that even the simplest perceptual learning involves hundreds of neurons widely dispersed in the brain and is established only gradually by the development of neuronal interconnections. The perception of a given event activates a certain pattern of sensory, associational and motor neurons. At first the pattern is a comparatively simple one and its durability is precarious. But as the perception is repeated and the neurons involved become more practiced in firing as a team, their functional interconnections become more firmly established. In time additional neurons are recruited, alternate pathways develop and the system becomes less and less vulnerable to disruption.

Hebb's model helps to explain the well-known fact that long-established memories are much less subject to obliteration by brain damage or stress than are the memories of recent events. Extending the analogy to the thirst-drive system, we can say that this system resists disruption because it is solidly established with a wealth of alternate pathways. It differs from a memory pattern, however, in that most of the neuronal interconnections are present at birth, having been established by genetic inheritance rather than by perception and learning.

The complexity of the thirst-drive circuit also helps to explain how a drive is maintained over a period of time. Obviously a nerve circuit that mediates a primary drive must be able to dominate brain activity long enough to permit the organism to search for environmental stimuli that will satisfy the drive. The thirst-drive circuit shown in the illustration at the left exhibits both closed-loop and reciprocal pathways. Such a system is ideally designed to continue functioning over a period of time, even after the cessation of the input that triggered the activity. Messages can continue to circulate, or "reverberate," through such a system until an inhibitory brake is applied.

Another set of experimental facts emphasizes the complexity of the thirst-drive system. It is clear that thirst can be triggered by several different means. For example, Andersson in Sweden has found two types of specialized neurons in the hypothalamus that increase thirst. One type responds to increased osmotic pressure, the other is sensitive to a rise in temperature. There is also other evidence suggesting that thirst-triggering inputs come from other parts of the brain, including the amygdala and the reticular activating system. Our map of the thirst-drive system, picturing it as a complex circuit with many way stations, helps to explain how these various inputs may be fed into the system.

So far we have little information about the chemical substances and brain circuits that control the primary drives other than thirst. Evidence from electrical-stimulation experiments, however, suggests that the same structures and pathways are involved in these other drives. It looks more and more as if the primary-drive circuits all follow a roughly parallel course in the brain. Thus in our laboratory we are seeking to determine whether each is stimulated and modulated by specific chemicals. We recently tested a male rat by injecting three different chemicals, on separate occasions, into the same site in the brain. An injection of acetylcholine into this site stimulated the animal to drink, noradrenalin prompted him to eat and testosterone caused him to build nests! Coury and I are now trying to trace a hunger circuit through the brain. Curiously enough we had very little success until a mixture of chemicals was tried that both suppresses acetylcholine action and enhances the action of noradrenalin.

The Cat Is Not a Rat

I must point out that so far the only animal in which we have succeeded in tracing a brain circuit for a primary drive is the rat. The brain of the cat, for example, does not respond the same way when we inject acetylcholine into regions anatomically similar to those that stimulate thirst in the rat. Instead of stimulating cats to drink, these injections elicit anger, fear or a sleeplike trance. Independently, Raúl Hernández-Peón in Mexico City has reported tracing in the cat's brain a sleep circuit that follows much the same course as the thirst circuit in the rat. The chemical that induces sleep is acetylcholine. We interpret this to mean that there are species differences in the relations between specific chemicals and nerve circuits, but that the general principle of chemical specificity of separate functional systems still applies.

Whether or not our present theories are correct, chemical explorations of the brain have established at least two significant facts: first, that certain brain cells are stimulated selectively by specific chemicals and, second, that drive-oriented behavior can be triggered and sustained by chemical means. It seems safe to predict that chemical stimulation of the brain will become an increasingly important tool in the investigation of the neurophysiological bases of behavior.

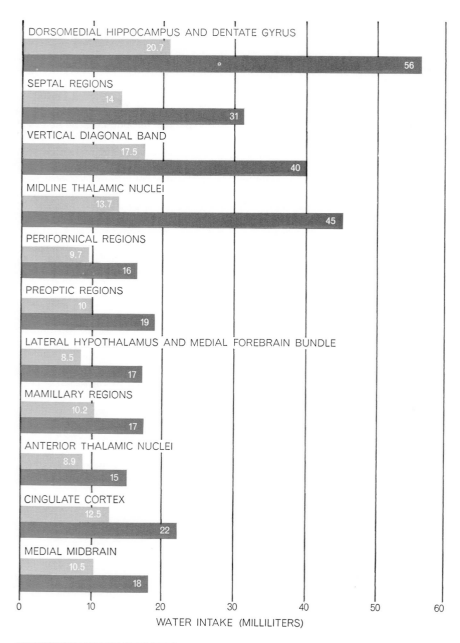

WATER INTAKE (MILLILITERS)

EXCESSIVE WATER INTAKE during the hour after stimulus is related to the area of the brain that was stimulated. The light bars show the mean amount of water consumed in the course of multiple tests with a series of rats. The dark bars show the maximum water intake by a single animal. Normally a rat will drink about 1.5 milliliters per hour. A greater intake is evidence that the stimulated structure is part of the brain's thirst-drive system.

20

STRESS AND BEHAVIOR

SEYMOUR LEVINE
January 1971

Hans Selye's concept of the general "stress syndrome" has surely been one of the fruitful ideas of this era in biological and medical research. He showed that in response to stress the body of a mammal mobilizes a system of defensive reactions involving the pituitary and adrenal glands. The discovery illuminated the causes and symptoms of a number of diseases and disorders. More than that, it has opened a new outlook on the functions of the pituitary-adrenal system. One can readily understand how the hormones of this system may defend the body against physiological insult, for example by suppressing inflammation and thus preventing tissue damage. It is a striking fact, however, that the system's activity can be evoked by all kinds of stresses, not only by severe somatic stresses such as disease, burns, bone fractures, temperature extremes, surgery and drugs but also by a wide range of psychological conditions: fear, apprehension, anxiety, a loud noise, crowding, even mere exposure to a novel environment. Indeed, most of the situations that activate the pituitary-adrenal system do not involve tissue damage. It appears, therefore, that these hormones in animals, including man, may have many functions in addition to the defense of tissue integrity, and as a psychologist I have been investigating possible roles of the pituitary-adrenal system in the regulation of behavior.

The essentials of the system's operation in response to stress are as follows. Information concerning the stress (coming either from external sources through the sensory system or from internal sources such as a change in body temperature or in the blood's composition) is received and integrated by the central nervous system and is presumably delivered to the hypothalamus, the basal area of the brain. The hypothalamus secretes a substance called the corticotropin-releasing factor (CRF), which stimulates the pituitary to secrete the hormone ACTH. This in turn stimulates the cortex of the adrenal gland to step up its synthesis and secretion of hormones, particularly those known as glucocorticoids. In man the glucocorticoid is predominantly hydrocortisone; in many lower animals such as the rat it is corticosterone.

The entire mechanism is exquisitely controlled by a feedback system. When the glucocorticoid level in the circulating blood is elevated, the central nervous system, receiving the message, shuts off the process that leads to secretion of the stimulating hormone ACTH. Two experimental demonstrations have most clearly verified the existence of this feedback process. If the adrenal gland is removed from an animal, the pituitary puts out abnormal amounts of ACTH, presumably because the absence of the adrenal hormone frees it from restriction of this secretion. On the other hand, if crystals of glucocorticoid are implanted in the hypothalamus, the animal's secretion of ACTH stops almost completely, just as if the adrenal cortex were releasing large quantities of the glucocorticoid.

Now, it is well known that a high level of either of these hormones (ACTH or glucocorticoid) in the circulating blood can have dramatic effects on the brain. Patients who have received glucocorticoids for treatment of an illness have on occasion suffered severe mental changes, sometimes leading to psychosis. And patients with a diseased condition of the adrenal gland that caused it to secrete an abnormal amount of cortical hormone have also shown effects on the brain, including changes in the pattern of electrical activity and convulsions.

Two long-term studies of my own, previously reported in *Scientific American* [see "Stimulation in Infancy," Offprint 436, and "Sex Differences in the Brain," Offprint 498], strongly indicated that hormones play an important part in the development of behavior. One of these studies showed that rats subjected to shocks and other stresses in early life developed normally and were able to cope well with stresses later, whereas animals that received no stimulation in infancy grew up to be timid and deviant in behavior. At the adult stage the two groups differed sharply in the response of the pituitary-adrenal system to stress: the animals that had been stimulated in infancy showed a prompt and effective hormonal response; those that had not been stimulated responded slowly and ineffectively. The other study, based on the administration or deprivation of sex hormones at a critical early stage of development in male and female rats, indicated that these treatments markedly affected the animals' later behavior, nonsexual as well as sexual. It is noteworthy that the sex hormones are steroids rather similar to those produced by the adrenal cortex.

Direct evidence of the involvement of the pituitary-adrenal system in overt behavior was reported by two groups of experimenters some 15 years ago. Mortimer H. Appley, now at the University of Massachusetts, and his co-workers were investigating the learning of an avoidance response in rats. The animals were placed in a "shuttle box" divided into two compartments by a barrier. An electric shock was applied, and if the animals crossed the barrier, they could avoid or terminate the shock. The avoidance response consisted in making the move

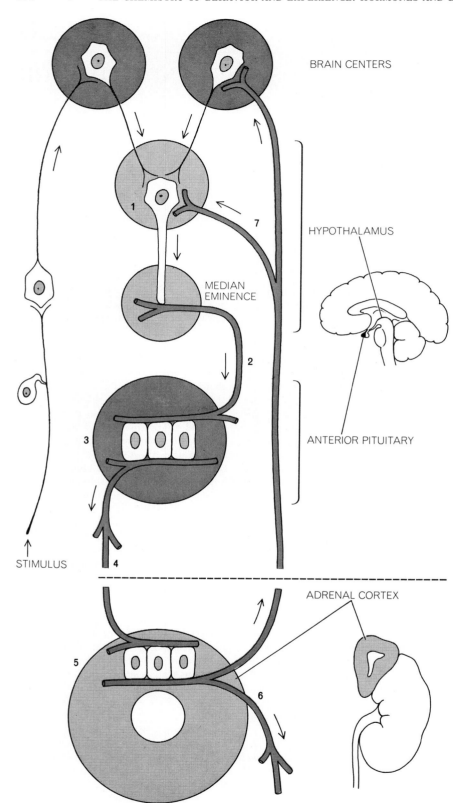

BRAIN CENTERS

HYPOTHALAMUS

MEDIAN EMINENCE

ANTERIOR PITUITARY

STIMULUS

ADRENAL CORTEX

PITUITARY-ADRENAL SYSTEM involves nerve cells and hormones in a feedback loop. A stress stimulus reaching neurosecretory cells of the hypothalamus in the base of the brain (1) stimulates them to release corticotropin-releasing factor (CRF), which moves through short blood vessels (2) to the anterior lobe of the pituitary gland (3). Pituitary cells thereupon release adrenocorticotrophic hormone (ACTH) into the circulation (4). The ACTH stimulates cells of the adrenal cortex (5) to secrete glucocorticoid hormones (primarily hydrocortisone in man) into the circulation (6). When glucocorticoids reach neurosecretory cells or other brain cells (it is not clear which), they modulate CRF production (7).

across the barrier when a conditioned stimulus, a buzzer signaling the onset of the shock, was sounded. Appley found that when the pituitary gland was removed surgically from rats, their learning of the avoidance response was severely retarded. It turned out that an injection of ACTH in pituitary-deprived rats could restore the learning ability to normal. At about the same time Robert E. Miller and Robert Murphy of the University of Pittsburgh reported experiments showing that ACTH could affect extinction of the avoidance response. Normally if the shocks are discontinued, so that the animal receives no shock when it fails to react to the conditioned stimulus (the buzzer in this case), the avoidance response to the buzzer is gradually extinguished. Miller and Murphy found that when they injected ACTH in animals during the learning period, the animals continued to make the avoidance response anyway, long after it was extinguished in animals that had not received the ACTH injection. In short, ACTH inhibited the extinction process.

These findings were not immediately followed up, perhaps mainly because little was known at the time about the details of the pituitary-adrenal system and only rudimentary techniques were available for studying it. Since then purified preparations of the hormones involved and new techniques for accurate measurement of these substances in the circulating blood have been developed, and the system is now under intensive study. Most of the experimental investigation is being conducted at three centers: in the Institute of Pharmacology at the University of Utrecht under David de Wied, in the Institute of Physiology at the University of Pecs in Hungary under Elemér Endroczi and in our own laboratories in the department of psychiatry at Stanford University.

The new explorations of the pituitary-adrenal system began where the ground had already been broken: in studies of the learning and extinction of the avoidance response, primarily by use of the shuttle box. De Wied verified the role of ACTH both in avoidance learning and in inhibiting extinction of the response. He did this in physiological terms by means of several experiments. He verified the fact that removal of the pituitary gland severely retards the learning of a conditioned avoidance response. He also removed the adrenal gland from rats and found that the response was then not extinguished, presumably because adrenal hormones were no longer present to restrict the pituitary's output of ACTH. When he excised the pituitary, thus eliminating the secretion of ACTH, the animals returned to near-normal behavior in the extinction of the avoidance response.

In further experiments De Wied injected glucocorticoids, including corticosterone, the principal steroid hormone of the rat's adrenal cortex, into animals that had had the adrenal gland, but not the pituitary, removed; as expected, this had the effect of speeding up the extinction of the avoidance response. Similarly, the administration to such animals of dexamethasone, a synthetic glucocorticoid that is known to be a potent inhibitor of ACTH, resulted in rapid extinction of the avoidance response; the larger the dose, the more rapid the extinction. Curiously, De Wied found that corticosterone and dexamethasone promoted extinction even in animals that lacked the pituitary gland, the source of ACTH. This indicated that the glucocorticoid can produce its effect not only through suppression of ACTH but also, in some way, by acting directly on the central nervous system. It has recently been found, on the other hand, that there may be secretions from the pituitary other than ACTH that can affect learning and inhibit extinction of the avoidance response. The inhibition can be produced, for example, by a truncated portion of the ACTH molecule consisting of the first 10 amino acids in the sequence of 39 in the rat's ACTH—a molecular fragment that has no influence on the adrenal cortex. The same fragment, along with other smaller peptides recently isolated by De Wied, can also overcome the deficit in avoidance learning that is produced by ablation of the pituitary.

With an apparatus somewhat different from the shuttle box we obtained further light in our laboratory on ACTH's effects on behavior. We first train the animals to press a bar to obtain water. After this learning has been established the animal is given an electric shock on pressing the bar. This causes the animal to avoid approaching the bar (called "passive avoidance") for a time, but after several days the animal will usually return to it in the effort to get water and then will quickly lose its fear of the bar if it is not shocked. We found, however, that if the animal was given doses of ACTH after the shock, it generally failed to return to the bar at all, even though it was very thirsty. That is to say, ACTH suppressed the bar-pressing response, or, to put it another way, it strengthened the passive-avoidance response. In animals with the pituitary gland removed, injections of ACTH suppressed a return to bar-pressing after a shock but injections of hydrocortisone did not have this effect.

The experiments I have described so far have involved behavior under the stress of fear and anxiety. Our investigations with the bar-pressing device go on to reveal that the pituitary-adrenal system also comes into play in the regulation of behavior based on "appetitive" responses (as opposed to avoidance responses). Suppose we eliminate the electric shock factor and simply arrange that after the animal has learned to press the bar for water it fails to obtain water on later trials. Normally the animal's bar-pressing behavior is then quickly extinguished. We found, however, that when we injected ACTH in the animals in these circumstances, the extinction of bar-pressing was delayed; the rats went on pressing the bar for some time although they received no water as reinforcement. Following up this finding, we measured the corticosterone levels in the blood of normal, untreated rats both when they were reinforced and when they were not reinforced on pressing the

"SHUTTLE BOX" used for studying avoidance behavior is a two-compartment cage. The floor can be electrically charged. A shock is delivered on the side occupied by the rat (detected by the photocell). The rat can avoid the shock by learning to respond to the conditioned stimulus: a light and noise delivered briefly before the shock. The avoidance response, once learned, is slowly "extinguished" if the conditioned stimulus is no longer accompanied by a shock. Injections of ACTH inhibited the extinction process.

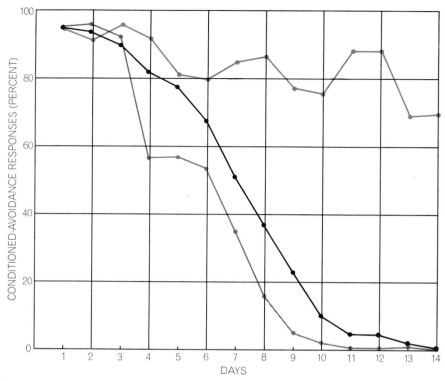

EXTINCTION of the avoidance response was studied by David de Wied of the University of Utrecht. Removal of the adrenal gland inhibited extinction (*color*); the rats responded to the conditioned stimulus in the absence of shock, presumably because adrenal hormones were not available to restrict ACTH output. When the pituitary was removed, the rate of extinction (*gray*) was about the same as in rats given only a sham operation (*black*).

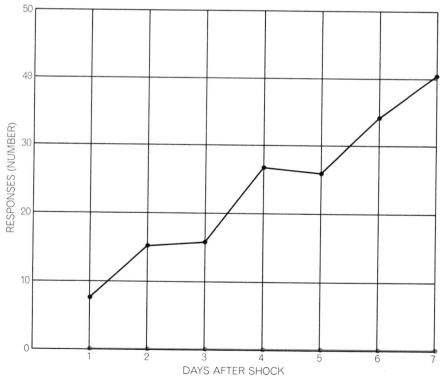

PASSIVE AVOIDANCE BEHAVIOR is studied by observing how rats, trained to press a bar for water, avoid the bar after they get a shock on pressing it. Before being shocked rats pressed the bar about 75 times a day. After the shock the control animals returned to the bar and, finding they were not shocked, gradually increased their responses (*black curve*). Rats injected with ACTH stayed away (*color*): ACTH strengthens the avoidance response.

bar. The animals that received no water reinforcement, with the result of rapid extinction of bar-pressing, showed a marked rise in activity of the pituitary-adrenal system during this period, whereas in animals that received water each time they pressed the bar there was no change in the hormonal output. In short, the extinction of appetitive behavior in this case clearly involved the pituitary-adrenal system.

Further investigations have now shown that the system affects a much wider range of behavior than learning and extinction. One of the areas that has been studied is habituation: the gradual subsidence of reactions that had appeared on first exposure to a novel stimulus when the stimulus is repeated. An organism presented with an unexpected stimulus usually exhibits what Ivan Pavlov called an orientation reflex, which includes increased electrical activity in the brain, a reduction of blood flow to the extremities, changes in the electrical resistance of the skin, a rise in the level of adrenal-steroid hormones in the blood and some overt motor activity of the body.

If the stimulus is repeated frequently, these reactions eventually disappear; the organism is then said to be habituated to the stimulus. Endroczi and his co-workers recently examined the influence of ACTH on habituation of one of the reactions in human subjects—the increase of electrical activity in the brain, as indicated by electroencephalography. The electrical activity evoked in the human brain by a novel sound or a flickering light generally subsides, after repetition of the stimulus, into a pattern known as electroencephalogram (EEG) synchronization, which is taken to be a sign of habituation. Endroczi's group found that treatment of their subjects with ACTH or the 10-amino-acid fragment of ACTH produced a marked delay in the appearance of the synchronization pattern, indicating that the hormone inhibits the process of habituation.

Experiments with animals in our laboratory support that finding. The stimulus we used was a sudden sound that produces a "startle" response in rats, which is evidenced by vigorous body movements. After a number of repetitions of the sound stimulus the startle response fades. It turned out that rats deprived of the adrenal gland (and consequently with a high level of ACTH in their circulation) took significantly longer than intact animals to habituate to the sound stimulus. An implant of the adrenal hormone hydrocortisone in the hy-

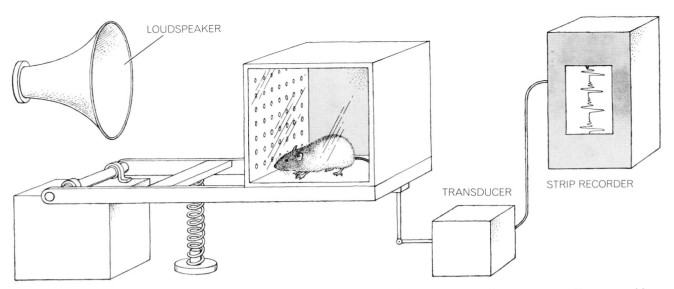

"STARTLE" RESPONSE is measured by placing a rat in a cage with a movable floor and exposing it to a sudden, loud noise. The rat tenses or jumps, and the resulting movement of the floor is transduced into movement of a pen on recording paper. After a number of repetitions of the noise the rat becomes habituated to it and the magnitude of the animal's startle response diminishes.

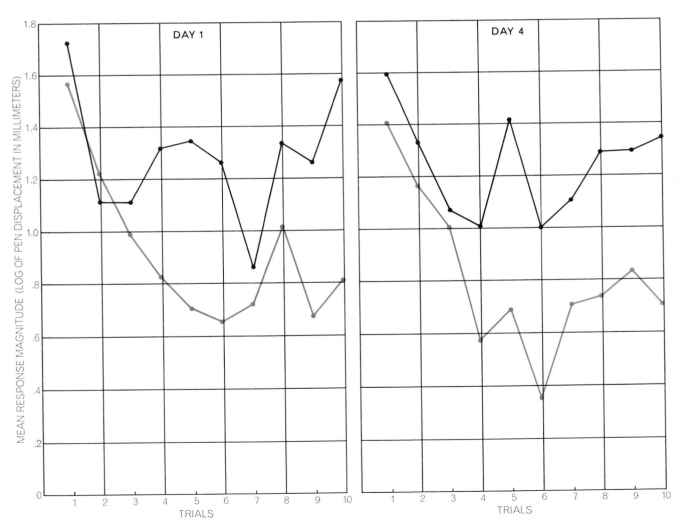

HABITUATION is affected by the pituitary-adrenal system. If a crystal of the adrenal hormone hydrocortisone is implanted in a rat's hypothalamus, preventing ACTH secretion, habituation is speeded up, as shown here. The mean startle response (shown as the logarithm of the recording pen's movement) falls away more rapidly in implanted rats (*color*) than in control animals (*black*).

pothalamus, on the other hand, speeded up habituation.

A series of studies by Robert I. Henkin of the National Heart Institute has demonstrated that hormones of the adrenal cortex play a crucial role in the sensory functions in man. Patients whose adrenal gland has been removed surgically or is functioning poorly show a marked increase in the ability to detect sensory signals, particularly in the senses of taste, smell, hearing and proprioception (sensing of internal signals). On the other hand, patients with Cushing's syndrome, marked by excessive secretion from the adrenal cortex, suffer a considerable dulling of the senses. Henkin showed that sensory detection and the integration of sensory signals are regulated by a complex feedback system involving interactions of the endocrine system and the nervous system. Although patients with a deficiency of adrenal cortex hormones are extraordinarily sensitive in the detection of sensory signals, they have difficulty integrating the signals, so that they cannot evaluate variations in properties such as loudness and tonal qualities and have some difficulty understanding speech. Proper treatment with steroid hormones of the adrenal gland can restore normal sensory detection and perception in such patients.

Henkin has been able to detect the effects of the adrenal corticosteroids on sensory perception even in normal subjects. There is a daily cycle of secretion of these steroid hormones by the adrenal cortex. Henkin finds that when adrenocortical secretion is at its highest level, taste detection and recognition is at its lowest, and vice versa.

In our laboratory we have found that the adrenal's steroid hormones can have a truly remarkable effect on the ability of animals to judge the passage of time. Some years ago Murray Sidman of the Harvard Medical School devised an experiment to test this capability. The animal is placed in an experimental chamber and every 20 seconds an electric shock is applied. By pressing a bar in the chamber the animal can prevent the shock from occurring, because the bar resets the triggering clock to postpone the shock for another 20 seconds. Thus the animal can avoid the shock altogether by appropriate timing of its presses on the bar. Adopting this device, we found that rats learned to press the bar at intervals averaging between 12 and 15 seconds. This prevented a majority of the shocks. We then gave the animals glucocorticoids and found that they became significantly more efficient!

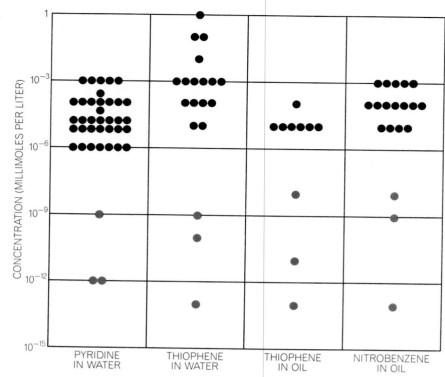

SENSORY FUNCTION is also affected by adrenocortical hormones. Robert I. Henkin of the National Heart Institute found that patients whose adrenal-hormone function is poor are much more sensitive to odor. Placing various chemicals in solution, he measured the detection threshold: the concentration at which an odor could be detected in the vapor. The threshold was much lower in the patients (*color*) than in normal volunteers (*black*).

They lengthened the interval between bar presses and took fewer shocks. Evidently under the influence of the hormones the rats were able to make finer discriminations concerning the passage of time. Monkeys also showed improvement in timing performance in response to treatment with ACTH.

The mechanism by which the pituitary-adrenal hormones act to regulate or influence behavior is still almost completely unknown. Obviously they must do so by acting on the brain. It is well known that hormones in general are targeted to specific sites and that the body tissues have a remarkable selectivity for them. The uterus, for instance, picks up and responds selectively to estrogen and progesterone among all the hormones circulating in the blood, and the seminal vesicles and prostate gland of the male select testosterone. There is now much evidence that organs of the brain may be similarly selective. Bruce Sherman McEwen of Rockefeller University has recently reported that the hippocampus, just below the cerebral cortex, appears to be a specific receptor site for hormones of the adrenal cortex, and other studies indicate that the lateral portion

of the hypothalamus may be a receptor site for gonadal hormones. We have the inviting prospect, therefore, that exploration of the brain to locate the receptor sites for the hormones of the pituitary-adrenal system, and studies of the hormones' action on the cells of these sites, may yield important information on how the system regulates behavior. Bela Bohun in Hungary has already demonstrated that implantation of small quantities of glucocorticoids in the reticular formation in the brain stem facilitates extinction of an avoidance response.

Since this system plays a key role in learning, habituation to novel stimuli, sensing and perception, it obviously has a high adaptive significance for mammals, including man. Its reactions to moderate stress may contribute greatly to the behavioral effectiveness and stability of the organism. Just as the studies of young animals showed, contrary to expectations, that some degree of stress in infancy is necessary for the development of normal, adaptive behavior, so the information we now have on the operations of the pituitary-adrenal system indicates that in many situations effective behavior in adult life may depend on exposure to some optimum level of stress.

21

MARIHUANA

LESTER GRINSPOON
December 1969

The earliest record of man's use of marihuana is a description of the drug in a Chinese compendium of medicines, the herbal of Emperor Shen Nung, dated 2737 B.C. Marihuana was a subject of extravagant social controversy even in ancient times: there were those who warned that the hemp plant lined the road to Hades, and those who thought it led to paradise. Its use as an intoxicant spread from China to India, then to North Africa and from there, about A.D. 1800, to Europe, perhaps primarily through troops of Napoleon's army returning from the Egyptian campaign. In the Western Hemisphere marihuana has been known for centuries in South and Central America, but it did not begin to be used in the U.S. to any significant extent until about 1920. Since the hemp plant *Cannabis sativa*, the source of the drug in its various forms, is a common weed growing freely in many climates, there is no way of knowing precisely how extensive the world usage of the drug may be today. A United Nations survey in 1950 estimated that its users then numbered some 200 million people, principally in Asia and Africa.

Cannabis sativa has a long history of use as a source of fiber, as a drug in tribal religious ceremonies and as medicine, particularly in India. In the 19th century the drug was widely prescribed in the Western world for various ailments and discomforts, such as cough-

ing, fatigue, rheumatism, asthma, delirium tremens, migraine headache and painful menstruation. Although its use was already declining somewhat because of the introduction of synthetic hypnotics and analgesics, it remained in the U.S. *Pharmacopoeia* until 1937. The difficulties imposed on its use by the Tax Act of 1937 completed its medical demise.

In any case, throughout history the principal interest in the hemp plant has been in its properties as an agent for achieving euphoria. The name marihuana is said to be a corruption of the Portuguese word *mariguango*, meaning intoxicant. The drug's ubiquity is evidenced in the multitude of vernacular terms by which it is known; in the U.S. it is variously called the weed, stuff, Indian hay, grass, pot, tea, maryjane and other names. In this country it is almost invariably smoked (usually as a cigarette called a reefer or a joint), but elsewhere the drug is often taken in the form of a drink or in foods such as sweetmeats.

Drug preparations from the hemp plant vary widely in quality and potency, depending on the climate, soil, cultivation and method of preparation. The drug is obtained almost exclusively from the female plant. When the cultivated plant is fully ripe, a sticky, golden yellow resin with a minty fragrance covers its flower clusters and top leaves. The plant's resin contains the active substances. Preparations of the drug come

in three grades, identified by Indian names. The cheapest and least potent, called bhang, is derived from the cut tops of uncultivated plants and has a low resin content. Most of the marihuana smoked in the U.S. is of this grade. To the discriminating Hindu bhang is a crude substitute for ganja, a little like the difference between beer and fine Scotch, and it is scorned by all but the very poorest in India. Ganja is obtained from the flowering tops and leaves of carefully selected, cultivated plants, and it has a higher quality and quantity of resin. The third and highest grade of the drug, called charas in India, is made from the resin itself, carefully scraped from the tops of mature plants. Only this version of the drug is properly called hashish; the common supposition that hashish refers to all varieties of cannabis drugs is incorrect. Charas, or hashish, is five to eight times stronger in effect than the most potent marihuana regularly available in the U.S.

The chemistry of the cannabis drugs is extremely complex and not completely understood. In the 1940's it was determined that the active constituents are various isomers of tetrahydrocannabinol. Recently one of these isomers, called the delta-1 form, has been synthesized and is believed to be the primary active component of marihuana. The drug's effects, however, probably also involve other components and the

SEPALS

MALE

STAMENS

PISTILS

BRACT

FEMALE

HEMP PLANT (*CANNABIS SATIVA*) is a common weed grow-ing freely in many parts of the world, where it is used as a medi-cine, an intoxicant and a source of fiber. It is classified as a dioe-cious plant, that is, the male reproductive parts are on one individ- ual (*left*) and the female parts are on another (*right*). Details of the two types of flower are shown at bottom. The active substances in the drug are contained in a sticky yellow resin that covers the flower clusters and top leaves of the female plant when it is ripe.

form in which it is taken. About 80 derivatives of cannabinol have been prepared, and some of these have been tested for effects in animals or in human volunteers.

The effects of cannabis (used here as a general term for the various forms of the psychoactive products of the plant) in animals are confined to the central nervous system. The drug does not noticeably affect the gross behavior of rats or mice or simple learning in rats; it does, however, calm mice that have been made aggressive by isolation, and in dogs it induces a dreamy, somnolent state reminiscent of the last stage of a human "high." In large doses cannabis produces in animals symptoms such as vomiting, diarrhea, fibrillary tremors and failure of muscular coordination. Lethal doses have been established for a few animals; given by mouth, the lethal dose for cats, for example, is three grams of charas, eight grams of ganja or 10 grams of bhang per kilogram of body weight. Huge doses have been given to dogs without causing death, and there has been no reported case of a fatality from the drug in man.

The psychic effects of the drug have been described in a very extensive literature. Hashish long ago acquired a lurid reputation through the writings of literary figures, notably the group of French writers (Baudelaire, Gautier, Dumas *père* and others) who formed Le Club des Hachichins (hashish smokers) in Paris in the 1850's. Their reports, written under the influence of large amounts of hashish, must be discounted as exaggerations that do not apply to moderate use of the drug. Hashish is supposed to have been responsible for Baudelaire's psychosis and death, but the story overlooks the fact that he had been an alcoholic and suffered from tertiary syphilis.

Bayard Taylor, the American writer, lecturer and traveler best known for his translation of Goethe's *Faust*, wrote one of the first accounts of a cannabis experience in terms that began to approach a clinical description. He tried the drug in a spirit of inquiry during a visit to Egypt in 1854 and related the effects as follows: "The sensations it then produced were . . . physically of exquisite lightness and airiness—mentally of a wonderfully keen perception of the ludicrous in the most simple and familiar objects. During the half hour in which it lasted, I was at no time so far under its control that I could not, with the clearest perception, study the changes through which I passed. I noted with careful attention the fine sensations which spread throughout the whole tissue of my nervous fibers, each thrill helping to divest my frame of its earthly and material nature, till my substance appeared to me no grosser than the vapours of the atmosphere, and while sitting in the calm of the Egyptian twilight I expected to be lifted up and carried away by the first breeze that should ruffle the Nile. While this process was going on, the objects by which I was surrounded assumed a strange and whimsical expression. . . . I was provoked into a long fit of laughter. The Hallucination died away as gradually as it came, leaving me overcome with a soft and pleasant drowsiness, from which I sank into a deep, refreshing sleep."

Perhaps the most detailed clinical account is that of the noted New York psychiatrist Walter Bromberg, who in 1934 described the psychic effects on the basis of many observations and talks with people while they were under the influence of marihuana and of his own experience with the drug. "The intoxication," he wrote, "is initiated by a period of anxiety within 10 to 30 minutes after smoking, in which the user sometimes . . . develops fears of death and anxieties of vague nature associated with restlessness and hyper-activity. Within a few minutes he begins to feel more calm and soon develops definite euphoria; he becomes talkative . . . is elated, exhilarated . . . begins to have . . . an astounding feeling of lightness of the limbs and body . . . laughs uncontrollably and explosively . . . without at times the slightest provocation . . . has the impression that his conversation is witty, brilliant. . . . The rapid flow of ideas gives the impression of brilliance of thought and observation [but] confusion appears on trying to remember what was thought . . . he may begin to see visual hallucinations . . . flashes of light or amorphous forms of vivid color which evolve and develop into geometric figures, shapes, human faces and pictures of great complexity. . . . After a longer or shorter time, lasting up to two hours, the smoker becomes drowsy, falls into a dreamless sleep and awakens with no physiologic after-effects and with a clear memory of what had happened during the intoxication."

Most observers confirm Bromberg's account as a composite description of marihuana highs. They find that the effects from smoking marihuana last for two to four hours, and from ingestion of the drug, for five to 12 hours. For a new user the initial anxiety that sometimes occurs is alleviated if supportive friends are present; experienced users occasionally describe it as "happy anxiety." It is contended that the intoxication heightens sensitivity to external stimuli, reveals details that would ordinarily be overlooked, makes colors seem brighter and richer, brings out values in works of art that previously had little or no meaning to the viewer and enhances the appreciation of music. Many jazz musicians have said they perform better under the influence of marihuana, but this has not been objectively confirmed.

The sense of time is distorted: 10 minutes may seem like an hour. Curiously, there is often a splitting of consciousness, so that the smoker, while experiencing the high, is at the same time an objective observer of his own intoxication. He may, for example, be afflicted with paranoid thoughts yet at the same time be reasonably objective about them and even laugh or scoff at them and in a sense enjoy them. The ability to retain a degree of objectivity may explain the fact that many experienced users of marihuana manage to behave in a perfectly sober fashion in public even when they are highly intoxicated.

Marihuana is definitely distinguishable from other hallucinogenic drugs such as LSD, DMT, mescaline, peyote and psilocybin. Although it produces some of the same effects, it is far less potent than these other drugs. It does not alter consciousness to nearly so great an extent as they do nor does it lead to increasing tolerance to the drug dosage. Moreover, marihuana smokers can usually gauge the effects accurately and thus control the intake of the drug to the amount required to produce the desired degree of euphoria.

Let us consider now what has been learned from attempts to obtain objective measurements of the effects of the use of marihuana: psychological, physiological, psychic and social. There is a large literature on these studies, extending over a century or more and particularly voluminous in the 1960's. Although most of the studies leave much to be desired methodologically, many nonetheless add to the total of our knowledge about the drug.

An intensive investigation exploring various aspects of the marihuana problem was conducted in the 1930's by a committee appointed by Mayor Fiorello La Guardia of New York. In this inquiry Robert S. Morrow examined the effects of the drug on psychomotor functions and certain sensory abilities. He found that even in large doses marihuana did

202

CANNABINOL

Δ^1-TRANS-TETRAHYDROCANNABINOL

Δ^6-TRANS-TETRAHYDROCANNABINOL

CANNABICHROMENE

CANNABIDIOL

CANNABIDIOLIC ACID

ACTIVE CONSTITUENTS of the cannabis drugs include various derivatives of cannabinol, only a few of which are represented by the molecular diagrams on these two pages. One of the isomers of tetrahydrocannabinol, called the delta-1 form (*second from left in*

not affect performance on tests of the speed of tapping or the quickness of response to simple stimuli. Nor did it impair hearing acuity, musical ability or the ability to judge short time periods or short distances accurately. The drug did affect steadiness of the hand and body and the reaction time for complex stimuli.

More recently Lincoln D. Clark and Edwin N. Nakashima of the University of Utah College of Medicine used eight tests of perception, coordination and learning to examine subjects who received doses of marihuana by mouth. They found that performance on six of the eight tests was not impaired even by high doses of the drug. The two tasks on which performance was affected were reaction time and learning of a digit code; however, in the case of the former this conclusion was based on data from only two subjects and in the latter test it was based on data from five subjects, one of whom actually showed improvement while receiving the drug.

Andrew T. Weil, Norman E. Zinberg and Judith M. Nelsen of the Boston University School of Medicine recently applied other tests to two different groups of subjects, one group consisting of chronic users of marihuana, the other of

persons experiencing the drug for the first time. In ability to maintain sustained attention (the "Continuous Performance Test") the performance of both groups was unaffected either by a low dose or by a high dose of the drug. In cognitive functioning (the "Digit Symbol Substitution Test") the drug-naïve group showed some impairment during the high, but the performance of experienced users of marihuana showed no significant impairment and in fact on the higher doses revealed a trend toward improvement. In muscular coordination and attention (the "Pursuit Rotor Test") the results were the same as in the DSST, but in this case the improvement in the chronic users' performance may have been due simply to practice at the task. Nine subjects receiving the drug for the first time were also tested for the effect on their time sense. Before taking the drug the subjects had shown that in the undrugged state they could come within two minutes of estimating a five-minute interval correctly. After receiving a placebo no subject changed his guess of a five-minute time span. While intoxicated on a low dose three subjects roughly doubled their estimate of a five-minute time span, and while on a high dose four increased their estimates.

In the La Guardia study Florence Halpern investigated marihuana's effects on intellectual functioning. She found that the subjects' scores on intelligence tests, particularly where number concepts were involved, tended to decline during the mature stages of a high. Their performance returned to normal afterward. In some tests of memory and of verbal facility the performances either were not impaired or actually were improved under the influence of low doses of the drug. She concluded that where intellectual performance was reduced the lowered scores were due to a loss of speed and accuracy during the intoxication.

A number of investigators, including members of the La Guardia study, Weil's group and others, have examined the physical and physiological effects of marihuana intoxication. Occasionally there may be nausea, vomiting and diarrhea, particularly if the drug is taken by mouth. Usually, however, the bodily symptoms accompanying the high are slight. There is only very slight, if any, dilatation of the pupils accompanied by a sluggish pupillary response to light, slight tremors and a mild lack of coordination. A consistently observed physiological effect is increase in the pulse rate

Δ¹-TRANS-TETRAHYDROCANNABINOLIC ACID

CANNABINOLIC ACID

CANNABIGEROL

CANNABIGEROLIC ACID

top row), has been synthesized and is believed to be the primary active component of mari-huana. The drug's intoxicating effects, however, probably involve other components as well.

[*see illustration on page 205*]; in addition there may be a slight rise in the blood pressure. Urination tends to increase in frequency and perhaps in amount. Often the mouth and throat feel dry, causing thirst. One of the most striking results of the intoxication is a sense of hunger. It generates a high appreciation of food, so that a person under the influence may approach an ordinary dish with the anticipation of a gourmet confronting a special treat. This effect suggests that the drug might be useful in the treatment of the pathological loss of appetite known as anorexia nervosa.

There is now an abundance of evidence that marihuana is not an addictive drug. Cessation of its use produces no withdrawal symptoms, nor does a user feel any need to increase the dosage as he becomes accustomed to the drug. Investigators have found that habituation to marihuana is not as strong as to tobacco or to alcohol. Bromberg concluded that marihuana is not habit-forming, and that it is used to serve "the hedonistic elements of the personality." It is certainly possible that in some people this desire may develop into a dependency on the drug for the experience of pleasure or respite from psychic pain.

Can such a use be called abuse of the drug? The term "abuse" is difficult to define; its interpretation varies from culture to culture and from custom to custom. If abuse is measured in terms of the danger to the individual and society, then it must be pointed out that although the dangers of alcoholism and even of social drinking are well established, social drinking is not considered abuse in the U.S. The dangers of the use of marihuana, on the other hand, have not yet been clearly determined.

The prevailing public attitude toward marihuana in the U.S. is charged with a hyperemotional bias. In part this is the product of an "educational campaign" initiated in the 1930's by the Federal Bureau of Narcotics (since renamed the Bureau of Narcotics and Dangerous Drugs), a campaign that has disseminated much distortion and misinformation about the drug [*see illustration on next page*]. There are also cultural and social factors that contribute to the public apprehension about marihuana. The still powerful vestige of the Protestant ethic in this country condemns marihuana as an opiate used solely for the pursuit of pleasure (whereas alcohol is accepted because it lubricates the wheels of commerce and catalyzes social

intercourse). Marihuana's effect in producing a state of introspection and bodily passivity is repellent to a cultural tradition that prizes activity, aggressiveness and achievement. And it may well be that social prejudices enter into the public alarm concerning the drug: prejudice on the part of the older generation, which sees marihuana as a symbol of the alienation of the young, and on the part of the white population, which, perhaps largely unconsciously, regards marihuana as a nonwhite drug that is rapidly invading the white community, because until fairly recently the smoking of marihuana took place mainly in the ghettos of Negroes, Puerto Ricans and people of Mexican origin. It is perhaps no accident that some of the Southern states have most severe laws against the distribution of marihuana, carrying penalties of life imprisonment or even death in some cases.

If we are to find a rational and effective approach to the problem of the increasing use of marihuana in the U.S., we obviously need to reduce the emotionalism surrounding the subject and replace myths with facts as far as they can be determined. Let us examine the current suppositions about the drug.

Does marihuana lead its users to the use of narcotics? The 1937 Federal law that made the cannabis drugs illegal led to a rise in price that provided an incentive to pushers of narcotics to also handle marihuana without any additional legal risk. The resulting potential for the exposure of users to both types of drugs might have been expected to lead to an increase in the use of narcotics that was significantly related to the increasing use of marihuana. No such relation has been found in several studies that have looked into this question, including the La Guardia study and a U.S. Presidential task force investigation of narcotics and drug abuse. It is true that the Federal study showed that among heroin users about 50 percent had had experience with marihuana; the study also found, however, that most of the heroin addicts had been users of alcohol and tobacco. There is no evidence that marihuana is more likely than alcohol or tobacco to lead to the use of narcotics.

Does marihuana incite people to aggression and violent criminal behavior, as some investigators have maintained? In an intensive study of the marihuana problem in Manhattan, Bromberg found no indication of such a relation. "No cases of murder or sexual crime due to marihuana were established." Reviewing a case that had been cited by the Federal Bureau of Narcotics, of a man who was alleged to have confessed to murdering a friend while under the influence of marihuana, Bromberg found on examination of the individual that he was a psychopathic liar and that there was "no indication in the examination or history" that he had ever used marihuana or any other drug. A psychiatric investigator in Nigeria, T. Asuni, noted that an underprivileged community had a high incidence both of crime and of the use of hashish, but he concluded that these statistics were attributable to the frustrations of the people's lives rather than to a relation between the drug and crime. Indeed, two investigators of the use of the drug in India, R. N. Chopra and G. S. Chopra, have contended that instead of inciting criminal behavior cannabis tends to suppress it; the intoxication induces a lethargy that is not conducive to any physical activity, let alone

the committing of crimes. The release of inhibitions results in verbal rather than behavioral expression. During the high the marihuana user may say things he would not ordinarily say, but he generally will not do things that are foreign to his nature. If he is not normally a criminal, he will not commit a crime under the influence of the drug.

Does marihuana induce sexual debauchery? This popular impression may owe its origin partly to the fantasies of dissolute writers and partly to the fact that in times past users in the Middle East laced the drug with aphrodisiacs. There is no evidence that cannabis stimulates sexual desire or power; this is conceded even by Ahmed Benabud, a Moroccan psychiatrist and investigator of the drug who condemns it severely on psychological grounds. There are those, on the other hand, who contend that marihuana weakens sexual desire—with equally little substantiation. Some marihuana users report that the high en-

hances the enjoyment of sexual intercourse. This may be true in the same sense that the enjoyment of art and music is apparently enhanced. It is questionable, however, that the intoxication breaks down moral barriers that are not already broken.

Does marihuana lead to physical and mental degeneracy? Reports from many investigators, particularly in Egypt and in parts of the Orient, indicate that long-term users of the potent versions of cannabis are indeed typically passive, nonproductive, slothful and totally lacking in ambition. It is possible that chronic use of the drug in its stronger forms may in fact have debilitating effects, as prolonged heavy drinking does. There is another possible explanation, however. Many of those who take up cannabis are people who are hungry, sick, hopeless or defeated, seeking through this inexpensive drug to soften the impact of an otherwise unbearable reality. In most situations one cannot be certain which came

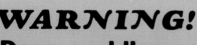
ANTIMARIHUANA POSTER is part of the "educational campaign describing the drug, its identification and evil effects" supported in the U.S. since the 1930's by the Federal Bureau of Narcotics (since renamed the Bureau of Narcotics and Dangerous Drugs).

first: the drug on the one hand or the depression or personality disorder on the other. This question applies to many of the "potheads" in the U.S. An intensive study of college students who had taken to marihuana showed that many of them had suffered serious conflicts or depression long before they began to use the drug.

There is a substantial body of evidence that moderate use of marihuana does not produce physical or mental deterioration. One of the earliest and most extensive studies of this question was an investigation conducted by the British Government in India in the 1890's. The real motive for the inquiry is suspected to have been to establish that cannabis was more dangerous than Scotch whisky, from whose sale the government could obtain a great deal more tax revenue. Nevertheless, the investigation was carried out with typical British impartiality and thoroughness. The investigating agency, called the Indian Hemp Drug Commission, interviewed some 800 persons, including cannabis users and dealers, physicians, superintendents of insane asylums, religious leaders and a variety of other authorities, and in 1894 published a report running to more than 3,000 pages. It concluded that there was no evidence that moderate use of the cannabis drugs produced any disease or mental or moral damage or that it had any more tendency to lead to excess than the moderate use of whisky did.

In the La Guardia study in New York City an examination of chronic users who had averaged about seven marihuana cigarettes a day (a comparatively high dosage) over a long period (the mean was eight years) showed that they had suffered no mental or physical decline as a result of their use of the drug. A similar study by H. L. Freedman and M. J. Rockmore, examining 310 Army men who had used marihuana for an average of seven years, produced the same finding.

In the effort to obtain a rational perspective on the marihuana problem one is inevitably drawn repeatedly to comparisons between this drug and alcohol and to the public attitudes toward the two drugs. The habit called social drinking is considered as American as apple pie, and it receives about as much public acceptance. Yet even this kind of drinking carries clearly demonstrated hazards and consequences of a most serious nature. Life insurance statistics show that social drinkers have considerably higher than average mortality rates from all the leading causes of

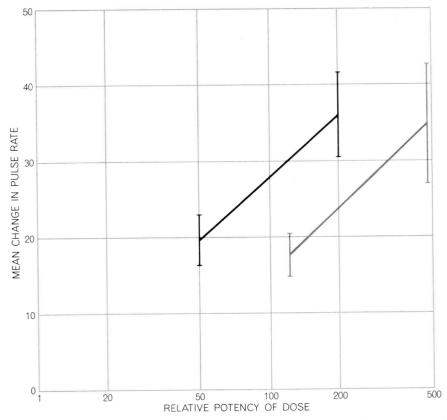

INCREASE IN PULSE RATE is the most consistently reported physiological effect of marihuana intoxication. In this graph, based on the work of Harris Isbell and his colleagues at the University of Kentucky, the two lines show the pulse responses to varying doses of pure synthetic delta-1-tetrahydrocannabinol, taken both by smoking (*left*) and orally (*right*). In most cases the physiological effects of a marihuana "high" are slight.

death: diseases of the heart and circulatory system, cancer, diseases of the digestive system, homicides, suicides and motor-vehicle and other accidents. A majority of drivers killed in vehicle accidents are found to have been drinking. In contrast, there has been no evidence so far that marihuana contributes to the development of any organic disease, and in the only investigation to date of the effect on driving, a controlled study conducted recently by the Bureau of Motor Vehicles of the state of Washington, it was found that marihuana causes significantly less impairment of driving ability than alcohol does [*see illustration on page 207*].

Perhaps the weightiest charge made against cannabis is that it may lead to psychosis or at least to personality disorders. There is a vast literature on this subject, and it divides into all shades of opinion. Many psychiatrists in India, Egypt, Morocco and Nigeria have declared emphatically that the drug can produce insanity; others insist that it does not. One of the authorities most

often quoted in support of the indictment is Benabud of Morocco. He believes that the drug produces a specific syndrome, called "cannabis psychosis." His description of the identifying symptoms is far from clear, however, and other investigators dispute the existence of such a psychosis. The symptoms said to be characteristic of this syndrome are also common to other acute toxic states including, particularly in Morocco, those associated with malnutrition and endemic infections. Benabud estimates that the number of kif (marihuana) smokers suffering from all types of psychosis is not more than five per 1,000; this rate, however, is lower than the estimated total incidence of all psychoses in populations of other countries. Thus one would have to assume either that there is a much lower prevalence of psychoses other than "cannabis psychosis" among kif smokers in Morocco or that there is no such thing as a "cannabis psychosis," and that the drug is contributing little or nothing to the prevalence rate for psychoses.

The American psychiatrist Bromberg,

in a report of one of his studies, listed 31 patients whose psychoses he attributed to the toxic effects of marihuana. Of these 31, however, seven patients were already predisposed to functional psychoses that were only precipitated by the drug, seven others were later found to be schizophrenics, one was later diagnosed as a manic-depressive and a number of others may have had an acute and temporary attack of psychosis (the "five-day schizophrenia") that could have been mistaken for a drug reaction.

Bromberg found no psychotics among 67 imprisoned criminals who had been users of marihuana. Freedman and Rockmore found none among the 310 marihuana-smoking soldiers they studied, and similar findings have been reported in several other studies of sizable samples. The Chopras in India, in examinations of a total of 1,238 cannabis users, found only 13 to be psychotic, which is about the usual rate of incidence of psychosis in the total population in Western countries. In the La Guardia study nine out of 77 subjects who were studied intensively had a history of psychosis; this high rate could be attributed, however,

to the fact that all the subjects were patients in hospitals or institutions. Samuel Allentuck and K. H. Bowman, the psychiatrists who examined this group, concluded that "marihuana will not produce psychosis *de novo* in a well-integrated, stable person."

This is not to say that the drug may not precipitate an acute anxiety state with paranoid thoughts or even a temporary psychosis in a susceptible person. A drug that alters the state of consciousness and distorts perception and the body image may well tip a delicately balanced ego, already overburdened with anxiety, into a schizophrenic reaction. In our clinical research program at the Massachusetts Mental Health Center in Boston we surveyed the cases of 41 patients who had been admitted in an acute state of schizophrenia. Six of the patients had used marihuana at one time or another, but in four cases the drug experience had occurred long before the schizophrenic breakdown. In the other two cases a careful study of the entire history failed to indicate definitely whether the drug had or had not precipitated the psychosis.

Very little research attention has been given to the possibility that marihuana might *protect* some people from psychosis. Among users of the drug the proportion of people with neuroses or personality disorders is usually higher than in the general population; one might therefore expect the incidence of psychoses also to be higher in this group. The fact that it is not suggests that for some mentally disturbed people the escape provided by the drug may serve to prevent a psychotic breakdown.

A century ago a French physician, Jacques Joseph Moreau de Tours, reported that he had successfully treated melancholia and other chronic mental illnesses with an extract of cannabis. Several other physicians in France, Germany and England tried the drug, with conflicting results. In the 1940's some interest developed in synhexyl, a synthetic tetrahydrocannabinol, as an apparently promising treatment for depressive psychoses; in the only controlled study, however, this particular drug was found to be no more effective than a placebo.

Tests of the use of cannabis to help

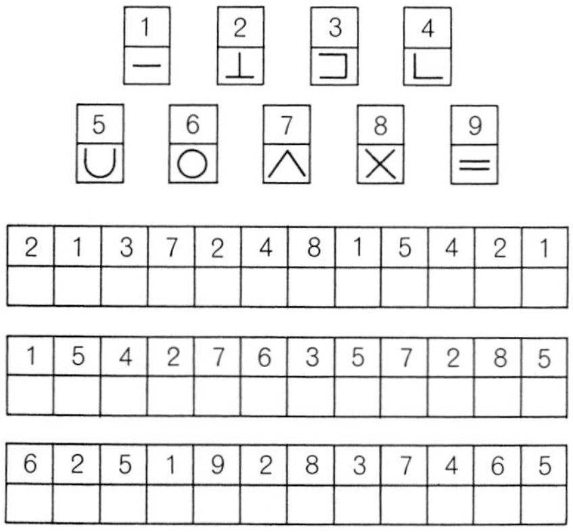

NAÏVE SUBJECTS	15 MINUTES			90 MINUTES		
	PLACEBO	LOW DOSE	HIGH DOSE	PLACEBO	LOW DOSE	HIGH DOSE
1	−3	−	+5	−7	+4	+8
2	+10	−8	−17	−1	−15	−5
3	−3	+6	−7	−10	+2	−1
4	+3	−4	−3		−7	
5	+4	+1	−7	+6		−8
6	−3	−1	−9	+3	−5	−12
7	+2	−4	−6	+3	−5	−4
8	−1	+3	+1	+4	+4	−3
9	−1	−4	−3	+6	−1	−10
MEAN	+0.9	−1.2	−5.1	+0.4	−2.6	−3.9
STANDARD ERROR	1.4	1.4	2.1	1.9	2.0	2.0
CHRONIC USERS			HIGH DOSE			HIGH DOSE
10			−4			−16
11			+1			+6
12			+11			+18
13			+3			+4
14			−2			−3
15			−6			+8
16			−4			
17			+3			
MEAN			+0.25			+2.8
STANDARD ERROR			1.9			4.7

TEST OF COGNITIVE FUNCTIONING (called "Digit Symbol Substitution Test") was administered recently by Andrew T. Weil, Norman E. Zinberg and Judith M. Nelsen of the Boston University School of Medicine to two different groups of subjects, one group consisting of chronic users of marihuana, the other of persons experiencing the drug for the first time. A sample of the test is shown at left; the results of the study are summarized at right. On a signal from the examiner the subject was required to fill as many of the empty spaces as possible with the appropriate symbols. The code was always available to the subject during the 90-second administration of the test. The results were tabulated in terms of the change in scores from a base-line score (number correct before smoking marihuana) both 15 minutes and 90 minutes after the smoking session. On the average Weil and his colleagues found that the drug-naïve group showed some impairment during the high (*top right*), but the performance of experienced users of marihuana showed no significant impairment and in fact on the higher doses revealed a slight trend toward improvement (*bottom right*).

drug addicts withdraw from the use of narcotics have yielded more promising results. The first medical use for this purpose was reported in 1889 by an English physician, Edward Birch, who treated a chloral hydrate addict and an opium addict by replacing their drugs with cannabis and found they were then able to discontinue the cannabis without withdrawal symptoms. Similar successes were obtained more recently in two notable trials: one reported in 1942 by Allentuck and Bowman, who tapered off opiate addicts with a marihuana derivative, and another in 1953 by two North Carolina physicians, L. S. Thompson and R. C. Proctor, who withdrew patients from addiction to narcotics, barbiturates and alcohol by the use of pyrahexyl, a tetrahydrocannabinol.

Curiously, these encouraging results have not been followed up by large-scale clinical trials or basic research. It seems that research on the possible medical uses of marihuana is discouraged by the lingering common impression that it is addictive and by the fact that the drug is outlawed and difficult to obtain legally even for research purposes.

Indispensable to an understanding of marihuana's effects and of the present burgeoning spread of its use is the study in depth of people's motivations for using it. In India, where the use is not illegal and therefore not complicated by anxieties arising from that cause, cannabis serves the clear-cut purpose of simple relief from the dreariness and hardships of poverty. The Chopras note that during the harvest season the consumption of the drug increases by 50 percent among farmers in some areas. These authors observe: "A common practice amongst laborers engaged in building or excavation work is to have a few pulls at a ganja pipe or to drink a glass of bhang toward the evening. This produces a sense of well-being, relieves fatigue, stimulates the appetite and induces a feeling of mild stimulation which enables the worker to bear more cheerfully the strain of the daily routine of life."

This simple motivation goes far to explain the fact that in the U.S. marihuana first came into wide use in the ghettos. Several studies of population samples in the Army have shown that 87 percent or more of the marihuana users there were Negroes. Inquiring into the motivations of the 310 marihuana smokers they studied, Freedman and Rockmore found that the responses generally ran in this vein: the drug gave its users "a good feeling"; it was a substi-

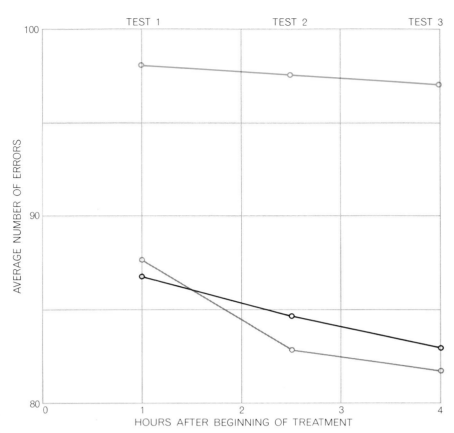

COMPARATIVE STUDY of the effects of marihuana and alcohol on simulated driving performance was conducted by the Bureau of Motor Vehicles of the state of Washington. The graph shows average number of errors on tests administered at three stages after treatment with alcohol (*color*), marihuana (*black*) and a placebo (*gray*). In general it was found that marihuana causes significantly less impairment of driving ability than alcohol does.

tute for whisky; "I feel bad all the time—weeds make me feel better"; "It makes me sleep and eases my pain"; "It makes me feel like I'm a man." For many the drug was evidently an escape from feelings of inadequacy, personal frustrations, anxiety and/or depression.

One must look beyond personal factors, however, to account for the current vogue of marihuana among large portions of the U.S. population. A study of 54 psychiatric patients who were white, middle-class college graduates, for example, elicited the responses that they took up marihuana out of curiosity, to go along with friends, for stimulation or for an unusual experience. Among the youth of this country marihuana has a powerful attraction for those who have a tendency to introspection and meditation or an urge to retire from involvement in society. For many the use of the illegal drug is an act of defiance of the "establishment."

As C. P. Snow has observed: "Uneasiness seems to be becoming part of the climate of our time." It is difficult to

avoid the conclusion that the increasing use of marihuana is in part related to the fearful threats of overpopulation, racial conflict and nuclear war. Conversely, the same threats may indirectly be contributing to the emotional campaign against this drug. It is conceivable that some of the affect generated in the population by the violence and martial spirit of our time is being displaced onto issues such as marihuana. Regarded as essentially evil and dangerous, adopted by hippies, yippies and others who demonstrate and call attention to the aspects of reality and the threats of doom that most of us find too distressing to confront, marihuana is a natural target as a scapegoat.

In short, the anxiety and sense of helplessness generated by the dangers of our time may be focused in some degree on marihuana, driving some people to protective immersion in the drug and arousing others to a crusade against it. Although either of these responses may have some adaptive value for the individual psyche, neither contributes toward the development of a more secure world.

22

THE HALLUCINOGENIC DRUGS

FRANK BARRON, MURRAY E. JARVIK AND STERLING BUNNELL, JR.
April 1964

Human beings have two powerful needs that are at odds with each other: to keep things the same, and to have something new happen. We like to feel secure, yet at times we like to be surprised. Too much predictability leads to monotony, but too little may lead to anxiety. To establish a balance between continuity and change is a task facing all organisms, individual and social, human and non-human.

Keeping things predictable is generally considered one of the functions of the ego. When a person perceives accurately, thinks clearly, plans wisely and acts appropriately—and represses maladaptive thoughts and emotions—we say that his ego is strong. But the strong ego is also inventive, open to many perceptions that at first may be disorganizing. Research on the personality traits of highly creative individuals has shown that they are particularly alert to the challenge of the contradictory and the unpredictable, and that they may even court the irrational in their own make-up as a source of new and unexpected insight. Indeed, through all recorded history and everywhere in the world men have gone to considerable lengths to seek unpredictability by disrupting the functioning of the ego. A change of scene, a change of heart, a change of mind: these are the popular prescriptions for getting out of a rut.

Among the common ways of changing "mind" must be reckoned the use of intoxicating substances. Alcohol has quite won the day for this purpose in the U.S. and much of the rest of the world. Consumed at a moderate rate and in sensible quantities, it can serve simultaneously as a euphoriant and tranquilizing agent before it finally dulls the faculties and puts one to sleep. In properly disposed individuals it may dissolve sexual inhibitions, relieve fear and anxiety, or stimulate meditation on the meaning of life. In spite of its costliness to individual and social health when it is used immoderately, alcohol retains its rank as first among the substances used by mankind to change mental experience. Its closest rivals in popularity are opium and its derivatives and various preparations of cannabis, such as hashish and marijuana.

This article deals with another group of such consciousness-altering substances: the "hallucinogens." The most important of these are mescaline, which comes from the peyote cactus *Lophophora williamsii;* psilocybin and psilocin, from such mushrooms as *Psilocybe mexicana* and *Stropharia cubensis;* and d-lysergic acid diethylamide (LSD), which is derived from ergot (*Claviceps purpurea*), a fungus that grows on rye and wheat. All are alkaloids more or less related to one another in chemical structure.

Various names have been applied to this class of substances. They produce distinctive changes in perception that are sometimes referred to as hallucinations, although usually the person under the influence of the drug can distinguish his visions from reality, and even when they seem quite compelling he is able to attribute them to the action of the drug. If, therefore, the term "hallucination" is reserved for perceptions that the perceiver himself firmly believes indicate the existence of a corresponding object or event, but for which other observers can find no objective basis, then the "hallucinogens" only rarely produce hallucinations. There are several other names for this class of drugs. They have been called "psychotomimetic" because in some cases the effects seem to mimic psychosis [see "Experimental Psychoses," by six staff members of the Boston Psychopathic Hospital; SCIENTIFIC AMERICAN, June, 1955]. Some observers prefer to use the term "psychedelic" to suggest that unsuspected capacities of the imagination are sometimes revealed in the perceptual changes.

The hallucinogens are currently a subject of intense debate and concern in medical and psychological circles. At issue is the degree of danger they present to the psychological health of the person who uses them. This has become an important question because of a rapidly increasing interest in the drugs among laymen. The recent controversy at Harvard University, stemming at first from methodological disagreements

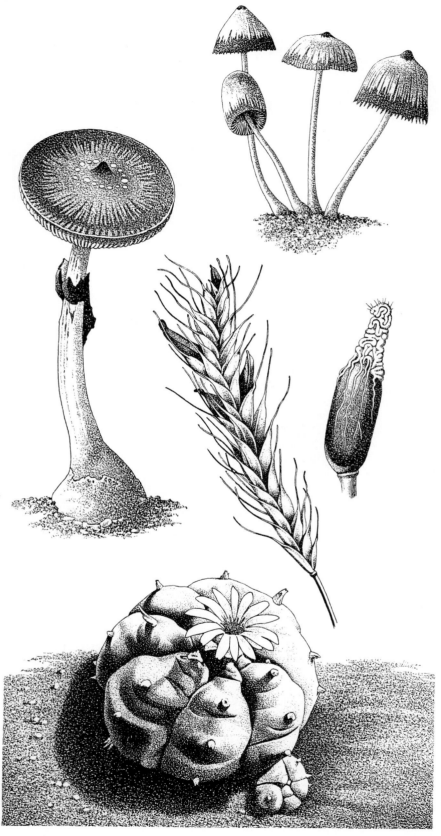

NATURAL SOURCES of the main hallucinogens are depicted. Psilocybin comes from the mushrooms *Stropharia cubensis* (*top left*) and *Psilocybe mexicana* (*top right*). LSD is synthesized from an alkaloid in ergot (*Claviceps purpurea*), a fungus that grows on cereal grains; an ergot-infested rye seed head is shown (*center*) together with a larger-scale drawing of the ergot fungus. Mescaline is from the peyote cactus *Lophophora williamsii* (*bottom*).

among investigators but subsequently involving the issue of protection of the mental health of the student body, indicated the scope of popular interest in taking the drugs and the consequent public concern over their possible misuse.

There are, on the other hand, constructive uses of the drugs. In spite of obvious differences between the "model psychoses" produced by these drugs and naturally occurring psychoses, there are enough similarities to warrant intensive investigation along these lines. The drugs also provide the only link, however tenuous, between human psychoses and aberrant behavior in animals, in which physiological mechanisms can be studied more readily than in man. Beyond this many therapists feel that there is a specialized role for the hallucinogens in the treatment of psychoneuroses. Other investigators are struck by the possibility of using the drugs to facilitate meditation and aesthetic discrimination and to stimulate the imagination. These possibilities, taken in conjunction with the known hazards, are the bases for the current professional concern and controversy.

In evaluating potential uses and misuses of the hallucinogens, one can draw on a considerable body of knowledge from such disciplines as anthropology, pharmacology, biochemistry, psychology and psychiatry.

In some primitive societies the plants from which the major hallucinogens are derived have been known for millenniums and have been utilized for divination, curing, communion with supernatural powers and meditation to improve self-understanding or social unity; they have also served such mundane purposes as allaying hunger and relieving discomfort or boredom. In the Western Hemisphere the ingestion of hallucinogenic plants in pre-Columbian times was limited to a zone extending from what is now the southwestern U.S. to the northwestern basin of the Amazon. Among the Aztecs there were professional diviners who achieved inspiration by eating either peyote, hallucinogenic mushrooms (which the Aztecs called *teo-nanacatyl*, or "god's flesh") or other hallucinogenic plants. *Teo-nanacatyl* was said to have been distributed at the coronation of Montezuma to make the ceremony seem more spectacular. In the years following the conquest of Mexico there were reports of communal mushroom rites among the Aztecs and other Indians of southern Mexico. The communal use has almost died out today, but in several

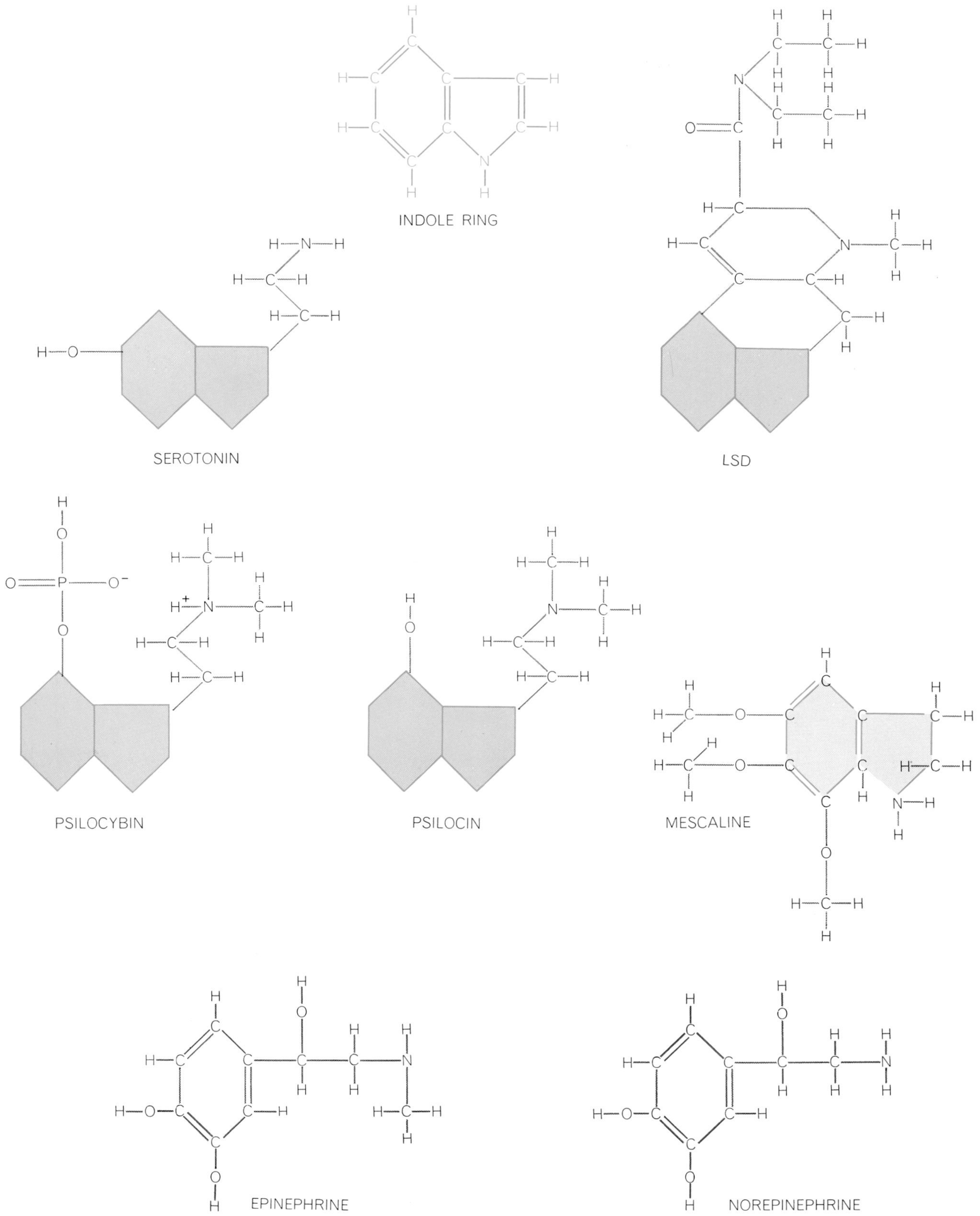

INDOLE RING

SEROTONIN

LSD

PSILOCYBIN

PSILOCIN

MESCALINE

EPINEPHRINE

NOREPINEPHRINE

CHEMICAL RELATIONS among several of the hallucinogens and neurohumors are indicated by these structural diagrams. The indole ring (*in color at top*) is a basic structural unit; it appears, as indicated by the colored shapes, in serotonin, LSD, psilocybin and psilocin. Mescaline does not have an indole ring but, as shown by the light color, can be represented so as to suggest its relation to the ring. The close relation between mescaline and the two catechol amines epinephrine and norepinephrine is also apparent here.

212

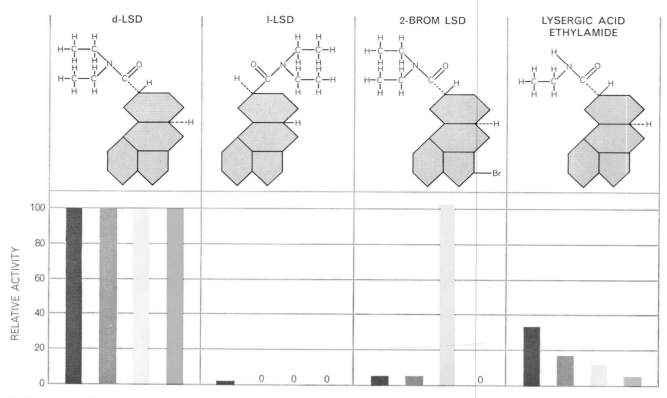

| d-LSD | l-LSD | 2-BROM LSD | LYSERGIC ACID ETHYLAMIDE |

SLIGHT CHANGES in LSD molecule produce large changes in its properties. Here LSD (*left*) is used as a standard, with a "relative activity" of 100 in toxicity (*dark gray bar*), fever-producing effect (*light gray*), ability to antagonize serotonin (*light color*) and typical psychotomimetic effects (*dark color*). The stereoisomer of LSD (*second from left*) in which the positions of the side chains are reversed, shows almost no activity; the substitution of a bromine atom (*third from left*) reduces the psychotomimetic effect but not the serotonin antagonism; the removal of one of the two ethyl groups (*right*) sharply reduces activity in each of the areas.

tribes the medicine men or women (*curanderos*) still partake of *Psilocybe* and *Stropharia* in their rituals.

In the arid region between the Rio Grande and central Mexico, where the peyote cactus grows, the dried tops of the plants ("peyote buttons") were eaten by Indian shamans, or medicine men, and figured in tribal rituals. During the 19th century the Mescalero Apaches acquired the plant and developed a peyote rite. The peyotism of the Mescaleros (whence the name mescaline) spread to the Comanches and Kiowas, who transformed it into a religion with a doctrine and ethic as well as ritual. Peyotism, which spread rapidly through the Plains tribes, became fused with Christianity. Today its adherents worship God as the great spirit who controls the universe and put some of his power into peyote, and Jesus as the man who gave the plant to the Indians in a time of need. Saturday-night meetings, usually held in a traditional tepee, begin with the eating of the sacramental peyote; then the night is spent in prayer, ritual singing and introspective contemplation, and in the morning there is a communion breakfast of corn, game and fruit.

Recognizing the need for an effective organization to protect their form of worship, several peyote churches joined in 1918 to form the Native American Church, which now has about 225,000 members in tribes from Nevada to the East Coast and from the Mexican border to Saskatchewan. It preaches brotherly love, care of the family, self-reliance and abstinence from alcohol. The church has been able to defeat attempts, chiefly by the missionaries of other churches, to outlaw peyote by Federal legislation, and it has recently brought about the repeal of antipeyote legislation in several states.

The hallucinogens began to attract scholarly interest in the last decade of the 19th century, when the investigations and conceptions of such men as Francis Galton, J. M. Charcot, Sigmund Freud and William James introduced a new spirit of serious inquiry into such subjects as hallucination, mystical experience and other "paranormal" psychic phenomena. Havelock Ellis and the psychiatrist Silas Weir Mitchell wrote accounts of the subjective effects of peyote, or Anhalonium, as it was then called. Such essays in turn stimulated

the interest of pharmacologists. The active principle of peyote, the alkaloid called mescaline, was isolated in 1896; in 1919 it was recognized that the molecular structure of mescaline was related to the structure of the adrenal hormone epinephrine.

This was an important turning point, because the interest in the hallucinogens as a possible key to naturally occurring psychoses is based on the chemical relations between the drugs and the neurohumors: substances that chemically transmit impulses across synapses between two neurons, or nerve cells, or between a neuron and an effector such as a muscle cell. Acetylcholine and the catechol amines epinephrine and norepinephrine have been shown to act in this manner in the peripheral nervous system of vertebrates; serotonin has the same effect in some invertebrates. It is frequently assumed that these substances also act as neurohumors in the central nervous system; at least they are present there, and injecting them into various parts of the brain seems to affect nervous activity.

The structural resemblance of mescaline and epinephrine suggested a possible link between the drug and mental illness: Might the early, excited stage of schizophrenia be produced or at least triggered by an error in metabolism that produced a mescaline-like substance? Techniques for gathering evidence on this question were not available, however, and the speculation on an "M-substance" did not lead to serious experimental work.

When LSD was discovered in 1943, its extraordinary potency again aroused interest in the possibility of finding a natural chemical activator of the schizophrenic process. The M-substance hypothesis was revived on the basis of reports that hallucinogenic effects were produced by adrenochrome and other breakdown products of epinephrine, and the hypothesis appeared to be strengthened by the isolation from human urine of some close analogues of hallucinogens. Adrenochrome has not, however, been detected in significant amounts in the human body, and it seems unlikely that the analogues could be produced in sufficient quantity to effect mental changes.

The relation between LSD and serotonin has given rise to the hypothesis that schizophrenia is caused by an imbalance in the metabolism of serotonin, with excitement and hallucinations resulting from an excess of serotonin in certain regions of the brain, and depressive and catatonic states resulting from a deficiency of serotonin. The idea arose in part from the observation that in some laboratory physiological preparations LSD acts rather like serotonin but in other preparations it is a powerful antagonist of serotonin; thus LSD might facilitate or block some neurohumoral action of serotonin in the brain.

The broad objection to the serotonin theory of schizophrenia is that it requires an oversimplified view of the disease's pattern of symptoms. Moreover, many congeners, or close analogues, of LSD, such as 2-brom lysergic acid, are equally effective or more effective antagonists of serotonin without being significantly active psychologically in man. This does not disprove the hypothesis, however. In man 2-brom LSD blocks the mental effects of a subsequent dose of LSD, and in the heart of a clam it blocks the action of both LSD and serotonin. Perhaps there are "keyholes" at the sites where neurohumors act; in the case of those for serotonin it may be that LSD fits the hole and opens the lock, whereas the psychologically inactive analogues merely occupy the keyhole, blocking the action of serotonin or LSD without mimicking their effects. Certainly the re-semblance of most of the hallucinogens to serotonin is marked, and the correlations between chemical structure and pharmacological action deserve intensive investigation. The serotonin theory of schizophrenia is far from proved, but there is strong evidence for an organic factor of some kind in the disease; it may yet turn out to involve either a specific neurohumor or an imbalance among several neurohumors.

The ingestion of LSD, mescaline or psilocybin can produce a wide range of subjective and objective effects. The subjective effects apparently depend on at least three kinds of variable: the properties and potency of the drug itself; the basic personality traits and current mood of the person ingesting it, and the social and psychological context, including the meaning to the individual of his act in taking the drug and his interpretation of the motives of those who made it available. The discussion of subjective effects that follows is compiled from many different accounts of the drug experience; it should be considered an inventory of possible effects rather than a description of a typical episode.

One subjective experience that is frequently reported is a change in visual perception. When the eyes are open, the perception of light and space is affected: colors become more vivid and seem to glow; the space between objects becomes more apparent, as though space itself had become "real," and surface details appear to be more sharply defined. Many people feel a new awareness of the physical beauty of the world, particularly of visual harmonies, colors, the play of light and the exquisiteness of detail.

The visual effects are even more striking when the eyes are closed. A constantly changing display appears, its content ranging from abstract forms to dramatic scenes involving imagined people or animals, sometimes in exotic lands or ancient times. Different individuals have recalled seeing wavy lines, cobweb or chessboard designs, gratings, mosaics, carpets, floral designs, gems, windmills, mausoleums, landscapes, "arabesques spiraling into eternity," statuesque men of the past, chariots, sequences of dramatic action, the face of Buddha, the face of Christ, the Crucifixion, "the mythical dwelling places of the gods," the immensity and blackness of space. After taking peyote Silas Weir Mitchell wrote: "To give the faintest idea of the perfectly satisfying intensity and purity of these gorgeous color fruits

WATER COLORS were done, while under the influence of a relatively large dose of a hallucinogenic drug, by a person with no art training. Originals are bright yellow, purple, green and red as well as black.

214

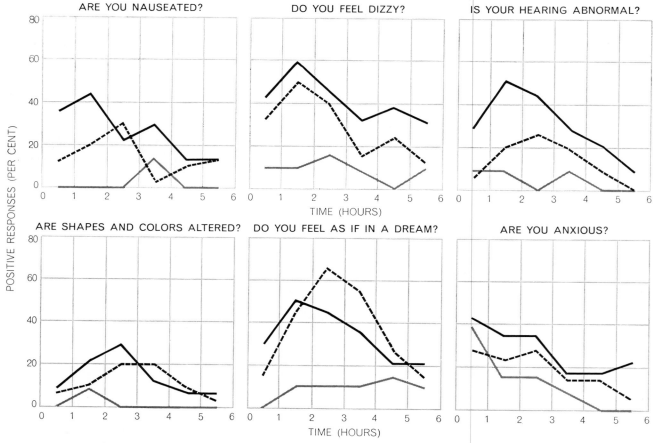

ARE YOU NAUSEATED?

DO YOU FEEL DIZZY?

IS YOUR HEARING ABNORMAL?

ARE SHAPES AND COLORS ALTERED?

DO YOU FEEL AS IF IN A DREAM?

ARE YOU ANXIOUS?

POSITIVE RESPONSES (PER CENT)

TIME (HOURS)

SUBJECTIVE REPORT on physiological and perceptual effects of LSD was obtained by means of a questionnaire containing 47 items, the results for six of which are presented. Volunteers were questioned at one-hour intervals beginning half an hour after they took the drug. The curves show the per cent of the group giving positive answers at each time. The gray curves are for those given an inactive substance, the broken black curves for between 25 and 75 micrograms and the solid black curves for between 100 and 225.

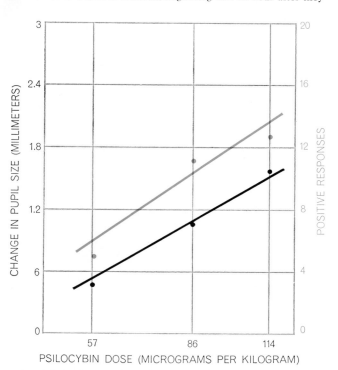

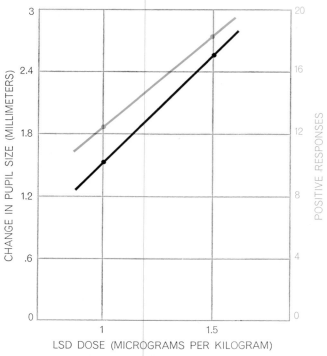

OBJECTIVE AND SUBJECTIVE effects vary with dosage as shown here. The data plotted in black are for the increase in size of pupil; the number of positive responses to questions like the ones at the top of the page are shown in color. The objective and subjective measures vary in a similar manner. The data are from an experiment done by Harris Isbell of the University of Kentucky.

is quite beyond my power." A painter described the waning hours of the effects of psilocybin as follows: "As the afternoon wore on I felt very content to simply sit and stare out of the window at the snow and the trees, and at that time I recall feeling that the snow, the fire in the fireplace, the darkened and book-lined room were so perfect as to seem almost unreal."

The changes in visual perception are not always pleasant. Aldous Huxley called one of his books about mescaline *Heaven and Hell* in recognition of the contradictory sensations induced by the drug. The "hellish" experiences include an impression of blackness accompanied by feelings of gloom and isolation, a garish modification of the glowing colors observed in the "heavenly" phase, a sense of sickly greens and ugly dark reds. The subject's perception of his own body may become unpleasant: his limbs may seem to be distorted or his flesh to be decaying; in a mirror his face may appear to be a mask, his smile a meaningless grimace. Sometimes all human movements appear to be mere puppetry, or everyone seems to be dead. These experiences can be so disturbing that a residue of fear and depression persists long after the effects of the drug have worn off.

Often there are complex auditory hallucinations as well as visual ones: lengthy conversations between imaginary people, perfectly orchestrated musical compositions the subject has never heard before, voices speaking foreign languages unknown to the subject. There have also been reports of hallucinatory odors and tastes and of visceral and other bodily sensations. Frequently patterns of association normally confined to a single sense will cross over to other senses: the sound of music evokes the visual impression of jets of colored light, a "cold" human voice makes the subject shiver, pricking the skin with a pin produces the visual impression of a circle, light glinting on a Christmas tree ornament seems to shatter and to evoke the sound of sleigh bells. The time sense is altered too. The passage of time may seem to be a slow and pleasant flow or to be intolerably tedious. A "sense of timelessness" is often reported; the subject feels outside of or beyond time, or time and space seem infinite.

In some individuals one of the most basic constancies in perception is affected: the distinction between subject and object. A firm sense of personal identity depends on knowing accurately the borders of the self and on being able to distinguish what is inside from what is outside. Paranoia is the most vivid pathological instance of the breakdown of this discrimination; the paranoiac attributes to personal and impersonal forces outside himself the impulses that actually are inside him. Mystical and transcendental experiences are marked by the loss of this same basic constancy. "All is one" is the prototype of a mystical utterance. In the mystical state the distinction between subject and object disappears; the subject is seen to be one with the object. The experience is usually one of rapture or ecstasy and in religious terms is described as "holy." When the subject thus achieves complete identification with the object, the experience seems beyond words.

Some people who have taken a large dose of a hallucinogenic drug report feelings of "emptiness" or "silence," pertaining either to the interior of the self or to an "interior" of the universe— or to both as one. Such individuals have a sense of being completely undifferentiated, as though it were their personal consciousness that had been "emptied," leaving none of the usual discriminations on which the functioning of the ego depends. One man who had this experience thought later that it had been an anticipation of death, and that the regaining of the basic discriminations was like a remembrance of the very first days of life after birth.

The effect of the hallucinogens on sexual experience is not well documented. One experiment that is often quoted seemed to provide evidence that mescaline is an anaphrodisiac, an inhibitor of sexual appetite; this conclusion seemed plausible because the drugs have so often been associated with rituals emphasizing asceticism and prayer. The fact is, however, that the drugs are probably neither anaphrodisiacs nor aphrodisiacs—if indeed any drug is. There is reason to believe that if the drug-taking situation is one in which sexual relations seem appropriate, the hallucinogens simply bring to the sexual experience the same kind of change in perception that occurs in other areas of experience.

The point is that in all the hallucinogen-produced experiences it is never the drug alone that is at work. As in the case of alcohol, the effects vary widely depending on when the drug is taken, where, in the presence of whom, in what dosage and—perhaps most important of all—by whom. What happens to the individual after he takes the drug, and his changing relations to the setting and the people in it during the episode, will further influence his experience.

Since the setting is so influential in these experiments, it sometimes happens that a person who is present when someone else is taking a hallucinogenic drug, but who does not take the drug himself, behaves as though he were under the influence of a hallucinogen. In view of this effect one might expect that a person given an inactive substance he thought was a drug would respond as though he had actually received the drug. Indeed, such responses have sometimes been noted. In controlled experiments, however, subjects given an inactive substance are readily distinguishable from those who take a drug; the difference is apparent in their appearance and behavior, their answers to questionnaires and their physiological responses. Such behavioral similarities as are observed can be explained largely by a certain apprehension felt by a person who receives an inactive substance he thinks is a drug, or by anticipation on the part of someone who has taken the drug before.

In addition to the various subjective effects of the hallucinogens there are a number of observable changes in physiological function and in performance that one can measure or at least describe objectively. The basic physiological effects are those typical of a mild excitement of the sympathetic nervous system. The hallucinogens usually dilate the pupils, constrict the peripheral arterioles and raise the systolic blood pressure; they may also increase the excitability of such spinal reflexes as the knee jerk. Electroencephalograms show that the effect on electrical brain waves is usually of a fairly nonspecific "arousal" nature: the pattern is similar to that of a normally alert, attentive and problem-oriented subject, and if rhythms characteristic of drowsiness or sleep have been present, they disappear when the drug is administered. (Insomnia is common the first night after one of the drugs has been taken.) Animal experiments suggest that LSD produces these effects by stimulating the reticular formation of the midbrain, not directly but by stepping up the sensory input.

Under the influence of one of the hallucinogens there is usually some reduction in performance on standard tests of reasoning, memory, arithmetic, spelling and drawing. These findings may not indicate an inability to perform well; after taking a drug many people simply refuse to co-operate with the tester. The very fact that someone should want to

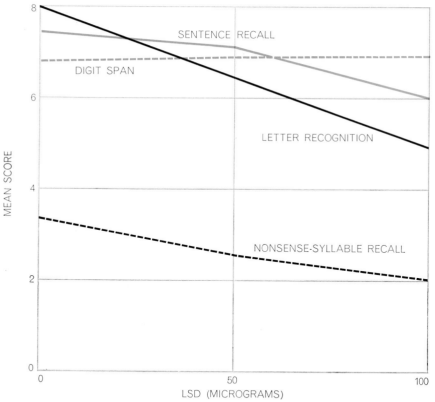

EFFECT OF LSD on memory was determined with standard tests. Curves show results of four tests for subjects given an inactive substance, 50 micrograms of the drug and 100 micrograms respectively. Effect of LSD was to decrease scores except in a test of digit-recall ability.

test them may seem absurd and may arouse either hostility or amusement. Studies by one of the authors in which tests of attention and concentration were administered to subjects who had been given different doses of LSD indicated that motivation was perhaps as important in determining scores as the subject's intellectual capacity.

The hallucinogenic drugs are not addictive—if one means by addiction that physiological dependence is established and the drug becomes necessary, usually in increasing amounts, for satisfactory physiological functioning. Some individuals become psychologically dependent on the drugs, however, and develop a "habit" in that sense; indeed, there is a tendency for those who ingest hallucinogens habitually to make the drug experience the center of all their activities. LSD, mescaline and psilocybin do produce physiological tolerance. If the same quantity of LSD is administered on three successive days, for example, it will not suffice by the third day to produce the same subjective or physiological effects; tolerance develops more slowly and less completely with mescaline and psilocybin. When an individual becomes tolerant to a given dos-

age of LSD, the ordinarily equivalent dose of psilocybin produces reduced effects. This phenomenon of cross-tolerance suggests that the two drugs have common pathways of action. Any tolerance established by daily administration of the drugs wears off rather rapidly, generally being dissipated within a few days if the drug is not taken.

The three major hallucinogens differ markedly in potency. The standard human doses—those that will cause the average adult male weighing about 150 pounds to show the full clinical effects—are 500 milligrams of mescaline, 20 milligrams of psilocybin and .1 milligram of LSD. It is assumed that in a large enough dose any of the hallucinogens would be lethal, but there are no documented cases of human deaths from the drugs alone. Death has been brought on in sensitive laboratory animals such as rabbits by LSD doses equivalent to 120 times the standard human dose. Some animals are much less susceptible; white rats have been given doses 1,000 times larger than the standard human dose without lasting harm. The maximum doses known by the authors to have been taken by human beings are 900 milligrams of mescaline, 70 milligrams

of psilocybin and two milligrams of LSD. No permanent effects were noted in these cases, but obviously no decisive studies of the upper limits of dosage have been undertaken.

There are also differences among the hallucinogens in the time of onset of effects and the duration of intoxication. When mescaline is given orally, the effects appear in two or three hours and last for 12 hours or more. LSD acts in less than an hour; some of its effects persist for eight or nine hours, and insomnia can last as long as 16 hours. Psilocybin usually acts within 20 or 30 minutes, and its full effect is felt for about five hours. All these estimates are for the standard dose administered orally; when any of the drugs is given intravenously, the first effects appear within minutes.

At the present time LSD and psilocybin are treated by the U.S. Food and Drug Administration like any other "experimental drug," which means that they can be legally distributed only to qualified investigators who will administer them in the course of an approved program of experimentation. In practice the drugs are legally available only to investigators working under a Government grant or for a state or Federal agency.

Nevertheless, there has probably been an increase during the past two or three years in the uncontrolled use of the drugs to satisfy personal curiosity or to experience novel sensations. This has led a number of responsible people in government, law, medicine and psychology to urge the imposition of stricter controls that would make the drugs more difficult to obtain even for basic research. These people emphasize the harmful possibilities of the drugs; citing the known cases of adverse reactions, they conclude that the prudent course is to curtail experimentation with hallucinogens.

Others—primarily those who have worked with the drugs—emphasize the constructive possibilities, insist that the hallucinogens have already opened up important leads in research and conclude that it would be shortsighted as well as contrary to the spirit of free scientific inquiry to restrict the activities of qualified investigators. Some go further, questioning whether citizens should be denied the opportunity of trying the drugs even without medical or psychological supervision and arguing that anyone who is mentally competent should have the right to explore the varieties of conscious experience if he can do so without harming himself or others.

The most systematic survey of the incidence of serious adverse reactions to hallucinogens covered nearly 5,000 cases, in which LSD was administered on more than 25,000 occasions. Psychotic reactions lasting more than 48 hours were observed in fewer than two-tenths of 1 per cent of the cases. The rate of attempted suicides was slightly over a tenth of 1 per cent, and these involved psychiatric patients with histories of instability. Among those who took the drug simply as subjects in experiments there were no attempted suicides and the psychotic reactions occurred in fewer than a tenth of 1 per cent of the cases.

Recent reports do indicate that the incidence of bad reactions has been increasing, perhaps because more individuals have been taking the hallucinogens in settings that emphasize sensation-seeking or even deliberate social delinquency. Since under such circumstances there is usually no one in attendance who knows how to avert dangerous developments, a person in this situation may find himself facing an extremely frightening hallucination with no one present who can help him to recognize where the hallucination ends and reality begins. Yet the question of what is a proper setting is not a simple one. One of the criticisms of the Harvard experiments was that some were conducted in private homes rather than in a laboratory or clinical setting. The experimenters defended this as an attempt to provide a feeling of naturalness and "psychological safety." Such a setting, they hypothesized, should reduce the likelihood of negative reactions such as fear and hostility and increase the positive experiences. Controlled studies of this hypothesis have not been carried out, however.

Many psychiatrists and psychologists who have administered hallucinogens in a therapeutic setting claim specific benefits in the treatment of psychoneuroses, alcoholism and social delinquency. The published studies are difficult to evaluate because almost none have employed control groups. One summary of the available statistics on the treatment of alcoholism does indicate that about 50 per cent of the patients treated with a combination of psychotherapy and LSD abstained from alcohol for at least a year, compared with 30 per cent of the patients treated by psychotherapy alone.

In another recent study the results of psychological testing before and after LSD therapy were comparable in most respects to the results obtained when conventional brief psychotherapy was employed. Single-treatment LSD therapy was significantly more effective, however, in relieving neurotic depression. If replicated, these results may provide an important basis for more directed study of the treatment of specific psychopathological conditions.

If the hallucinogens do have psychotherapeutic merit, it seems possible that they work by producing a shift in personal values. William James long ago noted that "the best cure for dipsomania is religiomania." There appear to be religious aspects of the drug experience that may bring about a change in behavior by causing a "change of heart." If this is so, one might be able to apply the hallucinogens in the service of moral regeneration while relying on more conventional techniques to give the patient insight into his habitual behavior patterns and motives.

In the light of the information now available about the uses and possible abuses of the hallucinogens, common sense surely decrees some form of social control. In considering such control it should always be emphasized that the reaction to these drugs depends not only on their chemical properties and biological activity but also on the context in which they are taken, the meaning of the act and the personality and mood of the individual who takes them. If taking the drug is defined by the group or individual, or by society, as immoral or criminal, one can expect guilt and aggression and further social delinquency to result; if the aim is to help or to be helped, the experience may be therapeutic and strengthening; if the subject fears psychosis, the drug could induce psychosis. The hallucinogens, like so many other discoveries of man, are analogous to fire, which can burn down the house or spread through the house life-sustaining warmth. Purpose, planning and constructive control make the difference. The immediate research challenge presented by the hallucinogens is a practical question: Can ways be found to minimize or eliminate the hazards, and to identify and develop further the constructive potentialities, of these powerful drugs?

NATIVE AMERICAN CHURCH members take part in a peyote ceremony in Saskatchewan, Canada. Under the influence of the drug, they gaze into the fire as they pray and meditate.

VI

SENSORY PROCESSES AND PERCEPTION

VI

SENSORY PROCESSES AND PERCEPTION

INTRODUCTION

A basic issue confronting man and confounding philosophers is the perception of reality: How is it that we see and experience the world as we do? It is clear that our perceptions of the world must have some relationship to the "real" world, otherwise we would long ago have been devoured by jungle predators, who seem not to be bothered by the issue. The problem is quite fundamental—the physicist tells us the world is made up of collections of atomic particles and waves of energy, but it most certainly does not *look* like that. It is a comforting fact that even the atomic physicist must depend upon the very same perceptions of color, form, position, and so forth, that all of us use in everyday life to construct reality. Our sensory systems—particularly touch, hearing, and vision—are the bridge between the real world and our experience of it. Sensory receptors transform the energy of physical stimuli into nerve impulses, which travel to the brain to produce sensations and perceptions. Our experience of the world corresponds much more closely to the patterns of activity of neurons in the brain (particularly of those in the thalamus and the cerebral cortex) than it does to the patterns of impinging stimulus energy: it bears a *relation* to the latter, but the relation is not linear.

In the first article in this section, "The Perception of Pain," Ronald Melzack discusses what is surely the most immediate and compelling of all our subjective experiences. Pain is unique in having no particular type or category of appropriate physical stimuli. Any type of stimulus—pressure, light, sound, chemical substances—can induce pain under certain conditions, particularly if the stimulus is strong. In biological terms, pain is clearly adaptive. Under normal circumstances, any stimulus that causes tissue damage will be felt as painful. Pain, of course, is only one aspect of the somatic sensory system, which conveys information to the brain about stimulation of the skin, the positions of the limbs, and the tension on muscles and tendons.

The auditory system has been much underrated in discussions of the importance of sensory systems. Although the visual system handles more information, one of the most important aspects of human behavior, the use of language, depends upon hearing. Perhaps because reading has become so important in human affairs, we tend to forget that language is basically an auditory phenomenon. Language developed many thousands of years before writing, and every normal human child learns language purely through hearing, long before he learns to read. The receptive apparatus of the auditory system is described in "The Ear," an article by Georg von Békésy, who received the Nobel prize in 1961 for his work on the basilar membrane, the basic receptor system in the ear that encodes the nature of sounds.

Roughly 80 percent of the information that we process about our world is provided by vision. Charles R. Michael, in his article "Retinal Processing of Visual Images," discusses the extent to which visual stimuli are encoded at the retina, the layer of light-sensitive cells and neurons at the back of the eye. Lower organisms, such as the frog, which do not have much in the way of a cerebral cortex, accomplish a surprising amount of encoding at the retina. The receptor cells themselves, the rods and cones, simply respond when light falls on them—the rods to the entire visible spectrum of wavelengths and the cones, which are responsible for color vision, only to certain ranges of wavelengths. In the frog, the nerve cells within the retina transform this simple information into a surprisingly complex code of the visual world. The situation is quite different in mammals, as described by David H. Hubel in his article "The Visual Cortex of the Brain." In higher animals, at least from cat to man, complex stimulus encoding occurs not in the retina but rather in the visual cortex. Hubel and his colleague Torsten N. Wiesel first made the remarkable discovery that individual nerve cells in the visual region of the cerebral cortex encode complex aspects of the visual world, ranging from edges and lines to right angles, tongues, and other dimensional stimuli. The manner in which these complex feature-detector neurons are activated to yield complex coding is described by Hubel. A critically important recent observation by Hubel and Wiesel and others is that this complex wiring seems to be present at birth. We do not learn to see complex visual stimuli, we see them because the capacity to see them is wired into our brains.

The importance of behavioral responses to perception is emphasized in the article "Eye Movements and Visual Perception" by David Noton and Lawrence Stark. The article deals with the eye movements that occur when a person looks at a stationary picture or drawing. There are actually two sorts of eye movements: very rapid but very small *nystagmic* movements that occur continuously and seem to be necessary for normal vision, and *saccadic* movements, which are rapid and extensive sweeps of the eyes as they shift from one fixation point to another when looking at a stationary scene. The authors describe these movements and develop a most interesting theory of visual memory in relation to the serial pattern of eye movements that a subject makes when looking at a picture.

A basic topic in sensory perception is the development of perception through experience. As indicated above in our discussion of visual coding, the capacity for complex visual perceptions appears to be wired into the brain. In the last article in this section, "Plasticity in Sensory-Motor Systems," Richard Held describes some fascinating experiments that indicate that behavioral interaction with the environment may be necessary for the development of accurate responses to visual stimuli. These observations are not necessarily contradictory, but they do suggest that what is learned in complex perception may relate more to the performance of responses than the initial brain analysis of stimuli.

23

THE PERCEPTION OF PAIN

RONALD MELZACK
February 1961

Even though pain is a private and personal experience, we rarely pause to define it in ordinary conversation. Indeed, no one who has worked on the problem of pain has ever been able to define pain to the satisfaction of all his colleagues. When compared with vision or hearing, for example, the perception of pain seems simple, urgent and primitive. We expect the nerve signals evoked by injury to "get through," unless we are unconscious or anesthetized. But experiments show that pain is not always perceived after injury even when we are fully conscious and alert. Thus a knowledge of pain perception goes beyond the problem of pain itself: it helps us to understand the enormous plasticity of the nervous system and how each of us responds to the world in a unique fashion.

A vast amount of study has been devoted to the perception of pain, especially in the last decade, and from it is emerging a concept of pain quite different from the classical view. Research shows that pain is much more variable and modifiable than many people have believed in the past. Moreover, direct recordings of nerve signals are helping us to see, in physiological detail, why pain is such a complex experience.

Anyone who has suffered prolonged, severe pain comes to regard it as an evil, punishing affliction that is harmful in its own right. Yet everyone recognizes the positive aspect of pain. It warns us that something biologically harmful is happening. The occasional reports of people who are born without the ability to feel pain provide convincing testimony on the value of pain. Such a person sustains extensive burns and bruises during childhood, frequently bites deep into his tongue while chewing food, and learns only with difficulty to avoid inflicting severe wounds on himself.

It is the obvious biological significance of pain that leads most of us to expect that it must always occur after injury and that the intensity of pain we feel is proportional to the amount and extent of the damage. Actually, in higher species at least, there is much evidence that pain is not simply a function of the amount of bodily damage alone. Rather, the amount and quality of pain we feel are also determined by our previous experiences and how well we remember them, by our ability to understand the cause of the pain and to grasp its consequences. Even the significance pain has in the culture in which we have been brought up plays an essential role in how we feel and respond to it.

In our culture, for example, childbirth is widely regarded as a painful experience. Yet anthropologists have observed cultures in which the women show virtually no distress during childbirth. In some of these cultures a woman who is going to have a baby continues to work in the fields until the child is about to be born. Her husband then gets into bed and groans as though he were in great pain while she bears the child. The husband stays in bed with the baby to recover from the terrible ordeal he has just gone through, and the mother almost immediately returns to attend the crops.

Can this mean that all women in our culture are making up their pain? Not at all. It happens to be part of our culture to recognize childbirth as possibly endangering the life of the mother, and young girls learn to fear it in the course of growing up. Books on "natural childbirth" ("childbirth without fear") stress the extent to which fear increases the amount of pain felt during labor and birth and point out how difficult it is to dispel it.

The influence of early experience on the perception of pain was demonstrated a few years ago in experiments my colleagues and I conducted at McGill University [see "Early Environment," by William R. Thompson and Ronald Melzack; SCIENTIFIC AMERICAN Offprint 469]. We raised Scottish terriers in isolation from infancy to maturity so that they were deprived of normal environmental stimuli, including the bodily knocks and scrapes that young animals get in the course of growing up. We were surprised to find that when these dogs grew up they failed to respond normally to a flaming match. Some of them repeatedly poked their noses into the flame and sniffed at it as long as it was present. If they snuffed it out, they reacted similarly to a second flaming match and even to a third. Others did not sniff at the match but made no effort to get away when we touched their noses with the flame repeatedly. These dogs also endured pinpricks with little or no evidence of pain. In contrast, littermates that had been reared in a normal environment recognized potential harm so quickly that we were usually unable to touch them with the flame or pin more than once.

This astonishing behavior of dogs reared in isolation cannot be attributed to a general failure of the sensory conducting systems. Intense electric shock elicited violent excitement. Moreover, reflex movements made by the dogs during contact with fire and pinprick indicate that they may have felt something during stimulation; but the lack of any observable emotional disturbance, apart from reflex movements, suggests that

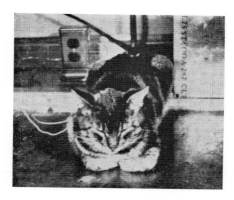

ATTENTIVE CAT (*middle*) watching mouse in a jar presumably does not hear a click as loudly as when it is in repose (*top and bottom*). Assumption is based on shape of nerve-signal recordings picked up by electrode implanted in auditory pathway. Clicks were sounded at the dots. This experiment was performed at the School of Medicine of the University of California at Los Angeles by Raúl Hernández-Peon and his associates.

their perception of actual damage to the skin was highly abnormal.

We have considerable evidence to show that people too attach variable meanings to pain-producing situations and that these meanings greatly influence the degree and quality of pain they feel. During World War II Henry K. Beecher of the Harvard Medical School observed the behavior of soldiers severely wounded in battle. He was astonished to find that when the wounded were carried into combat hospitals, only one out of three complained of enough pain to require morphine. Most of the soldiers either denied having pain from their extensive wounds or had so little that they did not want any medication to relieve it. These men, Beecher points out, were not in a state of shock, nor were they totally unable to feel pain, for they complained as vigorously as normal men at an inept vein puncture. When Beecher returned to clinical practice as an anesthesiologist, he asked a group of civilians who had just undergone major surgery and who had incisions similar to the wounds received by the soldiers whether they wanted morphine to alleviate their pain. In contrast with the wounded soldiers, four out of five claimed they were in severe pain and pleaded for a morphine injection.

Beecher concluded from his study that "the common belief that wounds are inevitably associated with pain, that the more extensive the wound the worse the pain, was not supported by observations made as carefully as possible in the combat zone." He goes on to say: "The data state in numerical terms what is known to all thoughtful clinical observers: There is no simple direct relationship between the wound per se and the pain experienced. The pain is in very large part determined by other factors, and of great importance here is the significance of the wound.... In the wounded soldier [the response to injury] was relief, thankfulness at his escape alive from the battlefield, even euphoria; to the civilian, his major surgery was a depressing, calamitous event."

The importance of the meaning associated with a pain-producing situation is made particularly clear in conditioning experiments carried out by the Russian physiologist Ivan Pavlov. Dogs normally react violently when they are given strong electric shocks to a paw. Pavlov found, however, that if he consistently presented food to a dog after each shock, the dog developed an entirely new response. Immediately after a shock the dog would salivate, wag its tail and turn

eagerly toward the food dish. The electric shock now failed to evoke any responses indicative of pain and became instead a signal meaning that food was on the way. The dog's conditioned behavior persisted when Pavlov increased the intensity of the electric shocks and even when he supplemented them by burning and wounding the dog's skin. Jules H. Masserman of Northwestern University carried the experiment still further. After cats had been taught to respond to electric shock as a signal for feeding, they were trained to administer the shock themselves by walking up to a switch and closing it.

It is well known that prize fighters, football players and other athletes can sustain severe injuries without being aware that they have been hurt. In fact, almost any situation that attracts intense, prolonged attention may diminish or abolish pain perception. Formal recognition of this fact has led to increasing medical interest in hypnosis. Like pain itself, the hypnotic state eludes precise definition. But loosely speaking hypnosis

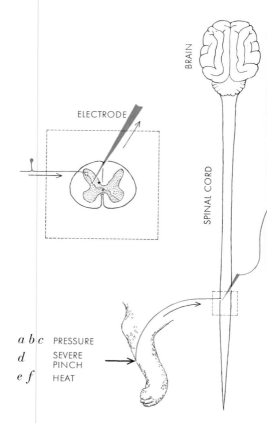

NEURON-FIRING PATTERNS, recorded from single cells in the spinal cord of a cat, show the initial response in the central nervous system to various stimuli applied to the cat's leg. Pattern *a* was caused by

is a trance state in which the subject's attention is focused intensely on the hypnotist while attention to other stimuli is markedly diminished. Evidently a small percentage of people can be hypnotized deeply enough to undergo surgery entirely without anesthesia. For a larger number of people hypnosis reduces the amount of pain-killing drug required to produce successful analgesia.

If, however, the subject's attention is focused on a potentially painful experience, he will tend to perceive pain more intensely than he would normally. K. R. L. Hall and E. Stride in England found that the simple appearance of the word "pain" in a set of instructions made anxious subjects report as painful a level of electric shock they did not regard as painful when the word was absent from the instructions. Thus the mere anticipation of pain is sufficient to raise the level of anxiety and thereby the intensity of perceived pain. Similarly, experiments carried out by Harris E. Hill and his colleagues at the U. S. Public Health Service Hospital in Lexington, Ky., have shown that if anxiety is dispelled (by re-

assuring a subject that he has control over the pain-producing stimulus), a given level of electric shock or burning heat is perceived as significantly less painful than the same stimulus under conditions of high anxiety. Hill was also able to show that morphine diminishes pain if the anxiety level is high but has no demonstrable effect if the subject's anxiety has been dispelled.

The influence of psychological processes such as anxiety, attention and suggestion on the intensity of perceived pain is further demonstrated by studies of the effectiveness of placebos. Clinical investigators have found that severe pain (such as postsurgical pain) can be relieved in some patients by giving them a placebo, such as sugar solution or saline solution, in place of morphine or other analgesic drugs. About 35 per cent of the patients report marked relief from pain after being given a placebo. Since morphine, even in large doses, will relieve severe pain in only some 75 per cent of patients, one can conclude that nearly half of the drug's effectiveness is really a placebo effect. This is not to imply that

people who are helped by a placebo do not have real pain; no one will deny the reality of postsurgical pain. Rather, it illustrates the powerful contribution of psychological processes to the perception of pain.

Taken together, the observations described so far indicate that the same injury can have different effects on different people or even on the same person at different times. A stimulus may be painful in one situation and not in another. How can we account for such variability in terms of what we know about the nervous system? First, we must recast the psychological facts into physiological terms. We must assume that psychological processes such as memories of previous experiences, thoughts, emotions and the focusing of attention are in some way functions of the higher areas of the brain—that they represent the actual activities of nerve impulses. What the psychological data suggest, then, is that these higher brain functions are able to modify the patterns of nerve impulses produced by an injury. Re-

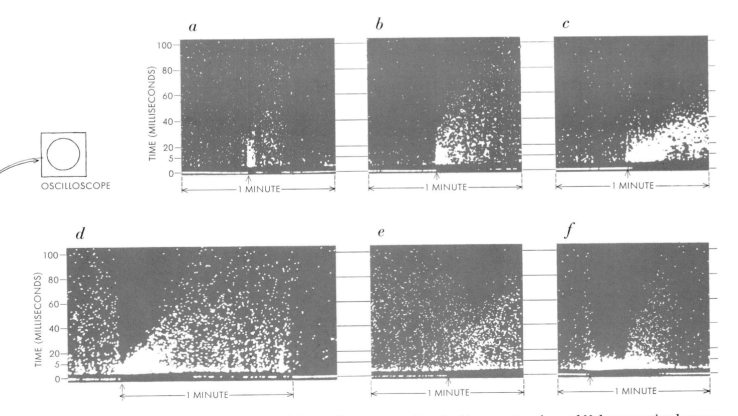

hanging a two-gram weight on a single hair; *b* shows effect of a 20-gram weight; *c* is effect of a mild pinch. All three stimuli start at arrows and continue for duration of the recording. In *d* the skin was severely pinched for one minute. In *e* and *f* a heat lamp was directed at the skin for 15 seconds after the arrows, raising the skin temperature four and 12 degrees centigrade respectively. Each dot in the recordings represents a single nerve impulse; height above base line represents time interval between recorded impulse and preceding one. These experiments were performed by Patrick D. Wall at Massachusetts Institute of Technology.

markable evidence for such complex neural interplay has recently been observed in physiological laboratories.

When energy from the environment stimulates the skin, a message is transmitted along nerve bundles to the spinal cord of the central nervous system. Until recently it was believed that the message, once fed in, was relayed without interference direct to a particular area of the brain cortex; the arrival of the message at this cortical area produced the sensation of pain, touch, warmth or cold, depending entirely on the physical characteristics of the initial stimulus. We now know that this is only a part of the picture. Investigators in a number of countries have recently demonstrated the presence of systems of nerve fibers that run from the higher areas of the brain downward to make connection with the message-carrying nerve pathways in the spinal cord. Electrical activity induced in these higher brain areas is capable of suppressing or modifying the message; it may never get beyond the lower levels of the central nervous system or an entirely different message may reach the brain [see illustration on opposite page].

There is no longer any doubt that these message-modifying fibers exist; it has been found that electrical stimulation of widespread regions of the brain is able to modify the messages transmitted through every major sensory system. The origins and terminations of these message-controlling fibers have not yet been fully established. But even at this stage it is reasonable to speculate that the fibers provide the mechanism whereby higher brain activities such as memories, thoughts and emotions can modify the sensory messages after injury. We can assume, moreover, that this modification can occur throughout the entire axis of the central nervous system, at every junction at which nerve messages are relayed from one neuron to the next in the course of their ascent to the highest areas of the brain. If this view is right, we have a conceptual physiological model to account for the fact that psychological events play an essential role in determining the quality and intensity of the ultimate perceptual experience.

We may ask at this point: What is the nature of the sensory nerve signals or messages traveling to the brain after injury that permits them to be modified in the course of their transmission? Let us say we have burned a finger; what is the sequence of events that follows in the nervous system? To begin with, the intense heat energy is converted into a code of electrical nerve impulses. These

energy conversions occur in nerve endings in the skin called receptors, of which there are many different types. It was once popular to identify one of these types as the specific "pain receptor." We now believe that receptor mechanisms are more complicated. There is general agreement that the receptors that respond to noxious stimulation are widely branching, bushy networks of fibers that penetrate the layers of the skin in such a way their receptive fields heavily overlap with one another. Thus damage at any point on the skin will activate at least two or more of these networks and initiate the transmission of trains of nerve impulses along bundles of sensory nerve fibers that run from the finger into the spinal cord. What enters the spinal cord of the central nervous system is a coded pattern of nerve impulses, traveling along many fibers and moving at different speeds and with different frequencies [see illustration on preceding page].

Before the nerve-impulse pattern can begin its ascent to the brain, a portion of it must first pass through a pool of short, densely packed nerve fibers that are dif-

fusely interconnected. The fibers comprising these pools, found throughout the length of the spinal cord, are called internuncial neurons. It is in the course of transmission from the sensory fibers to the ascending spinal cord neurons that the pattern of signals may be modified. Patrick D. Wall of the Massachusetts Institute of Technology has been able to insert microelectrodes into single spinal cord neurons in cats and record the patterns of neural firing evoked when painful stimuli are applied to the skin. He has shown that these patterns of firing can be altered and limited in duration by subjecting the surrounding skin to a vibratory stimulus [see illustration below]. Wall has directly confirmed with human subjects that normally painful electric shocks and pinpricks are not perceived as painful when the surrounding skin is stimulated with a rapidly vibrating device.

Once the sensory patterns or signals have entered the spinal cord neurons they are transmitted to the brain along nerve bundles that occupy the anterolateral (front and side) portions of the spinal cord. Many fibers belonging to

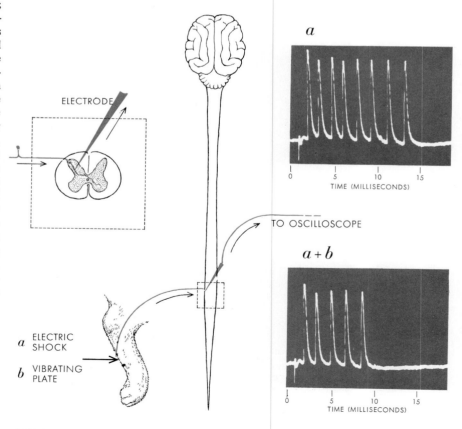

MODIFICATION OF SENSORY MESSAGES can take place within the spinal cord under certain conditions. In experiment at left, performed by Wall, the long train of nerve impulses following a single shock (a) is shortened when the skin around the shocked region is simultaneously vibrated by a metal plate (b). In experiment at right an afferent nerve

these bundles continue to the thalamus, forming the spinothalamic tract. The majority of the fibers, however, penetrate a tangled thicket of short, diffusely interconnected nerve fibers that form the central core of the lower part of the brain. Out of this formation of "reticulated" cells there emerges a series of pathways, so that the sensory patterns now stream along multiple routes to the higher regions of the brain.

When I was working with W. K. Livingston at the University of Oregon Medical School, our group found that electrical impulses evoked by painful stimuli are transmitted through the lower part of the brain along five distinct routes [*see illustrations on next two pages*]. Three of them—the spinothalamic tract, the central tegmental tract and the central gray pathway—appear to represent major conduction systems for sensory pain patterns since their electrical activity is significantly depressed by analgesic agents (such as nitrous oxide) that are capable of abolishing the awareness of pain in human patients without similarly affecting vision and hear-

ing. Analgesic drugs also produce a striking reduction in the electrical activity in the fourth region, the central core of reticulated cells, which has been shown by other investigators to have the role of arousing the whole brain into alert activity. The final pathway, a major sensory system called the lemniscal tract, plays an undetermined role in the total pain process since its transmission capacity is unaffected by anesthetic or analgesic drugs.

In order to determine the role played by these various ascending pathways in the perception of pain, we studied the behavior of cats in which some of the pathways had been selectively destroyed [*see illustration on page 231*]. We found that cats with lesions of the spinothalamic tract often failed to respond to normally painful stimuli, confirming earlier evidence that had demonstrated the importance of this pathway in the sensory pain process. But we found that it is not the only pathway involved. Cats with lesions in the central gray pathway also failed to respond to the stimuli. In contrast, cats with the lemniscal tract made inactive responded immediately to the stimuli.

To our surprise, the picture turned out to be even more complex than this. Lesions of the central tegmental tract had the opposite effect of making the cats excessively responsive to some kinds of painful stimuli, and many of these cats showed behavior suggesting "spontaneous pain" in the absence of external stimulation.

A recent development in the surgical control of pain in human patients lends striking confirmation to the results obtained in the cat study. Frank R. Ervin and Vernon H. Mark of the departments of psychiatry and neurosurgery at the Massachusetts General Hospital have found that patients suffering unbearable pain from cancer and other pathological sources may obtain excellent relief from pain after a small surgical lesion is made in that part of the human thalamus which receives fibers from the spino-thalamic tract as well as from the pathways that stem from the reticular formation. If, however, the lesion is made just a few millimeters in front of this area, destroying the thalamic fibers of the lemniscal pathway, the experience of pain remains unchanged. Direct obser-

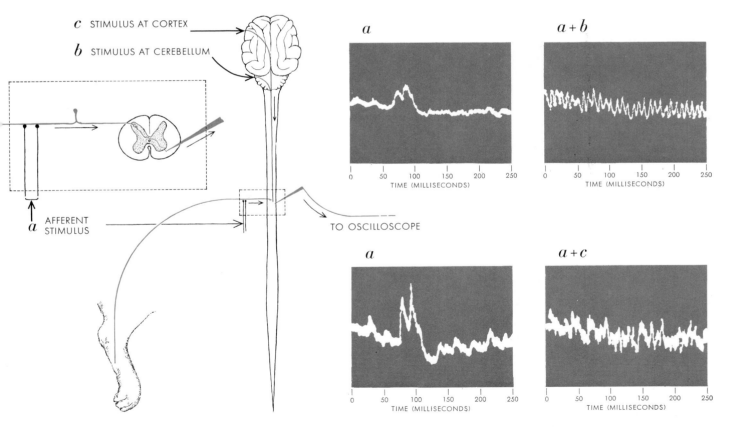

fiber entering the spinal cord is electrically stimulated directly (*a*). The signal passes through a pool of neurons and is recorded on the other side of the cord (whence it ascends to the brain), producing tracing *a*. If the cerebellum (*b*) or cortex (*c*) is stimulated simultaneously, the afferent signal is almost completely suppressed, as shown in tracings *a* + *b* and *a* + *c*. These experiments were performed at the School of Medicine of the University of California at Los Angeles by K.-E. Hagbarth and D. I. B. Kerr.

STIMULATION OF BRAIN STEM impels a cat to rotate a paddle wheel that turns off the weak electric stimulus. The stimulus was turned on between top and middle photographs. The cat's quickly learned behavior has all the characteristics of pain avoidance. These are frames from a motion picture made by **Neal E. Miller of Yale University.**

vations such as these on the sensory mechanisms of the pain process have provided us with valuable information on the nature of pain.

But we still cannot account for the complexity of many pain phenomena, especially bizarre pain syndromes sometimes encountered in hospital clinics. One in particular—phantom-limb pain—is both fascinating and terrible. In 1552 Ambroise Paré described it thus: "Verily it is a thing wondrous strange and prodigious, and which will scarce be credited, unless by such as have seen with their eyes, and heard with their ears, the patients who have many months after the cutting away of the leg, grievously complained that they yet felt exceeding great pain of that leg so cut off."

The majority of amputees report feeling a phantom limb soon after amputation and it may remain for years without bothering them. About 30 per cent, however, have the misfortune to develop pains in their phantom limbs, and in about 5 per cent the pain is severe. These pains may be occasional or continuous, but they are felt in definite parts of the phantom limb. W. K. Livingston reports the case of a young woman who described her phantom hand as being clenched, fingers bent over the thumb and digging into the palm of her hand, so that the whole hand became tired and painful. When she was able to open her phantom hand as a result of her physician's treatment, the pain vanished.

Phantom-limb pain tends to decrease and eventually disappear in most amputees. There are a few, however, for whom the pain increases in severity over the years. In addition, the disturbance spreads and other regions of the body may become so sensitized that merely touching them will evoke spasms of severe pain in the phantom limb. Even emotional upsets such as seeing a disturbing film may sharply increase the pain. Still worse, the conventional surgical procedures, such as cutting the spino-thalamic tract, usually fail to bring permanent relief, so that these patients may undergo a series of such operations without any decrease in the severity of the pain. Phenomena such as these defy explanation in terms of our present physiological knowledge. A few psychiatrists have been tempted simply to label these amputees as neurotic, but the evidence argues against such an explanation for all cases.

So far we can only speculate on the nature of phantom-limb pain. We know that irritation of the nerves of the remaining part of the limb contributes to the pain process, since stimulation of

these nerves can trigger severe pain. But the spread of the trigger sites and the frequent failure of conventional surgical procedures make it clear that this is not the whole story. All the evidence suggests that the primary focus of physiological disturbance lies in the central nervous system itself. Livingston believes that the initial damage to the limb, or perhaps the trauma associated with its removal, disturbs the patterning of neural activity in the internuncial pools of the spinal cord, creating reverberating, abnormally patterned activity. Even minor irritations to the skin or nerves near the site of the operation can then feed into these active pools of neurons and keep them in an abnormal, disturbed state over periods of years. Im-

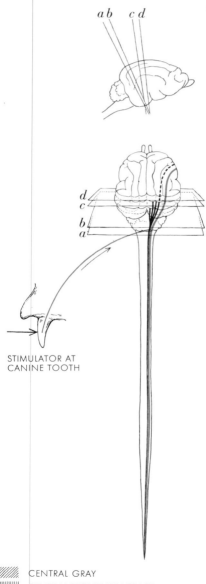

STIMULATOR AT CANINE TOOTH

CENTRAL GRAY
CENTRAL TEGMENTAL TRACT
RETICULAR FORMATION
SPINOTHALAMIC TRACT
LEMNISCAL TRACT

pulse patterns that would normally be interpreted as touch may now trigger these neuron pools into greater activity, thereby sending volleys of abnormal patterns of impulses to the higher areas of the brain and bringing about the perception of pain. Although there is no direct evidence that the internuncial pools play this role in phantom-limb pain, the concept helps us to understand facts that are otherwise difficult to explain.

So far we have been discussing pain primarily as a sensory experience somewhat similar to sight or hearing. But there is something missing. Pain has a unique, distinctly unpleasant quality that wells up in consciousness and obliterates anything we may have been

thinking or doing at the time. It becomes overwhelming and demands immediate attention. Pain has a strong emotional quality that drives us into doing something about it. We seek desperately to stop the pain as quickly as we can by whatever means we can.

Introspectionist psychologists at the turn of the century made a sharp distinction between the sensory and the emotional, or affective, dimensions of pain. The psychologist Edward B. Titchener was convinced that there is a continuum of *feeling* in conscious experience, distinctly different from sensation, that ranges through all the degrees of pleasantness and unpleasantness. "The pain of a toothache," Titchener wrote, "is localized at a particular place, 'in the

tooth'; but the unpleasantness of it suffuses the whole of present experience, is as wide as consciousness. The word 'pain' . . . often means the whole toothache experience."

These two dimensions, the sensory and the affective, are brought clearly into focus by clinical studies on prefrontal lobotomy, a neurosurgical operation for intense pain in which the connections between the prefrontal lobes and the rest of the brain are severed. Typically, these patients report after the operation that they still have pain but it does not bother them; they simply no longer care about the pain and often forget it is there. When they are questioned more closely, they frequently say that they still have the "little" pain, but the "big" pain, the

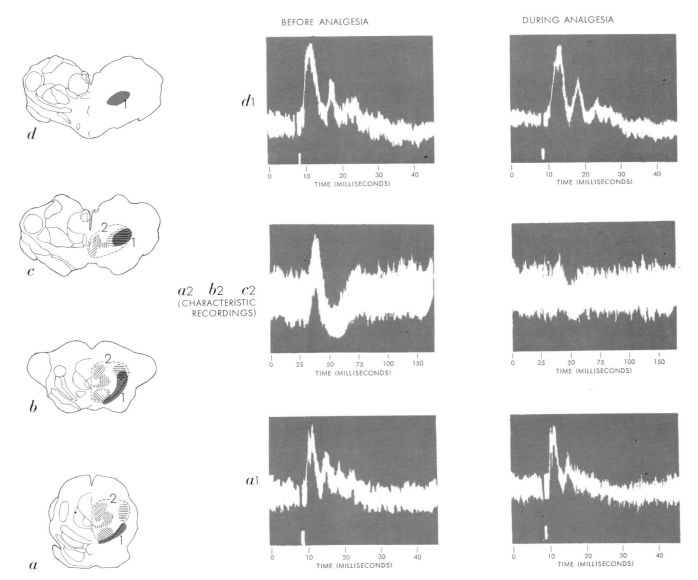

BEFORE ANALGESIA   DURING ANALGESIA

$d1$

$a2 \quad b2 \quad c2$
(CHARACTERISTIC RECORDINGS)

$a1$

FIVE PATHWAYS in the brain stem transmit signals evoked by stimulating the nerve of a cat's tooth. The sections *a, b, c* and *d* show how the pathways progress through the midbrain and thalamus; two of the pathways, the spinothalamic and lemniscal, send projections to the cortex [*see also illustration on next page*]. An analgesic mixture of nitrous oxide and oxygen largely blocks the signals in four (*2*) of the five pathways. The signal is not blocked, however, in the lemniscal pathway (*1*), which projects to the cortex. These experiments were performed by D. I. B. Kerr, Frederick P. Haugen and the author at the University of Oregon Medical School.

suffering, the anguish are gone. Yet they complain vociferously about pinprick and mild burn. It is certain that the operation does not stop pain perception entirely, since the sensory component is still present. Its predominant effect appears to be on the emotional coloring of the total pain experience; the terribly unpleasant quality of the pain has been abolished.

How are we to account for these effects? It is known that prefrontal lobotomy lowers the anxiety associated with pain to a striking degree: the fear of death is greatly diminished as well as the patient's preoccupation with his painful disease. It is often suggested that the reduction of anxiety brings about a concomitant reduction of pain intensity; specifically that the brain's prefrontal lobes, which are presumably involved in higher psychological processes, fail to elaborate the sensory nerve patterns as they ascend from the source of the pain. Such an explanation is consistent with the perceptual approach to pain that we have been discussing.

But is it only this? The emotional quality of the pain experience and its remarkable capacity for acting as a drive are both so different from touch, warmth or cold that to explain its psychological and neural basis seems to require something more than different patterns of nerve impulses arriving at the higher sensory areas of the brain. We might infer that distinctly different parts of the brain are involved in addition to the sensory areas.

Where, then, do the streams of sensory nerve impulses go after they are transmitted through the lower portions of the brain? We know that the spinothalamic tract has a relay station in the thalamus and there is good evidence that at least a portion of its impulse patterns is transmitted upward to the sensory cortex. The central gray neurons and the central tegmental tract, however, make connection with other neural systems, so that impulse patterns produced by painful stimuli have access to large areas of the brain that lie beneath the cortex.

Various experiments suggest that some of these subcortical areas are particularly concerned with the "driving" or motivating aspects of behavior. Neal E. Miller and other investigators at Yale University have used implanted electrodes to make a systematic exploration of areas deep within the brains of cats and other animals. When certain areas are stimulated, the animals cry out and behave exactly as if they were in pain [see illustration on page 228]. To call these areas "pain centers" would be misleading, since the evidence we have been discussing points to a complex interaction of sensory and cognitive processes involving other major portions of the brain. But there can be little doubt that these subcortical areas make a major contribution to the total pain process. Is it possible that the activities in these areas provide the neural substrate for the affective, "driving" component of pain perception? There is great temptation to speculate that they do—but in fact we do not know. All we can say for the present is that the ascending sensory patterns arouse activities in the brain that somehow subserve the broad category

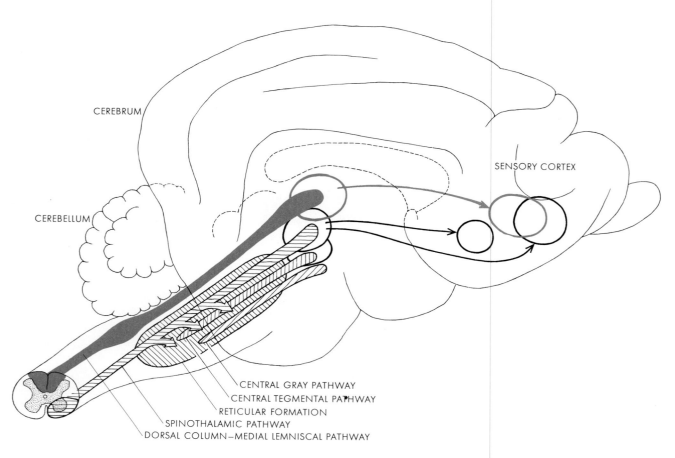

CEREBRUM

SENSORY CORTEX

CEREBELLUM

CENTRAL GRAY PATHWAY
CENTRAL TEGMENTAL PATHWAY
RETICULAR FORMATION
SPINOTHALAMIC PATHWAY
DORSAL COLUMN—MEDIAL LEMNISCAL PATHWAY

SIGNALS REACH THE CORTEX via projections from at least two of the five pathways ascending through the brain stem: the spinothalamic and the dorsal column — medial lemniscal pathways. Fibers from the former also penetrate the brain stem reticular formation, which is capable of arousing the whole cortex into activity. Surgical experiments [see illustration on opposite page] and analgesia experiments, suggest that pain perception is associated least with signals reaching cortex from lemniscal pathway.

of perceptions we describe as "pain."

It is now almost eight years since W. K. Livingston attempted to answer in these pages the question "What Is Pain?" [see SCIENTIFIC AMERICAN Offprint 407]. He argued against the classical conception that the intensity of pain sensation is always proportional to the stimulus. He proposed instead that pain, like all perceptions, is "subjective, individual and modified by degrees of attention, emotional states and the conditioning influence of past experience." Since that time we have moved still further away from the classical assumptions of specific "pain receptors," "pain pathways" and a "pain center" in the brain, all of which implied that stimulation of a "pain receptor" will invariably produce pain, that the pain will have only one specific quality and that it can vary only in intensity.

Pain, we now believe, refers to a category of complex experiences, not to a single sensation produced by a specific stimulus. In her essay "On Being Ill" Virginia Woolf touches on precisely this point. "English," she writes, "which can express the thoughts of Hamlet and the tragedy of Lear, has no words for the shiver and the headache.... The merest schoolgirl, when she falls in love, has Shakespeare and Keats to speak for her; but let a sufferer try to describe a pain in his head to a doctor and language at once runs dry."

We are beginning to recognize the poverty of language for describing the many different qualities of sensory and affective experience that we simply categorize under the broad heading of "pain." We are more and more aware of the plasticity and modifiability of events occurring in the central nervous system. We are aware that in the lower part of the brain, at least, the patterns of impulses produced by painful stimuli travel over multiple pathways going to widespread regions of the brain and not along a single path going to a "pain center." The psychological evidence strongly supports the view of pain as a perceptual experience whose quality and intensity is influenced by the unique past history of the individual, by the meaning he gives to the pain-producing situation and by his "state of mind" at the moment. We believe that all these factors play a role in determining the actual patterns of nerve impulses ascending to the brain and traveling within the brain itself. In this way pain becomes a function of the whole individual, including his present thoughts and fears as well as his hopes for the future.

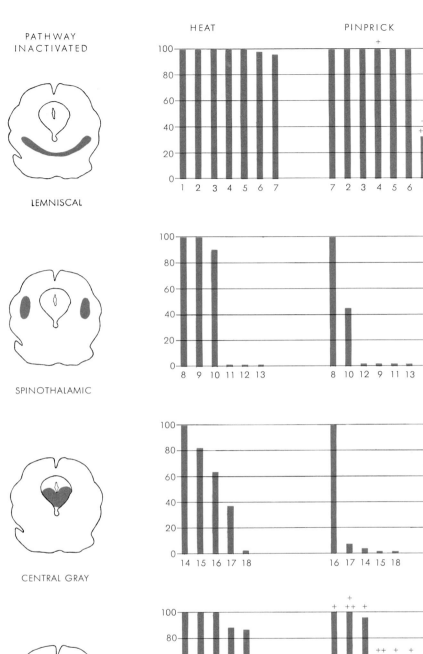

SURGICAL INACTIVATION OF BRAIN STEM PATHWAYS gives added evidence of complexity of pain perception. The surgery was performed on cats that had been trained to jump out of a box to avoid having their paws pricked or burned. Brain sections at left indicate the pathways inactivated in various animals. After surgery the animals were retested. The code number of each animal appears at the bottom of the bar graphs. Height of bar indicates percentage of avoidance responses when paws were pricked or heated. The marks + and ++ indicate, respectively, animals that became hyperresponsive to pain or that gave evidence of "spontaneous" pain. Inactivation of the spinothalamic and central gray pathways reduced the behavioral evidence of pain; inactivation of the lemniscal path had little or no effect. Inactivation of the central tegmental pathway seemed to heighten pain sensitivity.

24

THE EAR

GEORG VON BÉKÉSY
August 1957

Even in our era of technological wonders, the performances of our most amazing machines are still put in the shade by the sense organs of the human body. Consider the accomplishments of the ear. It is so sensitive that it can almost hear the random rain of air molecules bouncing against the eardrum. Yet in spite of its extraordinary sensitivity the ear can withstand the pounding of sound waves strong enough to set the body vibrating. The ear is equipped, moreover, with a truly impressive selectivity. In a room crowded with people talking, it can suppress most of the noise and concentrate on one speaker. From the blended sounds of a symphony orchestra the ear of the conductor can single out the one instrument that is not performing to his satisfaction.

In structure and in operation the ear is extraordinarily delicate. One measure of its fineness is the tiny vibrations to which it will respond. At some sound frequencies the vibrations of the eardrum are as small as one billionth of a centimeter—about one tenth the diameter of the hydrogen atom! And the vibrations of the very fine membrane in the inner ear which transmits this stimulation to the auditory nerve are nearly 100 times smaller in amplitude. This fact alone is enough to explain why hearing has so long been one of the mysteries of physiology. Even today we do not know how these minute vibrations stimulate the nerve endings. But thanks to refined electro-acoustical instruments we do know quite a bit now about how the ear functions.

What are the ear's abilities? We can get a quick picture of the working condition of an ear by taking an audiogram, which is a measure of the threshold of hearing at the various sound frequencies. The hearing is tested with pure tones at various frequencies, and the audiogram tells how much sound pressure on the eardrum (*i.e.*, what intensity of sound) is necessary for the sound at each frequency to be just barely audible. Curiously, the audiogram curve often is very much the same for the various members of a family; possibly this is connected in some way with the similarity in the shape of the face.

The ear is least sensitive at the low frequencies: for instance, its sensitivity for a tone of 100 cycles per second is 1,000 times lower than for one at 1,000 cycles per second. This comparative insensitivity to the slower vibrations is an obvious physical necessity, because otherwise we would hear all the vibrations of our own bodies. If you stick a finger in each ear, closing it to air-borne sounds, you hear a very low, irregular tone, produced by the contractions of the muscles of the arm and finger. It is interesting that the ear is just insensitive enough to low frequencies to avoid the disturbing effect of the noises produced by muscles, bodily movements, etc. If it were any more sensitive to these frequencies than it is, we would even hear the vibrations of the head that are produced by the shock of every step we take when walking.

On the high-frequency side the range that the ear covers is remarkable. In childhood some of us can hear well at frequencies as high as 40,000 cycles per second. But with age our acuteness of hearing in the high-frequency range steadily falls. Normally the drop is almost as regular as clockwork: testing several persons in their 40s with tones at a fixed level of intensity, we found that over a period of five years their upper limit dropped about 80 cycles per second every six months. (The experiment was quite depressing to most of the participants.) The aging of the ear is not difficult to understand if we assume that the elasticity of the tissues in the inner ear declines in the same way as that of the skin: it is well known that the skin becomes less resilient as we grow old—a

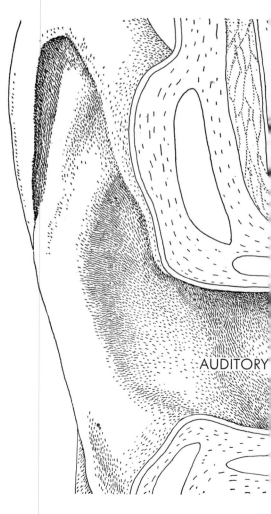

AUDITORY

PARTS OF THE EAR are illustrated in somewhat simplified cross section. Be-

phenomenon anyone can test by lifting the skin on the back of his hand and measuring the time it takes to fall back.

However, the loss of hearing sensitivity with age may also be due to nerve deterioration. Damage to the auditory nervous system by extremely loud noises, by drugs or by inflammation of the inner ear can impair hearing. Sometimes after such damage the hearing improves with time; sometimes (*e.g.*, when the damaging agent is streptomycin) the loss is permanent. Unfortunately a physician cannot predict the prospects for recovery of hearing loss, because they vary from person to person.

Psychological factors seem to be involved. Occasionally, especially after an ear operation, a patient appears to improve in hearing only to relapse after a short time. Some reports have even suggested that operating on one ear has improved the unoperated ear as well. Since such an interaction between the two ears would be of considerable neuro-

logical interest, I have investigated the matter, but I have never found an improvement in the untreated ear that could be validated by an objective test.

Structure of the Ear

To understand how the ear achieves its sensitivity, we must take a look at the anatomy of the middle and the inner ear. When sound waves start the eardrum (tympanic membrane) vibrating, the vibrations are transmitted via certain small bones (ossicles) to the fluid of the inner ear. One of the ossicles, the tiny stirrup (weighing only about 1.2 milligrams), acts on the fluid like a piston, driving it back and forth in the rhythm of the sound pressure. These movements of the fluid force into vibration a thin membrane, called the basilar membrane. The latter in turn finally transmits the stimulus to the organ of Corti, a complex structure which contains the endings of the auditory nerves. The question im-

mediately comes up: Why is this long and complicated chain of transmission necessary?

The reason is that we have a formidable mechanical problem if we are to extract the utmost energy from the sound waves striking the eardrum. Usually when a sound hits a solid surface, most of its energy is reflected away. The problem the ear has to solve is to absorb this energy. To do so it has to act as a kind of mechanical transformer, converting the large amplitude of the sound pressure waves in the air into more forceful vibrations of smaller amplitude. A hydraulic press is such a transformer: it multiplies the pressure acting on the surface of a piston by concentrating the force of the pressure upon a second piston of smaller area. The middle ear acts exactly like a hydraulic press: the tiny footplate of the stirrup transforms the small pressure on the surface of the eardrum into a 22-fold greater pressure on the fluid of the inner ear. In this way the

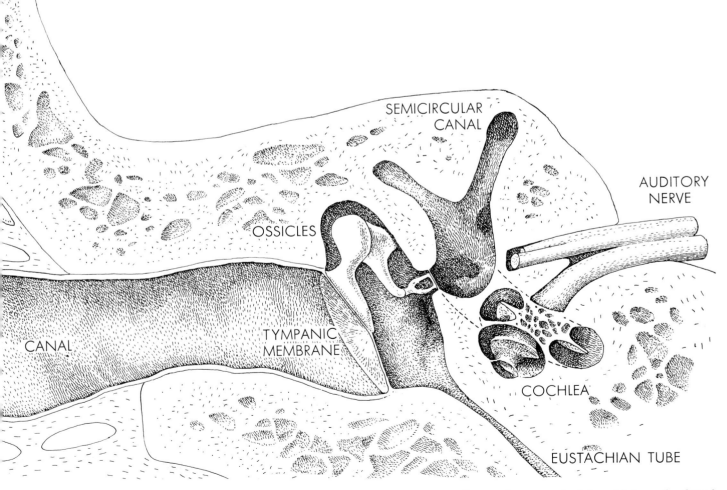

tween the eardrum (tympanic membrane) and the fluid-filled inner ear are the three small bones (ossicles) of the middle ear. The auditory nerve endings are in an organ (*not shown*) between the plate of bone which spirals up the cochlea and the outer wall of the cochlea.

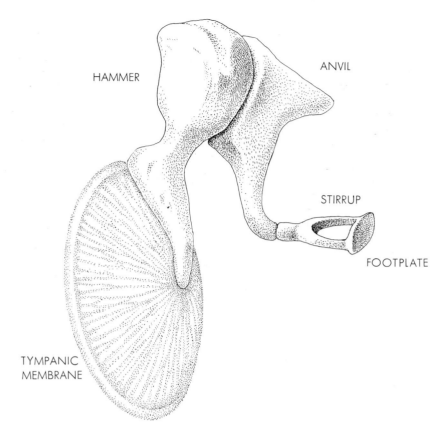

THREE OSSICLES transmit the vibrations of the tympanic membrane to the inner ear. The footplate of stirrup, surrounded by a narrow membrane, presses against inner-ear fluid.

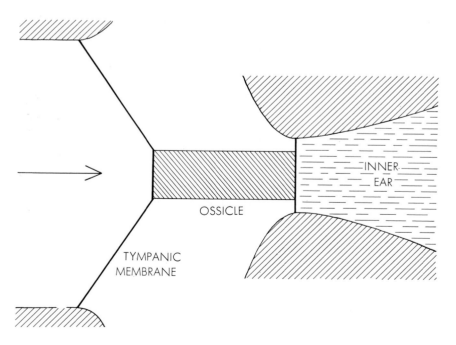

HOW OSSICLES ACT as a piston pressing against the fluid of the inner ear is indicated by this drawing. Pressure of the vibrations of tympanic membrane are amplified 22 times.

ear absorbs the greater part of the sound energy and transmits it to the inner ear without much loss.

But it needs another transformer to amplify the pressure of the fluid into a still larger force upon the tissues to which the nerves are attached. I think the ear's mechanism for this purpose is very ingenious indeed. It is based on the fact that a flat membrane, stretched to cover the opening of a tube, has a lateral tension along its surface. This tension can be increased tremendously if pressure is applied to one side of the membrane. And that is the function of the organ of Corti. It is constructed in such a way that pressure on the basilar membrane is transformed into shearing forces many times larger on the other side of the organ [*see diagram at bottom of opposite page*]. The enhanced shearing forces rub upon extremely sensitive cells attached to the nerve endings.

The eardrum is not by any means the only avenue through which we hear. We also hear through our skull, which is to say, by bone conduction. When we click our teeth or chew a cracker, the sounds come mainly by way of vibrations of the skull. Some of the vibrations are transmitted directly to the inner ear, by-passing the middle ear. This fact helps in the diagnosis of hearing difficulties. If a person can hear bone-conducted sounds but is comparatively deaf to air-borne sounds, we know that the trouble lies in the middle ear. But if he hears no sound by bone conduction, then his auditory nerves are gone, and there is no cure for his deafness. This is an old test, long used by deaf musicians. If a violin player cannot hear his violin even when he touches his teeth to the vibrating instrument, then he knows he suffers from nerve deafness, and there is no cure.

Speaking and Hearing

Hearing by bone conduction plays an important role in the process of speaking. The vibrations of our vocal cords not only produce sounds which go to our ears via the air but also cause the body to vibrate, and the vibration of the jawbone is transmitted to the ear canal. When you hum with closed lips, the sounds you hear are to a large degree heard by bone conduction. (If you stop your ears with your fingers, the hum sounds much louder.) During speaking and singing, therefore, you hear two different sounds—one by bone conduction and the other by air conduction. Of course another listener hears only the air-conducted sounds. In these sounds

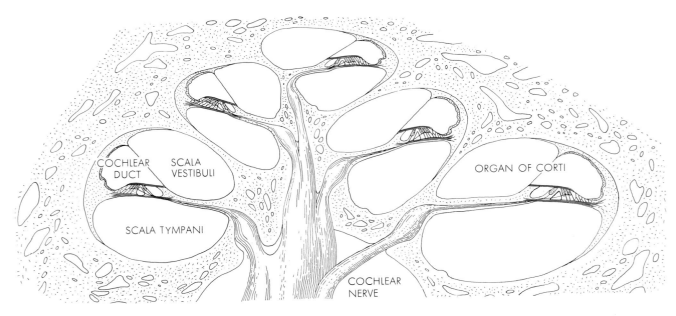

TUBE OF THE COCHLEA, coiled like the shell of a snail, is depicted in cross section. The plate of bone which appears in the cross section on pages 232–233 juts from the inside of the tube. Between it and the outside of the tube is the sensitive organ of Corti.

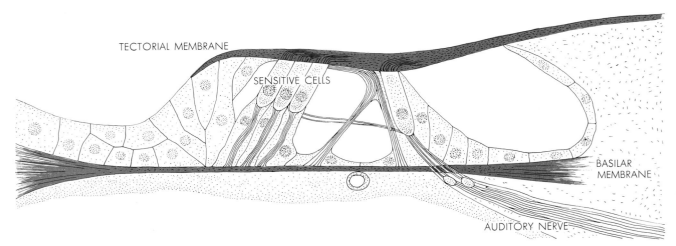

ORGAN OF CORTI lies between the basilar and tectorial membranes. Within it are sensitive cells which are attached to a branch of the auditory nerve (*lower right*). When fluid in scala tympani (*see drawing at top of page*) vibrates, these cells are stimulated.

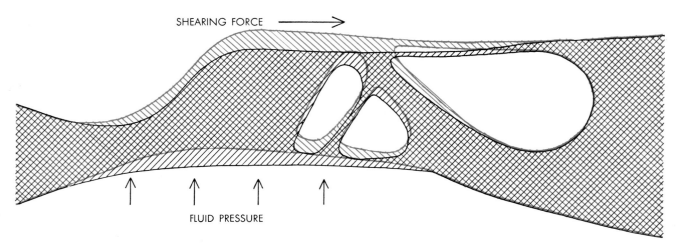

HOW VIBRATION FORCES ARE AMPLIFIED by the organ of Corti is indicated by this drawing. When the vibration of the fluid in the scala tympani exerts a force on the basilar membrane, a larger shearing force is brought to bear on tectorial membrane.

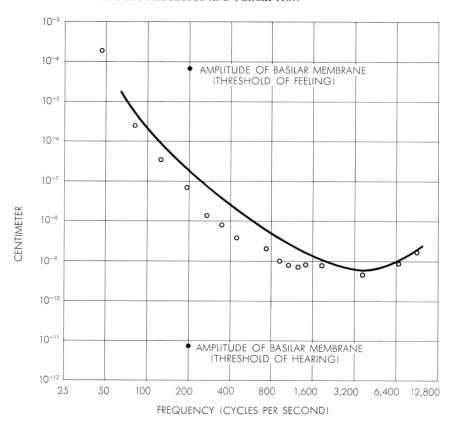

SENSITIVITY OF THE EAR is indicated by this curve, in which the amplitude of the vibrations of the tympanic membrane in fractions of a centimeter is plotted against the frequency of sound impinging on the membrane. Diameter of hydrogen atom is 10^{-8} centimeter.

cording of our voice may strike us as very thin and disappointing. From this point of view we have to admire the astonishing performance of an opera singer. The singer and the audience hear rather different sounds, and it is a miracle to me that they understand each other so well. Perhaps young singers would progress faster if during their training they spent more time studying recordings of their voices.

Feedback to the Voice

The control of speaking and singing involves a complicated feedback system. Just as feedback between the eyes and the muscles guides the hand when it moves to pick up an object, so feedback continually adjusts and corrects the voice as we speak or sing. When we start to sing, the beginning of the sound tells us the pitch, and we immediately adjust the tension of the vocal cords if the pitch is wrong. This feedback requires an exceedingly elaborate and rapid mechanism. How it works is not yet entirely understood. But it is small wonder that it takes a child years to learn to speak, or that it is almost impossible for an adult to learn to speak a foreign language with the native accents.

Any disturbance in the feedback immediately disturbs the speech. For instance, if, while a person is speaking, his speech is fed back to him with a time delay by means of a microphone and receivers at his ears, his pronunciation and accent will change, and if the delay interval is made long enough, he will find it impossible to speak at all.

some of the low-frequency components of the vocal cords' vibrations are lost. This explains why one can hardly recognize his own voice when he listens to a recording of his speech. As we normally hear ourselves, the low-frequency vibrations of our vocal cords, conducted to our own ears by the bones, make our speech sound much more powerful and dynamic than the pure sound waves heard by a second person or through a recording system. Consequently the re

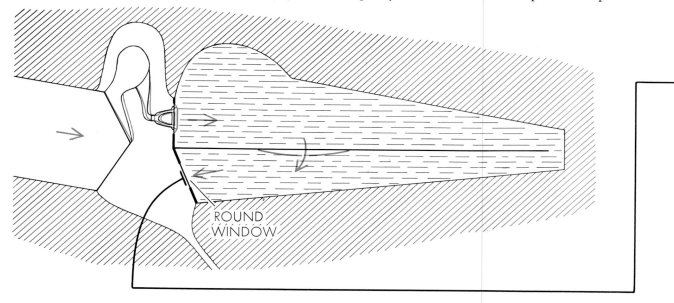

ELECTRICAL POTENTIALS of the microphonic type generated by the inner ear of an experimental animal can be detected by this arrangement. At left is a highly schematic diagram of the ear; the cochlea is represented in cross section by the fluid-filled chamber and the organ of Corti by the horizontal line in this chamber. When the vibrations of the eardrum are transmitted to the organ of Corti,

This phenomenon affords an easy test for exposing pretended deafness. If the subject can continue speaking normally in the face of a delayed feedback through the machine to his ears, we can be sure that he is really deaf.

The same technique can be used to assess the skill of a pianist. A piano player generally adjusts his touch to the acoustics of the room: if the room is very reverberant, so that the music sounds too loud, he uses a lighter touch; if the sound is damped by the walls, he strengthens his touch. We had a number of pianists play in a room where the damping could be varied, and recorded the amplitude of the vibrations of the piano's sounding board while the musicians played various pieces. When they played an easy piece, their adjustment to the acoustics was very clear: as the sound absorption of the room was increased, the pianist played more loudly, and when the damping on the walls was taken away, the pianist's touch became lighter. But when the piece was difficult, many of the pianists concentrated so hard on the problems of the music that they failed to adjust to the feedback of the room. A master musician, however, was not lost to the sound effects. Taking the technical difficulties of the music in stride, he was able to adjust the sound level to the damping of the room with the same accuracy as for an easy piece. Our rating of the pianists by this test closely matched their reputation among musical experts.

In connection with room acoustics, I should like to mention one of the ear's most amazing performances. How is it

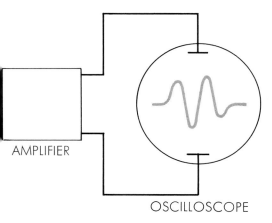

AMPLIFIER

OSCILLOSCOPE

INDIFFERENT ELECTRODE IN THE MUSCLE

its microphonic potentials can be picked up at the round window of the cochlea and displayed on the face of an oscilloscope (*right*).

that we can locate a speaker, even without seeing him, in a bare-walled room where reflections of his voice come at us from every side? This is an almost unbelievable performance by the ear. It is as if, looking into a room completely lined with mirrors, we saw only the real figure and none of the hundreds of reflected images. The eye cannot suppress the reflections, but the ear can. The ear is able to ignore all the sounds except the first that strikes it. It has a built-in inhibitory mechanism.

Suppressed Sounds

One of the most important factors that subordinate the reflected sounds is the delay in their arrival; necessarily they come to the ear only after the sound that has traveled directly from the speaker to the listener. The reflected sounds reinforce the loudness and tone volume of the direct sound, and perhaps even modify its localization, but by and large, they are not distinguishable from it. Only when the delay is appreciable does a reflected sound appear as a separate unit—an echo. Echoes often are heard in a large church, where reflections may lag more than half a second behind the direct sound. They are apt to be a problem in a concert hall. Dead walls are not desirable, because the music would sound weak. For every size of concert room there is an optimal compromise on wall reflectivity which will give amplification to the music but prevent disturbing echoes.

In addition to time delay, there are other factors that act to inhibit some sounds and favor others. Strong sounds generally suppress weaker ones. Sounds in which we are interested take precedence over those that concern us less, as I pointed out in the examples of the speaker in a noisy room and the orchestra conductor detecting an errant instrument. This brings us to the intimate collaboration between the ear and the nervous system.

Any stimulation of the ear (*e.g.*, any change in pressure) is translated into electrical messages to the brain via the nerves. We can therefore draw information about the ear from an analysis of these electrical impulses, now made possible by electronic instruments. There are two principal types of electric potential that carry the messages. One is a continuous, wavelike potential which has been given the name microphonic. In experimental animals such as guinea pigs and cats the microphonics are large enough to be easily measured (they range up to about half a millivolt). It

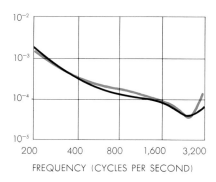
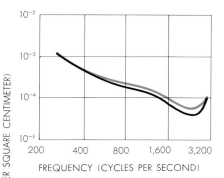
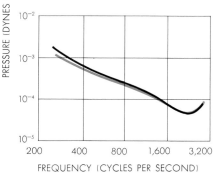
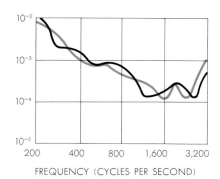

AUDIOGRAMS plot the threshold of hearing (in terms of pressure on the tympanic membrane) against the frequency of sound. The first three audiograms show the threshold for three members of the same family; the fourth, the threshold for an unrelated person. The black curves represent the threshold for one ear of the subject; the colored curves, for the other ear of the same subject. The audiogram curves indicate that in normal hearing the threshold in both ears, and the threshold in members of the same family, are remarkably similar.

238

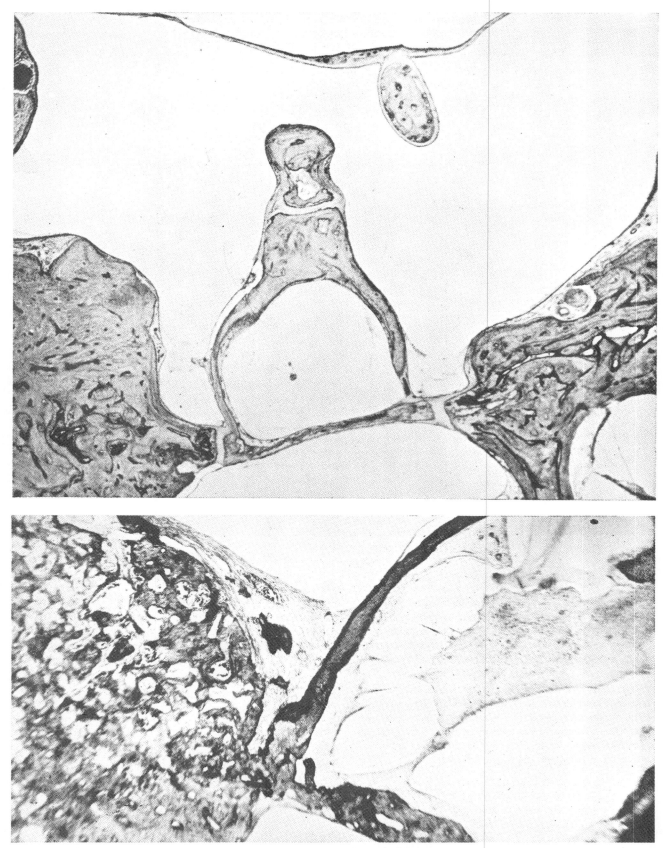

STIRRUP of the normal human ear is enlarged 19 times in the photograph at the top of this page. The thin line at the top of the photograph is the tympanic membrane seen in cross section. The hammer and anvil do not appear. The narrow membrane around the footplate of the stirrup may be seen as a translucent area between the footplate and the surrounding bone. The photograph at the bottom shows the immobilized footplate of an otosclerotic ear. In this photograph only the left side of the stirrup appears; the footplate is the dark area at the bottom center. The membrane around the footplate has been converted into a rigid bony growth.

has turned out that the magnitude of the microphonics produced in the inner ear is directly proportional to the displacements of the stirrup footplate that set the fluid in the inner ear in motion. The microphonics therefore permit us to determine directly to what extent the sound pressure applied to the eardrum is transmitted to the inner ear, and they have become one of the most useful tools for exploring sound transmission in the middle ear. For instance, there used to be endless discussion of the simple question: Just how much does perforation of the eardrum affect hearing? The question has now been answered with mathematical precision by experiments on animals. A hole of precisely measured size is drilled in the eardrum, and the amount of hearing loss is determined by the change in the microphonics. This type of observation on cats has shown that a perforation about one millimeter in diameter destroys hearing at the frequencies below 100 cycles per second but causes almost no impairment of hearing in the range of frequencies above 1,000 cycles per second. From studies of the physical properties of the human ear we can judge that the findings on animals apply fairly closely to man also.

The second type of electric potential takes the form of sharp pulses, which appear as spikes in the recording instrument. The sound of a sharp click produces a series of brief spikes; a pure tone generates volleys of spikes, generally in the rhythm of the period of the tone. We can follow the spikes along the nerve pathways all the way from the inner ear up to the cortex of the brain. And when we do, we find that stimulation of specific spots on the membrane of the inner ear seems to be projected to corresponding spots in the auditory area of the cortex. This is reminiscent of the projection of images on the retina of the eye to the visual area of the brain. But in the case of the ear the situation must be more complex, because there are nerve branches leading to the opposite ear and there seem to be several auditory projection areas on the surface of the brain. At the moment research is going on to find out how the secondary areas function and what their purpose is.

Detecting Pitch

The orderly projection of the sensitive area of the inner ear onto the higher brain levels is probably connected with the resolution of pitch. The ear itself can analyze sounds and separate one tone from another. There are limits to this

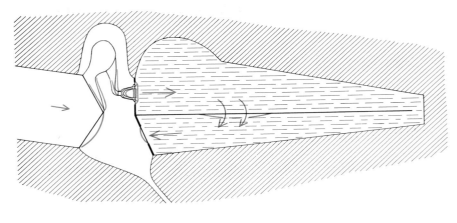

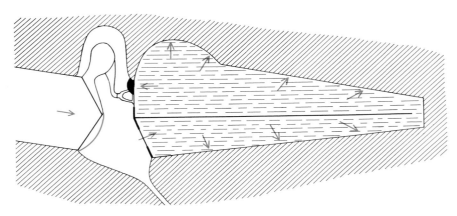

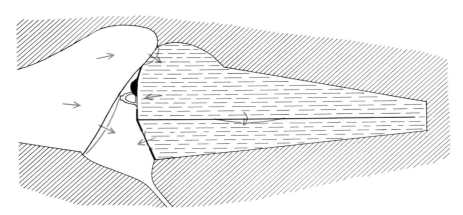

FENESTRATION OPERATION can alleviate the effects of otosclerosis. The drawing at the top schematically depicts the normal human ear as described in the caption for the illustration on page 236 and 237. The pressure on the components of the ear is indicated by the colored arrows. The drawing in the middle shows an otosclerotic ear; the otosclerotic growth is represented as a black protuberance. Because the stirrup cannot move, the pressure on the tympanic membrane is transmitted to the organ of Corti only through the round window of the cochlea; and because the fluid in the cochlea is incompressible, the organ of Corti cannot vibrate. The drawing at the bottom shows how the fenestration operation makes a new window into the cochlea to permit the organ of Corti to vibrate freely.

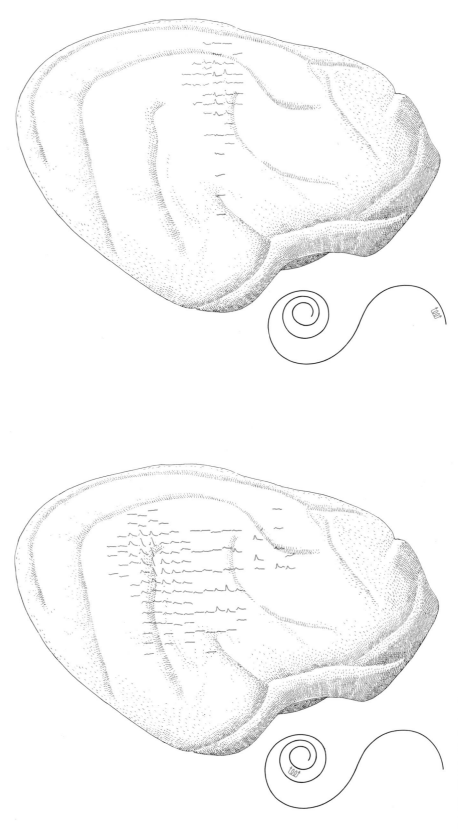

NERVE IMPULSES due to the electrical stimulation of the organ of Corti were localized on the surface of the brain of a cat. The spirals below each of these drawings of a cat's brain represent the full length of the organ of Corti. The pairs of colored arrows on each spiral indicate the point at which the organ was stimulated. The colored peaks superimposed on the brains represent the electrical potentials detected by an electrode placed at that point.

ability, but if the frequencies of the tones presented are not too close together, they are discriminated pretty well. Long ago this raised the question: How is the ear able to discriminate the pitch of a tone? Many theories have been argued, but only within the last decade has it been possible to plan pertinent experiments.

In the low-frequency range up to 60 cycles per second the vibration of the basilar membrane produces in the auditory nerve volleys of electric spikes synchronous with the rhythm of the sound. As the sound pressure increases, the number of spikes packed into each period increases. Thus two variables are transmitted to the cortex: (1) the number of spikes and (2) their rhythm. These two variables alone convey the loudness and the pitch of the sound.

Above 60 cycles per second a new phenomenon comes in. The basilar membrane now begins to vibrate unequally over its area: each tone produces a maximal vibration in a different area of the membrane. Gradually this selectivity takes over the determination of pitch, for the rhythm of the spikes, which indicates the pitch at low frequencies, becomes irregular at the higher ones. Above 4,000 cycles per second pitch is determined entirely by the location of the maximal vibration amplitude along the basilar membrane. Apparently there is an inhibitory mechanism which suppresses the weaker stimuli and thus sharpens considerably the sensation around the maximum. This type of inhibition can also operate in sense organs such as the skin and the eye. In order to see sharply we need not only a sharp image of the object on the retina but also an inhibitory system to suppress stray light entering the eye. Otherwise we would see the object surrounded by a halo. The ear is much the same. Without inhibitory effects a tone would sound like a noise of a certain pitch but not like a pure tone.

We can sum up by saying that the basilar membrane makes a rough, mechanical frequency analysis, and the auditory nervous system sharpens the analysis in some manner not yet understood. It is a part of the general functioning of the higher nerve centers, and it will be understood only when we know more about the functioning of these centers. If the answer is found for the ear, it will probably apply to the other sense organs as well.

Deafness

Now let us run briefly over some of

the types of hearing disorders, which have become much more understandable as a result of recent experimental researches.

Infections of the ear used to be responsible for the overwhelming majority of the cases of deafness. Ten years ago in a large city hospital there was a death almost every day from such infections. Thanks to antibiotics, they can now be arrested, and, if treated in time, an ear infection is seldom either fatal or destructive of hearing, though occasionally an operation is necessary to scoop out the diseased part of the mastoid bone.

The two other principal types of deafness are those caused by destruction of the auditory nerves and by otosclerosis (a tumorous bone growth). Nerve deafness cannot be cured: no drug or mechanical manipulation or operation can restore the victim's hearing. But the impairment of hearing caused by otosclerosis can usually be repaired, at least in part.

Otosclerosis is an abnormal but painless growth in a temporal bone (*i.e.*, at the side of the skull, near the middle ear). If it does not invade a part of the ear that participates in the transmission of sound, no harm is done to the hearing. But if the growth happens to involve the stirrup footplate, it will reduce or even completely freeze the footplate's ability to make its piston-like movements; the vibrations of the eardrum then can no longer be transmitted to the inner ear. An otosclerotic growth can occur at any age, may slow down for many years, and may suddenly start up again. It is found more often in women than in men and seems to be accelerated by pregnancy.

Immobilization of the stirrup blocks the hearing of air-borne sound but leaves hearing by bone conduction unimpaired. This fact is used for diagnosis. A patient who has lost part of his hearing ability because of otosclerosis does not find noise disturbing to his understanding of speech; in fact, noise may even improve his discrimination of speech. There is an old story about a somewhat deaf English earl (in France it is a count) who trained his servant to beat a drum whenever someone else spoke, so that he could understand the speaker better. The noise of the drum made the speaker raise his voice to the earl's hearing range. For the hard-of-hearing earl the noise of the drum was tolerable, but for other listeners it masked what the speaker was saying, so that the earl enjoyed exclusive rights to his conversation.

Difficulty in hearing air-borne sound can be corrected by a hearing aid. Theoretically it should be possible to compensate almost any amount of such hearing loss, because techniques for amplifying sound are highly developed, particularly now with the help of the transistor. But there is a physiological limit to the amount of pressure amplification that the ear will stand. Heightening of the pressure eventually produces an unpleasant tickling sensation through its effect on skin tissue in the middle ear. The sensation can be avoided by using a bone-conduction earphone, pressed firmly against the surface of the skull, but this constant pressure is unpleasant to many people.

Operations

As is widely known, there are now operations (*e.g.*, "fenestration") which can cure otosclerotic deafness. In the 19th century physicians realized that if they could somehow dislodge or loosen the immobilized stirrup footplate, they might restore hearing. Experimenters in France found that they could sometimes free the footplate sufficiently merely by pressing a blunt needle against the right spot on the stirrup. Although it works only occasionally, the procedure seems so simple that it has recently had a revival of popularity in the U. S. If the maneuver is successful (and I am told that 30 per cent of these operations are) the hearing improves immediately. But unfortunately the surgeon cannot get a clear look at the scene of the operation and must apply the pushing force at random. This makes the operation something of a gamble, and the patient's hearing may not only fail to be improved but may even be reduced. Moreover, the operation is bound to be ineffectual when a large portion of the footplate is fixed. There are other important objections to the operation. After all, it involves the breaking of bone, to free the adhering part of the stirrup. I do not think that bone-breaking can be improved to a standard procedure. In any case, precision cutting seems to me always superior to breaking, in surgery as in mechanics. This brings us to the operation called fenestration.

For many decades it has been known that drilling a small opening, even the size of a pinhead, in the bony wall of the inner ear on the footplate side can produce a remarkable improvement in hearing. The reason, now well understood, is quite simple. If a hole is made in the bone and then covered again with a flexible membrane, movements of the fluid in, for instance, the lateral canal of the vestibular organ can be transmitted to the fluid of the inner ear, and so vibrations are once again communicable from the middle to the inner ear. In the typical present fenestration operation the surgeon bores a small hole in the canal wall with a dental drill and then covers the hole with a flap of skin. The operation today is a straightforward surgical procedure, and all its steps are under accurate control.

Hazards to Hearing

I want to conclude by mentioning the problem of nerve deafness. Many cases of nerve deafness are produced by intense noise, especially noise with high-frequency components. Since there is no cure, it behooves us to look out for such exposures. Nerve deafness creeps up on us slowly, and we are not as careful as we should be to avoid exposure to intense noise. We should also be more vigilant about other hazards capable of producing nerve deafness, notably certain drugs and certain diseases.

We could do much to ameliorate the tragedy of deafness if we changed some of our attitudes toward it. Blindness evokes our instant sympathy, and we go out of our way to help the blind person. But deafness often goes unrecognized. If a deaf person misunderstands what we say, we are apt to attribute it to lack of intelligence instead of to faulty hearing. Very few people have the patience to help the deafened. To a deaf man the outside world appears unfriendly. He tries to hide his deafness, and this only brings on more problems.

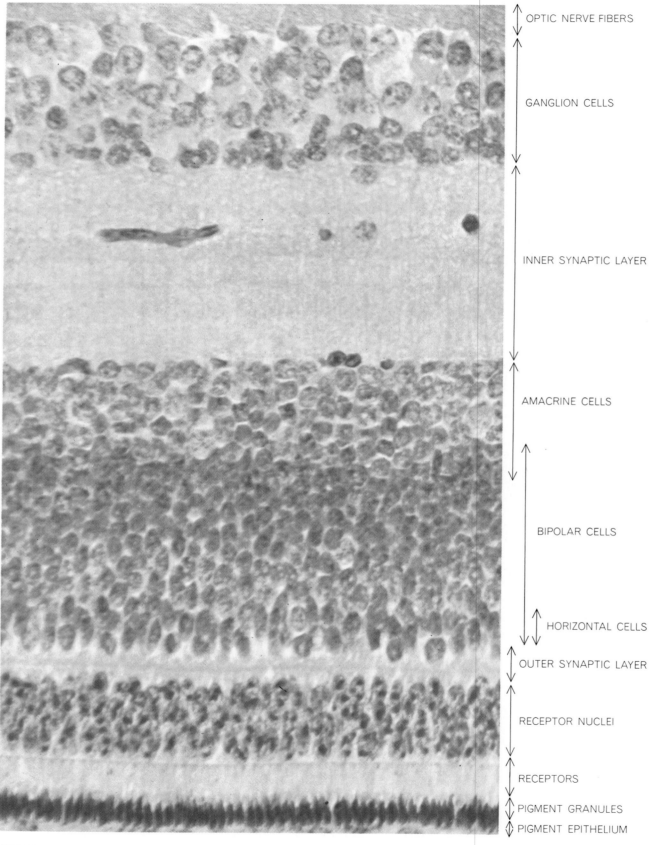

OPTIC NERVE FIBERS

GANGLION CELLS

INNER SYNAPTIC LAYER

AMACRINE CELLS

BIPOLAR CELLS

HORIZONTAL CELLS

OUTER SYNAPTIC LAYER

RECEPTOR NUCLEI

RECEPTORS

PIGMENT GRANULES

PIGMENT EPITHELIUM

RETINA of the ground squirrel is enlarged 800 diameters in a photomicrograph made by John E. Dowling of the Johns Hopkins University School of Medicine from a section prepared by Richard L. Sidman of the Harvard Medical School. Light striking the retina passes back (*down in the micrograph*) through the cell layers and is absorbed by visual pigments in the receptors. Depending on the pattern of retinal synapses, the resulting nerve activity excites or inhibits horizontal, bipolar and amacrine cells and ultimately the ganglion cells. The output of the ganglion cells constitutes all the information that is conducted to the brain along the optic nerve.

25

RETINAL PROCESSING OF VISUAL IMAGES

CHARLES R. MICHAEL
May 1969

In the eye of vertebrate animals an image of the external world is focused on the retina by the cornea and the lens. The light is absorbed by the visual pigments of the retinal receptor cells, the electrical activity of which varies with the quantity of light they receive. The conversion of light into electrical activity is not the only function of the retina, however. The retina is more than just the biological equivalent of a photographic emulsion. The transformation of the visual image into nerve impulses traveling along the optic nerve calls for a considerable amount of processing. Activity in the optic nerve is not related simply to the intensity of illumination falling on each retinal receptor but rather to specific aspects of the visual image, and some aspects are emphasized at the expense of others. The information transmitted to the brain is related not so much to patterns of light and dark as to such properties as contrast at borders, the movement of an object or its color.

It is now clear that the degree of retinal transformation varies among species. Curiously, the degree of transformation does not parallel the evolutionary development of the vertebrates. For example, the retina of primates (monkeys, apes and man) is simpler in terms of both anatomy and physiology than the retina of the frog. On the other hand, some mammals, such as the rabbit and the ground squirrel, have retinas that are almost as complex as the frog's. In each species there is a close correlation between the anatomy and the physiology of the retina. Furthermore, there appears to be a direct relation between the complexity of an animal's retina and the development of the visual centers of its brain.

A brief description of the structure and interactions of neurons, or nerve cells, is necessary for a clear understanding of the retina's organization and operation. A number of fine processes called dendrites radiate from the cell body of each neuron [*see illustration below*]. In addition there usually is a single long process—an axon—that extends some distance from the cell body. Messages, in the form of brief electrical nerve impulses that vary in frequency but not in amplitude, travel from the cell body along the axon to its endings, which come in contact with the dendrites or the cell body of another neuron at junctions known as synapses. Information is transmitted from one neuron to another at the synapses, usually by the release of a chemical substance from tiny vesicles, or sacs, in the axon endings. The release of the chemical is initiated by the arrival of a nerve impulse.

There are two basic types of chemical synapse. In one type the substance diffusing from the axon has an excitatory effect on the dendrite or cell body beyond the synapse and makes it more likely that the postsynaptic cell will discharge. In the other type the chemical has an inhibitory effect on the postsynaptic process and renders the cell less likely to discharge. The interplay of the excitatory and the inhibitory synaptic activity impinging on a single cell strongly influences its pattern of discharge.

In the vertebrate retina the cell bodies of the neurons are arrayed in three distinct layers [*see illustration on opposite page*]. The outermost layer (the one farthest from the lens of the eye) consists of the receptor cells containing the light-absorbing visual pigments. The next layer includes the bipolar cells (which conduct messages from the receptors to the cells in the third layer) and the horizontal and amacrine cells, which appear to be involved in the lateral transmission of information. The third layer contains the ganglion cells, whose axons form the optic nerve, the sole output of the retina. In between the three layers of cell bodies are two synaptic layers in which the different cell processes come in close contact. One might think a system containing only two layers of synapses and five types of cell could not accomplish much in terms of the analysis of the retinal image. The richness of the synaptic connections in the retina, however, makes possible a variety of integrative mechanisms.

John E. Dowling of the Wilmer Ophthalmological Institute of the Johns Hopkins University School of Medicine has

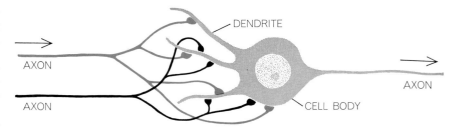

INFORMATION is transmitted from an axon ending of one nerve cell to the cell body or dendrite of another by a chemical transmitter substance that diffuses across the synaptic gap. Impulses from an excitatory cell (*color*) tend to make the cell beyond the synapse (*gray*) fire. Impulses from inhibitory endings (*black*) make it less likely that the cell will fire.

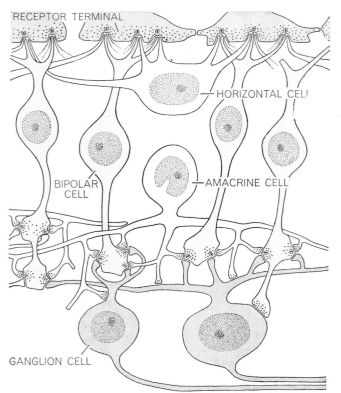

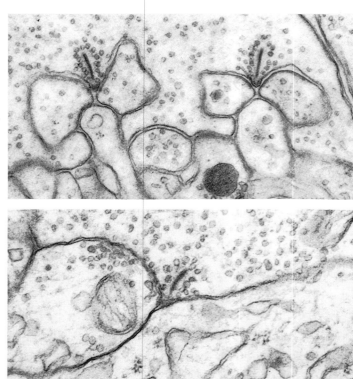

PRIMATE RETINA'S synaptic organization is diagrammed (*left*) on the basis of electron micrographs made by Dowling, two of which are reproduced (*middle*) and mapped (*right*). Two "ribbon" synapses in the base of a receptor in a monkey's retina are enlarged 45,000 diameters (*top*); at each of them a bipolar-cell dendrite and two horizontal-cell processes make contact. The small spheroidal objects are sacs containing transmitter substances. An axon ending of a bipolar cell in a human retina, enlarged 35,000

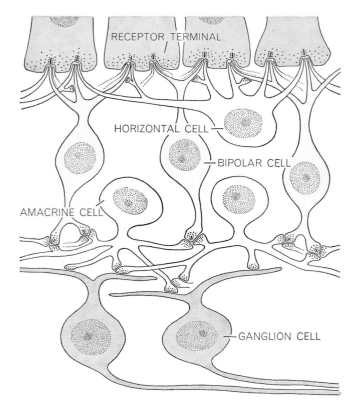

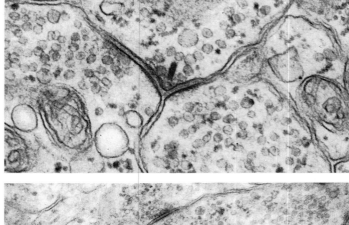

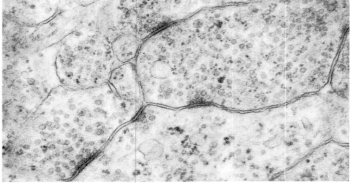

FROG RETINA'S synaptic contacts are illustrated. In the two electron micrographs a bipolar-cell axon (enlarged 60,000 diameters) synapses with two amacrine-cell processes (*top*), and four amacrine cells (enlarged 30,000 diameters) synapse serially with one another (*bottom*). In the frog's retina horizontal cells not only connect receptors but also synapse on bipolar-cell processes.

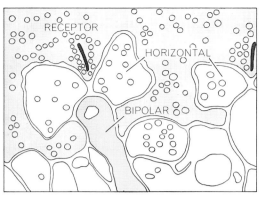

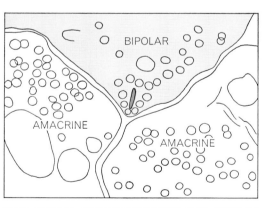

diameters (*bottom*), synapses with processes from an amacrine cell and a ganglion cell. In the primate retina the signal from a receptor is conducted directly to a ganglion cell.

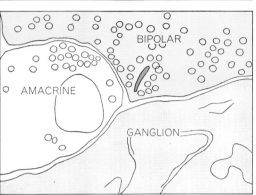

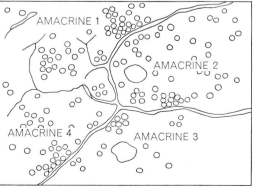

Signals from receptors are conducted not directly to ganglion cells but rather to amacrine cells and from them to ganglion cells.

carried out a detailed electron-microscope study of the synaptic organization of the retina [*see illustrations on these two pages*]. In the outer synaptic layer of all the retinas he has studied the terminals in the bases of the receptors form synapses with bipolar-cell dendrites and horizontal-cell processes. The horizontal cells connect neighboring receptors; the bipolar cells send information to the inner synaptic layer. In the retinas of the frog, the pigeon and the rabbit there are additional connections: horizontal-cell processes also form synapses with other horizontal cells and with bipolar-cell dendrites.

In the inner synaptic layer of the primate retina each bipolar terminal forms synapses with two processes, a ganglion-cell dendrite and an amacrine-cell process. The tangential processes of the amacrine cells extend as much as one millimeter along the inner synaptic layer and are most likely involved in the lateral transmission of information across the retina. In the inner synaptic layer of the frog's retina the bipolar terminals make contact only with amacrine cells, which in turn form synapses with ganglion cells; the frog's ganglion cells are therefore primarily influenced by amacrine rather than by bipolar cells. In fact, in the frog's retina anywhere from one to five amacrine cells may be interposed between a given bipolar cell and the ganglion cell with which it is associated. Through these serially arranged amacrine cells there is the possibility of considerable neural interaction in the inner synaptic layer of the frog.

It appears that it is primarily the pattern of organization in the two synaptic layers that distinguishes the retinas of different species. How is it that the retina of primates is simpler than that of the frog, an animal much lower on the evolutionary scale, and that the frog and the pigeon, which are widely separated in terms of overall development, have remarkably similar retinas? As we shall see, the synaptic complexity of these retinas is reflected in their analytical capacity.

By some unknown mechanism the absorption of light produces an electrical response in the receptors that is transmitted to the bipolar cells. These neurons in turn transmit information to the retinal ganglion cells, whose axons form the optic nerve. Since the optic nerve is the only connection between the retina and the brain, the information it carries represents the total integrative capacity of the retina. It would be ideal if one could study the electrical activity

of each of the five types of neuron in the retina and thus learn the function of each and how they interact with one another. Unfortunately it is difficult to record the electrical activity of any individual neurons in the retina other than the ganglion cells. Most investigators have therefore studied ganglion cells or their axons, the individual fibers of the optic nerve. This type of study enables one to determine the overall analytical powers of a retina, and in some cases to deduce the individual steps of the processing.

A given retinal ganglion cell receives information from a rather small population of receptor cells. The area covered by these receptors is called the receptive field of that ganglion cell. In other words, the receptive field of a cell in the visual system is the area of the retina that, when stimulated, influences the electrical activity of the cell in either an excitatory or an inhibitory manner. In an experiment a microelectrode is inserted into the retina or the optic nerve of an anesthetized animal until the electrical activity of a single ganglion cell or optic nerve fiber is recorded. The eye is presented with a series of test stimuli, projected directly onto the retina or onto a white screen the animal is facing, while the microelectrode is simultaneously advanced through the optic nerve or the retina. Often it is necessary to try a large variety of stimuli before finding the one that will evoke the strongest response from a cell. The search may take several hours, but in all cases it is eventually possible to map a cell's receptive field and define precisely the type of stimulus to which it responds.

In 1938 H. K. Hartline, working at the University of Pennsylvania, studied the receptive fields of the frog's ganglion cells and for the first time succeeded in mapping the receptive fields of cells in a visual system. (For such pioneering investigations Hartline received a Nobel prize in 1967.) In 1953 Stephen W. Kuffler, then at the Wilmer Institute, found that the receptive fields of the cat's retinal ganglion cells were organized in a concentric manner, with a circular central area surrounded by a ring-shaped outer zone. In some instances a spot of light in the central region excited a cell (an "on" response), whereas light falling on the surround inhibited any spontaneous discharge and a burst of impulses followed when the illumination ceased (an "off" response). In other cells the situation was reversed: illumination of the center produced an "off" response, and stimulation of the surround an "on" response. Stimuli that simultaneously covered both the center and the surround had little effect on a cell's discharge. What each of these ganglion cells was doing, in other words, was comparing the illumination of the center of its receptive field with that of the surround. Ganglion cells with this type of receptive field have been found in the retinas of every vertebrate that has been studied.

Several years later Jerome Y. Lettvin and his colleagues at the Massachusetts Institute of Technology decided to re-examine the receptive fields of ganglion cells in the retina of the frog. They found that the frog's retina is much more complex than the cat's. It appears to have at least five classes of ganglion cells, including some that respond only to convex edges or only to changes in contrast. For example, the convex-edge detectors re-spond to the positive curvature of an edge that is darker than the background. Straight edges are poor stimuli, but any perceptible convexity or projecting angle evokes a discharge; in general, the great-er the curvature of the edge, the larger the response.

These cells respond to moving stimuli as well as to those that are stationary within the receptive field. The response to a stationary dark spot lasts for many minutes, but it ceases immediately when the background light is turned off and does not appear again when it is turned on. Similarly, when a stimulus is brought into the receptive field in total darkness and the background light is then turned on, there is no response. Apparently an additional requirement for the discharge of these cells is that the object be "seen" during its movement into the field.

The frog is primarily interested in catching flying insects, and so most of its ganglion cells, including the convex-edge detectors, are organized to respond to small moving objects. Cells with such sophisticated discriminatory properties have never been seen in the cat's retina. The complexity of the ganglion cells' be-havior in the frog may be related to the extensive serial synapses among ama-crine cells interposed between the bi-polar axons and the ganglion-cell den-drites.

For the past 10 years David H. Hubel and Torsten N. Wiesel of the Harvard Medical School have been studying the receptive fields of cells in the visual sys-tem of cats and monkeys [see the article "The Visual Cortex of the Brain," by David H. Hubel beginning on page 253].

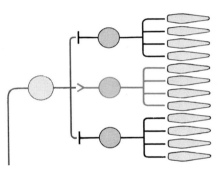
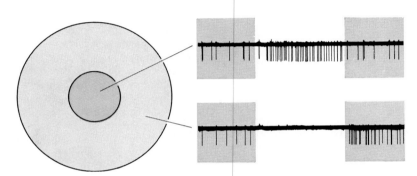

CONTRAST-SENSITIVE ganglion cells in the cat's retina have fields with a concentric organization. The oscilloscope records (*right*) show that a spot of light in the center of the receptive field (*middle*) of this "on"-center ganglion cell excites the cell; stimu-lation of the surround inhibits it. (The responses would be re-versed if this were an "off"-center cell.) Presumably there are two types of bipolar cell, excitatory (*color*) and inhibitory (*black*), that collect information from receptors in the two parts of the field (*left*).

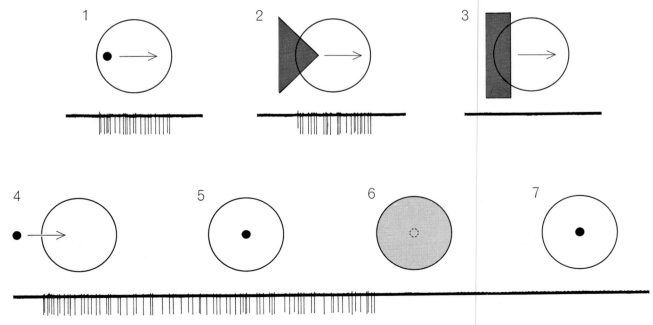

CONVEX-EDGE DETECTORS in the frog's retina respond to a moving stimulus that has a positive curvature (1) or contains an angle (2) but not to a moving straight edge (3). The response to an object entering the field (4) continues when the object stops within the field (5). The response ceases when the background light goes off (6) and does not recur if the light goes on again (7).

In the course of their investigations farther along the visual pathway they have found that the receptive fields of neurons in the visual cortex of the brain are organized so that the cells are most sensitive to line stimuli, such as white or black bars or straight edges separating light areas from dark ones. In all cases the size, shape, position and orientation of the stimulus is highly critical for an optimum response.

So far Hubel and Wiesel have identified three major classes of form-sensitive cortical cells [see illustrations at right]. The first, called simple cells, have receptive fields that can be mapped with stationary stimuli. The fields are subdivided into excitatory and inhibitory regions separated by boundaries that are straight and parallel. The neurons next highest in order, the complex cells, have receptive fields that cannot be mapped into "on" and "off" regions and are best studied with moving stimuli. Unlike the simple cells, the complex ones respond with sustained firing to movement throughout their receptive fields, and the response is usually directionally selective.

The highest order of cortical neurons studied, the hypercomplex cells, are most effectively activated by a properly oriented line stimulus that is limited in its length at one end or both ends. The receptive fields consist of a central orientation-sensitive "activation" area flanked on one side or on opposite sides by orientation-sensitive "antagonistic" regions. The hypercomplex cells respond only to moving stimuli, again usually in a directionally selective manner. Cells with receptive fields of these three types occur only in the cortex of the cat and the monkey, not in the retina. Moreover, of these three types of cortical cell only the hypercomplex ones have functional properties that approach in sophistication the retinal ganglion cells of the frog.

From the work of Kuffler, Lettvin, Hubel and Wiesel one might have concluded that it is only in lower animals such as frogs that the visual image is analyzed to a significant extent in the retina, and that cells with complicated response properties and receptive fields are found only at the cortical level in the mammalian visual system. Recent investigations—by Horace B. Barlow and William R. Levick at the University of California at Berkeley on the rabbit's retina and by me at Harvard University and Johns Hopkins on the retina of the ground squirrel—make it clear that such a conclusion is not justified. In certain mammals complex analysis of sensory information does occur in the retina, be-

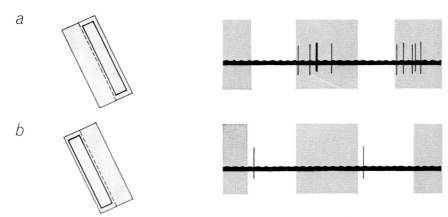

SIMPLE CELL in the cat's visual cortex has a field with excitatory (color) and inhibitory regions separated by straight, parallel boundaries. This one gives an "off" response to a slit stimulus in one region (a) and a small "on" response to a stimulus in the other region (b).

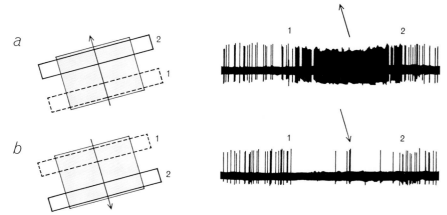

COMPLEX CELL in the cat's cortex responds continuously to a properly oriented stimulus moving across its entire field. This spontaneously active cell responds vigorously to movement in one direction (a) and is largely inhibited by movement in the other direction (b).

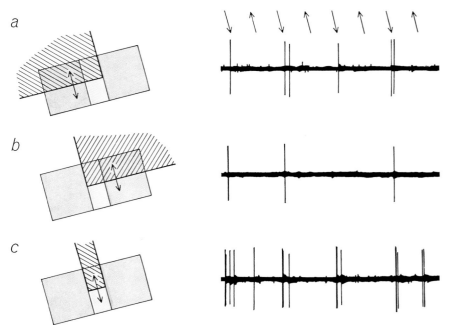

HYPERCOMPLEX CELL has a field with a central activation region (color) and antagonistic flanks (gray). It responds best to stimuli that are limited in length. Here the longer stimuli affect both kinds of region (a, b), the most limited one only the activation area (c).

fore the neural activity moves on to the higher nervous centers. Some mammalian retinas, in fact, appear to be capable of a complexity of neural integration that in the cat and the monkey is attained only in the visual cortex.

We find that the retina of the rabbit and that of the ground squirrel (*Citellus mexicanus*) contain many types of ganglion cell, each specifically sensitive to a particular aspect of the stimulus such as color, convex edges or oriented lines. The most thoroughly investigated of these cells are the directionally selective neurons found in both animals. They are vigorously excited by a stimulus moving in one direction (the "preferred" direction) across their receptive fields and are inhibited by motion in the reverse direction (the "null" direction). The directionally selective response is independent of the velocity of movement of the stimulus, its shape, the contrast between it and the background and the level of the background illumination [*see upper illustration below*]. Smaller stimuli are more effective than larger ones, indicating that a powerful antagonistic region surrounds the center of the receptive field. The activity of these cells would seem to provide a basis for discriminating the direction of motion of small objects in the animal's visual field.

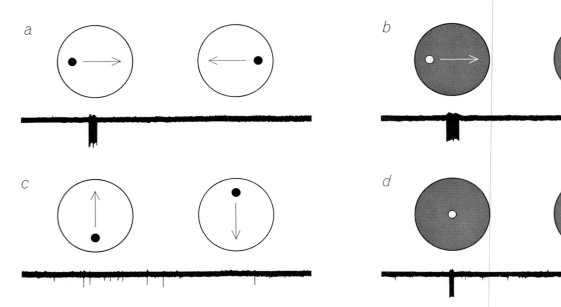

DIRECTIONALLY SELECTIVE ganglion cells in the ground squirrel's retina respond to movement in one direction but not in the opposite direction (*a*). A change in contrast makes no difference (*b*). Movement at a right angle does not produce a clear response (*c*). A stationary spot evokes a brief discharge when the light goes on and another discharge when the light goes off (*d*).

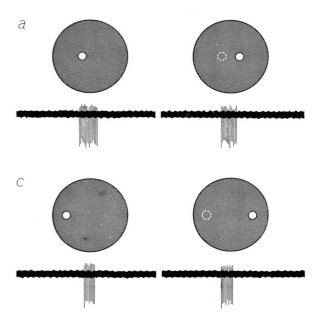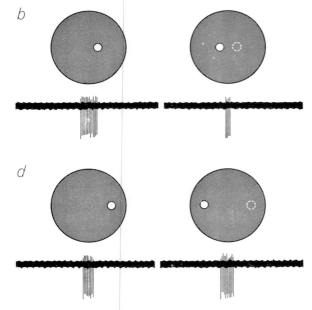

SEQUENCE-DISCRIMINATION is the basis of directional selectivity. When two spots close together are flashed sequentially in the preferred direction, there is a good "on-off" response to each flash (*a*). (In this illustration only "on" responses are shown.) When they are flashed in the opposite direction, the response to the second flash is much weakened (*b*), apparently because of inhibition from the first flash. When the two spots are farther apart, however, the sequence of illumination makes no difference (*c*, *d*).

We have established that this directional selectivity is accomplished primarily by an inhibitory mechanism. The most direct evidence for inhibition was the cessation of the discharge of spontaneously active units during null movements. Most of the directionally sensitive ganglion cells are not spontaneously active, however. For such "quiet" cells a light spot anywhere in the field center produced a short burst of impulses when it was turned on and another when it was turned off; if the same spot was moved in the null direction, it produced no such response—even though the movement of its leading and trailing edges should be equivalent to the turning on and off of a stationary spot. Apparently a wave of inhibition precedes the null-moving stimulus, preventing or counteracting an excitatory response that would occur if the spot were stationary.

By working with two independent stationary stimuli instead of one moving stimulus we learned more about the inhibitory mechanism and its spatial extent. When two small white spots were positioned next to each other on the directional axis, each spot by itself produced the expected "on-off" response [see bottom illustration on opposite page]. When the spots were flashed sequentially in the preferred direction, the response to the second spot was as large as or larger than the response to the first one. When they were flashed sequentially in the null direction, however, only the first spot produced a strong "on-off" discharge; the second response was weak or absent. Apparently any potential response to the second spot was partially or completely inhibited by the first flash. It must therefore be the sequence of changes in the illumination of points along the directional axis that determines the response to a moving stimulus.

The next step was to move the two white spots away from each other. When the separation was small, there was a clear indication of inhibition for the null sequence of illumination. When the separation reached 20 minutes of arc, however, the second response was as strong as the first regardless of the sequence of illumination. This showed that the complete mechanism for discriminating the sequence of excitation is contained within an area extending about 15 minutes of arc along the directional axis, a distance corresponding to about 30 microns (30 thousandths of a millimeter) on the retina. Since the diameter of the field centers ranged between 30 and 60 minutes of arc, the mechanism

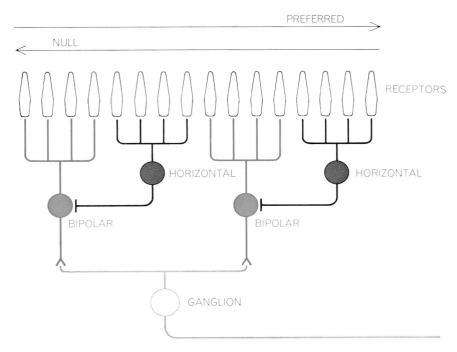

MECHANISM for directional selectivity is suggested. Each bipolar cell is connected to two groups of receptors—to one directly and to the other by way of an inhibitory horizontal cell. A stimulus moving to the right (preferred direction) excites the bipolar cells, which in turn excite the ganglion cell. A stimulus moving to the left (null direction), however, first excites the horizontal cells, inhibiting any subsequent response from the bipolar cells.

for directional selectivity clearly does not require movement over the entire center in order to operate effectively.

Barlow and Levick proposed a mechanism to explain the directional selectivity of these cells, and their conclusions were confirmed and extended by my own work on the ground squirrel's retina. The results from both laboratories suggest that a directionally selective ganglion cell must be excited by a group of sequence-discriminating subunits that share the same preferred direction of motion. This must be the case because the experiments with two spots showed that sequence discrimination involved distances considerably smaller than the size of the ganglion cell's field center. The directionally selective mechanism must therefore be located at an earlier stage than the retinal ganglion cells, and it seems likely that the bipolar cells are the subunits.

Suppose a given bipolar cell is connected to two groups of receptors, to one set directly and to the other by way of an interneuron, probably a horizontal cell [see illustration above]. The receptors have an excitatory effect on the horizontal or bipolar cell with which they are in contact, but the horizontal cell makes an inhibitory synapse with the bipolar cell. The sequence of excitation of the two populations of receptors will

determine the response of the bipolar cell. A stimulus moving in the preferred direction will first excite the bipolar cell through the directly connected receptors. Although the horizontal cell will subsequently be activated, its inhibitory effect will be too late to prevent the bipolar cell's excitatory response. A spot moving in the null direction, on the other hand, will first stimulate the receptors connected to the horizontal cell, thereby inhibiting the bipolar-cell activity that would otherwise be excited by the directly connected receptors. Thus the bipolar cells distinguish between the null and the preferred sequences of excitation of the two neighboring receptor populations with which they are associated. A ganglion cell receives excitatory inputs from a number of these sequence-discriminating bipolar cells and therefore is itself excited by preferred motion. Since any spontaneous discharges by ganglion cells are inhibited by null movement, such spontaneous activity is probably produced by a constant excitatory bombardment from the bipolar cells. Any null movement inhibits the bipolar cells, and so the spontaneous activity of the ganglion cell ceases.

This proposed mechanism needs further study, but so far it is supported by all the physiological experiments performed independently in Barlow's laboratory and in my own. Moreover, the theory's requirement of connections between horizontal and bipolar cells receives anatomical confirmation from Dowling's discovery of horizontal-cell processes in the rabbit's retina that synapse on the dendrites and cell bodies of the bipolar cells. The lateral extent of these processes is in the same range as the dimensions of the subunit systems, measured physiologically. To be sure, these are preliminary microscopic observations, but the organization of the rabbit's outer synaptic layer does seem to support the proposed mechanism for directional selectivity.

Let us now turn to another aspect of the visual image, the perception of color. It is surely one of the most fascinating sensory capacities man possesses,

and he shares it with few other animals. Among the mammals only man and some of the Old World monkeys have complete color vision as we know it; some New World monkeys, the tree shrew and the ground squirrel have partial color vision. Any animal that does see color must have two or more visual pigments in its retina. These pigments are contained in the receptors called cones. (The other photoreceptor cells of vertebrates, the rods, function in dim illumination and their visual pigment is not involved in color perception.) Since the ground squirrel's retina contains only cones, it is not surprising that many of its ganglion cells code and relay color information.

The ground squirrel appears to have two cone visual pigments, one that absorbs maximally in the green region of

the spectrum and another that is most sensitive in the blue. The ganglion cells concerned with color coding are "opponent color" cells. They are either excited by green light and inhibited by blue or excited by blue light and inhibited by green. It seems probable that a given ganglion cell receives information from two classes of bipolar cells, one connected only with cones containing the green-sensitive pigment and the other only with cones containing the blue-sensitive pigment. Presumably one type of bipolar cell excites the ganglion cell and the other inhibits it. As one would expect, these ganglion cells are poorly responsive to white light, which contains all wavelengths and therefore stimulates both the excitatory and the inhibitory inputs.

A series of experiments revealed that

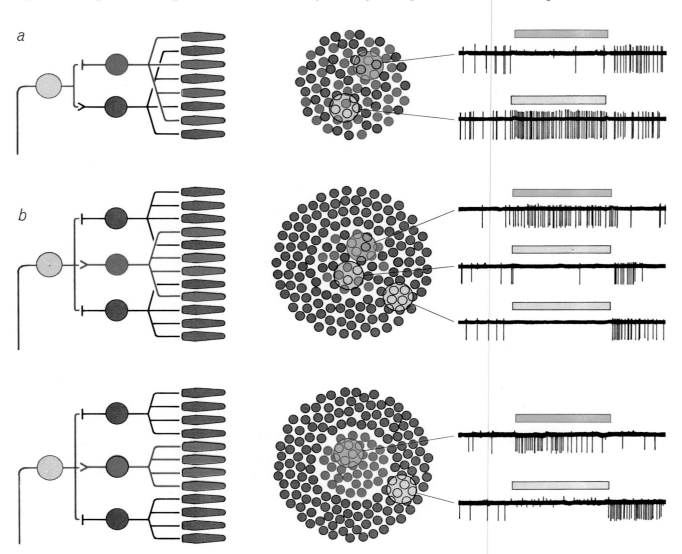

GROUND SQUIRREL'S RETINA seems to have two cone pigments, one more sensitive to green light and the other to blue (*shown here as gray*). Three types of color-coded ganglion cell (*left*) have been identified: some with receptive fields (*middle*) in which two cone populations overlap completely (*a*), some in which they are partially segregated (*b*) and some in which they are completely segregated (*c*). Probably each ganglion cell receives information from some bipolar cells connected to green-sensitive cones and others connected to blue-sensitive cones. The bipolar cells have opposite effects: one excites a ganglion cell and the other inhibits it.

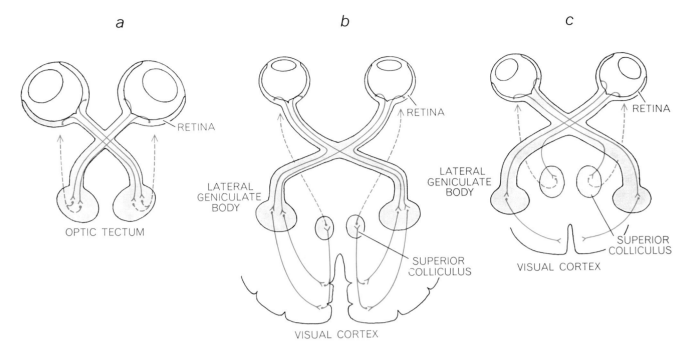

a

RETINA

OPTIC TECTUM

b

RETINA

LATERAL
GENICULATE
BODY

SUPERIOR
COLLICULUS

VISUAL CORTEX

c

RETINA

LATERAL
GENICULATE
BODY

SUPERIOR
COLLICULUS

VISUAL CORTEX

OPTIC NERVE FIBERS have different destinations in different species. The frog and the pigeon have no cortex, and almost all the fibers project to the optic tectum (*a*). In the cat and primates almost all the fibers go to the lateral geniculate nucleus, where signals are relayed to the well-developed visual cortex (*b*). The ground squirrel may be a special intermediate case. Some fibers (the more sophisticated, directionally selective ones) go to the superior colliculus; the remainder go to the lateral geniculate, which projects to the cortex (*c*). From the colliculus (or tectum) signals travel to the muscles controlling eye movement (*broken arrows*).

the receptive fields of the ground squirrel's opponent-color cells are divided into several classes [*see illustration on opposite page*]. In many cases the field seemed not to be organized into a center and a surround but instead gave opponent-color responses throughout its extent; apparently the green-sensitive and the blue-sensitive cones feeding into these cells had identical spatial distributions. Another class of cells had a field center and a surround; only the center received inputs from green-sensitive cones, whereas both the center and the surround were influenced by blue-sensitive cones. The third group also had a center-surround organization, but here the center was driven only by green-sensitive cones and the surround only by blue-sensitive ones; in this last type of field there was complete spatial separation of the two color systems.

The color-coded responses of ganglion cells were first studied in the goldfish by Edward F. MacNichol, Jr., of Johns Hopkins and Henry G. Wagner and Myron L. Wolbarsht of the Naval Medical Research Institute [see "Three-Pigment Color Vision," by Edward F. MacNichol, Jr.; SCIENTIFIC AMERICAN Offprint 197]. Recently Hubel and Wiesel have mapped the receptive fields of several types of opponent-color cells in the monkey's lateral geniculate nucleus, the neu-

ral way station between the retina and the visual cortex. In all the animals studied the receptive fields of most of the color-coded cells are organized in such a way that they can deal with both color and contrast information. In other words, there are opponent-color and opponent-spatial mechanisms influencing the activity of a single cell. This means that the optimum stimulus must be specified not only in terms of color but also in size and shape.

It appears to be a general rule that the retinal processing of information involves a comparison by a ganglion cell of the signals from two sets of receptors. What the contrast-sensitive units in the cat are doing is comparing the information received from receptors in the field center with information from other receptors located in the surround. The directionally selective cells in the rabbit's and the ground squirrel's retina are collecting data from subunits sensitive to the sequence in which two separate sets of receptors are illuminated. Finally, the opponent-color units in the ground squirrel are comparing the excitatory and inhibitory signals from two populations of cones that have different spectral sensitivities and often different spatial distributions. For each type of cell there is an antagonistic interaction of the excitatory and inhibitory effects of two groups

of receptors, and so a generalized stimulus is far less effective than one that is quite specific in contrast, movement or color.

One can see, then, that there are two principal types of visual system. The first is typified in the frog, the rabbit and the ground squirrel. (The work of Humberto R. Maturana in Chile on the pigeon's retina indicates that it too belongs in this group.) The individual ganglion cells of these animals are usually highly specialized in terms of stimulus requirements, and such fundamental variables as edges, color, contrast, orientation and directional movement are processed intensively within the retina. The second type of visual system is the one found in cats, monkeys and presumably man. Here the ganglion cells at the retinal level are concerned only with the simultaneous contrast between the centers and the surrounds of their receptive fields, and in some cases with color information. The aspects of edge detection, orientation and directional selectivity are dealt with only later in the visual cortex, and there in a most detailed and precise manner.

Why should some animals process visual information so intensively within the retina whereas others put off this integration until farther along the visual pathway? One major factor may be the presence or absence of a visual cortex and, if it is present, its level of development. The frog and the pigeon, for instance, have no visual cortex; almost all their optic nerve fibers go to the optic tectum. The cat and the monkey have a highly developed cortex; almost all their optic nerve fibers go to the lateral geniculate nucleus, whose neurons in turn project their axons to the visual cortex. The ground squirrel has a visual cortex, but it is one that lacks the extensive convoluted surface characteristic of the cat's and the primate's cortex and presumably has not developed functionally to the same degree as it has in the higher mammals. And, as one might have predicted, in the ground squirrel about half of the optic nerve fibers project to the lateral geniculate nucleus and the rest go to the superior colliculus, the mammalian ana-logue of the optic tectum [*see illustration on page 251*].

The ground squirrel, then, represents an interesting intermediate situation. It has some highly specialized retinal ganglion cells, the directionally selective neurons. These, I have found, project to the superior colliculus just as the sophisticated neurons of the frog's and the pigeon's retina go to the analogous optic tectum. On the other hand, the ground squirrel's retina also contains some simpler ganglion cells, the contrast-sensitive and opponent-color neurons. As in the cat and primates, these cells project to the lateral geniculate nucleus, where the information is relayed to the visual cortex. It appears that, regardless of the presence or absence of a visual cortex or of its degree of development, highly specialized retinal ganglion cells always project to the superior colliculus (or the optic tectum). Since the superior colliculus is associated with eye movements, it is not surprising that the information on directional movement is sent there. Nor is it surprising that the contrast and color information goes to the cortex, which is involved in the conscious perception of the visual image.

This parceling out of information occurs in a different way in the cat and the primate, whose retinas are simpler. In these animals one of the major outputs of the visual cortex is to the superior colliculus, perhaps providing a route for information related to the voluntary control of eye movements. This suggests a functional unity amid anatomical diversity. The colliculus has not lost its importance with the extensive development of the cortex in higher mammals; rather, its relative position in the visual system has simply been shifted.

26

THE VISUAL CORTEX OF THE BRAIN

DAVID H. HUBEL
November 1963

An image of the outside world striking the retina of the eye activates a most intricate process that results in vision: the transformation of the retinal image into a perception. The transformation occurs partly in the retina but mostly in the brain, and it is, as one can recognize instantly by considering how modest in comparison is the achievement of a camera, a task of impressive magnitude.

The process begins with the responses of some 130 million light-sensitive receptor cells in each retina. From these cells messages are transmitted to other retinal cells and then sent on to the brain, where they must be analyzed and interpreted. To get an idea of the magnitude of the task, think what is involved in watching a moving animal, such as a horse. At a glance one takes in its size, form, color and rate of movement. From tiny differences in the two retinal images there results a three-dimensional picture. Somehow the brain manages to compare this picture with previous impressions; recognition occurs and then any appropriate action can be taken.

The organization of the visual system —a large, intricately connected population of nerve cells in the retina and brain —is still poorly understood. In recent years, however, various studies have begun to reveal something of the arrangement and function of these cells. A decade ago Stephen W. Kuffler, working with cats at the Johns Hopkins Hospital, discovered that some analysis of visual patterns takes place outside the brain, in the nerve cells of the retina. My colleague Torsten N. Wiesel and I at the Harvard Medical School, exploring the first stages of the processing that occurs in the brain of the cat, have mapped the visual pathway a little further: to what appears to be the sixth step from the retina to the cortex of the cerebrum. This kind of work falls far short of providing a full understanding of vision, but it does convey some idea of the mechanisms and circuitry of the visual system.

In broad outline the visual pathway is clearly defined [*see bottom illustration on following page*]. From the retina of each eye visual messages travel along the optic nerve, which consists of about a million nerve fibers. At the junction known as the chiasm about half of the nerves cross over into opposite hemispheres of the brain, the other nerves remaining on the same side. The optic nerve fibers lead to the first way stations in the brain: a pair of cell clusters called the lateral geniculate bodies. From here new fibers course back through the brain to the visual area of the cerebral cortex. It is convenient, although admittedly a gross oversimplification, to think of the pathway from retina to cortex as consisting of six types of nerve cells, of which three are in the retina, one is in the geniculate body and two are in the cortex.

Nerve cells, or neurons, transmit messages in the form of brief electrochemical impulses. These travel along the outer membrane of the cell, notably along the membrane of its long principal fiber, the axon. It is possible to obtain an electrical record of impulses of a single nerve cell by placing a fine electrode near the cell body or one of its fibers. Such measurements have shown that impulses travel along the nerves at velocities of between half a meter and 100 meters per second. The impulses in a given fiber all have about the same amplitude; the strength of the stimuli that give rise to them is reflected not in amplitude but in frequency.

At its terminus the fiber of a nerve cell makes contact with another nerve cell (or with a muscle cell or gland cell), forming the junction called the synapse. At most synapses an impulse on reaching the end of a fiber causes the release of a small amount of a specific substance, which diffuses outward to the membrane of the next cell. There the substance either excites the cell or inhibits it. In excitation the substance acts to bring the cell into a state in which it is more likely to "fire"; in inhibition the substance acts to prevent firing. For most synapses the substances that act as transmitters are unknown. Moreover, there is no sure way to determine from microscopic appearances alone whether a synapse is excitatory or inhibitory.

It is at the synapses that the modification and analysis of nerve messages take place. The kind of analysis depends partly on the nature of the synapse: on how many nerve fibers converge on a single cell and on how the excitatory and inhibitory endings distribute themselves. In most parts of the nervous system the anatomy is too intricate to reveal much about function. One way to circumvent this difficulty is to record impulses with microelectrodes in anesthetized animals, first from the fibers coming into a structure of neurons and then from the neurons themselves, or from the fibers they send onward. Comparison of the behavior of incoming and outgoing fibers provides a basis for learning what the structure does. Through such exploration of the different parts of the brain concerned with vision one can hope to build up some idea of how the entire visual system works.

That is what Wiesel and I have undertaken, mainly through studies of the visual system of the cat. In our experiments the anesthetized animal faces a wide screen 1.5 meters away, and we shine various patterns of white light on the screen with a projector. Simultane-

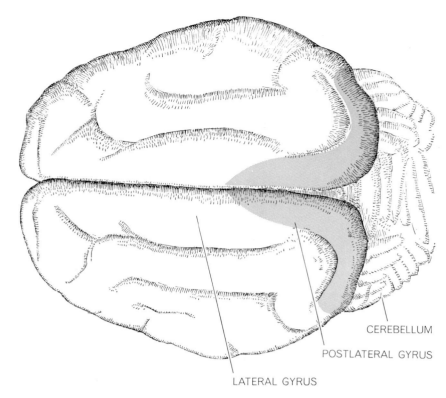

CORTEX OF CAT'S BRAIN is depicted as it would be seen from the top. The colored region indicates the cortical area that deals at least in a preliminary way with vision.

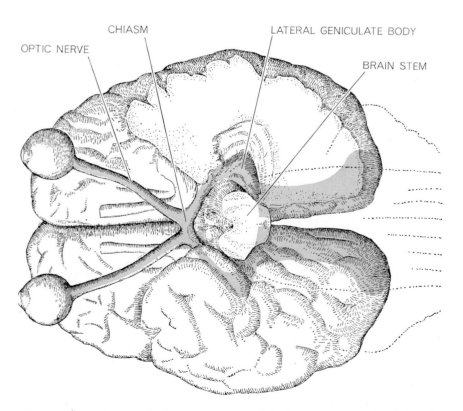

VISUAL SYSTEM appears in this representation of the human brain as viewed from below. Visual pathway from retinas to cortex via the lateral geniculate body is shown in color.

ously we penetrate the visual portion of the cortex with microelectrodes. In that way we can record the responses of individual cells to the light patterns. Sometimes it takes many hours to find the region of the retina with which a particular visual cell is linked and to work out the optimum stimuli for that cell. The reader should bear in mind the relation between each visual cell—no matter how far along the visual pathway it may be—and the retina. It requires an image on the retina to evoke a meaningful response in any visual cell, however indirect and complex the linkage may be.

The retina is a complicated structure, in both its anatomy and its physiology, and the description I shall give is highly simplified. Light coming through the lens of the eye falls on the mosaic of receptor cells in the retina. The receptor cells do not send impulses directly through the optic nerve but instead connect with a set of retinal cells called bipolar cells. These in turn connect with retinal ganglion cells, and it is the latter set of cells, the third in the visual pathway, that sends its fibers—the optic nerve fibers—to the brain.

This series of cells and synapses is no simple bucket brigade for impulses: a receptor may send nerve endings to more than one bipolar cell, and several receptors may converge on one bipolar cell. The same holds for the synapses between the bipolar cells and the retinal ganglion cells. Stimulating a single receptor by light might therefore be expected to have an influence on many bipolar or ganglion cells; conversely, it should be possible to influence one bipolar or retinal ganglion cell from a number of receptors and hence from a substantial area of the retina.

The area of receptor mosaic in the retina feeding into a single visual cell is called the receptive field of the cell. This term is applied to any cell in the visual system to refer to the area of retina with which the cell is connected—the retinal area that on stimulation produces a response from the cell.

Any of the synapses with a particular cell may be excitatory or inhibitory, so that stimulation of a particular point on the retina may either increase or decrease the cell's firing rate. Moreover, a single cell may receive several excitatory and inhibitory impulses at once, with the result that it will respond according to the net effect of these inputs. In considering the behavior of a single cell an observer should remember that it is just one of a huge popu-

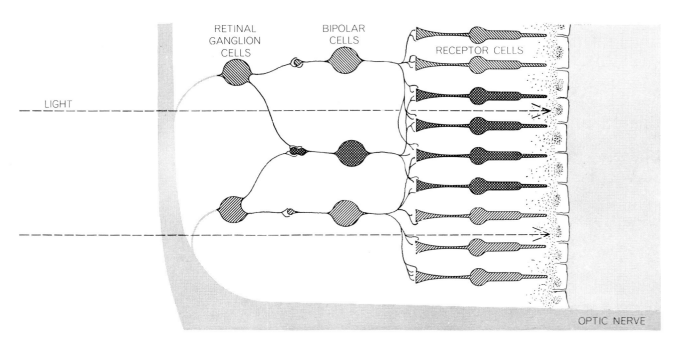

STRUCTURE OF RETINA is depicted schematically. Images fall on the receptor cells, of which there are about 130 million in each retina. Some analysis of an image occurs as the receptors transmit messages to the retinal ganglion cells via the bipolar cells. A group of receptors funnels into a particular ganglion cell, as indicated by the shading; that group forms the ganglion cell's receptive field. Inasmuch as the fields of several ganglion cells overlap, one receptor may send messages to several ganglion cells.

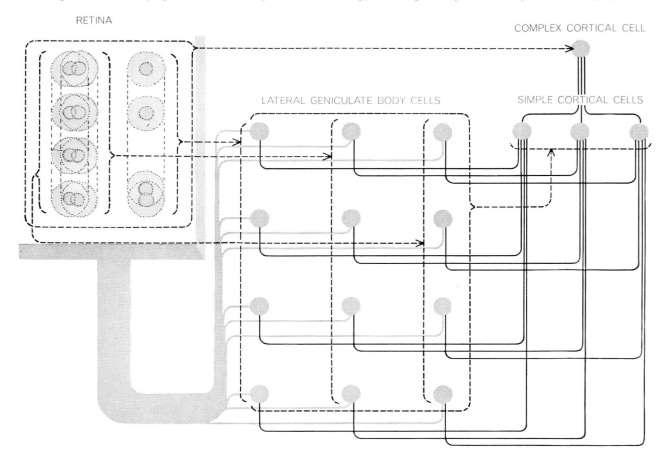

VISUAL PROCESSING BY BRAIN begins in the lateral geniculate body, which continues the analysis made by retinal cells. In the cortex "simple" cells respond strongly to line stimuli, provided that the position and orientation of the line are suitable for a particular cell. "Complex" cells respond well to line stimuli, but the position of the line is not critical and the cell continues to respond even if a properly oriented stimulus is moved, as long as it remains in the cell's receptive field. Broken lines indicate how receptive fields of all these cells overlap on the retina; solid lines, how several cells at one stage affect a single cell at the next stage.

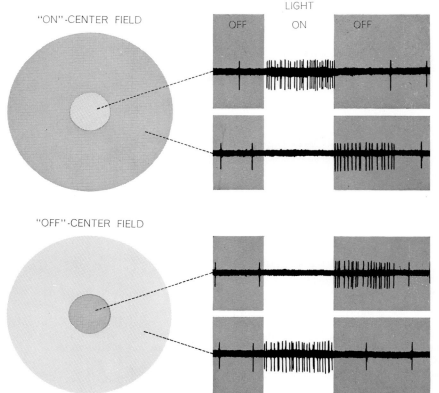

CONCENTRIC FIELDS are characteristic of retinal ganglion cells and of geniculate cells. At top an oscilloscope recording shows strong firing by an "on"-center type of cell when a spot of light strikes the field center; if the spot hits an "off" area, the firing is suppressed until the light goes off. At bottom are responses of another cell of the "off"-center type.

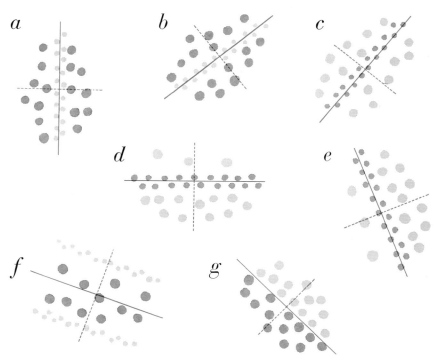

SIMPLE CORTICAL CELLS have receptive fields of various types. In all of them the "on" and "off" areas, represented by colored and gray dots respectively, are separated by straight boundaries. Orientations of fields vary, as indicated particularly at *a* and *b*. In the cat's visual system such fields are generally one millimeter or less in diameter.

lation of cells: a stimulus that excites one cell will undoubtedly excite many others, meanwhile inhibiting yet another array of cells and leaving others entirely unaffected.

For many years it has been known that retinal ganglion cells fire at a fairly steady rate even in the absence of any stimulation. Kuffler was the first to observe how the retinal ganglion cells of mammals are influenced by small spots of light. He found that the resting discharges of a cell were intensified or diminished by light in a small and more or less circular region of the retina. That region was of course the cell's receptive field. Depending on where in the field a spot of light fell, either of two responses could be produced. One was an "on" response, in which the cell's firing rate increased under the stimulus of light. The other was an "off" response, in which the stimulus of light decreased the cell's firing rate. Moreover, turning the light off usually evoked a burst of impulses from the cell. Kuffler called the retinal regions from which these responses could be evoked "on" regions and "off" regions.

On mapping the receptive fields of a large number of retinal ganglion cells into "on" and "off" regions, Kuffler discovered that there were two distinct cell types. In one the receptive field consisted of a small circular "on" area and a surrounding zone that gave "off" responses. Kuffler termed this an "on"-center cell. The second type, which he called "off"-center, had just the reverse form of field—an "off" center and an "on" periphery [see top illustration on this page]. For a given cell the effects of light varied markedly according to the place in which the light struck the receptive field. Two spots of light shone on separate parts of an "on" area produced a more vigorous "on" response than either spot alone, whereas if one spot was shone on an "on" area and the other on an "off" area, the two effects tended to neutralize each other, resulting in a very weak "on" or "off" response. In an "on"-center cell, illuminating the entire central "on" region evoked a maximum response; a smaller or larger spot of light was less effective.

Lighting up the whole retina diffusely, even though it may affect every receptor in the retina, does not affect a retinal ganglion cell nearly so strongly as a small circular spot of exactly the right size placed so as to cover precisely the receptive-field center. The main concern of these cells seems to be the contrast in illumination between one retinal region and surrounding regions.

Retinal ganglion cells differ greatly in the size of their receptive-field centers. Cells near the fovea (the part of the retina serving the center of gaze) are specialized for precise discrimination; in the monkey the field centers of these cells may be about the same size as a single cone—an area subtending a few minutes of arc at the cornea. On the other hand, some cells far out in the retinal periphery have field centers up to a millimeter or so in diameter. (In man one millimeter of retina corresponds to an arc of about three degrees in the 180-degree visual field.) Cells with such large receptive-field centers are probably specialized for work in very dim light, since they can sum up messages from a large number of receptors.

Given this knowledge of the kind of visual information brought to the brain by the optic nerve, our first problem was to learn how the messages were handled at the first central way station, the lateral geniculate body. Compared with the retina, the geniculate body is a relatively simple structure. In a sense there is only one synapse involved, since the incoming optic nerve fibers end in cells that send their fibers directly to the visual cortex. Yet in the cat many optic nerve fibers converge on each geniculate cell, and it is reasonable to expect some change in the visual messages from the optic nerve to the geniculate cells.

When we came to study the geniculate body, we found that the cells have many of the characteristics Kuffler described for retinal ganglion cells. Each geniculate cell is driven from a circumscribed retinal region (the receptive field) and has either an "on" center or an "off" center, with an opposing periphery. There are, however, differences between geniculate cells and retinal ganglion cells, the most important of which is the greatly enhanced capacity of the periphery of a geniculate cell's receptive field to cancel the effects of the center. This means that the lateral geniculate cells must be even more specialized than retinal ganglion cells in responding to spatial differences in retinal illumination rather than to the illumination itself. The lateral geniculate body, in short, has the function of increasing the disparity—already present in retinal ganglion cells—between responses to a small, centered spot and to diffuse light.

In contrast to the comparatively simple lateral geniculate body, the cerebral cortex is a structure of stupendous complexity. The cells of this great plate of

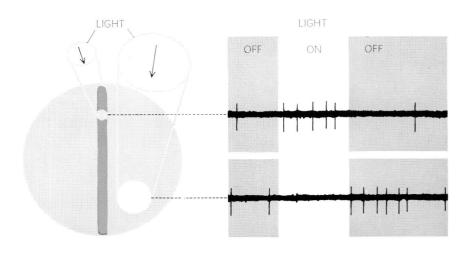

RESPONSE IS WEAK when a circular spot of light is shone on receptive field of a simple cortical cell. Such spots get a vigorous response from retinal and geniculate cells. This cell has a receptive field of type shown at *a* in bottom illustration on preceding page.

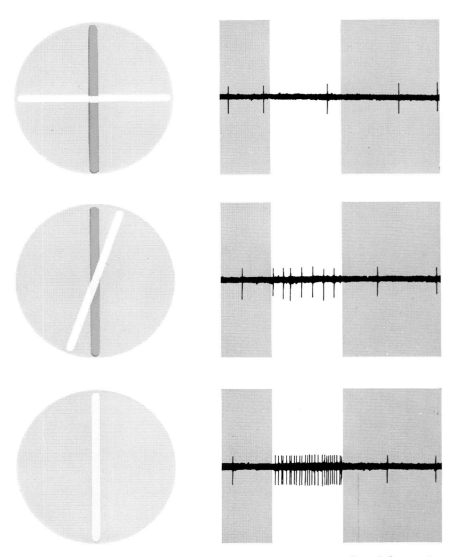

IMPORTANCE OF ORIENTATION to simple cortical cells is indicated by varying responses to a slit of light from a cell preferring a vertical orientation. Horizontal slit *(top)* produces no response, slight tilt a weak response, vertical slit a strong response.

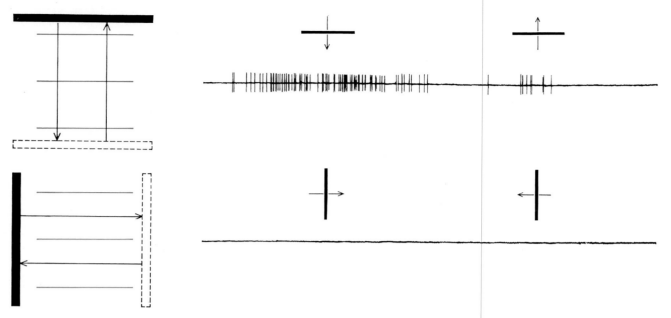

COMPLEX CORTICAL CELL responded vigorously to slow downward movement of a dark, horizontal bar. Upward movement of bar produced a weak response and horizontal movement of a vertical bar produced no response. For other shapes, orientations and movements there are other complex cells showing maximum response. Such cells may figure in perception of form and movement.

gray matter—a structure that would be about 20 square feet in area and a tenth of an inch thick if flattened out— are arranged in a number of more or less distinct layers. The millions of fibers that come in from the lateral geniculate body connect with cortical cells in the layer that is fourth from the top. From here the information is sooner or later disseminated to all layers of the cortex by rich interconnections between them. Many of the cells, particularly those of the third and fifth layers, send their fibers out of the cortex, projecting to centers deep in the brain or passing over to nearby cortical areas for further processing of the visual messages. Our problem was to learn how the information the visual cortex sends out differs from what it takes in.

Most connections between cortical cells are in a direction perpendicular to the surface; side-to-side connections are generally quite short. One might therefore predict that impulses arriving at a particular area of the cortex would exert their effects quite locally. Moreover, the retinas project to the visual cortex (via the lateral geniculate body) in a systematic topologic manner; that is, a given area of cortex gets its input ultimately from a circumscribed area of retina. These two observations suggest that a given cortical cell should have a small receptive field; it should be influenced from a circumscribed retinal region only, just as a geniculate or retinal ganglion cell is. Beyond this the anatomy provides no hint of what the cortex does

with the information it receives about an image on the retina.

In the face of the anatomical complexity of the cortex, it would have been surprising if the cells had proved to have the concentric receptive fields characteristic of cells in the retina and the lateral geniculate body. Indeed, in the cat we have observed no cortical cells with concentric receptive fields; instead there are many different cell types, with fields markedly different from anything seen in the retinal and geniculate cells.

The many varieties of cortical cells may, however, be classified by function into two large groups. One we have called "simple"; the function of these cells is to respond to line stimuli—such shapes as slits, which we define as light lines on a dark background; dark bars (dark lines on a light background), and edges (straight-line boundaries between light and dark regions). Whether or not a given cell responds depends on the orientation of the shape and its position on the cell's receptive field. A bar shone vertically on the screen may activate a given cell, whereas the same cell will fail to respond (but others will respond) if the bar is displaced to one side or moved appreciably out of the vertical. The second group of cortical cells we have called "complex"; they too respond best to bars, slits or edges, provided that, as with simple cells, the shape is suitably oriented for the particular cell under observation. Complex cells, how-

ever, are not so discriminating as to the exact position of the stimulus, provided that it is properly oriented. Moreover, unlike simple cells, they respond with sustained firing to moving lines.

From the preference of simple and complex cells for specific orientation of light stimuli, it follows that there must be a multiplicity of cell types to handle the great number of possible positions and orientations. Wiesel and I have found a large variety of cortical cell responses, even though the number of individual cells we have studied runs only into the hundreds compared with the millions that exist. Among simple cells, the retinal region over which a cell can be influenced—the receptive field—is, like the fields of retinal and geniculate cells, divided into "on" and "off" areas. In simple cells, however, these areas are far from being circularly symmetrical. In a typical example the receptive field consists of a very long and narrow "on" area, which is adjoined on each side by larger "off" regions. The magnitude of an "on" response depends, as with retinal and geniculate cells, on how much either type of region is covered by the stimulating light. A long, narrow slit that just fills the elongated "on" region produces a powerful "on" response. Stimulation with the slit in a different orientation produces a much weaker effect, because the slit is now no longer illuminating all the "on" region but instead includes some of the antagonistic "off" region. A slit at right angles to the optimum orientation for a cell of this type is usually completely ineffective.

In the simple cortical cells the process of pitting these two antagonistic parts of a receptive field against each other is carried still further than it is in the lateral geniculate body. As a rule a large spot of light—or what amounts to the same thing, diffuse light covering the whole retina—evokes no response at all in simple cortical cells. Here the "on" and "off" effects apparently balance out with great precision.

Some other common types of simple receptive fields include an "on" center with a large "off" area to one side and a small one to the other; an "on" and an "off" area side by side; a narrow "off" center with "on" sides; a wide "on" center with narrow "off" sides. All these fields have in common that the border or borders separating "on" and "off" regions are straight and parallel rather than circular [*see bottom illustration on page 256*]. The most efficient stimuli—slits, edges or dark bars—all involve straight lines. Each cell responds best to a particular orientation of line; other orientations produce less vigorous responses, and usually the orientation perpendicular to the optimum evokes no response at all. A particular cell's optimum, which we term the receptive-field orientation is thus a property built into the cell by its connections. In general the receptive-field orientation differs from one cell to the next, and it may be vertical, horizontal or oblique. We have no evidence that any one orientation, such as vertical or horizontal, is more common than any other.

How can one explain this specificity of simple cortical cells? We are inclined to think they receive their input directly from the incoming lateral geniculate fibers. We suppose a typical simple cell has for its input a large number of lateral geniculate cells whose "on" centers are arranged along a straight line; a spot of light shone anywhere along that line will activate some of the geniculate cells and lead to activation of the cortical cell. A light shone over the entire area will activate all the geniculate cells and have a tremendous final impact on the cortical cell [*see bottom illustration on page 255*].

One can now begin to grasp the significance of the great number of cells in the visual cortex. Each cell seems to have its own specific duties; it takes care of one restricted part of the retina, responds best to one particular shape of stimulus and to one particular orientation. To look at the problem from the

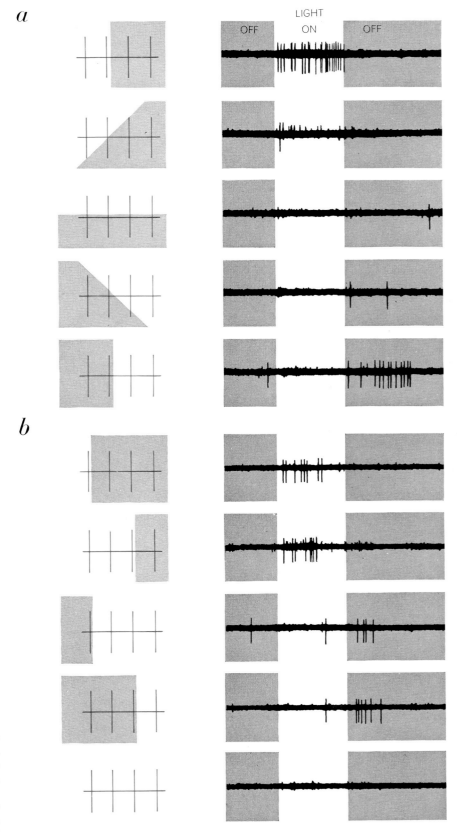

SINGLE COMPLEX CELL showed varying responses to an edge projected on the cell's receptive field in the retina. In group *a* the stimulus was presented in differing orientations. In group *b* all the edges were vertical and all but the last evoked responses regardless of where in the receptive field the light struck. When a large rectangle of light covered entire receptive field, however, as shown at bottom, cell failed to respond.

opposite direction, for each stimulus—each area of the retina stimulated, each type of line (edge, slit or bar) and each orientation of stimulus—there is a particular set of simple cortical cells that will respond; changing any of the stimulus arrangements will cause a whole new population of cells to respond. The number of populations responding successively as the eye watches a slowly rotating propeller is scarcely imaginable.

Such a profound rearrangement and analysis of the incoming messages might seem enough of a task for a single structure, but it turns out to be only part of what happens in the cortex. The next major transformation involves the cortical cells that occupy what is probably the sixth step in the visual pathway: the complex cells, which are also present in this cortical region and to some extent intermixed with the simple cells.

Complex cells are like simple ones in several ways. A cell responds to a stimulus only within a restricted region of retina: the receptive field. It responds best to the line stimuli (slits, edges or dark bars) and the stimulus must be oriented to suit the cell. But complex fields, unlike the simple ones, cannot be mapped into antagonistic "on" and "off" regions.

A typical complex cell we studied happened to fire to a vertical edge, and it gave "on" or "off" responses depending on whether light was to the left or to the right. Other orientations were almost completely without effect [*see illustration on preceding page*]. These re-

sponses are just what could be expected from a simple cell with a receptive field consisting of an excitatory area separated from an inhibitory one by a vertical boundary. In this case, however, the cell had an additional property that could not be explained by such an arrangement. A vertical edge evoked responses anywhere within the receptive field, "on" responses with light to the left, "off" responses with light to the right. Such behavior cannot be understood in terms of antagonistic "on" and "off" subdivisions of the receptive field, and when we explored the field with small spots we found no such regions. Instead the spot either produced responses at both "on" and "off" or evoked no responses at all.

Complex cells, then, respond like simple cells to one particular aspect of the stimulus, namely its orientation. But when the stimulus is moved, without changing the orientation, a complex cell differs from its simple counterpart chiefly in responding with sustained firing. The firing continues as the stimulus is moved over a substantial retinal area, usually the entire receptive field of the cell, whereas a simple cell will respond to movement only as the stimulus crosses a very narrow boundary separating "on" and "off" regions.

It is difficult to explain this behavior by any scheme in which geniculate cells project directly to complex cells. On the other hand, the findings can be explained fairly well by the supposition

that a complex cell receives its input from a large number of simple cells. This supposition requires only that the simple cells have the same field orientation and be all of the same general type. A complex cell responding to vertical edges, for example, would thus receive fibers from simple cells that have vertically oriented receptive fields. All such a scheme needs to have added is the requirement that the retinal positions of these simple fields be arranged throughout the area occupied by the complex field.

The main difficulty with such a scheme is that it presupposes an enormous degree of cortical organization. What a vast network of connections must be needed if a single complex cell is to receive fibers from just the right simple cells, all with the appropriate field arrangements, tilts and positions! Yet there is unexpected and compelling evidence that such a system of connections exists. It comes from a study of what can be called the functional architecture of the cortex. By penetrating with a microelectrode through the cortex in many directions, perhaps many times in a single tiny region of the brain, we learned that the cells are arranged not in a haphazard manner but with a high degree of order. The physiological results show that functionally the cortex is subdivided like a beehive into tiny columns, or segments [*see illustration on next page*], each of which extends from the surface to the white matter lower in the brain. A column is de-

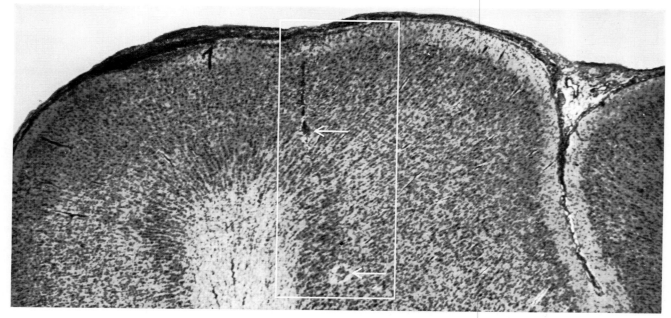

SECTION OF CAT'S VISUAL CORTEX shows track of microelectrode penetration and, at arrows, two points along the track where lesions were made so that it would be possible to ascertain later where the tip of the electrode was at certain times. This section of cortex is from a single gyrus, or fold of the brain; it was six millimeters wide and is shown here enlarged 30 diameters.

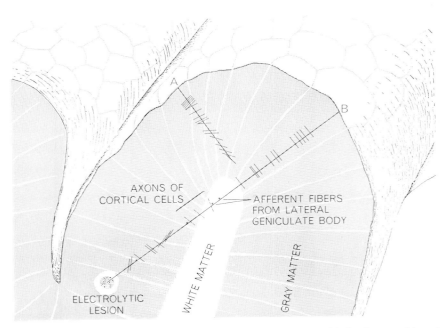

AXONS OF
CORTICAL CELLS

AFFERENT FIBERS
FROM LATERAL
GENICULATE BODY

WHITE MATTER

GRAY MATTER

ELECTROLYTIC
LESION

FUNCTIONAL ARRANGEMENT of cells in visual cortex resembled columns, although columnar structure is not apparent under a microscope. Lines *A* and *B* show paths of two microelectrode penetrations; colored lines show receptive-field orientations encountered. Cells in a single column had same orientation; change of orientation showed new column.

fined not by any anatomically obvious wall—no columns are visible under the microscope—but by the fact that the thousands of cells it contains all have the same receptive-field orientation. The evidence for this is that in a typical microelectrode penetration through the cortex the cells—recorded in sequence as the electrode is pushed ahead—all have the same field orientation, provided that the penetration is made in a direction perpendicular to the surface of the cortical segment. If the penetration is oblique, as we pass from column to column we record several cells with one field orientation, then a new sequence of cells with a new orientation, and then still another.

The columns are irregular in cross-sectional shape, and on the average they are about half a millimeter across. In respects other than receptive-field orientation the cells in a particular column tend to differ; some are simple, others complex; some respond to slits, others prefer dark bars or edges.

Returning to the proposed scheme for explaining the properties of complex cells, one sees that gathered together in a single column are the very cells one should expect to be interconnected: cells whose fields have the same orientation and the same general retinal position, although not the same position. Furthermore, it is known from

the anatomy that there are rich interconnections between neighboring cells, and the preponderance of these connections in a vertical direction fits well with the long, narrow, more or less cylindrical shape of the columns. This means that a column may be looked on as an independent functional unit of cortex, in which simple cells receive connections from lateral geniculate cells and send projections to complex cells.

It is possible to get an inkling of the part these different cell types play in vision by considering what must be happening in the brain when one looks at a form, such as, to take a relatively simple example, a black square on a white background. Suppose the eyes fix on some arbitrary point to the left of the square. On the reasonably safe assumption that the human visual cortex works something like the cat's and the monkey's, it can be predicted that the near edge of the square will activate a particular group of simple cells, namely cells that prefer edges with light to the left and dark to the right and whose fields are oriented vertically and are so placed on the retina that the boundary between "on" and "off" regions falls exactly along the image of the near edge of the square. Other populations of cells will obviously be called into action by the other three edges of the square. All the cell populations will change if the eye strays from the point fixed on, or if

the square is moved while the eye remains stationary, or if the square is rotated.

In the same way each edge will activate a population of complex cells, again cells that prefer edges in a specific orientation. But a given complex cell, unlike a simple cell, will continue to be activated when the eye moves or when the form moves, if the movement is not so large that the edge passes entirely outside the receptive field of the cell, and if there is no rotation. This means that the populations of complex cells affected by the whole square will be to some extent independent of the exact position of the image of the square on the retina.

Each of the cortical columns contains thousands of cells, some with simple fields and some with complex. Evidently the visual cortex analyzes an enormous amount of information, with each small region of visual field represented over and over again in column after column, first for one receptive-field orientation and then for another.

In sum, the visual cortex appears to have a rich assortment of functions. It rearranges the input from the lateral geniculate body in a way that makes lines and contours the most important stimuli. What appears to be a first step in perceptual generalization results from the response of cortical cells to the orientation of a stimulus, apart from its exact retinal position. Movement is also an important stimulus factor; its rate and direction must both be specified if a cell is to be effectively driven.

One cannot expect to "explain" vision, however, from a knowledge of the behavior of a single set of cells, geniculate or cortical, any more than one could understand a wood-pulp mill from an examination of the machine that cuts the logs into chips. We are now studying how still "higher" structures build on the information they receive from these cortical cells, rearranging it to produce an even greater complexity of response.

In all of this work we have been particularly encouraged to find that the areas we study can be understood in terms of comparatively simple concepts such as the nerve impulse, convergence of many nerves on a single cell, excitation and inhibition. Moreover, if the connections suggested by these studies are remotely close to reality, one can conclude that at least some parts of the brain can be followed relatively easily, without necessarily requiring higher mathematics, computers or a knowledge of network theories.

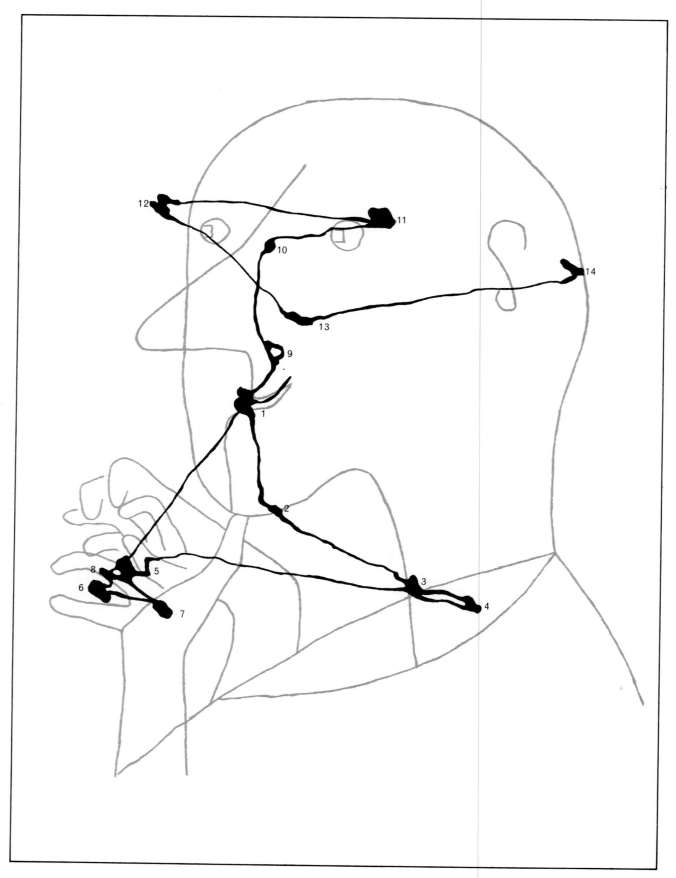

EYE MOVEMENTS made by a subject viewing for the first time a drawing adapted from Paul Klee's "Old Man Figuring" appear in black. Numbers show the order of the subject's visual fixations on the picture during part of a 20-second viewing. Lines between them represent saccades, or rapid movements of eyes from one fixation to the next. Saccades occupy about 10 percent of viewing time.

27

EYE MOVEMENTS AND VISUAL PERCEPTION

DAVID NOTON AND LAWRENCE STARK
June 1971

The eyes are the most active of all human sense organs. Other sensory receptors, such as the ears, accept rather passively whatever signals come their way, but the eyes are continually moving as they scan and inspect the details of the visual world. The movements of the eyes play an important role in visual perception, and analyzing them can reveal a great deal about the process of perception.

We have recently been recording the eye movements of human subjects as they first inspected unfamiliar objects and then later recognized them. In essence we found that every person has a characteristic way of looking at an object that is familiar to him. For each object he has a preferred path that his eyes tend to follow when he inspects or recognizes the object. Our results suggest a new hypothesis about visual learning and recognition. Before describing and explaining our experiments more fully we shall set the stage by outlining some earlier experiments that have aided the interpretation of our results.

Eye movements are necessary for a physiological reason: detailed visual information can be obtained only through the fovea, the small central area of the retina that has the highest concentration of photoreceptors. Therefore the eyes must move in order to provide information about objects that are to be inspected in any detail (except when the object is quite small in terms of the angle it subtends in the visual field). The eye-movement muscles, under the control of the brain, aim the eyes at points of interest [see "Control Mechanisms of the Eye," by Derek H. Fender, SCIENTIFIC AMERICAN Offprint 187, and "Movements of the Eye," by E. Llewellyn Thomas, SCIENTIFIC AMERICAN Offprint 516].

During normal viewing of stationary objects the eyes alternate between fixa-tions, when they are aimed at a fixed point in the visual field, and rapid movements called saccades. Each saccade leads to a new fixation on a different point in the visual field. Typically there are two or three saccades per second. The movements are so fast that they occupy only about 10 percent of the viewing time.

Visual learning and recognition involve storing and retrieving memories. By way of the lens, the retina and the optic nerve, nerve cells in the visual cortex of the brain are activated and an image of the object being viewed is formed there. (The image is of course in the form of neural activity and is quite unlike the retinal image of the object.) The memory system of the brain must contain an internal representation of every object that is to be recognized. Learning or becoming familiar with an object is the process of constructing this representation. Recognition of an object when it is encountered again is the process of matching it with its internal representation in the memory system.

A certain amount of controversy surrounds the question of whether visual recognition is a parallel, one-step process or a serial, step-by-step one. Psychologists of the Gestalt school have maintained that objects are recognized as wholes, without any need for analysis into component parts. This argument implies that the internal representation of each object is a unitary whole that is matched with the object in a single operation. More recently other psychologists have proposed that the internal representation is a piecemeal affair—an assemblage of parts or features. During recognition the features are matched serially with the features of the object step by step. Successful matching of all the features completes recognition.

The serial-recognition hypothesis is supported mainly by the results of experiments that measure the time taken by a subject to recognize different objects. Typically the subject scans an array of objects (usually abstract figures) looking for a previously memorized "target" object. The time he spends considering each object (either recognizing it as a target object or rejecting it as being different) is measured. That time is normally quite short, but it can be measured in various ways with adequate accuracy. Each object is small enough to be recognized with a single fixation, so that eye movements do not contribute to the time spent on recognition.

Experiments of this kind yield two general results. First, it is found that on the average the subject takes longer to recognize a target object than he does to reject a nontarget object. That is the result to be expected if objects are recognized serially, feature by feature. When an object is compared mentally with the internal representation of the target object, a nontarget object will fail to match some feature of the internal representation and will be rejected without further checking of features, whereas target objects will be checked on all features. The result seems inconsistent with the Gestalt hypothesis of a holistic internal representation matched with the object in a single operation. Presumably in such an operation the subject would take no longer to recognize an object than he would to reject it.

A second result is obtained by varying the complexity of the memorized target object. It is found that the subject takes longer to recognize complex target objects than to recognize simple ones. This result too is consistent with the serial-recognition hypothesis, since more features must be checked in the more complex object. By the same token the result also appears to be inconsistent with the Gestalt hypothesis.

It would be incorrect to give the impression that the serial nature of object recognition is firmly established to the exclusion of the unitary concept advanced by Gestalt psychologists. They have shown convincingly that there is indeed some "primitive unity" to an object, so that the object can often be singled out as a separate entity even before true recognition begins. Moreover, some of the recognition-time experiments described above provide evidence, at least with very simple objects, that as an object becomes well known its internal representation becomes more holistic and the recognition process correspondingly becomes more parallel. Nonetheless, the weight of evidence seems to support the serial hypothesis, at least for objects that are not notably simple and familiar.

If the internal representation of an object in memory is an assemblage of features, two questions naturally suggest themselves. First, what are these features, that is, what components of an object does the brain select as the key items for identifying the object? Second, how are such features integrated and related to one another to form the complete internal representation of the object? The study of eye movements during visual perception yields considerable evidence on these two points.

In experiments relating to the first question the general approach is to present to a subject a picture or another object that is sufficiently large and close to the eyes so that it cannot all be registered on the foveas in one fixation. For example, a picture 35 centimeters wide and 100 centimeters from the eyes subtends a horizontal angle of 20 degrees at each eye—roughly the angle subtended by a page of this magazine held at arm's length. This is far wider than the one to two degrees of visual field that are brought to focus on the fovea.

Under these conditions the subject must move his eyes and look around the picture, fixating each part he wants to see clearly. The assumption is that he looks mainly at the parts of the picture he regards as being its features; they are the parts that hold for him the most information about the picture. Features are tentatively located by peripheral vision and then fixated directly for detailed inspection. (It is important to note that in these experiments and in the others we shall describe the subject is given only general instructions, such as "Just look at the pictures," or even no instructions at all. More specific instructions, requiring him to inspect and describe some specific aspect of the picture, usually result in appropriately directed fixations, as might be expected.)

When subjects freely view simple pictures, such as line drawings, under these conditions, it is found that their fixations tend to cluster around the angles of the picture. For example, Leonard Zusne and Kenneth M. Michels performed an experiment of this type at Purdue University, using as pictures line drawings of simple polygons [see illustration on

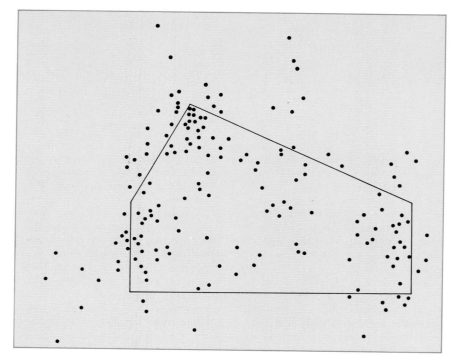

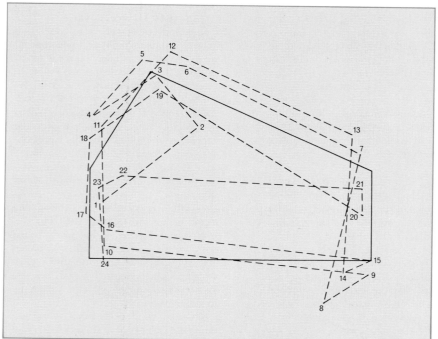

IMPORTANCE OF ANGLES as features that the brain employs in memorizing and recognizing an object was apparent in experiments by Leonard Zusne and Kenneth M. Michels at Purdue University. They recorded fixations while subjects looked at drawings of polygons for eight seconds. At top is one of the polygons; the dots indicate the fixations of seven subjects. Sequence of fixations by one subject in an eight-second viewing appears at bottom.

opposite page]. From the fixations made by their subjects in viewing such figures it is clear that the angles of the drawings attracted the eyes most strongly.

Our tentative conclusion is that, at least with such line drawings, the angles are the principal features the brain employs to store and recognize the drawing. Certainly angles would be an efficient choice for features. In 1954 Fred Attneave III of the University of Oregon pointed out that the most informative parts of a line drawing are the angles and sharp curves. To illustrate his argument he presented a picture that was obtained by selecting the 38 points of greatest curvature in a picture of a sleeping cat and joining the points with straight lines [*see top illustration at right*]. The result is clearly recognizable.

Additional evidence that angles and sharp curves are features has come from electrophysiologists who have investigated the activity of individual brain cells. For example, in the late 1950's Jerome Y. Lettvin, H. R. Maturana, W. S. McCulloch and W. H. Pitts of the Massachusetts Institute of Technology found angle-detecting neurons in the frog's retina. More recently David H. Hubel and Torsten N. Wiesel of the Harvard Medical School have extended this result to cats and monkeys (whose angle-detecting cells are in the visual cortex rather than the retina). And recordings obtained from the human visual cortex by Elwin Marg of the University of California at Berkeley give preliminary indications that these results can be extended to man.

Somewhat analogous results have been obtained with pictures more complex than simple line drawings. It is not surprising that in such cases the features are also more complex. As a result no formal description of them has been achieved. Again, however, high information content seems to be the criterion. Norman H. Mackworth and A. J. Morandi made a series of recordings at Harvard University of fixations by subjects viewing two complex photographs. They concluded that the fixations were concentrated on unpredictable or unusual details, in particular on unpredictable contours. An unpredictable contour is one that changes direction rapidly and irregularly and therefore has a high information content.

We conclude, then, that angles and other informative details are the features selected by the brain for remembering and recognizing an object. The next question concerns how these

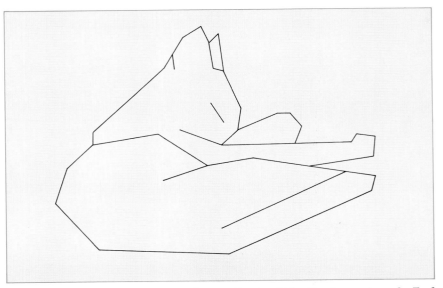

SHARP CURVES are also important as features for visual identification, as shown by Fred Attneave III of the University of Oregon in a picture made by selecting the 38 points of greatest curvature in a picture of a sleeping cat and joining them with straight lines, thus eliminating all other curves. The result is still easily recognizable, suggesting that points of sharp curvature provide highly useful information to the brain in visual perception.

features are integrated by the brain into a whole—the internal representation—so that one sees the object as a whole, as an object rather than an unconnected sequence of features. Once again useful evidence comes from recordings of eye movements. Just as study of the locations of fixations indicated the probable nature of the features, so analysis of the order of fixations suggests a format for the interconnection of features into the overall internal representation.

The illustration below shows the fixations made by a subject while viewing a photograph of a bust of the Egyptian queen Nefertiti. It is one of a series of recordings made by Alfred L. Yarbus of the Institute for Problems of Information Transmission of the Academy of Sciences of the U.S.S.R. The illustration

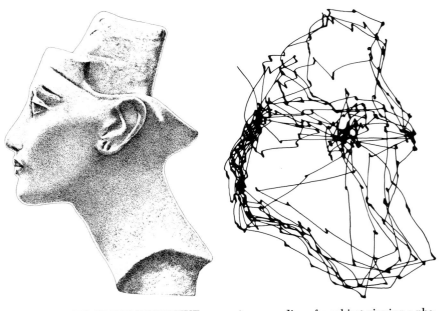

REGULARITIES OF EYE MOVEMENT appear in a recording of a subject viewing a photograph of a bust of Queen Nefertiti. At left is a drawing of what the subject saw; at right are his eye movements as recorded by Alfred L. Yarbus of the Institute for Problems of Information Transmission in Moscow. The eyes seem to visit the features of the head cyclically, following fairly regular pathways, rather than crisscrossing the picture at random.

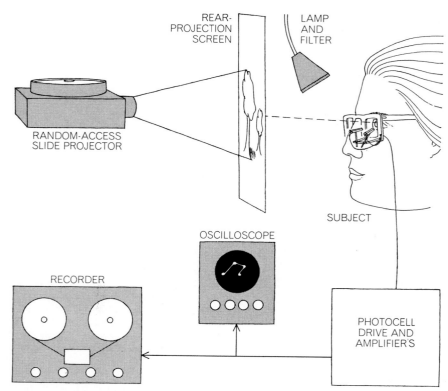

REAR-
PROJECTION
SCREEN

LAMP
AND
FILTER

RANDOM-ACCESS
SLIDE PROJECTOR

SUBJECT

OSCILLOSCOPE

RECORDER

PHOTOCELL
DRIVE AND
AMPLIFIER'S

EXPERIMENTAL PROCEDURE employed by the authors is depicted schematically. The subject viewed pictures displayed on a rear-projection screen by a random-access slide projector. Diffuse infrared light was shined on his eyes; his eye movements were recorded by photocells, mounted on a spectacle frame, that detected reflections of the infrared light from one eyeball. Eye movements were displayed on oscilloscope and also recorded on tape.

shows clearly an important aspect of eye movement during visual perception, namely that the order of the fixations is by no means random. The lines representing the saccades form broad bands from point to point and do not crisscross the picture at random as would be expected if the eyes visited the different features repetitively in a random order. It appears that fixation on any one feature, such as Nefertiti's eye, is usually followed by fixation on the same next feature, such as her mouth. The overall record seems to indicate a series of cycles; in each cycle the eyes visit the main features of the picture, following rather regular pathways from feature to feature.

Recently at the University of California at Berkeley we have developed a hypothesis about visual perception that predicts and explains this apparent regularity of eye movement. Essentially we propose that in the internal representation or memory of the picture the features are linked together in sequence by the memory of the eye movement required to look from one feature to the next. Thus the eyes would tend to move from feature to feature in a fixed order, scanning the picture.

Most of Yarbus' recordings are summaries of many fixations and do not contain complete information on the ordering of the fixations. Thus the regularities of eye movements predicted by our hypothesis could not be definitely confirmed from his data. To eliminate this constraint and to subject our hypothesis to a more specific test we recently made a new series of recordings of eye movements during visual perception.

Our subjects viewed line drawings of simple objects and abstract symbols as we measured their eye movements (using photocells to determine the movements of the "white" of the eye) and recorded them on magnetic tape [see illustration above]. We thereby obtained a permanent record of the order of fixations made by the subjects and could play it back later at a lower speed, analyzing it at length for cycles and other regularities of movement. As in the earlier experiments, the drawings were fairly large and close to the subject's eyes, a typical drawing subtending about 20 degrees at the eye. In addition we drew the pictures with quite thin lines and displayed them with an underpowered slide projector, throwing a dim

image on a screen that was fully exposed to the ordinary light in the laboratory. In this way we produced an image of low visibility and could be sure that the subject would have to look directly (foveally) at each feature that interested him, thus revealing to our recording equipment the locus of his attention.

Our initial results amply confirmed the previous impression of cycles of eye movements. We found that when a subject viewed a picture under these conditions, his eyes usually scanned it following—intermittently but repeatedly—a fixed path, which we have termed his "scan path" for that picture [see illustration on opposite page]. The occurrences of the scan path were separated by periods in which the fixations were ordered in a less regular manner.

Each scan path was characteristic of a given subject viewing a given picture. A subject had a different scan path for every picture he viewed, and for a given picture each subject had a different scan path. A typical scan path for our pictures consisted of about 10 fixations and lasted for from three to five seconds. Scan paths usually occupied from 25 to 35 percent of the subject's viewing time, the rest being devoted to less regular eye movements.

It must be added that scan paths were not always observed. Certain pictures (one of a telephone, for example) seemed often not to provoke a repetitive response, although no definite common characteristic could be discerned in such pictures. The commonest reaction, however, was to exhibit a scan path. It was interesting now for us to refer back to the earlier recordings by Zusne and Michels, where we observed scan paths that had previously passed unnoticed. For instance, in the illustration on page 264 fixations No. 4 through No. 11 and No. 11 through No. 18 appear to be two occurrences of a scan path. They are identical, even to the inclusion of the small reverse movement in the lower right-hand corner of the figure.

This demonstration of the existence of scan paths strengthened and clarified our ideas about visual perception. In accordance with the serial hypothesis, we assume that the internal representation of an object in the memory system is an assemblage of features. To this we add a crucial hypothesis: that the features are assembled in a format we have termed a "feature ring" [see illustration on page 268]. The ring is a sequence of sensory and motor memory traces, alternately recording a feature of the object and the eye movement required to reach the next feature. The feature ring establishes a fixed ordering of features and eye movements, corresponding to a scan path on the object.

Our hypothesis states that as a subject views an object for the first time and becomes familiar with it he scans it with his eyes and develops a scan path for it. During this time he lays down the memory traces of the feature ring, which records both the sensory activity and the motor activity. When he subsequently encounters the same object again, he recognizes it by matching it with the feature ring, which is its internal representation in his memory. Matching consists in verifying the successive features and carrying out the intervening eye

movements, as directed by the feature ring.

This hypothesis not only offers a plausible format for the internal representation of objects—a format consistent with the existence of scan paths—but also has certain other attractive features. For example, it enables us to draw an interesting analogy between perception and behavior, in which both are seen to involve the alternation of sensory and motor activity. In the case of behavior, such as the performance of a learned sequence of activities, the sensing of a situation alternates with motor activity designed to bring about an expected new situation. In the case of perception (or, more specifically, recognition) of an object the verification of features alternates with

movement of the eyes to the expected new feature.

The feature-ring hypothesis also makes a verifiable prediction concerning eye movements during recognition: The successive eye movements and feature verifications, being directed by the feature ring, should trace out the same scan path that was established for the object during the initial viewing. Confirmation of the prediction would further strengthen the case for the hypothesis. Since the prediction is subject to experimental confirmation we designed an experiment to test it.

The experiment had two phases, which we called the learning phase and the recognition phase. (We did not, of

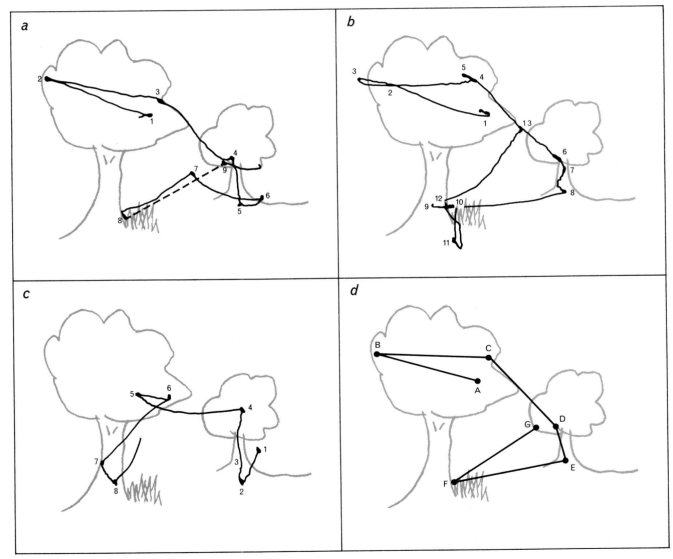

REGULAR PATTERN of eye movement by a given subject viewing a given picture was termed the subject's "scan path" for that picture. Two of five observed occurrences of one subject's scan path as he looked at a simple drawing of trees for 75 seconds are shown here (a, b). The dotted line between fixations 8 and 9 of a indicates that the recording of this saccade was interrupted by a blink. Less regular eye movements made between these appearances of the scan path are at c. Subject's scan path is idealized at d.

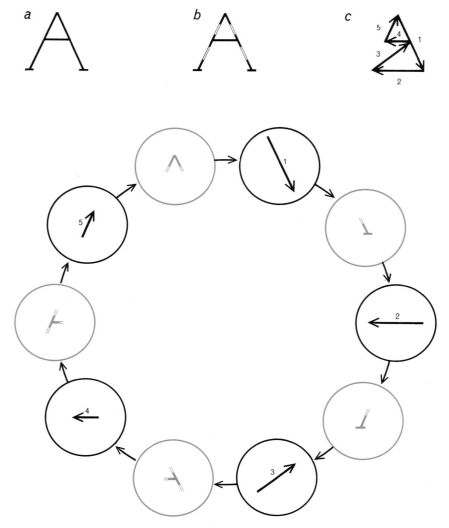

FEATURE RING is proposed by the authors as a format for the internal representation of an object. The object (a) is identified by its principal features (b) and is represented in the memory by them and by the recollection of the scan path (c) whereby they were viewed. The feature ring therefore consists of sensory memory traces (color) recording the features and motor memory traces (black) of the eye movements from one feature to the next.

ing-phase occurrences of the scan path; in the recognition phase he was matching the feature ring with the picture, following the scan path dictated by the feature ring.

An additional result of this experiment was to demonstrate that different subjects have different scan paths for a given picture and, conversely, that a given subject has different scan paths for different pictures [see illustration on page 270]. These findings help to discount certain alternative explanations that might be advanced to account for the occurrence of scan paths. The fact that a subject has quite different scan paths for different pictures suggests that the scan paths are not the result of some fixed habit of eye movement, such as reading Chinese vertically, brought to each picture but rather that they come from a more specific source, such as learned feature rings. Similarly, the differences among subjects in scan paths used for a given picture suggest that the scan paths do not result from peripheral feature detectors that control eye movements independent of the recognition process, since these detectors might be expected to operate in much the same way in all subjects.

Although the results of the second experiment provided considerable support for our ideas on visual perception, certain things remain unexplained. For example, sometimes no scan path was observed during the learning phase. Even when we did find a scan path, it did not always reappear in the recognition phase. On the average the appropriate scan path appeared in about 65 percent of the recognition-phase viewings. This is a rather strong result in view of the many possible paths around each picture, but it leaves 35 percent of the viewings, when no scan path appeared, in need of explanation.

Probably the basic idea of the feature ring needs elaboration. If provision were made for memory traces recording other eye movements between features not adjacent in the ring, and if the original ring represented the preferred and habitual order of processing rather than the inevitable order, the occasional substitution of an abnormal order for the

course, use any such suggestive terms in briefing the subjects; as before, they were simply told to look at the pictures.) In the learning phase the subject viewed five pictures he had not seen before, each for 20 seconds. The pictures and viewing conditions were similar to those of the first experiment. For the recognition phase, which followed immediately, the five pictures were mixed with five others the subject had not seen. This was to make the recognition task less easy. The set of 10 pictures was then presented to the subject three times in random order; he had five seconds to look at each picture. Eye movements were recorded during both the learning phase and the recognition phase.

When we analyzed the recordings, we were pleased to find that to a large

extent our predictions were confirmed. Scan paths appeared in the subject's eye movements during the learning phase, and during the recognition phase his first few eye movements on viewing a picture (presumably during the time he was recognizing it) usually followed the same scan path he had established for that picture during the learning phase [see illustration on opposite page]. In terms of our hypothesis the subject was forming a feature ring during the learn-

RECURRENCE OF SCAN PATH during recognition of an object is predicted by the feature-ring hypothesis. A subject viewed the adaptation of Klee's drawing (a). A scan path appeared while he was familiarizing himself with the picture (b, c). It also appeared (d, e) during the recognition phase each time he identified the picture as he viewed a sequence of familiar and unfamiliar scenes depicted in similar drawings. This particular experimental subject's scan path for this particular picture is presented in idealized form at f.

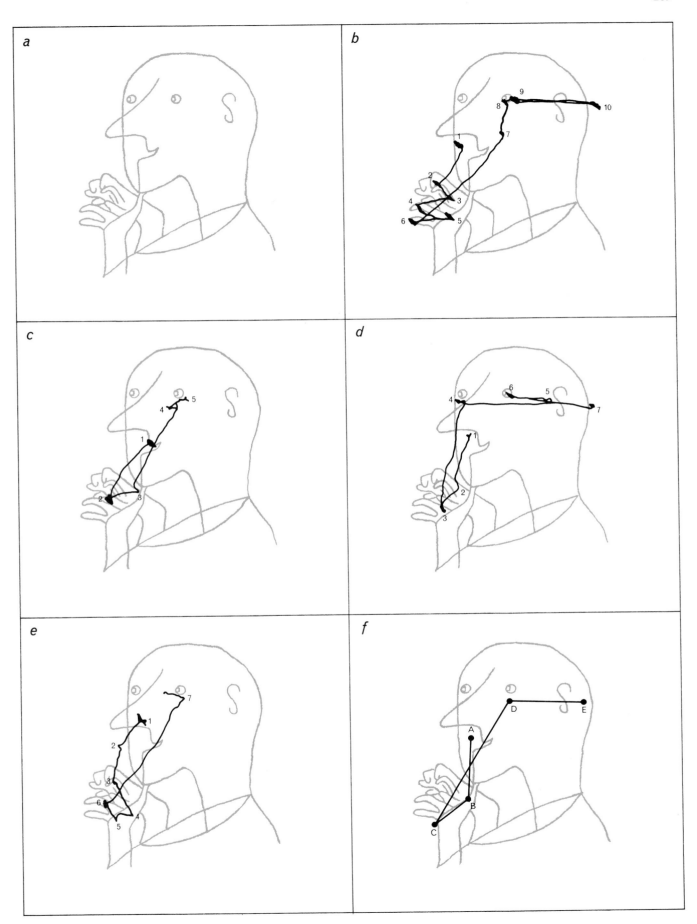

scan path would be explained [*see top illustration on opposite page*].

It must also be remembered that the eye-movement recordings in our experiments were made while the subjects viewed pictures that were rather large and close to their eyes, forcing them to look around in the picture to see its features clearly. In the more normal viewing situation, with a picture or an object small enough to be wholly visible with a single fixation, no eye movements are necessary for recognition. We assume

that in such a case the steps in perception are parallel up to the point where an image of the object is formed in the visual cortex and that thereafter (as would seem evident from the experiments on recognition time) the matching of the image and the internal representation is carried out serially, feature by feature. Now, however, we must postulate instead of eye movements from feature to feature a sequence of internal shifts of attention, processing the features serially and following the scan

path dictated by the feature ring. Thus each motor memory trace in the feature ring records a shift of attention that can be executed either externally, as an eye movement, or internally, depending on the extent of the shift required.

In this connection several recordings made by Lloyd Kaufman and Whitman Richards at M.I.T. are of interest. Their subjects viewed simple figures, such as a drawing of a cube, that could be taken in with a single fixation. At 10 randomly chosen moments the subject was asked

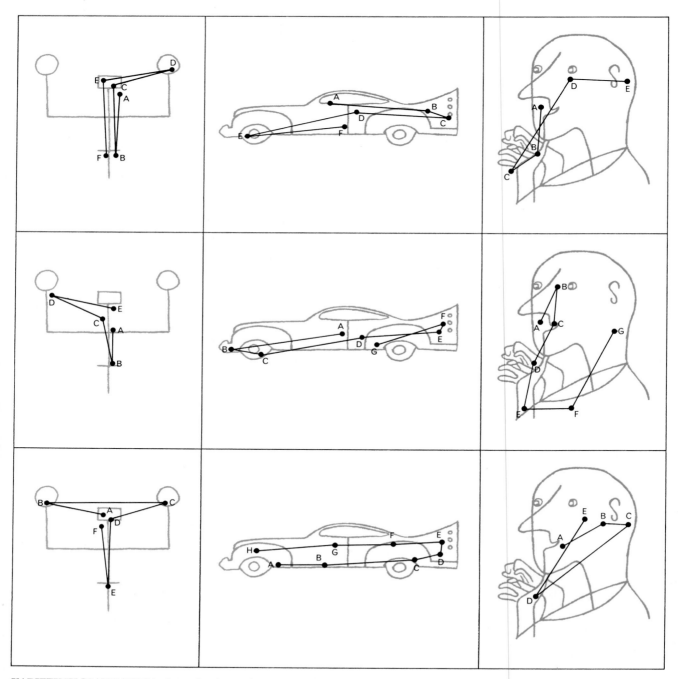

VARIETY IN SCAN PATHS is shown for three subjects and three pictures. Each horizontal row depicts the scan paths used by one subject for the three pictures. Vertically one sees how the scan paths of the three subjects for any one picture also varied widely.

to indicate where he thought he was looking. His answer presumably showed what part of the picture he was attending to visually. His actual fixation point was then recorded at another 10 randomly selected moments [*see bottom illustration at right*]. The results suggest that the subject's attention moved around the picture but his fixation remained fairly steady near the center of the picture. This finding is consistent with the view that smaller objects too are processed serially, by internal shifts of attention, even though little or no eye movement is involved.

It is important to note, however, that neither these results nor ours prove that recognition of objects and pictures is necessarily a serial process under normal conditions, when the object is not so large and close as to force serial processing by eye movements. The experiments on recognition time support the serial hypothesis, but it cannot yet be regarded as being conclusively established. In our experiments we provided a situation that forced the subject to view and recognize pictures serially with eye movements, thus revealing the order of feature processing, and we assumed that the results would be relevant to recognition under more normal conditions. Our results suggest a more detailed explanation of serial processing—the feature ring producing the scan path—but this explanation remains conditional on the serial hypothesis.

In sum, we believe the experimental results so far obtained support three main conclusions concerning the visual recognition of objects and pictures. First, the internal representation or memory of an object is a piecemeal affair: an assemblage of features or, more strictly, of memory traces of features; during recognition the internal representation is matched serially with the object, feature by feature. Second, the features of an object are the parts of it (such as the angles and curves of line drawings) that yield the most information. Third, the memory traces recording the features are assembled into the complete internal representation by being connected by other memory traces that record the shifts of attention required to pass from feature to feature, either with eye movements or with internal shifts of attention; the attention shifts connect the features in a preferred order, forming a feature ring and resulting in a scan path, which is usually followed when verifying the features during recognition.

Clearly these conclusions indicate a

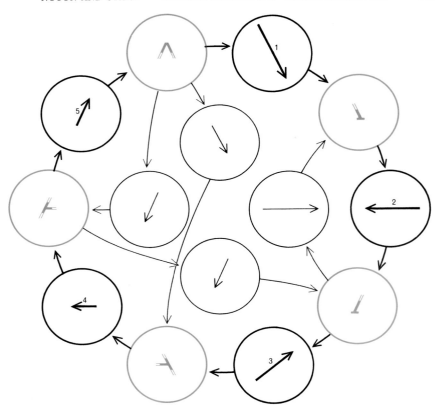

MODIFIED FEATURE RING takes into account less regular eye movements that do not conform to scan path. Several movements, which appeared in 35 percent of recognition viewings, are in center of this ring. Outside ring, consisting of sensory (*color*) and motor memory traces (*black*), represents scan path and remains preferred order of processing.

distinctly serial conception of visual learning and recognition. In the trend to look toward serial concepts to advance the understanding of visual perception one can note the influence of current work in computerized pattern recognition, where the serial approach has long been favored. Indeed, computer and information-processing concepts, usually serial in nature, are having an increasing influence on brain research in general.

Our own thoughts on visual recognition offer a case in point. We have developed them simultaneously with an analogous system for computerized pattern recognition. Although the system has not been implemented in working form, a somewhat similar scheme is being used in the visual-recognition system of a robot being developed by a group at the Stanford Research Institute. We believe this fruitful interaction between biology and engineering can be expected to continue, to the enrichment of both.

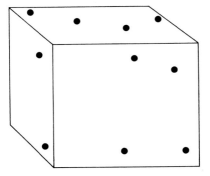
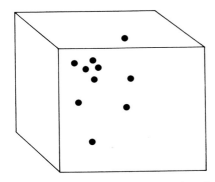

INTERNAL SHIFTS OF ATTENTION apparently replace eye movements in processing of objects small enough to be viewed with single fixation. A subject's attention, represented by statements of where he thought he was looking, moved around picture (*left*), whereas measured fixation point (*right*) remained relatively stationary. Illustration is based on work by Lloyd Kaufman and Whitman Richards at the Massachusetts Institute of Technology.

28

PLASTICITY IN SENSORY-MOTOR SYSTEMS

RICHARD HELD
November 1965

Anyone who has worn eyeglasses is likely to have experienced distorted vision the first time he put them on. The distortion may have been severe enough to cause him trouble in motor coordination, as in reaching out to touch something or in being sure of where he stepped. Such a person will also recall, however, that in a day or two the distortion disappeared. Evidently his central nervous system had made some adjustment so that the things he saw through the glasses looked normal again and he could have renewed confidence in his touch and step.

This process of adjustment, particularly as it operates in recovery from radical transformations of vision (as when the world is made to appear upside down or greatly shifted to one side by special goggles), has attracted the attention of scientists at least since the time of the great 19th-century investigator Hermann von Helmholtz. What has intrigued us all is the finding that correct perception of space and accurate visually guided action in space are in the long run not dependent on unique and permanently fixed optical properties of the paths taken by light rays traveling from object to eye. This finding, however, must be squared with the normally high order of precision in spatial vision and its stability over a period of time. How can the visual control of spatially coordinated action be stable under normal circumstances and yet sufficiently modifiable to allow recovery from transformation? Recovery takes time and renewed contact with the environment. Adaptation must result from information drawn from this contact with the environment. If the end product of adaptation is recovery of the former stability of perception, then the information on which that recovery is

based must be as reliable and unvarying as its end product. The investigations my colleagues and I have undertaken (first at Brandeis University and more recently at the Massachusetts Institute of Technology) have been directed toward discovering this source of information and elucidating the mechanism of its use by the perceiving organism. A useful tool in our work has been deliberate distortion of visual and auditory signals, a technique we call rearrangement.

Visual rearrangement can be produced experimentally with prisms [see "Experiments with Goggles," by Ivo Kohler; SCIENTIFIC AMERICAN Offprint 465]. Similarly, the apparent direction of sounds can be distorted in the laboratory by suitable apparatus. We have used such devices to show that in many cases the viewer or the listener subjected to these distortions soon adapts to them, provided that during the experiment he has been allowed to make voluntary use of his muscles in a more or less normal way.

The proviso suggests that there is more to the mechanism of perceptual adaptation than a change in the way the sensory parts of the central nervous system process data from the eyes and ears. The muscles and motor parts of the nervous system are evidently involved in the adaptation too—a revelation that has been very important in our efforts to discover the responsible source of information. The concept of a relation between sensory and motor activities in the adaptive process is reinforced by what happens when humans and certain other mammals undergo sensory deprivation through prolonged isolation in monotonous environments, or motor deprivation through prolonged immobilization. Their performance on perceptual

and motor tasks declines. By the same token, the young of higher mammals fail to develop normal behavior if they undergo sensory or motor deprivation.

Taken together, these findings by various experimenters suggested to us that a single mechanism is involved in three processes: (1) the development of normal sensory-motor control in the young, (2) the maintenance of that control once it has developed and (3) the adaptation to changes or apparent changes in the data reported by the senses of sight and hearing. A demonstration that such a mechanism exists would be of value in understanding these processes. Moreover, it would help to explain a phenomenon that otherwise could be accounted for only by the existence of enormous amounts of genetically coded information. That phenomenon is the adjustment of the central nervous system to the growth of the body—on the sensory side to the fact that the afferent, or input, signals must change with the increasing separation between the eyes and between the ears, and on the motor side to the fact that the growth of bone and muscle must call for a gradual modification of the efferent, or output, signals required to accomplish a particular movement. This problem is especially critical for animals that grow slowly and have many jointed bones. The possibility that the need for genetically coded information has been reduced by some such mechanism is of course contingent on the assumption that the animal's environment is fairly stable. For these reasons it is not surprising that clear evidence for adaptation to rearrangement and for dependence of the young on environmental contact in developing coordination has been found only in primates and in cats.

Such, in brief, is the background of

our effort to discover the operating conditions of the suspected mechanism. Our conclusion has been that a key to its operation is the availability of "reafference." This word was coined by the German physiologists Erich von Holst and Horst Mittelstädt to describe neural excitation following sensory stimulation that is systematically dependent on movements initiated by the sensing animal; von Holst and Mittelstädt also used the word "exafference" to describe the result of stimulation that is inde-

pendent of self-produced movement. "Afference" alone refers to any excitation of afferent nerves. These concepts should become clearer to the reader from the remainder of this article.

Among the contributions von Helmholtz made to science were many that were later incorporated into psychology. His experiments included work on the displacement of visual images by prisms. He was the first to report that the misreaching caused by such a dis-

placement is progressively reduced during repeated efforts and that on removal of the prism the subject who has succeeded in adapting to this displacement will at first misreach in the opposite direction.

Helmholtz' findings and those of similar experiments by many other workers have often been interpreted as resulting from recognition of error and consequent correction. We doubted this interpretation because of our conviction that a single mechanism underlies both

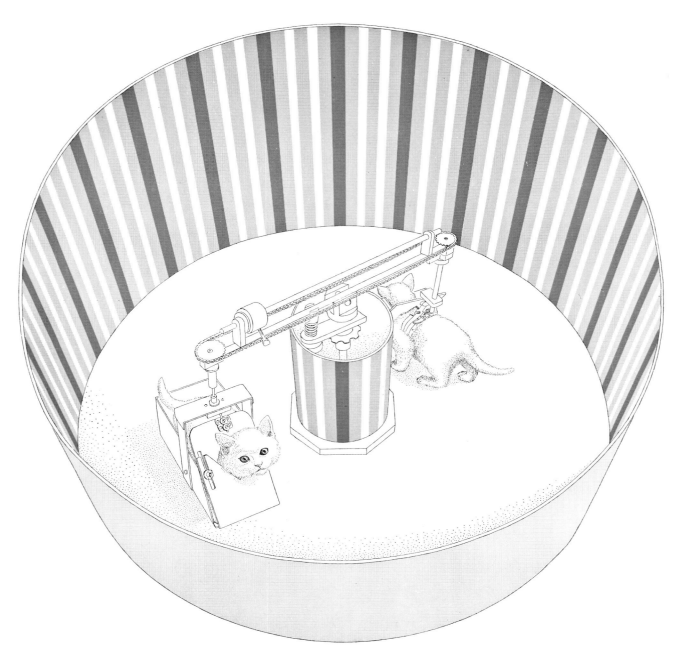

ACTIVE AND PASSIVE MOVEMENTS of kittens were compared in this apparatus. The active kitten walked about more or less freely; its gross movements were transmitted to the passive kitten by the chain and bar. The passive kitten, carried in a gondola, received essentially the same visual stimulation as the active kitten because of the unvarying pattern on the wall and on the center post. Active kittens developed normal sensory-motor coordination; passive kittens failed to do so until after being freed for several days.

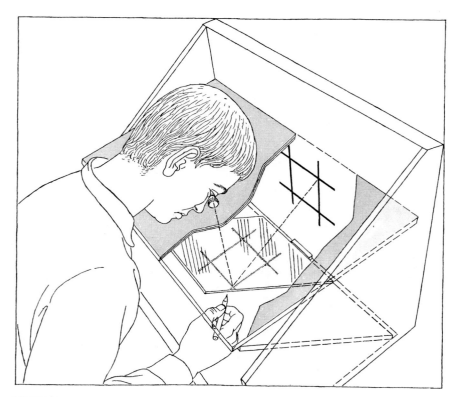

MIRROR APPARATUS tests subject's ability to guide his unseen hand to a visible target. Subject first marks under the mirror the apparent location of the corners of the square as he sees them in the mirror. He then looks through a prism, as depicted in the illustration below, after which he makes more marks. They show his adaptation to the prism effect.

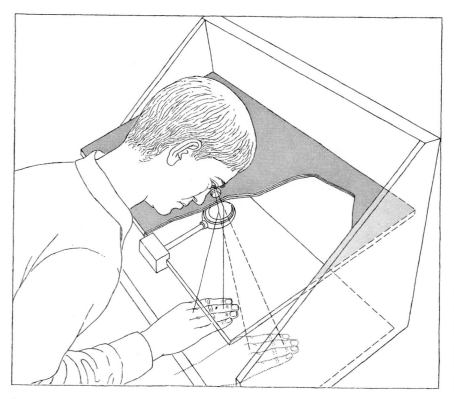

VIEW THROUGH PRISM displaces a visual image. Some subjects looked at their motionless hand, some moved the arm back and forth in a left-right arc, and some had the arm moved passively in a similar arc. They then made marks under the mirror as shown in the illustration at the top of the page. Typical results appear in illustrations on opposite page.

adaptation to rearrangement in the adult and the development of the young. An error-correcting process could hardly explain the original acquisition of coordination. If an infant initially has no sense of the spatial relation between his efforts to move his hand and their visual consequences, he cannot recognize a visible error in reaching. Yet infants do acquire eye-hand coordination in their earliest months. Hence we suspected that error recognition was no more necessary for adaptation in the adult than it was in the development of the infant's coordination. To test this assumption we designed an experiment that prevented the subject from recognizing his error. If he still managed to correct his reach to allow for a displaced image, it would be evident that there was more to the matter of adaptation than the simple fact that the subject could see his error directly.

With this objective in mind we designed the apparatus shown in the top illustration at the left. In this apparatus the subject saw the image of a square target reflected by a mirror and was asked to mark on a piece of paper under the mirror the apparent position of the corners of the square. Because of the mirror, he could see neither the marks nor his hand. After he had marked each point 10 times, withdrawing his hand between markings so that he would have to position it anew each time, the mirror and marking sheet were removed and a prism was substituted. Looking through the prism, the subject then spent several minutes moving his hand in various ways, none of which involved deliberate reaching for a target. Thereafter the original situation was restored and the subject made more marks under the mirror. These marks revealed that each of the subjects was making some correction for the displacement of image that had been caused by the prism.

Having thus established that at least partial adaptation can occur in the absence of direct recognition of error, we used the apparatus to test the role of motor-sensory feedback in adaptation. Our main purpose was to see what degree of adaptation would occur under the respective conditions of active and passive movement—in other words, under conditions of reafference and exafference in which the afference was equivalent. In these experiments the subject's writing arm was strapped to a board pivoted at his elbow to allow left and right movement. He then looked at his hand through a prism under three conditions: (1) no movement, (2) active movement, in which he moved the arm back and forth himself, and (3) passive movement, in which he kept his arm limp and it was moved back and forth by the experimenter. In each case he marked the apparent location of points under the mirror before and after looking through the prism.

Comparison of these marks showed that a few minutes of active movement produced substantial compensatory shifts [see *illustrations at right*]. Indeed, many of the subjects showed full adaptation, meaning exact compensation for the displacement caused by the prism, within half an hour. In contrast, the subjects in the condition of passive movement showed no adaptation. Even though the eye received the same information from both active and passive conditions, the evidently crucial connection between motor output and sensory input was lacking in the passive condition. These experiments showed that movement alone, in the absence of the opportunity for recognition of error, does not suffice to produce adaptation; it must be self-produced movement. From the point of view of our approach this kind of movement, with its contingent reafferent stimulation, is the critical factor in compensating for displaced visual images.

What about an adaptive situation involving movements of the entire body rather than just the arm and hand? We explored this situation in two ways, using an apparatus in which the subject judged the direction of a target only in reference to himself and not to other visible objects [see top illustration on next page]. This kind of direction-finding is sometimes called egocentric localization.

The apparatus consisted initially of a drum that could be rotated by the experimenter, after which the subject, sitting in a chair that he could rotate, was asked to position himself so that a target appeared directly in front of him. Later we dispensed with the drum and merely put the subject in a rotatable chair in a small room. After the experimenter had randomly positioned the target, which was a dimly illuminated slit, the subject rotated himself to find the target.

The first of the two ways in which we tested the role of reafferent stimulation involving movement of the whole body was an experiment in adaptation to short-term exposure to prisms. After several trials at locating the target, the subject put on prism goggles. He then

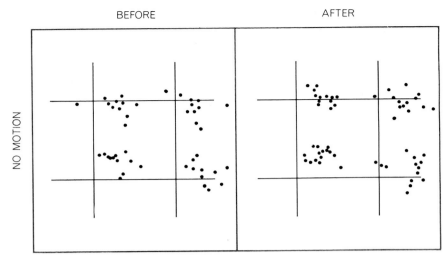

BEFORE — AFTER — NO MOTION

MARKINGS made by a subject before and after looking through a prism as described in illustrations on opposite page are shown. He kept hand still while viewing it through prism.

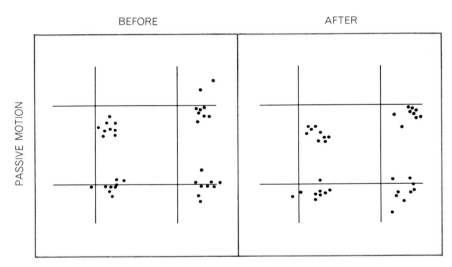

BEFORE — AFTER — PASSIVE MOTION

PASSIVE MOVEMENT of subject's hand as he viewed it through prism produced these marks. They show no adaptation to horizontal displacement of images caused by the prism.

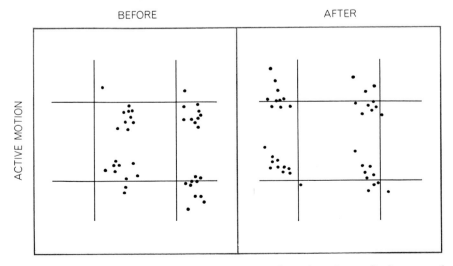

BEFORE — AFTER — ACTIVE MOTION

ACTIVE MOVEMENT of subject's hand produced a clear adaptation to displacement of images by prism. Tests showed importance of such movement in sensorimotor coordination.

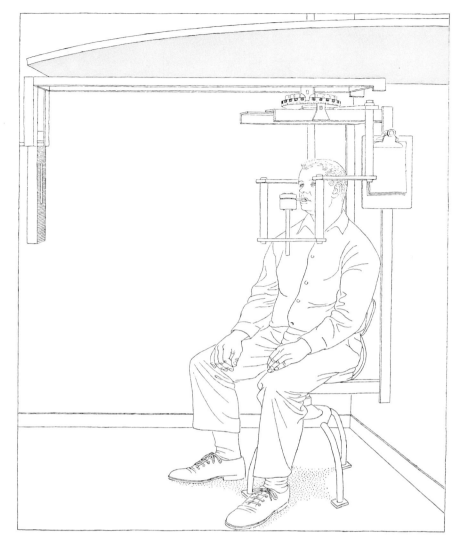

DIRECTION-FINDING by egocentric localization, in which a subject judges the direction of a target only in relation to himself and not to other visual cues, uses this apparatus. Target is randomly positioned at subject's eye level; he then rotates himself so that the target is directly in front of him. He does this before and after wearing prism goggles with which he either walks on an outdoor path or is pushed along the same path in a wheelchair. Change in direction-finding after wearing prisms measures adaptation to the prisms.

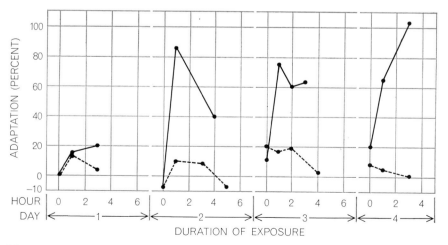

PROLONGED EXPOSURE to prisms produced varying degrees of adaptation to them depending on whether a subject's movement was active (*solid lines*) or passive (*broken lines*).

walked for an hour along an outdoor path or sat in a wheelchair that was pushed along the same path for the same length of time. Thereupon he removed the goggles and went back to the target-finding apparatus for more tests. Any error in target-finding after wearing the prism goggles would be a measure of the adaptation the subject had made to the visual displacements produced by the prisms.

Again the degree of adaptation achieved by the subjects who had been involved in active movement was far greater than that of the subjects who had been carried in the wheelchair. This was true both when one subject had been exposed to the active condition and another to the passive and when a single subject had been exposed successively to each condition. Even more striking contrasts appeared in our second test, which involved wearing prisms for several hours at a time under conditions of active and passive movement. In these circumstances several of the subjects who were able to move voluntarily achieved full adaptation, whereas subjects whose movements were passive achieved virtually no adaptation.

In this connection it will be useful to mention an experiment we conducted on directional hearing. The sound emanating from a localized source reaches the listener's nearer ear a fraction of a second sooner than it reaches his farther ear. This small difference in the time of arrival of the sound at the two ears is the first stage in ascertaining the direction from which the sound comes. If, then, a subject's ears could be in effect displaced around the vertical axis of his head by a small angle, he would err by an equivalent angle in his location of the sound. This effect can be produced artificially by a device called the pseudophone, in which microphones substitute for the external ears. Subjects who have worn a pseudophone for several hours in a normally noisy environment show compensatory shifts in locating sounds, provided that they have been able to move voluntarily. In addition they occasionally report that they hear two sources of sound when only one is present. When measurements are made of the two apparent directions of the source, they differ by approximately the angle at which the ears were displaced around the center of the head during the exposure period. I have called the effect diplophonia.

The reports of doubled localization

following adaptation suggest that compensation for rearrangement consists in the acquisition of a new mode of coordination that is objectively accurate for the condition of rearrangement but that coexists along with the older and more habitual mode. If this is true, the

gradual and progressive course of adaptation usually found in experiments must be considered the result of a slow shift by the subject from the older direction of localization to the newer direction.

All these experiments strongly suggested the role in adaptation of the

close correlation between signals from the motor nervous system, producing active physical movement, and the consequent sensory feedback. This correlation results from the fact that the feedback signals are causally related to movement and that in a stable environ-

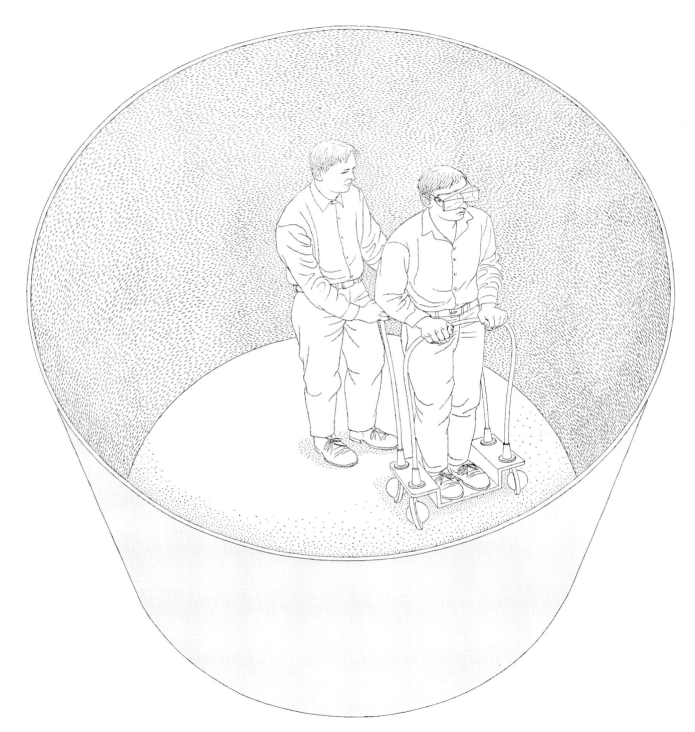

PASSIVE TRANSPORT of a subject wearing prism goggles while viewing a random scene is depicted. Purpose of the apparatus was to test the hypothesis that subjects moving actively through such a scene, which looks the same with or without prisms, would show a degree of adaptation to the prisms whereas subjects moved passively would not. That is what happened. Tests showed a link between visual and motor processes in the central nervous system by altering the correlation between motor outflow and visual feedback.

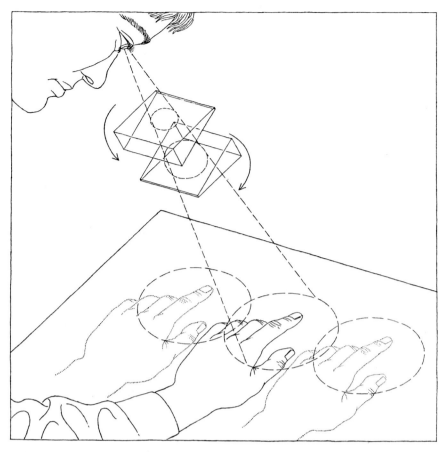

VERIFICATION EXPERIMENT sought to show role of correlation of sensory feedback and active physical movement by impairing it. Means of decorrelation was the rotating-prism apparatus shown here. It produces apparently continuous movement of subject's hand in one dimension, thus breaking the link between actual movement and visual feedback.

	VERTICAL DISPLACEMENT		HORIZONTAL DISPLACEMENT	
BEFORE EXPOSURE				
AFTER EXPOSURE				

RESULTS OF DECORRELATION are shown in markings made by a subject before and after looking through rotating prism. In one condition (*left*) prisms displaced images vertically; in another (*right*), horizontally. Markings after long exposure are spread out in the direction of displacement, showing a loss of precision in visual-motor coordination.

ment there is a unique feedback signal for any particular movement. The correlation is reduced by environmental instability: the presence either of objects that themselves move or of passive movements of the body that are produced by external forces. Under these conditions more than one feedback signal may accompany any particular movement.

From a theoretical point of view the importance of body movement and particularly of self-produced movement derives from the fact that only an organism that can take account of the output signals to its own musculature is in a position to detect and factor out the decorrelating effects of both moving objects and externally imposed body movement. One way to verify the importance of the correlation would be to set up an experimental situation in which the correlation was impaired or deliberately decorrelated. If the consequence was a loss of coordination, evidence for the role of normally correlated reafference in maintaining normal coordination would be strengthened.

We conducted such an experiment in visual perception by means of an apparatus that provided a prism effect of continually varying power [*see top illustration at left*]. In such an apparatus an object such as the hand seems to move constantly, and the movement perceived is wholly independent of whatever actual motion may be taking place. The same arm movement made at different times will produce different retinal feedbacks. Since the subject does not control the continual changes in his visual input that are produced by the prism, his nervous system has no means of distinguishing these changes in the input from those that are self-initiated.

With this apparatus we conducted various experiments, again including active and passive arm movements of the type described previously. We found that the coordination between eye and hand was significantly degraded under conditions of active movement but not under conditions of passive movement. Similar results appeared in tests made by Sanford Freedman of Tufts University of the effect of decorrelation on hearing. Again the performance of subjects who were allowed to move actively during decorrelation deteriorated badly, whereas the performance of subjects whose bodily movements were restricted did not deteriorate. Both the visual and the auditory experiments confirmed the importance of the correlation between movement and sensory feedback in maintaining accurate coordination.

In another test of our hypothesis about reafference we undertook to see what would happen when subjects looked through prisms at a random scene, lacking in the lines and curves that provide normal visual cues. The straight lines characteristic of normal scenes look curved when viewed through a prism. When the prism is removed, such lines seem to curve in the opposite direction. What if straight lines looked curved after a subject had removed prism goggles through which he had viewed a random scene?

Our hypothesis was that such an effect would be produced in subjects who moved actively while viewing the random field but not in those whose movements were passive. If such a result occurred, we would have shown that the subjective geometry of the visual field can be altered by reafference. This finding would have the surprising implication that a motor factor is involved in a process traditionally regarded as purely visual. We would have demonstrated in another way the close, one-to-one correlation between movement and visual feedback and would have further evidence of a link between motor and visual mechanisms in the central nervous system.

Our apparatus for testing this hypothesis consisted of a large drum that had on its inside surface an irregular array of small spots [see illustration on page 277]. These spots looked the same whether viewed with a prism or not. Each subject, before putting on prism goggles and entering the drum, was tested for his perception of a vertical line; we did this by having him indicate when a grating of bars given varying curvatures by prisms appeared straight. Thereafter, entering the drum with the goggles on, the subject either walked around in the drum or was transported on a cart. He stayed in the drum for half an hour and then, after removing the goggles, again took the test with the grating of bars. Without exception the active subjects perceived curvature when looking at lines that were actually straight, whereas the passive subjects perceived little or none.

Having established by these various means the role of reafference in adaptation to changed sensory inputs, we decided to examine its role in the development of visually controlled coordination in the newborn. The contribution of experience to the development

of perceived space and of spatially oriented behavior has been debated for some centuries. During the past few decades a number of experimental approaches to the issue have been made. The technique most often used involves depriving very young animals of sensory contact with the environment. It has been hoped that the procedure would decide whether or not sensory experience, as opposed to maturation alone in the absence of such experience, is required for the development of spatial discrimination.

In certain species of higher mammals, including man, various forms of visual deprivation ranging from total absence of light to mere absence of gross movement in a normally illuminated environment have all resulted in deficiencies in visually guided behavior. Unfortunately these deficiencies are not easily interpreted. They can be attributed, at least in part, to several alternative causes, including pathological changes in the anatomy of the retina and its projections to the brain. Since our findings implicated movement-produced stimulation, they enabled us to test this factor without depriving animals of normal visual stimulation.

The experiments my colleague Alan Hein and I have performed to study the earliest development of vision originated from observations made by Austin H. Riesen of the University of California at Riverside and his collaborators. Riesen's research demonstrated that kittens restrained from walking from the time of their earliest exposure to light develop marked deficiencies in the visual control of behavior compared with unrestrained animals reared normally. The deficiencies of Riesen's animals may have resulted either from the lack of variation in visual stimulation, which was the explanation he preferred, or from the lack of visual stimulation correlated with movement, which was our own hypothesis.

To decide between these alternatives we devised an apparatus in which the gross movements of a kitten moving more or less normally were transmitted to a second kitten that was carried in a gondola [see illustration on page 273]. These gross movements included turns to left and right, circular progress around the center post of the apparatus and any up-and-down motions made by the first kitten. The second kitten was allowed to move its head, since prior experimenters had reported that head movement alone was not sufficient to

produce normal behavior in kittens, and it could also move its legs inside the gondola. Both kittens received essentially the same visual stimulation because the pattern on the walls and the center post of the apparatus was unvarying.

Eight pairs of kittens were reared in darkness until the active member of each pair had enough strength and coordination to move the other kitten in the apparatus; the ages at which that state was attained ranged from eight to 12 weeks. Two other pairs were exposed to patterned light for three hours a day between the ages of two and 10 weeks; during exposure they were in a holder that prevented locomotion. Thereafter all 10 pairs spent three hours a day in the apparatus under the experimental condition; when they were not in the apparatus, they were kept with their mothers and littermates in unlighted cages.

After an average of about 30 hours in the apparatus the active member of each pair showed normal behavior in several visually guided tasks. It blinked at an approaching object; it put out its forepaws as if to ward off collision when gently carried downward toward a surface, and it avoided the deep side of a visual cliff—an apparatus in which two depths, one shallow and the other a sharp drop, appear beneath a sheet of glass [see "The 'Visual Cliff,' " by Eleanor J. Gibson and Richard D. Walk; SCIENTIFIC AMERICAN Offprint 402]. After the same period of exposure each of the passive kittens failed to show these types of behavior. The passive kittens did, however, develop such types of behavior within days after they were allowed to run about in a normal environment.

In sum, the experiments I have described have led us to conclude that the correlation entailed in the sensory feedback accompanying movement—reafference—plays a vital role in perceptual adaptation. It helps the newborn to develop motor coordination; it figures in the adjustment to the changed relation between afferent and efferent signals resulting from growth; it operates in the maintenance of normal coordination, and it is of major importance in coping with altered visual and auditory inputs. The importance of the correlation in all these functions has been revealed by experiments that tamper with its normal operation. In the process these experiments have uncovered a fundamental role of the motor-sensory feedback loop.

VII

DRIVE, MOTIVATION, AND EMOTION

VII

DRIVE, MOTIVATION, AND EMOTION

INTRODUCTION

The concepts of drive and motivation are so basic to behavior that they almost defy definition. Men and other higher animals behave purposively; they act as though they have reasons or motives for their acts. Motivation is defined by many scientists as the driving force that impels behavior. Motivation is a general term; drive is sometimes used more specifically—as when a hungry animal is said to exhibit hunger drive. Others also use drive in a more general sense (for example, a hungry animal is said to be in a high drive state because of hunger). These complexities of definition derive in part from differing theoretical views about the psychological meaning of motivation. In a sense, the problem is simpler for physiological psychology—our task is to determine the biological structures, systems, and mechanisms that generate or impel behavior. It is possible that when we fully understand these mechanisms we will no longer have need of such general terms as drive and motivation.

The first article, "Electrically Controlled Behavior" by Erich von Holst and Ursula von Saint Paul, illustrates the problem of determining what motivates behavior. Walter R. Hess, working in Zurich in the 1930s, first demonstrated that what appeared to be highly motivated behaviors—such as rage, eating, fear, and pleasure—could be elicited in cats by electrical stimulation of certain regions of the brain, particularly in the vicinity of the hypothalamus. Here, von Holst and von Saint Paul demonstrate that a wide range of "motivated" behavior patterns can be elicited in the chicken by electrical stimulation of the brain. Such well-coordinated and seemingly purposive acts as approaching an object and pecking at it, crowing, attacking an "enemy" —indeed, virtually all the normal behavior repertory of the bird—can be evoked by appropriate brain stimulation. The major difference between electrically controlled behavior and normal behavior is that, in the former, a given response sequence, such as attack, occurs mechanically and in isolation, rather than in relation to the normal ongoing interaction between the bird and its environment. The authors discuss their findings and how they relate to the meaning of drive and motivation.

The next article, "Pleasure Centers in the Brain" by James Olds, describes one of the most dramatic and important discoveries about the substrates of motivation in the brain. Olds and Peter Milner found that if a shock is delivered to certain regions of the brain, an animal will attempt to elicit the shock again. Olds combined this observation with Skinner's operant lever-press technique—an animal will press literally thousands of times to deliver shocks to his own brain. One of the "hottest" regions for this phenomenon is in the lateral hypothalamus, an area also connected with such basic drives as eating and drinking. The more general significance of Olds' work is, of course, that such electrical self-stimulation seems to tap directly into brain mechanisms of reward and reinforcement.

Curiosity and the desire to explore are fundamental aspects of behavior, as noted by Robert A. Butler in his article "Curiosity in Monkeys." This work has profound implications for our understanding of motivation. The need to receive stimuli appears to be as strong or stronger than such "basic" drives as hunger and thirst. If a monkey is kept in a dark test box and given the opportunity of looking out of the box briefly by pushing a lever, he will push and look almost endlessly. As Butler suggests, "curiosity" may be largely responsible for the extensive early learning that is such a powerful factor in the biological success of the primates, particularly man.

"Emotion" is familiar to all of us, and at the same time it is a source of some confusion in psychology. Emotion can be measured in terms of behavior, as well as in terms of subjective feeling. Eckhard Hess, in his article entitled "Attitude and Pupil Size," discusses one such measure as an illustration of an experimental approach to the study of emotion. The changes in pupil size of men and women looking at male and female "pinup" pictures are a dramatic example. Pupil diameter is, of course, regulated by the autonomic nervous system, the system controlling the smooth muscles and glands that play such an important role in the expression of emotions. Emotional behavior is considered by many to reflect the drive or motivational state of an organism. It is clear that learned emotional behavior can serve as a very strong source of motivation. Conditioned fear, resulting from pairing of neutral stimuli with shock or other severe punishment, yields highly motivated behavior in rat and man. The issue of emotional conditioning is discussed further in Section IX.

The biology of motivation is not limited to brain mechanisms connected with eating, reward, and emotional responses—in higher animals, social factors play a critical role. In the last article in this section, "Social Deprivation in Monkeys," Harry F. and Margaret Kuenne Harlow describe the importance of such factors. From the time of Freud, adult motives have been traced to the child's relations with his parents. As the Harlows demonstrate, opportunity for normal interaction with age peers is essential for the normal emotional development of monkeys. If deprived of this interaction, they grow up to become severely disturbed, even psychotic, adults.

29

ELECTRICALLY CONTROLLED BEHAVIOR

ERICH VON HOLST AND URSULA VON SAINT PAUL
March 1962

We all recognize that many human actions are controlled by drives, which we can steer but which we cannot easily ignore. We become hungry, thirsty, sleepy; we crave affection; sometimes we are angry or frightened. If we classify an action as controlled by drives when it is not planned or directed by conscious intelligence, then we can maintain that nearly all kinds of animal behavior, and rather large portions of human behavior, are drive-controlled. Often we are not aware of why we act as we do. This lack of awareness takes a number of forms.

A boy who stops in front of several grocery stores on his way home from school may not realize that it is hunger that makes the window displays so attractive to him. He may remember only later that he has missed his lunch that day. In this example the drive accentuates whatever is most important among the things that can be perceived.

A man who is kept waiting by a young lady may approach a complete stranger, thinking her to be the person he is expecting. He does not realize that it is his longing that transforms the stranger into the person he is expecting; he is only annoyed by his poor eyesight. Here the drive has led to a change in perception, an illusion.

A child who wakes up crying with fear in a strange room, quite sure that he sees a tiger, does not know it is his own fear that creates the animal, which disappears as soon as the light is turned on. Here the drive produced a hallucination.

Thus our moods, feelings, drives and wishes constantly color and change the so-called objective world around us. Our actions are guided by a variety of unconscious drives on which are superimposed those needs and wishes of which we are aware.

Presumably animals other than man have no awareness of drives. Moreover, if a drive in an animal is fully satisfied, it cannot be elicited by any stimulus. On the other hand, the longer a drive is held in check, the more urgent it becomes and the wider is the range of stimuli that will elicit the corresponding behavior, be it eating, sexual activity, flight or care of another animal of the same species. In many kinds of behavior if the drive is held in check too long, the behavior pattern will begin in the total absence of the appropriate stimulus.

An example is described by the eminent student of animal behavior Konrad Z. Lorenz. When a captive starling accustomed to receiving its food from a dish was allowed to fly freely, it performed, as if in pantomime, the entire pent-up cycle of catching an insect in the air. It would appear to fixate on an insect, swoop down on it, catch it and

URGE TO FLEE is elicited by a weak electric current delivered by an electrode implanted in the brain stem of a rooster. Before stimulation (*left*) the rooster feeds calmly. On stimulation (*center*) the rooster fixates intently on a nonexistent object approaching from

swallow it—all in the absence of an insect. It is hard to believe that in such cases an animal does not have a hallucinatory perception of the absent prey.

We know from observations of people with brain damage, from electrical stimulation of regions of the brain in patients undergoing brain surgery while conscious, and particularly from the celebrated experiments on cats by Walter R. Hess of Zurich, that in mammals the chief center for the regulation of drives lies in a part of the brain stem called the diencephalon. When various areas of the brain of a surgical patient are stimulated, a number of spontaneous desires and feelings and their corresponding perceptions are elicited. Hess implanted electrodes in the brain stem of cats and found that in the presence of the appropriate object he could stimulate the cats to eat, attack or flee. If the stimulation was very intense, the animal would chew inedible objects or attack a human observer instead of a natural enemy. The cats behaved as they would have if the corresponding drives had been abnormally pent up. Perceptual accentuation, illusion and hallucination all seem to have been involved in these experiments.

Hess began his pioneering studies in the early 1930's and in 1949 shared the Nobel prize for medicine and physiology. His methods allowed him to identify many reactive regions in the brain stem. He sacrificed his animals following stimulation, cut their brains into serial sections and mapped the points of effective stimulation, which had been stained. Certain moods or drives, such as fatigue, turned out to be associated with specific zones, whereas others were related to larger regions or interspersed with the locations associated with other drives. Unfortunately simple spatial separation into discrete centers, each representing one specific function, is not to be found.

Such localization of function in the nervous system has considerable importance for the physician. The physiologist, however, must remember that localization studies answer the question of "where" but not the questions of "how" and "why." In order to answer these physiological questions one must try to penetrate into the dynamics of the drive mechanism. It is on this topic that I wish to report.

There are two methods of studying the way in which animal behavior is controlled by drives. The first is careful observation of one species over many years and under various conditions. In this way one acquires expert knowledge that enables one to predict with some certainty how an animal of this species will behave in a particular situation. Predictive ability of this sort is largely intuitive; it cannot be reduced to its components or used to make measurements. Analysis and measurement become possible, however, with the second method, namely the technical mastery of electrical stimulation of regions in the brain stem. Even with this method a detailed understanding of the species and its behavior remains indispensable. To recognize the delicate interplay of drives one must be able to judge the significance of individual behavior sequences, as seen under normal conditions, and to appreciate their place within the animal's behavioral repertory.

The richest inventory of behavior can be found among animals that form social groups. In addition to the egoistic drives that every organism needs for survival, these animals display a variety of altruistic drives for regulating their social interactions, which are not unlike

a distance; the object gets closer as the stimulus increases in strength and duration. (The stimulus voltage can be read on the meter at right.) Finally (*right*) the rooster jumps away fearfully. On repeated stimulation the frightening object always seems to come from the same direction. These photographs were made by the authors at the Max Planck Institute for the Physiology of Behavior.

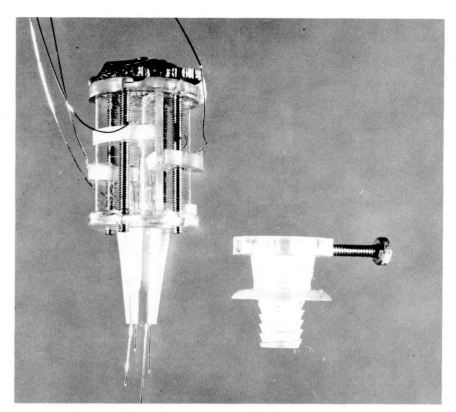

STIMULATING APPARATUS consists of a plastic fitting (*right*), which heals in place after being threaded into the skull of an animal, and an electrode carrier (*left*), which goes into the fitting. The carrier holds four electrodes, the lengths of which are adjustable.

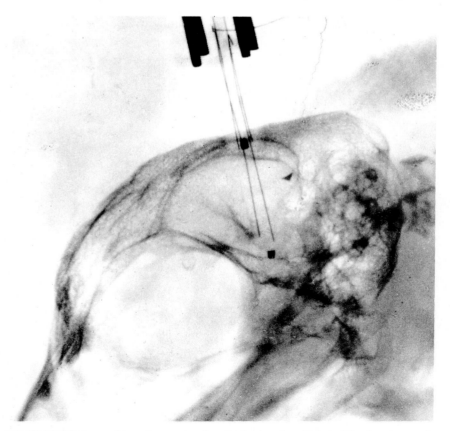

X-RAY VIEW shows electrodes penetrating the brain of a chicken. The drawing at the bottom left on the opposite page delineates the brain and the brain stem region. The electrodes and the stimuli they carry cause no pain, and the experiments do the animal no harm.

human social behavior. Such a species, the domestic chicken, has served as our experimental subject at the Max Planck Institute for the Physiology of Behavior in Seewiesen, Germany.

Chickens have a large repertory of gestures and a language consisting of several dozen "words." To be sure, their language is not learned, as is the language of man; their sounds and the understanding of these sounds are inborn. In the chicken yard there is a definite "pecking order" among the hens, which has been established as the result of fights in early youth. The hen of highest rank is entitled to the best sleeping place and the best food; the others take what is left in sequence. Transgression by a hen of lower rank is punished by pecking and the pulling of feathers.

The rooster is both ruler and cavalier. He warns the others with several distinct sounds against approaching enemies on the ground or in the air. He defends the hens against attackers, announces the presence of food, seeks out a nesting place for the young hen who is ready to mate and summons her with gentle, whispering sounds. Half-asleep, he watches over the sleeping flock. The call "cock-a-doodle-doo," which each rooster emits in his own distinctive fashion, may be freely translated to mean: "Here I am, ready to stand by you as mate and defender." Rival males are threatened and fought with vigor; the defeated rooster leaves the scene and may hide for days. All these forms of behavior, which I have merely sketched, are accompanied or preceded by specific gestures or sounds that tell the expert much about what is happening. It takes years to recognize and appreciate the complex social activity of the chicken yard. But until one understands chicken society there is no point in using electrical stimulation methods to study the role of drives in behavior.

At our institute these methods begin with anesthetizing a chicken and inserting in its skull a small threaded plastic fitting that remains in place permanently. To conduct an experiment we introduce into an opening in the fitting a small device bearing four electrode wires, each of which can be positioned in the brain by a screw [*see top illustration at left*]. The electrodes can be inserted while the animal is conscious, since the brain itself is totally insensitive to touching or probing. The damage done by this procedure is so slight that the experimental animal remains normal and healthy after 100 or more experiments extending over a period of years.

The initial experiment is to advance an electrode slowly into the brain stem, applying at intervals a low-voltage alternating current (usually of 50 cycles). We observe the animal's reaction closely and record, often with motion pictures, the behavior that is elicited as the tip of the electrode reaches different levels. When the electrode tip is still some distance away from a reactive structure, a relatively strong current will be needed to evoke a particular response. As the electrode tip penetrates deeper, the response can be evoked with less and less current: the threshold decreases. As the electrode tip moves away from this response zone the threshold increases again. One thereby obtains, on traversing the brain stem, a varying number of threshold curves for different types of behavior [*see illustration at right below*]. If an interesting reaction is encountered, the electrode is left at this depth and is allowed to remain for hours or days in the animal's skull.

The chickens are kept on a table to which they have become accustomed before testing, and they are connected with fine wires to the stimulating apparatus. Alternatively the animals are equipped with a tiny radio receiver, weighing about 25 grams, and are permitted to wander about freely. The remote-control procedure is valuable for studying behavior within a social group.

By stimulating the brain stem in this way we have evoked almost all the forms of activity and vocalization familiar to those acquainted with chickens. We have also obtained various composite forms of behavior, some of which do not occur in nature. The natural modes of behavior can be classified provisionally into simple movements and complex behavior sequences. Simple movements are, for example, sitting, standing, preening, grooming, looking about alertly, and stretching the neck as if peering at something in the distance. The last response is sometimes accompanied by a special call used to warn against airborne predators. Other simple responses are scratching with one foot, which is part of a courtship sequence, and the various orienting attitudes such as turning the head to the right or left or moving it up or down.

More complex behavior sequences include seeking and eating food, seeking and drinking water, escaping from predators on the ground, escaping from flying predators, the sequence of settling down and falling asleep and the sequence of guiding a hen to a nest, which is of course performed only by the rooster. These complex activities consist of a chain of different individual movements that are all related to a single goal. For example, a series of steps is interposed between an initiating stimulus, delivered to the "sleep" region in a waking and active rooster, and the final stage of deep sleep. The animal stops eating, looks around and walks; it flutters its eyelids, yawns and sits down; it fluffs its plumage, retracts its head and closes its eyes. All these effects—each of which, incidentally, can be evoked individually from other foci—are subordinated to a single drive, that associated with fatigue or the desire to sleep. Another meaningful series, having to do with disgust, is depicted at top of page 290. Here also individual components can be evoked by stimulating other specific regions of the brain stem.

The ability to evoke at will either individual movements or complex drive sequences has theoretical significance. In the case of individual movements

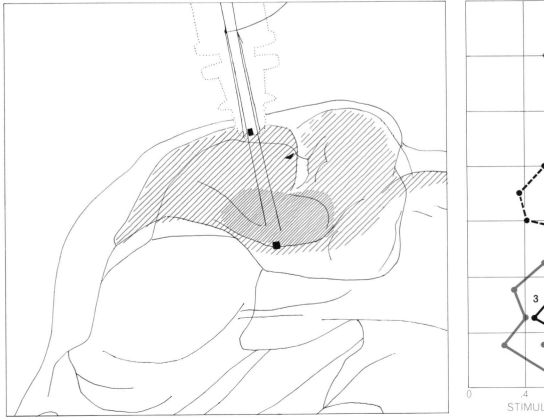
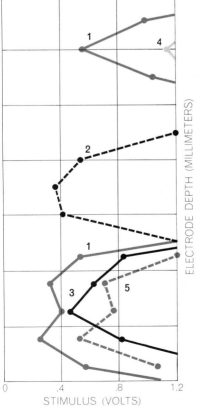

REGION STIMULATED AND RESPONSES are shown in these two illustrations. The brain is indicated (*left*) by colored hatching, and the brain stem, the region actually stimulated, is doubly hatched. As an electrode is lowered gradually to different depths and activated, the animal may respond in various ways. The charted responses (*right*) are: *1*, alertness; *2*, watchful staring; *3*, shaking the head; *4*, turning to left; *5*, turning to right. Overlapping represents responses at the same depth but at different sites.

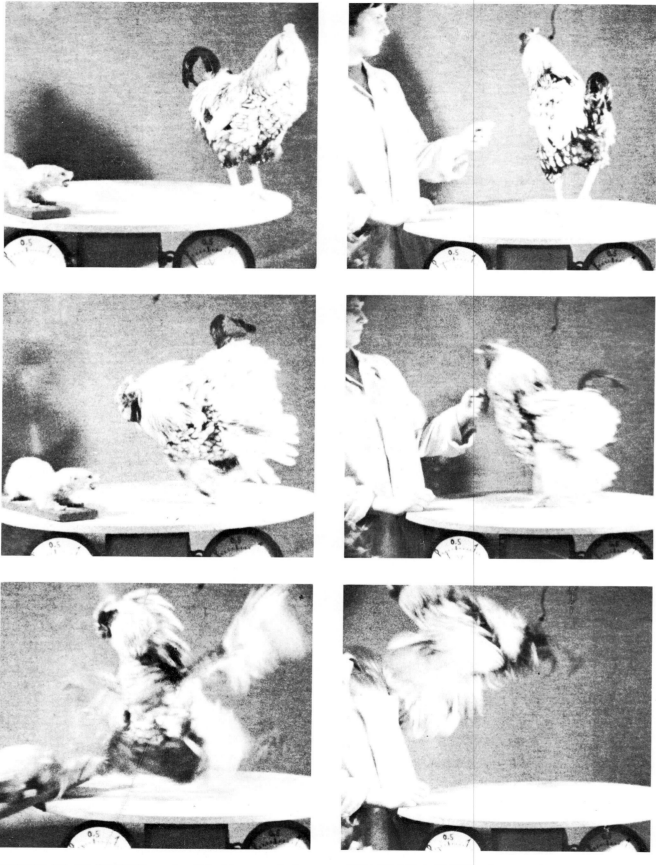

ATTACK ON AN "ENEMY" can be elicited by a particular stimulus. In the absence of the stimulus (*top*) the rooster ignores the stuffed predator. When the stimulus is applied, the bird turns on the stuffed animal and attacks it furiously, spurs flying.

ATTACK ON A FRIEND, the rooster's keeper, is provoked if the natural "enemy" is absent and if the stimulus used in the film sequence shown at left is prolonged. The rooster prefers to aim its attack at the keeper's face rather than at her hand

the stimulus merely furnishes an impulse for a particular movement; in the case of the drives the stimulus sets up a goal that can be attained in different ways, depending on external circumstances. It is not always easy to decide, however, whether a stimulus activates an isolated movement or an entire drive sequence. Many complex behavior sequences occur in their entirety only under certain external circumstances. To be sure, escape reactions can be evoked in the absence of the appropriate external object (or its substitute) if the brain stimulation is sufficiently intense. In such cases it is probable that the absent object of fear is being hallucinated. Hallucination, or apparent hallucination, does not seem to occur, however, when aggressive behavior is evoked by stimulation. Let me explain further.

Chickens exhibit different kinds of attack behavior. For example, stimulation of a certain region of the brain activates the characteristic attack that one hen makes against another hen of lower rank. If the stimulated hen is confronted with another hen (alive or stuffed), it pecks at the other hen and pulls its feathers. When a human hand is proffered as a substitute object, it is pecked in the same way if the stimulation has been increased somewhat. When no object is provided, however, and if the brain stimulation is strong, the hen looks about in great excitement and pecks the ground several times, much as an angry man may hit a table with his fist if the object of his anger is out of reach. But the other part of this form of natural attack, the plucking of feathers, is missing.

A totally different form of aggression is directed against natural enemies of the species. The behavior that accompanies this drive never arises unless an enemy, real or artificial, is present. The three photographs at the left on the opposite page, taken from a motion picture, shows an electrically stimulated rooster attacking a small stuffed predator. Before stimulation the rooster had hardly noticed that an "enemy" was present The stimulation brought out the full behavioral sequence: alertness, visual fixation, approach, attitude of rage, attack with spurs and triumphant call.

The second series of motion-picture frames on the opposite page shows the behavior of the same rooster toward a keeper who had always been treated as a friend. After sustained stimulation the rooster flew up and attacked the keeper's face with its spurs. (The human face is apparently a better substitute for an enemy than the human hand.) If all substitutes for an enemy are lacking—when

there is, so to speak, no hook on which to hang an illusion—the rooster exhibits only motor restlessness. Moreover, the same motor restlessness is observed if one stimulates brain areas associated with hunger, thirst, courtship or fighting under conditions in which the environment does not permit the unreeling of the entire behavior sequence. For this reason it is often necessary to vary the external conditions to be sure which particular behavior sequence—which complex drive—has in fact been activated.

Simple behavior patterns other than motor restlessness can be observed in a variety of complex drive systems. Sitting down occurs whether the hen simply wants to sit down, to incubate eggs or to

go to sleep. Standing up marks the onset of all those behavior sequences that entail a change in position. A particular excited cackling (poh-poh-poh) accompanies a number of behavior sequences that involve a mood of anxious tension. Another kind of cackling that sounds oddly like scolding (cock-cock-cock-colay) accompanies various forms of relaxation of function, such as landing after a brief flight or "relief" after laying an egg. The frozen stance, with head pulled in, can be an element in the behavior toward a predator threatening from the air (in which case the chicken seems to feign death), or it can be an attitude of humility brought on by a rival of superior strength. Even the pecking

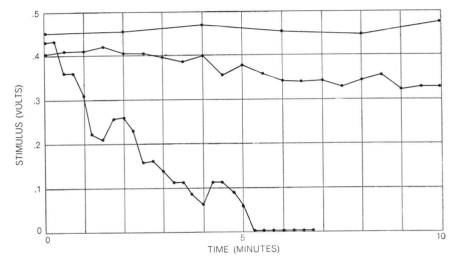

EFFECT OF STIMULATION FREQUENCY is found by plotting the threshold voltage needed to elicit "attentive reconnoitering" in a sleepy hen. The voltage is raised slowly; the dots indicate the voltage reached when the hen's head begins to move. If the stimuli are two minutes apart (*top curve*), the threshold voltage is virtually the same each time. If the stimuli are only 30 seconds apart (*middle curve*), the threshold voltage tends to drop. If the stimuli are closely spaced (*bottom*), the hen becomes fully awake in about five minutes.

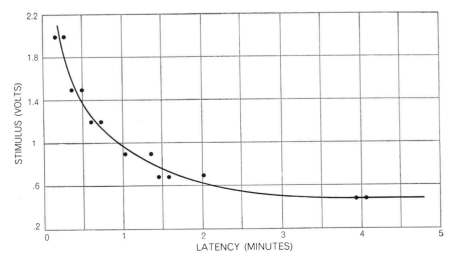

EFFECT OF VOLTAGE STRENGTH is found by plotting the interval between stimulus and response, called the latency. In this case the response is a warning call (clucking).

STIMULUS

——————→ TIME

"DISGUST REACTION" can be elicited by stimulating the hen's brain stem in the appropriate place. The hen, which has been eating, stops (*1*), spits out the food in its beak (*2*), shakes its head (*3*) and wipes its beak on the ground before eating again (*4*).

of food on the ground can be either an element in the behavior associated with hunger or an element of fights between rivals. Fighting cocks tend to peck hastily at food or, if a rival is present, they peck the bare ground. The latter form of pecking, known as displacement pecking, is a threatening gesture [see "The Fighting Behavior of Animals," by Irenäus Eibl-Eibesfeldt; SCIENTIFIC AMERICAN Offprint 470].

From such observations we can conclude that a fairly large number of movements or behavior elements are subordinated to a smaller number of more complex drives. The drives employ the repertory of simple movements as a means of reaching various goals. The existence of such a hierarchic system of drives is well supported by the observation that only the complex "high level" drives give the impression of completely spontaneous activity. In contrast, the individual acts induced by stimulation, such as particular sounds, head-turning, sitting down, pecking, swallowing and the like, all have a certain mechanical character, as if they did not concern the animal as a whole.

Before turning to our experimental attempts to combine drives, I should say something about thresholds and the variation in the strength of the current needed to evoke particular forms of activity. During and after stimulation there are conspicuous changes in behavior. When a particular behavior is evoked in a given brain region for the first time, the threshold is usually quite high; that is, one has to apply a strong stimulus in order to elicit the behavior. With rapidly repeated or protracted stimulation the threshold decreases markedly and may even fall to zero, in which case the activity may continue for a fairly long time without further stimulation [*see upper illustration on preceding page*]. Later on, if the stimulus is maintained over a

COMBINATION OF TWO STIMULI may result in the suppression of the weaker response, followed by its delayed expression. One stimulus causes the hen to flatten its feathers and stretch out its neck (*a*). A different stimulus induces it to fluff its feathers (*b*). Combination of the two elicits the two responses in succession, but the second does not appear until all stimulation has ended (*c*).

period of time, the threshold gradually rises again and often becomes so high that, for several minutes or as much as an hour afterward, the particular behavior cannot be elicited.

By combining brain stimuli in certain ways we have found that the initial decline in threshold and its subsequent rise are attributable to two different processes. The initial decline in threshold represents a change in what can be called central set, or predisposition, so that it favors a particular activity to which the animal was initially more or less indifferent. Simultaneously there is a rise in threshold for other activities that are antagonistic to the one evoked. For instance, if by stimulation one makes a sleepy animal hungry and it begins to eat, the threshold for inducing sleep has been concurrently increased. Similarly, if an animal that spontaneously exhibits a slight tendency toward flight is made sleepy by the appropriate brain stimulation, the threshold for flight is simultaneously increased. These shifts in central set represent a shift in dynamic balance. In contrast, the kind of increase in threshold that occurs after prolonged activation of a particular behavior represents a form of central blocking, or central adaptation, that makes the animal in-

creasingly less sensitive to the continuing stimulation. This blocking occurs in the brain stem close to the stimulated region, whereas the central change of set seems to take place higher in the brain, closer to the cortical regions associated with motor activity.

In addition to these quantitative changes in behavior, qualitative changes also appear. I shall cite only one striking example. In roosters a number of behavioral states manifest a certain underlying depressive quality, such states as the desire to escape, crying, "freezing," warning, reconnoitering, scolding. If, through appropriate stimulation, one of these activities is maintained over a period of time, there is usually a change five to 10 seconds after the end of the stimulation that transforms the depressive mood into a euphoric, self-assured one. The rooster stands up alertly, flaps its wings and crows. In much the same way, people often feel happy and cheerful after a prolonged depression.

The foregoing illustrates the necessity for controlling conditions carefully if one hopes to discover exact relationships between stimulus and response. Fortunately such control is attainable, and it is possible to maintain a desired mood

over long periods without change. Clear stimulus-response relationships then become evident. For many types of behavior we have been able to draw simple curves showing the interval between onset of the stimulus and onset of the response—that is, showing latency as a function of stimulus strength [*see lower illustration on page 289*]. For example, with a stimulus current of about .5 volt the latency in a given response may be four seconds; with four times the voltage the latency may be only about .2 second. In general we find a simple reciprocal relationship between stimulus intensity and stimulus duration.

In addition to latency we can measure such variables as the speed of a motor sequence, the frequency of a rhythmic repetitive movement or the length of time a given kind of behavior continues beyond the end of the stimulation. Reproducible quantitative relationships can be observed in all these cases. The freely moving animal, steered by the experimenter in its spontaneous activities, proves to be a complicated yet precisely functioning physical apparatus.

All this had to be considered before we could turn to the problem of combining different drives. Such a combination is achieved by means of two differ-

STIMULUS 1

STIMULUS 2

STIMULUS 1

→ TIME

ANOTHER COMBINATION OF STIMULI leads to suppression of certain components of one of the responses. Gradual activation of an urge to flee in a sitting hen (*a*) causes the hen to stand and look about alertly before it finally jumps. When a continuous stimulus for sitting is applied at the same time (*b*), the hen becomes restless but keeps sitting until it finally jumps away.

ent electrodes that activate different drives concurrently in different regions of the brain. For safety's sake this is done by stimulating one region intermittently and the other region during the intervals. In this way only one region is physically stimulated at a time, although two drives are activated simultaneously. If the alternation of the two stimuli is between four and 10 per second, the physiological effects in both regions become perfectly continuous.

When two drives are intermingled in this way, several types of interplay can be observed. The simplest type results when two different elementary movements are stimulated: one movement is simply added to the other without mutual influence. If, for example, one stimulus makes the chicken sit down and the other makes it look to the left, then the chicken does both simultaneously. Similarly, one can combine pecking and head-turning, rising and cackling, sitting down and preening, and so on.

More interesting is a combination in which the animal strikes a balance, so to speak, between the two forms of behavior. For instance, one can combine reconnoitering (peering into the distance, with neck stretched and head immobile) with a totally different searching gesture (in which the head sweeps quickly back and forth). This combination results in a compromise movement in which the neck protrudes only a little and the head moves only slightly.

In a fairly rare type of combined reaction both forms of behavior appear in full strength but alternate rhythmically. An example would be eating and reconnoitering: the animal makes a few pecking movements, then raises its head abruptly to look about, pecks and looks about again. When two responses are mutually antagonistic, an attempt to evoke them together will lead to mutual cancellation, provided that the two brain stimuli have been properly adjusted. Thus a stimulus to turn to the left can be exactly canceled by a stimulus to turn to the right.

In an even rarer type of combined reaction two stimuli lead to a new type of behavior containing elements not normally evoked by either stimulus alone. So far we have found only one particularly clear example of this reaction. One of two stimuli induces the hen to peck aggressively; the other induces it to take flight, with its feathers smoothed down. Both stimuli together, if properly balanced, induce neither attack nor flight. Instead the hen emits piercing cries and rushes frantically back and forth with its feathers raised and its wings spread. In nature this behavior would occur if the hen were confronted by an antagonist of superior strength near its nest, where it would not be inclined to flee.

A frequent result of combining two stimuli is that the stronger drive suppresses the weaker one, even though more voltage is applied to evoke the

weaker drive. One can often show that the weaker drive has been activated but that its expression has somehow been blocked. One stimulus makes the hen appear anxious, stretch out its neck and flatten its plumage; the other stimulus induces it to fluff up its plumage (a component of grooming). If the relative strength of the two stimuli is appropriate, the animal acts, on simultaneous delivery of both stimuli, as if only the first stimulus were present. If both stimuli are stopped at the same time, the fluffed-up plumage appears afterward. Evidently this response too must have been activated during the period of stimulation, although it remained latent.

The phenomenon of suppression exhibits still other peculiarities. Complex drive systems, which consist of several behavior elements, are rarely suppressed as a whole; instead their components are eliminated successively, as if they had different thresholds for suppression. If one slowly activates a tendency to flee in a chicken that has been sitting quietly on the ground, there appear successively, like links in a chain, the following movements: attentive alertness, getting up, walking about, freezing and finally jumping away. The sequence mimics flight from an air-borne predator. Let us now deliver to another region of the brain in the same chicken a stimulus inducing a strong tendency to sit while simultaneously activating the tendency to flee. At first nothing happens, until the urge to flee becomes quite intense. Then

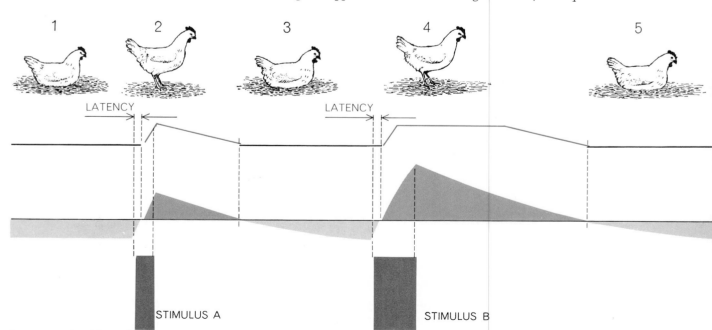

URGE TO STAND, induced by electrical stimulation, can be made to override a spontaneous urge to sit. If the stimulus (A) is strong but brief, the chicken stands up quickly and promptly sits down again (1, 2, 3). If the stimulus is repeated at the same strength but is maintained twice as long (B), the chicken remains standing for an appreciable time (4). With a weaker but longer stimulus (C), the bird gets up more slowly and remains standing for a still longer time (6). Note, however, that the time the bird

the chicken suddenly jumps away as the last phase of the suppressed escape sequence erupts explosively. This behavior resembles the natural behavior of a bird that continues to incubate its eggs in the nest as an enemy comes gradually closer. The bird jumps from the nest only at the last moment.

So far I have discussed only those drive combinations that result from two kinds of brain stimulation. It is possible, however, to activate and combine two different drives by inducing one form of behavior through an environmental stimulus (visual or auditory) and letting it interact with an artificially induced drive. One can say that there is no essential difference between these two methods, and the situation is no different when brain stimulation is combined with a spontaneous drive. It is easier, however, to make measurements if both drives are associated with voltages. These facts strongly suggest that stimulation of the brain stem indeed sets off, in the responding centers, what are essentially complete and normal processes. The effects of stimulation are therefore not mere imitations of natural processes. They are not "pseudoaffective" states but genuine drives.

I shall now attempt to give a somewhat more detailed theoretical interpretation of what goes on within the nervous system when two drives interact. Let us consider a simple case of antagonism between drives, for example the one found

in a hen that has a spontaneous urge to sit (because it is in the "incubating mood") but that can be induced to get up by stimulation of a particular brain region. The illustration on the bottom of these two pages depicts the situation. We stimulate such a hen, which sits spontaneously, three separate times to make it stand. The three stimuli differ in intensity and duration.

We record all those aspects of resulting behavior that can be measured: the latency, the speed with which the animal gets up and the length of time that the animal continues to stand after cessation of the stimulus. All these values are represented schematically in the upper curve of the illustration. One can see how the latency depends on the strength of the stimulus, as already discussed. One can also see how the speed with which the animal gets up (steepness of the curve) depends on strength and duration of the stimulus. In theory one could reduce all these data by ascribing them to a single process, which is depicted by the intermediate curve. The horizontal zero line should represent that central condition in which standing and sitting are in equilibrium. Below this line the central drive to sit is dominant; above the line the drive to stand is dominant. The stimulus for getting up alters this central state; when the drive for sitting becomes zero, the threshold has been reached and the animal begins to stand up.

If the stimulus for getting up is in-

tense, the threshold is reached rapidly and the latency is short. If the stimulus for standing is weak, the curve rises less steeply, intersects the zero line later, and the latency is prolonged. The steepness of this rising curve similarly determines the speed with which the animal gets up. The length of time it remains standing after the stimulus to stand up has been turned off depends only on the height reached by the central drive level for standing.

The intermediate curve shown in the illustration may seem to be nothing but a hypothetical construct. But if we now fit the chicken with a second electrode to activate sitting, we can see that the intermediate curve does in fact represent something real. We deliver a stimulus for sitting, at various times, while the animal is spontaneously standing and measure the strength of the stimulus needed to induce the animal to sit down at any given moment. The values obtained are in complete agreement with the intermediate curve, which had at first been based on mere conjecture. In other words, there must be, within the central nervous system, some kind of process that takes the course described by the form of our intermediate curve. It is too early to say anything about the nature of this process, whether it is chemical or electrical or whether it is a combination of both (which is the most likely).

As one can see, it is possible to measure the inner dynamics of drives in a rather complicated animal and thereby measure processes that ordinarily elude us when we simply observe behavior; so far as we are concerned an animal that sits is merely sitting; a rooster that crows is merely crowing; a hen that eats is merely eating. But observation alone cannot as a rule tell us how strongly the animal "feels inclined" to sit, crow or eat. We do not know how strong the inner drives are at any given instant or what other drives may be operating. A more detailed analysis of these central phenomena is likely to reveal a complicated interplay of forces. It is only infrequently the case that two drives, such as those that involve sitting and standing, are mutually antagonistic. On the whole the momentary situation within the brain is much more like a knot of numerous threads that pull in the most diverse directions. The organism comprises a bundle of drives, which support one another or oppose one another to greater or lesser extent. "Spontaneous" activity is the result of a continual and shifting interplay of forces in the central nervous system.

LATENCY

STIMULUS C

remains standing when the stimulus has been turned off is about the same after each of the last two stimuli. Evidently some process in the central nervous system of the chicken takes the form of the intermediate curve. The colored area above the "zero line" symbolizes the urge to stand; the gray area below the line symbolizes the urge to sit.

30

PLEASURE CENTERS IN THE BRAIN

JAMES OLDS
October 1956

The brain has been mapped in various ways by modern physiologists. They have located the sensory and motor systems and the seats of many kinds of behavior—centers where messages of sight, sound, touch and action are received and interpreted. Where, then, dwell the "higher feelings," such as love, fear, pain and pleasure? Up to three years ago the notion that the emotions had specific seats in the brain might have been dismissed as naive—akin perhaps to medieval anatomy or phrenology. But recent research has brought a surprising turn of affairs. The brain does seem to have definite loci of pleasure and pain, and we shall review here the experiments which have led to this conclusion.

The classical mapping exploration of the brain ranged mainly over its broad, fissured roof—the cortex—and there localized the sensory and motor systems and other areas which seemed to control most overt behavior. Other areas of the brain remained mostly unexplored, and comparatively little was known about their functions. Particularly mysterious was the series of structures lying along the mid-line of the brain from the roof down to the spinal cord, structures which include the hypothalamus and parts of the thalamus [*see diagram on page 296*]. It was believed that general functions of the brain might reside in these structures. But they were difficult

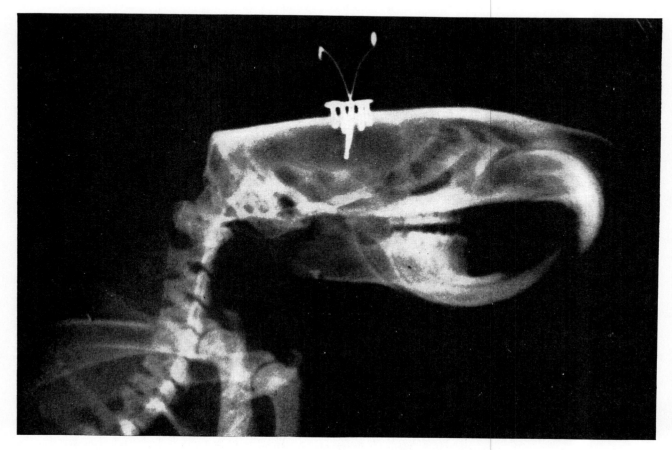

IMPLANTED ELECTRODES in the brain of a rat are shown in this X-ray photograph. The electrodes are held in a plastic carrier screwed to the skull. They can be used to give an electrical stimulus to the brain or to record electrical impulses generated by the brain.

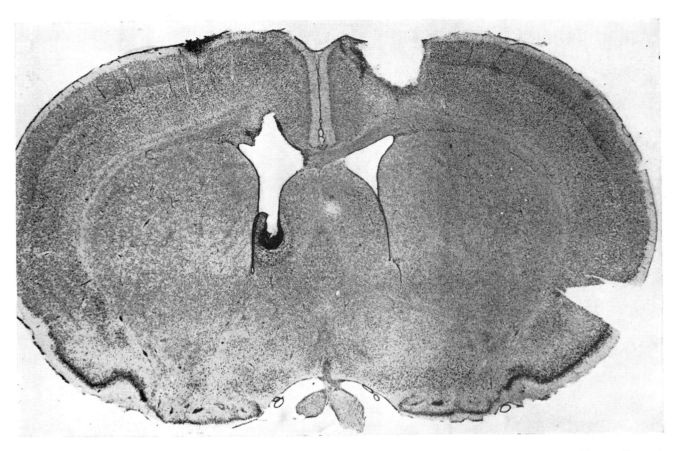

RAT'S BRAIN in a photomicrographic cross section shows a black spot to left of center, marking the point where electrical stimulus was applied. Such cross sections make it possible to tell exactly which center in the brain was involved in the animal's response.

to investigate, for two reasons. First, the structures were hard to get at. Most of them lie deep in the brain and could not be reached without damaging the brain, whereas the cortex could be explored by electrical stimulators and recording instruments touching the surface. Secondly, there was a lack of psychological tools for measuring the more general responses of an animal. It is easy to test an animal's reaction to stimulation of a motor center in the brain, for it takes the simple form of flexing a muscle, but how is one to measure an animal's feeling of pleasure?

The first difficulty was overcome by the development of an instrument for probing the brain. Basically the instrument is a very fine needle electrode which can be inserted to any point of the brain without damage. In the early experiments the brain of an animal could be probed only with some of its skull removed and while it was under anesthesia. But W. R. Hess in Zurich developed a method of studying the brain for longer periods and under more normal circumstances. The electrodes were inserted through the skull, fixed in position

and left there; after the skin healed over the wound, the animal could be studied in its ordinary activities.

Using the earlier technique, H. W. Magoun and his collaborators at Northwestern University explored the region known as the "reticular system" in the lower part of the mid-brain [see page 296]. They showed that this system controls the sleep and wakefulness of animals. Stimulation of the system produced an "alert" electrical pattern, even from an anesthetized animal, and injury to nerve cells there produced more or less continuous sleep.

Hess, with his new technique, examined the hypothalamus and the region around the septum (the dividing membrane at the mid-line), which lie forward of the reticular system. He found that these parts of the brain play an important part in an animal's automatic protective behavior. In the rear section of the hypothalamus is a system which controls emergency responses that prepare the animal for fight or flight. Another system in the front part of the hypothalamus and in the septal area apparently controls rest, recovery, diges-

tion and elimination. In short, these studies seemed to localize the animal's brain responses in situations provoking fear, rage, escape or certain needs.

There remained an important part of the mid-line region of the brain which had not been explored and whose functions were still almost completely unknown. This area, comprising the upper portion of the middle system, seemed to be connected with smell, and to this day it is called the rhinencephalon, or "smell-brain." But the area appeared to receive messages from many organs of the body, and there were various other reasons to believe it was not concerned exclusively or even primarily with smell. As early as 1937 James W. Papez of Cornell University suggested that the rhinencephalon might control emotional experience and behavior. He based this speculation partly on the observation that rabies, which produces profound emotional upset, seems to attack parts of the rhinencephalon.

Such observations, then, constituted our knowledge of the areas of the brain until recently. Certain areas had

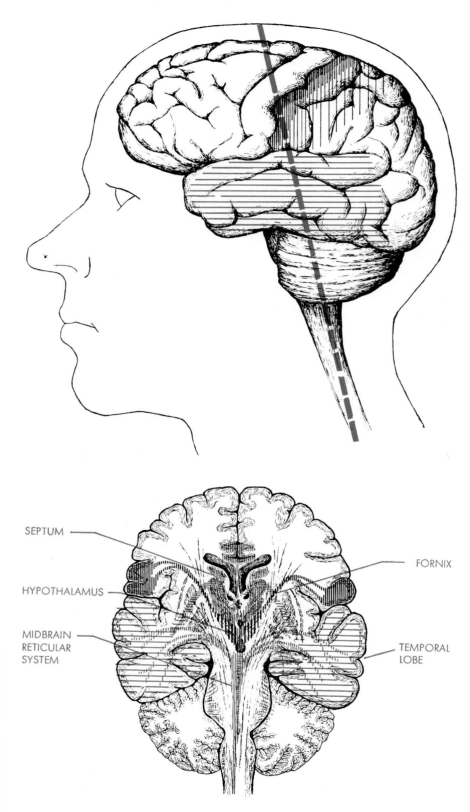

SEPTUM

HYPOTHALAMUS

MIDBRAIN
RETICULAR
SYSTEM

FORNIX

TEMPORAL
LOBE

LOCATIONS OF FUNCTION in the human brain are mapped in these two diagrams. The white areas in both diagrams comprise the motor system; the black crosshatched areas, the sensory system. Crosshatched in color are the "nonspecific" regions now found to be involved in motivation of behavior. The diagram at bottom shows the brain from behind, dissected along the heavy dashed line at top. The labels here identify the centers which correspond to those investigated in the rat. The fornix and parts of the temporal lobes, plus associated structures not labeled, together constitute the rhinencephalon or "smell-brain."

been found to be involved in various kinds of emotional behavior, but the evidence was only of a general nature. The prevailing view still held that the basic motivations—pain, pleasure and so on—probably involved excitation or activity of the whole brain.

Investigation of these matters in more detail became possible only after psychologists had developed methods for detecting and measuring positive emotional behavior—pleasure and the satisfaction of specific "wants." It was B. F. Skinner, the Harvard University experimental psychologist, who produced the needed refinement. He worked out a technique for measuring the rewarding effect of a stimulus (or the degree of satisfaction) in terms of the frequency with which an animal would perform an act which led to the reward. For example, the animal was placed in a bare box containing a lever it could manipulate. If it received no reward when it pressed the lever, the animal might perform this act perhaps five to 10 times an hour. But if it was rewarded with a pellet of food every time it worked the lever, then its rate of performing the act would rise to 100 or more times per hour. This increase in response frequency from five or 10 to 100 per hour provided a measure of the rewarding effect of the food. Other stimuli produce different response rates, and in each case the rise in rate seems to be a quite accurate measure of the reward value of the given stimulus.

With the help of Hess's technique for probing the brain and Skinner's for measuring motivation, we have been engaged in a series of experiments which began three years ago under the guidance of the psychologist D. O. Hebb at McGill University. At the beginning we planned to explore particularly the midbrain reticular system—the sleep-control area that had been investigated by Magoun.

Just before we began our own work, H. R. Delgado, W. W. Roberts and N. E. Miller at Yale University had undertaken a similar study. They had located an area in the lower part of the mid-line system where stimulation caused the animal to avoid the behavior that provoked the electrical stimulus. We wished to investigate positive as well as negative effects—that is, to learn whether stimulation of some areas might be sought rather than avoided by the animal.

We were not at first concerned to hit very specific points in the brain, and in fact in our early tests the electrodes did not always go to the particular areas in the mid-line system at which they were aimed. Our lack of aim turned out to be a fortunate happening for us. In one animal the electrode missed its target and landed not in the mid-brain reticular system but in a nerve pathway from the rhinencephalon. This led to an unexpected discovery.

In the test experiment we were using, the animal was placed in a large box with corners labeled A, B, C and D. Whenever the animal went to corner A, its brain was given a mild electric shock by the experimenter. When the test was performed on the animal with the electrode in the rhinencephalic nerve, it kept returning to corner A. After several such returns on the first day, it finally went to a different place and fell asleep. The next day, however, it seemed even more interested in corner A.

At this point we assumed that the stimulus must provoke curiosity; we did not yet think of it as a reward. Further experimentation on the same animal soon indicated, to our surprise, that its response to the stimulus was more than curiosity. On the second day, after the animal had acquired the habit of returning to corner A to be stimulated, we began trying to draw it away to corner B, giving it an electric shock whenever it took a step in that direction. Within a matter of five minutes the animal was in corner B. After this, the animal could be directed to almost any spot in the box at the will of the experimenter. Every step in the right direction was paid with a small shock; on arrival at the appointed place the animal received a longer series of shocks.

Next the animal was put on a T-shaped platform and stimulated if it turned right at the crossing of the T but not if it turned left. It soon learned to turn right every time. At this point we reversed the procedure, and the animal had to turn left in order to get a shock. With some guidance from the experimenter it eventually switched from the right to the left. We followed up with a test of the animal's response when it was hungry. Food was withheld for 24 hours. Then the animal was placed in a T both arms of which were baited with mash. The animal would receive the electric stimulus at a point halfway down the right arm. It learned to go there, and it always stopped at this point, never going on to the food at all!

After confirming this powerful effect of stimulation of brain areas by experiments with a series of animals, we set out to map the places in the brain where

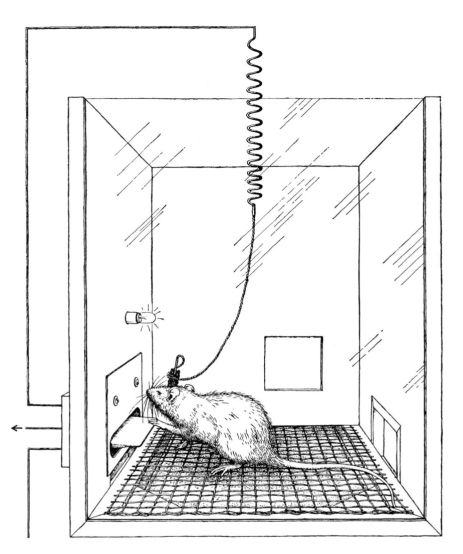

SELF-STIMULATION CIRCUIT is diagrammed here. When the rat presses on treadle it triggers an electric stimulus to its brain and simultaneously records action via wire at left.

such an effect could be obtained. We wanted to measure the strength of the effect in each place. Here Skinner's technique provided the means. By putting the animal in the "do-it-yourself" situation (i.e., pressing a lever to stimulate its own brain) we could translate the animal's strength of "desire" into response frequency, which can be seen and measured.

The first animal in the Skinner box ended all doubts in our minds that electric stimulation applied to some parts of the brain could indeed provide reward for behavior. The test displayed the phenomenon in bold relief where anyone who wanted to look could see it. Left to itself in the apparatus, the animal (after about two to five minutes of learning) stimulated its own brain regularly about once every five seconds, taking a

stimulus of a second or so every time. After 30 minutes the experimenter turned off the current, so that the animal's pressing of the lever no longer stimulated the brain. Under these conditions the animal pressed it about seven times and then went to sleep. We found that the test was repeatable as often as we cared to apply it. When the current was turned on and the animal was given one shock as an *hors d'oeuvre*, it would begin stimulating its brain again. When the electricity was turned off, it would try a few times and then go to sleep.

The current used to stimulate was ordinary house current reduced by a small transformer and then regulated between one and five volts by means of a potentiometer (a radio volume control). As the resistance in the brain was approximately 12,000 ohms, the current ranged from about .000083 to .000420 of an ampere. The shock lasted up to about a second, and the animal had to release the lever and press again to get more.

We now started to localize and quantify the rewarding effect in the brain by planting electrodes in all parts of the brain in large numbers of rats. Each rat had a pair of electrodes consisting of insulated silver wires a hundredth of an inch in diameter. The two stimulating tips were only about one 500th of an inch apart. During a test the animal was placed in a Skinner box designed to produce a chance response rate of about 10 to 25 bar-presses per hour. Each animal was given about six hours of testing with the electric current turned on and one hour with the current off. All responses were recorded automatically, and the animal was given a score on the basis of the amount of time it spent stimulating its brain.

When electrodes were implanted in the classical sensory and motor systems, response rates stayed at the chance level of 10 to 25 an hour. In most parts of the mid-line system, the response rates rose to levels of from 200 to 5,000 an hour, definitely indicative of a rewarding effect of the electric stimulus. But in some of the lower parts of the mid-line system there was an opposite effect: the animal would press the lever once and never go back. This indicated a punishing effect in those areas. They appeared to be the same areas where Delgado, Roberts and Miller at Yale also had discovered the avoidance effect—and where Hess and others had found responses of rage and escape.

The animals seemed to experience the strongest reward, or pleasure, from stimulation of areas of the hypothalamus and certain mid-brain nuclei—regions which Hess and others had found to be centers for control of digestive, sexual, excretory and similar processes. Animals with electrodes in these areas would stimulate themselves from 500 to 5,000 times per hour. In the rhinencephalon the effects were milder, producing self-stimulation at rates around 200 times per hour.

Electric stimulation in some of these regions actually appeared to be far more rewarding to the animals than an ordinary satisfier such as food. For example, hungry rats ran faster to reach an electric stimulator than they did to reach food. Indeed, a hungry animal often ignored available food in favor of the pleasure of stimulating itself electrically. Some rats with electrodes in these places stimulated their brains more than 2,000 times per hour for 24 consecutive hours!

Why is the electric stimulation so rewarding? We are currently exploring this question, working on the hypothesis that brain stimulation in these regions must excite some of the nerve cells that would be excited by satisfaction of the basic drives—hunger, sex, thirst and so forth. We have looked to see whether some parts of the "reward system" of the brain are specialized; that is, there may be one part for the hunger drive, another for the sex drive, etc.

In experiments on hunger, we have found that an animal's appetite for electric stimulation in some brain regions increases as hunger increases: the animal will respond much faster when hungry than when full. We are performing similar tests in other places in the brain with variations of thirst and sex hormones. We have already found that there are areas where the rewarding effects of a brain stimulus can be abolished by castration and restored by injections of testosterone.

Our present tentative conclusion is that emotional and motivational mechanisms can indeed be localized in the brain; that certain portions of the brain are sensitive to each of the basic drives. Strong electrical stimulation of these areas seems to be even more satisfying than the usual rewards of food, etc. This finding contradicts the long-held theory that strong excitation in the brain means punishment. In some areas of the brain it means reward.

The main question for future research is to determine how the excited "reward" cells act upon the specific sensory-motor systems to intensify the rewarded

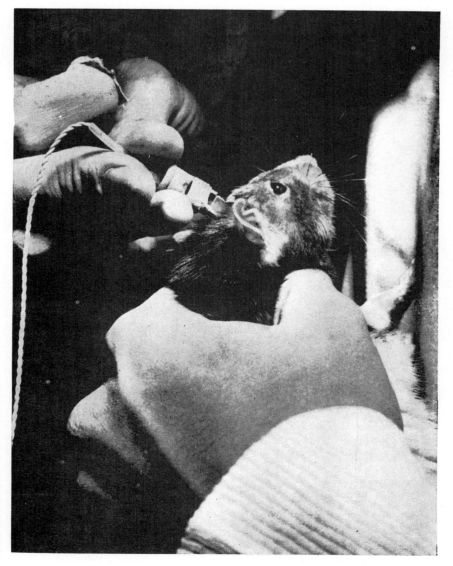

RAT IS CONNECTED to electrical circuit by a plug which can be disconnected to free the animal during rest periods. Presence of electrodes does not pain or discommode the rat.

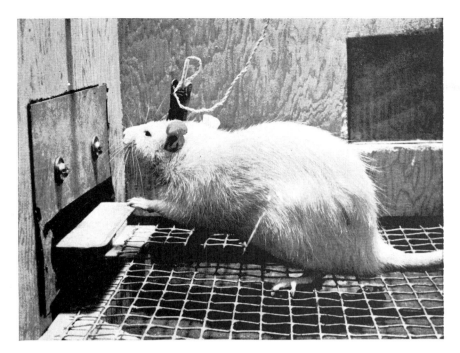

RAT SEEKS STIMULUS as it places its paw on the treadle. Some of the animals have been seen to stimulate themselves for 24 hours without rest and as often as 5,000 times an hour.

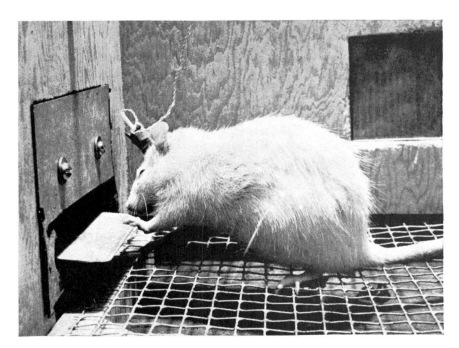

RAT FEELS STIMULUS as it presses on treadle. Pulse lasts less than a second; the current is less than .0005 ampere. The animal must release lever and press again to renew the stimulus.

behavior.

At the moment we are using the self-stimulating technique to learn whether drugs will selectively affect the various motivational centers of the brain. We hope, for example, that we may eventually find one drug that will raise or lower thresholds in the hunger system, another for the sex-drive system, and so forth. Such drugs would allow control of psychological disorders caused by surfeits or deficits in motivational conditions.

Enough of the brain-stimulating work has been repeated on monkeys by J. V. Brady and J. C. Lilly (who work in different laboratories in Washington, D. C.) to indicate that our general conclusions can very likely be generalized eventually to human beings—with modifications, of course.

31

CURIOSITY IN MONKEYS

ROBERT A. BUTLER
February 1954

Curiosity is certainly one of the strongest motives in human behavior. Children begin very early to explore the world around them: they are excited by new sights and sounds, continually manipulate and investigate their toys or other small objects, and in general are extremely responsive to new things and events in their environment. Indeed, severe deprivation of environmental stimulation may permanently retard a child's development.

Until recently little or no research has been conducted on the curiosity motives, for reasons which are not hard to discover. A current theory in psychology has reduced human motivations to the biological drives of hunger, thirst and sex and the conditioned drive to avoid pain, and it has maintained that all learning is based on these drives. Curiosity was dismissed by the behaviorists as an "instinct," beyond the scope of experi-

mental investigation. But in recent years psychologists have found a great deal of experimental evidence that the behavior of human beings and other primates cannot be explained adequately in terms of biological or pain-avoidance drives. Some experimental study has been given to the curiosity motives in monkeys, and this article will review those studies.

The everyday behavior of monkeys seems plainly to be motivated in considerable part by something akin to curiosity. Monkeys, not unlike children, persist in examining things in their immediate environment by close inspection and manipulation. Every object presented to a monkey is at one time or another handled, fondled, scratched, rubbed, bent, picked at, bitten and pulled apart before finally being discarded. A monkey will tamper with the lock on his cage door and will invariably confiscate any objects left on accessible

shelves. In short, a monkey spends a considerable portion of his life "monkeying around" with anything he can get his hands on.

To prove that monkeys have a fundamental curiosity drive, or drive to manipulate, we must demonstrate three things: (1) that they will work for long periods with the manipulatory behavior itself as the sole reward; (2) that the manipulation drive will produce learning, in the same way as the hunger or pain-avoidance drives, and (3) that no drives other than curiosity are significantly influencing the experimental results.

Harry F. Harlow and his associates at the University of Wisconsin were the first to investigate manipulatory behavior in monkeys. Their experiments were designed to determine whether monkeys can learn how to solve a me-

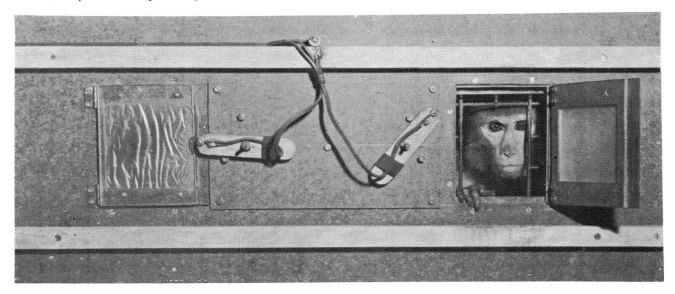

CURIOUS MONKEY stares out into the busy laboratory. Tirelessly the monkey in this experiment would push open the door with the blue card on its back when it learned that this and not the adjacent yellow door afforded a glimpse from its cage.

EAGER to peer out of its cage, the monkey shown from without on page 301 is about to open the blue door. All these photographs were made at the University of Wisconsin.

chanical puzzle with no reward other than the working of it. The puzzle consisted of three interlocking devices—a metal pin, a hook-and-eye and a hasp. The three items could be disengaged if the monkey first removed the pin, then took the hook out of the eye and finally lifted the hasp. If the monkey touched any of the items out of order, it was counted as an error. After a few training sessions the monkeys' score was nearly perfect. Then the puzzle was made harder by adding more devices, but it was just as readily solved. Another study investigated the persistence of this behavior. Every six minutes the puzzle was reset. The monkeys went on disassembling it repeatedly for 10 hours, at which point the experimenters, rather than the subjects, had had enough.

Recently Wisconsin's Primate Laboratory devised a puzzle that involves learning to discriminate between stimuli. The usual procedure in such a test is to give a reward, such as food, for the correct response in a choice between two different stimuli. But in this experiment the only reward was the opportunity to manipulate objects. Ten screw eyes were mounted in two vertical rows on a metal panel. Five of them, colored red, were removable; the other five, colored green, were firmly fixed. The screw eyes were randomly placed so that the only clue to whether they were removable was color. The monkeys soon learned that the red screw eyes could be removed to play with, and they almost unerringly touched only those.

These experiments yielded two important findings: that the opportunity to manipulate objects is reward enough to motivate monkeys to learn, and that an external stimulus, like an internal, biological one, can evoke a drive. The curiosity motives apparently are initiated by external stimuli.

What kinds of stimuli are most effective in eliciting the manipulation drive? Wallace Welker of the Yerkes Laboratories of Primate Biology has just completed experiments on chimpanzees which bear directly on this problem. On a table before the chimp's cage he placed a pair of objects. One of the pair would be movable and the other fixed, or the handling of one would produce a sound and the other not. Like monkeys, the chimpanzees showed a strong preference for movable objects over fixed ones and for objects that produced a sound or triggered a light over those that yielded no change in the environment. After 30 minutes with a pair of objects the animals became bored and stopped handling them, but their interest could be maintained if new stimuli were introduced periodically. Young chimpanzees consistently displayed more manipulatory behavior than older ones.

Monkeys and apes watch closely everything that goes on around them. Perhaps this expression of curiosity in monkeys accounts for their popularity with man. At the zoo or in the laboratory, man and monkey seem to observe each other with great interest. Which one derives more information from the experience remains an enigma. It is as if man as an observer meets his first real competitor in the monkey. Sometimes this competition becomes rather unnerving. I had such an experience during the course of a series of experiments at the Wisconsin laboratories. I was testing monkeys on a food-rewarded problem. The monkey worked behind a screen where it could not see the experimenter. By the same token, the experimenter could not see the monkey, and there was a great temptation to peek to find out what the animal was doing. I first made a small peephole in the panel, but the monkey quickly discovered it and thereafter spied on me as often as I did on him. I next tried placing a small mirror in a position that enabled me to watch the animal constantly. The monkey turned the tables by dropping its work and watching me through the mirror!

Taking advantage of this lead, we designed an experiment to investigate monkeys' visual exploratory behavior. The apparatus was essentially an enclosure with a built-in color discrimination problem. Monkeys were rewarded by a view of the surroundings outside the enclosure, provided they responded correctly on the problem. The monkey was placed in a large box with two doors. The animal was given preliminary training to familiarize it with the apparatus: first it was given a look through the open doors into the laboratory, where considerable activity was going on, and then the experimenter closed the doors. Soon the monkey learned to open the doors within a few seconds.

Then the main part of the experiment began. One door was locked, and it was identifiable by a yellow card on the inside. The other door, marked by a blue card, was unlocked. The experimenter raised a screen that had been lowered between the monkey and the doors, exposing the two doors with their differently colored cards. If the monkey pushed against the door with the blue card, the door opened and it could look outside. After 30 seconds the experi-

PUZZLE SOLVING indicates the extent of the curiosity drive in monkeys. Learning to discriminate, monkey pulls only red, removable screw eyes (*left*). In another test with no reward other than doing it, monkey repeatedly works puzzle of pin, hook and eye, hasp.

TOY TRAIN proved to be a strong visual incentive for monkeys to open the door repeatedly in order to be able to view it. An even stronger one was the sight of another monkey.

BOWL OF FRUIT turned out to be less of a stimulus for the monkeys than either the toy train or another monkey as an inducement to push open the door of its cage to view it.

menter lowered the screen and the trial was over. If the animal pushed against the door holding the yellow card, it automatically flashed on a light which signaled its error; the experimenter immediately lowered the screen, denying the subject a glimpse of the outside world. Twenty trials a day were given for 20 days, and each test session lasted from 25 to 45 minutes. The experimenter recorded the number of correct responses and the length of time that elapsed between the raising of the screen and the monkey's attack on one of the doors. The speed of response provided a measure of the strength of the monkey's motivation to look outside.

The results of the experiment left no doubt about the strength of the monkeys' curiosity or its power in promoting learning. Throughout the 20 days of testing the animals worked away eagerly at the problem (the colored cards were shifted at random from door to door). Without tiring of the game, they went on pushing the doors enthusiastically to get a look at the people working in the laboratory outside the box. In a second study that ran for 57 days and presented various color-discrimination problems, the subjects worked just as unflaggingly.

These data strongly suggest that the drive to explore visually is indeed a fundamental drive in monkeys. To measure its strength and persistence further, two monkeys were tested for four continuous hours each day for five days. The animals worked as fast on Day Five as they did on Day One. A second experiment yielded still more surprising results. Three monkeys were put to the door-opening test hour after hour, with 30 seconds between trials, until they quit. One monkey performed for nine continuous hours, another worked for 11 and the third for more than 19 hours! The response time of this marathon performer was actually shortest during the final hour of the test.

That monkeys would work as long and as persistently for a food reward is highly unlikely. The tenacity and rapidity with which these subjects performed on the task of opening a door in order to see outside clearly indicated that the activities in the laboratory were extremely effective in exciting their curiosity.

To find out what specific kinds of visual stimuli excited them, we presented to the monkeys three different sights: a fellow monkey, an operating toy electric train and an array of fresh fruit and monkey chow. As a standard for comparison the test was arranged so that the monkeys would sometimes see nothing but an empty room. The apparatus was the same as before except that this time the box had only one door. Upon opening the door, the monkey saw a large chamber which contained a monkey, the running train, the array of food or nothing at all. The monkeys were allowed a five-second view, and the trials were repeated at 10-second intervals. Eight monkeys were tested 30 minutes a day, five days a week for a period of four weeks. Each week the visual incentive was changed. The strongest incentive turned out to be, not surprisingly, the sight of another monkey; the electric train ran a close second.

We next investigated the relative effectiveness of different sounds. A highly vocal monkey and the noise of the electric train were the incentives. Sometimes the subjects, after opening the door, could see the source of the sound, sometimes not. Ten of the youngest monkeys in the colony participated in the study. All of them opened the door frequently and rapidly, through five weeks of testing, irrespective of which sound they heard or whether they were rewarded with the sight of the sound-maker. Although the experiment failed to show any clear-cut differences among the incentives, it provided valuable evidence on the strength of the curiosity drive in young monkeys.

These researches with monkeys and apes are the beginnings of what promises to be a most fascinating and important area of investigation. The strong tendency of monkeys and apes to explore all things and situations provides an extremely serviceable mechanism for acquainting these animals with the intricacies of their environment. That this tendency is most marked in the younger animals suggests that the curiosity motives are largely responsible for the early and extensive learning which unquestionably contributes to the biological success of the primates.

32

ATTITUDE AND PUPIL SIZE

ECKHARD H. HESS
April 1965

One night about five years ago I was lying in bed leafing through a book of strikingly beautiful animal photographs. My wife happened to glance over at me and remarked that the light must be bad—my pupils were unusually large. It seemed to me that there was plenty of light coming from the bedside lamp and I said so, but she insisted that my pupils were dilated. As a psychologist who is interested in visual perception, I was puzzled by this little episode. Later, as I was trying to go to sleep, I recalled that someone had once reported a correlation between a person's pupil size and his emotional response to certain aspects of his environment. In this case it was difficult to see an emotional component. It seemed more a matter of intellectual interest, and no increase in pupil size had been reported for that.

The next morning I went to my laboratory at the University of Chicago. As soon as I got there I collected a number of pictures—all landscapes except for one seminude "pinup." When my assistant, James M. Polt, came in, I made him the subject of a quick experiment. I shuffled the pictures and, holding them above my eyes where I could not see them, showed them to Polt one at a time and watched his eyes as he looked at them. When I displayed the seventh picture, I noted a distinct increase in the size of his pupils; I checked the picture, and of course it was the pinup he had been looking at. Polt and I then embarked on an investigation of the relation between pupil size and mental activity.

The idea that the eyes are clues to emotions—"windows of the soul," as the French poet Guillaume de Salluste wrote—is almost commonplace in literature and everyday language. We say "His eyes were like saucers" or "His eyes were pinpoints of hate"; we use such terms as "beady-eyed" or "bug-eyed" or "hard-eyed." In his *Expressions of Emotion in Man and Animals* Charles Darwin referred to the widening and narrowing of the eyes, accomplished by movements of the eyelids and eyebrows, as signs of human emotion; he apparently assumed that the pupil dilated and contracted only as a physiological mechanism responsive to changes in light intensity.

This light reflex is controlled by one of the two divisions of the autonomic nervous system: the parasympathetic system. Later investigators noted that pupil size is also governed by the other division of the autonomic system—the sympathetic system—in response to strong emotional states and that it can vary with the progress of mental activity. On a less sophisticated level some people to whom it is important to know what someone else is thinking appear to have been aware of the pupil-size phenomenon for a long time. It is said that magicians doing card tricks can identify the card a person is thinking about by watching his pupils enlarge when the card is turned up, and that Chinese jade dealers watch a buyer's pupils to know when he is impressed by a specimen and is likely to pay a high price. Polt and I have been able to study the pupil response in detail and to show what a remarkably sensitive indicator of certain mental activities it can be. We believe it can provide quantitative data on the effects of visual and other sensory stimulation, on cerebral processes and even on changes in fairly complex attitudes.

Most of our early experiments related pupil size to the interest value and "emotionality" of visual stimuli. Our techniques for these studies are quite simple. The subject peers into a box, looking at a screen on which we project the stimulus picture. A mirror reflects the image of his eye into a motion-picture camera. First we show a control slide that is carefully matched in overall brightness to the stimulus slide that will follow it; this adapts the subject's eyes to the light intensity of the stimulus slide. At various points on the control slide are numbers that direct the subject's gaze to the center of the field. Meanwhile the camera, operating at the rate of two frames per second, records the size of his pupil. After 10 seconds the control slide is switched off and the stimulus slide is projected for 10 seconds; as the subject looks at it the camera continues to make two pictures of his eye per second. The sequence of control and stimulus is repeated about 10 or 12 times a sitting. To score the response to a stimulus we compare the average size of the pupil as photographed during the showing of the control slide with its average size during the stimulus period. Usually we simply project the negative image of the pupil, a bright spot of light, on a screen and measure the diameter with a ruler; alternatively we record the changes in size electronically by measuring the area of the pupil spot with a photocell.

In our first experiment, before we were able to control accurately for brightness, we tested four men and two women, reasoning that a significant difference in the reactions of subjects of different sex to the same picture would be evidence of a pupil response to something other than light intensity. The results confirmed our expectations: the men's pupils dilated more at the sight of a female pinup than the women's

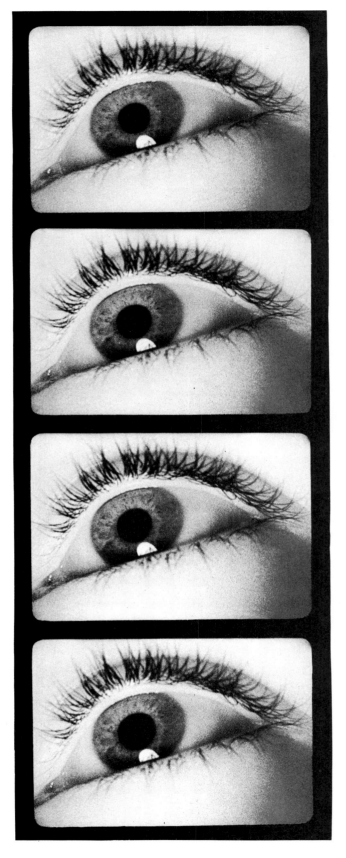

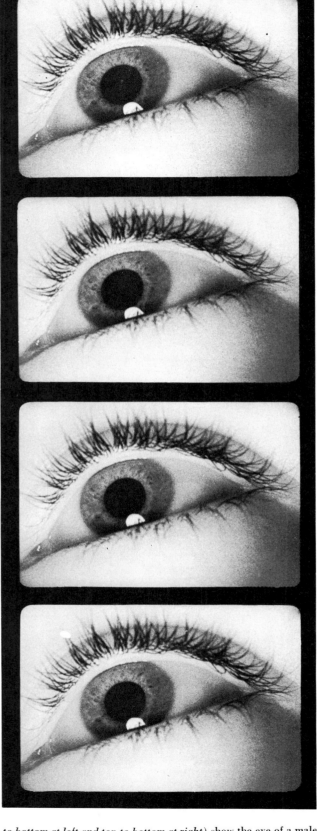

PUPIL SIZE varies with the interest value of a visual stimulus. In the author's laboratory a subject's eye is filmed as he looks at slides flashed on a screen. These consecutive frames (*top to bottom at left and top to bottom at right*) show the eye of a male subject during the first four seconds after a photograph of a woman's face appeared. His pupil increased in diameter 30 percent.

SUBJECT in pupil-response studies peers into a box, looking at a rear-projection screen on which slides are flashed from the projector at right. A motor-driven camera mounted on the box makes a continuous record of pupil size at the rate of two frames a second.

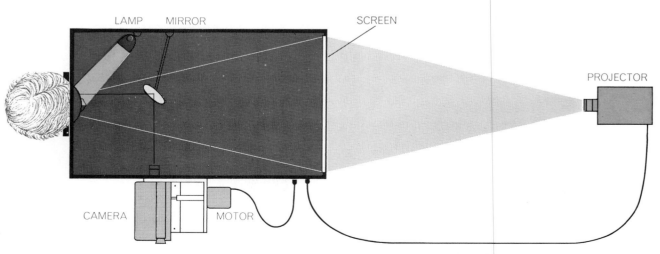

PUPIL-RESPONSE APPARATUS is simple. The lamp and the camera film work in the infrared. A timer advances the projector every 10 seconds, flashing a control slide and a stimulus slide alternately. The mirror is below eye level so that view of screen is clear.

did; the women showed a greater response than the men did to a picture of a baby or of a mother and baby and to a male pinup [*see illustration at right*]. We interpreted dilation in these cases as an indication of interest.

We then undertook another demonstration designed to eliminate the role of brightness. In this experiment we did not show a control slide; only the general room lighting illuminated the rear-projection screen of the apparatus during the control period. When the stimulus slide came on, every part of the screen was therefore at least somewhat brighter than it had been during the control period. If the eye responded only to changes in light intensity, then the response by all subjects to any stimulus ought to be negative; that is, the pupil should constrict slightly every time. This was not the case; we got positive responses in those subjects and for just those stimuli that would have been expected, on the basis of the results of the first study, to produce positive responses. We also got constriction, but only for stimuli that the person involved might be expected to find distasteful or unappealing.

These negative responses, exemplified by the reaction of most of our female subjects to pictures of sharks, were not isolated phenomena; constriction is as characteristic in the case of certain aversive stimuli as dilation is in the case of interesting or pleasant pictures. We observed a strong negative response, for example, when subjects were shown a picture of a cross-eyed or crippled child; as those being tested said, they simply did not like to look at such pictures. One woman went so far as to close her eyes when one of the pictures was on the screen, giving what might be considered the ultimate in negative responses. The negative response also turned up in a number of subjects presented with examples of modern paintings, particularly abstract ones. (We were interested to note that some people who insisted that they liked modern art showed strong negative responses to almost all the modern paintings we showed them.) The results are consistent with a finding by the Soviet psychologist A. R. Shachnowich that a person's pupils may constrict when he looks at unfamiliar geometric patterns.

We have come on one special category of stimuli, examples of which are pictures of dead soldiers on a battlefield, piles of corpses in a concentration camp and the body of a murdered gang-

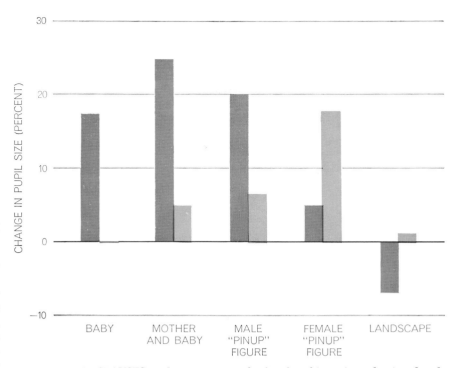

DIFFERENT RESPONSES to the same picture by female subjects (*gray bars*) and male (*colored bars*) established that the pupil response was independent of light intensity. The bars show changes in average area of pupils from the control period to the stimulus period.

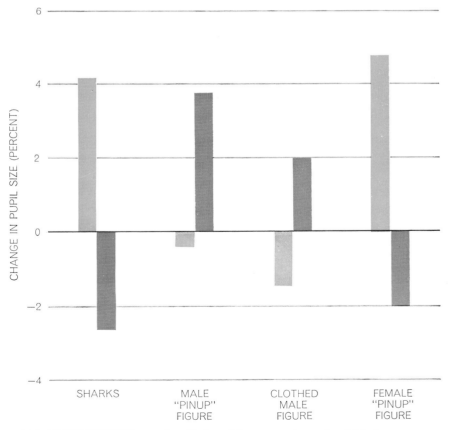

ROLE OF BRIGHTNESS was also eliminated in an experiment in which the screen was unlighted before the stimulus appeared. Whereas responses to light alone would therefore have resulted in constriction, some pictures caused dilation in men (*colored bars*) and women (*gray*). In this experiment pupil diameter was tabulated rather than area.

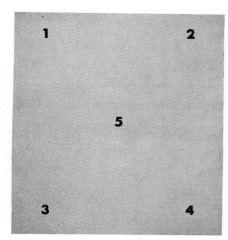

CONTROL SLIDE provides calibration for experiments involving direction of gaze (*opposite page*). The subject looks at the five numbers in sequence and the camera records the resulting movements of his pupil.

ster. One might expect these to be "negative," and indeed they do produce extreme pupil constriction in some subjects, but they elicit a very different pattern of responses in others. On initial exposure the subject often responds with a large increase, rather than a decrease, in pupil size. Then, with repeated presentations, there is a shift to a negative response; the shift is usually accomplished after three to five exposures, and the time interval between those exposures seems to make little difference. Our impression was that these were negative stimuli with an additional "shock" content that prompted a strong emotional reaction. To check this hypothesis we attached electrodes to the hands of some of our volunteers and recorded their galvanic skin response, a measure of the electrical resistance of the skin that has been correlated with emotional level and is a component of most so-called lie-detector tests. As we had anticipated, stimuli we had classified as "shocking" got a high galvanic skin response along with the initial high pupil response in most subjects. After repeated presentations the skin response decreased rapidly as the pupil response shifted from dilation to constriction.

Although we have dealt primarily with positive stimuli, the evidence suggests that at least with respect to visual material there is a continuum of responses that ranges from extreme dilation for interesting or pleasing stimuli to extreme constriction for material that is unpleasant or distasteful to the viewer. In the presence of uninteresting

or boring pictures we find only slight random variations in pupil size.

One of the most interesting things about the changes in pupil size is that they are extremely sensitive, sometimes revealing different responses to stimuli that at the verbal level seem to the person being tested quite similar. We once demonstrated this effect with a pair of stimulus photographs that in themselves provided an interesting illustration of the relation between pupil size and personality. In a series of pictures shown to a group of 20 men we included two photographs of an attractive young woman. These two slides were identical except for the fact that one had been retouched to make the woman's pupils extra large and the other to make them very small. The average response to the picture with the large pupils was more than twice as strong as the response to the one with small pupils; nevertheless, when the men were questioned after the experimental session, most of them reported that the two pictures were identical. Some did say that one was "more feminine" or "prettier" or "softer." None noticed that one had larger pupils than the other. In fact, they had to be shown the difference. As long ago as the Middle Ages women dilated their pupils with the drug belladonna (which means "beautiful woman" in Italian). Clearly large pupils are attractive to men, but the response to them—at least in our subjects—is apparently at a nonverbal level. One might hazard a guess that what is appealing about large pupils in a woman is that they imply extraordinary interest in the man she is with!

Pupillary activity can serve as a measure of motivation. We have investigated the effect of hunger, which is a standard approach in psychological studies of motivation. It occurred to us that a person's physiological state might be a factor in the pupil response when we analyzed the results of a study in which several of the stimulus slides were pictures of food—rather attractive pictures to which we had expected the subjects to respond positively. The general response was positive, but about half of the people tested had much stronger responses than the others. After puzzling over this for a while we checked our logbook and found that about 90 percent of the subjects who had evinced strong responses had been tested in the late morning or late afternoon—when, it seemed obvious, they should have been hungrier than the people tested soon after breakfast or lunch.

To be sure, not everyone is equally hungry a given number of hours after eating, but when we tested two groups controlled for length of time without food, our results were unequivocal: the pupil responses of 10 subjects who were "deprived" for four or five hours were more than two and a half times larger than those of 10 subjects who had eaten a meal within an hour before being tested. The mean responses of the two groups were 11.3 percent and 4.4 percent respectively.

Interestingly enough the pupils respond not only to visual stimuli but also to stimuli affecting other senses. So far our most systematic research on nonvisual stimuli has dealt with the sense of taste. The subject places his head in a modified apparatus that leaves his mouth free; he holds a flexible straw to which the experimenter can raise a cup of the liquid to be tasted. During the test the taster keeps his eyes on an X projected on the screen, and the camera records any changes in pupil size.

Our first study involved a variety of presumably pleasant-tasting liquids—carbonated drinks, chocolate drinks and milk—and some unpleasant-tasting ones, including concentrated lemon juice and a solution of quinine. We were surprised to find that both the pleasant and the unpleasant liquids brought an increase in pupil size compared with a "control" of water. Then we decided to test a series of similar liquids, all presumably on the positive side of the "pleasant-unpleasant" continuum, to see if, as in the case of visual material, some of the stimuli would elicit greater responses than others. We selected five "orange" beverages and had each subject alternate sips of water with sips of a beverage. One of the five orange beverages caused a significantly larger average increase in pupil size than the others did; the same drink also won on the basis of verbal preferences expressed by the subjects after they had been through the pupil-size test. Although we still have a good deal of work to do on taste, particularly with regard to the response to unpleasant stimuli, we are encouraged by the results so far. The essential sensitivity of the pupil response suggests that it can reveal preferences in some cases in which the actual taste differences are so slight that the subject cannot even articulate them—a possibility with interesting implications for market research.

We have also had our volunteers listen to taped excerpts of music while

DIRECTIONAL ANALYSIS reveals where a subject was looking when each frame of film was made as well as how large his pupil was. Superposed on the upper reproduction of Leon Kroll's "Morning on the Cape" are symbols showing the sequence of fixations by a female subject looking at the painting; a man's responses are shown below. The light-color symbols indicate a pupil size about the same as during the preceding control period; open symbols denote smaller responses and dark-color symbols larger responses. The experimenters determine the direction of gaze by shining light through the film negative; the beam that passes through the image of the pupil is projected on a photograph of the stimulus (in this case the painting) and its position is recorded.

the camera monitors their pupil size. We find different responses to different compositions, apparently depending on individual preference. As in the case of the taste stimuli, however, the response to music seems always to be in a positive direction: the pupil becomes larger when music of any kind is being played. We have begun to test for the effect of taped verbal statements and individual words, which also seem to elicit different pupil responses. Research in these areas, together with some preliminary

work concerning the sense of smell, supports the hypothesis that the pupil is closely associated not only with visual centers in the brain but also with other brain centers. In general it strongly suggests that pupillary changes reflect ongoing activity in the brain.

It is not surprising that the response of the pupil should be intimately associated with mental activity. Embryologically and anatomically the eye is an extension of the brain; it is almost

as though a portion of the brain were in plain sight for the psychologist to peer at. Once it is, so to speak, "calibrated" the pupil response should make it possible to observe ongoing mental behavior directly and without requiring the investigator to attach to his subject electrodes or other equipment that may affect the very behavior he seeks to observe.

More than 50 years ago German psychologists noted that mental activity (solving arithmetical problems, for ex-

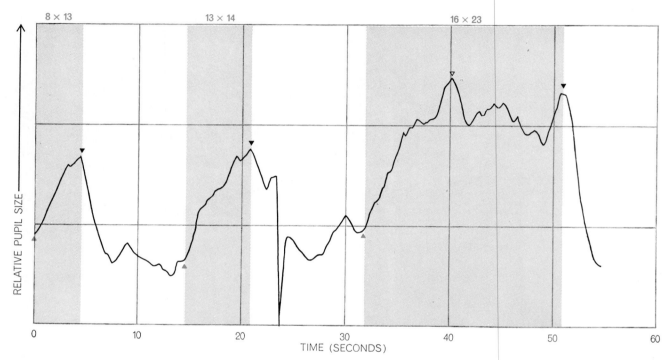

CHANGES IN PUPIL SIZE are traced in a subject doing the three mental-arithmetic problems shown at the top. Beginning when the problem is posed (*colored triangles*), the pupil dilates until the answer is given (*solid black triangles*). This subject appears to have reached a solution of the third problem (*open triangle*) and then to have reconsidered, checking his answer before giving it.

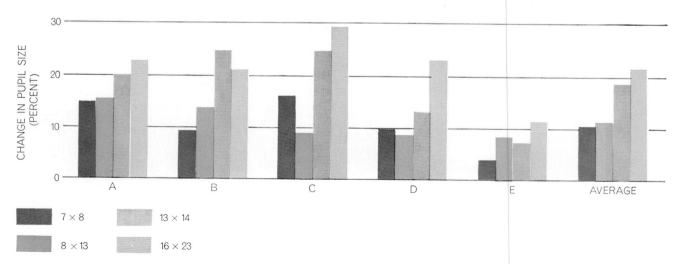

INDIVIDUAL DIFFERENCES in pupil response while solving multiplication problems reflect the fact that two of the five subjects, *D* and *E*, could do mental arithmetic with less effort than the others. The change in pupil size was computed by comparing the average size in the five frames before the problem was posed with the average in the five frames just before the answer was given.

ample) caused a gross increase in pupil size. We decided this would be a good area for detailed study in an effort to see how precise and differentiated an indicator the response could be. We present mental-arithmetic problems of varying difficulty to volunteers and then obtain a continuous trace of their pupil response by measuring the filmed images of the pupil with a photocell [*see upper illustration on opposite page*]. As soon as the problem is presented the size of the pupil begins to increase. It reaches a maximum as the subject arrives at his solution and then immediately starts to decrease, returning to its base level as soon as the answer is verbalized. If the subject is told to solve the problem but not give the answer, there is some decrease at the instant of solution but the pupil remains abnormally large; then, when the experimenter asks for the solution, the pupil returns to its base level as the subject verbalizes the answer.

In one study we tested five people, two who seemed to be able to do mental arithmetic easily and three for whom even simple multiplication required a lot of effort. The pupil-response results reflect these individual differences [*see lower illustration on opposite page*] and also show a fairly consistent increase in dilation as the problems increase in difficulty. Individual differences of another kind are revealed by the trace of a subject's pupil size. Most subjects do have a response that drops to normal as soon as they give the answer. In some people, however, the size of the pupil decreases momentarily after the answer is given and then goes up again, sometimes as high as the original peak, suggesting that the worried subject is working the problem over again to be sure he was correct. Other people, judging by the response record, tend to recheck their answers before announcing them.

We have found a similar response in spelling, with the maximum pupil size correlated to the difficulty of the word. The response also appears when a subject is working an anagram, a situation that is not very different from the kind of mental activity associated with decision-making. We believe the pupil-response technique should be valuable for studying the course of decision-making and perhaps for assessing decision-making abilities in an individual.

It is always difficult to elicit from someone information that involves his private attitudes toward some person or concept or thing. The pupil-

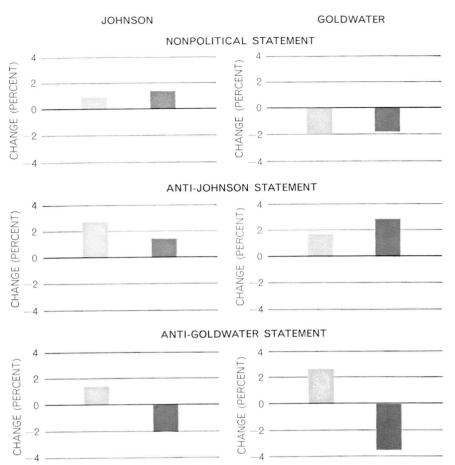

ATTITUDE CHANGES are revealed by responses to Johnson (*left*) and Goldwater (*right*) before (*light bars*) and after (*dark bars*) subjects read a statement supplied by the experimenter. Nonpolitical material had no appreciable effect. The anti-Johnson material had the expected effect. Bitter anti-Goldwater material made response to both candidates negative.

response technique can measure just such attitudes. We have established that the correlation between a person's expressed attitude and his "measured pupil" attitude can vary widely, depending on the topic. For example, we tested 64 people with five pictures of foods and also asked them to rank the foods from favorite to least preferred. When we matched each person's verbal report with his pupil response, we obtained 61 positive correlations—a result one could expect to get by chance only once in a million times.

The correlation is poor in an area that involves social values or pressures, however. For example, we do not get such good agreement between pupillary and verbal responses when we show women pictures of seminude men and women. Nor did we get good correlation when we did a political study last fall. We showed photographs of President Johnson and Barry Goldwater to 34 University of Chicago students, faculty members and employees. Everyone professed to be in favor of Johnson and

against Goldwater. The pupil-response test, however, had indicated that about a third of these people actually had a slightly more positive attitude toward Goldwater than toward Johnson.

To be sure, the pupil test may overemphasize the effect of physical appearance; certainly our data do not prove that a third of the subjects went on to vote for Goldwater. But the results do raise the interesting possibility that at least some of them did, and that in the liberal atmosphere of the university these people found it difficult to utter any pro-Goldwater sentiment. The results suggest that our technique, by which we measure a response that is not under the control of the person being tested, may yield more accurate representations of an attitude than can be obtained with even a well-drawn questionnaire or with some devious "projective" technique in which a person's verbal or motor responses are recorded in an effort to uncover his real feelings.

For me the most interesting aspect

TWO PHOTOGRAPHS, almost identical, elicited very different responses from a group of male subjects. One in which a girl's eyes were retouched, as at left, to make the pupils large got a greater response than one in which the pupils were made small (*right*).

of our work has been the measurement of changes in attitude. We begin by determining the pupil response of one of our volunteers to someone's picture. Then we have the subject read some kind of informative material, we retest for the response and compare the "before" and "after" scores. In one case the reading material consisted of a passage indicating that the man whose picture had been displayed was the former commandant of the concentration camp at Auschwitz. When we then remeasured the subject's pupil response to the man in question, we found that a more negative attitude had clearly developed as a result of the intervening reading.

Take another and more hypothetical example: Suppose a patient seeking psychotherapy has a fear of people with beards. We ought to be able to get a pupillary measure of his attitude by showing him photographs of bearded men, among others, and then be able to check on the course of treatment by repeating the test later. Regardless of whether what intervenes is straightforward information, psychotherapy, political propaganda, advertising or any other material intended to change attitudes, it should be possible to monitor the effectiveness of that material by measuring changes in pupil size, and to

do this with a number of people at any desired interval.

One recent study along these lines will illustrate the possibilities. We showed five different photographs of President Johnson and five of Goldwater, along with a single photograph of former presidents Kennedy and Eisenhower, to three groups of people. One group thereupon read anti-Johnson material, another read anti-Goldwater material and the third read some excerpts from a psychology journal that had no political content. Then each group was retested.

Now the people who had read the anti-Johnson material showed a slightly smaller response than before to Johnson and a slightly larger response than before to Goldwater. Some extremely negative anti-Goldwater material, which one of my assistants apparently found very easy to write, had a different kind of effect. It did cause the expected decrease in the response to Goldwater, but it also caused a large drop in the response to Johnson and even to Eisenhower! The only person who was unaffected was Kennedy. This may indicate that bitter campaign propaganda can lower a person's attitude toward politicians in general, Kennedy alone being spared for obvious reasons.

The pupil response promises to be

a new tool with which to probe the mind. We are applying it now in a variety of studies. One deals with the development in young people of sexual interest and of identification with parents from preschool age to high school age. In an attempt to establish personality differences, we are tabulating the responses of a number of subjects to pictures of people under stress and pictures of the same people after they have been released from the stressful situation. Our other current study deals with volunteers who are experiencing changes in perception as the result of hypnotic suggestion. In the perception laboratory of Marplan, a communications-research organization that has supported much of our work, Paula Drillman is studying responses to packages, products and advertising on television and in other media. Several laboratories at Chicago and elsewhere are employing our techniques to study such diverse problems as the process of decision-making, the effect of certain kinds of experience on the attitudes of white people toward Negroes and the efficacy of different methods of problem-solving. Those of us engaged in this work have the feeling that we have only begun to understand and exploit the information implicit in the dilations and constrictions of the pupil.

33

SOCIAL DEPRIVATION IN MONKEYS

HARRY F. AND MARGARET KUENNE HARLOW

November 1962

In *An Outline of Psychoanalysis*, published posthumously in 1940, Sigmund Freud was able to refer to "the common assertion that the child is psychologically the father of the man and that the events of his first years are of paramount importance for his whole subsequent life." It was, of course, Freud's own historic investigations, begun a half-century before, that first elucidated the role of infantile experiences in the development of the personality and its disorders. The "central experience of this period of childhood," he found, is the infant's relation to his mother. Freud's ideas have now shaped the thinking of two generations of psychologists, psychiatrists and psychoanalysts. Much evidence in support of his deep insights has been accumulated, particularly from clinical studies of the mentally ill. Contemporary writers stress inadequate or inconsistent mothering as a basic cause of later disorders such as withdrawal, hostility, anxiety, sexual maladjustment, alcoholism and, significantly, inadequate maternal behavior!

The evidence from clinical studies for this or any other view of human personality development is qualified, however, by an inherent defect. These studies are necessarily retrospective: they start with the disorder and work backward in time, retracing the experiences of the individual as he and his relatives and associates recall them. Inevitably details are lost or distorted, and the story is often so confounded as to require a generous exercise of intuition on the part of the investigator. Nor does evidence obtained in this manner exclude other possible causes of personality disorder. Against arguments in favor of a biochemical or neurological causation of mental illness, for example, there is no way to show that the patient began life with full potentiality for normal development. Given

the decisive influence ascribed to the mother-infant relation, there may be a tendency in the reconstruction of the past to overlook or suppress evidence for the influence of other significant early relations, such as the bonds of interaction with other children. Little attention has been given, in fact, to child-to-child relations in the study of personality development. Yet it can be supposed that these play a significant part in determining the peer relations and the sexual role of the adult. Plainly there is a need to study the development of per-

ABNORMAL MOTHER, raised with a cloth surrogate instead of her mother, rejects her infant, refusing to let it nurse. Infants of four such mothers, raised under same conditions as infants of good mothers, developed relatively normally in spite of poor maternal care.

INFANTS PLAY in one of the playpens used in experiments described in two preceding illustrations. Both infants, photographed when they were six months old, had normal mothers.

sonality forward in time from infancy. Ideally the study should be conducted under controlled laboratory conditions so that the effects of single variables or combinations of variables can be traced.

Acceding to the moral and physical impossibility of conducting such an investigation with human subjects, we have been observing the development of social behavior in large numbers of rhesus monkeys at the Primate Laboratory of the University of Wisconsin. Apart from this primate's kinship to man, it offers a reasonable experimental substitute because it undergoes a relatively long period of development analogous to that of the human child and involving intimate attachment to its mother and social interaction with its age-mates. With these animals we have been able to observe the consequences of the deprivation of all social contact for various lengths of time. We have also raised them without mothers but in the company of age-mates and with mothers but without age-mates.

We have thereby been able to make some estimate of the contribution of each of these primary affectional systems to the integrated adult personality. Our observations sustain the significance of the maternal relation, particularly in facilitating the interaction of the infant with other infants. But at the same time we have found compelling evidence that opportunity for infant-infant interaction under optimal conditions may fully compensate for lack of mothering, at least in so far as infant-infant social and heterosexual relations are concerned. It seems possible—even likely—that the infant-

mother affectional system is dispensable, whereas the infant-infant system is the *sine qua non* for later adjustment in all spheres of monkey life. In line with the "paramount importance" that Freud assigned to experience in the first years of life, our experiments indicate that there is a critical period somewhere between the third and sixth months of life during which social deprivation, particularly deprivation of the company of its peers, irreversibly blights the animal's capacity for social adjustment.

Our investigations of the emotional development of our subjects grew out of the effort to produce and maintain a colony of sturdy, disease-free young animals for use in various research programs. By separating them from their mothers a few hours after birth and placing them in a more fully controlled regimen of nurture and physical care we were able both to achieve a higher rate of survival and to remove the animals for testing without maternal protest. Only later did we realize that our monkeys were emotionally disturbed as well as sturdy and disease-free. Some of our researches are therefore retrospective. Others are in part exploratory, representing attempts to set up new experimental situations or to find new techniques for measurement. Most are incomplete because investigations of social and behavioral development are long-term. In a sense, they can never end, because the problems of one generation must be traced into the next.

Having separated the infant from its mother, our procedure was to keep it alone in a bare wire cage in a large room with other infants so housed. Thus each

little monkey could see and hear others of its kind, although it could not make direct physical contact with them. The 56 animals raised in this manner now range in age from five to eight years. As a group they exhibit abnormalities of behavior rarely seen in animals born in the wild and brought to the laboratory as preadolescents or adolescents, even after the latter have been housed in individual cages for many years. The laboratory-born monkeys sit in their cages and stare fixedly into space, circle their cages in a repetitive stereotyped manner and clasp their heads in their hands or arms and rock for long periods of time. They often develop compulsive habits, such as pinching precisely the same patch of skin on the chest between the same fingers hundreds of times a day; occasionally such behavior may become punitive and the animal may chew and tear at its body until it bleeds. Often the approach of a human being becomes the stimulus to self-aggression. This behavior constitutes a complete breakdown and reversal of the normal defensive response; a monkey born in the wild will direct such threats and aggression at the approaching person, not at itself. Similar symptoms of emotional pathology are observed in deprived children in orphanages and in withdrawn adolescents and adults in mental hospitals.

William A. Mason, now at the Yerkes Laboratories of Primate Biology, compared the behavior of six of these animals, which were then two years old and had been housed all their lives in individual cages, with a matched group of rhesus monkeys that had been captured in the wild during their first year of life and housed together in captivity for a while before being individually housed in the laboratory. The most striking difference was that all the animals that had been born in the wild—and not one of the laboratory-born animals—displayed normal sex behavior. That the laboratory-born animals were not lacking in sex drive was indicated by the fact that the males frequently approached the females and the females displayed part of the pattern of sexual presentation. But they did not orient themselves correctly and they did not succeed in mating. Moreover, the monkeys born in the wild had apparently learned to live with others in a stable hierarchy of dominance, or "pecking order"; consequently in the pairing test they fought one another less and engaged more often in social grooming. They would also release a companion from a locked cage more frequently than did the laboratory-born animals, which usually ignored their caged partner's plight.

The severity of the affliction that grips these monkeys raised in the partial isolation of individual wire cages has become more apparent as they have grown older. They pay little or no attention to animals in neighboring cages; those caged with companions sit in opposite corners with only rare interaction. No heterosexual behavior has ever been observed between male and female cagemates, even between those that have lived together for as long as seven years.

When efforts have been made to bring about matings, by pairing animals during the female's estrus, they have sometimes fought so viciously that they have had to be parted. Attempts to mate the socially deprived animals with sexually adequate and experienced monkeys from

MOTHERLESS INFANTS, raised from birth by cloth surrogates, play in a specially constructed playroom supplied with equipment for climbing and swinging. These animals, plus one other not seen in this photograph, were kept in individual cages and brought together in the playroom for 20 minutes a day. Although they had no maternal care whatever, they developed normally in every respect.

the breeding colony have been similarly frustrated.

In the summer of 1960 we undertook to devise a group-psychotherapy situation for 19 of these animals—nine males and 10 females—by using them to stock the monkey island in the municipal zoo in Madison, Wis. This was their first experience outside the laboratory, and they had much to learn in order to survive. They had to learn to drink water from an open trough instead of from a tube in the wall of a cage, to compete for food in a communal feeding situation, to huddle together or find shelter from inclement weather, to climb rocks and avoid the water surrounding the island. Most difficult of all, they had to learn to live together. Within the first few days they made all the necessary physical adjustments. The three casualties—a male that

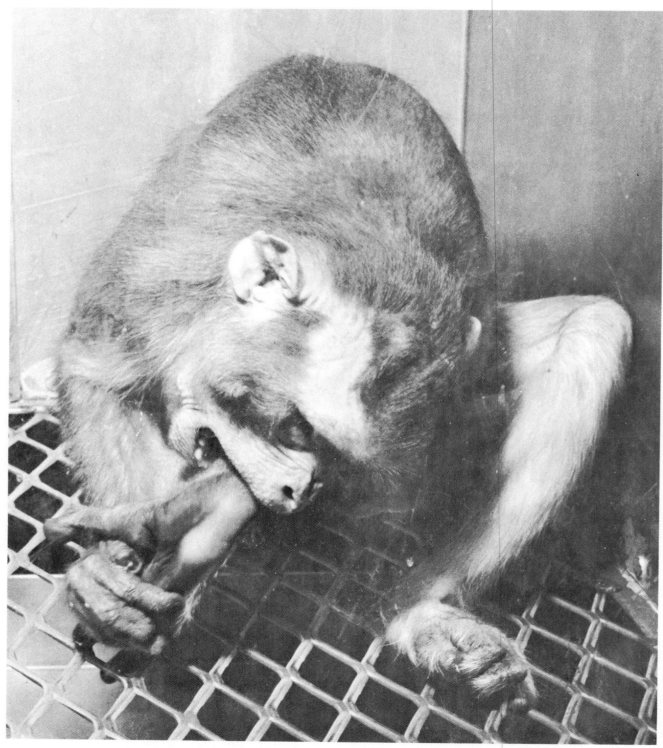

MONKEYS RAISED IN PARTIAL ISOLATION from birth to six months develop severe abnormalities of behavior. This animal, now full-grown, bites itself at the approach of the photographer. Animals raised in isolation often display such self-punishing behavior when a human being appears. They defend themselves adequately, however, against other monkeys and are often extremely aggressive.

EXPERIMENTAL CONDITION	PRESENT AGE	BEHAVIOR				
		NONE	LOW	ALMOST NORMAL	PROBABLY NORMAL	NORMAL
RAISED IN ISOLATION						
TOTAL — CAGE-RAISED FOR 2 YEARS	4 YEARS	■□▪				
TOTAL — CAGE-RAISED FOR 6 MONTHS	14 MONTHS	□▪	■			
TOTAL — CAGE-RAISED FOR 80 DAYS	10½ MONTHS			■□▪		
PARTIAL — CAGE-RAISED FOR 6 MONTHS	5 TO 8 YEARS	■		□		
PARTIAL — SURROGATE-RAISED FOR 6 MONTHS	3 TO 5 YEARS	■		□		
RAISED WITH MOTHER						
NORMAL MOTHER; NO PLAY WITH PEERS	1 YEAR	▪■				□
MOTHERLESS MOTHER; PLAY IN PLAYPEN	14 MONTHS		□		▪■	
NORMAL MOTHER; PLAY IN PLAYPEN	2 YEARS				■□	▪
RAISED WITH PEERS						
FOUR RAISED IN ONE CAGE; PLAY IN PLAYROOM	1 YEAR				■	□▪
SURROGATE-RAISED; PLAY IN PLAYPEN	2 YEARS				▪■□	▪
SURROGATE-RAISED; PLAY IN PLAYROOM	21 MONTHS				■□	▪

■ PLAY
□ DEFENSE
▪ SEX

RESULTS OF EXPERIMENTS are summarized. The monkey's capacity to develop normally appears to be determined by the seventh month of life. Animals isolated for six months are aberrant in every respect. Play with peers seems even more necessary than mothering to the development of effective social relations.

drowned and two females that were injured and had to be returned to the laboratory—resulted from the stress of social adjustment. Fighting was severe at first; it decreased as effective dominance relations were established and friendship pairs formed. Grooming appeared in normal style and with almost normal frequency. A limited amount of sex behavior was observed, but it was infantile in form, with inadequate posturing by both females and males. In the hope of promoting therapy along this line we introduced our largest, strongest and most effective breeding-colony male to the island around the middle of summer. He immediately established himself at the head of the dominance order. But in spite of his considerable persistence and patience he did not succeed in starting a single pregnancy.

Back in the laboratory these animals ceased to groom and fought more frequently. In pairings with breeding-colony monkeys, not one male has achieved a normal mount or intromission and only one female has become pregnant. After two years we have had to conclude that the island experience was of no lasting value.

As the effects of the separation of these monkeys from their mothers in infancy were first becoming apparent in 1957 we were prompted to undertake a study of the mother-infant affectional bond. To each of one group of four animals separated from their mothers at birth we furnished a surrogate mother: a welded wire cylindrical form with the nipple of the feeding bottle protruding from its "breast" and with a wooden head surmounting it. The majority of the animals, 60 in all, were raised with cozier surrogate mothers covered by terry cloth. In connection with certain experiments some of these individuals have had both a bare-wire and a cloth-covered mother. The infants developed a strong attachment to the cloth mothers and little or none to the wire mothers, regardless of which one provided milk. In fright-inducing situations the infants showed that they derived a strong sense of security from the presence of their cloth mothers [see the article "Love in Infant Monkeys," by Harry F. Harlow, beginning on page 78]. Even after two years of separation they exhibit a persistent attachment to the effigies.

In almost all other respects, however, the behavior of these monkeys at ages ranging from three to five years is indistinguishable from that of monkeys raised in bare wire cages with no source of contact comfort other than a gauze diaper pad. They are without question socially and sexually aberrant. No normal sex behavior has been observed in the living cages of any of the animals that have been housed with a companion of the opposite sex. In exposure to monkeys from the breeding colony not one male and only one female has shown normal mating behavior and only four females have been successfully impregnated. Compared with the cage-raised monkeys, the surrogate-raised animals seem to be less aggressive, whether toward themselves or other monkeys. But they are also younger on the average, and their better dispositions can be attributed to their lesser age.

Thus the nourishment and contact comfort provided by the nursing cloth-covered mother in infancy does not produce a normal adolescent or adult. The surrogate cannot cradle the baby or communicate monkey sounds and gestures. It cannot punish for misbehavior or attempt to break the infant's bodily attachment before it becomes a fixation. The entire group of animals separated from their mothers at birth and raised in individual wire cages, with or without surrogate, must be written off as potential breeding stock. Apparently their early social deprivation permanently impairs their ability to form effective relations with other monkeys, whether the opportunity was offered to them in the second six months of life or in the second to the fifth year of life.

One may correctly assume that total social isolation, compared with the partial isolation in which these subjects were reared, would produce even more devastating effects on later personality development. Such disastrous effects have been reported in the rare cases of children who have been liberated after months or years of lonely confinement in a darkened room. We have submitted a few monkeys to total isolation. Our purpose was to establish the maximum of social deprivation that would allow survival and also to determine whether or not there is a critical period in which social deprivation may have irreversible effects.

In our first study a male and a female were housed alone from birth for a period of two years, each one in its own cubicle with solid walls. Their behavior could be observed through one-way vision screens and tested by remote control. The animals adapted to solid food slowly, but they had normal weight and good coats when they were removed from the isolation boxes at the end of two years. Throughout this period nei-

ther animal had seen any living being other than itself.

They responded to their liberation by the crouching posture with which monkeys typically react to extreme threat. When placed together, each one crouched and made no further response to the other. Paired with younger monkeys from the group raised in partial isolation, they froze or fled when approached and made no effort to defend themselves from aggressive assaults. After another two years, in which they were kept together in a single large cage in the colony room, they showed the same abnormal fear of the sight or sound of other monkeys.

We are now engaged in studying the effects of six months of total social isolation. The first pair of monkeys, both males, has been out of isolation for eight months. They are housed, each monkey in its own cage, in racks with other monkeys of their age that were raised in the partial isolation of individual wire cages. For 20 minutes a day, five days a week, they are tested with a pair of these monkeys in the "playroom" of the laboratory. This room we designed to stimulate the young monkeys to a maximum of activity. It was not until the 12th and 27th week respectively that the two totally deprived monkeys began to move and climb about. They now circulate freely but not as actively as the control animals. Although frequently attacked by the

controls, neither one has attempted to defend itself or fight back; they either accept abuse or flee. One must be characterized as extremely disturbed and almost devoid of social behavior. The other resembles a normal two-month-old rhesus infant in its play and social behavior, and the indications are that it will never be able to make mature contacts with its peers.

A considerably more hopeful prognosis is indicated for two groups of four monkeys raised in total isolation for the much shorter period of 80 days. In their cubicles these animals had the contact comfort of a cloth-covered surrogate. They were deficient in social behavior during the first test periods in the playroom. But they made rapid gains; now, eight months later, we rate them as "almost normal" in play, defense and sex behavior. At least seven of the eight seem to bear no permanent scars as the result of early isolation.

Our first few experiments in the total isolation of these animals would thus appear to have bracketed what may be the critical period of development during which social experience is necessary for normal behavior in later life. We have additional experiments in progress, involving a second pair that will have been isolated for six months and a first pair that will have been isolated for a full year. The indications are that six months of isolation will render the animals per-

"TOGETHER-TOGETHER" EXPERIMENT involved raising four motherless infants in one cage and giving them 20 minutes a day in the playroom. At one year of age they are normal, but during their early months they spent most of the time huddled in this position.

manently inadequate. Since the rhesus monkey is more mature than the human infant at birth and grows four times more rapidly, this is equivalent to two or three years for the human child. On the other hand, there is reason to believe that the effects of shorter periods of early isolation, perhaps 60 to 90 days or even more, are clearly reversible. This would be equivalent to about six months in the development of the human infant. The time probably varies with the individual and with the experiences to which it is exposed once it is removed from isolation. Beyond a brief period of neonatal grace, however, the evidence suggests that every additional week or month of social deprivation increasingly imperils social development in the rhesus monkey. Case studies of children reared in impersonal institutions or in homes with indifferent mothers or nurses show a frightening comparability. The child may remain relatively unharmed through the first six months of life. But from this time on the damage is progressive and cumulative. By one year of age he may sustain enduring emotional scars and by two years many children have reached the point of no return.

In all of these experiments in partial and total isolation, whether unwitting or deliberate, our animals were deprived of the company of their peers as well as of their mothers. We accordingly undertook a series of experiments designed to distinguish and compare the roles of mother-infant and infant-infant relations in the maturation of rhesus monkey behavior. Our most privileged subjects are two groups of four monkeys each, now two years old, that were raised with their mothers during the first 18 and 21 months respectively and with peers from the first weeks. Each mother-infant pair occupied a large cage that gave the infant access to one cell of a four-unit playpen. By removing the screens between the playpens we enabled the infants to play together in pairs or as foursomes during scheduled observation periods each day. In parallel with these two groups we raised another group of four in a playpen setup without their mothers but with a terrycloth surrogate in each home cage.

From the time the mothers let them leave their home cages, after 20 or 30 days, the mothered infants entered into more lively and consistent relations with one another than did the four motherless ones. Their behavior evolved more rapidly through the sequence of increasingly complex play patterns that reflects the maturation and learning of the infant

GROUP PSYCHOTHERAPY for monkeys raised in isolation in the laboratory was attempted by removing them to the semiwild conditions of the zoo after they reached maturity. Here their behavior improved; they began to play together and groom one another. But when they were returned to the laboratory, they reverted to their earlier abnormal behavior.

monkey and is observed in a community of normal infants. The older they grew and the more complex the play patterns became, the greater became the observable difference between the mothered and the motherless monkeys. Now, at the end of the second year, the 12 animals are living together in one playpen setup, with each original group occupying one living cage and its adjoining playpen. All are observed in daily interaction without the dividing panels. The early differences between them have all but disappeared. Seven of the eight mothered animals engage in normal sexual activity and assume correct posture. The deviant is a male, and this animal was the social reject in its all-male group of four. Of the two motherless males, one has recently achieved full adult sexual posture and the other is approaching it. The two motherless females appear normal, but it remains to be seen whether or not their maternal behavior will reflect their lack of mothering.

Observation of infants with their mothers suggests reasons for the differences in the early social and sexual behavior of these playpen groups. From early in life on the infant monkey shows a strong tendency to imitate its mother; this responding to another monkey's behavior carries over to interaction with its peers. It is apparent also that sexual activity is stimulated by the mother's grooming of the infant. Finally, as the mother begins occasionally to reject its offspring in the third or fourth month,

the infant is propelled into closer relations with its peers. These observations underlie the self-evident fact that the mother-infant relation plays a positive role in the normal development of the infant-infant and heterosexual relations of the young monkey.

That the mother-infant relation can also play a disruptive role was demonstrated in another experiment. Four females that had been raised in the partial isolation of individual wire cages—and successfully impregnated in spite of the inadequacy of their sexual behavior—delivered infants within three weeks of one another. This made it possible to set up a playpen group composed of these "motherless" mothers and their infants. The maternal behavior of all four mothers was completely abnormal, ranging from indifference to outright abuse. Whereas it usually requires more than one person to separate an infant from its mother, these mothers paid no attention when their infants were removed from the cages for the hand-feeding necessitated by the mothers' refusal to nurse. Two of the mothers did eventually permit fairly frequent nursing, but their apparently closer maternal relations were accompanied by more violent abuse. The infants were persistent in seeking contact with their mothers and climbed on their backs when they were repulsed at the breast. In play with one another during the first six months, the infants were close to the normally mothered animals in maturity of play, but they played less.

NORMAL MOTHER-INFANT RELATION among monkeys involves close bodily contact between the two. This pair and three similar pairs were used in a study of the relative importance of maternal and peer relations in the social development of the young. Each pair was housed alone, but the infants had access to a common playpen. In this situation the young developed normally.

In sexual activity, however, they were far more precocious. During the eight months since they have been separated from their mothers, they have exhibited more aggression and day-to-day variability in their behavior than have the members of other playpen groups. The two male offspring of the most abusive mothers have become disinterested in the female and occupy the subordinate position in all activities.

More study of more babies from motherless mothers is needed to determine whether or not the interrelations that characterize this pilot group will characterize others of the same composition. There is no question about the motherless mothers themselves. The aberration of their maternal behavior would have ensured the early demise of their infants outside the laboratory. As for the infants, the extremes of sexuality and aggressiveness observed in their behavior evoke all too vivid parallels in the behavior of disturbed human children and adolescents in psychiatric clinics and institutions for delinquents.

Another pilot experiment has shown that even normal mothering is not enough to produce socially adequate offspring. We isolated two infants in the exclusive company of their mothers to the age of seven months and then brought the mother-infant pairs together in a playpen unit. The female infant took full advantage of the play apparatus provided, but in three months the male was never seen to leave its home cage, and its mother would not permit the female to come within arm's reach. Social interaction of the infants was limited to an occasional exchange of tentative threats. For the past two months they have been separated from their mothers, housed in individual cages and brought together in the playroom for 15 minutes each day. In this normally stimulating environment they have so far shown no disposition to play together. Next to the infants that have been raised in total isolation, these are the most retarded of the infants tested in the playroom.

It is to the play-exciting stimulus of the playroom that we owe the unexpected outcome of our most suggestive experiment. The room is a relatively spacious one, with an eight-foot ceiling and 40 square feet of floor space. It is equipped with movable and stationary toys and a wealth of climbing devices, including an artificial tree, a ladder and a burlap-covered climbing ramp that leads to a platform. Our purpose in constructing the playroom was to provide the monkeys with opportunities to move about in the three-dimensional world to which, as arboreal animals, they are much more highly adapted than man. To assess the effects of different histories of early social experience we customarily turn the animals loose in the room in groups of four for regularly scheduled periods of observation each day.

The opportunities afforded by the playroom were most fully exploited by two groups of four infants that otherwise spent their days housed alone in their cages with a cloth surrogate. In terms of "mothering," therefore, these monkeys were most closely comparable to the four that were raised with surrogates in the playpen situation. These animals were released in the playroom for 20 minutes a day from the first month of life through the 11th, in the case of one group, and through the second year in the case of the other. In contrast with all the other groups observed in the playroom, therefore, they did their "growing up" in this environment. Even though their exposure to the room and to one another was limited to 20 minutes a day, they enacted with great spirit the entire growth pattern of rhesus-monkey play behavior.

They began by exploring the room and each other. Gradually over the next two or three months they developed a game of rough-and-tumble play, with jumping, scuffling, wrestling, hair-pulling and a little nipping, but with no real damage, and then an associated game of flight and pursuit in which the participants are alternately the threateners and the threatened. While these group activities evolved, so did the capacity for individual play exploits, with the animals running, leaping, swinging and climbing, heedless of one another and apparently caught up in the sheer joy of action. As their skill and strength grew, their social play involved shorter but brisker episodes of free-for-all action, with longer chases between bouts. Subsequently they developed an even more complex pattern of violent activity, performed with blinding speed and integrating all objects, animate and inanimate, in the room. Along with social play, and possibly as a result or by-product, they began to exhibit sexual posturing—immature and fleeting in the first six months and more frequent and adult in form by the end of the year. The differences in play activity that distinguish males and females became evident in the first two or three months, with the females threatening and initiating rough contact far less frequently than the males and withdrawing from threats and approaches far more frequently.

Thus in spite of the relatively limited opportunity for contact afforded by their daily schedule, all the individuals in these two groups developed effective infant-infant play relations. Those observed into the second year have shown the full repertory of adult sexual behavior. At the same chronological age these motherless monkeys have attained as full a maturity in these respects as the infants raised with their mothers in the playpen.

Another group of four motherless animals raised together in a single large cage from the age of two weeks is yielding similar evidence of the effectiveness of the infant-infant affectional bond. During their first two months these animals spent much of their time clinging together, each animal clutching the back of the one just ahead of it in "choo-choo" fashion. They moved about as a group of three or four; when one of them broke away, it was soon clutched by another to form the nucleus of a new line. In the playroom the choo-choo linkage gave way to individual exploratory expeditions. During periods of observation, whether in their home cage or in the playroom, these animals have consistently scored lower in play activity than the most playful groups. We think this is explained, however, by the fact that they are able to spread their play over a 24-hour period. At the age of one year they live amicably together. In sex behavior they are more mature than the mother-raised playpen babies. No member of the group shows any sign of damage by mother-deprivation.

Our observations of the three groups of motherless infants raised in close association with one another therefore indicate that opportunity for optimal infant-infant interaction may compensate for lack of mothering. This is true at least in so far as infant-infant and sexual relations are concerned. Whether or not maternal behavior or later social adjustment will be affected remains to be seen.

Of course research on nonhuman animals, even monkeys, will never resolve the baffling complex roles of various kinds of early experience in the development of human personality. It is clear, however, that important theoretical and practical questions in this realm of interest can be resolved by the use of monkeys. The close behavioral resemblance of our disturbed infants to disturbed human beings gives us the confidence that we are working with significant variables and the hope that we can point the way to reducing the toll of psychosocial trauma in human society.

VIII

SLEEP, DREAMING, AND AROUSAL

VIII

SLEEP, DREAMING, AND AROUSAL

INTRODUCTION

Rhythmic variations in levels of arousal and activity are a universal characteristic of higher organisms; sleeping and waking are the normal extremes. The study of sleep has achieved a genuine breakthrough with the discovery that there are two sleep states, the deeper state being associated with dreaming. For the first time, we now have instruments and measurements with which we can characterize the dream state. Sleep itself still remains something of a mystery—it is not yet known why sleep is necessary. A great deal has been learned, however, about the brain mechanisms underlying sleep. The level of arousal and activity also varies markedly in the waking state. Studies of the effects of arousal on behavior indicate that humans perform best at some level of arousal intermediate between agitation and boredom. Sensory deprivation produces marked pathology in human experience and performance.

In his article "The States of Sleep," Michael Jouvet summarizes our current knowledge on the subject. Light sleep shows the characteristic alpha waves, or slow waves, in the EEG, and was earlier thought to be *the* sleep state. We now know that higher animals, including man, spend a substantial portion of each night's sleep in a deeper state called paradoxical sleep. It is termed paradoxical because, although stronger external stimuli are required to awaken a person from it than from light sleep, the EEG shows the same pattern as in the waking state. Paradoxical sleep is associated with dreaming and is characterized by rapid eye movements, hence the term "REM" sleep. "Patterns of Dreaming," an article by one of the pioneering scientists in the field of sleep, Nathaniel Kleitman, is next in this section. In a typical night's sleep, Kleitman points out, a normal person shows regular cyclic variations between light sleep and deep sleep. Although many people assert that they never dream, they will almost invariably admit to having been dreaming if they are awakened directly from the deep-sleep state. The content of dreams can have a significant impact on waking behavior, as did Joseph's prophetic dream in the Old Testament. Calvin S. Hall has spent many years analyzing dream content. His intriguing observations are summarized in the article "What People Dream About."

The properties of arousal in the waking state are examined by Daniel E. Berlyne in "Conflict and Arousal." Performance in learning and motor skills is clearly improved by a certain degree of arousal. Berlyne also describes experiments where he has increased the level of arousal in his subjects by inducing a certain degree of conflict in them. Within limits, conflict seems to improve performance. The opposite extreme is considered by Woodburn Heron in his article "The Pathology of Boredom." Heron describes the now famous experiments on sensory deprivation at McGill University, wherein human volunteers with their hands wrapped in cotton were kept for periods of a few days in rooms shielded from light and sound. They were literally deprived of most sensory experience. The subjects developed abnormal brain waves and reported a variety of hallucinations.

34

THE STATES OF SLEEP

MICHEL JOUVET
February 1967

Early philosophers recognized that there are two distinctly different levels of sleep. An ancient Hindu tale described three states of mind in man: (1) wakefulness (*vaiswanara*), in which a person "is conscious only of external objects [and] is the enjoyer of the pleasures of sense"; (2) dreaming sleep (*taijasa*), in which one "is conscious only of his dreams [and] is the enjoyer of the subtle impressions in the mind of the deeds he has done in the past," and (3) dreamless sleep (*prajna*), a "blissful" state in which "the veil of unconsciousness envelops his thought and knowledge, and the subtle impressions of his mind apparently vanish."

States 2 and 3 obviously are rather difficult to investigate objectively, and until very recently the phases of sleep remained a subject of vague speculation. Within the past few years, however,

studies with the aid of the electroencephalograph have begun to lift the veil. By recording brain waves, eye movements and other activities of the nervous system during the different sleep states neurophysiologists are beginning to identify the specific nervous-system structures involved, and we are now in a position to analyze some of the mechanisms responsible.

Brain Activities in Sleep

Lucretius, that remarkably inquisitive and shrewd observer of nature, surmised that the fidgetings of animals during sleep were linked to dreaming. Some 30 years ago a German investigator, R. Klaue, made a significant discovery with the electroencephalograph. He found that sleep progressed in a characteristic sequence: a period of light sleep, during

which the brain cortex produced slow brain waves, followed by a period of deep sleep, in which the cortical activity speeded up. Klaue's report was completely overlooked at the time. In the 1950's, however, Nathaniel Kleitman and his students at the University of Chicago took up this line of investigation. Kleitman and Eugene Aserinsky found (in studies of infants) that periods of "active" sleep, alternating with quiescent periods, were marked by rapid eye movements under the closed lids. Later Kleitman and William C. Dement, in studies of adults, correlated the eye movements with certain brain-wave patterns and definitely linked these activities and patterns to periods of dreaming [see the article "Patterns of Dreaming," by Nathaniel Kleitman, beginning on page 337]. In 1958 Dement showed that cats may have periods of sleep similarly marked by rapid eye movement and fast cortical activity. He called such periods "activated sleep."

Meanwhile at the University of Lyons, François Michel and I had been conducting a series of experiments with cats. In the cat, which spends about two-thirds of its time sleeping, the process of falling asleep follows a characteristic course, signaled by easily observable external signs. Typically the animal curls up in a ball with its neck bent. The flexing of the nape of its neck is a clear sign that the muscles there retain some tonus, that is, they are not completely relaxed. In this position the cat lapses into a light sleep from which it is easily awakened.

After about 10 to 20 minutes there comes a constellation of changes that mark passage over the brink into deep sleep. The cat's neck and back relax their curvature, showing that the muscles have completely lost tonus: they are now altogether slack. At the same time there

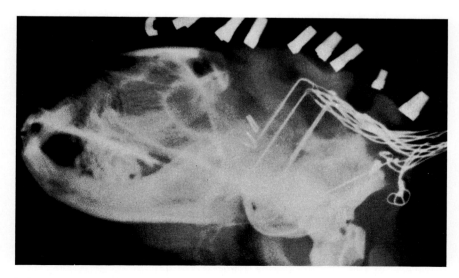

X RAY OF CAT'S HEAD shows a cluster of electrodes with which the author obtained a record of the electrical signals from various parts of the cat's brain. The cat's mouth is at the left; one electrode at far right measures the changes in the animal's neck-muscle tension.

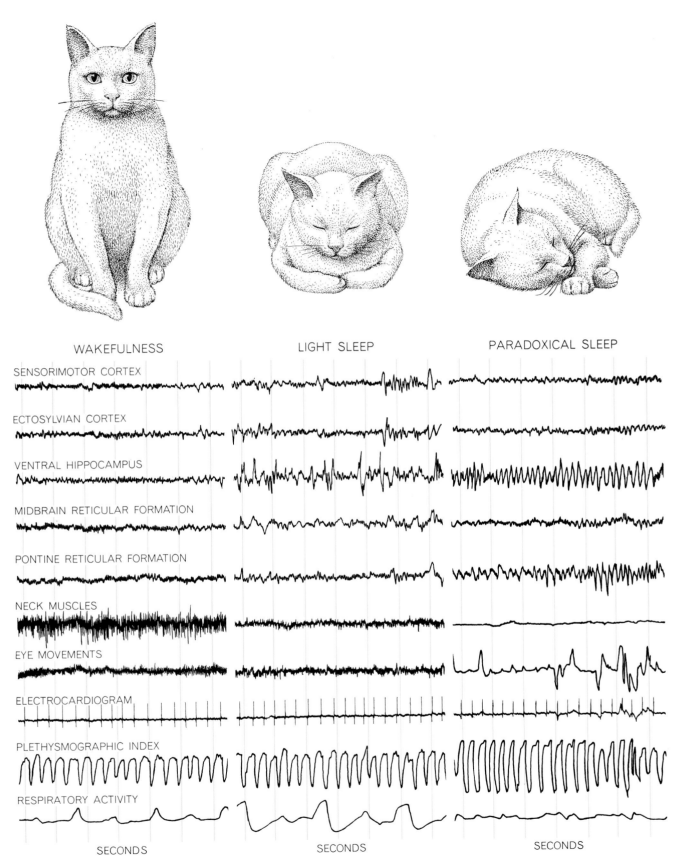

WAKEFULNESS   LIGHT SLEEP   PARADOXICAL SLEEP

SENSORIMOTOR CORTEX

ECTOSYLVIAN CORTEX

VENTRAL HIPPOCAMPUS

MIDBRAIN RETICULAR FORMATION

PONTINE RETICULAR FORMATION

NECK MUSCLES

EYE MOVEMENTS

ELECTROCARDIOGRAM

PLETHYSMOGRAPHIC INDEX

RESPIRATORY ACTIVITY

SECONDS   SECONDS   SECONDS

CHARACTERISTIC RHYTHMS associated with deep sleep in a cat (*group of traces at right*) are so much like those of wakefulness (*left group*) and so different from those of light sleep (*middle group*) that the author has applied the term "paradoxical" to deep sleep. Normal cats spend about two-thirds of the time sleeping. They usually begin each sleep period with 25 minutes of light sleep, followed by six or seven minutes of paradoxical sleep. In the latter state they are hard to wake and their muscles are relaxed.

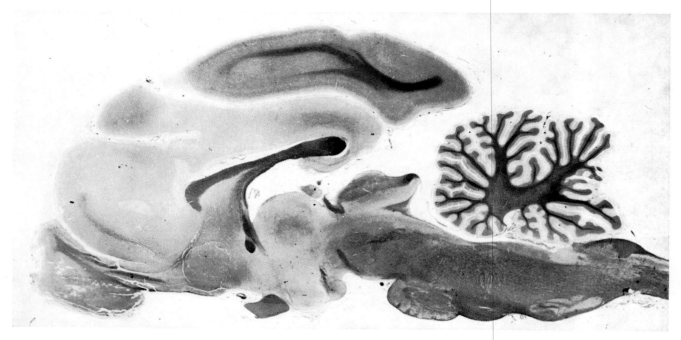

CAT'S BRAIN, seen in front-to-back section, has a number of segments. Some of the principal ones are identified in the illustration at the top of the opposite page. Many segments of the cat's brain, such as the cerebellum (*top right*), have no role to play in sleep.

are bursts of rapid eye movements (eight to 30 movements in each burst) in either the side-to-side or the up-and-down direction, like the movements in visual use of the eyes. Occasionally these eyeball movements behind the closed eyelids are accompanied by a sudden dilation of the pupils, which in the main are tightly constricted during sleep. Along with the eye movements go events involving many other parts of the body: small tremors of muscles at the ends of the extremities, causing rapid flexing of the digits and now and then small scratching motions; very rapid movements of the ears, the whiskers, the tail and the tongue, and an episode of fast and irregular breathing.

It is somewhat startling to realize that all this activity goes on during a period in which the animal's muscular system is totally atonic (lacking in tension). The activities are also the accompaniment of deep sleep, as is indicated by the fact that it takes an unusually high level of sound or electrical stimulation to arouse the cat during this phase. The state of deep sleep lasts about six or seven minutes and alternates with periods of lighter sleep that last for an average of about 25 minutes.

To obtain more objective and specific information about events in the brain during sleep we implanted electrodes in the muscles of the neck and in the midbrain of cats. We used animals that

were deprived of the brain cortex, since we wished to study the subcortical activities. In the course of extended recordings of the electrical events we were surprised to find that the electrical activity of the neck muscles disappeared completely for regular periods (six minutes long), and the condition persisted when sharp spikes of high voltage showed up now and then in the pontine reticular formation, situated just behind the "arousal center" of the midbrain. These electrical signs were correlated with eye movements of the sleeping animal. Further, we noted that in cats with intact brains both the abolition of muscle tonus and the sharp high-voltage spikes were strikingly correlated with the rapid eye

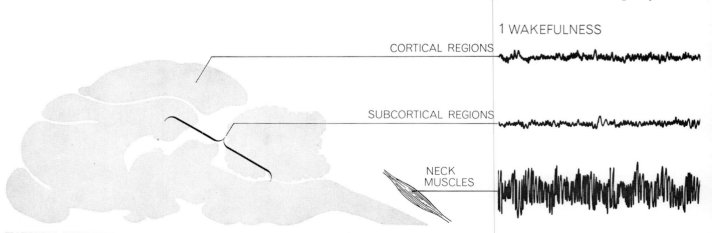

1 WAKEFULNESS

CORTICAL REGIONS

SUBCORTICAL REGIONS

NECK
MUSCLES

VARYING RHYTHMS are identified with the various states of sleep. From left to right, a wakeful cat (*1*) shows high-speed alternations in electric potential in both cortical and subcortical regions of the brain, as well as neck-muscle tension. In light sleep (*2*) the cat shows a slower rhythm in the traces from the cortical and subcortical regions, but neck-muscle tension continues. The phasic, or

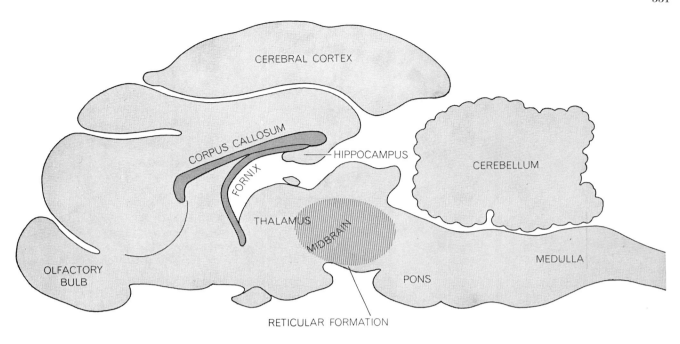

BRAIN SEGMENTS associated with sleep include the reticular formation, which controls wakefulness. This region is under the control of an area in the lower brain. When the control is blocked by making a cut through the pons, a normal cat becomes insomniac.

movement and fast cortical activity Dement had described. These findings presented a paradox. It was surely strange to find fast cortical activity (generally a sign of wakefulness) coupled with complete muscular atony (invariably a sign of deep sleep)!

The Two Sleep States

We named this strange state "paradoxical sleep." It is also called deep sleep, fast-wave sleep, rapid-eye-movement (REM) sleep and dreaming sleep, whereas the lighter sleep that precedes it is often called slow-wave sleep. We consider paradoxical sleep a qualitatively distinct state, not simply a deepened version of the first stage of sleep. Very schematically (for the cat) we can describe the three states—wakefulness, light sleep and paradoxical sleep—in the following physiological terms. Wakefulness is accompanied by fast, low-voltage electrical activity in the cortex and the subcortical structures of the brain and by a significant amount of tonus in the muscular system. The first stage of sleep, or light sleep, is characterized by a slackening of electrical activity in the cortex and subcortical structures, by the occurrence of "spindles," or groups of sharp jumps, in the brain waves and by retention of the muscular tension. Paradoxical sleep presents a more complex picture that we must consider in some detail.

We can classify the phenomena in paradoxical sleep under two heads: tonic (those having to do with continuous phenomena) and phasic (those of a periodic character). The principal tonic phenomena observed in the cat are fast electrical waves (almost like those of wakefulness) in the cortex and subcortical structures, very regular "theta" waves at the level of the hippocampus (a structure running from the front to the rear of the brain) and total disappearance of electrical activity in the muscles of the neck. The principal phasic phenomena are high-voltage spikes, isolated or grouped in volleys, that appear at the level of the pons and the rear part of the cortex (which is associated with the visual sys-

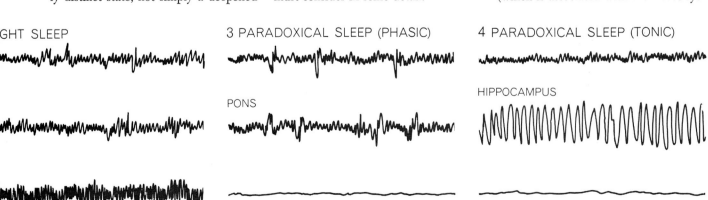

periodic, aspects of paradoxical sleep (3) are marked by isolated spike discharges from the rear of the cortex and the pons, as well as by rapid eye movement and limb movements. Loss of neck-muscle tension is a tonic (4) rather than a phasic phenomenon. Other tonic, or continuous, aspects of paradoxical sleep are high-speed cortical rhythms and regular "theta" waves from hippocampus.

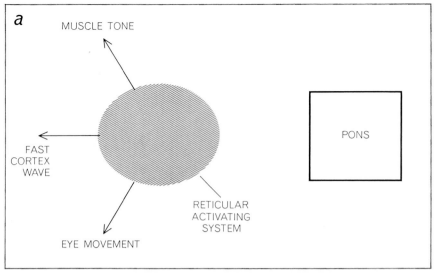

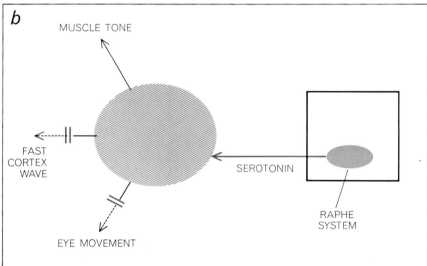

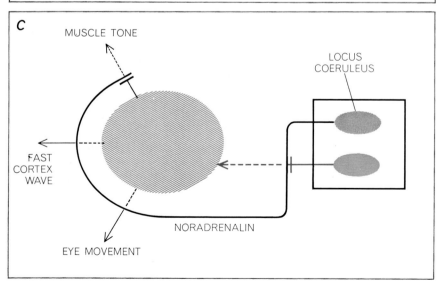

WORKING HYPOTHESIS, proposed by the author to provide a bridge between the neurophysiology and the biochemistry of sleep, suggests that the normal state of wakefulness (*a*) is transformed into light sleep (*b*) when a secretion produced by the nuclei of raphe modifies many effects of the reticular activating system. Paradoxical sleep follows (*c*) when a second secretion, produced by the locus coeruleus, supplants the raphe secretion and produces effects that resemble normal wakefulness except for the loss of muscle tension.

tem). These spikes make their appearance about a minute before the tonic phenomena. Just as the latter show up, the peripheral phasic phenomena come into evidence: rapid eye movements, clawing movements of the paws and so on. The high-voltage spikes during paradoxical sleep in the cat come at a remarkably constant rate: about 60 to 70 per minute.

Our continuous recordings around the clock in a soundproofed cage have shown that cats spend about 35 percent of the time (in the 24-hour day) in the state of wakefulness, 50 percent in light sleep and 15 percent in paradoxical sleep. In most cases the three states follow a regular cycle from wakefulness to light sleep to paradoxical sleep to wakefulness again. An adult cat never goes directly from wakefulness into paradoxical sleep.

Thus we find that the two states of sleep have well-defined and clearly distinct electrical signatures. Equipped with this information, we are better prepared to search for the nervous structures and mechanisms that are responsible for sleep and dreaming.

The Suppression of Wakefulness

The first and most important question we must answer is this: Does the nervous system possess a specific sleep-producing mechanism? In other words, should we not rather confine our research to the operations of the mechanism that keeps us awake? Kleitman has put the issue very clearly; he observes that to say one falls asleep or is put to sleep is not the same as saying one ceases to stay awake. The first statement implies that an active mechanism suppresses the state of wakefulness—a mechanism analogous to applying the brakes in an automobile. The second statement implies that the wakefulness-producing mechanism simply stops operating—a situation analogous to removing the foot from the accelerator. Thus the mechanism responsible for sleep would be negative or passive, not active.

Now, it has been known for nearly two decades that the brain contains a center specifically responsible for maintaining wakefulness. This was discovered by H. W. Magoun of the U.S. and Giuseppe Moruzzi of Italy, working together at Northwestern University [see the article "The Reticular Formation," by J. D. French, beginning on page 102]. They named this center, located in the midbrain, the reticular activating system (RAS). Stimulation of the RAS center in a slumbering animal arouses the animal; conversely, destruction of the center causes the animal to go into a permanent coma. To explain normal sleep, then, we must find out what process or mechanism brings about a deactivation of the RAS for the period of sleep.

On the basis of the known facts about the RAS there seemed at first no need to invoke the idea of a braking mechanism to account for deactivation of the system. The Belgian neurophysiologist Frédéric Bremer suggested that the RAS could simply lapse into quiescence as a result of a decline of stimuli (such as disturbing noise) from the surroundings [see "Sleep," by Nathaniel Kleitman; SCIENTIFIC AMERICAN Offprint 431].

Several years ago, however, explorations of the brain by the Swiss neurophysiologist W. R. Hess and others began to produce indications that the brain might contain centers that could suppress the activity of the RAS. In these experiments, conducted with cats, the cats fell asleep after electrical stimulation of various regions in the thalamus and elsewhere or after the injection of chemicals into the cerebrum. Interesting as these findings were, they were not very convincing on the question at issue. After all, since a cat normally sleeps about two-thirds of the time anyway, how could one be sure that the applied treatments acted through specific sleep-inducing centers? Moreover, the experiments seemed to implicate nearly all the nerve structures surrounding the RAS, from the cerebral cortex all the way down to the spinal cord, as being capable of inducing sleep. It was implausible that a sleep-inducing system could be so diffuse. Nevertheless, in spite of all these doubts, the experiments at least pointed to the possibility that the RAS might be influenced by other brain centers.

Moruzzi and his group in Italy proceeded to more definitive experiments. Seeking to pin down the location of a center capable of opposing the action of the RAS, they focused their search on the lower part of the brainstem. They chose a site at the middle of the pons in front of the trigeminal nerve, and with cats as subjects they cut completely through the brainstem at that point. The outcome of this operation was that the cats became insomniac: they slept only 20 percent of the time instead of 65 percent! The brain cortex showed the characteristic electrical activity of wakefulness (fast, low-voltage activity), and the eye movements also were those of a wakeful animal pursuing moving objects. The experiments left no doubt that the cut had disconnected the RAS from some structure in the lower part of the brainstem that normally exercised con-

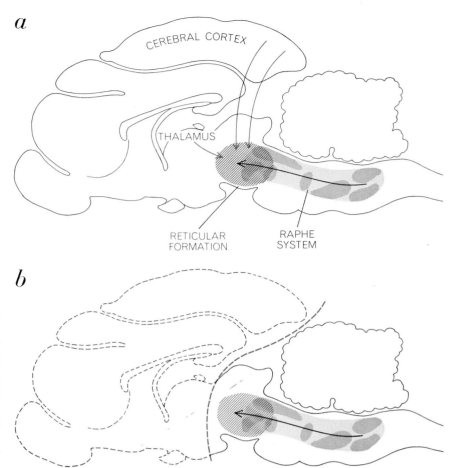

BRAIN STRUCTURES involved in light sleep include the raphe system, which, by producing the monoamine serotonin, serves to counteract the alerting effects of the brain's reticular formation ("*a*," *color at left*). The author suggests that raphe system structures act to modulate the fast wave pattern of the alert cortex into the slower pattern typical of light sleep. Such slow activity, however, depends on higher as well as lower brain structures (*b*); when a cat is deprived of its cerebral cortex and thalamus, the brain stem wave pattern characteristic of light sleep disappears. The reason for this is not yet understood.

trol over the waking center. It was as if a brake had been removed, so that the RAS was essentially unrestricted and kept the animal awake most of the time.

The new evidence leads, therefore, to the conclusion that sleeping is subject to both active and passive controls. The active type of control consists in the application of a brake on the RAS by some other brain structure or structures; the passive type corresponds to a letup on the accelerator in the RAS itself.

Sleep Centers

What, and where, are the sleep-inducing centers that act on the RAS? Our suspicions are now focused on a collection of nerve cells at the midline of the brainstem that are known as the "nuclei of raphe" (from a Greek word meaning "seam" and signifying the juncture of the two halves of the brain). In Sweden, Annica Dahlström and Kzell Fuxe have

shown that under ultraviolet light these cells emit a yellow fluorescence that shows they are rich in the hormone-like substance serotonin, which is known to have a wide spectrum of powerful effects on the brain and other organs of the body [see "Serotonin," by Irvine H. Page; SCIENTIFIC AMERICAN, December, 1957]. Suspecting from various preliminary pharmacological experiments that serotonin might play a role in sleep, we decided to test the effects of destroying the raphe cells, which are the principal source of the serotonin supply in the brain. We found that when we destroyed 80 percent of these cells at the level of the medulla in cats (the animals could not have survived destruction of a larger percentage), the cats became even more sleepless than those on which Moruzzi had performed his operation. In more than 100 hours of continuous observation with electrical recording instruments, our animals slept less than 10 percent of the time. Our results were closely related to those of Moruzzi's. His operation dividing the brainstem cut through the raphe system. We found that when we destroyed only the raphe cells on one side or the other of the site of his cut, our animals were reduced to the same amount of sleep (20 percent) as those on which he had performed his experiment. This gives us further reason to believe the raphe system may indeed be the main center responsible for bringing on sleep in cats.

These new developments bring serotonin into a prominent place in the research picture and offer an avenue for biochemical attack on the mysteries of sleep. The fact that the raphe cells are chiefly notable for their production of serotonin seems to nominate this substance for an important role in producing the onset of sleep. We have recently been able to demonstrate a significant correlation between the extent of the lesion of the raphe system, the decrease in sleep and the decrease in the amount of serotonin in the brain as measured by means of spectrofluorescent techniques.

In physiological terms we can begin to see the outlines of the system of brain structures involved in initiating the onset of sleep and maintaining the first stage of light slumber. At the level of the brainstem, probably within the raphe system, there are structures that apparently counteract the RAS and by their braking action cause the animal to fall asleep. Associated with these structures there presumably are nearby structures that account for the modulations of electrical activity (notably the slow brain waves) that have been observed to accompany light sleep. This slow activity seems to depend primarily, however, on the higher brain structures, particularly the cortex and the thalamus; in a decorticated animal the pattern characteristic of light sleep does not make its appearance. We must therefore conclude that the set of mechanisms brought into play during the process of falling asleep is a complicated one and that a number of steps in the process still remain to be discovered.

Paradoxical Sleep

In searching for the structures involved in paradoxical, or deep, sleep we are in a somewhat better position. When an animal is in that state, we have as clues to guide us not only the electrical activities in the brain but also conclusive and readily observable signs such as the disappearance of tonus in the muscles of the neck. This is the single most reliable mark of paradoxical sleep. Furthermore, it enables us to study animals that have been subjected to drastic operations we cannot use in the study of light sleep because they obliterate the electrical activities that identify the falling-asleep stage.

A cat whose brainstem has been cut through at the level of the pons, so that essentially all the upper part of the brain has been removed, still exhibits the cycle of waking and deep sleep. Such an animal can be kept alive for several months, and with the regularity of a biological clock it oscillates between wakefulness and the state of paradoxical sleep, in which it spends only about 10 percent of the time. This state is signaled, as in normal animals, by the typical slackness of the neck muscles, by the electroencephalographic spikes denoting electrical activity in the pons structures and by lateral movements of the eyeballs.

When, however, we sever the brainstem at a lower level, in the lower part of the pons just ahead of the medulla, the animal no longer falls into paradoxical sleep. The sign that marks this cyclical state—periodic loss of muscle tonus—disappears. It seems, therefore, that the onset of paradoxical sleep must be triggered by the action of structures somewhere in the middle portion of the pons. Further experiments have made it possible for us to locate these structures rather precisely. We have found that paradoxical sleep can be abolished by destroying certain nerve cells in a dorsal area of the pons known as the locus coeruleus. Dahlström and Fuxe have shown that these cells have a green fluorescence under ultraviolet light and that they contain noradrenalin. Hence it seems that noradrenalin may play a role in producing paradoxical sleep similar to the one serotonin apparently plays in bringing about light sleep.

What mechanism is responsible for the elimination of muscular tonus that accompanies paradoxical sleep? It seems

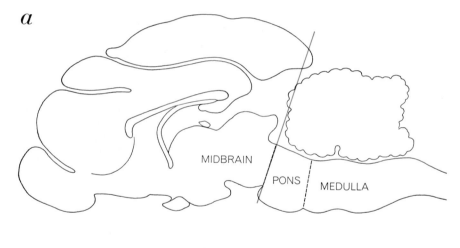

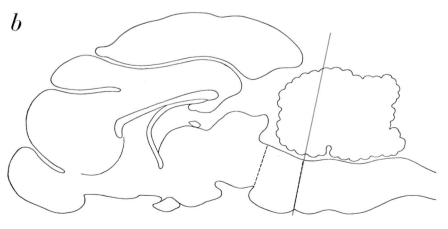

PARADOXICAL-SLEEP STRUCTURES evidently lie far back along the brainstem. A cat deprived of all its higher brain function by means of a cut through the pons (*a*) will live for months, alternately awake and in paradoxical sleep. If a cut is made lower (*b*) along the brainstem, however, the cat will no longer fall into paradoxical sleep, because the cut destroys some brain cells in that region, which produce another monoamine, noradrenalin.

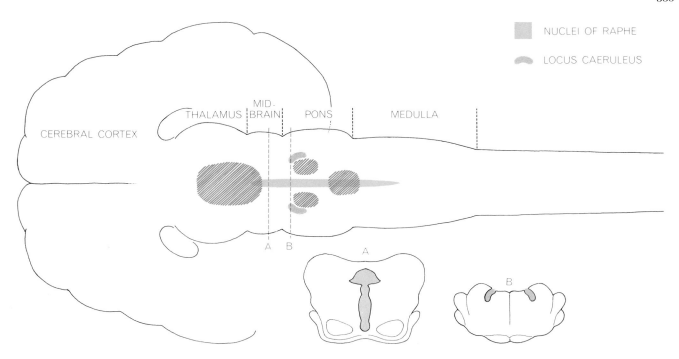

THALAMUS | MID-BRAIN | PONS | MEDULLA

CEREBRAL CORTEX

A B

A

B

CAT'S BRAINSTEM is the site of the two groups of cells that produce the substances affecting light and paradoxical sleep. The nuclei of raphe (*color*) secrete serotonin; another cell group in the pons, known as the locus coeruleus (*gray*), secretes noradrenalin.

most likely that the source of this inhibition lies in the spinal cord, and Moruzzi and his colleague Ottavio Pompeiano are making a detailed investigation of this hypothesis.

The objective information about paradoxical sleep developed so far gives us some suggestions about the mechanisms involved in dreaming. The controlling structures apparently are located in the dorsal part of the pons. They give rise to spontaneous excitations that travel mainly to the brain's visual tracts, and it seems possible that this excitation is related to the formation of the images that one "sees" in dreams. Regardless of how strongly the brain is stimulated by these spontaneous impulses (as Edward V. Evarts of the National Institute of Mental Health and others have shown by means of microelectrode recordings of the visual system), during sleep the body's motor system remains inactive because a potent braking mechanism blocks electrical excitation of the motor nerves. This inhibitory mechanism seems to be controlled by the hormone-secreting nerves of the locus coeruleus structure. If this structure is destroyed, the animal may periodically exhibit a spasm of active behavior, which looks very much as if it is generated by the hallucinations of a dream. In such episodes the cat, although it evinces the unmistakable signs of deep sleep and does not respond to external stimuli, will sometimes perform bodily movements of rage,

fear or pursuit for a minute or two. The sleeping animal's behavior may even be so fierce as to make the experimenter recoil.

All in all the experimental evidence from mammals obliges us to conclude that sleep has a fundamental duality; deep sleep is distinctly different from light sleep, and the duality is founded on physiological mechanisms and probably on biochemical ones as well. Can we shed further light on the subject by examining animal evolution?

The Evolution of Sleep

Looking into this question systematically in our laboratory, we failed to find any evidence of paradoxical sleep in the tortoise and concluded that probably reptiles in general were capable only of light sleep. Among birds, however, we start to see a beginning of paradoxical sleep, albeit very brief. In our subjects—pigeons, chicks and other fowl—this state of sleep lasts no longer than 15 seconds at a time and makes up only .5 percent of the total sleeping time, contrasted with the higher mammals' 20 to 30 percent. In the mammalian order all the animals that have been studied, from the mouse to the chimpanzee, spend a substantial portion of their sleeping time in paradoxical sleep. We find a fairly strong indication that the hunting species (man, the cat, the dog) enjoy more deep sleep than the hunted (rabbits, ruminants). In

our tests the former average 20 percent of total sleep time in paradoxical sleep, whereas the latter average only 5 to 10 percent. Further studies are needed, however, to determine if what we found in our caged animals is also true of their sleep in their natural environments.

The evolutionary evidence shows, then, that the early vertebrates slept only lightly and deep sleep came as a rather late development in animal evolution. Curiously, however, it turns out that the opposite is true in the development of a young individual; in this case ontogeny does not follow phylogeny. In the mammals (cat or man) light sleep does not occur until the nervous system has acquired a certain amount of maturity. A newborn kitten in its first days of life spends half of its time in the waking state and half in paradoxical sleep, going directly from one state into the other, whereas in the adult cat there is almost invariably a transitional period of light sleep. By the end of the first month the kitten's time is divided equally among wakefulness, light sleep and paradoxical sleep (that is, a third in each); thereafter both wakefulness and light sleep increase until adulthood stabilizes the proportions of the three states at 35, 50 and 15 percent respectively.

Considering these facts of evolution and development, we are confronted with the question: What function does paradoxical sleep serve after all? As Kleitman reported in his article "Patterns

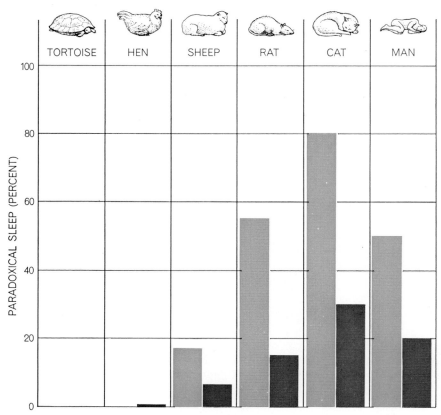

PARADOXICAL SLEEP among three vertebrate classes of increasing evolutionary complexity is shown as a percentage of each animal's time spent in light sleep. None is known in the case of the reptile, a tortoise; in the case of the hen it is only two-tenths of 1 percent of the total. In the case of each of the four mammal species shown, the newborn spend at least twice as much time in paradoxical sleep (*color*) as do their adult counterparts (*black*).

of Dreaming," Dement found that when he repeatedly interrupted people's dreams by waking them, this had the effect of making them dream more during their subsequent sleep periods. These results indicated that dreaming fulfills some genuine need. What that need may be remains a mystery. Dement's subjects showed no detectable disturbances of any importance—emotional or physiological—as a result of their deprivation of dreaming.

We have found much the same thing to be true of the deprivation of paradoxical sleep in cats. For such a test we place a cat on a small pedestal in a pool of water with the pedestal barely topping the water surface. Each time the cat drops off into paradoxical sleep the relaxation of its neck muscles causes its head to droop into the water and this wakes the animal up. Cats that have been deprived of paradoxical sleep in this way for several weeks show no profound disturbances, aside from a modest speeding up of the heart rate. They do, however, have a characteristic pattern of aftereffects with respect to paradoxical sleep. For several days following their removal from the pedestal they spend

much more than the usual amount of time (up to 60 percent) in paradoxical sleep, as if to catch up. After this rebound they gradually recover the normal rhythm (15 percent in deep sleep), and only then does the heart slow to the normal rate. The recovery period depends on the length of the deprivation period: a cat that has gone without paradoxical sleep for 20 days takes about 10 days to return to normal.

The Chemistry of Sleep

All of this suggests that some chemical process takes place during the recovery period. Let us suppose that the deprivation of paradoxical sleep causes a certain substance related to the nervous system to accumulate. The excess of paradoxical sleep during the recovery period will then be occupied with elimination of this "substance," presumably through the agency of "enzymatic" factors that act only during paradoxical sleep.

There is reason to believe that certain enzymes called monoamine oxidases, which oxidize substances having a single amine group, play a crucial role in bringing about the transition from light sleep

to paradoxical sleep. We have found that drugs capable of inhibiting these enzymes can suppress paradoxical sleep in cats without affecting either light sleep or wakefulness. A single injection of the drug nialamide, for example, will eliminate paradoxical sleep from the cycle for a period of hundreds of hours. We have also found that this potent drug can suppress paradoxical sleep in cats that have first been deprived of such sleep for a long period in the pool experiment.

The findings concerning the probable importance of the monoamine oxidases in the sleep mechanism raise the hope that it may soon be possible to build a bridge between neurophysiology and biochemistry in the investigation of sleep. If it is indeed a fact that these enzymes play an important role in sleep, this tends to strengthen the hypothesis that serotonin and noradrenalin, which are monoamines, are involved in the two states of sleep—serotonin in light sleep and noradrenalin in paradoxical sleep. There are other bits of chemical evidence that support the same view. For example, the drug reserpine, which is known to prevent the accumulation of monoamines at places where these compounds are usually deposited, has been found to be capable of producing some specific electrical signs of paradoxical sleep in experimental animals. Further, the injection of certain precursors involved in the synthesis of serotonin in the brain can produce a state resembling light sleep, whereas drugs that selectively depress the serotonin level in the brain produce a state of permanent wakefulness.

We can put together a tentative working hypothesis about the brain mechanisms that control sleep. It seems that the raphe system is the seat responsible for the onset of light sleep, and that it operates through the secretion of serotonin. Similarly, the locus coeruleus harbors the system responsible for producing deep sleep, and this uses noradrenalin as its agent. In cyclic fashion these two systems apply brakes to the reticular activating system responsible for wakefulness and also influence all the other nerve systems in the brain, notably those involved in dreaming.

Dreaming itself, particularly the question of its evolutionary origin and what function it serves, is still one of the great mysteries of biology. With the discovery of its objective accompaniments and the intriguing phenomenon of paradoxical sleep, however, it seems that we have set foot on a new continent that holds promise of exciting explorations.

35

PATTERNS OF DREAMING

NATHANIEL KLEITMAN
November 1960

Dreams have troubled the waking hours as well as the sleep of men since time immemorial. These hallucinatory experiences have inspired soothsayers and psychiatrists alike, and their bizarre contents, variously interpreted as prophetic insights and clues to personality, are the subject of a considerable body of literature. The scientific value of even the most recent contributions to this literature, however, is seriously qualified: The sole witness to the dream is the dreamer himself. The same limitation confronts the investigator who would inquire into the process of dreaming, as distinguished from the contents of dreams. Only the awakened sleeper can testify that he has dreamed. If he reports that he has not, it may be that he fails to recall his dreaming.

Nonetheless, in the course of our long-term investigation of sleep at the University of Chicago, we found ourselves venturing into research in the hitherto subjective realm of dreaming. We discovered an objective and apparently reliable way to determine whether a sleeper is dreaming—in the sense, of course, of his "reporting having dreamed" when he wakes up or is awakened. The objective indicator of dreaming makes it possible to chart the onset and duration of dreaming episodes throughout the night without disturbing the sleeper. One can also awaken and interrogate him at the beginning of a dream, in the middle, at the end, or at any measured interval after the end. By such means it has been determined that there is periodicity in dreaming, and the consequences of efforts to disturb this periodicity have been observed. The results indicate that dreaming as a fundamental physiological process is related to other rhythms of the body. As for the folklore that surrounds the process, this work has answered such questions as: Does everyone dream? How often does one dream in the course of a night's sleep? Is the "plot" of a dream really compressed into a moment of dreaming? Do external and internal stimuli—light, noise, hunger or thirst—affect the content of dreams?

As so often happens in research, the objective indicator of dreaming was discovered by accident. During a study of the cyclic variations of sleep in infants, a graduate student named Eugene Aserinsky observed that the infant's eyes continued to move under its closed lids for some time after all major body movement had ceased with the onset of sleep. The eye movements would stop and then begin again from time to time, and were the first movements to be seen as the infant woke up. Aserinsky found that eye movements provided a more reliable means of distinguishing between the active and quiescent phases of sleep than did gross body movements.

These observations suggested that eye movements might be used to follow similar cycles in the depth of sleep in adults. Disturbance to the sleeper was minimized by monitoring the eye movements remotely with an electroencephalograph, a device that records the weak electrical signals generated continuously by the brain. A potential difference across the eyeball between the cornea and the retina makes it possible to detect movements of the eyes by means of electrodes taped to the skin above and below or on either side of one eye. Other channels of the electroencephalograph recorded the sleeper's brain waves, his pulse and respiration rates and the gross movements of his body.

The tracings of the electroencephalograph showed not only the slow movements of the eyes that Aserinsky had observed in infants but also rapid eye-movements that came in clusters. Each individual eye-movement took a fraction of a second, but a cluster often lasted, with interruptions, as long as 50 minutes. The first rapid eye-movements usually began about an hour after the onset of sleep, and clusters appeared in cyclic fashion through the night [*see illustration on page 340*].

Coincident with this cycle of eye movement the electroencephalograph recorded a fluctuation in the brain-wave pattern. As each series of movements began, the brain waves changed from the pattern typical of deep sleep to one indicating lighter sleep. The pulse and respiration rates also increased, and the sleeper lay motionless.

Considered together, these observations suggested an emotionally charged cerebral activity—such as might occur in dreaming. This surmise was tested by the only possible means: arousing and questioning the sleepers. Those awakened in the midst of a cluster of rapid eye-movements testified they had been dreaming. Those awakened in the apparently deeper phases of sleep said they had not. Thus the objective indicator of dreaming came into use.

It is clear that such an indicator can reveal nothing about the content of dreams. But the process of dreaming is no more bound up with dream content than thinking is with what one is thinking about. The hallucinatory content of dreams would appear, in this light, to be nothing more than the expression of a crude type of activity carried on in the cerebral cortex during a certain phase of sleep. The contrast with the kind of cerebral activity that characterizes the waking state in healthy adults and older children is instructive. Responding to the impulses that stream in from the various receptor organs of the sensory system, the cortex first subjects them to analysis. It refers the present moment of experience to its memory of the past and projects past and present into the future, weighing the consequences of action not yet taken. A decision is reached, and the cortex generates an integrated response. This is manifested in the action of the effector organs (mostly muscles) or in the deliberate inhibition of action. (A great deal of civilized behavior consists in not doing what comes naturally.) In dreaming, the same kind of cortical activity proceeds at a lower level of per-

formance. The analysis of events is faulty; the dreamer recognizes a deceased friend but accepts his presence without surprise. The memory is full of gaps and brings the past to the surface in confusion. In consequence the integration of the cortical response is incomplete, and the dreamer is often led into the phantom commission of antisocial acts. Fortunately the impulses from the sleeping cortex die out on the way to the effector organs, and no harm is done.

Such protoplasmic poisons as alcohol may reduce cortical activity to an equally low level of performance. A markedly

intoxicated person misjudges the situation, assumes unwarranted risks in action and later does not recall what happened. Even when quite drunk, however, some persons stop short of foolish and dangerous extremes of behavior. So, also, a dreamer will accept absurdities in the imaginary series of events until they become too painful and ludicrous; he then wakes up to the comforting discovery that he was dreaming. The fantasizing of very young children, senile aged people and of persons suffering certain disorders of the central nervous system may also be likened to dreaming. After sudden awakening, even normal people may

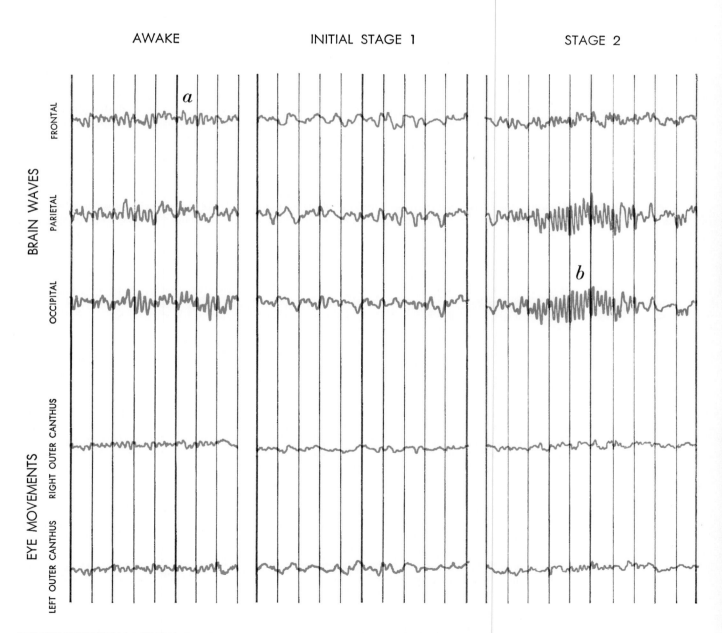

| | AWAKE | INITIAL STAGE 1 | STAGE 2 |

BRAIN WAVES — FRONTAL, PARIETAL, OCCIPITAL

EYE MOVEMENTS — RIGHT OUTER CANTHUS, LEFT OUTER CANTHUS

ELECTROENCEPHALOGRAMS show the patterns of brain waves (*top three tracings*) and eye-movement potentials (*bottom two tracings*) that are characteristic of each level of sleep. Labels at left indicate region of head to which recording electrodes are at-

tached. Vertical lines are time-scale; 10 lines represent an interval of four seconds. A subject who is awake but resting with his eyes closed shows the brain-wave pattern known as alpha rhythm (*a*). As sleep begins, pattern known as Initial Stage 1 electroen-

be bewildered and act in a deranged manner for some time. The content of dreams, explicit or hidden, may indeed have inherent interest. But for the purpose of an investigation of dreaming, it is sufficient to recognize the dream itself as a manifestation of low-grade thinking.

The objective indicator that a sleeper is dreaming, it must be admitted, is not infallible. Some subjects reported they had been dreaming during periods when they showed no rapid eye-movements. Others moved their bodies restlessly when the records on the other channels of the electroencephalograph indicated they were dreaming. Sometimes the heart and respiration rate slowed down instead of speeding up. Occasionally a subject claimed to have been dreaming when his brain waves indicated a deeper phase of sleep. William Dement, another student in our laboratory who is now at Mount Sinai Hospital in New York City, showed that of the four criteria the most reliable is the brain-wave pattern.

A person who is awake but resting with his eyes closed shows the so-called alpha rhythm—brain waves with a relatively large amplitude and a frequency of eight to 13 cycles per second [see illustration on these two pages]. As he falls asleep, the amplitude of the waves decreases, and the rhythm slows to four to six cycles per second. Dement called this pattern the Stage 1 electroencephalogram (Stage 1 EEG). Deeper sleep is characterized by the appearance of "sleep spindles"—short bursts of waves that progressively increase and decrease in amplitude and have a frequency of 14 to 16 cycles per second; Dement divided this level of sleep into two stages (Stage 2 and Stage 3 EEG). The deepest level of sleep is characterized by the appearance of large, slow waves (Stage 4 EEG). During a typical night of sleep,

STAGE 3 · STAGE 4 · EMERGENT STAGE 1 (DREAMING)

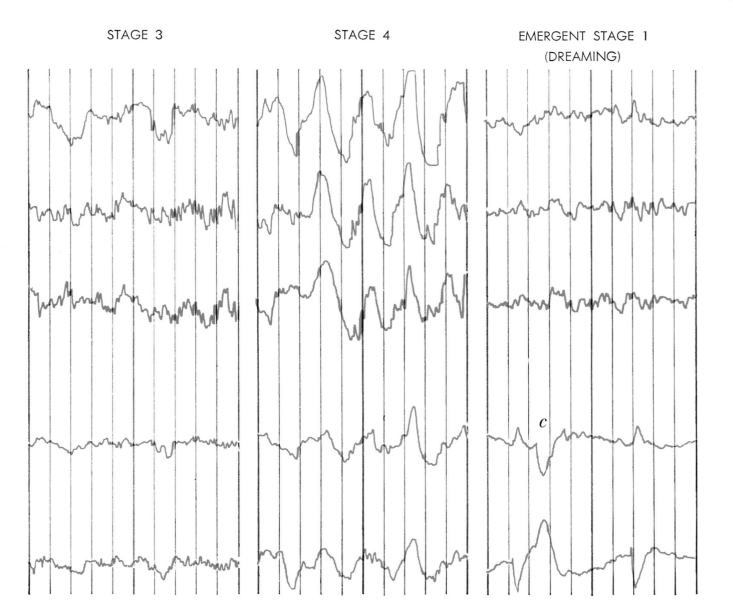

cephalogram (Initial Stage 1 EEG) appears. During deeper sleep subject shows short bursts of waves called sleep spindles (*b*). Deepest level of sleep (Stage 4 EEG) is characterized by the appearance of large, slow waves. EEG pattern changes from Stage 1 through Stage 4, then swings back to Stage 1. This "emergent" Stage 1 is accompanied by rapid eye-movements, as indicated by peaks in tracings of eye-movement potentials (*c*). Similar peaks during Stage 4 are not eye movements but brain waves that spread to eye electrodes.

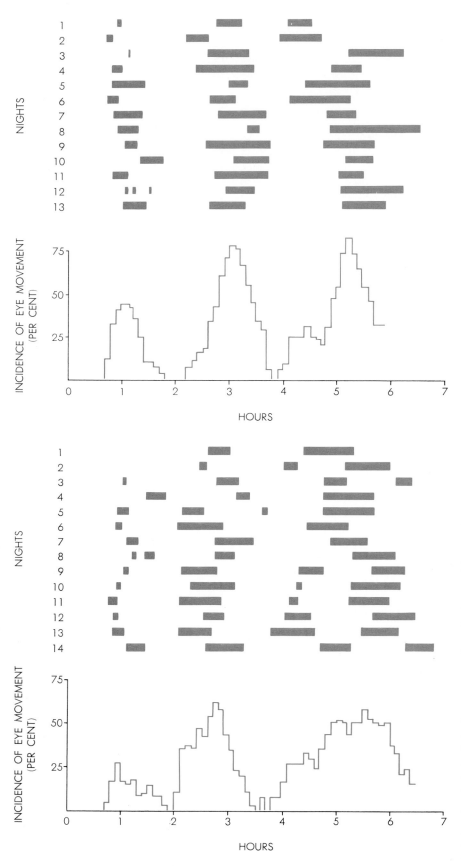

the depth of sleep fluctuates on a cycle lasting roughly 90 minutes. The EEG pattern passes from Stage 1 through Stage 4, then swings back to Stage 1. During later cycles the sleep may not be so deep; the EEG pattern may dip no farther than the intermediate stages before it returns to Stage 1 [*see illustration on page 342*].

Dement found that dreaming occurs during the Stage 1 EEG, but not when this brain-wave pattern first appears at the onset of sleep. Only when the cycle returns to the Stage 1 EEG from a deeper EEG level does it mark a dreaming episode. During this "emergent" Stage 1 it is much more difficult to awaken the sleeper than during the "initial" Stage 1 EEG.

The inconsistencies between the EEG record and the other criteria may be largely explained by the relationship of these other activities to the dream episode. For example, most of the rapid eye-movements are horizontal, and it is apparent that these movements represent a busy scanning of the scene of dream action. On the infrequent occasions when the rapid eye-movements were vertical, the sleepers reported dreams that involved the upward or downward motion of objects or persons. When the record showed few or no rapid eye-movements, and the EEG denoted dreaming, the subjects reported that they had been watching some distant point in their dreams. In other words, the amount and direction of the eye movements correspond to what the dreamer is looking at or following with his eyes. Moreover, rapid eye-movements seem to be related to the degree to which the dreamer participates in the events of the dream. An "active" dream, in which the dreamer is greatly involved, is more likely to be accompanied by rapid eye-movements than is a "passive" one.

The absence of gross body movements during dreaming seemed more difficult to explain. One would assume that a sleeper would begin to move about as his sleep lightens and that a good deal of activity would occur during dreaming. Actually the exact opposite was observed. Dreaming often began just after a series of body movements ceased. The sleeper usually remained almost motionless, showing only the telltale rapid eye-movements, and stirred again when the eye movements stopped. We were indebted to Georg Mann, a public-information officer at the University of Chicago, for the metaphor that captured the essence of this situation. He compared the dreamer to a spectator at a theater:

RAPID EYE-MOVEMENTS (*horizontal colored bars*) occur several times each night. Each horizontal row of bars represents a single night of sleep; one subject was studied for 13 nights (*top graph*), the other for 14 (*bottom graph*). Histograms at bottom of each graph show composite cycles of subject's eye movements during entire series of nights.

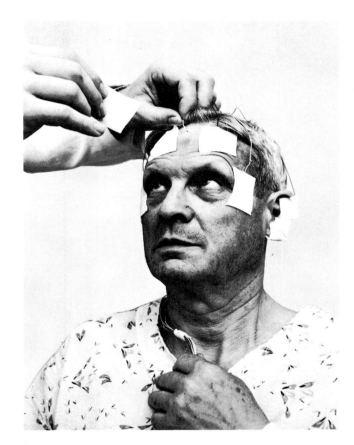

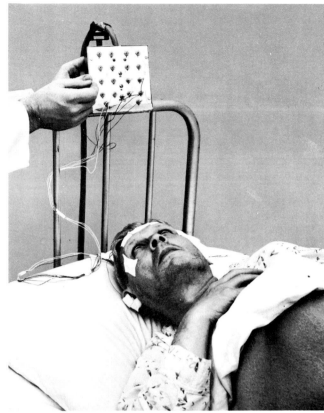

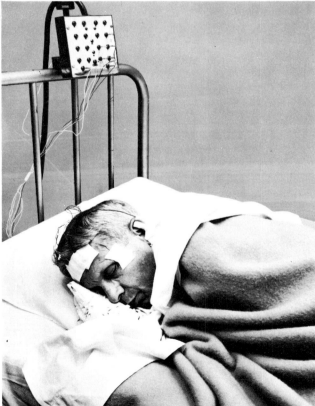

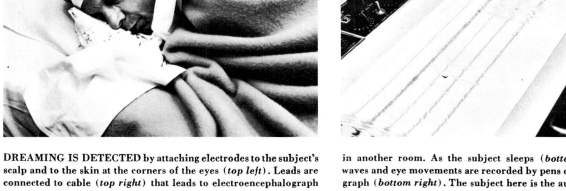

DREAMING IS DETECTED by attaching electrodes to the subject's scalp and to the skin at the corners of the eyes (*top left*). Leads are connected to cable (*top right*) that leads to electroencephalograph in another room. As the subject sleeps (*bottom left*), his brain waves and eye movements are recorded by pens of electroencephalograph (*bottom right*). The subject here is the author of this article.

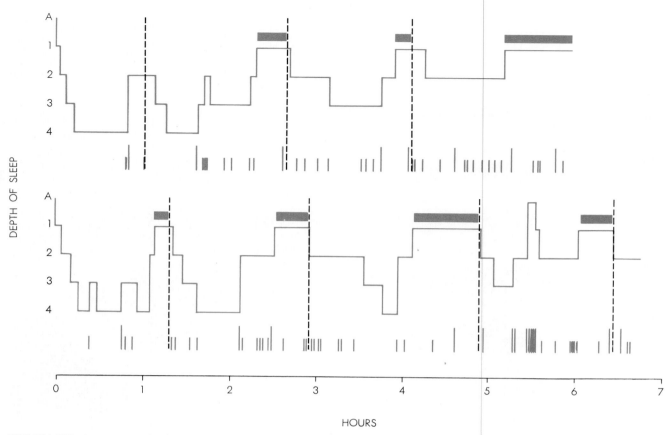

DEPTH OF SLEEP

HOURS

EEG STAGES of two subjects show a cyclic variation during typical night of sleep. Measured in terms of EEG stages, depth of sleep fluctuates on a 90-minute cycle. Cycle begins when subject who is awake (A) falls into light sleep (EEG Stage 1), then into successively deeper levels of sleep (EEG Stages 2, 3 and 4). Cycle ends with swing back to Stage 1. Periods of rapid eye-movement (*horizontal colored bars*) occur during this stage. Vertical broken lines indicate when next cycle begins. Vertical colored lines at bottom of each graph indicate when body movements occurred; longer lines represent major movements; shorter lines, minor ones.

fidgeting in his seat before the curtain goes up; then sitting quietly, often "spellbound" by the action, following the motions of the actors with his eyes; then stirring again when the curtain falls.

Some body movement may be related to dream content. Edward A. Wolpert of the University of Chicago attached electrodes to the limbs of sleeping subjects and recorded the electrical "action" potentials of the muscles. The record of one of his subjects showed a sequence of motor activity first in the right hand, then in the left, and finally in one leg (only one leg was wired for recording). When aroused immediately thereafter, the sleeper reported dreaming that he lifted a bucket with his right hand, transferred it to his left, and then started to walk. Sleepwalking may be an extreme expression of such motor outflow to extremities. Occasionally a subject would vocalize when he stirred, mumbling and even talking distinctly, but such activity usually occurred between episodes of dreaming.

Some people assert that they seldom or never dream. But all of the subjects—

and all of those observed in other laboratories that employ the objective indicator—reported dreaming upon being awakened at appropriate times. It can be stated with some assurance, therefore, that everybody dreams repeatedly every night. Donald R. Goodenough and his associates at the Downstate Medical Center of the State University of New York compared one group of subjects who said they never dreamed with another group who said they always dreamed. Certain unexplained differences showed up in the EEG records of the two groups, and the "dreamers" were more likely to report dreaming in correspondence with rapid eye-movements than the "nondreamers." Rapid eye-movements were observed with the same frequency, however, in both groups. The evidence is overwhelming that the two groups should be classified as "recallers" and "nonrecallers."

These studies have also upset the notion that a long series of events can be compressed into a moment of dreaming. Whether the subject was loquacious or laconic in recounting his dream, the

time-span of the narrative was consistent with dreaming time as indicated by our objective criteria. It appears that the course of time in dreaming is about the same as in the waking state.

It is often said that external events in the sleeper's immediate environment may suggest or affect the content of dreams. To test this idea Dement and Wolpert exposed a number of subjects to the stimuli of sound, light and drops of water during periods of dreaming. Elements suggestive of such stimuli appeared in only a minority of the dreams recounted thereafter. Drops of water, falling on the skin, proved to be the most suggestive. Falling water showed up in six dream reports out of 15 that followed arousal by this stimulus, and water had a place in 14 narratives out of 33 when the sleepers were subjected to the stimulus but not awakened by it. An electric bell used routinely to awaken the subjects found its way into 20 out of 204 dreams, most commonly as the ringing of a telephone or doorbell.

Internal stimuli from the viscera have

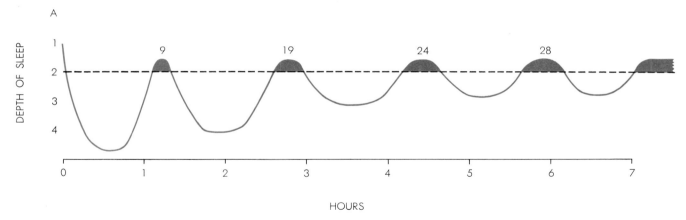

EPISODES OF DREAMING (*colored areas*) alternate with periods of deeper sleep. Dreaming and rapid eye-movements begin when sleeper emerges from deep sleep to level of EEG Stage 1. Numbers over colored areas show length of successive periods of dreaming.

been held to cause, or at least influence, dreams. Dreams about eating are said to be stimulated by contractions of an empty stomach. Dement and Wolpert had three subjects go without fluids for 24 hours on five occasions; only five of 15 dream narratives contained elements that could be related to thirst. In no case did the narrative involve an awareness of thirst or descriptions of drinking, although the subjects were very thirsty when they went to bed.

Most of the dream experience in normal sleep is never recalled. Recollection is best when the sleepers are awakened during the dreaming episode and becomes progressively poorer the longer they are permitted to sleep after a dream has ended. At the University of Chicago, Wolpert and Harry Trosman found that 25 out of 26 subjects had no memory of dreaming when they were roused for questioning more than 10 minutes after the Stage 2 EEG had superseded the Stage 1.

Once the objective indicator had shown itself to be a reliable measure of dreaming, it was employed to enact the pattern of dreaming through many nights of uninterrupted sleep. In a sampling of 71 nights of sleep, with 33 different subjects, the first emergent Stage 1 EEG—plus the accompanying rapid eye-movements and cardiac and respiratory changes—appeared a little over an hour after sleep had begun. This episode of dreaming lasted on the average less than 10 minutes. Three, four and even five dreaming periods followed at intervals of about 90 minutes. These lasted 20 to 35 minutes and added up to a total of one or two hours of dreaming for an average night's sleep. All of the subjects exhibited the cycle of alternate periods of dreaming and deeper sleep, some on

a more constant schedule than others.

The mechanism that spaces the episodes of dreaming is unknown, but it may be related to the cycle of rest and activity which Aserinsky found in infants. The mean length of that cycle is approximately an hour, and at the end of a cycle the infants stir, either to awaken fully or to go back to sleep for another cycle. In infants on a self-demand feeding schedule, the duration of the period between feedings tends to be roughly whole multiples of the length of this cycle. Apparently the cycle lengthens with age, extending to the 90-minute dreaming cycles observed in adults. A similar increase occurs in the length of the cardiac, respiratory and gastric cycles, indicating that the dream cycle is in line with the basic physiological rhythms of the body.

What happens if the dreaming cycle is disturbed? This interesting question has been taken up by Dement and his associates. Monitoring the subject's cycle, they awaken him as soon as he starts to dream and thus keep him from dreaming. Since one must be certain that dreaming has started before attempting to stop it, such interference cannot completely deprive the subject of his dreaming, but total dreaming time can be reduced by 75 to 80 per cent. Dement established that the mean normal dreaming time of his eight male subjects was 20 per cent, or about 82 minutes in about seven hours of sleep. Attempts to curtail their dreaming in the course of three to seven consecutive nights required in each case a progressively larger number of awakenings—in some cases three times as many. During the "recovery" period after this ordeal, the dreaming time of five of the subjects went up to 112 minutes, or 27 per cent of the sleeping time,

on the first night and gradually fell back to normal on succeeding nights. In six of the subjects arousal in the midst of nondreaming periods during "control" nights of sleep had no effect on dreaming during the recovery nights that followed. The curtailment of dreaming time produced anxiety, irritability, a greater appetite and a gain in body weight; the control awakenings had no such effects. As soon as the subjects of the experiment were allowed their usual dreaming time, they regained their emotional composure.

Dement tentatively interprets his findings as indicating that "a certain amount of dreaming is a necessity." Charles Fisher, a psychiatrist at Mount Sinai Hospital in New York, adds that "the dream is the normal psychosis and dreaming permits each and every one of us to be quietly and safely insane every night of our lives."

From the same evidence, however, one may equally well argue that the curtailment of dreaming engenders irritability and anxiety simply because it interferes with an acquired habit. Animals (and some people) that have acquired a "sweet tooth" may be similarly upset by deprivation of sugar. They will also consume excessive quantities of sugar after the supply is restored, just as Dement's subjects sought to make up for "missed" dreaming. In other words, the low-grade cerebral activity that is dreaming may serve no significant function whatever.

Further observation and experiment will have to decide which of these conflicting views is sound. The objective indicator is now available to help investigators find the answer to this and other questions about the nature and meaning of dreaming.

36

WHAT PEOPLE DREAM ABOUT

CALVIN S. HALL
May 1951

MAN'S DREAMS have always interested and perplexed him. From ancient times and from every civilization and culture, we have evidence of man's concern about the meaning of dreams. They have been interpreted variously as divine messages, as the experiences of disembodied souls roaming heaven and earth during sleep, as visitations from the dead, as prophecies of the future, as the sleeping person's perceptions of external stimuli or bodily disturbances (what Thomas Hobbes called "the distemper of inward parts"), as fulfillments or attempted fulfillments of wishes (Freud), as attempts by the dreamer to discern his psychic development in order to plan for the future (Jung), as expressions of one's style of life (Adler), as attempted resolutions of conflicts (Stekel).

Probably all of these theories, however ancient their origin and however nebulous their validity, have their votaries today. Dream books based on the theory that dreams foretell the future are undoubtedly as widely consulted today as they were during the Renaissance, when the dream book compiled by the second-century soothsayer Artemidorus was republished in many languages and editions, and was plagiarized and elaborated by numerous opportunists, who in that day as in this knew a good thing when they saw it.

Even in modern times speculations about dreams have been long on theory and short on observation. What do people dream about? What is the content and character of their dreams? As far as I know, no one has made an extensive and systematic study of these questions. To be sure, psychoanalysts have given much careful analysis to the dreams of deranged and disturbed persons, but even for this unrepresentative segment of mankind there are no large-scale surveys of the content of their dreams.

The writer has undertaken to make such a survey, for the purpose of obtaining some empirical facts as a foundation for theorizing. He has collected more than 10,000 dreams thus far, not from mental patients but from essentially normal people. They were asked to record their recollection of each dream on a printed form which included questions requesting certain specific information, such as the setting of the dream, the age and sex of the characters appearing in it, the dreamer's emotions and whether the dream was in color. Obviously we cannot know how faithfully the subjects' recollections mirrored their actual dreams, so strictly speaking we should call our project a study of what people *say* they dream about. This has ever been the case and probably always will be, for no one has discovered a means of transcribing a dream while it is being dreamed.

We classified the dream material so that it could be studied statistically. From the many possible methods of classification we chose, as a beginning,

ACTIONS that are performed by the dreamer, which in the author's study come under the heading of plot, were divided into categories. The five categories shown from left on these pages were movement (34 per cent), verbal

a simple breakdown into five fundamental categories: 1) the dream setting, 2) its cast of characters, 3) its plot, in terms of actions and interactions, 4) the dreamer's emotions, and 5) color.

WHAT are the most common settings in people's dreams? An analysis of 1,000 dreams reported by a group of educated adults provided 1,328 different settings. These could be classified into 10 general categories. The most frequent scene was a part of a dwelling or other building; this accounted for 24 per cent of all dreams. The other settings, in order of frequency, were: a conveyance of some kind, most commonly an automobile, 13 per cent; an entire building, 11 per cent; a place of recreation, 10 per cent; a street or road, 9 per cent; a rural or other outdoor area, 9 per cent; a store or shop, 4 per cent; a classroom, 4 per cent; an office or factory, 1 per cent; miscellaneous (including restaurants, bars, battlefields, hospitals, churches, and so on), 14 per cent. In dreams occurring in part of a dwelling the most popular room is the living room, with the bedroom, kitchen, stairway and basement following in order.

The outstanding feature of these dream settings is their commonplaceness. The typical dream occurs in prosaic surroundings—a living room, an automobile, a street, a classroom, a grocery store, a field. The dreamer may not always recognize the details of the place, but usually it is a type of scene with which he is familiar; seldom does he dream of a bizarre or exotic environment. Yet dream settings apparently are not entirely representative of waking life, as far as frequency is concerned. Considering the amount of time that people spend in places of work, such as offices, factories and classrooms, these places appear with disproportionately low frequency in dreams. On the other hand, conveyances and recreational places occupy a larger share in dreams than they do in waking life experiences. In other words, in our dreams we tend to show an aversion toward work, study and commercial transactions and an affinity for recreation, riding and residences.

FOR a study of characters appearing in dreams, we divided our subjects into two groups according to age, since it seemed likely that older people might differ from younger ones in the persons they dreamed about. The younger group was aged 18 to 28, the older 30 to 80. Let us consider the younger group first. They furnished a total of 1,819 dreams. In 15 per cent of these the only character was the dreamer. In the remaining 85 per cent, in which two or more characters appeared, the average number was two persons besides the dreamer.

Who are these characters? Of the persons other than the dreamer, 43 per cent appeared to be strangers, 37 per cent were identified as friends or acquaintances of the dreamer, 19 per cent were family members, relatives or in-laws, 1 per cent were famous or prominent public figures. The relatively infrequent appearance of prominent persons in dreams supports other evidence possessed by the writer that dreams rarely concern themselves with current events. Among the members of the family, the character that appears in dreams most often is mother (34 per cent); then come father (27 per cent), brother (14 per cent) and sister (12 per cent).

We also classified the characters in dreams by sex and age. It turns out that men dream about males twice as often as they do about females, whereas women dream almost equally about both sexes. In the dreams of both men and women 21 per cent of the characters are not identified as to sex.

The analysis showed, as is not surprising, that people dream most often about other people of their own age. In the sample of dreams from the subjects in the 18-to-28 age group, 42 per cent of the dream characters were the dreamers' peers in age, 20 per cent were older, 3 per cent were younger and 35 per cent were of unspecified age.

We found that in general there were no very pronounced differences between the characters in the dreams of the young and older groups. Older people dream more about family and relatives and less about friends and acquaintances, which is not very surprising, since the younger dreamers were for the most part unmarried. Older people also dream more about younger characters and less about older characters and peers than do younger dreamers. We may generalize our findings by saying that while children are dreaming about their parents, their parents are dreaming about them, and while husbands are dreaming about their wives, their wives are dreaming about them.

We come now to actions or behavior: What do people do in their dreams? We

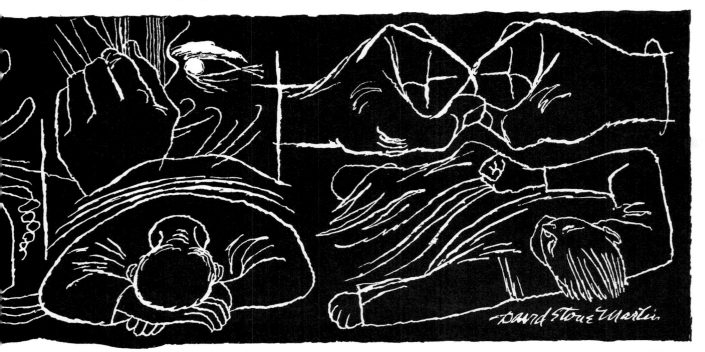

(11), sedentary (7), visual (7) and antagonistic (3). The categories of appreciable size that are not illustrated were social (6 per cent), recreational (5), manual (4), mental (4), endeavor (4) and obtaining (3).

classified 2,668 actions in 1,000 dreams. By far the largest proportion (34 per cent) fall into the category of movement—walking, running, riding or some other gross change in bodily position. We found that, contrary to popular belief, falling or floating in dreams is not very common. After movement, the next most common activities were talking (11 per cent), sitting (7 per cent), watching (7 per cent), socializing (6 per cent), playing (5 per cent), manual work (4 per cent), thinking (4 per cent), striving (4 per cent), quarreling or fighting (3 per cent) and acquiring (3 per cent). From this it can be seen that passive or quiet activities occupy a large part of dreams, while manual activities are surprisingly infrequent. Such common waking occupations as typing, sewing, ironing and fixing things are not represented in these thousand dreams at all; cooking, cleaning house, making beds and washing dishes occur only once each. But strenuous recreational activities, such as swimming, diving, playing a game and dancing, are fairly frequent. In short, dreamers go places more than they do things; they play more than they work; their activities are more passive than active.

WHAT of the relations between the dreamer and the other characters in his dream? We classified the interactions in a sample of 1,320 dreams in various categories according to degrees of friendliness or hostility. In general, hostile acts (by or against the dreamer) outnumbered friendly ones 448 to 188. In the hostile sphere the acts of aggression ranged from murder (2 per cent) and physical attack (28 per cent) to denunciation (27 per cent) and mere feelings of hostility (8 per cent). The friendly acts ranged from an unexpressed feeling of friendliness to the giving of an expensive gift.

The emotions felt by dreamers during their dreams were recorded in five classes: 1) apprehension, including fear, anxiety and perplexity; 2) anger, including frustration; 3) sadness; 4) happiness, and 5) excitement, including surprise. Apprehension predominated, accounting for 40 per cent of all dream emotions; anger, happiness and excitement were tied with 18 per cent each, and sadness was the least frequent, 6 per cent. Thus 64 per cent of all dream emotions were negative or unpleasant (apprehension, anger, sadness) and only 18 per cent (happiness) were positively pleasant.

Yet paradoxically in the judgment of the dreamers themselves the dreams as a whole were rated pleasant much more often than unpleasant. They found 41 per cent of the dreams pleasant, 25 per cent unpleasant, 11 per cent mixed and 23 per cent without feeling tone. Older dreamers reported more unpleasant dreams than younger ones, but the difference was not great.

A question that has puzzled many students of dreams is why some of them are seen wholly or partly in natural colors ("technicolor"). I am afraid I have little to contribute to the solution of this puzzle beyond a few figures and a few negative conclusions. In a survey of over 3,000 dreams 29 per cent were colored or had some color in them and the rest were completely colorless. Women report color in dreams more often (31 per cent) than do men (24 per cent). There is a slight tendency for people over 50 to have fewer colored dreams than those under that age. Many people never experience color in dreams; on the other hand, a few have all their dreams in color.

What is the psychological significance of technicolored dreams? We have compared the dreams of people who dream entirely in color with those of people who never dream in color and have found no difference in any aspect of their dreams. We have compared the colored with the colorless dreams of the same person without discovering any way in which they differed. Nor can we find any single specific symbolic meaning in a particular color. We are forced to conclude on the basis of our present evidence that color in dreams is merely an embellishment, signifying nothing in itself.

WHAT do all these facts on the content of dreams mean? I shall present my general theory of dreams and show how some of the foregoing findings fit into this theory.

Dreaming is thinking that occurs during sleep. It is a peculiar form of thinking in which the conceptions or ideas are expressed not in the form of words or drawings, as in waking life, but in the form of images, usually visual images. In other words, the abstract and invisible ideas are converted into concrete and visible images. By an odd process which we do not understand, the sleeping person can see his own thoughts embodied in the form of pictures. When he communicates his dream to another person, he is communicating his thoughts, whether he knows it or not.

During sleep we think about our problems and predicaments, our fears and hopes. The dreamer thinks about himself: what kind of person he is and how well fitted he is to deal with his conflicts and anxieties. He thinks about other people who touch his life intimately. His conceptions are purely egocentric; there appears to be no place in dreams for impersonal, detached thoughts. Accordingly the interpretation of dreams—the translation of the dreamer's images into his ideas—gives us an inner view of him, as though we were inside looking out and seeing the world as he sees it. We see how he looks to himself, how others look to him, and how he conceives of life. This is the heart of the matter, and the reason why dreams are important data for the psychologist.

How a person sees himself is expressed in dreams by the parts the dreamer plays. He may play the part of a victim or an aggressor or both; he may conceive of himself as winning in spite of adverse circumstances, or losing because of these same adversities. He may assume the role of a saint or a sinner, a dependent person or an independent one, a miser or a philanthropist. As Emerson said, "A skillful man reads his dreams for his self-knowledge."

Although the characters in his dreams are many and varied, they probably all have one thing in common—they are all emotionally involved in the dreamer's life. If this is so, one may well ask, why do we dream so often about strangers? The answer is that they are not really strangers but personifications of our conceptions of people we know. A person who conceives of his father as stern and autocratic, for example, may in his dreams turn his father into an army officer or a policeman or a schoolteacher or some other symbol of strict discipline. Very likely he will also have other conceptions of his father, and for each conception he finds an appropriate older figure who personifies the particular father conception uppermost in his mind at the time of the dream. Many of these father figures will be strangers to the dreamer, although the qualities expressed will be familiar enough to him.

Similarly the dream setting may portray the ways in which the dreamer looks at the world. If he feels that the world is closing in on him, he dreams of cramped places; if the world appears bleak, the dream setting is bleak. Tumultuous and tempestuous scenery—raging seas, milling crowds, exploding bombs, thunderstorms—betokens an outlook of insecurity and chaos. In one series of dreams studied by the writer there was a plethora of dirty, dank and dismal settings—a visible projection of the dreamer's conception of a world decaying.

DREAMS are filled with the gratification or attempted gratification of impulses, particularly sexual and aggressive impulses. They tell us how the dreamer regards these impulses. If he thinks of sex or aggression as wicked, the expression of these impulses in his dreams will be followed by some form of punishment or misfortune. If he conceives of sex as a mechanical matter, he may have a dream like that of one young man who reported a nocturnal emission dream in which a lady plumber turned on a faucet for the dreamer. We study dreams, therefore, not to discover the wish motivating the dream, as Freud did, but rather to determine how the dreamer conceives of his wishes.

Dreams also provide a vista of the dreamer's conceptions of his conflicts. The dramatic quality of a dream—its plot, tensions and resolutions—is derived from an underlying conflict in whose grip the dreamer feels himself to be. In a series of dreams from the same individual we can see his conflict running like Ariadne's thread through the labyrinth of his dreams. The conflict may hang on with surprising tenacity over a period of years. Apparently the conflicts that motivate dreams are basic ones which rarely become resolved. We suspect that these internal wars have their origins early in life and are not easily, if ever, brought to a satisfactory conclusion.

In our studies of many dream series, a few conflicts stand out as being shared by many people. One such inner tug-of-war is that between the progressive pull of maturity, growth and independence and the regressive pull of infantile security, passivity and dependence. This conflict is particularly acute during adolescence and the late teens and early twenties, but in a large proportion of people it persists through later ages and returns to prominence in old age.

Another ubiquitous inner conflict is that between conceptions of good and evil—the moral conflict. The opposing forces are those of impulse and conscience. The dreamer impulsively kills a dream character and is then punished for his crime. Or he is driven to express sexuality for which he suffers some misfortune.

A third conflict arises out of the tug between the opposing tendencies toward integration and disintegration. By integration is meant all of the life-maintaining and love-encompassing aims of man; by disintegration, the forces of death, hate, fear and anxiety which produce disunity and dissolution. One pole affirms life and love, the other affirms death and hate. Anxiety dreams and nightmares express the conception of personal disintegration.

WE study dreams in order to enlarge our understanding of man. They yield information that is not readily obtained from other sources. This information consists of man's most personal and intimate conceptions, conceptions of which not even the person himself is aware. It is important to know these conceptions, for they are the foundation of man's conduct. How we view ourselves and the world around us determines in large measure how we will behave.

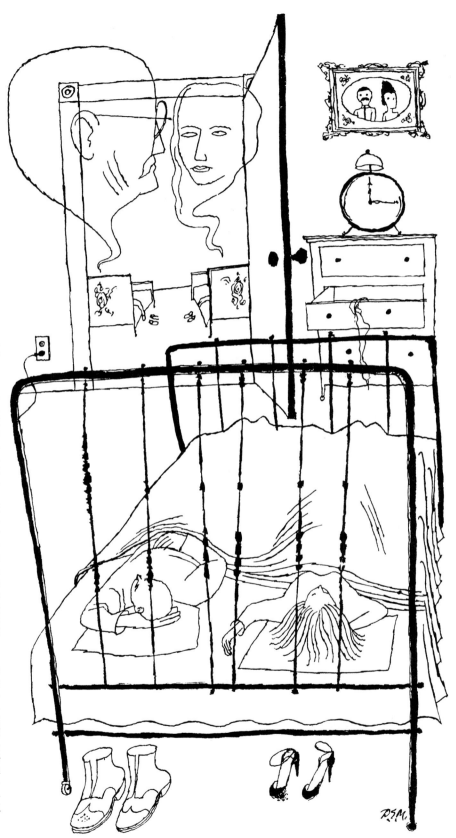

PARENTS AND CHILDREN revealed a significant dream pattern. The parents tended to dream about the children and the children tended to dream about the parents. The same appeared to be true of husbands and wives.

37

CONFLICT AND AROUSAL

DANIEL E. BERLYNE
August 1966

Ever since psychology became a scientific discipline the experimental psychologist has sought to relate human and animal behavior to properties of objects and events in the environment. He has concentrated on different kinds of properties at different times. A century ago, when experimental psychology began, the "psychophysicists" measured human reactions to the weight of an object held in the hand, the loudness or pitch of a tone, the length of a black line on a white background, and the like. These stimulus properties all depend on how energy is distributed in space and time, and energy had been a powerful unifying concept in the science of the early 19th century. Later, under the influence of the theory of evolution, experimental investigators of behavior focused on the kinds of factors that govern natural selection. They examined the psychological effects of stimuli that are beneficial or harmful, satisfying or annoying, rewarding or punishing.

In the 20th century the measurement of information and of its opposite—uncertainty—is revealing new interrelations in many different areas of science. Psychologists are now becoming interested in certain aspects of behavior that hinge on how novel, surprising, complex, puzzling or ambiguous a stimulus is. Such characteristics are closely bound up with how much information or uncertainty attaches to the stimulus. The term "collative stimulus properties" has been proposed as a convenient device for referring to all these characteristics collectively. They involve collation or comparison: they are all a matter of how far a particular environmental feature resembles or differs from others that are presented at the same time or that have been experienced in the past.

These factors can have a wide variety of motivational effects on behavior. An extremely strange phenomenon, especially if it consists of a mixture of familiar and unfamiliar elements, can induce fear and flight. D. O. Hebb of McGill University discovered several harmless but novel or surprising sights that would terrify a chimpanzee. They included a model of a chimpanzee's head without the body and a familiar attendant wearing another attendant's coat. Charlotte Bühler's experiments, conducted in Vienna in the 1920's, similarly showed how infants could be distressed by the sound of a strange voice coming from a familiar face or by a familiar voice coming from a strange mask. Animals and young children will often stand gazing in frozen fascination

CONFLICT APPARATUS consists of a panel on which four pairs of lights form a diamond pattern (*rear*). A switch (*front*), operated by the subject, can be moved in four directions that correspond to the four corners of the diamond. The subject is told that whenever any light is lit on the panel he is to move the switch to the corresponding position. In each trial two lights are lit. When both are at the same corner of the diamond, the subject can make an unequivocal movement of the switch; this is a "low conflict" trial. When the lights are lit at different corners of the diamond, the subject is told to move the switch toward whichever of the two lights he may choose. This kind of trial contains "high conflict."

at something they have never seen before, or vacillate between moving toward or away from it. By the same token the appreciation of art and humor turns quite subtly on the degree of novelty, surprise and complexity. If a joke is too predictable or too simple, it falls flat; if its content is too farfetched or too intricate, it seems labored or ponderous.

Moderate amounts of unpredictable change are, however, sought out and welcomed. The kinds of behavior that we label as "play" or "recreation" are cases in point. An environment where stimulation is kept to a minimum or is unduly monotonous will generally become intolerable before long. As numerous experiments on sensory deprivation have demonstrated, boredom can impair several perceptual and intellectual functions. It seems that the nervous system of a higher animal is made to cope with environments that present a fair amount of challenge to its capacities. It is not at its best when the demands that are made on it are either too exacting or not exacting enough.

Perhaps the most interesting psychological effects of novelty and complexity, and certainly the ones that have received the most investigation so far, are those that belong under such headings as "attention" and "curiosity." A term current among psychologists is "exploratory behavior." In one of our experiments pictures of animals were exposed two at a time and side by side on a screen and the subject's eye movements were observed. The same picture was presented trial after trial on one side, while pictures of different animals were successively exposed on the other side. In such a situation a human subject will spend an increasing proportion of the time looking at the side on which the pictures vary from trial to trial. In other words, novel stimuli attract more inspection than familiar stimuli. Similarly, human subjects will spend more time looking at more complex or more incongruous pictures, unless complexity becomes extreme [see bottom illustration on next two pages].

What do such properties as novelty, surprisingness, complexity, puzzlingness and ambiguity have in common to give them their motivational significance? Various answers have been proposed, but the most satisfactory one, which covers the diversity of collative stimulus properties most adequately, seems to be that they all give rise to conflict. Environmental events that pos-

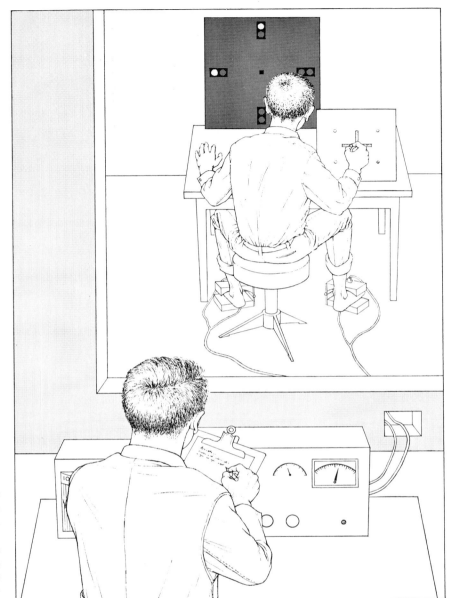

CONFLICT EXPERIMENT puts a barefoot subject at the switch of the conflict apparatus (*top and in illustration on opposite page*). An observer (*bottom*) records variations in the galvanic skin response of the subject's feet as he reacts to a series of low-conflict and high-conflict trials. The response, produced by sweating, gives an index of increased arousal.

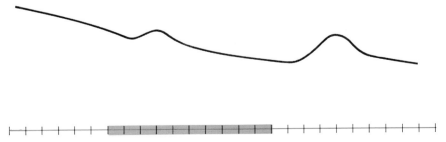

SAMPLE RESPONSE to a conflict trial is shown by the two peaks in the curve of the graph (*top*). The solid bar (*color*) on the bottom line indicates the 10-second interval in which the lights of the conflict apparatus are lit. The first of the peaks, each of which marks an increase in the conductance of the subject's skin, is a response to the start of the trial. Changes in the size of this peak enabled the author and his colleagues to compare the degree of arousal that each subject experienced in the face of high-conflict and low-conflict stimuli.

	1	2	3	4	5	6	7	8	9	10	11	12	13	14	15	16	17	18	19	20
GROUP I	A	B	A	B	A	B	A	B	A	B	A	B	A	B	A	A	A	B	A	B
GROUP II	B	A	B	A	B	A	B	A	B	A	B	A	B	A	B	A	B	A	A	A

EFFECTS OF SURPRISE were measured in an experiment that put the conflict apparatus to a different use. Two groups of subjects were told that the top and right-hand lights of the diamond would blink alternately (just as the letter *A* alternates with the letter *B* in the two sequences above). This was true until Trial 16 for Group I and Trial 19 for Group II, when the top lights went on three times in succession (*color*). The conductance of the "surprised" group then became substantially greater than the skin

sess such properties to a high degree do not bring one predominant reaction immediately to the fore. They initiate discordant and mutually interfering processes in the central nervous system. Different aspects or components of the stimulus tend to evoke several competing bodily movements. It is not clear how the stimulus event should be classified, what its hidden characteristics are like, what is likely to follow it. If the nervous system did not have means of dealing with conflict due to collative stimulus properties, a chaotic melee of disparate responses, each prevented by its competitors from reaching fruition, would soon make adaptive behavior impossible. Fortunately there are several resources on which we can call to forestall this danger. Perceptual and thought processes impose order on the external world by classifying, interrelating, interpreting and organizing the informa-

tion that comes in through sense organs. But often this incoming information is not enough. Further information may then be sought through exploratory behavior. If, however, the disturbance is too severe and too threatening, the organism may be inclined to withdraw attention, or even to flee, from the troublesome stimulus, and signs of fear and stress may appear.

Psychologists are becoming more and more impressed with the crucial role played by curiosity and other motivational effects of conflict in human emotional and intellectual development. Jean Piaget of the University of Geneva, the outstanding figure in contemporary developmental psychology, believes that "disequilibrium," or discomfort arising from inconsistency and lack of certainty in judgment, is the main force pushing the child toward mature, logical ways of organizing thoughts and perceptions.

Some of the new techniques of instruction being tried out in schools expose children to experiences designed to make them aware of the gaps and contradictions in their knowledge or understanding. There are indications that learning motivated by curiosity can give rise not only to particularly rapid and lasting acquisition of knowledge but also, above all, to knowledge in which ideas are fruitfully pieced together in coherent structures.

These developments, and others pointing in the same direction, have encouraged a reappraisal and broadening of the concept of "drive," which has dominated discussions of motivation for about 40 years. A condition of high drive has usually been regarded as a condition of discomfort, tension and restlessness. It manifests itself in three principal ways: (1) it activates or energizes the organism as a whole, making

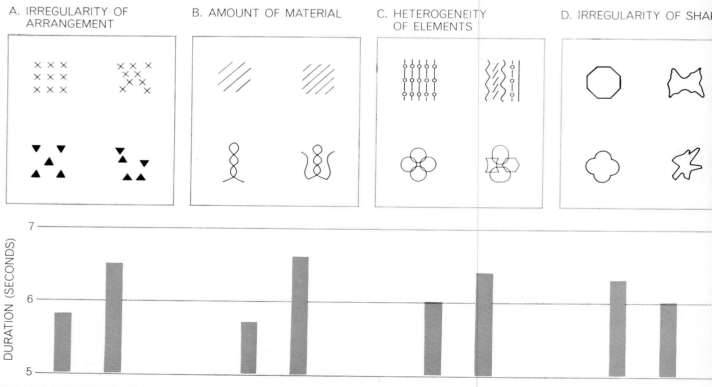

A. IRREGULARITY OF ARRANGEMENT   B. AMOUNT OF MATERIAL   C. HETEROGENEITY OF ELEMENTS   D. IRREGULARITY OF SHA

DURATION (SECONDS)

IMPACT OF IRREGULARITY was studied by the author in an experiment that recorded subjects' brain rhythms with an electro-encephalograph as they viewed first one and then another of the paired diagrams reproduced here. In each pair the left figure is the

SURPRISING STIMULI

.739

COMPARISON STIMULI

.236

conductance of the "unsurprised" group during the corresponding trial (*see matching white letter A*). The two bars (*above*) compare the mean amplitudes of both responses.

responses more vigorous and intensifying trial-and-error behavior; (2) it inclines an organism toward a particular class of behavior that is likely to relieve the drive—food-seeking in hunger, aggressive behavior in rage, and so on—and (3) it enhances learning by making the organism particularly sensitive to appropriate reinforcing events. Ivan Pavlov found it difficult, if not impossible, to condition a dog to salivate at the sound of a bell when the dog was not hungry. Neal E. Miller and Richard C. DeBold of Yale University, using a device that forces rats to swallow water, have determined that drinking will act as a reward only when rats are thirsty. In short, the level of drive and the particular kind of drive that is operating play a large part in determining what an animal will do, and how energetically, and what new responses it will acquire, and how effectively, through learning.

Over the years there have been many unsolved problems regarding the nature of drive: how it operates and what physiological mechanisms underlie it. Recently new findings and ideas with a bearing on these problems have come from progress in brain physiology. One especially significant body of work has been concerned with the processes on which "arousal" depends.

A higher animal's arousal level—how wide-awake, attentive or excited the animal is—fluctuates from moment to moment. It can range between sleep or coma at one extreme and frenzy at the other. It is manifested by changes in almost every system of the body: by the brain's electrical activity, the heart rate, the pattern of respiration, the electrical properties and temperature of the skin, the dilation and constriction of peripheral blood vessels, even the diameter of the pupil of the eye [see the article "Attitude and Pupil Size," by Eckhard H. Hess, beginning on page 306]. With increasing arousal the body mobilizes and sharpens all its functions, including the readiness of the skeletal muscles for action, the acuteness of the sense organs and the ability of the central nervous system to analyze and process incoming information. A great deal of knowledge is accumulating about the parts of the brain that control arousal level. The essential role of the reticular formation of the brainstem has been

demonstrated by many experimental findings [see the article "The Reticular Formation," by J. D. French, beginning on page 102]. It has more recently become apparent, however, that interactions of the reticular formation with other brain structures (particularly the hypothalamus and the cerebral cortex) are of crucial importance.

Considering the entire picture, one can find good grounds for concluding that arousal and drive are closely related. Many of the conditions that produce high drive—hunger, thirst, sexual receptivity, pain, cold—also produce bodily signs of high arousal and activate the reticular formation. A highly aroused animal displays the excitability and intensity of behavior that have long been associated with high drive. Furthermore, when arousal becomes inordinately high, performance is impaired, which recalls the deleterious effects that have long been ascribed to "overmotivation." The justification for equating drive and arousal is most apparent when we consider the first of the three aspects of drive discussed earlier, namely the general activating or energizing effects. As far as the other two functions of drive are concerned—direction toward particular forms of behavior and sensitization to particular kinds of reinforcement—the situation is less clear, and more research is needed. There are,

NCONGRUITY   F. NUMBER OF INDEPENDENT UNITS   G. ASYMMETRY   H. RANDOM REDISTRIBUTION

 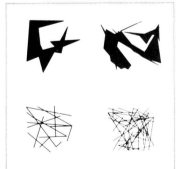 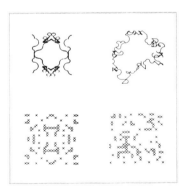 

simpler or more congruous and the right figure the more complex or incongruous one. The bars below each pair of figures show in seconds the time during which subjects switched from the standard waking "alpha" rhythm to a wave pattern indicative of alertness.

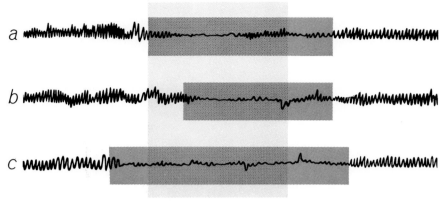

DIFFERING RESPONSES by subjects to the stimulus of visual patterns are indicated in three electroencephalograph tracings. In *a* the break from alpha rhythm to desynchronization (which indicates alertness) starts simultaneously with the start of stimulus (*light color*). In *b* there is a delay before the alertness pattern appears. In *c*, however, a conditioned response appears; the subject's pattern of alertness begins before the stimulus is received. All subjects' brains resume the alpha rhythm soon after the stimulus is halted.

however, already indications that different centers in the brainstem control different kinds of arousal, corresponding to different biological needs, and that changes in arousal are intimately connected with the reinforcement of learned responses.

What has all this to do with conflict-producing stimuli? For one thing, there appears to be a close relation between arousal and the exploratory activities that are so often evoked by novel, complex or ambiguous stimuli. Some investigators, particularly those in the U.S.S.R., have found that exploratory responses form part of a comprehensive network of psychophysiological processes called the "orientation reaction." This represents a broadened usage of a term introduced in Pavlov's laboratory. The orientation reaction includes, in addition to processes that direct sense organs toward the source of stimulation and raise their sensitivity, most of the bodily signs of heightened arousal.

We are therefore tempted to ask whether or not the motivational effects of stimuli that produce conflict work through increases in arousal. The implications reach beyond exploratory behavior. If we may conclude that conflict can increase arousal and if arousal may be equated with drive, conflict will have to be added to the list of conditions from which high drive can result. Heretofore internal physiological disturbances (such as those associated with hunger, thirst or sexual appetite) and external irritants (such as painful stimulation and excessive heat or cold) have been recognized as sources of primary drive. Neutral stimuli that have frequently accompanied these conditions can, through a conditioned-response mechanism, come to induce secondary drive (for example learned fear or anger). Our view of motivation will be broadened considerably if we are obliged to accept conflict as an additional source of drive. This will imply that animals can be impelled to action and, if necessary, to the learning of new responses not only by visceral disturbances and noxious external stimulation but also by conditions that set up discordant processes in the central nervous system.

With several collaborators, first at the National Institute of Mental Health and later at Boston University and at the University of Toronto, I have been engaged in experiments designed to verify that conflict and collative stimulus properties can heighten arousal in human subjects. The first experiment was concerned with conflict, and we attempted to separate conflict from other factors with which it is often combined in everyday life.

The subject sat before a panel bearing eight lights, two at each corner of a diamond. "Low conflict" and "high conflict" trials were interspersed. A low-conflict trial consisted of turning on two lights at one corner of the diamond, whereupon the subject was to press a key in the direction of that corner. For high-conflict trials two lights appeared at two corners, and the subject had to press the key one way or the other.

In order to make sure that the results would be due to differing degrees of conflict and not simply to the two kinds of lighting pattern, there was a prelimi-

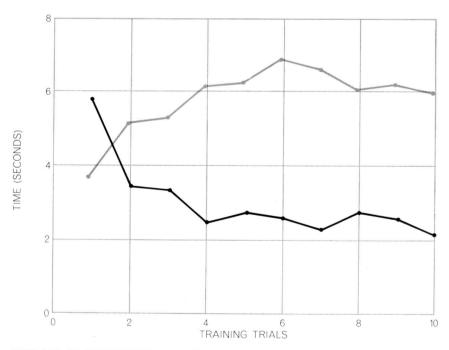

EFFECTS OF MONOTONY are evident in this record of a subject's eye movements as he viewed 10 consecutive pairs of pictures. One picture in each pair was the same throughout the 10 trials; the other one was different at each trial. This varying stimulus (*color*) soon attracted the subject's attention (measured by the attention given to each 10-second exposure) more than the recurring stimulus, which came to be ignored.

nary run in which pairs of lights at the same corner and at different corners appeared in a random order but no key-pressing response was required of the subject or even mentioned.

Changes in arousal were measured by means of the galvanic skin response (a transient rise in the conductance of the skin), recorded from electrodes attached to the soles of the feet. If the subject had been instructed to act as soon as the lights appeared, the resulting galvanic skin response would have reflected the joint influence of the stimulation and the bodily movement. To obviate this difficulty the lights were always on for 10 seconds, and the subject was instructed to move the key as soon as they went off. Two galvanic skin responses generally appeared, one just after the illumination of the stimulus lights and one just after their extinction. The first response was the one of interest, since it reflected the impact of a stimulus pattern associated with a greater or lesser degree of conflict. The mean amplitude of the galvanic skin response immediately after the onset of the stimulus was significantly higher for high-conflict trials than for low-conflict trials, confirming the prediction. The difference did not appear when we examined the galvanic skin response that followed the pressing of the key at the termination of the stimulus or the galvanic skin response that occurred during the preliminary phase when the combinations of lights were presented without requiring manual responses. We can conclude that this was due to differences in degree of conflict.

We went on to test effects of the principal collative stimulus properties one by one. There was no need to demonstrate that novelty affects arousal. Many previous experiments had shown that, say, a monotonously repeated tone gradually loses its power to cause arousal, whereas as soon as it is replaced by a tone of a different pitch the orientation reaction revives.

Accordingly our next experiment focused on surprisingness. In everyday life surprising stimuli are often novel and novel stimuli are often surprising, but we had to find a way of inducing surprise without novelty. This was done by breaking an expected sequence. Using the apparatus described above, we told the subject in advance that the two lights at the top of the diamond and the two lights at the right-hand corner would light up alternately. This alternation was maintained until a stage toward the end of the experiment, when

lights appeared at the same corner for two successive trials. The second of these trials thus presented a stimulus that was surprising (since it violated the subject's expectation) without being novel. The results of this experiment, which was carefully designed to control for spatial and temporal position, showed a galvanic skin response to be more intense with surprising stimuli than with nonsurprising stimuli that were otherwise identical. This was so whether or not the subject was instructed to respond by pressing a key.

At Toronto we later studied effects of complexity and incongruity on arousal. Some of the visual patterns that had been used in the experiments on exploratory behavior served as stimuli. Our subjects sat in a comfortable chair in a dark room watching a screen. Different subjects saw the patterns in different orders, so that effects of temporal position could be counterbalanced. This time the patterns were drawn in white on a black background, because the dazzling effects of a white rectangular background would have overwhelmed the effects we were seeking.

In these experiments changes in arousal were measured through electro-encephalographic (EEG) recordings of brain waves. In a relatively relaxed but waking state the brain produces regular "alpha" waves at a frequency of about 10 cycles per second. In response to arousing stimulation these waves are

usually replaced by a flatter, more irregular, predominantly high-frequency tracing: the "desynchronization" pattern. The duration of desynchronization can be taken as a measure of the intensity of the orientation reaction. It turned out that the more complex, irregular or incongruous stimuli evoked, on the average, significantly longer-lasting desynchronizations than the others. Hence we have some evidence that the arousal system is responsive to the complexity or incongruity of an incoming stimulus as well as to its novelty, surprisingness and in general its potentiality for inducing conflict.

These findings are only part of much evidence, coming in from many different areas of research in psychology and neurophysiology, with convergent implications. It is becoming clear that we must enlarge and refine our view of the motivational aspects of human and animal behavior. We must recognize and study an entire new spectrum of sources of motivation, depending on conflict, uncertainty and collative stimulus properties. Corresponding to them there must be a range of powerful and hitherto neglected factors that can provide reinforcement for learning. When we have investigated them further, we shall have a better understanding of how learning works. We may also be in a better position to produce it effectively in the classroom.

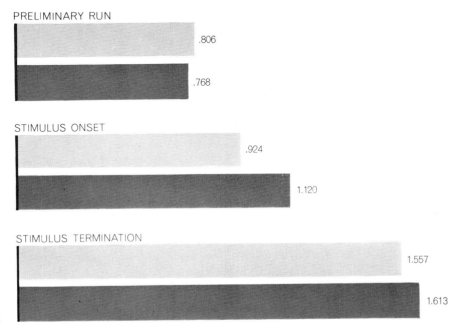

PRELIMINARY RUN

.806

.768

STIMULUS ONSET

.924

1.120

STIMULUS TERMINATION

1.557

1.613

EFFECTS OF CONFLICT are shown in the average of 25 subjects' skin responses during trials involving low conflict (*light bars*) and high conflict (*dark bars*). The latter produced significantly greater response than the former only at the onset of stimulus (*center bars*).

38

THE PATHOLOGY OF BOREDOM

WOODBURN HERON
January 1957

If you shake the surface on which a snail is resting, it withdraws into its shell. If you shake it repeatedly, the snail after a while fails to react. In the same way a sea anemone which is disturbed by a drop of water falling on the water surface above it ceases to be disturbed if drops continue to fall; a bird stops flying away from a rustling motion if the motion is steadily repeated. Most organisms stop responding to a stimulus repeated over and over again (unless the response is reinforced by reward or avoidance of punishment). Indeed, the higher organisms actively avoid a completely monotonous environment. A rat in a maze will use different routes to food, if they are available, rather than the same one all the time. It will tend to avoid areas in which it has spent considerable time and to explore the less familiar areas.

Monotony is an important and enduring human problem. Persons who have to work for long periods at repetitive tasks often complain of being bored and dissatisfied with their jobs, and frequently their performance declines. During the last war N. H. Mackworth of England made a series of researches for the Royal Air Force to find out why radar operators on antisubmarine patrol sometimes failed to detect U-boats. The operators usually worked in isolation, watching a radar screen hour after hour. Mackworth set up a comparable laboratory situation, requiring subjects to watch a pointer moving around a graduated dial and to press a button whenever the pointer made a double jump. The subjects' efficiency declined in the surprisingly short time of half an hour. As a result of this and other research the radar operators' tour of duty was shortened.

In this age of semi-automation, when not only military personnel but also many industrial workers have little to do but keep a constant watch on instruments, the problem of human behavior in monotonous situations is becoming acute. In 1951 the McGill University psychologist D. O. Hebb obtained a grant from the Defence Research Board of Canada to make a systematic study of the effects of exposure for prolonged periods to a rigidly monotonous environment. Hebb's collaborators in the project were B. K. Doane, T. H. Scott, W. H. Bexton and the writer of this article.

The aim of the project was to obtain basic information on how human beings would react in situations where

EXPERIMENTAL CUBICLE constructed at McGill University in Montreal to study the effects of perceptual isolation is at the right in this semischematic drawing from above. The subject lies on a bed 24 hours a day, with time out for meals and going to the bathroom. The room is always lighted. The visual perception of the subject is restricted by a translu-

nothing at all was happening. The purpose was not to cut individuals off from any sensory stimulation whatever, but to remove all patterned or perceptual stimulation, so far as we could arrange it.

The subjects were male college students, paid $20 a day to participate. They lay on a comfortable bed in a lighted cubicle 24 hours a day for as long as they cared to stay, with time out only for meals (which they usually ate sitting on the edge of the bed) and going to the toilet. They wore translucent plastic visors which transmitted diffuse light but prevented pattern vision. Cotton gloves and cardboard cuffs extending beyond the fingertips restricted perception by touch. Their auditory perception was limited by a U-shaped foam rubber pillow on which their heads lay and by a continuous hum of air-conditioning equipment which masked small sounds.

When we started the research we were not at all sure what aspects of behavior it would be most profitable to investigate. Accordingly we began with a preliminary run in which we merely observed the subjects' behavior and interviewed them afterward. Most of these subjects had planned to think about their work: some intended to review their studies, some to plan term papers, and one thought that he would organize a lecture he had to deliver. Nearly all of them reported that the most striking thing about the experience was that they were unable to think clearly about anything for any length of time and that their thought processes seemed to be affected in other ways. We therefore decided that the first thing to do was to test effects on mental performance.

We used three main methods of investigating this. One was a battery of oral tests involving simple arithmetic, anagrams, word association and so on. This battery was given before the experiment, at 12, 24 and 48 hours during the isolation and finally three days afterward. Another battery of tests, given two days before and immediately after the isolation period, included copying a design with blocks, speed of copying a prose paragraph, substituting symbols for numbers, picking out what was odd in each of a series of pictures (for instance, one picture showed a man in a canoe using a broom instead of a paddle) and recognizing patterns embedded in a complex background. The third test used a recording of a talk arguing for the reality of ghosts, poltergeists and other supernatural phenomena. It was played to each subject during his isolation. We examined the individual's attitude toward supernatural phenomena before he entered isolation and after he had emerged.

On almost every test the subjects' performance was impaired by their isolation in the monotonous environment (and was poorer than that of a control group of students). The isolation experience also tended to make the subjects susceptible to the argument for the existence of supernatural phenomena. Some of them reported that for several days after the experiment they were afraid that they were going to see ghosts.

As the subjects lay in isolation, cut off from stimulation, the content of their thought gradually changed. At first

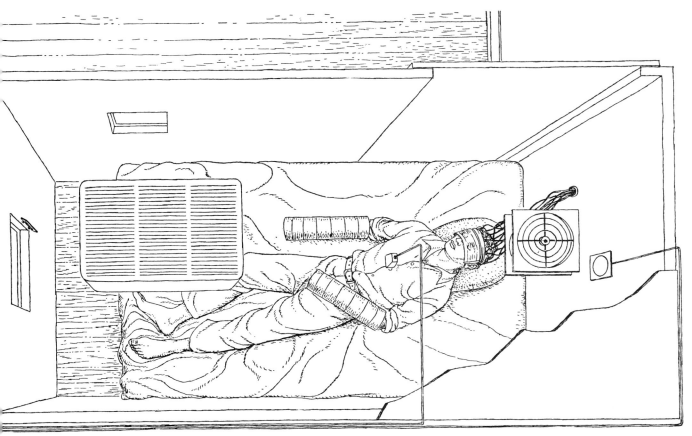

cent plastic visor; his auditory perception, by a U-shaped pillow covering his ears and by the noise of an air conditioner and a fan (*ceiling of cubicle*). In the experiment depicted here a flat pillow is used to leave room for the wires attached to the subject's scalp, which are connected to an electroencephalograph in an adjacent room. The subject's sense of touch is restricted by cotton gloves and long cardboard cuffs. The experimenter and the subject can communicate by means of a system of microphones and loud speakers.

they tended to think about their studies, about the experiment, about their personal problems. After a while they began to reminisce about past incidents, their families, their friends and so on. To pass the time some tried to remember in detail a motion picture they had seen; others thought about traveling from one familiar place to another and would try to imagine all the events of the journey; some counted numbers steadily into the thousands. (Incidentally, such experiences are commonly reported by persons who have been in solitary confinement for long periods.) Eventually some subjects reached a state in which it took too much effort to concentrate, and they became "content to let the mind drift," as one subject put it. Others said: "My mind just became full of sounds and colors, and I could not control it"; "I just ran out of things to think of"; "I couldn't think of anything to think about." Several subjects experienced "blank periods" when they did not seem to be thinking at all.

Not surprisingly, the subjects became markedly irritable as time went on and often expressed their irritation. Yet they also had spells when they were easily amused. In the interview afterward many of the subjects expressed surprise that their feelings could have oscillated so much, and that they could have behaved in such a childish way. They also said that they seemed to lose their "sense of perspective" while in the cubicle, and some subjects mentioned that at times they felt that the experimenters were against them, and were trying to make things exceptionally tough for them.

The subjects reported something else to which we at first paid no particular attention, but which was to emerge as the most striking result of the experiments. Many of them, after long isolation, began to see "images." One man repeatedly saw a vision of a rock shaded by a tree; another kept on seeing pictures of babies and could not get rid of them. Several subjects seemed to be "having dreams" while they were awake. Not until one of the experimenters himself went through the isolation experience for a long period did we realize the power and strangeness of the phenomenon. His report, and a review of the literature on other experiments in monotony, made clear that the experimental situation induced hallucinations.

The visual phenomena were similar to those experienced after taking the intoxicating drug of the mescal plant (mescal buttons), which is a ceremonial practice of some Indian tribes in the Southwest. They have also been reported in experiments in which subjects were exposed for long periods to blank visual fields or flickering light.

Our subjects' hallucinations usually began with simple forms. They might start to "see" dots of light, lines or simple geometrical patterns. Then the visions became more complex, with abstract patterns repeated like a design on wallpaper, or recognizable figures, such as rows of little yellow men with black caps on and their mouths open. Finally there were integrated scenes: *e.g.*, a procession of squirrels with sacks over their shoulders marching "purposefully" across the visual field, prehistoric animals walking about in a jungle, processions of eyeglasses marching down a street. These scenes were frequently distorted, and were described as being like animated movie cartoons. Usually the subjects were at first surprised and amused by these phenomena, looked forward eagerly to see what was going to happen next and found that the "pictures" alleviated their boredom. But after a while the pictures became disturbing, and so vivid that they interfered with sleep. Some of the subjects complained that their eyes became tired from "focusing" on the pictures. They found sometimes that they could even scan the "scene," taking in new parts as they moved their eyes, as if they were looking at real pictures.

The subjects had little control over the content of the hallucinations. Some kept seeing the same type of picture no matter how hard they tried to change it. One man could see nothing but dogs, another nothing but eyeglasses of various types, and so on. Some subjects were able to realize visions of objects suggested by the experimenter, but not always in the way they were instructed. One man, trying to "get" a pen, saw first an inkblot on a white tablecloth, then a pencil, then a green horse, finally a pen.

The hallucinations were not confined to vision. Occasionally a subject heard people in the "scene" talking, and one man repeatedly heard a music box playing. Another saw the sun rising over a church and heard a choir singing "in full stereophonic sound." Several subjects reported sensations of movement or touch. One had a feeling of being hit in the arm by pellets fired from a miniature rocket ship he saw; another, reaching out to touch a doorknob in his vision, felt an electric shock. Some subjects reported that they felt as if another body were lying beside them in the cubicle; in one case the two bodies overlapped, partly occupying the same space. Some reported feelings of "otherness" or "bodily strangeness"; trying to describe their sensations, they said, "my mind seemed to be a ball of cotton wool floating above my body," or "something seemed to be sucking my mind out through my eyes."

After emerging from isolation, our subjects frequently reported that "things looked curved," "near things looked large and far things looked small," "things seemed to move," and so on. We therefore made some systematic tests of their visual perception. The most striking finding was that when subjects emerged after several days of isolation, the whole room appeared to be in motion. In addition there was a tendency for surfaces to appear curved, and for objects to appear to be changing their size and shape. Asked to match a disk that was handed to them to one in a row of disks of various sizes 12 feet away, the subjects consistently chose a larger disk than did control subjects.

We recorded changes in the electrical activity of the brain in these subjects by means of electroencephalograms made before, during and after the isolation period. There was a tendency for some slow waves, which are normally present in sleep but not when an adult is awake, to appear after a period of isolation. In addition, the frequencies in the region of the principal brain rhythm slowed down [*see charts on opposite page*].

The overt behavior of the subjects during the experiment was, of course, carefully recorded. Most of the subjects went to sleep fairly soon after they had been placed in the cubicle. After waking they showed increasing signs of restlessness. This restlessness was not continuous but came in more and more intense spells, which were described as being very unpleasant. The subjects appeared eager for stimulation, and would talk to themselves, whistle, sing or recite poetry. When they came out for meals, they tended to be garrulous and attempted to draw the experimenters into conversation. In moving about, as when they were led to the toilet, they appeared dazed and confused, and had increasing difficulty in finding their way about the washroom.

As an outgrowth of the general experiment, we have begun some tests to find out the effects of restriction of just one sense. We tested six subjects who wore the frosted visors constantly but who otherwise were allowed to pursue

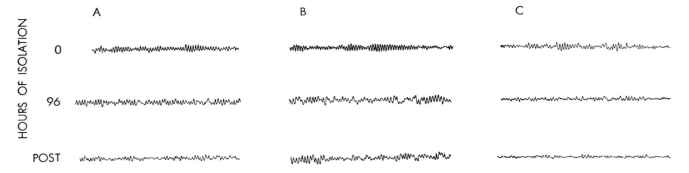

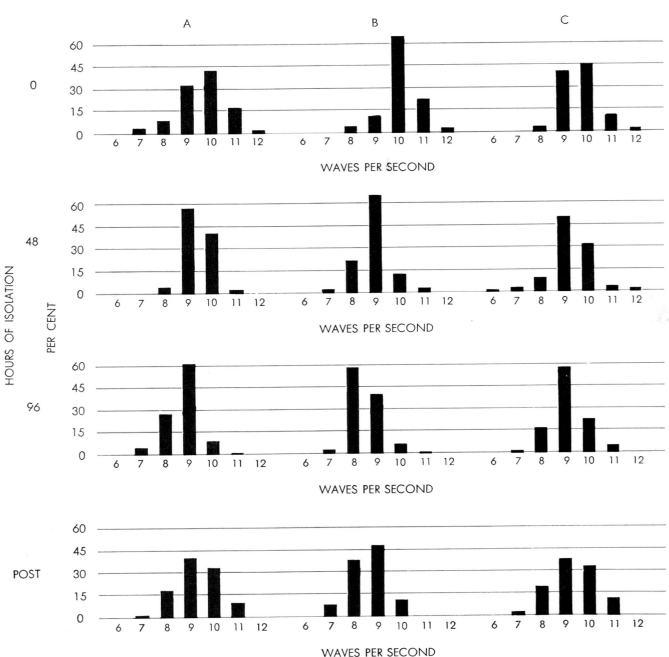

BRAIN WAVES from the occipital region of three subjects of the McGill University experiments (*above*) showed some change after 96 hours of isolation and three hours after the subject had emerged from isolation (POST). Similar changes in three other subjects are reflected in the bar charts (*bottom*). Below each bar is the number of waves counted in each one-second interval over a period of 300 seconds. The height of each bar is the percentage of all the waves during that period. Thus it indicates wave frequencies.

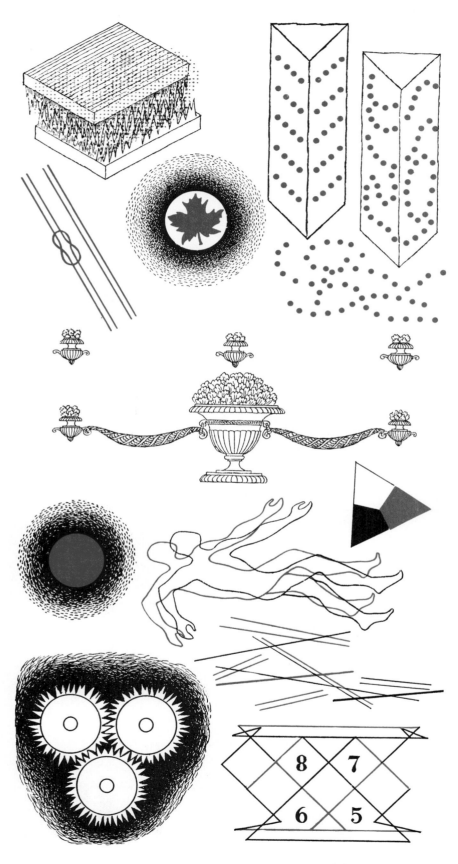

HALLUCINATIONS of isolated subjects are depicted. The drawings are based on descriptions by the subjects during the experiment and on sketches made after isolation period.

comparatively "normal" activities. Unfortunately the results of this experiment are not "pure," because the restriction of vision greatly restricted their movements and opportunity for other stimulation. These subjects developed visual hallucinations and also experienced some disorders of visual perception when the visors were removed.

Prolonged exposure to a monotonous environment, then, has definitely deleterious effects. The individual's thinking is impaired; he shows childish emotional responses; his visual perception becomes disturbed; he suffers from hallucinations; his brain-wave pattern changes. These findings are in line with recent studies of the brain, especially of the reticular formation in the midbrain [see the article "Pleasure Centers in the Brain," by James Olds, beginning on page 294]. In some way the reticular formation regulates the brain's activity. The recent studies indicate that normal functioning of the brain depends on a continuing arousal reaction generated in the reticular formation, which in turn depends on constant sensory bombardment. It appears that, aside from their specific functions, sensory stimuli have the general function of maintaining this arousal, and they rapidly lose their power to do so if they are restricted to the monotonously repeated stimulation of an unchanging environment. Under these circumstances the activity of the cortex may be impaired so that the brain behaves abnormally.

The results of our experiments seem to throw light on a number of practical problems. For instance, studies in France and at Harvard University have indicated that hallucinations are fairly common among long-distance truck drivers. After many hours on the road they may begin to see apparitions such as giant red spiders on the windshield and non-existent animals running across the road, which frequently cause accidents. Similar phenomena have been reported by aviators on long flights: Charles Lindbergh described some in his autobiography. It is not improbable that some unexplained airplane and railroad accidents have been occasioned by effects of prolonged monotonous stimulation.

A changing sensory environment seems essential for human beings. Without it, the brain ceases to function in an adequate way, and abnormalities of behavior develop. In fact, as Christopher Burney observed in his remarkable account of his stay in solitary confinement: "Variety is not the spice of life; it is the very stuff of it."

IX

LEARNING AND MEMORY

IX

LEARNING AND MEMORY

INTRODUCTION

The neural basis of learning is considered by many to be the most fundamental topic in the biology of behavior. As the articles in the earlier sections demonstrated, we have a good understanding of the basic processes of communication among neurons, and at least a beginning glimpse of the mechanisms underlying perception, motivation, and sleep. However, we still have no clear view of the biological mechanisms of learning. It is convenient to distinguish between learning and memory: learning refers to the acquisition or development of new behaviors, and memory, to the retention or recall of the learned behaviors. If anything characterizes higher animals, and distinguishes man from other primates, it is learning. Knowledge, culture, and society—not to mention crime and war—are products of human learning.

In the first article, "Learning in the Autonomic Nervous System," Leo V. DiCara provides a very clear discussion of two basic types of learning, classical and instrumental conditioning. He describes fascinating experiments that he has done with Neal E. Miller and his associates on instrumental conditioning of the autonomic nervous system. It had long been thought that such autonomic behaviors as heartbeat, intestinal contractions, and blood flow could be trained only by classical conditioning. Thus, by pairing a sound stimulus with a strong electrical shock that elicits increased heartbeat, an experimenter can condition a subject to respond with increased heart rate to the sound stimulus alone. But DiCara reports that instrumental learning of autonomic responses—in which, for example, increased heart rate leads to a positive reward—can occur both rapidly and extensively under certain conditions. In addition to its basic importance, this work may have considerable implications for clinical treatment of physiological disorders.

Ralph W. Gerard, a leading neural scientist, is the author of the next article, "What Is Memory?" As Gerard emphasizes, there appear to be two kinds of memory processes. One has been called short-term memory—it develops immediately after a learning experience, is very sensitive to interference by trauma or electroconvulsive shock, and can be facilitated by certain drugs. The other, long-term memory, seems almost impervious to interference and probably involves permanent physicochemical alterations in the brain. Bernard W. Agranoff considers the biochemical mechanisms of long-term memory in his article "Memory and Protein Synthesis." Goldfish trained to cross a barrier in order to avoid electrical shock were given substances that interfere with the manufacture of proteins in the brain. Under certain conditions, this treatment appears to have abolished the learned response. Agranoff concludes that protein synthesis is a necessary substrate for the establishment of long-term memory.

Karl H. Pribram, an eminent neuropsychologist, is the author of "The Neurophysiology of Remembering." Pribram addresses the basic issue first raised in 1929 by K. S. Lashley in his search for the "engram." Lashley's work indicated that, although it very clearly occurred in the cerebral cortex, learning could not be localized in engrams, or specific local circuits. Thus, visual memory is retained as long as some small piece of visual cortex remains intact, regardless of the location of that piece. Pribram suggests that holography may provide the missing clue. He summarizes a number of studies from his laboratory that bear on this critical issue of how the brain stores memory.

VISCERAL RESPONSES of active rats were measured with this experimental setup. The necessary tubes and wires (in this case including a plastic catheter to sense blood pressure in an abdom- inal artery) are led from the rat's skull through a protective steel spring to a mercury connector, a fluid swivel that permits free movement. The platform is wired to record the rat's activity.

39

LEARNING IN THE AUTONOMIC NERVOUS SYSTEM

LEO V. DiCARA
January 1970

The heart beats and the stomach digests food without any obvious training, effort or even attention. That may be the basis of a curious prejudice against the visceral responses—the responses of glands, of cardiac muscle and of the smooth muscle of the alimentary canal and blood vessels—and against the autonomic nervous system, which controls them. Such responses are assumed to be quite different from, and somehow inferior to, the highly coordinated voluntary responses of skeletal muscles and the cerebrospinal nervous system that controls them. A corollary of this attitude has been the assumption that visceral responses can be "conditioned" but cannot be learned in the same way as skeletal responses. It turns out that these long-standing assumptions are not valid. There is apparently only one kind of learning; supposedly involuntary responses can be genuinely learned. These findings, which have profound significance for theories of learning and the biological basis of learning, should lead to better understanding of the cause and cure of psychosomatic disorders and of the mechanisms whereby the body maintains homeostasis, or a stable internal environment.

Learning theorists distinguish between two types of learning. One type, which is thought to be involuntary and therefore inferior, is classical, or Pavlovian, conditioning. In this process a conditioned stimulus (a signal of some kind) is presented along with an innate unconditioned stimulus (such as food) that normally elicits a certain innate unconditioned response (such as salivation); after a time the conditioned stimulus elicits the same response. The other type of learning—clearly subject to voluntary control and therefore considered superior—is instrumental, or trial-and-

error, learning, also called operant conditioning. In this process a reinforcement, or reward, is given whenever the desired conditioned response is elicited by a conditioned stimulus (such as a certain signal). The possibilities of learning are limited in classical conditioning, because the stimulus and response must have a natural relationship to begin

with. In instrumental learning, on the other hand, the reinforcement strengthens any immediately preceding response; a given response can be reinforced by a variety of rewards and a given reward can reinforce a variety of responses.

Differences in the conditions under which learning occurs through classical

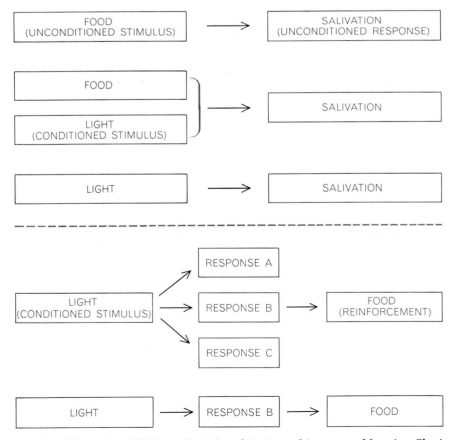

TWO TYPES OF LEARNING are classical conditioning and instrumental learning. Classical conditioning (*top*) begins with an unconditioned stimulus. The conditioned stimulus that is paired with it comes to substitute for it in producing the unconditioned response. In instrumental learning (*bottom*) a conditioned stimulus is presented along with an opportunity to respond in various ways. The correct response is reinforced, or rewarded. After several reinforcements the stimulus serves as a signal to perform the learned response.

conditioning and through instrumental learning have been cited to show that the two processes are two distinct phenomena that operate through different neurophysiological mechanisms. The traditional belief has been that the involuntary and inferior visceral responses can be modified only by the correspondingly inferior type of learning—classical conditioning—and not by the superior and voluntary instrumental learning, which has been thought to modify only voluntary, skeletal responses.

Not all learning theorists accepted this distinction. For many years Neal E. Miller of Rockefeller University has held that classical conditioning and instrumental learning are not two basically different phenomena but rather two manifestations of the same phenomenon under different conditions—that there is, in fact, only one kind of learning. To support such a position he had to show that instrumental training procedures can produce learning of any visceral responses that can be acquired through classical conditioning, and the demonstration had to be very clear and convincing in the face of the ingrained belief that such learning is simply not possible.

Research on the instrumental modification of visceral responses comes up against a basic problem: most such responses can be affected by voluntary activities such as the tensing of muscles or changes in the rate or pattern of breathing. It is therefore hard to rule out completely the possibility that the experimental subject has not directly learned to control a visceral response through the autonomic system but rather has learned to execute some subtle and undetectable skeletal response that in turn modifies the visceral behavior. (A skilled disciple of yoga, for example, can stop his heart sounds by controlling his rib cage and diaphragm muscles so that pressure within the chest is increased to the point where the venous return of blood to the heart is considerably retarded.)

To guard against the contamination of experimental results by such "cheating," careful controls and detailed statistical analysis of data are required. The primary control Miller and I apply in our animal experiments is paralysis of the subject's skeletal muscles. This is accomplished by administering a drug of the curare family (such as d-tubocurarine) that blocks acetylcholine, the chemical transmitter by which cerebrospinal nerve impulses are delivered to skeletal muscles, but does not interfere with consciousness or with the transmitters that mediate autonomic responses. A curarized animal cannot breathe and must therefore be maintained on a mechanical respirator. Moreover, it cannot eat or drink, and so the possibilities of rewarding it are limited. We rely on two methods of reinforcement. One is electrical stimulation of a "pleasure center" in the brain, the medial forebrain bundle in the hypothalamus, and the other is the avoidance of or escape from a mildly unpleasant electric shock.

Utilizing these techniques, we have shown that animals can learn visceral responses in the same way that they learn skeletal responses. Specifically, we have produced, through instrumental training, increases and decreases in heart rate, blood pressure, intestinal contractions, control of blood-vessel diameter and rate of formation of urine. Other investigators have demonstrated significant instrumental learning of heart-rate and blood-pressure control by human beings and have begun to apply the powerful techniques developed in animal experiments to the actual treatment of human cardiovascular disorders.

After Miller and his colleagues Jay Trowill and Alfredo Carmona had achieved promising preliminary results (including the instrumental learning of salivation in dogs, the classical response of classical conditioning), he and I undertook in 1965 to show that there are no real differences between the two kinds of learning: that the laws of learning observed in the instrumental training of skeletal responses all apply also to the instrumental training of visceral responses. We worked with curarized rats, which we trained to increase or to decrease their heart rate in order to obtain pleasurable brain stimulation. First we rewarded small changes in the desired direction that occurred during "time in" periods, that is, during the presentation of light and tone signals that indicated when the reward was available. Then we set the criterion (the level required to obtain a reward) at progressively higher levels and thus "shaped" the rats to learn increases or decreases in heart rate of about 20 percent in the course of a 90-minute training period [see illustration on page 366].

These changes were largely overall increases or decreases in the "base line" heart rate. We were anxious to demonstrate something more: that heart rate, like skeletal responses, could be brought under the control of a discriminative stimulus, which is to say that the rats could learn to respond specifically to the light and tone stimuli that indicated when a reward was available and not to respond during "time out" periods when they would not be rewarded. To this end we trained rats for another 45 minutes at the highest criterion level. When we began discrimination training, it took the

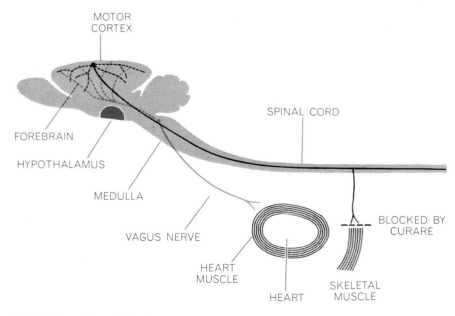

CURARE paralyzes skeletal muscles. It ensures, for example, that a change in heart rate has been controlled by autonomic impulses from the vagus nerve and not by cerebrospinal impulses to skeletal muscles. The two nervous systems are not completely separate: visceral responses have representation at higher brain centers in the cortex (*broken lines*).

rats some time after the beginning of each stimulus period to meet the criterion and get the reward; by the end of the training they were changing their heart rate in the rewarded direction almost immediately after the time-in period began [*see illustration on page 367*].

In skeletal instrumental training discrimination is also learned between a positive stimulus, response to which is rewarded, and a negative stimulus, response to which is not rewarded. Our animals learned to respond with the proper visceral behavior to one stimulus (such as a light) and not to respond to another (such as a tone). Moreover, once an animal has learned to discriminate between positive and negative cues for a given skeletal response, it is easier for it to respond similarly with a different response for the same reward. We found that this phenomenon of transfer also appeared in visceral training: rats that showed the best discrimination between a positive and a negative stimulus for a skeletal response (pressing a bar) also showed the best discrimination when the same stimuli were used for increased or decreased heart rate.

Two other properties of instrumental training are retention and extinction. To test for retention we gave rats a single training session and then returned them to their home cages for three months. When they were again curarized and tested, without being reinforced, rats in both the increase group and the decrease group showed good retention by exhibiting reliable changes in the direction for which they had been rewarded three months earlier. Although learned skeletal responses are remembered well, they can be progressively weakened, or experimentally extinguished, by prolonged trials without reward. We have observed this phenomenon of extinction in visceral learning also. To sum up, all the phenomena of instrumental training that we have tested to date have turned out to be characteristic of visceral as well as skeletal responses.

The experiments I have described relied on electrical stimulation of the brain as a reinforcement. In order to be sure that there was nothing unique about brain stimulation as a reward for visceral learning, Miller and I did an experiment with electric-shock avoidance, the other of the two commonly used rewards that can conveniently be administered to paralyzed rats. A shock signal was presented to the curarized rats. After it had been on for five seconds it was accompanied by brief pulses of mild

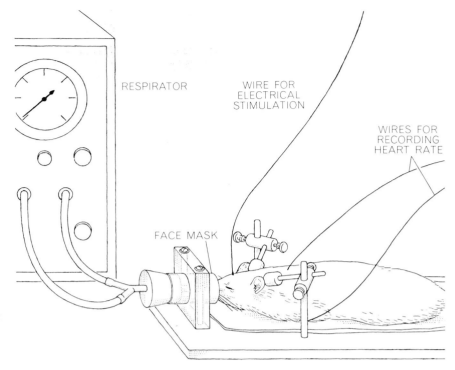

CURARIZED RATS cannot breathe and must be fitted with a face mask connected to a respirator. Such usual instrumental-learning rewards as food and water cannot be used.

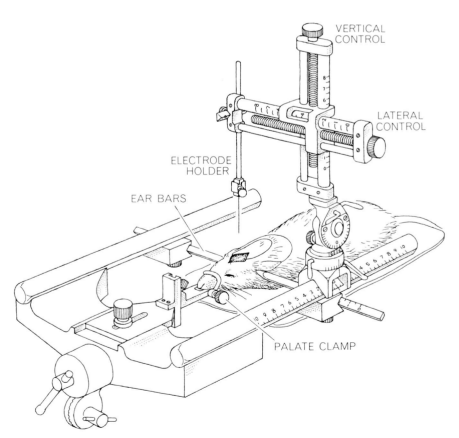

REWARD for visceral learning is either electrical stimulation of the brain or avoidance of electric shock. For brain stimulation an electrode implanted in the brain of an anesthetized rat is guided to a "pleasure center" in the hypothalamus with the aid of a stereotactic device.

shock delivered to the rat's tail. During the first five seconds the animal could turn off the shock signal and avoid the shock by making the correct heart-rate response; failing that, it could escape the shock by making the correct response and thus turning off both the signal and the shock.

In the course of a training session we mixed shock trials with "safe" trials and "blank" trials at random. During a safe trial we presented a different signal and did not administer a shock; during a blank trial there was no signal or shock. For half of the rats the shock signal was a tone and the safe signal a flashing light; for the other half the stimuli were reversed. The rats that were rewarded for increasing their heart rate learned to increase it and those that were rewarded for decreasing the rate learned to decrease it. In part the learning represented a general change in base line, as indicated by the trend of the heart rate during blank trials. Beyond this, however, the rats clearly learned to discriminate. As their training progressed, the shock signal began to elicit a greater change in the rewarded direction than the blank trials did. Conversely, the safe signal elicited a trend in the opposite direction—toward the base line represented by the data for the blank trials [see illustration on page 368].

At this point we had shown that instrumental learning of visceral responses follows the laws of skeletal instrumental training and that it is not limited to a particular kind of reward. We also showed that the response itself is not limited: we trained rats to raise and lower their systolic blood pressure in much the same way. These results were all obtained, however, with animals that were paralyzed. Would normal, active animals also learn a visceral response? If so, could that response be shown to be independent of skeletal activity? We designed a special experimental cage and the necessary equipment to make possible the recording of various responses of active rats [see illustration on page 362], and we established that heart-rate and blood-pressure changes could be learned by noncurarized animals. The heart-rate learning persisted in subsequent tests during which the same animals were paralyzed by curare, indicating that it had not been due to the indirect effects of overt skeletal responses. This conclusion was strengthened when, on being retrained without curare, the two groups of animals displayed increasing differences in heart rate, whereas any differences in respiration and general level of activity continued to decrease.

We noted with interest that initial learning in the noncurarized state was slower and less effective than it had been in the previous experiments under curare. Moreover, a single training session under curare facilitated later learning in the noncurarized state. It seems likely that paralysis eliminated "noise" (the confusing effects of changes in heart action and blood-vessel tone caused by skeletal activity) and perhaps also made it possible for the animal to concentrate on and sense the small changes accomplished directly by the autonomic system.

In all these studies the fact that the same reward could produce changes in opposite directions ruled out the possibility that the visceral learning was caused by some innate, unconditioned effect of the reward. Furthermore, the fact that the curarized rats were completely paralyzed, which was confirmed by electromyographic traces that would have recorded any activity of the skeletal muscles, ruled out any obvious effect of the voluntary responses. It was still possible, however, that we were somehow inducing a general pattern of arousal or were training the animals to initiate impulses from the higher brain centers that would have produced skeletal movements were it not for the curare, and that it was the innate effect of these central commands to struggle and relax that were in turn changing the heart rate. Such possibilities made it desirable to discover whether or not changes in heart rate could be learned independently of changes in other autonomic responses that would occur as natural concomitants of arousal.

To this end Miller and Ali Banuazizi compared the instrumental learning of heart rate with that of intestinal contraction in curarized rats. They chose these two responses because the vagus nerve innervates both the heart and the gut, and the effect of vagal activation on both organs is well established. In order to record intestinal motility they inserted a water-filled balloon in the large intestine. Movement of the intestine wall caused fluctuations in the water pressure that were changed into electric voltages by a pressure transducer attached to the balloon.

The results were clear-cut. The rats rewarded (by brain stimulation) for increases in intestinal contraction learned an increase and those rewarded for decreases learned a decrease, but neither

HEART-RATE CHANGES are shown for rats rewarded for increasing the rate (*color*) and for decreasing it (*black*). Animals were curarized and rewarded with brain stimulation.

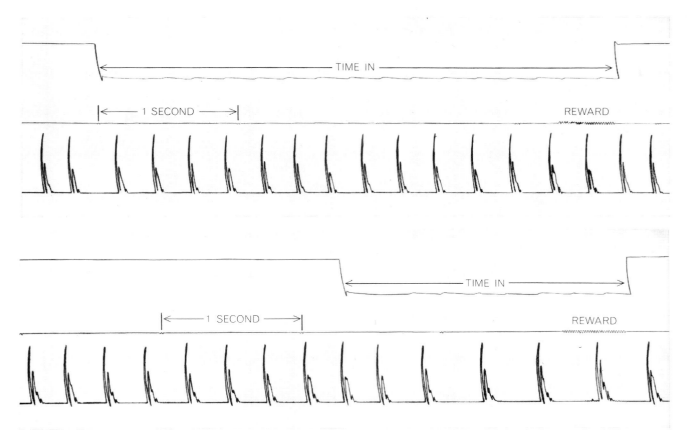

ELECTROCARDIOGRAMS made at the beginning and at the end of an extra period of training demonstrate discrimination. At first the rat takes some time after the onset of stimulus ("time in") to respond (by slowing its heartbeat) and earn a reward (*top*). After 45 minutes of discrimination training the rat responds more directly: it slows its heartbeat soon after time-in period begins (*bottom*).

group showed an appreciable change in heart rate. The group that was rewarded for increases in heart rate learned an increase and the group rewarded for decreases learned a decrease, but neither heart-rate group showed an increase in intestinal contraction [*see illustrations on page 370*]. Moreover, the heart-rate and intestinal learning were negatively correlated: the better the response being rewarded was learned, the less change there was in the unrewarded response. These results showed that the instrumental learning of two visceral responses can occur independently of each other and that what is learned is specifically the rewarded response. They ruled out the possibility that the learning was mediated by a general reaction such as arousal.

There was still a remote possibility to be eliminated: The central impulses I mentioned might be initiated selectively toward muscles that affect the intestines when intestinal changes are rewarded and toward muscles that affect heart rate when heart-rate changes are rewarded. Miller and I therefore trained curarized rats to increase or decrease their heart rate and then tested them in the noncurarized state for transfer of learning. We reasoned that if heart-rate changes were not directly learned under curare but rather were mediated by the learning of central impulses to skeletal muscles, movement of such muscles would betray the fact if the learning was transferred to the noncurarized state. We found that learned increases and decreases of about 10 percent did transfer independently of muscle movement: the differences between the two groups in heart rate were too large to be accounted for by the differences between them in respiration or general level of activity.

The strongest argument against attempts to explain visceral learning as a response to skeletal movement or central motor impulses is this kind of specificity. As more and more different visceral responses are recorded and the learning of them is shown to be specific, it becomes harder to think of enough different voluntary responses to account for them all. We have shown, for example, that curarized rats can learn to make changes in the dilation and constriction of blood vessels in the skin and to make these vasomotor changes independently of changes in heart rate and blood pressure. Indeed, the rats can be trained to make these changes specific to a single structure: they can dilate the blood vessels in one ear more than those in the other ear! This could not be the result of heart-rate or blood-pressure changes, which would affect both ears equally. We also obtained instrumental learning in the rate of urine formation by the kidneys, independent of blood pressure or heart rate. The increases and decreases in the amount of urine produced were achieved by specific changes in the arteries of the kidneys that resulted in an increase or decrease in the blood flow through the kidneys.

In addition to buttressing the case for instrumental learning of visceral responses, these striking results suggest that vasomotor responses, which are mediated by the sympathetic division of the autonomic nervous system, are capable of much greater specificity than was believed possible. This specificity is compatible with an increasing body of evidence that various visceral responses have specific representation at the cerebral cortex, that is, that they have neural connections of some kind to higher brain centers.

Some recent experiments indicate that not only visceral behavior but also the electrical activity of these higher brain centers themselves can be modified by direct reinforcement of changes in brain activity. Miller and Carmona trained noncurarized cats and curarized rats to change the character of their electroencephalogram, raising or lowering the voltage of the brain waves. A. H. Black of McMaster University in Canada trained dogs to alter the activity of one kind of brain wave, the theta wave. More recently Stephen S. Fox of the University of Iowa used instrumental techniques to modify, both in animals and in human subjects, the amplitude of an electrical event in the cortex that is ordinarily evoked as a visual response.

We are now trying to apply similar techniques to modify the electrical activity of the vagus nerve at its nucleus in the lowermost portion of the brain. Preliminary results suggest that this is possible. The next step will be to investigate the visceral consequences of such modi-

fication. This kind of work may open up possibilities for modifying the activity of specific parts of the brain and the functions they control and thereby learning more about the functions of different parts of the brain.

Controlled manipulation of visceral responses by instrumental training also makes it possible to investigate the mechanisms that underlie visceral learning. We have made a beginning in this direction by considering the biochemical consequences of heart-rate training and specifically the role of the catecholamines, substances such as epinephrine and norepinephrine that are synthesized in the brain and in sympathetic-nerve tissues. Norepinephrine serves as a nerve-impulse transmitter in the central nervous system. Both substances play roles in the coordination of neural and glandular activity, influencing the blood vessels, the heart and several other organs. Alterations in heart rate produced by increased sympathetic-nerve activity in the heart, for example, are accompanied by changes in the synthesis, uptake and utilization of catecholamines in the heart, suggesting that it may be possible to influence cardiac catecholamine me-

tabolism through instrumental learning of heart-rate responses. This would be important in view of the possible role of norepinephrine in essential hypertension (high blood pressure) and congestive heart failure; it might also help to establish the role of learning and experience in the development of certain psychosomatic disorders.

Eric Stone and I found that the level of catecholamines in the heart varies with heart-rate training. After three hours of training under curare, rats trained to increase their heart rate have a significantly higher concentration of cardiac catecholamines than rats trained to decrease their heart rate. Experiments are now under way to determine how long such biochemical differences between the two groups persist after training and whether the heart-rate conditioning has long-range effects on the heart and on the excitability of the sympathetic nerves. When we examined the brains of rats in the two groups we found a similar biochemical difference: the animals trained to increase their heart rate had a significantly higher level of norepinephrine in the brain stem than rats trained to decrease heart rate. Brain norepinephrine helps to determine the excitability of the central nervous system and is involved in emotional behavior. We have therefore started experiments to see whether or not changes in sympathetic excitability obtained by cardiovascular instrumental training are related to changes in the metabolism of norepinephrine and, if so, in which areas of the brain these metabolic changes are most apparent.

Is the capacity for instrumental learning of autonomic responses just a useless by-product of the capacity for cerebrospinal, skeletal-muscle learning? Or does it have a significant adaptive function in helping to maintain homeostasis, a stable internal environment? Skeletal responses operate on the external environment; there is obvious survival value in the ability to learn a response that brings a reward such as food, water or escape from pain. The responses mediated by the autonomic system, on the other hand, do not have such direct effects on the external environment. That was one of the reasons for the persistent belief that they are not subject to instrumental learning. Yet the experiments I have described demonstrate that visceral responses are indeed subject to instrumental training. This forces us to think of the internal behavior of the visceral organs in the same way we think of the external,

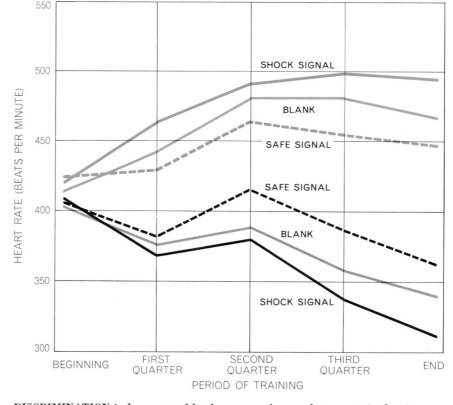

DISCRIMINATION is demonstrated by these curves for rats that were trained to increase (*color*) and decrease (*black*) heart rate and were rewarded by avoidance of shock. The results for blank trials (no signal or shock) show "base line" learning. The results for shock-signal and safe-signal trials show discriminating responses to more specific stimuli.

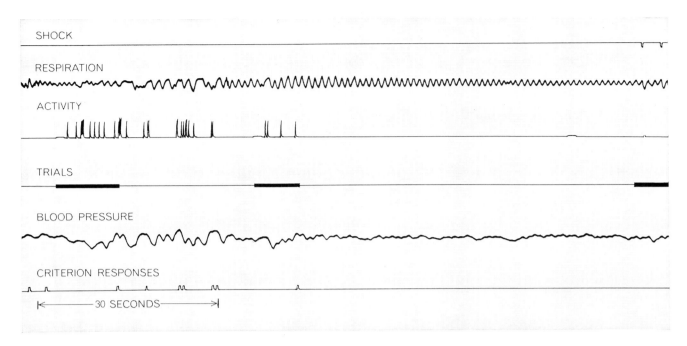

SHOCK

RESPIRATION

ACTIVITY

TRIALS

BLOOD PRESSURE

CRITERION RESPONSES

|←————— 30 SECONDS —————→|

POLYGRAPH RECORD, a small portion of which is reproduced, records a free-moving rat's respiration, activity and systolic blood pressure. It also shows when trials took place, whether the blood-pressure increase met the criterion and whether, not having met criterion, the animal received an electric shock. This record was made by an animal being tested as in the illustration on page 362.

observable behavior of the skeletal muscles, and therefore to consider its adaptive value to homeostasis.

In a recent experiment George Wolf, Miller and I found that the correction of a deviation from homeostasis by an internal, glandular response (rather than by an external response such as eating or drinking) can serve as a reward to reinforce learning. We injected albino rats with an antidiuretic hormone (ADH) if they chose one arm of a T-shaped maze and with a control solution (a minute amount of isotonic saline solution) if they chose the other arm. Before running the maze each rat had been given an excess of water through a tube placed in the stomach, so that the antidiuretic hormone was maladaptive: it interfered with the kidney response that was necessary to get rid of the excess water and restore homeostasis, whereas the control solution did not interfere. The rats learned to select the side of the maze that ensured an injection of saline solution, so that their own glandular response to the excess water could restore homeostasis. Then we did the same experiment with rats that suffered from diabetes insipidus, a disorder in which too much urine is passed and it is insufficiently concentrated. These rats had been tube-fed an excess of a highly concentrated salt solution. Now the homeostatic effects of the two injections were reversed: the ADH was adaptive, tend-

ing to concentrate the urine and thereby get rid of the excess salt, whereas the control solution had no such effect. This time the rats selected the ADH side of the maze. As a control we tested normal rats that were given neither water nor concentrated saline solution, and we found they did not learn to choose either side of the maze in order to obtain or avoid the antidiuretic hormone.

In many experiments a deficit in water or in salt has been shown to serve as a drive to motivate learning; the external response of drinking water or saline solution—thus correcting the deficit—functions as a reward to reinforce learning. What our experiment showed was that the return to a normal balance can be effected by action that achieves an internal, glandular response rather than by the external response of drinking.

Consider this result along with those demonstrating that glandular and visceral responses can be instrumentally learned. Taken together, they suggest that an animal can learn glandular and visceral responses that promptly restore a deviation from homeostasis to the proper level. Whether such theoretically possible learning actually takes place depends on whether innate homeostatic mechanisms control the internal environment so closely and effectively that deviations large enough to serve as a drive are not allowed. It may be that innate controls are ordinarily accurate

enough to do just that, but that if abnormal circumstances such as disease interfere with innate control, visceral learning reinforced by a return to homeostasis may be available as an emergency replacement.

Are human beings capable of instrumental learning of visceral responses? One would think so. People are smarter than rats, and so anything rats can do people should be able to do better. Whether they can, however, is still not completely clear. The reason is largely that it is difficult to subject human beings to the rigorous controls that can be applied to animals (including deep paralysis by means of curare) and thus to be sure that changes in visceral responses represent true instrumental learning of such responses.

One recent experiment conducted by David Shapiro and his colleagues at the Harvard Medical School indicated that human subjects can be trained through feedback and reinforcement to modify their blood pressure. Each success (a rise in pressure for some volunteers and a decrease for others) was indicated by a flashing light. The reward, after 20 flashes, was a glimpse of a nude pinup picture. (The volunteers were of course male.) Most subjects said later they were not aware of having any control over the flashing light and did not in fact know what physiological function was being

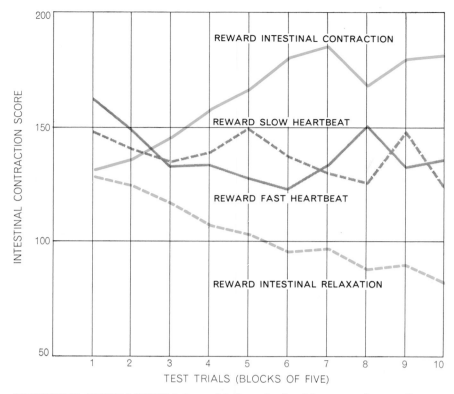

INTESTINAL CONTRACTION is learned independently of heart-rate changes. Contractions are increased by rats rewarded for increases (*colored line*) and decreased by rats rewarded for decreases (*broken colored line*). The intestinal-contraction score does not change appreciably, however, in rats rewarded for increasing or decreasing heart rate (*gray*).

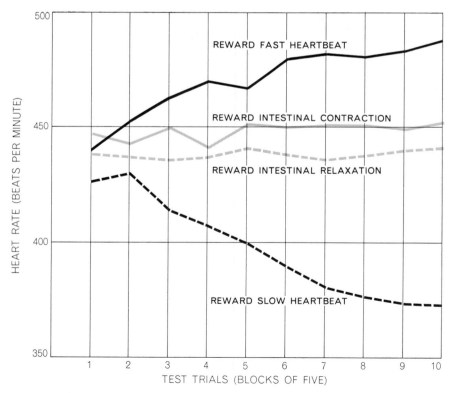

SPECIFICITY of learning is shown by this graph and the one at the top of the page. Here the results for heart rate rather than intestinal contraction are shown for the same animals. Rats rewarded for changing their heart rate change it in the appropriate direction (*black lines*). Rats rewarded for intestinal changes do not change heart rate (*light colored lines*).

measured, and so they presumably had not exerted any voluntary effort (at least not consciously and deliberately) to modify the response.

Whatever is actually being learned by such subjects, the extent of learning is clearly less than can be achieved in animals. In one of our experiments the average difference in blood pressure between the two groups of curarized rats was 58 millimeters of mercury. Shapiro's two human groups, in contrast, yielded a comparable difference of about four millimeters. Clearly curarized rats do better than noncurarized people, but that is not really surprising. The difference between the noncurarized rats and the noncurarized human subjects is much smaller [*see bottom illustration on opposite page*].

The curare effect here is in line with what is seen in experiments with a single species. What does it mean? I mentioned above that initial training under curare facilitated further training in the noncurarized state. Perhaps the curare keeps the animal from being confused (as it may be in the noncurarized state) when a small change in the correct direction that is produced by direct control of the visceral response is obscured by a larger change in the opposite direction that is accomplished through skeletal activity and is therefore not rewarded. It is also possible that the curare helps to eliminate variability in the stimulus and to shift the animal's attention from distracting skeletal activity to the relevant visceral activity. It may be possible to facilitate visceral learning in humans by training people (perhaps through hypnosis) to breathe regularly, to relax and to concentrate in an attempt to mimic the conditions produced by curarization.

The evidence for instrumental learning of visceral responses suggests that psychosomatic symptoms may be learned. John I. Lacey of the Fels Research Institute has shown that there is a tendency for each individual to respond to stress with his own rather consistent sequence of such visceral responses as headache, queasy stomach, palpitation or faintness. Instrumental learning might produce such a hierarchy. It is theoretically possible that such learning could be carried far enough to create an actual psychosomatic symptom. Presumably genetic and constitutional differences among individuals would affect the susceptibility of the various organ systems. So would the extent to which reinforcement is available. (Does a child's mother keep him home from school when he complains of headache? When he looks pale?) So also would the extent to which visceral learning is effective in the various organ systems.

We are now trying to see just how far we can push the learning of visceral responses—whether it can be carried far enough in noncurarized animals to produce physical damage. We also want to see if there is a critical period in the animal's infancy during which visceral learning has particularly intense and long-lasting effects. Some earlier experiments bear on such questions. For example, during training under curare seven rats in a group of 43 being rewarded for slowing their heart rate died, whereas none of 41 being rewarded for an increase in heart rate died. This statistically reliable difference might mean one of two things. Either training to speed the heart rate helps a rat to resist the stress of curare or the reward for slowing the heart rate is strong enough to overcome innate regulatory mechanisms and induce cardiac arrest.

If visceral responses can be modified by instrumental learning, it may be possible in effect to "train" people with certain disorders to get well. Such therapeutic learning should be worth trying on any symptom that is under neural control, that can be continuously monitored and for which a certain direction of change is clearly advisable from a medical point of view. For several years Bernard Engel and his colleagues at the Gerontology Research Center in Baltimore have been treating cardiac arrhythmias (disorders of heartbeat rhythm) through instrumental training. Heart function has been significantly improved in several of their patients. Miller and his colleagues at the Cornell University Medical College treated a patient with long-standing tachycardia (rapid heartbeat). For two weeks the patient made almost no progress, but in the third week his learning improved; since then he has been able to practice on his own and maintain his slower heart rate for several months. Clark T. Randt and his colleagues at the New York University School of Medicine have had some success in training epileptic patients to suppress paroxysmal spikes, an abnormal brain wave.

It is far too early to promise any cures. There is no doubt, however, that the exciting possibility of applying these powerful new techniques to therapeutic education should be investigated vigorously at the clinical as well as the experimental level.

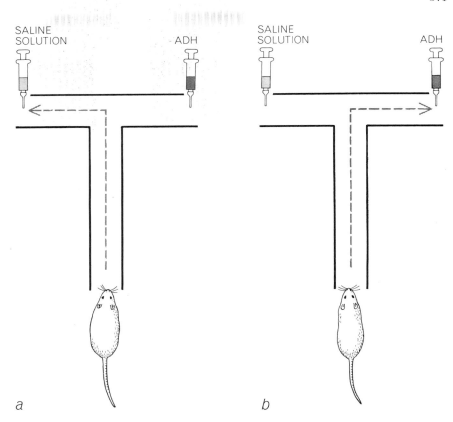

VISCERAL RESPONSE that adjusts the internal environment can serve as a reward to reinforce learning. Rats "loaded" with water (*a*) learned to choose the side of a *T*-maze that resulted in an injection of a control solution rather than one of antidiuretic hormone (ADH), which would interfere with water excretion. (The arms associated with each reward were changed at random.) Rats loaded with salt (*b*), on the other hand, for whom the hormone would induce the proper kidney response, learned to pick the ADH-associated arm.

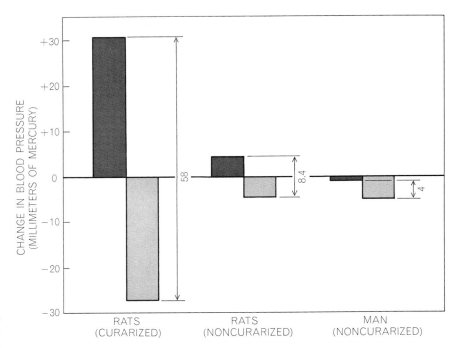

COMPARISON of blood-pressure learning in rats and humans rewarded for increasing (*dark gray bars*) and for decreasing (*light gray*) blood pressure shows that the difference between curarized and noncurarized subjects is greater than the difference between species.

40

WHAT IS MEMORY?

RALPH W. GERARD
September 1953

A textbook of biochemistry widely used early in this century had a famous passage on the memory of linseed oil. Exposure to light makes the oil turn gummy. A brief exposure may not cause any observable change. But on later illumination the oil will change more rapidly than if it had not already been exposed. The oil "remembers" its past experience and behaves differently because of it. Its memory consists in the fact that light produces, among other things, substances which aid the light-induced oxidations that make it gummy.

However far removed this may be from remembering the Gettysburg address, it clearly points up one way in which memory can work—by means of material traces of the past—and the difficulty of defining what memory is. Actually the behavior of the oil and of a human being memorizing the Gettysburg address are but extremes of a spectrum of such behavior in nature. Between these extremes there is a pretty smooth continuity, and any concept which defines memory much more narrowly than "the modification of behavior by experience" will run into trouble. Consciousness, for example, is not necessary to memory, for men remember, and recall under hypnosis, innumerable details never consciously perceived.

Where, then, shall we draw the line? A pebble, rubbed smooth in a stream, rolls differently from the original angular stone. Experience has here modified behavior; the past has been stored in a changed structure. Yet this does not greatly interest us as an instance of memory. Perhaps we should restrict the notion of memory to changes in systems which participate actively in causing the change. Then linseed oil "remembers," and so does the bulging calf muscle of a ballet dancer. Does a developing embryo "remember" the major steps, and missteps, in the long evolution of the species? Do trees "remember" good and bad seasons in the thickness of their rings? Is a film a memory of light in chemicals and a tape recording a memory of sound in magnetism? Is a library a memory of thoughts in books and a brain a memory of thoughts in protoplasm? Even to identify memory, let alone explain it, is no simple matter.

Without memory the past would vanish; intelligence, often called the ability to learn by experience, would be absent, and life would indeed be "a tale told by an idiot, full of sound and fury, signifying nothing." Today the search for the fundamental mechanisms of memory in the nervous system is being pressed with hopeful enthusiasm. The smell of success is in the air and great developments seem to wait just over the next ridge.

Let us consider as memory only that exhibited in man and in such sophisticated behavior as is usually close to conscious awareness. One great problem is: Why do certain impressions become conscious upon reception while others do not; why does awareness accompany some acts, not others; what, in general, invests certain neural events with a phosphorescence of subjective recognition? This question remains unanswered, but the answer is likely to come in terms of the evolution of awareness of certain types of neural events as useful to the organism.

Memory involves the making of an impression by an experience, the retention of some record of this impression and the re-entry of this record into consciousness (or behavior) as recall and recognition. The initial impression need not have entered awareness in order to be retained and recalled. Anyone asked to recall what he has just seen in a room or in a picture does a less complete job than a subject under hypnosis even years later. I have been told of a bricklayer who, under hypnosis, described correctly every bump and grain on the top surface of a brick he had laid in a wall 20 years before!

Guesses have been made as to how many items might be accumulated in memory over a lifetime. Some tests of perception suggest that each tenth of a second is a single "frame" of experience for the human brain. In that tenth of a second it can receive perhaps a thousand units of information, called bits. In 70 years, not allowing for any reception during sleep, some 15 trillion bits might pour into the brain and perhaps be stored there. Since this number is more than 1,000 times larger than the total of nerve cells, the problem of storage is not exactly simple.

Whether or not all incoming sensations are preserved as potential memories, there is an important time factor in their fixation. Youthful, repeated or vivid experiences seem most firmly fixed. They are the last to survive disrupting conditions—old age, brain damage, concussion or mental shock—and the first to return after a period of amnesia. A goose seems to fix upon the first moving object it sees as its mother and thereafter follows it about. An infant, suddenly frightened by a barking dog, may fear dogs for the rest of its life.

More often experiences force themselves into attention and memory only gradually. Even learning to perceive is a long, troublesome matter. Adults gaining vision for the first time must labor for months to learn to recognize a circle and to distinguish it from a triangle, let alone to see letters and words.

After any experience, apparently considerable time must elapse between the arrival of the incoming nerve impulses and the fixing of the trace. If a photographic plate acted similarly, it could not be developed at once after exposure but only some time later. Recent experiments in our laboratory have emphasized this phenomenon. Hamsters daily were run in a maze and were given an electric shock afterward. When the shock was given four hours or more after the run, it did not influence the learning curve. (The question of cumulative damage is irrelevant here.) A shock one hour after the run impaired learning a little, and as the shock was brought closer it interfered more and more, until at one minute after the run, it destroyed learning completely. Clearly some process of fixing continues for at least an hour.

The nature of the fixing process must be left for the moment, while some related phenomena of memory are noted. One is a type of erasing. A memory wizard who can glance through a newspaper and then name the word at any position in any column on any page makes an effort to forget this mass of information at the close of a performance so as not to "clutter up" his memory. Perhaps similar is the removal by a pre-suggested signal of an instruction to a hypnotized subject to perform some act after arousal. In such instances stored experience traces seem to be expunged, but whether they are really irrecoverable is perhaps not fully established. Recall alone may be at fault, as in simple forgetting.

A second phenomenon has to do with the alteration of memory traces. The memory left by an experience can change progressively. Memory, as has been well said, is reconstructive rather than reduplicative. It is also highly associative. Pictures redrawn from memory at intervals become more regular (details are smoothed out) or more exaggerated (some salient feature is caricatured) or an object different from the original (a chair looks more like a horse at each redrawing).

Besides fixation and storage, there remain recall and recognition. Failure to recall does not imply loss of the trace: witness the frequent experience of temporary inability to say a familiar name "just on the tip of my tongue." The most intriguing problem about memory, however, is not the existence but the tremendous specificity of recall. Both in its positive and negative aspects—as seen in dreams, in amnesia, in suppression and repression, in hypnosis, in hysteria and dual personality—recall offers bizarre phenomena, formidable to explain.

One day not long ago, as I left a lecture room I caught a fleeting glimpse of the head and shoulders of a person half-silhouetted against a window over a hundred feet away. I knew at once with certainty the name of the person standing there, although he had not crossed my path nor his name my mind for more than 15 years. A chord, a note, a word, a line can recall a long past experience. Or it may reawaken an intense emotion without the connected experience; I know of a young man who invariably faints at the sight of a stethoscope, yet has no general fear of doctors or illness and no idea of why he reacts so uncontrollably.

Recall may sometimes be disguised, seemingly to protect the subject from the anguish of fear or shame or pain. Parts of a story that touch upon a personal problem are often "forgotten" only to appear, modified, in a dream. A man who was unable to recall the telephone number of a girl friend while visiting her city dreamed of red objects that night and recognized in the morning that the numerical position of the letters r, e, d in the alphabet gave the missing number. This opens the door to the whole edifice of symbols. An unsophisticated youngster, directed under hypnosis to dream about bed-wetting, may report his dream in Freudian symbols which only an experienced psychoanalyst—or another naive youngster under hypnosis!—can recognize as referring to bed-wetting.

Finally, what of the compulsive neurotic whose affliction is banished when some infant experience is dredged up during psychotherapy? What of the psychoneurotic soldier, unable to recall a battle beyond a certain point, who relives under pentothal all the horror of seeing a companion's head blown off and is then able to remember and talk about it? What of aphasics, who can recognize words by sight or by sound but not both? And what of dream experiences, not actually sensed but presumably due to intrinsic brain activity, which may be recalled in wakefulness or only in other dreams, if at all? The problem of recall and its specificity is the real challenge to neurophysiology.

The human brain is composed of some 10 billion nerve cells, more or less alike, which interact in various ways. Each cell contributes to behavior, and

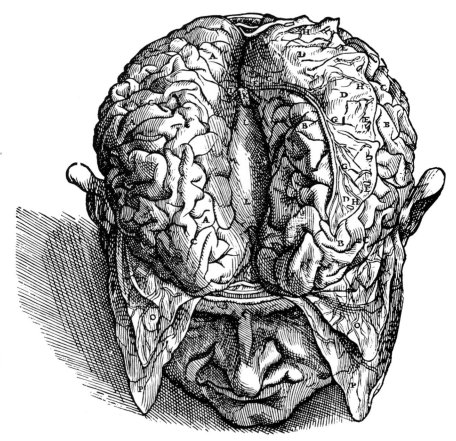

THE BRAIN was dissected by early anatomists seeking clues to its function. This woodcut is from the famous *De Humani Corporis Fabrica* of the pioneer Andreas Vesalius.

HAMSTER RUNS THROUGH MAZE as part of a memory experiment conducted by Robert E. Ransmeier at the University of Chicago. Each barrier in the maze has two doors, one open and one locked. After training hamster reaches food (*right*) in a few seconds.

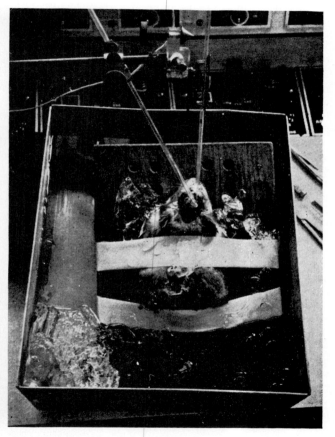

HAMSTER IS CHILLED in a refrigerator. When its temperature is 40 degrees Fahrenheit, the electrical pulse of its brain ceases.

ANOTHER HAMSTER IS TESTED by electroencephalograph to determine the temperature at which the electrical activity stops.

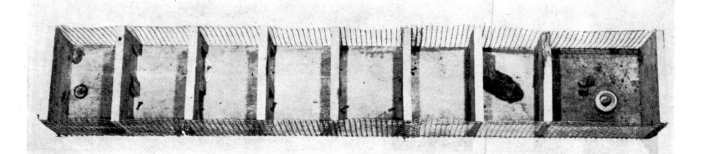

HAMSTER RUNS THROUGH THE MAZE AGAIN after it has been chilled to wipe out the electrical activity of its brain. The investigators discovered that hamsters trained to run through the maze suffered no impairment of this ability because of the chilling.

presumably to mental activity, by firing impulses or failing to fire. All the phenomena of memory must be explained in terms of the temporal and spatial patterns of these discharges.

If experience is to modify behavior, the activity of neurons connected with an experience must alter their subsequent activity patterns. Two general questions regarding the neural trace must be asked, and both can be given a reasonable, if not a certain, answer today. The first is: Does memory depend on a continuing activity or on some static residue, some structural alteration, left behind by past activity? Is a river the water flowing in it or the channel the water cuts? The answer today is tending strongly toward the latter. The second question is: Is the structural trace (or dynamic process) for each memory located in a particular region, or are memory traces suffused through the brain in some way? Are memories marks placed on violin strings or are they wave trains playing over these strings? The latter would imply dynamic memory, but the trace could still be structural, like the wiggled groove on a phonograph record. Whether the trace is localized or diffuse, its exact nature is a third, if somewhat subsidiary question. Current investigations suggest that there are multiple patterns of local traces rather than a single well-localized one, but the nature of the trace is almost pure guess.

A dynamic memory would depend on the continuous passage of nerve impulses or on the maintenance of some active metabolic or potential change in neurons, presumably reinforced by the repeated arrival of impulses. A nerve impulse traveling around a closed loop of connecting neurons would be a mechanism for such a dynamic memory, each remembered item depending on the activity of a particular loop or net of neurons. (Actually, since there are more memories than neurons, different memories would have to share portions of path, but this is physiologically possible without snarling traffic.) Such a memory device would, however, be metabolically expensive, and if the impulses really left no long-enduring trace, memories would be completely and irrevocably lost once the activity stopped.

There is a simple way to test the question as to whether a memory is purely dynamic. One need only stop all nerve impulses in the brain momentarily and observe whether a memory is lost. The problem, of course, is to stop the impulses reversibly. In sleep or under anesthesia the brain slows down but remains electrically active, and memories are largely undisturbed. But the brain's electrical activity can be stopped in several ways. When a hibernating animal, such as the hamster, is cooled to a body temperature of 40 degrees Fahrenheit, needles thrust into its brain fail to pick up electrical activity; it seems reasonably certain that the reverberating impulses are frozen in their tracks.

Another way of stopping the circulating nerve messages is to stimulate the neurons simultaneously by a vigorous electric shock, so that all the neurons presumably are unable to respond to a normal impulse. Such a shock does produce a period of complete electrical silence, measured in seconds or minutes. If the lower brain, controlling respiration, is included, the normal messages for breathing are suspended. Brain neurons may also be made electrically inactive by withholding oxygen for some two minutes or by withholding sugar. In all these cases the animals recover rapidly after the temporary treatment, and their memory can be investigated.

The experiment is now straightforward. Hamsters are first taught a simple maze. They are then hibernated or given electric shock or made to breathe nitrogen for a few minutes. After recovering, they are tested for their retention of learning. If they remember the way through the maze, the memory did not depend upon reverberating circuits or upon any other purely dynamic process. They remember!

This by no means excludes the initial dependence of memory on neuron activity. The passage of impulses is necessarily involved in the initial experience that leaves a memory trace. The fact that repetition makes for better memory reminds us of the analogy of the river cutting a channel in its bed. Indeed, the reason it takes time to fix a memory trace in the brain may be that impulses must circulate over their selected pathways many times in order to leave behind an enduring material change.

What, then, is this enduring static trace? Muscle fibers react to continued exercise by increasing their content of hemoglobin-like pigment; the meat becomes darker. No one has described an enduring chemical change in nerve or brain as a result of activity, but it must be conceded that this is a difficult quest and has not been undertaken very seriously. Muscle fibers swell and become hypertrophied on exercise. It has been shown recently that nerve fibers also swell slightly as they conduct impulses, and the swelling persists at least for minutes and hours if not for days and

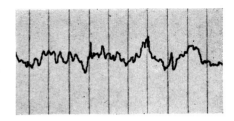

BRAIN WAVES of a hamster *(page 374)* are damped by chilling. Normal waves at top.

years. Nerve fibers also show alterations in potential which outlast the active period by many minutes. Any of these changes might occur at the critical junction between one neuron and the next—the synapse or gap across which conduction is considerably more precarious than it is along the uniform nerve fiber. The change might then make the passage of subsequent impulses easier or more difficult.

Certain it is that activity can facilitate and inactivity hinder the subsequent passage of an impulse across a synapse. This has been learned from experiments on simple spinal cord reflexes involving only one sensory neuron, one synapse and one motor neuron in each arc. If some of the sensory nerve fibers serving the knee-jerk reflex are stimulated, say a hundred times a second for 10 minutes, and are then tested with a single stimulus, the number of motor fibers responding (in effect, the size of the knee-jerk) is increased tenfold above the normal response to a single shock. The increased responsiveness dies out in two or three phases, one lasting for seconds and one certainly for hours. This suggests that the local trace left behind may have involved several changes. Conversely, when impulses are prevented from reaching the synapses of this reflex for days or weeks, by cutting the sensory nerve connections, the reflex elicited by a single shock is strikingly below normal. After a few shocks, however, the response begins to improve, and again the return toward normal seems to involve more than one phase.

Many suggestions have been made as to what kinds of changes may alter the response at a synapse. They must be structural—either in the fibers and contacts or at the molecular level, where displacement of ions might alter the electric potential or displacement of atoms change the chemistry. One observed change, already noted, is the swelling of fiber end-bulbs induced by activity. The swelling should favor the transmission of impulses. Actually this explanation is a modern version of one of the earliest theories of memory: that activity somehow causes a nerve fiber to sprout new twigs near its termination and so to increase its effective contact. Neurons from brains of older persons have in fact been reported to branch more extensively than those from the young, and the notoriously poor memory of old people for recent events might be attributed to the neurons' inability to grow more twigs or to accommodate more connections. A closely related suggestion, that electric-shock treatment of some psychoses is successful because it destroys certain existing connections and permits neurons to make "healthier" ones, is based upon the observation, made on transparent tadpole tails, that electric shocks cause nerve filaments to be torn off.

Another mechanism enjoying some current popularity is chemical. Since every type of cell of every individual of every species has its own chemical personality, and since this differentiation of cells depends on proteins, the specificity of memory might be due to changes in nerve proteins. Each trace could be limited to one or a few molecules in an end-bulb of a neuron. The body cells that manufacture and release antibodies against invading organisms "learn," as we know, from experience. When typhoid proteins, for instance, enter the body the first time, antibodies are produced slowly and in small amounts. But years later, when almost no antibody remains in the blood, a new invasion by this specific protein is met by a prompt and vigorous release of antibody that nips the disease before it gets started.

It is far from explained just how the passage of nerve impulses would alter protein molecules at a synapse, or how, in turn, an altered protein composition would aid or hinder the passage of a nerve impulse. Yet some such chemical mechanism cannot be discarded, for nerves and synapses can be highly specific and can change their specificity. For example, if an extra muscle is transplanted into the back of a salamander, the nerve to which it becomes attached will make the transplanted muscle contract simultaneously with the normal flexor if the transplant is a flexor muscle or with the normal extensor if it is an extensor. Somehow the central synapses have "discovered" what kind of muscle is attached at the far end of the motor neuron and they let through nerve impulses at the proper time for a muscle of this sort.

The essence of all these suggested mechanisms is that a given end-bulb of a neuron, initially ineffective, can become and remain effective as a result of activity. Indeed, mathematical theories of the behavior of complex nerve nets demand only such an assumption to account for the basic properties of memory. Moreover, the total number of end-bulbs on the neurons of the brain, some 10 trillion, about matches the number of bits of information the brain may store during a lifetime. But then each memory would have to have its exact microscopic spot in the brain, would have to stay put through life, and would somehow have to be deposited, once and once only, at a given end-bulb, despite the wide sweep of impulses through the brain during each experience. This raises sharply the problem of localization.

The degree of localization is probably the key problem of memory. If we could expect to find a given memory at a given place in the brain our experimental problem would be comparatively simple. We would locate the region and compare structural, chemical or physical changes there in animals with and without the appropriate experience. Some years ago there was an exciting report that electrical stimulation of a small spot in the cerebral cortex caused trained dogs to make a conditioned leg movement, while in unconditioned or deconditioned animals the same region was inactive. Alas, this claim has not been substantiated. There is, however, valid evidence of a kind of memory localization. When the exposed brain of a person under local anesthesia for a brain operation is stimulated electrically, various conscious effects are produced. Stimulating the occipital lobe, which receives the sensory fibers from the eyes, gives visual sensations. Similarly, stimulation of other specific regions produces sounds and skin sensations. These responses are not related to specific past experiences. However, other regions of the brain, particularly the temporal lobe, do respond to stimulation with the conscious recall of quite specific events from an individual's past.

The particularity, however, is at best only roughly localized, and localization largely vanishes when we look at the effects of brain damage. Large sections of nearly any part of the brain can be destroyed without loss of particular memories or, indeed, without disturbance of the memory function. Human brains have been extensively damaged by trauma, by tumors or abscesses, by loss of circulation, by operative removal, or by the shriveling away of extreme age. In these cases the ability to learn new things, to make sound judgments, to see new relations and to imagine new ideas may be profoundly disturbed, but the recollection of past experience is likely to remain reasonably intact. The frontal lobes of mental patients would not be amputated so freely as they are today if any serious defect in memory resulted.

So we are left with good reasons for believing that memories depend on static changes left behind by the passage of nerve impulses; that these changes occur somewhere along the paths the impulses traveled and are most likely at particular synapses; that the traces are to some extent gathered in certain regions, but that extensive brain damage is not accompanied by comparable losses of memories. One line of escape from the dilemma is to assume, as we can quite reasonably, that a given memory is not

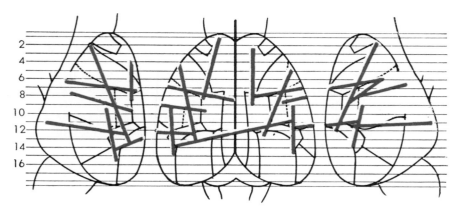

RAT'S BRAINS were incised by Karl S. Lashley of Harvard University and the Yerkes Laboratory of Primate Biology to determine the role of cortical connections in memory. This diagram shows the brain of the rat from the top (center) and both sides. Each red line represents an incision made in a single rat. None of the cuts impaired performance in maze.

represented by one specific local change but by a pattern of many changed loci—a pattern with sufficient redundancy so that if part of it is destroyed the rest will still suffice to represent the memory.

Such a view raises serious difficulties, but they do not appear to be insurmountable. For example, if thousands of neuron endings are involved in one memory, how can the brain store the huge number of memories we have assumed? Actually such indirect coding could greatly increase its storage capacity. Ten letters, each used to represent one item, give 10 items; but 10 letters used in groups as words give a vast number of items. Such patterned memory traces might also actually change with time, as particular neurons or synapses dropped out of the ensemble, and so permit the alteration of memories observed on successive recalls.

We come finally to the problem of recall. Recall is a matter of attention, a selecting or rejecting of particular memory traces. Here enter all the intriguing phenomena of specificity, suppression, symbolization and the like. The physiological explanation of these is certainly not yet at hand. Perhaps the best clue now available is the control of cortical activity and of conscious awareness by nerve centers in the older and deeper parts of the nervous system. Much recent experimentation has shown that these primitive jumbled masses of nerve cells in the upper part of the brain stem exercise a profound influence on the more recently evolved neurons of the cerebral cortex. Impulses from these deep cell groups continuously spray out to the cortex to regulate its activity. An excess of stimulation leads to cortical overactivity and convulsive seizures, followed by the unconsciousness of exhausted neurons. When the impulses are few and the cortex is comparatively inactive, the brain waves slow down and normal sleep results. One is tempted by the picture of an electron beam scanning the tube face of a television camera, picking up impressions left by the outside world from one tiny region after another. But whether such beams of nerve impulses, playing upon the cortex, do actually control attention, whether they are responsible for the evocation of specific memory traces, only the future can decide.

We are beginning to have some reasonable guesses as to the "gadgets" that would serve as a memory mechanism—guesses sufficiently concrete to permit testing by rigorous experimentation. I think it is realistic to hope for an understanding of memory precise enough to permit experimental modification of it in men.

41

MEMORY AND PROTEIN SYNTHESIS

BERNARD W. AGRANOFF
June 1967

What is the mechanism of memory? The question has not yet been answered, but the kind of evidence needed to answer it has slowly been accumulating. One important fact that has emerged is that there are two types of memory: short-term and long-term. To put it another way, the process of learning is different from the process of memory-storage; what is learned must somehow be fixed or consolidated before it can be remembered. For example, people who have received shock treatment in the course of psychiatric care report that they cannot remember experiences they had immediately before the treatment. It is as though the shock treatment had disrupted the process of consolidating their memory of the experiences.

In our laboratory at the University of Michigan we have demonstrated that there is a connection between the consolidation of memory and the manufacture of protein in the brain. Our experimental animal is the common goldfish (*Carassius auratus*). Basically what we do is train a large number of goldfish to perform a simple task and at various times before, during and after the training inject into their skulls a substance that interferes with the synthesis of protein. Then we observe the effect of the injections on the goldfish's performance.

Why seek a connection between memory and protein synthesis? For one thing, enzymes are proteins, and enzymes catalyze all the chemical reactions of life. It would seem reasonable to expect that memory, like all other life processes, is dependent on enzyme-catalyzed reactions. What is perhaps more to the point, the manufacture of new enzymes is characteristic of long-term changes in living organisms, such as growth and the differentiation of cells in the embryo. And long-term memory is by definition a long-term change.

The investigation of a connection between memory and protein synthesis is made possible by the profound advances in knowledge of protein synthesis that have come in the past 10 years. A molecule of protein is made from 20 differ-

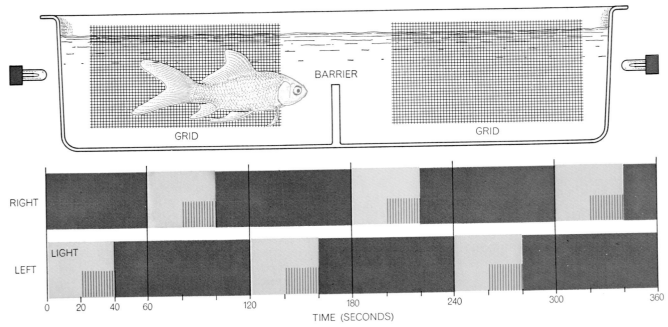

TRAINING TANK the author used was designed so that goldfish learned to swim from the light end to the dark end. A learning trial began with the illumination of the left end of the tank (*chart at bottom*), followed after a pause by mild electric shocks (*colored vertical lines*) from grids at that end. At first a fish would swim over the central barrier in response to shock; then increasingly the fish came to respond to light cue alone as sequence of light, shock and darkness was alternately repeated at each end of the tank.

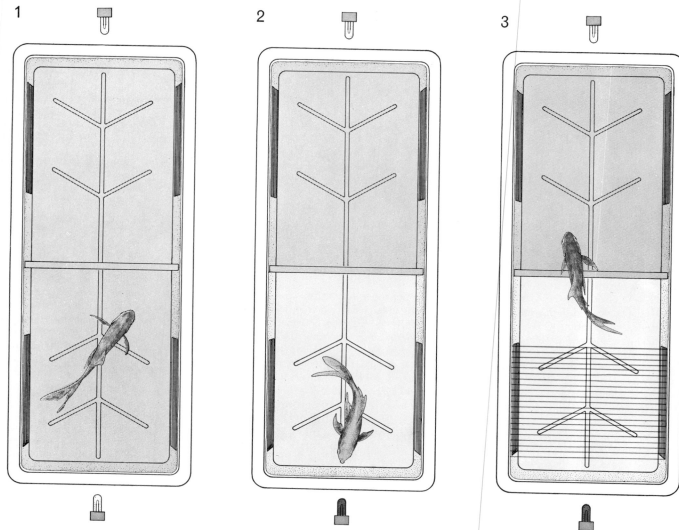

GOLDFISH LEARN in successive trials to solve the problem the shuttle box presents. Following 20 seconds of darkness (*1*) the end of the box where the fish is swimming is lighted for an equal period of time (*2*). The fish fails to respond, swimming over the barrier

ent kinds of amino acid molecule, strung together in a polypeptide chain. The stringing is done in the small bodies in the living cell called ribosomes. Each amino acid molecule is brought to the ribosome by a molecule of transfer RNA, a form of ribonucleic acid. The instructions according to which the amino acids are linked in a specific sequence are brought to the ribosome by another form of ribonucleic acid: messenger RNA. These instructions have been transcribed by the messenger RNA from deoxyribonucleic acid (DNA), the cell's central library of information.

With this much knowledge of protein synthesis one can begin to think of examining the process by interfering with it in selective ways. Such interference can be accomplished with antibiotics. Whereas some substances that interfere with the machinery of the cell, such as cyanide, are quite general in their ef-

fects, antibiotics can be highly selective. Indeed, some of them block only one step in cellular metabolism. As an example, the antibiotic puromycin simply stops the growth of the polypeptide chain in the ribosome. This it does by virtue of the fact that its molecule resembles one end of the transfer RNA molecule with an amino acid attached to it. Accordingly the puromycin molecule is joined to the growing end of the polypeptide chain and blocks its further growth. The truncated chain is released attached to the puromycin molecule.

Numerous workers have had the idea of using agents such as puromycin to block protein synthesis in animals and then observing the effects on the animals' behavior. Among them have been C. Wesley Dingman II and M. B. Sporn of the National Institutes of Health, who injected 8-azaguanine into rats; T. J. Chamberlain, G. H. Rothschild and

Ralph W. Gerard of the University of Michigan, who administered the same substance to rats, and Josefa B. Flexner, Louis B. Flexner and Eliot Stellar of the University of Pennsylvania, who injected puromycin into mice. Such experiments encouraged us to try our hand with the goldfish.

We chose the goldfish for our experiments because it is readily available and can be accommodated in the laboratory in large numbers. Moreover, a simple and automatically controlled training task for goldfish had already been developed by M. E. Bitterman of Bryn Mawr College. One might wonder if a fish has such a thing as long-term memory; in the opinion of numerous psychologists and anglers there can be no doubt of it.

Our training apparatus is called a shuttle box. It is an oblong plastic tank

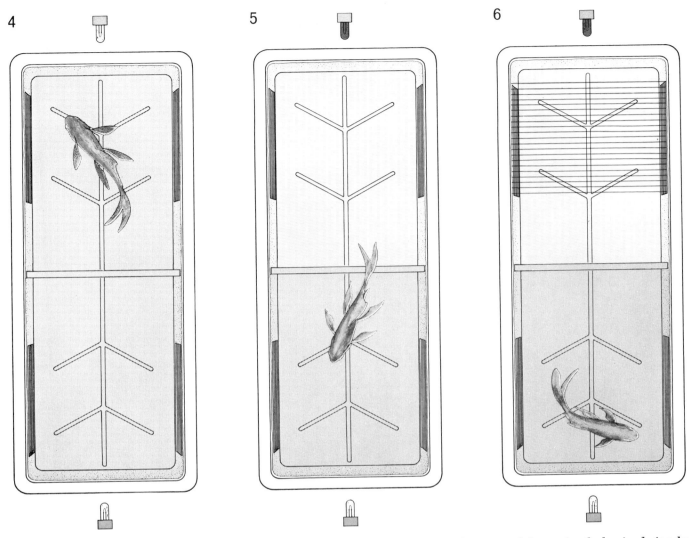

only after the shock period heralded by light has begun (3). When the same events are repeated at the other end of the box (4, 5 and 6), the fish shown here succeeds in crossing the barrier during the 20 seconds of light that precede the period of intermittent shock.

divided into two compartments by a barrier that comes to within an inch of the water surface [*see illustration on page 379*]. At each end of the box is a light that can be turned on and off. On opposite sides of each compartment are grids by means of which the fish can be given a mild electric shock through the water.

The task to be learned by the fish is that when it is in one compartment and the light goes on at that end of the box, it should swim over the barrier into the other compartment. In our initial experiments we left the fish in the dark for five minutes and then gave it five one-minute trials. Each trial consisted in (1) turning on the light at the fish's end of the box, (2) 20 seconds later intermittently turning on the shocking grids and (3) 20 seconds after that turning off both the shocking grids and the light. If the fish crossed the barrier into the other

compartment during the first 20 seconds, it *avoided* the shock; if it crossed the barrier during the second 20 seconds, it *escaped* the shock.

An untrained goldfish almost always escaped the shock, that is, it swam across the barrier only when the shock began. Whether the fish escaped the shock or avoided it, it crossed the barrier into the other compartment. Then, after 20 seconds of darkness, the light at that end was turned on to start the second trial. Thus the fish shuttled back and forth with each trial. If a fish failed to either avoid or escape, it missed the next trial. Such missed trials were rare and generally came only at the beginning of training.

In these experiments the goldfish went through five consecutive cycles of five minutes of darkness followed by five training trials; accordingly they received a total of 20 trials in 40 minutes. They

were then placed in individual "home" tanks—plastic tanks that are slightly smaller than the shuttle boxes—and kept there for three days. On the third day they were returned to the shuttle box, where they were given 10 more trials in 20 minutes.

The fish readily learned to move from one compartment to the other when the light went on, thereby avoiding the shock. Untrained fish avoided the shock in about 20 percent of the first 10 trials and continued to improve with further trials. If they were allowed to perform the task day after day, the curve of learning flattened out at about 80 percent correct responses.

What was even more significant for our experiments was what happened when we changed the interval between the first cycle of trials and the second, that is, between the 20th and the 21st of the 30 trials. If the second cycle was

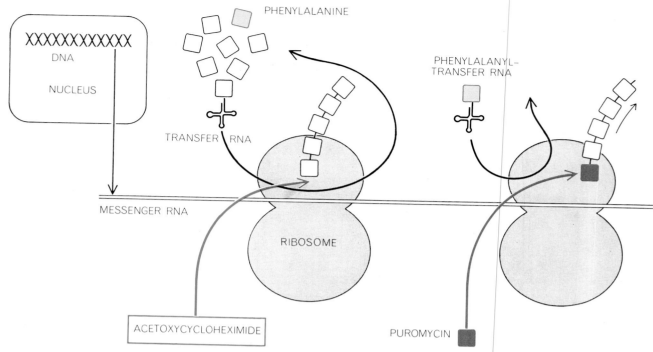

PHENYLALANINE

DNA

NUCLEUS

PHENYLALANYL-
TRANSFER RNA

TRANSFER RNA

MESSENGER RNA

RIBOSOME

ACETOXYCYCLOHEXIMIDE

PUROMYCIN

PROTEIN-BLOCKING AGENTS can interrupt the formation of molecules at the ribosome, where the amino acid units of protein are linked according to instructions embodied in messenger ribonucleic acid (mRNA). One agent, acetoxycycloheximide, interferes with the bonding mechanism that links amino acids brought to the ribosome by transfer RNA (tRNA). Puromycin, another agent, resembles the combination of tRNA and the amino acid phenylalanine. Thus it is taken into chain and prematurely halts its growth.

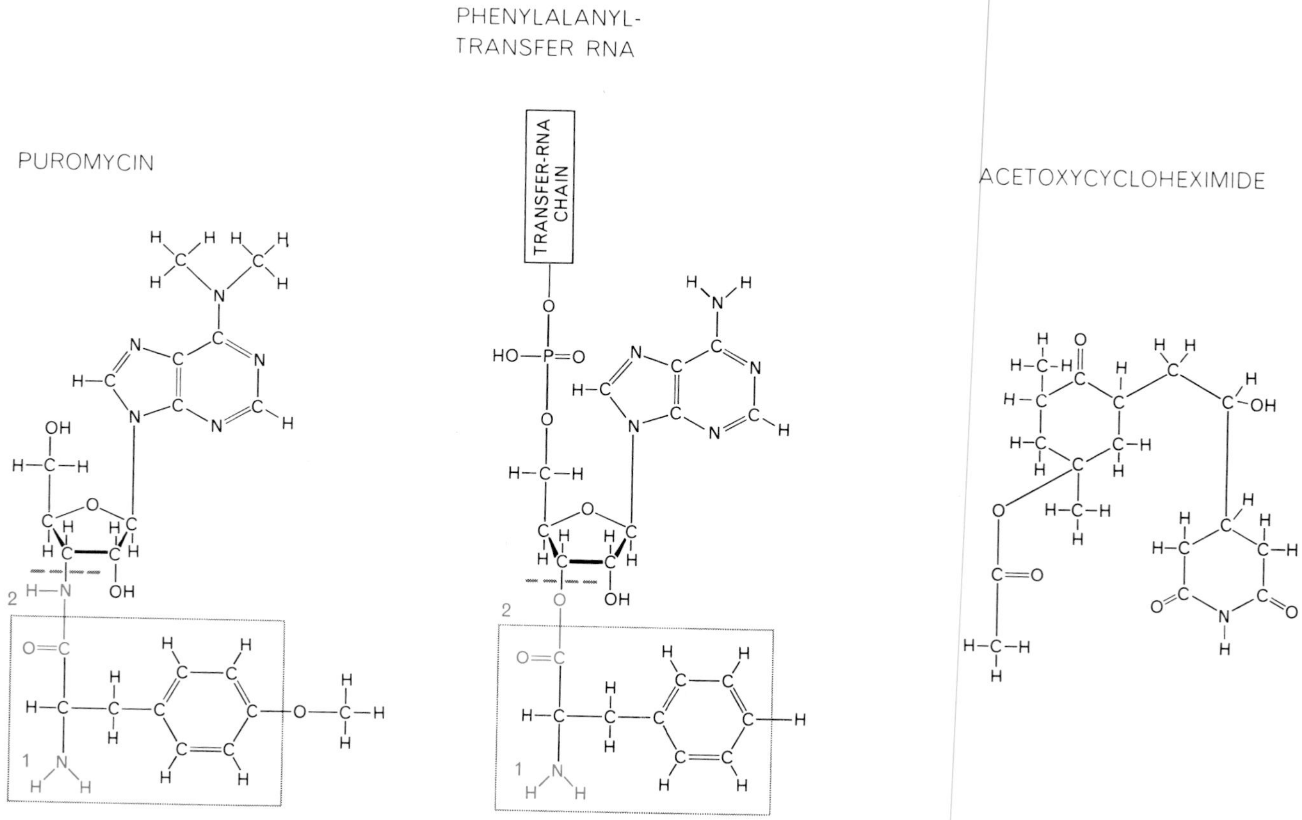

PHENYLALANYL-
TRANSFER RNA

PUROMYCIN

TRANSFER-RNA
CHAIN

ACETOXYCYCLOHEXIMIDE

MOLECULAR DIAGRAMS show the resemblance between puromycin and the combination phenylalanyl-tRNA. In both cases the portion of the molecule below the broken line is incorporated into a growing protein molecule, joining at the free amino group (1). But in puromycin the CONH group (2), unlike the corresponding group (COO) of phenylalanyl, will not accept another amino acid and the chain is broken. Acetoxycycloheximide does not resemble amino acid but slows rate at which the chain forms.

begun a full month after the first, the fish performed as well as they did on the third day. If the second cycle was begun on the day after the first, the fish performed equally well, as one would expect. In short, the fish had perfect memory of their training.

We found that we could predict the training scores of groups of fish on the third day on the basis of their scores on the first day. This made it easier for us to determine the effect of antibiotics on the fish's memory: we could compare the training scores of fish receiving antibiotics with the predicted scores. Since we conducted these initial experiments we have made several improvements in our procedure. We now record the escapes and avoidances automatically with photodetectors, and we have arranged matters so that a fish does not miss a trial if it fails to escape. We have altered the trial sequence and the time interval between the turning on of the light and the turning on of the shocking grid. The results obtained with these improved procedures are essentially the same as our earlier ones.

The principal antibiotic we use in our experiments is puromycin, whose effect on protein synthesis was described earlier. We inject the drug directly into the skull of the goldfish with a hypodermic syringe. A thin needle easily penetrates the skull; 10 microliters of solution is then injected over the fish's brain (not into it). In an early series of experiments we injected 170 micrograms of puromycin in that amount of solution at various stages in our training procedures.

We found that if the puromycin was injected immediately after training, memory of the training was obliterated. If the same amount of the drug was injected an hour after training, on the other hand, memory was unaffected. Injection 30 minutes after training produced an intermediate effect. Reducing the amount of puromycin caused a smaller loss of memory.

After the injection the fish seemed to swim normally. We were therefore encouraged to test whether or not puromycin interferes with the changes that occur in the brain as the fish is being trained. This we did by injecting the fish before their initial training. We found that they learned the task at a normal rate, that is, their improvement during the first 20 trials was normal. Fish tested three days later, however, showed a profound loss of memory. This indicated to us that puromycin did not block the short-term memory demonstrated during

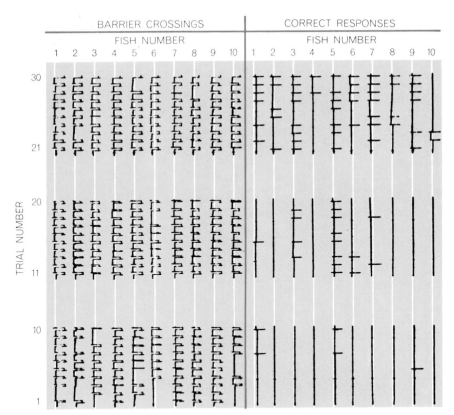

TRACE FROM RECORDER shows the performances of 10 goldfish in 30 trials. Each horizontal row represents a trial, beginning at the bottom with trial 1. A blip (left side) indicates that a fish either escaped or avoided the shock; a dash in the same row (right) signifies an avoidance, that is, a correct response for the trial. These fish learned at the normal rate.

learning but did interfere with the consolidation of long-term memory. And since an injection an hour after training has no effect on long-term memory, whereas an injection immediately after training obliterates it, it appears that consolidation can take place within an hour.

One observation puzzled us. The animals had received their initial training during a 40-minute period, 20 minutes of which was spent in the dark. Puromycin could erase all memory of this training; none of the memory was consolidated. Yet the experiment in which we injected puromycin 30 minutes after training had shown that more than half of the memory was consolidated during that period. How was it that no memory at all was consolidated at least toward the end of the 40-minute training period? To be sure, the fish that had been injected 30 minutes after the training period had been removed from the shuttle boxes and placed in their home tanks. But what was different about the time spent in the shuttle box and the time spent in the home tank that memory could be consolidated in the home tank

but could not be in the shuttle box?

Roger E. Davis of our laboratory undertook further experiments to clarify the phenomenon. He found that fish that were allowed to remain in the shuttle box for several hours after training and were then returned to their home tank showed no loss of memory when they were tested four days later. On the other hand, fish that were allowed to remain in the shuttle box for the same length of time and were then injected with puromycin and returned to their home tank had a marked memory loss! In other words, the fish in the first group did not consolidate memory of their training until after they had been placed in their home tank. It appears that simply being in the shuttle box prevents the fixation of memory. Subsequent studies have led us to the idea that memory fixation is blocked when the organism is in an environment associated with a high level of stimulation. This effect indicates that the formation of memory is environment-dependent, just as the consolidation of memory is time-dependent.

We conclude from all these experiments that long-term memory of training in the goldfish is formed by a puromycin-sensitive step that begins after training and requires that the animal be removed from the training environment. The initial acquisition of information by the fish is puromycin-insensitive and is a qualitatively different process. But what does the action of puromycin on memory formation have to do with its known biochemical effect: the inhibition of protein synthesis?

We undertook to establish that puromycin blocks protein synthesis in the goldfish brain under the conditions of our experiments. This we did in the following manner. First we injected puromycin into the skull of the fish. Next we injected into the abdominal cavity of the fish leucine that had been labeled with tritium, or radioactive hydrogen. Now, leucine is an amino acid, and if labeled leucine is injected into a goldfish's abdominal cavity, it will be incorporated into whatever protein is being synthesized throughout the goldfish's body. By measuring the amount of labeled leucine incorporated into protein after, say, 30 minutes, one can determine the rate of protein synthesis during that time.

We compared the amount of labeled leucine incorporated into protein in goldfish that had received an injection of puromycin with the amount incorporated in fish that had received either no

injection or an injection of inactive salt solution. We found that protein synthesis in the brain of fish that had been injected with puromycin was deeply inhibited. The effects of different doses of puromycin and the length of time it took the drug to act did not, however, closely correspond to what we had observed in our experiments involving the behavioral performance of the goldfish. In retrospect this result is not surprising. Various experiments, including our own, had shown that the rate of memory consolidation can be altered by changes in the conditions of training. Moreover, the rate of leucine incorporation can be affected by complex physiological factors.

Another way to check whether or not puromycin exerts its effects on memory by inhibiting protein synthesis would be to perform the memory experiments with a second drug known to inhibit such synthesis. Then if puromycin blocks long-term memory by some other mechanism, the second drug would have no effect on memory. It would be even better if the second drug did not resemble puromycin in molecular structure, so that its effect on protein synthesis would not be the same as puromycin's. Such a drug exists in acetoxycycloheximide. Where puromycin blocks the growth of the polypeptide chain by taking the place of an amino acid, acetoxycycloheximide simply slows down the rate at

which the amino acids are linked together. We found that a small amount of this drug (.1 microgram, or one 1,700th the weight of the amount of puromycin we had been using) produced a measurable memory deficit in goldfish. Moreover, it commensurately inhibited the synthesis of protein in the goldfish brain.

These experiments suggest that protein synthesis is required for the consolidation of memory, but they are not conclusive. Louis Flexner and his colleagues have found that puromycin can interfere with memory in mice. On the other hand, they find that acetoxycycloheximide has no such effect. They conclude that protein is required for the expression of memory but that experience acts not on protein synthesis directly but on messenger RNA. The conditions of their experiments and the fact that they are working with a different animal do not allow any ready comparison with our experiments.

Our studies of the goldfish have led us to view learning and memory as a form of biological development. One may think of the brain of an animal as being completely "wired" by heredity; all possible pathways are present, but not all are "soldered." It may be that in short-term memory, pathways are selected rapidly but impermanently. In that case protein synthesis would not be required, which may explain why puromycin has no effect on short-term memory. If the consolidation of memory calls for more permanent connections among pathways, it seems reasonable that protein synthesis would be involved. The formation of such connections, of course, would be blocked by puromycin and acetoxycycloheximide.

Another possibility is that the drugs block not the formation of permanent pathways but the transmission of a signal to fix what has just been learned. There is some evidence for this notion in what happens to people who suffer damage to certain parts of the brain (the mammillary bodies and the hippocampus). They retain older memories and are capable of new learning, but they cannot form new long-term memories. Experiments with animals also provide some evidence for a "fix" signal. We are currently doing experiments in the hope of determining which of these hypotheses best fits the effects of puromycin and acetoxycycloheximide on memory in the goldfish.

Quite apart from our own work, it has been suggested by others that it is possible to transfer patterns of behavior

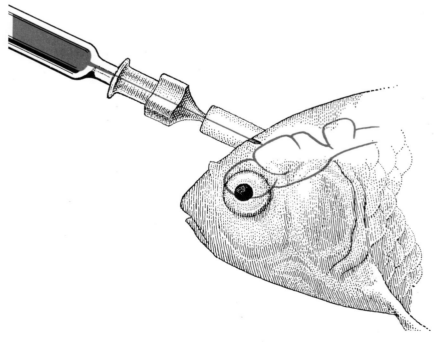

ANTIBIOTIC WAS INJECTED through the thin skull of a goldfish and over rather than into the brain. The antibiotic was puromycin, which inhibits protein synthesis. Following its injection the fish were able to swim normally. They could then be tested for memory loss.

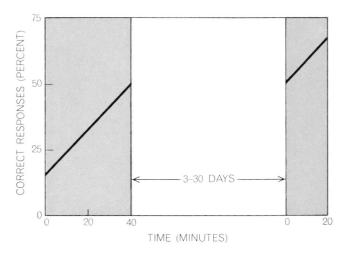

NORMAL LEARNING RATE of goldfish in 30 shuttle-box trials is shown by the black curve. Whether the last 10 trials were given three days after the first 20 (the regular procedure) or as much as a month later, fish demonstrated the same rate of improvement.

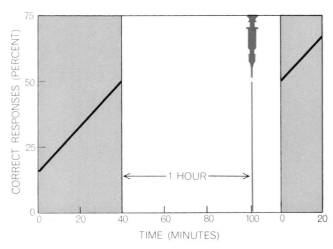

INJECTION WITH PUROMYCIN one hour after completion of 20 learning trials did not disrupt memory. Goldfish given the antibiotic at this point scored as well as those in the control group in the sequence of 10 trials that followed three days afterward.

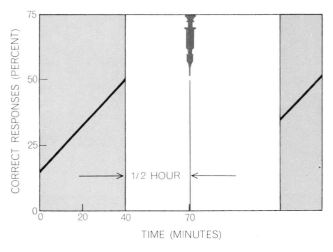

INJECTION HALF AN HOUR AFTER the first 20 trials cut the level of correct responses to half the level without such injection.

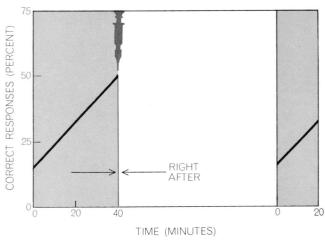

INJECTION IMMEDIATELY AFTER the first 20 trials erased all memory of training. The fish scored at the untrained level.

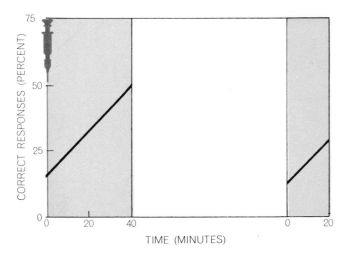

INJECTION PRIOR TO TRAINING did not affect the rate at which goldfish learned to solve the shuttle-box problem. But puromycin given at this point did suppress the formation of long-term memory, as shown by the drop in the scores three days afterward.

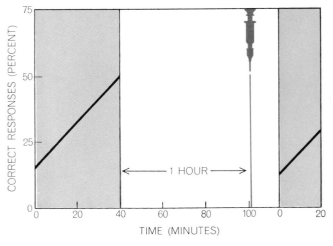

ENVIRONMENTAL FACTOR in the formation of lasting memory was seen when fish remained in training (instead of "home") tanks during the fixation period. Under these conditions fixation did not occur. Puromycin given at end of period still erased memory.

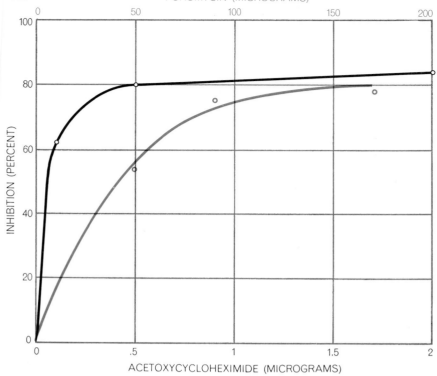

PUROMYCIN (MICROGRAMS)

INHIBITION (PERCENT)

ACETOXYCYCLOHEXIMIDE (MICROGRAMS)

SLOWED PROTEIN SYNTHESIS in the brain of goldfish is induced both by acetoxycyclo-heximide (*black line*) and the antibiotic puromycin (*colored line*), agents that block the fixation of memory. The author tested the effect on goldfish of various quantities of the two drugs; acetoxycycloheximide was found several hundred times more potent than puromycin.

from one animal to another (even to an animal of a different species) by injecting RNA or protein from the brain of a trained animal into the brain (or even the abdominal cavity) of an untrained one. If such transfers of behavior patterns can actually be accomplished, they imply that memory resides in molecules of RNA or protein. Nothing we have learned with the goldfish argues for or against the possibility that a behavior pattern is stored in such a molecule.

It can be observed, however, that there is no precedent in biology for such storage. What could be required would be a kind of somatic mutation: a change in the cell's store of information that would give rise to a protein with a new sequence of amino acids. It seems unlikely that such a process could operate at the speed required for learning.

It might also be that learning and memory involve the formation of short segments of RNA or protein that somehow label an individual brain cell. Richard Santen of our laboratory has calculated (on the basis of DNA content) the number of cells in the brain of a rat: it comes to 500 million. With this figure one can calculate further that a polypeptide chain of seven amino acids, arranged in every possible sequence, could provide each cell in the rat's brain with two unique markers.

The concept that each nerve cell has its own chemical marker is supported by experiments on the regeneration of the optic nerve performed by Roger W. Sperry of the California Institute of Technology. If the optic nerve of a frog is cut and the two ends of the nerve are put back together rotated 180 degrees with respect to each other, the severed fibers of the nerve link up with the same fiber as before. This of course suggests that each fiber has a unique marker that in the course of regeneration enables it to recognize its mate.

Is it possible, then, that a cell "turned on" by the learning process manufactures a chemical marker? And could such a process give rise to a substance that, when it is injected into another animal, finds its way to the exact location where it can effectuate memory? Thus far the evidence put forward in support of such ideas has not been impressive. In this exciting period of discovery in brain research clear-cut experiments are more important than theories. Certain long-term memories held by investigators in this area may be more of a hindrance than a help in exploring all its possibilities.

42

THE NEUROPHYSIOLOGY OF REMEMBERING

KARL H. PRIBRAM
January 1969

In 1950, toward the end of a busy life devoted to investigating the neurophysiology of memory, Karl S. Lashley wrote: "I sometimes feel, in reviewing the evidence on the localization of the memory trace, that the necessary conclusion is that learning just is not possible at all. Nevertheless, in spite of such evidence against it, learning does sometimes occur." That same year Edwin G. Boring, a leading psychologist of Lashley's generation, pointed out the deep impact that this failure to find physiological evidence for the memory trace had had on psychology. "Where or how," he asked, "does the brain store its memories? That is the great mystery. How can learning persist unreproduced, being affected by other learning while it waits? On the proper occasion what was learned reappears somewhat modified. Where was it in the meantime?... The physiology of memory has been so baffling a problem that most psychologists in facing it have gone positivistic, being content with hypothesized intervening variables or with empty correlations."

Hardly were these bleak observations in print before new research tools became available and were promptly applied in experiments on the neurophysiology of memory. As in all research that produces results important to workers in more than one discipline, however, dissemination across traditional boundaries is slowed by differences in vocabulary, in research technique and in the way a problem is subtly influenced by the subjects and materials employed by workers in different disciplines. As a result one finds even today that many psychologists (even those kindly disposed toward physiology) have the impression that little or no progress has been made in the effort to establish the neurophysiological basis of memory. This stems from the fact that psychologists have addressed themselves primarily to questions about *process*, whereas neurophysiologists and neurochemists have addressed themselves primarily to the question of how the brain achieves short-term and long-term *storage*.

My own research has sought to answer more directly the questions posed by psychologists: What kinds of memory process must exist in the brain to allow remembering to take place? The results of this research have cast doubt on at least some of the assumptions about brain mechanisms (explicit and implicit) that are held by both psychologists and physiologists and that in my view have impeded any coming to grips with the problem of process.

Neurophysiologists had over several decades extensively mapped the brain with electrical recording devices and with weak electric currents to trace nerve pathways. As a result of such experiments on cats, monkeys and even men (performed during neurosurgery) physiologists could speak with some confidence of visual, auditory and somesthetic and motor areas in the cerebral cortex. Although they remained baffled by the "memory trace," they still felt they could describe the nerve pathways from a stimulus input (say the flash of a light) to a muscular response. The success of these studies often blinded the investigators to the fact that many of these presumed pathways could hardly be reconciled with Lashley's experiments dating back to the 1920's, which showed that rats could remember and could perform complex activities even after major nerve pathways in the brain had been cut and after as much as 90 percent of the primary visual cortex had been surgically removed.

As a neurosurgeon I had no reason to challenge the prevailing views of physiologists until I met Lashley and was convinced that we knew less than we thought. I soon resolved to continue his general line of investigation, working with monkeys rather than with rats, and in addition to make an effort to follow recordable changes of the electrical activity of the brain as the animals were trained to perform various tasks. Although this work has gone slowly at times (one experiment I shall describe took seven years), my co-workers and I have now gathered neurophysiological data from more than 950 monkeys. The results of these experiments are forcing many revisions in traditional concepts of how the brain works when tasks are learned and later remembered.

Beyond this I believe there is now available a hypothesis about the nature of the memory trace that satisfies the known physiological requirements and that can be tested by experiment. It is perhaps not surprising that the brain may exploit, among other things, the most sophisticated principle of information storage yet known: the principle of the hologram. In a hologram the information in a scene is recorded on a photographic plate in the form of a complex interference, or diffraction, pattern that appears meaningless. When the pattern is illuminated by coherent light, however, the original image is reconstructed. What makes the hologram unique as a storage device is that every element in the original image is distributed over the entire photographic plate. The hypothesis is attractive because remembering or recollecting literally implies a reconstructive process—the assembly of dismembered mnemic events. In what follows, therefore, I shall give first the evidence for believing that

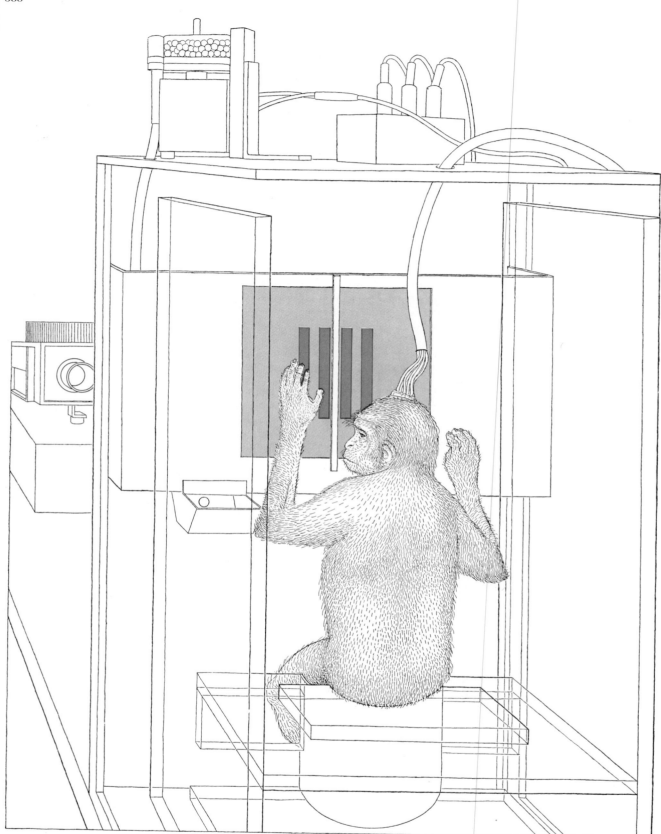

VISUAL-DISCRIMINATION TASK developed in the author's laboratory at Stanford University School of Medicine is depicted in this illustration. On the translucent panel in front of him the monkey sees either a circle or a series of vertical stripes, which have been projected from the rear. He is rewarded with a peanut, which drops into the receptacle at his left elbow, if he presses the right half of the panel when he sees the circle or the left half when he sees the stripes. Electrodes record the wave forms that appear in the monkey's visual cortex as he develops skill at this task. Early in the experiments the wave forms show whether the monkey sees the circle or stripes. Eventually they reveal in advance which half of the panel the monkey will press (*see illustration on page 390*).

mnemic events are distributed in the brain and then describe experiments that tell us something about the way these mnemic events become re-collected into useful memory processes.

The abuses that the brain can survive and still function successfully have been documented many times since Lashley's pioneering experiments. Human testimony is provided daily in the neurological clinic of every large hospital when diseased or damaged brain tissue has to be removed. In the laboratory the brain seems to mock the ingenuity of the experimenter. Robert Galambos of the University of California at San Diego has severed up to 98 percent of the optic tract of cats without seriously impairing the cats' ability to perform skillfully on tests requiring them to differentiate between highly similar figures. Roger W. Sperry of the California Institute of Technology has surgically cross-hatched sensory receiving areas in the cortex of monkeys without disturbing the presumed organization of the input system. In other experiments the system continued to function even when Sperry inserted strips of mica in the cross-hatched troughs in an effort to electrically insulate small squares of tissue from one another. Conversely, Lashley, Kao Liang Chow and Josephine Semmes tried, without success, to short-circuit the electrical activity of the brain by placing strips of gold foil over the receiving areas. To accomplish a similar end I injected a minute amount of aluminum hydroxide cream at a number of points within a receiving area of an animal's cerebral cortex to produce electrical discharges resembling those seen in electroencephalograms during an epileptic seizure. Although these multiple discharging foci sharply retarded the animal's ability to learn a task of pattern discrimination, they did not interfere with recognition of these patterns when the multiple lesions were produced after learning.

Such experiments have been interpreted as showing that each sensory system has considerable reserve capacity. Since it seems to make little difference in terms of performance which parts of the system are destroyed, it has been suggested that this reserve is distributed throughout the system, that the information needed to discriminate patterns is duplicated in many locations. According to this hypothesis, the discharging foci produced by injections of aluminum hydroxide cream interfere in some way with the reduplication that normally

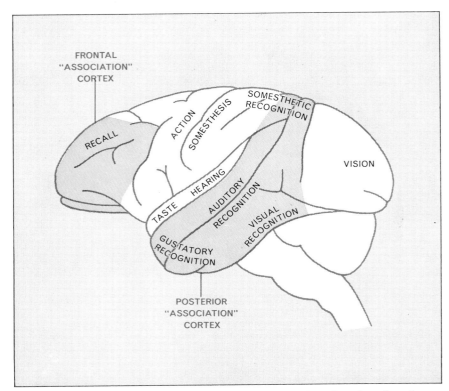

LOCALIZATIONS OF FUNCTION in the cerebral cortex of monkeys have been known in general for many years. The evidence has been supplied in part by anatomical tracing of nerve pathways and more recently by electrical recording of wave forms, both through the intact skull and by use of implanted electrodes. Somesthesis refers to the sense of touch.

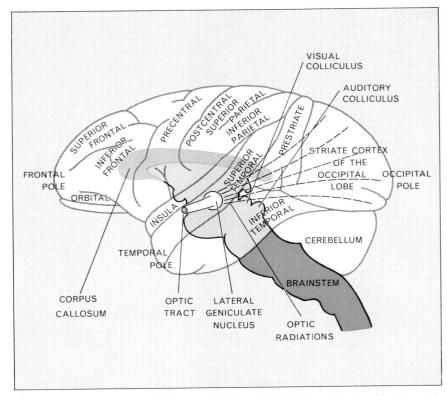

STRUCTURES IN CEREBRAL CORTEX AND BRAINSTEM mentioned in the text can be identified with the help of this illustration. Most of the cortical areas are labeled in adjectival form, the word "cortex" being omitted. The brainstem and its structures are shown in color. The corpus callosum is a bundle of nerve fibers that connects the two hemispheres of the brain. The lateral geniculate nucleus is the major relay station in the visual input system.

| DISCRIMINATION PANELS | STIMULUS EVENTS | RESPONSE EVENTS | | REINFORCING EVENTS |

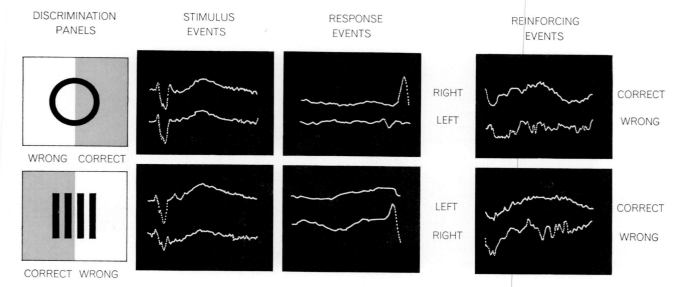

RESULTS OF VISUAL-DISCRIMINATION EXPERIMENT are shown in the wave forms recorded from the striate (visual) cortex of a monkey. The waves are those recorded after he has learned the task illustrated on page 388. The records under "Stimulus events" are wave forms that appear immediately after the monkey has been shown a circle or stripes. The records under "Response events" were generated just prior to the moment when the monkey actually responded by pressing either the left or the right half of the panel. The records under "Reinforcing events" were produced when the monkey was rewarded with a peanut if he was correct or not rewarded if he was wrong. The correct response was to press the right half of the panel on seeing a circle, the left half on seeing stripes.

A slight difference in the "stimulus" wave forms indicates whether the monkey has seen stripes or a circle. After he has learned his task well sharp differences appear in the response and reinforcing panels. The response wave forms, which are actually "intention" waves, show one pattern (the one with the sharp peak) whenever the monkey is about to press the right half of the panel, regardless of whether he has seen a circle or stripes. If he has actually seen stripes, of course, pressing the right half of the panel is the wrong response. Thus the wave forms reflect his intention to press a particular half of the panel. They could hardly reveal whether his response is going to be right or wrong because at this point he still "thinks" he is about to make the correct response.

takes place when information is being stored, but once storage is complete and the information is distributed all parts of the system are more or less "equipotent."

The correctness of this view has now been put to direct test. Over the past few years Nico Spinelli and I have shown that electrical activity recorded from widely distributed points in the striate, or visual, cortex of monkeys shows distinctive responses to different stimuli. Moreover, other widely distributed points within the cortex and brainstem give evidence that they have participated in storing information linked to the animal's response to particular stimuli. Let me describe the experiment more fully. (This is the one that took seven years to complete.)

Monkeys were placed in front of a translucent panel on which we could project either a circle or four vertical stripes [see illustration on page 388]. If, when the monkey saw the circle, he pressed the right half of the panel, he would be rewarded with a peanut. He would be similarly rewarded if he pressed the left side of the panel when the stripes appeared. Before the training begins we painlessly implant a num-

ber of tiny electrodes in the monkey's visual cortex. We then compare the electrical wave forms produced by the cortex during training with the wave forms produced after a high level of skill has been attained. We had expected that the wave forms would be different, and they were.

What we did not expect was that we would be able to tell from the waveform records whether the monkey saw a circle or vertical stripes, whether he responded correctly or made a mistake and, most surprising of all, whether he _intended_ to press the right half or the left half of the panel once he was presented with the problem and _before_ he initiated an overt response [see illustration above]. All these differing electrical responses arose in the visual cortex—the part of the brain that receives the visual input. We are forced to conclude that signals representing experience converge with and modify the input to the visual-input systems. We also found, however, that within the visual cortex different electrodes recorded different events.

Thus we now have direct evidence that signals become distributed within the input system. What we see (or at least what the monkey sees) is not a pure

and simple coding of the light patterns that are focused on the retina. Somewhere between the retina and the visual cortex the inflowing signals are modified to provide information that is already linked to a learned response, for example the monkey's intention to press one panel or another. Evidently what reaches the visual cortex is evoked by the external world but is hardly a direct or simple replica of it. Further, the information inherent in the input becomes distributed over wide regions of the visual cortex.

How might such a distribution of information occur? A possible clue to the puzzle came from an optical artifact, the hologram, which was then being made for the first time with the help of coherent laser light [see "Photography by Laser," by Emmett N. Leith and Juris Upatnieks; SCIENTIFIC AMERICAN Offprint 300]. The interference pattern of the hologram is created when a beam of coherent light is split so that a "reference" portion of the beam can interact with a portion reflected from a scene or an object. I reasoned (much as Lashley had) that neuronal events might interact in some way to produce complex patterns within the brain; the hologram now provided an explicit model.

Evidence for some such patterning of neuronal events, at least in the visual channels, has been provided by the work of R. W. Rodieck of the University of Sydney. He has shown that the initiating events in the visual channel that express the relations between the excitation of one receptor in the retina and the activity of neighboring points can be described mathematically through the use of "convolutional integrals," expressions somewhat similar to the familiar Fourier transformations. For example, the shape of the visual receptive field of a single retinal ganglion cell represents the convolution of a derivative of the shape of the retinal image produced at that point [*see illustration on this page*]. Convolutional integrals and Fourier transformations provide the mathematical basis on which holography was founded. Thus at least a first step has been taken to show that interference effects may operate in the central nervous system.

The question remains: How can interference effects be produced in the brain? One can imagine that when nerve impulses arrive at synapses (the junction between two nerve cells), they produce electrical events on the other side of the synapse that take the form of momentary standing wave fronts. Typically the junctions made by a nerve fiber number in the dozens, if not hundreds. The patterns set up by arriving nerve impulses presumably form a microstructure of wave forms that can interact with similar microstructures arising in overlapping junctional contacts. These other microstructures are derived from the spontaneous changes in electrical potential that ceaselessly occur in nerve tissue, and from other sources within the brain. Immediate cross-correlations result, and these can add in turn to produce new patterns of nerve impulses.

The hypothesis presented here is that the totality of this process has a more or less lasting effect on protein molecules and perhaps other macromolecules at the synaptic junctions and can serve as a neural hologram from which, given the appropriate input, an image can be reconstructed. The attractive feature of the hypothesis is that the information is distributed throughout the stored hologram and is thus resistant to insult. If even a small corner of a hologram is illuminated by the appropriate input, the entire original scene reappears. Moreover, holograms can be layered one on top of the other and yet be separately reconstructed.

The holographic hypothesis imme-

diately raises many questions. Do the mathematical expressions that interpret the shape of visual receptive fields at the ganglion-cell layer of the retina yield equally useful interpretations at more central stations in the visual system? What kind of neural reference mechanism plays the role of the coherent light source needed to make and display holograms? Perhaps a kind of coherence results from the anatomical fact that the retina and the visual cortex are linked by many thousands of fibers arranged in parallel pathways. Or it could be that the nerve cells in the visual channel achieve coherence by rhythmic firing. Still another possibility is that coherence results from the operation of the variety of detectors that respond to such simple aspects of stimuli as the tilt of a line and movement that have recently received so much attention [see the article "The Visual Cortex of the Brain,"

by David H. Hubel, beginning on page 253].

Other questions that flow from the holographic hypothesis are concerned with the storage of the memory trace. Two alternatives come to mind. The first involves a "tuning" of cell assemblies by changing synaptic characteristics so that a particular circuit will somehow resonate when it receives a familiar "note"; the second is some form of molecular storage, perhaps involving a change in structure at the synapses. Of course circuit-tuning may be secondary to just such structural changes, or the job may be done by a mechanism as yet unimagined. Such questions can be and are being investigated in the laboratory with techniques available today.

There is another line of investigation demonstrating that representations of

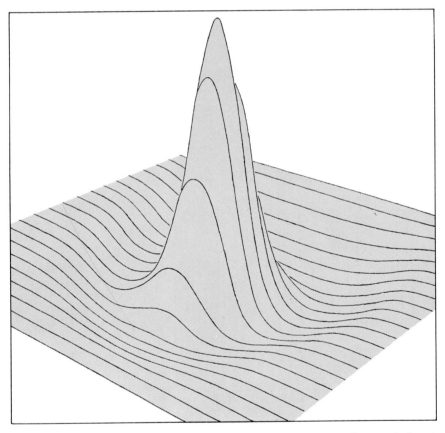

IDEALIZED MAP OF VISUAL RECEPTIVE FIELD represents recordings made from a single ganglion cell in the retina of the eye when a point source of light is presented in various parts of the visual field. The map contains smooth contour lines because the ganglion cell integrates the response of its neighbors, with which it is interconnected. The height of the contour at any point represents the number of times the individual nerve cell fires when the location of the point light source corresponds to that position on the map. Maximum firing occurs when the position of the light corresponds to that of the central peak. In mathematical terms, each contour line represents the "convolutional integral" of the first derivative of the shape of the stimulus figure. The interaction of many such convolutional integrals may produce hologram-like interference patterns within the visual system and elsewhere in the brain. Storage of such patterns could provide the basis of memory.

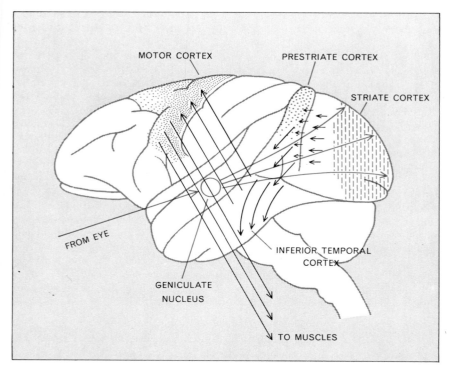

OLD VIEW OF VISUAL-RECOGNITION MECHANISM assumed that after visual information reached the striate cortex it was transferred to the prestriate cortex in two steps and from there to the inferior temporal cortex. Muscular response, according to the old view, then required that a message travel from the inferior temporal cortex to the precentral cortex (the motor cortex), which responded by sending signals down the brainstem to the muscles.

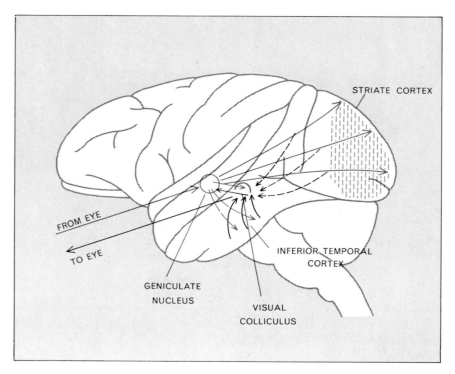

NEW VIEW OF VISUAL-RECOGNITION MECHANISM emphasizes the recent evidence that impulses from the inferior temporal cortex directly modify the visual input *before* it reaches the striate cortex *(see illustration on page 394)*. This modification takes place subcortically through tracts leading to the visual colliculus and through interactions between that part of the brainstem and the lateral geniculate nucleus. There is also some evidence for an indirect pathway from the retina to the inferior temporal cortex. Visual information also seems to flow from the visual cortex to the visual colliculus. In the new view the body's muscle responses are relatively independent of the visual-recognition mechanism.

experience are distributed after entering the brain. The experiments I have described thus far demonstrated a distribution in space. There is also distribution in time; there are mechanisms in the brain for temporally distributing, or holding, events long enough so that they can be firmly registered. The evidence comes from an important group of experiments showing how animals (including man) gradually become habituated to a novel stimulus. Until recently habituation was thought to be due to a fatiguing of the nervous system. Eugene Sokolov of the University of Moscow showed, however, that when one is habituated, one can be dishabituated, that is, "oriented" anew, by a lowering in the intensity of the stimulus or even by complete silence when stimuli are expected. I like to call it the "Bowery-el phenomenon." For many years there was an elevated railway line (the "el") on Third Avenue in New York that made a fearful racket; when it was torn down, people who had been living in apartments along the line awakened periodically out of a sound sleep to call the police about some strange occurrence they could not properly define. Many such calls came at the times the trains had formerly rumbled past. The strange occurrences were of course the deafening silence that had replaced the expected noise.

In laboratory studies of this phenomenon the physiological concomitants of the orienting reaction are recorded and their reduction allows habituation to be investigated. The orienting reaction includes, among other things, changes in the conductivity of the skin (the galvanic skin response), changes in heart rate and respiratory rate, and changes in the electroencephalogram. Muriel H. Bagshaw and I found that we had to separate these physiological indicators of the orienting reaction into two classes. This was necessary because after we had surgically removed the frontal lobes of a monkey's brain, or the brainstem region known as the amygdala, the orienting stimulus no longer evoked the galvanic skin response or changes in heart rate and respiratory rate. (The responses themselves were not destroyed, because they could be evoked under other conditions.) On the other hand, surgery did not eliminate certain changes in the electroencephalogram and certain behavioral changes that also occur as a part of the orienting reaction. Surgery also interfered with habituation: a monkey lacking his frontal lobes or his amygdala continued much longer to show the behavioral and electroencephalographic orienting reactions. These results suggested that the loss of

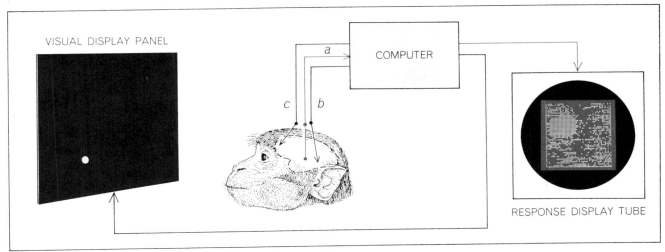

INVESTIGATION OF VISUAL RECEPTIVE FIELDS is carried out by presenting a monkey with a small source of light that is systematically moved from point to point in a raster-like pattern. At each point the response of a single cell in the lateral geniculate nucleus is recorded by a microelectrode (*a*). During this mapping a weak electrical stimulus can be delivered to other parts of the brain, such as the inferior temporal cortex (*b*) or the frontal cortex (*c*), to see if there is any effect. Some typical results are illustrated on the next page. The technique, which relies heavily on the computer, was developed by the author's colleague Nico Spinelli.

galvanic skin responses and heart and respiratory changes precluded habituation; when these indicators of orienting were not present, the stimulus, although perceived, failed to be registered in memory.

We have all had the experience of being preoccupied while a friend is recounting his experiences to us. Finally in exasperation he may say, "You aren't listening." Caught unaware, you may still be able quickly to repeat your friend's last sentence and from this even reconstruct what the "conversation" was about. If, however, your reverie is allowed to continue, much of what reached your ears will have been irretrievably lost; things just did not register. Thus there are two classes of indicators of orienting: the one concerned with just "sampling" the input, the other with its "registration," or storage.

E. D. Homskaya in the laboratory of A. R. Luria in Moscow and Mrs. Bagshaw in our laboratory at the Stanford University School of Medicine have also demonstrated that removal of the frontal lobes or the amygdala interferes with the indicators of registration when they appear in classical conditioning experiments. In normal animals the conditioning cue (such as a bell or a light) evokes changes in the galvanic skin response, in heart rate and in respiratory rate, as well as in the electroencephalogram. As the conditioning trials continue, these changes take place earlier and earlier until they actually precede the conditioning cue. It is as if the subject of the experiment were rehearsing the situation, anticipating what is coming next. After removal of the frontal lobes or the amyg-

dala, however, this rehearsal apparently ceases. Thus one can demonstrate that both anticipation and registration—a temporal distribution of mnemic events—take place in a normal subject, and that these processes are impaired by surgery in certain parts of the brain. There is as yet little evidence to indicate how these parts of the brain bring about this temporal distribution of mnemic events.

Given the fact that mnemic events become distributed in the brain, what happens during remembering? Some kind of organizing process is clearly required. Experimental data make it likely that this process involves the "association cortex" of primates such as monkeys and man [*see top illustration on page 389*]. These regions are not to be confused with the "polysensory association cortex" that immediately surrounds the sensory projection areas and that has been studied so intensively in cats. The primate association areas consist of two general classes: the frontal and the posterior. The posterior association areas are located among the various primary sensory areas and consist of subareas that are specific for each of the senses.

In operations on several hundred monkeys my colleagues and I have made many kinds of lesion in this posterior system; the type, the size and the location of the lesions were based on a variety of anatomical and physiological criteria. These monkeys have been tested for their ability to learn and to retain discrimination tasks involving four senses. Vision is studied with a variety of patterns, colors and brightnesses; touch, with unseen objects of different shapes

and textures; taste, with samples differing in bitterness or sweetness; hearing, with different sound patterns. From the results of such experiments we are able to subdivide the posterior association cortex into areas, each serving a particular sense. These investigations show that the parieto-occipital area is concerned with touch, the anterior temporal cortex with taste, the middle temporal region with hearing. The inferior temporal cortex is important to visual discrimination [*see illustrations on page 389*].

These results present a number of questions. Why, following the removal of the inferior temporal cortex, do monkeys fail completely to accomplish visual discriminations while being perfectly able to accomplish discriminations in other senses and to perform more complex tasks, such as tasks involving delayed reactions and alternation of response? The problem is complicated by the following facts. Visual information passes from the retina to a relay point called the lateral geniculate nucleus and thence to the occipital (or striate) cortex. It had long been taught that the occipital cortex then sends information out to the surrounding areas, and that the information finally reaches the inferior temporal cortex. Since our monkeys fail in visual discrimination tasks after the removal of the inferior temporal cortex, the classical teaching would seem to be supported. Other considerations nonetheless argue that the classical view must be wrong.

First of all, the anatomical evidence shows that nerve impulses would have to be relayed by three synapses in traveling from the occipital cortex to the inferior temporal region. Three synapses, however, can get a signal from anywhere to almost anywhere else in the brain, so that this is hardly sufficient evidence for a mechanism that demands strict sensory specificity. Second, Chow, in a series of experiments confirmed by my own, removed all the tissue surrounding the occipital cortex in monkeys, so that the primary visual receiving area is totally isolated from the inferior temporal cortex. Such animals show no loss of visual performance in spite of the fact that a lesion in the inferior temporal cortex only a third or a quarter the size of the one made in the disconnection experiment will cause serious impairment on the same tasks. This makes it most unlikely that impulses reaching the inferior temporal cortex from the upper regions of the visual system account for the importance of this cortex in vision.

What, then, is the mechanism that enables the inferior temporal cortex to play such a key role in the performance of visual tasks? Where does it get its information and where does it send it? The available evidence (much of which I have had to omit in this brief account) has led me to propose that the inferior temporal cortex exerts its control by organizing the traffic in the primary visual system. Recently the pathways from the inferior temporal cortex to the visual system have been traced. Applying the methods of electrophysiology, Spinelli and I have found, for example, that we can change the size and shape of visual receptive fields by stimulating the inferior temporal cortex [see illustration below]. These and other experiments demonstrate beyond doubt that the inferior temporal cortex is not the passive recipient of data relayed from the primary visual cortex, as was long believed, but actively influences what enters the visual cortex. Similar results have been obtained in the auditory system by James H. Dewson in my laboratory.

An experiment that tells us a little about the meaning of this control over input is currently being completed by my associate Lauren Gerbrandt. A monkey sits in a chair inside a box that can be opened, so that he can see out, or closed. He can be stimulated through an electrode placed in the lateral geniculate nucleus (the relay station in the visual input system) while we record the level of activity in the visual cortex. When the box is closed, geniculate stimulation evokes only a small response in the cortex. When the box is open, the response is large. Gerbrandt found, however, that he could augment the strength of the cortical response when the box is closed (and only then) by stimulation of

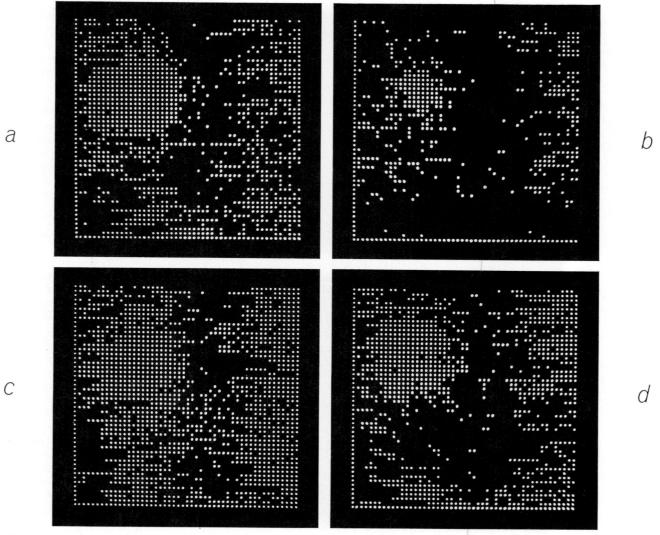

VISUAL-RECEPTIVE-FIELD MAPS, made by the technique illustrated on the preceding page, show how information flowing through the primary visual pathway is altered by stimulation elsewhere in the brain. Map *a* is the normal response of a cell in the geniculate nucleus when a light source is moved through a rasterlike pattern. Map *b* shows how the field is contracted by stimulation of the inferior temporal cortex. Map *c* shows the expansion produced by stimulation of the frontal cortex. Map *d* is a final control.

the inferior temporal cortex. The response is then as strong as when the monkey is alertly looking about, examining the world around him. This suggests to us that electrical stimulation of the association cortex crudely reproduces the neural activity that goes on naturally when the animal is actively engaged in sampling and attending his visual environment.

A detailed and satisfactory mechanism for explaining these results remains to be worked out. A tentative hypothesis supported by considerable anatomical evidence, and very recently by limited electrophysiological evidence, might go something like this. There is evidently an input from the visual pathway, rather separate from the primary visual pathway, that leads to the inferior temporal cortex. This visual input to the inferior temporal cortex triggers a process that feeds back into the primary visual system and there exercises a control over the flow of visual impulses to the visual cortex [see bottom illustration on page 392]. This view is based on such evidence as our ability to change the size and shape of the visual fields in the optic nerve and lateral geniculate nucleus by stimulation of the inferior temporal cortex.

This, however, can be only a part of the story. A satisfactory hypothesis also has to explain the first experiment I described, in which recordings from the visual cortex foreshadowed the monkey's intention to press either the right or the left panel when he was presented with a circle or vertical stripes. Here we have evidence that the frontal cortex and the amygdala, which are involved in registration, also affect the visual mechanism, often in a direction just opposite to what is produced by stimulation of the inferior temporal cortex.

Pathways from the visual cortex to the superior colliculus of the brainstem are well known. Recently we have traced similar pathways from the inferior temporal cortex to this same superior colliculus, which is an important structure in the visual system. (In birds the collicular region plays a role comparable to the role of the cerebral cortex in primates.) One can now begin to see how surgically isolating the visual cortex from the inferior temporal cortex does not destroy an animal's capacity to perform visual tasks. Evidently the communication link between the visual cortex and the inferior temporal cortex (which is essential to the retention of visual discriminations) is buried deep within the brainstem. Just as the brainstem serves

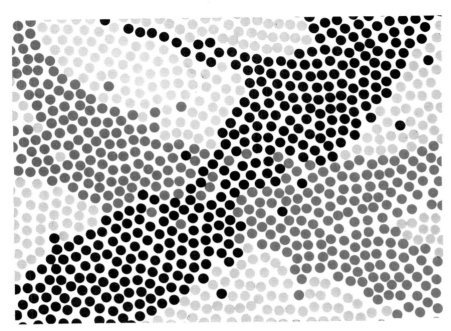

INTERSECTION OF NERVE PATHWAYS in the visual-input channel can be depicted schematically in two dimensions by an array of dots, each representing a single nerve cell. The response of each cell in turn can be visualized as corresponding to the patterns shown in the visual-receptive-field maps presented on page 394. At a given instant a stimulus arising in a particular part of the visual field will cause a certain group of cells (color) to respond. Simultaneously a stimulus in another part of the field will excite a different group (black). Gray cells are inactive at this instant. As long as the scene in the visual field remains constant, these same groups of cells will "flash" off and on many times a second. The interference patterns resulting from the interacting fields of the flashing cells may provide the opportunity for the formation of holographic patterns. This diagram first appeared in "The Physiology of Imagination," by John C. Eccles; SCIENTIFIC AMERICAN, September, 1958.

as a convergence station for the visual system, it serves (on the basis of Dewson's evidence) a similar function in hearing. The importance of such subcortical convergences, which in turn alter the input to the cortex, has been highlighted by these experiments.

Further evidence for this cortico-subcortical mode of operation of the brain (as opposed to a transcortical mode) comes from the same group of experiments in which our animals learned to distinguish between circles and stripes while a record of their brain waves was being made. The reason for doing these experiments in the first place was that I wanted to see how the wave forms recorded from various parts of the brain would be altered by making lesions in the inferior temporal cortex after the monkeys had learned their task. I fully expected that a lesion would selectively affect one of the wave forms and would leave others unchanged. Thus (I hoped) we would be able to identify the mechanism that accounted for the monkey's failure to perform satisfactorily after the lesion. We might conclude, for example, that the lesion had interfered with the monkey's capacity to differentiate between circles and stripes or that it had

interfered with some process linked to reinforcement or response. This is not what happened.

Instead of finding a selective change in one or another of these electrical waves, we found that the electrodes that provided the best differential recordings in advance of surgery subsequently showed no such differences; other electrodes whose wave forms had been undifferentiated now showed persistent and reliable differences. These differences turned out to be associated, for the most part, with responses, but in very peculiar ways that we have not as yet been able to decipher clearly.

It seems as if the frame of reference within which the brain activity had been working before the lesions were made was now shifted, and in fact was shifting from time to time. Judging by their behavior, the monkeys were as surprised by the effects of the surgery as we were. They approached their task confident of their ability to solve the problems, only to find they made errors (and hence received no peanut). This resulted in spurts, hesitations and variability in performance. It seemed as if they were completely baffled, not realizing, of course, that it was the inside of their

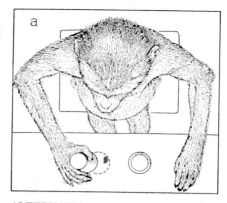 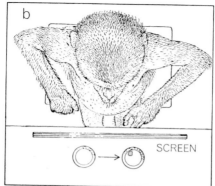 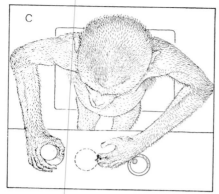

ALTERNATION TASK requires that a monkey remember which cup he lifted last in order to lift the correct one on his next trial and be rewarded with a peanut. Normally he is rewarded if he remembers to lift the cups in a simple alternating sequence: left, right, left and so on. After each trial a screen comes between him and the cups and remains there for periods that can be varied from seconds to many minutes. In part *c* of this sequence the monkey has forgotten to alternate his response. Experiments demonstrate that certain brain lesions interfere with a monkey's ability to remember what he did even a few seconds earlier. By changing the task only slightly, however, the author found that brain-damaged monkeys were no longer perplexed *(see illustration on page 397)*.

heads and not the situation that we had changed. What is the explanation?

Whatever the transformations of input (holographic or otherwise) that occur in the nervous system, such transformations are in effect coding operations. In order for a code to work, that is, to be decipherable, it must be framed within a context. This context must remain stable or the information conveyed by the code will be destroyed by successive transformations. Our reading of the recordings of the electrical brain activity of the monkeys who had their inferior temporal cortex removed is that the framework within which their discriminations had been made before surgery was now disrupted and shifting. The events observed by these monkeys no longer conveyed information because their brains had in a sense become unstable.

As a hypothesis this can be tested. We are about to investigate means of providing externally the stability that the brains of the brain-damaged monkeys evidently lack. Sandra Reitz, a student in my laboratory, recently suggested that this could be done simply by increasing the spatial redundancy of the visual cues (that is, the number of identical displays) that we present to our monkeys on a discrimination task. The expectation is, if our view is correct, that this change in the task will overcome the difficulty in discrimination experienced by the monkeys with lesions of the inferior temporal cortex.

Therefore a beginning has been made in specifying the structures that participate in the organization of memory inside the brain. The next task is to discover *how* these structures accomplish the physiological processes we call remembering, whether by holographic

representations or by some process even more subtle. In our concern with the storage mechanism, however, we should never overlook that aspect of memory which is of overriding importance to the process of effective remembering: the method of organizing or coding what is to be remembered.

In everyday life there are many homely examples to show that a given message is easier to remember in one form than in another. For example, rhymes are often employed in aphorisms ("A stitch in time saves nine"); many people cannot remember the number of days in the month without first recalling the jingle of their childhood. A more important example of the value of efficient coding is found in the 0–9 method of writing down numbers compared with the clumsy system of the Romans. By employing the concept of zero to indicate multiples of 10 our mathematical tasks are vastly simplified.

A coding mechanism need not necessarily be very complicated. Take, for example, the following "poem," which the neurophysiologist Warren McCulloch likes to intone with bishop-like solemnity: INMUDEELSARE/INCLAYNONEARE/INPINETARIS/INOAKNONEIS. When spaces are inserted where they belong, the message instantly becomes clear: IN MUD EELS ARE/IN CLAY NONE ARE/IN PINE TAR IS/IN OAK NONE IS. The passage has been decoded by the simple procedure of parsing, or what the psychologist George A. Miller, my sometime collaborator who is now at Rockefeller University, calls "chunking" [see "Information and Memory," by George A. Miller; SCIENTIFIC AMERICAN Offprint 419].

Many experiments with monkeys demonstrate that the frontal cortex—long regarded as the site of the "highest

mental faculties" in man and primates—plays an important role in short-term memory, whatever else it may be doing. When sufficiently complex tests, comparable to those used with monkeys, are given to lobotomized patients, they too show this memory disturbance. My experiments provide strong evidence that the primate frontal cortex performs its role by means of a coding operation that seems to resemble parsing, or chunking. When the frontal cortex of a monkey is damaged, the animal has difficulty performing tasks in which he has to remember what happened just a few seconds earlier.

Typical of such tasks is one in which the monkey faces two identical cups with lids that he must raise in a particular sequence to obtain a peanut [see illustration above]. In the simplest case he is rewarded with a peanut at each trial if he simply remembers to lift the lids alternately: left, right, left and so on. Then he must wait a specified interval, which can be varied from a few seconds to hours, between each trial, and while he is waiting an opaque screen is interposed between him and the cups. His task, then, is to remember which lid he lifted last so that he can lift the other one on the next trial. A monkey whose frontal cortex has been resected will fail at this simple task even when the interval between trials is reduced to three seconds.

It occurred to me that perhaps the task appears to these monkeys much as an unparsed passage does to us. I therefore changed the task so that the rewarded sequence became left-right (long interval), left-right (long interval) and so on. There was still a mandatory pause with the screen interposed of five seconds between each left-right trial, but now a longer interval of 15 seconds was inserted between *pairs* of trials. Immediately the monkeys with frontal cortex damage performed as successfully as the control animals whose brains were intact [*see illustration below*]. That time-parsing was the key to the success of the brain-damaged monkeys was shown by other experiments in which the interval between trials was held constant but some other clue, such as a red light or a buzzer, was presented at every other trial. The clues were ignored; the monkeys with frontal lobe resections still failed at the task.

The experiment is important in several respects. First, it demonstrates at least one function of the frontal lobes, a func-tion that may be basic to other func-tions. Second, it suggests that the diffi-culty the brain-damaged monkey has in recalling what he did last is not due sim-ply to a premature fading of the mem-ory trace; after all, he improved quickly when a longer interval was interposed, provided that the task was adequately structured. Third, this structuring, or-ganizing or coding is in fact crucial to the process of recall.

Other studies show that the frontal cortex, like the posterior association cortex, exercises control over sensory in-formation flowing into the cortical re-ceiving areas. In many instances, as I have noted, electrical stimulation of the frontal cortex produces effects that are opposite to those produced by posterior stimulation. Our studies are not ad-vanced enough as yet to specify which pathways from the frontal lobes may be involved. Recent work done by Donald B. Lindsley and Carmine D. Clemente at the Brain Research Institute of the Uni-versity of California at Los Angeles indi-cates that the pathway involved may be a large tract of fibers (running in the medial forebrain bundle) that carries in-hibitory impulses to the reticular forma-tion of the brainstem. I have on occa-sion attempted to spell out some possible relations between neural inhibitory proc-esses and short-term memory but such efforts are at best tentative.

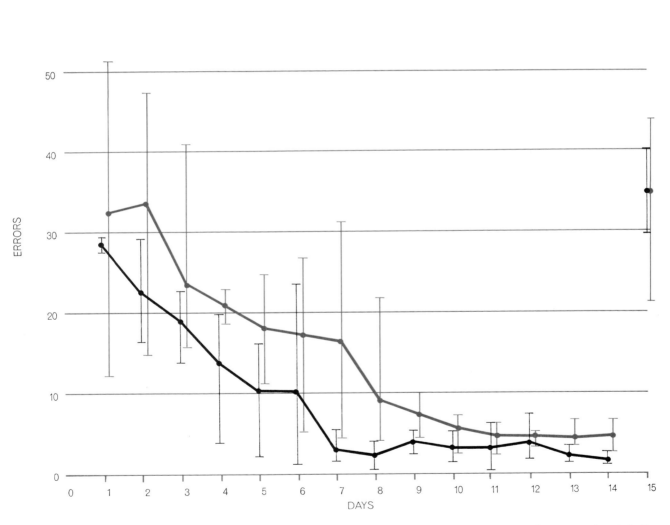

MODIFIED ALTERNATION TASK could be mastered as readily by monkeys with part of their frontal cortex removed *(colored curve)* as by normal monkeys *(black curve)*. The brain-damaged monkeys had been unable to solve the standard left-right alterna-tion task *(described in the illustration on page 396)* even when the interval between trials was only a few seconds. The task was then modified so that the interval between each left-and-right trial was kept brief (five seconds) but a 15-second pause was inserted after every right-hand trial. When this change was made, brain-damaged monkeys performed about as well as normal monkeys, as shown here. Errors are the number made each day before a monkey achieved 40 successful trials. Bars indicate the range of errors made by different monkeys. Data for the 15th day show the result when all the trials were again separated by equal intervals of five seconds.

Coding and recoding are thus found to be essential operations in both memory storage and remembering. I have described evidence showing clearly that storage is distributed throughout a sensory system. I have also mentioned some evidence suggesting that the transformations (coding operations) that are performed within the input channels can be described in terms of convolutional integrals. The basic premise involved is that neighboring neural elements do not work independently of one another. By virtue of lateral interactions, neural elements spatially superpose the excitatory and inhibitory electrical potentials that arise among neighboring nerve cells. These transformations generate a microstructure of postsynaptic events, which can be regarded as wave fronts that set up interference patterns with other (preexisting or internally generated) wave fronts, producing in their totality something resembling a hologram. Given a mechanism capable of storing this hologram, an image could be evoked at some later time by the appropriate input. In order to be effective as codes, transformations must take place within some stable framework. To an extent this framework can be provided by the stored microstructure itself, by the parallel pathways of the input system, by the specific detector sensitivities of units in the system and by the very redundancy of the external environment. (We have no trouble recognizing automobiles because there are so many of them and they are so much alike.)

For complex and novel events, however, a more powerful organizer must come into action. Experiments conducted in my laboratory and elsewhere suggest that this organizing mechanism critically involves the association areas of the cerebral cortex. The mechanism does not, however, seem to reside within these areas. Rather, the association areas exercise control on the input system by way of deeper structures in the brainstem. In short, the function of the association areas of the cortex turns out to be that of providing a major part of the organizing process necessary to remembering: the reconstruction of an image from distributed mnemic events.

X

COMPLEX PROCESSES:
THOUGHT, LANGUAGE, AND ATTENTION

X

COMPLEX PROCESSES: THOUGHT, LANGUAGE, AND ATTENTION

INTRODUCTION

Thought and language are the most complex and important human activities. In normal adults, the two processes cannot easily be separated. We tend to think in words, and, under normal circumstances, thinking is almost invariably accompanied by small responses of the vocal apparatus. Such peripheral responses, however, are not essential to thinking in man, and they are obviously absent in the thinking activities of nonhuman animals. Thinking is by no means the exclusive property of man—higher animals can think very well indeed and can solve complex problems. We are just beginning to have some idea of the behavioral properties and brain mechanisms of thinking—it is an area of research with a short past and a long future.

Language is truly the supreme and unique accomplishment of *Homo sapiens.* Many species of animals communicate: some with chemicals, as is common with fish and insects; some with elaborate behavior patterns, as in the nectar dance of the bee and the complex courting behavior of birds; and many with gestures and vocalizations, as is common among higher mammals, particularly the primates. (There is evidence, for example, that the hand-wave greeting is common to all higher primates, not just to man.) However, possession of language with syntax (that is, a formal structure for the sequences of sounds or symbols in communication) is unique to man. Linguistic studies of the "universal" properties of human language and the development of language in the individual suggest that, for normal individuals living in the company of others, language is an inevitable and universal consequence of possessing a human brain. The newly emerging discipline of neurolinguistics is concerned with these mechanisms. It is likely that within a very few years this will be a profoundly important field of study. Because we use language with such great ease and complexity, we tend to forget that it, like the other aspects of our behavior, is a biological phenomenon. It is an expression of the complex aspects of the organization and function of the brain.

In the first article in this, the last section, "Learning to Think," Harry F. and Margaret Kuenne Harlow analyze the fundamental problem of how thinking develops through past experience. They describe their now-classic discovery of the "learning set." When a monkey (or human child) is given a long series of similar problems to solve, he does not merely learn how to solve each problem in the same way, he also learns how to learn. His performance on successive problems becomes better, until he can solve each new problem in a single trial.

He acts as though he has insight into the nature of the problem. Adult humans exhibit "insight" very commonly. The point of the Harlow's work is that these insights, for monkey and man, come through vast experience with solving problems.

The next article, "The Functional Organization of the Brain," is by A. R. Luria, a leading Soviet brain scientist. Luria treats the functions of the association areas of the cerebral cortex. These are the areas of the brain that have developed most in primate evolution. The greater expansion of these areas in man is the primary neurological feature that distinguishes man from ape. Luria emphasizes the role of association cortex in language functions, particularly speech and writing; his article serves as an introduction to neurolinguistics, the study of the brain mechanisms of language. "The Origin of Speech," by Charles F. Hockett, is the next article in this section. Hockett compares communication throughout the animal kingdom in terms of a number of "design-features" that characterize language: it is clear that no infrahuman communication systems qualify as language. Hockett considers modern languages, including the historical development of modern Indo-European tongues, and emphasizes the fundamental and surprising fact that all human languages, no matter how primitive the culture, are equally rich, complex, and developed. His articles is an excellent survey of modern linguistics from a biological point of view.

The final article is Donald E. Broadbent's "Attention and the Perception of Speech." As Broadbent points out, the normal child learns language entirely through hearing it spoken. Reading, writing, and other elaborations of speech are secondary. Consequently, to understand language we must understand the biological mechanisms that underlie the perception of speech. Broadbent surveys the auditory system in terms of how it responds to speech sounds, and develops an analysis of how we perceive speech. A basic fact about speech is that we can really only attend to one voice message at a time. This observation raises the complex issue of what is meant by "attention." Although much has been written about brain mechanisms of attention, little is really known. Broadbent's article is concerned with the facts of selective response to multiple speech inputs—that is, comprehension of two different voice messages presented simultaneously, one in each ear. His work provides a solid empirical base of information about attentive behavior in the perception of language.

43

LEARNING TO THINK

HARRY F. AND MARGARET KUENNE HARLOW
August 1949

HOW does an infant, born with only a few simple reactions, develop into an adult capable of rapid learning and the almost incredibly complex mental processes known as thinking? This is one of psychology's unsolved problems. Most modern explanations are not much more enlightening than those offered by 18th-century French and English philosophers, who suggested that the mind developed merely by the process of associating ideas or experiences with one another. Even the early philosophers realized that this was not a completely adequate explanation.

The speed and complexity of a human being's mental processes, and the intricacy of the nerve mechanisms that presumably underlie them, suggest that the brain is not simply a passive network of communications but develops some kind of organization that facilitates learning and thinking. Whether such organizing principles exist has been a matter of considerable dispute. At one extreme, some modern psychologists deny that they do and describe learning as a mere trial-and-error process—a blind fumbling about until a solution accidentally appears. At the other extreme, there are psychologists who hold that people learn through an innate insight that reveals relationships to them.

To investigate, and to reconcile if possible, these seemingly antagonistic positions, a series of studies of the learning process has been carried out at the University of Wisconsin. Some of these have been made with young children, but most of the research has been on monkeys.

For two basic reasons animals are particularly good subjects for the investigation of learning at a fundamental level. One is that it is possible to control their entire learning history: the psychologist knows the problems to which they have been exposed, the amount of training they have had on each, and the record of their performance. The other reason is that the animals' adaptive processes are more simple than those of human beings, especially during the first stages of the attack on a problem. Often the animal's reactions throw into clear relief certain mechanisms that operate more

obscurely in man. Of course this is only a relative simplicity. All the higher mammals possess intricate nervous systems and can solve complex problems. Indeed, it is doubtful that man possesses any fundamental intellectual process, except true language, that is not also present in his more lowly biological brethren.

Tests of animal learning of the trial-and-error type have been made in innumerable laboratories. In the special tests devised for our experiments, we set out to determine whether monkeys could progress from trial-and-error learning to the ability to solve a problem immediately by insight.

One of the first experiments was a simple discrimination test. The monkeys were confronted with a small board on which lay two objects different in color, size and shape. If a monkey picked up the correct object, it was rewarded by finding raisins or peanuts underneath. The position of the objects was shifted on the board in an irregular manner from trial to trial, and the trials were continued until the monkey learned to choose the correct object. The unusual feature of the experiment was that the test was repeated many times, with several hundred different pairs of objects. In other words, instead of training a monkey to solve a single problem, as had been done in most previous psychological work of this kind, we trained the animal on many problems, all of the same general type, but with varying kinds of objects.

When the monkeys first faced this test, they learned by the slow, laborious, fumble-and-find process. But as a monkey solved problem after problem of the same basic kind, its behavior changed in a most dramatic way. It learned each new problem with progressively greater efficiency, until eventually the monkey showed perfect insight when faced with this particular kind of situation—it solved the problem in one trial. If it chose the correct object on the first trial, it rarely made an error on subsequent trials. If it chose the incorrect object on the first trial, it immediately shifted to the correct object, and subsequently responded almost perfectly.

Thus the test appeared to demonstrate that trial-and-error and insight are but

two different phases of one long continuous process. They are not different capacities, but merely represent the orderly development of a learning and thinking process.

A LONG series of these discrimination problems was also run on a group of nursery-school children two to five years of age. Young children were chosen because they have a minimum of previous experience. The conditions in the children's tests were only slightly different from those for the monkeys: they were rewarded by finding brightly colored macaroni beads instead of raisins and peanuts. Most of the children, like the monkeys, made many errors in the early stages of the tests and only gradually learned to solve a problem in one trial. As a group the children learned more rapidly than the monkeys, but they made the same types of errors. And the "smartest" monkeys learned faster than the "dullest" children.

We have called this process of progressive learning the formation of a "learning set." The subject learns an organized set of habits that enables him to meet effectively each new problem of this particular kind. A single set would provide only limited aid in enabling an animal to adapt to an ever-changing environment. But a host of different learning sets may supply the raw material for human thinking.

We have trained monkeys and children to solve problems much more complex than the ones thus far described. For instance, a deliberate attempt is made to confuse the subjects by reversing the conditions of the discrimination test. The previously correct object is no longer rewarded, and the previously incorrect object is always rewarded. When monkeys and children face this switch-over for the first time, they make many errors, persistently choosing the objects they had previously been trained to choose. Gradually, from problem to problem, the number of such errors decreases until finally the first reversal trial is followed by perfect performance. A single failure becomes the cue to the subject to shift his choice from the object which has been rewarded many times to the object

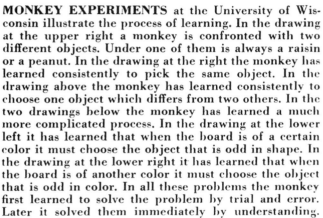

MONKEY EXPERIMENTS at the University of Wisconsin illustrate the process of learning. In the drawing at the upper right a monkey is confronted with two different objects. Under one of them is always a raisin or a peanut. In the drawing at the right the monkey has learned consistently to pick the same object. In the drawing above the monkey has learned consistently to choose one object which differs from two others. In the two drawings below the monkey has learned a much more complicated process. In the drawing at the lower left it has learned that when the board is of a certain color it must choose the object that is odd in shape. In the drawing at the lower right it has learned that when the board is of another color it must choose the object that is odd in color. In all these problems the monkey first learned to solve the problem by trial and error. Later it solved them immediately by understanding.

which has never been rewarded before. In this type of test children learn much more rapidly than monkeys.

A group of monkeys that had formed the discrimination-reversal learning set was later trained on a further refinement of the problem. This time the reward value of the objects was reversed for only one trial, and was then shifted back to the original relationship. After many problems, the monkeys learned to ignore the single reversal and treated it as if the experimenter had made an error!

The problem was made more complicated, in another test, by offering the subjects a choice among three objects instead of two. There is a tray containing three food wells. Two are covered by one kind of object, and the third is covered by another kind. The animal must choose the odd object. Suppose the objects are building blocks and funnels. In half the trials, there are two blocks and a funnel, and the correct object is the funnel. Then a switch is made to two funnels and one block. Now the correct object is the block. The animal must learn a subtle distinction here: it is not the shape of the object that is important, but its relation to the other two. The meaning of a specific object may change from trial to trial. This problem is something like the one a child faces in trying to learn to use the words "I," "you," and "he" properly. The meaning of the words changes according to the speaker. When the child is speaking, "I" refers to himself, "you" to the person addressed, and "he" to some third person. When the child is addressed, the child is no longer "I" but "you." And when others speak of him, the terms shift again.

Monkeys and children were trained on a series of these oddity problems, 24 trials being allowed for the solution of each problem. At first they floundered, but they improved from problem to problem until they learned to respond to each new problem with perfect or nearly perfect scores. And on this complex type of problem the monkeys did better than most of the children!

ONE of the most striking findings from these tests was that once the monkeys have formed these learning sets, they retain them for long periods and can use them appropriately as the occasion demands. After a lapse of a year or more, a monkey regains top efficiency, in a few minutes or hours of practice, on a problem that it may have taken many weeks to master originally.

All our studies indicate that the ability to solve problems without fumbling is not inborn but is acquired gradually. So we must re-examine the evidence offered in support of the theory that animals possess some innate insight that has nothing to do with learning.

The cornerstone of this theory is the work of the famous Gestalt psychologist Wolfgang Köhler on the behavior of chimpanzees. In a series of brilliant studies he clearly showed that these apes can use sticks to help them obtain bananas beyond their reach. They employed the sticks to knock the bananas down, to rake them in, to climb and to vault. The animals sometimes assembled short sticks to make a pole long enough to reach the food, and even used sticks in combination with stacked boxes to knock down high-dangling bait. That the chimpanzees frequently solved these problems suddenly, as if by a flash of insight, impressed Köhler as evidence of an ability to reason independently of learning. He even suggested that this ability might differentiate apes and men from other animals.

Unfortunately, since Köhler's animals had been captured in the jungle, he had no record of their previous learning. Recent studies on chimpanzees born in captivity at the Yerkes Laboratory of Primate Biology at Orange Park, Fla., throw doubt on the validity of Köhler's interpretations. Herbert Birch of the Yerkes Laboratory reported that when he gave sticks to four-year-old chimps in their cages, they showed little sign at first of ability to use them as tools. Gradually, in the course of three days, they learned to use the sticks to touch objects beyond their reach. Later the animals solved very simple stick problems fairly well, but they had difficulty with more complex problems.

Extending Birch's investigations, the late Paul Schiller presented a series of stick tasks to a group of chimpanzees from two to over eight years of age. The younger the animal, the more slowly it mastered the problems. Some young subjects took hundreds of trials to perform efficiently on even the simplest problems, while old, experienced animals solved them with little practice. None of the apes solved the tasks initially with sudden insight.

Even at the human level there is no evidence that children possess any innate endowment that enables them to solve tool problems with insight. Augusta Alpert of Columbia University tried some of Köhler's simple chimpanzee tests on bright nursery-school children. The younger children typically went through a trial-and-error process before solving the problems. Some of them failed to solve the easiest problem in the series in five experimental sessions.

Eunice Mathieson presented more difficult Köhler-type tasks to a group of University of Minnesota nursery-school children. The results were even more overwhelmingly against the notion that tool problems are solved by flashes of natural insight. The children rarely solved a problem without making many mistakes.

This research, then, supports our findings. In all clear-cut tests—that is, whenever the animals' entire learning history is known—monkeys, apes and children at first solve problems by trial and error. Only gradually does such behavior give way to immediate solutions.

WE began by pointing out that psychologists have sought to find in the higher mental processes some organizing mechanism or principle that would explain learning and thinking. We can now suggest such a mechanism: the learning set. Suppose we picture mental activity as a continuous structure built up, step by step, by the solution of increasingly difficult problems, from the simplest problem in learning to the most complex one in thinking. At each level the individual tries out various responses to solve each given task. At the lowest level he selects from unlearned responses or previously learned habits. As his experience increases, habits that do not help in the solution drop out and useful habits become established. After solving many problems of a certain kind, he develops organized patterns of responses that meet the demands of this type of situation. These patterns, or learning sets, can also be applied to the solution of still more complex problems. Eventually the individual may organize simple learning sets into more complex patterns of learning sets, which in turn are available for transfer as units to new situations.

Thus the individual learns to cope with more and more difficult problems. At the highest stage in this progression, the intelligent human adult selects from innumerable, previously acquired learning sets the raw material for thinking. His many years of education in school and outside have been devoted to building up these complex learning sets, and he comes to manipulate them with such ease that he and his observers may easily lose sight of their origin and development.

The fundamental role that language plays in the thinking process may be deduced easily from our experiments. They suggest that words are stimuli or signs that call forth the particular learning sets most appropriate for solving a given problem. If you listen to yourself "talk" while you are thinking, you will find that this is exactly what is happening. You review the different ways of solving a problem, and decide which is the best. When you ask a friend for advice, you are asking him to give you a word stimulus which will tell you the appropriate learning set or sets for the solution of your problem.

This principle is particularly well illustrated by some of our monkey experiments. Though monkeys do not talk, they can learn to identify symbols with appropriate learning sets. We have trained our monkeys to respond to signs in the form of differently colored trays on which the test objects appear. In one test the monkeys were presented with three different objects—a red U-shaped block, a green U-shaped block and a red cross-shaped block. Thus two of the objects were alike in form and two alike in color. When the objects were shown on an orange tray, the monkeys had to choose the green block, that is, the object that was odd in color. When they were shown on a cream-colored tray, the animals had to choose the cross-shaped block, that is, the object odd in form. After the monkeys had formed these two learning sets, the color cue of the tray enabled them to make the proper choice, trial after trial, without error. In a sense, the animals responded to a simple sign language. The difficulty of this test may be judged by the fact that the German neurologist Kurt Goldstein, using similar tests for human beings, found that people with organic brain disorders could not solve such tasks efficiently.

At the Wisconsin laboratories, Benjamin Winsten devised an even more difficult test for the monkeys. This problem tested the animals' ability to recognize similarities and differences, a kind of task frequently used on children's intelligence tests. Nine objects were placed on a tray and the monkey was handed one of them as a sample. The animal's problem was to pick out all identical objects, leaving all the rest on the tray. In the most complicated form of this test the monkey was given a sample which was not identical with the objects to be selected but was only a symbol for them. The animal was handed an unpainted triangle as a sign to pick out all red objects, and an unpainted circle as a sign to select all blue objects. One monkey learned to respond almost perfectly. Given a triangle, he would pick every object with any red on it; given a circle, he selected only the objects with blue on them.

All these data indicate that animals, human and subhuman, must learn to think. Thinking does not develop spontaneously as an expression of innate abilities; it is the end result of a long learning process. Years ago the British biologist, Thomas Henry Huxley, suggested that "the brain secretes thought as the liver secretes bile." Nothing could be further from the truth. The brain is essential to thought, but the untutored brain is not enough, no matter how good a brain it may be. An untrained brain is sufficient for trial-and-error, fumble-through behavior, but only training enables an individual to think in terms of ideas and concepts.

MORE COMPLICATED TEST involves teaching a monkey to choose certain objects not by matching but by response to a symbol. In the pair of drawings at the top of this page the monkey is shown a triangular object and pushes forward all the red objects. In drawings at bottom the monkey, shown a round object, pushes forward blue objects, here indicated by gray tone.

44

THE FUNCTIONAL ORGANIZATION OF THE BRAIN

A. R. LURIA
March 1970

The functional organization of the human brain is a problem that is far from solved. I shall describe in this article some recent advances in the mapping of the brain. They open up a new field of exploration having to do with the structures of the brain involved in complex forms of behavior.

So far as sensory and motor functions are concerned, the brain, as is well known, has been mapped in precise detail. Studies by neurologists and psychologists over the past century have defined the centers that are responsible for some elementary functions such as seeing, hearing, other sensory functions and the control of the various muscular systems of the body. From outward symptoms or simple tests disclosing a disturbance of one of these functions it is possible to deduce the location of the lesion (a tumor or a hemorrhage, for example) causing the disturbance. Such a finding is of major importance in neurology and neurosurgery. The sensory and motor centers, however, account for only a small part of the area of the cerebral cortex. At least three-quarters of the cortex has nothing to do with sensory functions or muscle actions. In order to proceed further with the mapping of the brain's functions we must look into the systems responsible for the higher, more complex behavioral processes.

It is obvious that these processes, being social in origin and highly complex in structure and involving the elaboration and storage of information and the programming and control of actions, are not localized in particular centers of the brain. Plainly they must be managed by an elaborate apparatus consisting of various brain structures. Modern psychological investigations have made it clear that each behavioral process is a complex functional system based on a plan or program of operations that leads to a definite goal. The system is self-regulating: the brain judges the result of every action in relation to the basic plan and calls an end to the activity when it arrives at a successful completion of the program. This mechanism is equally applicable to elementary, involuntary forms of behavior such as breathing and walking and to complicated, voluntary ones such as reading, writing, decision-making and problem-solving.

What is the organizational form of this system in the brain? Our present knowledge of neurology indicates that the apparatus directing a complex behavioral process comprises a number of brain structures, each playing a highly specific role and all under coordinated control. One should therefore expect that lesions of the structures involved might result in changes in the behavior, and that the nature of the change would vary according to the particular structure that is damaged.

A New Approach

This concept forms the basis of our new approach to exploration of the functional organization of the brain—a study we call neuropsychology. The study has two objectives. First, by pinpointing the brain lesions responsible for specific behavioral disorders we hope to develop a means of early diagnosis and precise location of brain injuries (including those from tumors or from hemorrhage) so that they can be treated by surgery as soon as possible. Second, neuropsychological investigation should provide us with a factor analysis that will lead to better understanding of the components of complex psychological functions for which the operations of the different parts of the brain are responsible.

The human brain can be considered to be made up of three main blocks incorporating basic functions. Let us examine the responsibilities of each block in turn.

The first block regulates the energy level and tone of the cortex, providing it with a stable basis for the organization of its various processes. The brilliant researches of Horace W. Magoun, Giuseppe Moruzzi, Herbert H. Jasper and Donald B. Lindsley located the components of the first block in the upper and lower parts of the brain stem and particularly in the reticular formation, which controls wakefulness. If an injury occurs in some part of the first block, the cortex goes into a pathological state: the stability of its dynamic processes breaks down, there is a marked deterioration of wakefulness and memory traces become disorganized.

I. P. Pavlov observed that when the normal tone of the cortex is lowered, the "law of force" is lost and much of the brain's ability to discriminate among stimuli suffers. Normally the cortex reacts powerfully to strong or significant stimuli and responds hardly at all to feeble or insignificant stimuli, which are easily suppressed. A weakened cortex, on the other hand, has about the same response to insignificant stimuli as to significant ones, and in an extremely weakened state it may react even more strongly to weak stimuli than to strong ones. We all know about this loss of the brain's selectivity from common experience. Recall how diffuse and disorganized our thoughts become when we are drowsy, and what bizarre associations the mind may form in a state of fatigue or in dreams.

Obviously the results of injury to the first block in the brain, namely the loss of the selectivity of cortical actions and of normal discrimination of stimuli, will bring about marked changes in behavior. The control of behavior becomes deranged. In our common work with Macdonald Critchley of England such disturbances have been observed in patients who had tumors of the middle parts of the frontal lobes, and other investigators in our laboratory in Moscow have since reported similar effects from lesions in deep parts of the brain.

The Second Block

The second block of the brain has received much more study, and its role in the organization of behavior is better known. Located in the rear parts of the cortex, it plays a decisive role in the analysis, coding and storage of information. In contrast to the functions of the first block, which are mainly of a general nature (for example controlling wakefulness), the systems of the second block have highly specific assignments.

We can easily identify areas in the second block that are respectively responsible for the analysis of optic, acoustic, cutaneous and kinesthetic stimuli. Each of these cortical areas has a hierarchical organization: a primary zone that sorts and records the sensory information, a secondary zone that organizes the information further and codes it and a tertiary zone where the data from different sources overlap and are combined to lay the groundwork for the organization of behavior.

Injuries to the parts of the second block produce much more specific effects than lesions in the first block do. An injury in a primary zone of the second block results in a sensory defect (in seeing or hearing, for example); it does not, however, bring about a marked change in complex forms of behavior. A lesion

in a secondary zone produces more complicated disturbances. It interferes with analysis of the sensory stimuli the zone receives and, because the coding function is impaired, the lesion leads to disorganization of all the behavioral processes that would normally respond to these particular stimuli. It does not disturb any other behavioral processes, however, which is an important aid for locating the lesion.

Of the various lesions in the second block of the brain those in the tertiary zones are particularly interesting to us as neuropsychologists. Since these zones are responsible for the synthesis of a collection of information inputs from different sources into a coherent whole, a lesion of a tertiary zone can cause such complex disturbances as visual disorientation in space. The lesion seriously im-

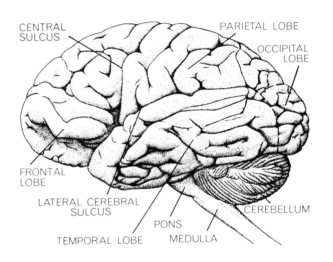

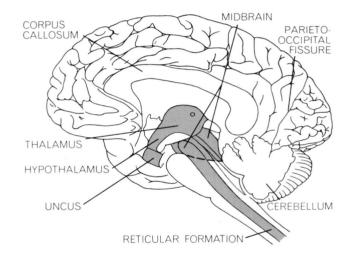

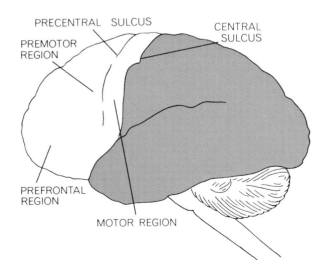

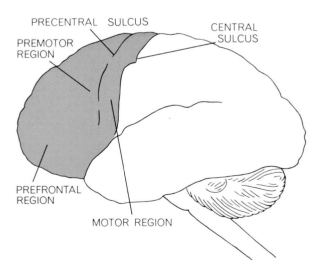

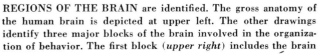

REGIONS OF THE BRAIN are identified. The gross anatomy of the human brain is depicted at upper left. The other drawings identify three major blocks of the brain involved in the organization of behavior. The first block (*upper right*) includes the brain stem and the old cortex. It regulates wakefulness and the response to stimuli. The second block (*lower left*) plays a key role in the analysis, coding and storage of information. The third block (*lower right*) is involved in the formation of intentions and programs.

pairs the ability to handle complex problems that entail an organization of input in simultaneous matrixes. That is why these lesions may render a person incapable of performing complex operations with numbers or of coping with a complexity in grammar logic or language structure.

The Third Block

The third block of the brain, comprising the frontal lobes, is involved in the formation of intentions and programs for behavior. Important contributions to elucidation of the functions of the frontal lobes have been made by S. I. Franz, L. Bianchi, Karl H. Pribram and Jerzy Konorski through studies of animals and by V. M. Bekhterev, C. Kleist and Derek E. Denny-Brown through clinical observations. We have devoted much study to the roles of the third block in our laboratory.

The frontal lobes perform no sensory or motor functions; sensation, movement, perception, speech and similar processes remain entirely unimpaired even after severe injury to these lobes. Nevertheless, the frontal lobes of the human brain are by no means silent. Our findings make it clear that they participate to a highly important degree in every complex behavioral process.

Intimately connected with the brain stem, including its reticular formation, the frontal lobes serve primarily to activate the brain. They regulate attention and concentration. W. Grey Walter showed a number of years ago that the activity of the brain could be measured by the appearance of certain slow brain waves in an electroencephalogram; these waves are evoked when a subject is stimulated to active expectancy and disappear when the subject's attention is exhausted [see "The Electrical Activity of the Brain," by W. Grey Walter; SCIENTIFIC AMERICAN Offprint 73]. At about the same time M. N. Livanov, a Russian investigator, found that mental activity is signaled by a complex of electrical excitations in the frontal cortex and that these excitations disappear when the subject subsides to a passive state or is lulled with tranquilizers.

Functional Systems

Now that we have reviewed the functions of the brain's basic blocks, let us see what we can learn about the location of specific parts of the various functional systems. It is clear that every complex form of behavior depends on the joint operation of several faculties located in different zones of the brain. A disturbance of any one faculty will affect the behavior, but each failure of a specific factor presumably will change the behavior in a different way. We have explored these effects in detail with a number of psychological experiments.

To illustrate our findings I shall discuss the results of a neuropsychological analysis of two processes. One is voluntary movement; the other is speech and in particular one of its forms, namely writing.

It was long supposed that voluntary movements are a function of the motor cortex, that is, the large pyramidal cells of the cortex of the anterior convolution of the brain. These cells, discovered by the Russian anatomist V. A. Betz more than 100 years ago, have exceptionally long axons that conduct the excitation toward the roots of the spinal cord. Impulses from these cells result in the constriction of muscles and are supposed to be the neurophysiological basis of voluntary movement.

Up to a certain point this is true, but the mechanism of the formation of a voluntary movement is much more complicated. To think that a voluntary action is formed in the narrow field of the motor cortex would be a mistake similar to an assumption that all the goods exported through a terminal are produced in the terminal. The system of cortical zones participating in the creation of a voluntary movement includes a complex of subcortical and cortical zones, each playing a highly specific role in the whole functional system. That is why lesions of different parts of the brain can result in the disturbance of different voluntary movements.

Let us examine the components of voluntary movement and see how it is affected differently by lesions in different parts of the brain. The first component is a precisely organized system of afferent (sensory) signals. The Russian physiologist N. A. Bernstein has shown in a series of studies that it is impossible to regulate a voluntary movement only by way of efferent impulses from the brain to the muscles. At every moment of the movement the position of the limb is different, and so is the density of the muscles. The brain has to receive feedback from the muscles and joints to correct the program of impulses directed to the motor apparatus. One can recognize the nature of the problem by recalling how difficult it is to start a leg movement if

VOLUNTARY MOVEMENT is controlled by a complex of cortical and subcortical zones. The classical theory was that voluntary movement originated with the large pyramidal cells (*arrowhead*) of the cortex; they have long axons that conduct impulses to the spinal cord. It is now known that other zones participating in voluntary movement are the postcentral zone (*1*), which deals with sensory feedback from the muscles; the parieto-occipital zone (*2*), which is involved in the spatial orientation of movement; the premotor zone (*3*), which deals with the separate links of motor behavior, and the frontal zone (*4*), which programs movements. Lesions in different zones give rise to different behavioral aberrations.

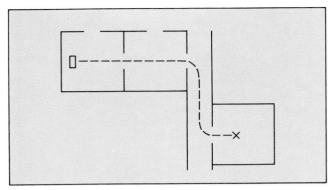

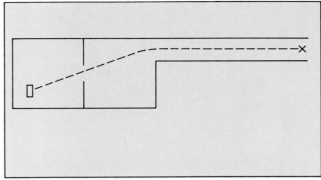

SPATIAL DISORGANIZATION is evident in a patient who had a gunshot wound of the right parieto-occipital part of the brain. The patient was asked to depict the layout of his hospital ward. His visualization is at right and the actual layout of the ward is at left.

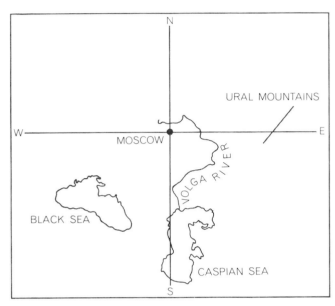

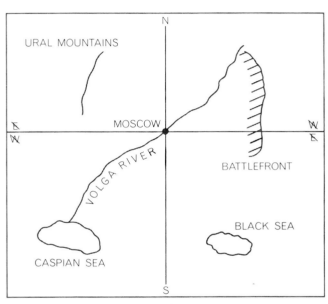

CONFUSION OVER DIRECTIONS was manifested by another patient with a gunshot wound of the right parieto-occipital zone. He was asked to draw a map of the region of the U.S.S.R. where he had been involved in fighting during World War II. The actual geographical relations are shown at left; the patient's view is at right. The line of battle represented on his map was in fact west of Moscow. In addition to reversing most of the locations, the patient could not make up his mind on the labeling of east and west.

the leg has become numb. This sensory or proprioceptive base is provided by a special part of the brain: the postcentral sensory cortex. If this part of the cortex is destroyed by a wound or other injury, the patient not only loses sensation in the limb but also is unable to fulfill a well-organized voluntary movement.

One of our co-workers has studied the physiological mechanism of such a disturbance and has shown that in lesions of the sensory part of the cortex every voluntary impulse loses its specific "address" and arrives equally at all muscles, both flexors and extensors. No organized movement can be elicited in such conditions. That is why neurologists have called this kind of motor disturbance afferent paresis.

A second component of voluntary movement is the spatial field. The movement has to be precisely oriented toward a certain point in space. Spatial analysis is done in another zone of the cortex: the tertiary parts of the parieto-occipital areas. Lesions of these highly complicated parts of the cortex result in a different kind of disturbance of voluntary movement. The sensory base of the movement remains intact, but the patient fails in a precise spatial organization of the movement. He loses the ability to evaluate spatial relations and confuses left and right. Such a patient may be unable to find his way in a familiar place or may be confused in such matters as evaluating the position of the hands of a watch or in distinguishing east and west on a map.

The sensory and spatial factors in the organization of a movement are basic but still insufficient to allow the completion of the movement. A voluntary movement is the result of a sequence of events. A skilled movement is really a kinetic melody of such interchangeable links. Only if one already fulfilled part of the movement is blocked and the impulse is shifted to another link can an organized skilled movement be made.

An important finding, first described by Karl S. Lashley and John F. Fulton and carefully studied in our laboratory for many years, is that a totally different part of the brain—the premotor cortex—is responsible for sequential interchanges of separate links of motor behavior. A skilled movement disintegrates when this part of the brain is injured. Such a patient still has sensory feedback and spatial orientation, but he loses the ability to arrest one of the steps of the movement and to make a transition from one step to the next.

Even now I have not fully described the brain's organization of a voluntary

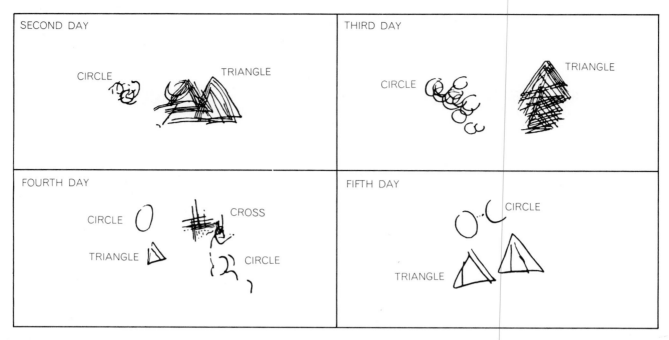

INFLUENCE OF PREMOTOR REGION on the organization of movement appears in drawings made by a patient after surgery for removal of a meningioma, which is a tumor arising from the meninges, from the left premotor region. On each of the days represented in the illustration the patient was asked to draw simple figures such as those shown here. Performance improved steadily.

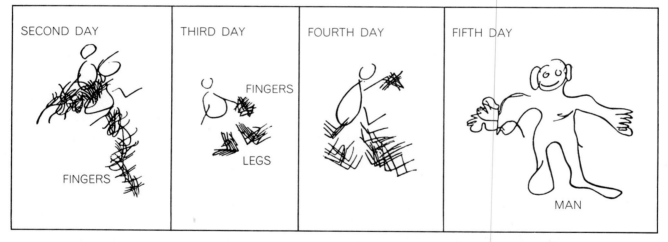

DRAWINGS OF A MAN were attempted by the same patient during the postoperative period. At first he drew a head and body, represented by the circles at top center in the drawing at left. Then he drew a second man, whose head is to the right of the first man's body. Then he made a series of stereotyped pen strokes. The ones that trail off at lower right in the first drawing were made on moving paper. On successive days the patient's work improved. Difficulty in stopping a movement often appears in premotor lesions.

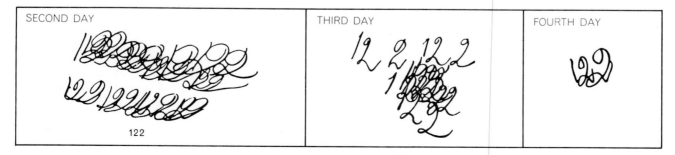

WRITING OF NUMBERS was attempted by the same patient on the second, third and fourth day after the operation. As in the other cases the patient at first showed a tendency to repeat part of the task, but the repetition diminished on the following days.

movement. Every movement has to be subordinated to a stable program or a stable intention. They are provided in the prefrontal lobes of the brain (included in the third block). If the frontal lobes are injured, the sensory base, spatial organization and plasticity of the movement remain but goal-linked actions are replaced by meaningless repetitions of already fulfilled movements or impulsive answers to outside stimuli. The whole purposive conduct of the patient is disturbed.

Speech and Writing

Let us now analyze a more complex psychological process: the ability to speak, and particularly the ability to write. It used to be thought that the operation of writing is controlled by a certain area (called Exher's center) in the middle of the premotor zone of the brain's left hemisphere (for a right-handed writer). It has since been learned, however, that this is not the case, and that a broad area of the left hemisphere is involved. We must therefore consider the effects of lesions in all parts of this region on writing.

Let us start by a psychological analysis of the processes involved in writing something in response to an instruction. Suppose one is asked to write a given word. The interpretation of the oral request turns out to be in itself a complex process. A word is composed of individual sounds, or phonemes, each coded by a letter or combination of letters. The recognition of a word may depend on the perception of very slight differences between phonemes, or acoustic cues. Consider, for example, "vine" and "wine," "special" and "spatial," "bull" and "pull," "bark" and "park." The practiced brain readily distinguishes between similar sounds, and to a person brought up in the English language the two words in these pairs sound quite different from each other. Obviously the brain must perform a sharp analysis of phonemes on the basis of learning. We become impressed with this fact when we see how difficult it is to sense distinctions in listening to a foreign language. To an English-speaking or French-speaking person, for example, three words in the Russian language—*pyl*, meaning "ardor," *pyl'* (with the *l* palatalized), meaning "dust," and *pil* (with a hard *l*), meaning "he drank"—sound almost exactly the same, yet a Russian has no difficulty distinguishing these words. Much more remarkable instances of subtle distinctions the mind is called on to make can be

cited in other languages. In Chinese *ma* and *ma* have the opposite meaning ("to buy" and "to sell"), although the only difference is in the tone of the vowel. In the Vietnamese language the phoneme *tü* has at least six different meanings, depending on the pitch of the voice!

What part of the brain is responsible for recognizing phonemes? Our observations on many hundreds of patients with local brain wounds or tumors who underwent word-writing tests established clearly that the critical region lies in the secondary zones of the left temporal lobe, which are intimately connected with other parts of the brain's speech area. People with lesions in this region cannot distinguish *b* from *p* or *t* from *d*, and they may write "pull" instead of "bull" or "tome" instead of "dome." Moreover, they may make unsuccessful attempts to find the contents of the sounds of words they try to write. Interestingly enough, Chinese patients with severe injury of the acoustic region have no such difficulty, because their writing is based on ideographs instead of on words that call for the coding of phonemes.

Continuing our dissection of the process of word recognition, we must note that people commonly pronounce an unfamiliar word before writing it, and in the case of an unfamiliar name they are likely to ask the person to spell it. Articulation of the sounds helps to clarify the word's acoustic structure. A class of Russian elementary schoolchildren during a lesson in the early stages of learning to write is generally abuzz with their mouthing of the words. To find out if this activity was really helpful, I asked one of my co-workers to conduct an ex-

periment. The children were instructed to hold their mouths open or to immobilize their tongues with their teeth while they wrote. In these circumstances, unable to articulate the words, the children made six times as many spelling mistakes!

It turns out that a separate area of the brain cortex, in the central (kinesthetic) region of the left hemisphere, controls the articulation of speech sounds. People with lesions in this area confuse the sound of *b* with that of *m* (both made with similar tongue and lip movements) and often cannot distinguish between *d, e, n* and *l*. A Russian with such a lesion may write *ston* ("groan") instead of *stol* ("table") and *khadat* (meaningless) instead of *khalat* ("dressing gown").

After evaluation of the speech sounds and recognition of the word, the next step toward writing the word is the coding of the sound units (phonemes) into the units of writing (letters). We find that this step calls into play still other parts of the brain cortex, in the visual and spatial zones. Patients with lesions in these zones (in the occipital and parietal lobes) have a perfectly normal ability to analyze speech sounds, but they show marked difficulty in recognizing and forming written letters. They find it difficult to visualize the required structure of a letter, to grasp the spatial relations among the parts of the letter and to put the parts together to form the whole.

The mental process for writing a word entails still another specialization: putting the letters in the proper sequence to form the word. Lashley discovered many years ago that sequential analysis

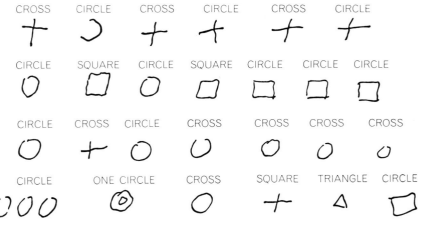

LESIONS OF FRONTAL LOBES interfere with the programming of actions and cause errors such as repetition. On each line of the illustration are drawings made by patients; printed words show what they were asked to draw. The first, second and fourth patient had tumors of the left frontal lobe; the third patient had an abscess of the right frontal lobe.

involved a zone of the brain different from that employed for spatial analysis. In the course of our extensive studies we have located the region responsible for sequential analysis in the anterior region of the left hemisphere. Lesions in the prefrontal region disturb the ability to carry out rhythmic movements of the body, and they also give patients difficulty in writing letters in the correct order. Such patients transpose letters, are unable to proceed serially from one letter to another and often replace the required letter with a meaningless stereotype. If the lesion is located deep in the brain where it interrupts connections between the basal ganglia and the cortex, the patient becomes incapable of writing words at all; he may merely repeat fragments of letters. Yet such a patient, with the higher parts of the cortex undamaged, can recognize phonemes and letters perfectly well.

Finally, there is an overall requirement for writing that involves the apparatuses of the third block of the brain as a whole. This is the matter of writing not merely letters or words but expressing thoughts and ideas. When the third block is damaged by severe lesions of the frontal lobes, the patient becomes unable to express his thoughts either orally or in writing. I shall never forget a letter written to the noted Russian neurosurgeon N. N. Burdenko by a woman with a severe lesion of the left frontal lobe. "Dear Professor," she wrote, "I want to tell you that I want to tell you that I want to tell you..." and so on for page after page!

The analysis of the writing process is just one of the tracers we have used in our psychological exploration of the functional organization of the brain. Over the past three decades investigators in our laboratory and our clinical associates have carried out similar analyses of the brain systems involved in perception, bodily movements, performance of planned actions, memorization and problem-solving. All these studies have demonstrated that detailed investigation of the nature of a behavioral disturbance can indeed guide one to the location of the causative lesion in the brain.

Factor Analyses

Obviously the neuropsychological approach provides a valuable means of dissecting mental processes as well as diagnosing illness. It is enabling us to search out the details of the brain's normal operations and capacities. A generation ago L. L. Thurstone of the University of Chicago and C. E. Spearman of the University of London learned some of the details by the statistical technique of factor analysis based on batteries of tests administered to great numbers of subjects. With the neuropsychological technique we can now make factor analyses in individual subjects. When a particular factor is incapacitated by a brain lesion, all the complex behavior processes that involve the factor are disturbed and all others remain normal. We find, for example, that an injury in the left temporal lobe causes the patient to have serious difficulty in analyzing speech sounds, in repeating verbal sounds, in naming objects and in writing, but the person retains normal capacities in spatial orientation and in handling simple computations. On the other hand, a lesion in the left parieto-occipital region that destroys spatial organization does not affect the patient's fluency of speech or sense of rhythm.

Sorting out the various factors and

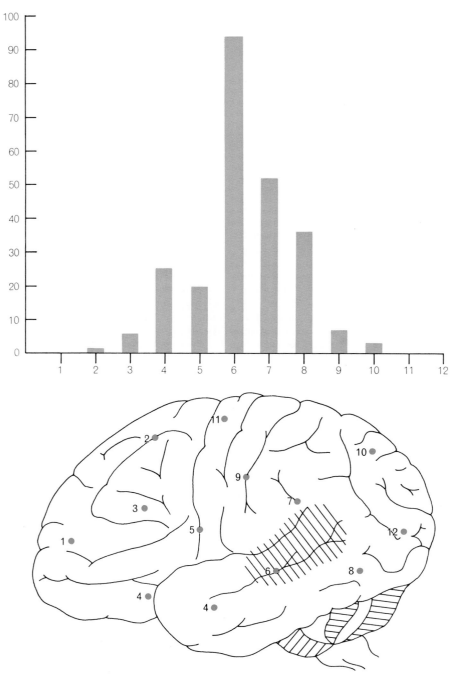

DISRUPTION OF HEARING in patients with bullet wounds in the left hemisphere of the cerebral cortex is charted. Affected areas of the brain are numbered, and the correspondingly numbered bars show the percent of patients who had difficulty recognizing sounds.

their effects, we arrive at some surprising findings. One is that behavioral processes that seem very similar or even identical may not be related to one another at all. For example, it turns out that the mechanism for perception of musical sounds is quite different from that for verbal sounds. A lesion of the left temporal lobe that destroys the ability to analyze phonemes leaves musical hearing undisturbed. I observed an outstanding Russian composer who suffered a hemorrhage in the left temporal lobe that deprived him of the ability to understand speech, yet he went on creating wonderful symphonies!

On the other hand, behavioral processes that seem to have nothing in common may actually be related through dependence on a particular brain factor. What can there be in common between the capacities for orientation in space, for doing computations and for dealing with complexities in grammar logic? Yet all three of these abilities are affected by the same lesion in the lower part of the left parietal lobe. Why so? A close analysis of the three processes suggests an explanation. Computation and the ability to handle language structure depend, like orientation, on the ability to grasp spatial relations. In order to subtract 7 from 31, for example, one first performs the operation $30 - 7 = 23$ and then adds the 1 to this preliminary result. There is a spatial factor here: one indicates unambiguously that the 1 is to be *added* by placing it to the right of the 23. A patient with a lesion disturbing his capacity for spatial organization is unable to cope with the problem because

he is at a loss whether to place the 1 to the left or the right—in other words, whether to add it or subtract it.

The same principle applies to understanding complex grammatical constructions. In order to grasp the difference between "father's brother" and "brother's father" or between "summer comes after spring" and "spring comes after summer," for example, one must make a clear analysis of the quasi-spatial relations between the elements in each expression.

Finally, the neuropsychological approach gives us a new insight into the effects of learning on the brain's processes. There is a well-known story of a patient of the 19th-century English neurologist Sir William Gowers who, after many unsuccessful attempts to repeat the word "no" in response to his instruction, at last burst out: "No, doctor, I can't say 'no.'" We have observed many cases of automatic performances of this kind in brain-injured patients who could not achieve a given task when they thought about it. One was an old lady who was unable to write a single word on instruction, but when she was asked to write a whole sentence quickly (a kinetic skill), she did so without hesitation. Patients who cannot write from dictation are often able to sign their names readily. It appears, therefore, that training or habituation changes the organization of the brain's activity, so that the brain comes to perform accustomed tasks without recourse to the processes of analysis. That is to say, the task may invoke a stereotype based on a network of cortical zones quite different from the one that was

(OKHO = OKNO)
(WINDOW)

(ИВАН = IVAN)

WRITING ABERRATION was shown by a patient with a tumor in the deep part of the brain's left premotor zone. He was asked to write the Russian words for window and Ivan, which are printed in Russian and in English transliteration below each example. Arrows show repetition or fragments.

called on originally when the performance required the help of the analytical apparatus.

Neuropsychology has put us on a new path in the investigation of how the brain functions, and we can suppose that it is likely to lead the way to substantial changes in the design of psychological research in the future.

каша — KASHA (PORRIDGE)
Гаша — GASHA (MEANINGLESS)

гора — GORA (MOUNTAIN)
Кара — KARA (PENALTY)

грибы — GRIBY (MUSHROOMS)
Криби — KRIBI (MEANINGLESS)

здоровье — ZDOROVIE (HEALTH)
Старове — STOROVE (MEANINGLESS)

WRITING DISTURBANCES appear in a patient with a lesion of the left temporal area. The patient was writing to dictation; the dictated Russian word, its transliteration and its English meaning are on the top line. The written response of the patient in each case appears below with its transliteration and English meaning in the single instance (*kara*) where the patient wrote a meaningful word.

т — m
Л — l

Л — l
н — n

халат — KHALAT (SMOCK)
ханат — KHANAT (MEANINGLESS)
хадат — KHADAT (MEANINGLESS)

большой — BOLSHOI (BIG)
бонишои — BONISHOI (MEANINGLESS)
бониш — BONISH (MEANINGLESS)

ERRORS IN WRITING also were shown by a patient with a lesion of the left parietal area. Again the dictated letter or word appears on the top line; the bottom lines show the written response by the patient. None of the words that the patient wrote were meaningful.

THREAT POSTURE of male stickleback is example of nonvocal communication in lower animals. In this picture, made by N. Tinbergen of the University of Oxford, the fish is responding to its mirror image by indicating readiness to fight "intruding" male.

45

THE ORIGIN OF SPEECH

CHARLES F. HOCKETT
September 1960

About 50 years ago the Linguistic Society of Paris established a standing rule barring from its sessions papers on the origin of language. This action was a symptom of the times. Speculation about the origin of language had been common throughout the 19th century, but had reached no conclusive results. The whole enterprise in consequence had come to be frowned upon—as futile or crackpot—in respectable linguistic and philological circles. Yet amidst the speculations there were two well-reasoned empirical plans that deserve mention even though their results were negative.

A century ago there were still many corners of the world that had not been visited by European travelers. It was reasonable for the European scholar to suspect that beyond the farthest frontiers there might lurk half-men or man-apes who would be "living fossils" attesting to earlier stages of human evolution. The speech (or quasi-speech) of these men (or quasi-men) might then similarly attest to earlier stages in the evolution of language. The search was vain. Nowhere in the world has there been discovered a language that can validly and meaningfully be called "primitive." Edward Sapir wrote in 1921: "There is no more striking general fact about language than its universality. One may argue as to whether a particular tribe engages in activities that are worthy of the name of religion or of art, but we know of no people that is not possessed of a fully developed language. The lowliest South African Bushman speaks in the forms of a rich symbolic system that is in essence perfectly comparable to the speech of the cultivated Frenchman."

The other empirical hope in the 19th century rested on the comparative method of historical linguistics, the discovery of which was one of the triumphs of the period. Between two languages the resemblances are sometimes so extensive and orderly that they cannot be attributed to chance or to parallel development. The alternative explanation is that the two are divergent descendants of a single earlier language. English, Dutch, German and the Scandinavian languages are related in just this way. The comparative method makes it possible to examine such a group of related languages and to construct, often in surprising detail, a portrayal of the common ancestor, in this case the proto-Germanic language. Direct documentary evidence of proto-Germanic does not exist, yet understanding of its workings exceeds that of many languages spoken today.

There was at first some hope that the comparative method might help determine the origin of language. This hope was rational in a day when it was thought that language might be only a few thousands or tens of thousands of years old, and when it was repeatedly being demonstrated that languages that had been thought to be unrelated were in fact related. By applying the comparative method to all the languages of the world, some earliest reconstructable horizon would be reached. This might not date back so early as the origin of language, but it might bear certain earmarks of primitiveness, and thus it would enable investigators to extrapolate toward the origin. This hope also proved vain. The earliest reconstructable stage for any language family shows all the complexities and flexibilities of the languages of today.

These points had become clear a half-century ago, by the time of the Paris ruling. Scholars cannot really approve of such a prohibition. But in this instance it had the useful result of channeling the energies of investigators toward the gathering of more and better information about languages as they are today. The subsequent progress in understanding the workings of language has been truly remarkable. Various related fields have also made vast strides in the last half-century: zoologists know more about the evolutionary process, anthropologists know more about the nature of culture, and so on. In the light of these developments there need be no apology for re-opening the issue of the origins of human speech.

Although the comparative method of linguistics, as has been shown, throws no light on the origin of language, the investigation may be furthered by a comparative method modeled on that of the zoologist. The frame of reference must be such that all languages look alike when viewed through it, but such that within it human language as a whole can be compared with the communicative systems of other animals, especially the other hominoids, man's closest living relatives, the gibbons and great apes. The useful items for this sort of comparison cannot be things such as the word for "sky"; languages have such words, but gibbon calls do not involve words at all. Nor can they be even the signal for "danger," which gibbons do have. Rather, they must be the basic features of design that can be present or absent in any communicative system, whether it be a communicative system of humans, of animals or of machines.

With this sort of comparative method it may be possible to reconstruct the communicative habits of the remote ancestors of the hominoid line, which may be called the protohominoids. The task, then, is to work out the sequence by which that ancestral system became language as the hominids—the man-apes and ancient men—became man.

A set of 13 design-features is presented in the illustration on the opposite page. There is solid empirical justification for the belief that all the languages of the world share every one of them. At first sight some appear so trivial that no one looking just at language would bother to note them. They become worthy of mention only when it is realized that certain animal systems—and certain human systems other than language—lack them.

The first design-feature—the "vocal-auditory channel"—is perhaps the most obvious. There are systems of communication that use other channels; for example, gesture, the dancing of bees or the courtship ritual of the stickleback. The vocal-auditory channel has the advantage—at least for primates—that it leaves much of the body free for other activities that can be carried on at the same time.

The next two design-features—"rapid fading" and "broadcast transmission and directional reception," stemming from the physics of sound—are almost unavoidable consequences of the first. A linguistic signal can be heard by any auditory system within earshot, and the source can normally be localized by binaural direction-finding. The rapid fading of such a signal means that it does not linger for reception at the hearer's convenience. Animal tracks and spoors, on the other hand, persist for a while; so of course do written records, a product of man's extremely recent cultural evolution.

The significance of "interchangeability" and "total feedback" for language becomes clear upon comparison with other systems. In general a speaker of a language can reproduce any linguistic message he can understand, whereas the characteristic courtship motions of the male and female stickleback are different, and neither can act out those appropriate to the other. For that matter in the communication of a human mother and infant neither is apt to transmit the characteristic signals or to manifest the typical responses of the other. Again, the speaker of a language hears, by total feedback, everything of linguistic relevance in what he himself says. In contrast, the male stickleback does not see the colors of his own eye and belly that are crucial in stimulating the female. Feedback is important, since it makes possible the so-called internalization of communicative behavior that

constitutes at least a major portion of "thinking."

The sixth design-feature, "specialization," refers to the fact that the bodily effort and spreading sound waves of speech serve no function except as signals. A dog, panting with his tongue hanging out, is performing a biologically essential activity, since this is how dogs cool themselves off and maintain the proper body temperature. The panting dog incidentally produces sound, and thereby may inform other dogs (or humans) as to where he is and how he feels. But this transmission of information is strictly a side effect. Nor does the dog's panting exhibit the design-feature of "semanticity." It is not a signal meaning that the dog is hot; it is part of being hot. In language, however, a message triggers the particular result it does because there are relatively fixed associations between elements in messages (e.g., words) and recurrent features or situations of the world around us. For example, the English word "salt" means salt, not sugar or pepper. The calls of gibbons also possess semanticity. The gibbon has a danger call, for example, and it does not in principle matter that the meaning of the call is a great deal broader and more vague than, say, the cry of "Fire!"

In a semantic communicative system the ties between meaningful message-elements and their meanings can be arbitrary or nonarbitrary. In language the ties are arbitrary. The word "salt" is not salty nor granular; "dog" is not "canine"; "whale" is a small word for a large object; "microorganism" is the reverse. A picture, on the other hand, looks like what it is a picture of. A bee dances faster if the source of nectar she is reporting is closer, and slower if it is farther away. The design-feature of "arbitrariness" has the disadvantage of being arbitrary, but the great advantage that there is no limit to what can be communicated about.

Human vocal organs can produce a huge variety of sound. But in any one language only a relatively small set of ranges of sound is used, and the differences between these ranges are functionally absolute. The English words "pin" and "bin" are different to the ear only at one point. If a speaker produces a syllable that deviates from the normal pronunciation of "pin" in the direction of that of "bin," he is not producing still a third word, but just saying "pin" (or perhaps "bin") in a noisy way. The hearer compensates if he can, on the basis of context, or else fails to under-

stand. This feature of "discreteness" in the elementary signaling units of a language contrasts with the use of sound effects by way of vocal gesture. There is an effectively continuous scale of degrees to which one may raise his voice as in anger, or lower it to signal confidentiality. Bee-dancing also is continuous rather than discrete.

Man is apparently almost unique in being able to talk about things that are remote in space or time (or both) from where the talking goes on. This feature—"displacement"—seems to be definitely lacking in the vocal signaling of man's closest relatives, though it does occur in bee-dancing.

One of the most important design-features of language is "productivity"; that is, the capacity to say things that have never been said or heard before and yet to be understood by other speakers of the language. If a gibbon makes any vocal sound at all, it is one or another of a small finite repertory of familiar calls. The gibbon call system can be characterized as closed. Language is open, or "productive," in the sense that one can coin new utterances by putting together pieces familiar from old utterances, assembling them by patterns of arrangement also familiar in old utterances.

Human genes carry the capacity to acquire a language, and probably also a strong drive toward such acquisition, but the detailed conventions of any one language are transmitted extragenetically by learning and teaching. To what extent such "traditional transmission" plays a part in gibbon calls or for other mammalian systems of vocal signals is not known, though in some instances the uniformity of the sounds made by a species, wherever the species is found over the world, is so great that genetics must be responsible.

The meaningful elements in any language—"words" in everyday parlance, "morphemes" to the linguist—constitute an enormous stock. Yet they are represented by small arrangements of a relatively very small stock of distinguishable sounds which are in themselves wholly meaningless. This "duality of patterning" is illustrated by the English words

THIRTEEN DESIGN-FEATURES of animal communication, discussed in detail in the text of this article, are symbolized on opposite page. The patterns of the words "pin," "bin," "team" and "meat" were recorded at Bell Telephone Laboratories.

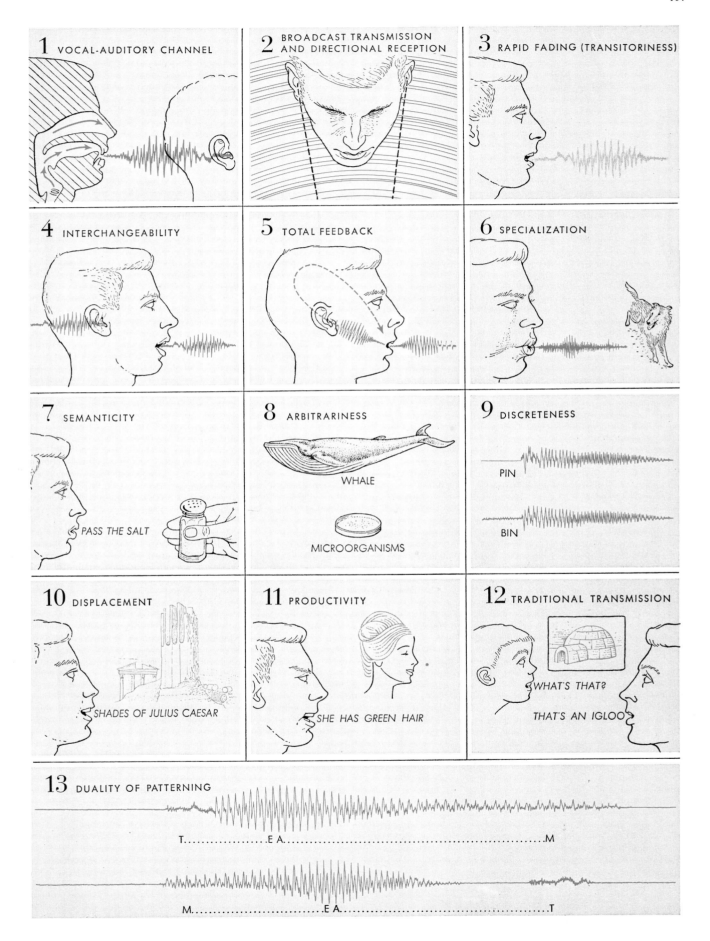

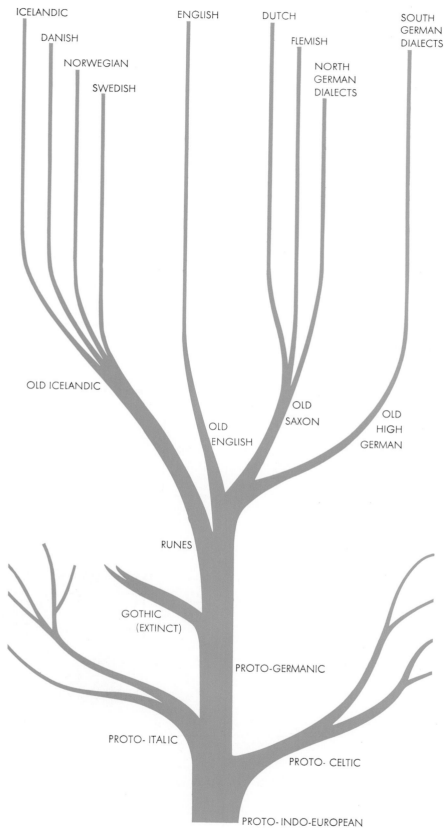

ICELANDIC

DANISH

NORWEGIAN

SWEDISH

ENGLISH

DUTCH

FLEMISH

NORTH
GERMAN
DIALECTS

SOUTH
GERMAN
DIALECTS

OLD ICELANDIC

OLD
ENGLISH

OLD
SAXON

OLD
HIGH
GERMAN

RUNES

GOTHIC
(EXTINCT)

PROTO-GERMANIC

PROTO- ITALIC

PROTO- CELTIC

PROTO- INDO-EUROPEAN

**ORIGIN OF MODERN GERMANIC LANGUAGES, as indicated by this "family tree,"
was proto-Germanic, spoken some 2,700 years ago. Comparison of present-day languages
has provided detailed knowledge of proto-Germanic, although no direct documentary evidence for the language exists. It grew, in turn, from the proto-Indo-European of 5000 B.C.
Historical studies cannot, however, trace origins of language back much further in time.**

"tack," "cat" and "act." They are totally
distinct as to meaning, and yet are composed of just three basic meaningless
sounds in different permutations. Few
animal communicative systems share this
design-feature of language—none among
the other hominoids, and perhaps none
at all.

It should be noted that some of these
13 design-features are not independent. In particular, a system cannot be
either arbitrary or nonarbitrary unless it
is semantic, and it cannot have duality
of patterning unless it is semantic. It
should also be noted that the listing does
not attempt to include all the features
that might be discovered in the communicative behavior of this or that species,
but only those that are clearly important
for language.

It is probably safe to assume that nine
of the 13 features were already present
in the vocal-auditory communication of
the protohominoids—just the nine that
are securely attested for the gibbons and
humans of today. That is, there were a
dozen or so distinct calls, each the appropriate vocal response (or vocal part
of the whole response) to a recurrent
and biologically important type of situation: the discovery of food, the detection of a predator, sexual interest, need
for maternal care, and so on. The problem of the origin of human speech, then,
is that of trying to determine how such a
system could have developed the four
additional properties of displacement,
productivity and full-blown traditional
transmission. Of course the full story involves a great deal more than communicative behavior alone. The development
must be visualized as occurring in the
context of the evolution of the primate
horde into the primitive society of food-
gatherers and hunters, an integral part,
but a part, of the total evolution of behavior.

It is possible to imagine a closed system developing some degree of productivity, even in the absence of the other
three features. Human speech exhibits a
phenomenon that could have this effect,
the phenomenon of "blending." Sometimes a speaker will hesitate between
two words or phrases, both reasonably
appropriate for the situation in which he
is speaking, and actually say something
that is neither wholly one nor wholly the
other, but a combination of parts of
each. Hesitating between "Don't shout
so loud" and "Don't yell so loud," he
might come out with "Don't shell so
loud." Blending is almost always involved in slips of the tongue, but it may

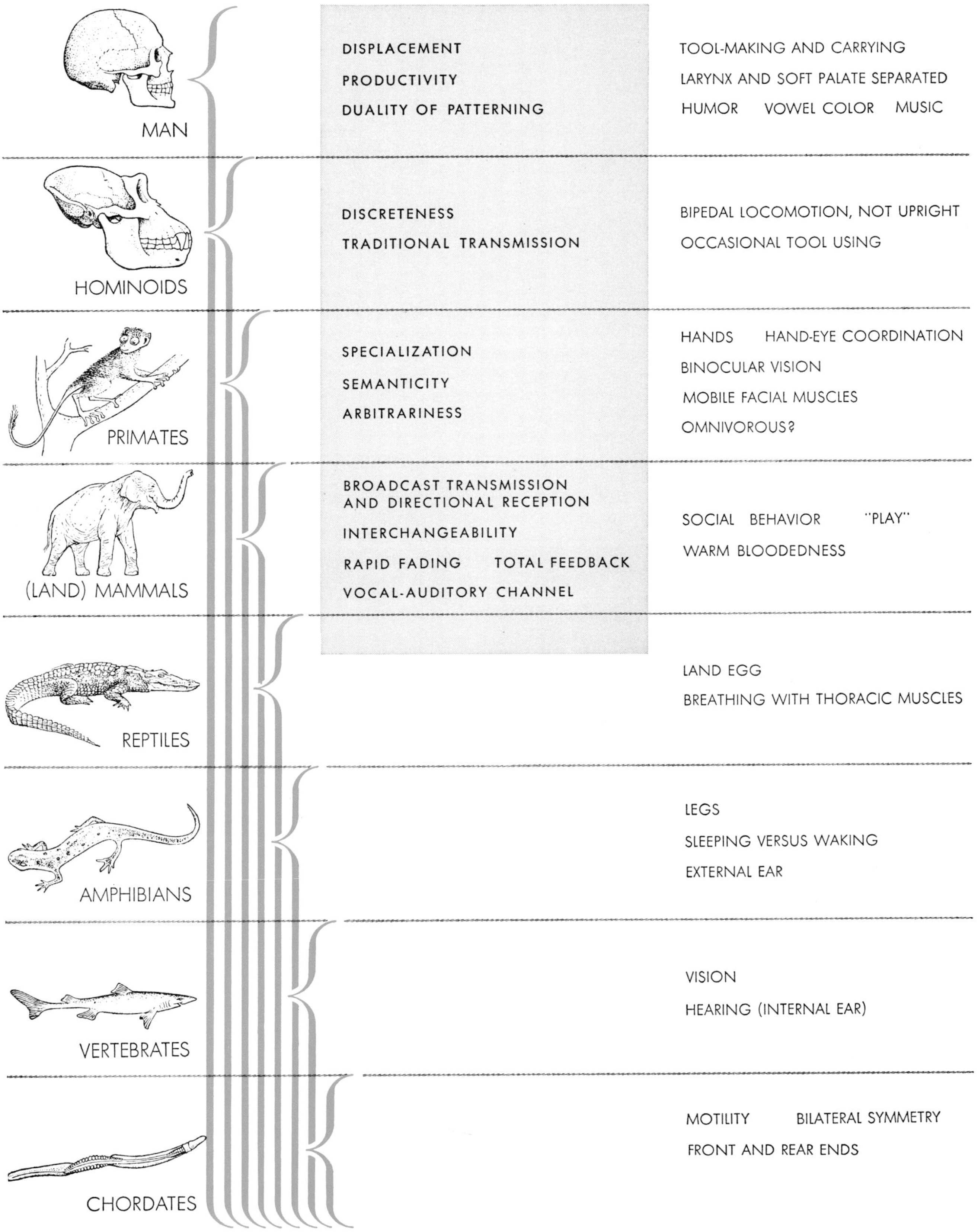

MAN

DISPLACEMENT

PRODUCTIVITY

DUALITY OF PATTERNING

TOOL-MAKING AND CARRYING

LARYNX AND SOFT PALATE SEPARATED

HUMOR   VOWEL COLOR   MUSIC

HOMINOIDS

DISCRETENESS

TRADITIONAL TRANSMISSION

BIPEDAL LOCOMOTION, NOT UPRIGHT

OCCASIONAL TOOL USING

PRIMATES

SPECIALIZATION

SEMANTICITY

ARBITRARINESS

HANDS   HAND-EYE COORDINATION

BINOCULAR VISION

MOBILE FACIAL MUSCLES

OMNIVOROUS?

(LAND) MAMMALS

BROADCAST TRANSMISSION
AND DIRECTIONAL RECEPTION

INTERCHANGEABILITY

RAPID FADING   TOTAL FEEDBACK

VOCAL-AUDITORY CHANNEL

SOCIAL   BEHAVIOR   "PLAY"

WARM BLOODEDNESS

REPTILES

LAND EGG

BREATHING WITH THORACIC MUSCLES

AMPHIBIANS

LEGS

SLEEPING VERSUS WAKING

EXTERNAL EAR

VERTEBRATES

VISION

HEARING (INTERNAL EAR)

CHORDATES

MOTILITY   BILATERAL SYMMETRY

FRONT AND REAR ENDS

EVOLUTION OF LANGUAGE and some related characteristics are suggested by this classification of chordates. The lowest form of animal in each classification exhibits the features listed at the right of the class. Brackets indicate that each group possesses or has evolved beyond the characteristics exhibited by all the groups below. The 13 design-features of language appear in the colored rectangle. Some but by no means all of the characteristics associated with communication are presented in the column at right.

also be the regular mechanism by which a speaker of a language says something that he has not said before. Anything a speaker says must be either an exact repetition of an utterance he has heard before, or else some blended product of two or more such familiar utterances. Thus even such a smooth and normal sentence as "I tried to get there, but the car broke down" might be produced as a blend, say, of "I tried to get there but couldn't" and "While I was driving down Main Street the car broke down."

Children acquiring the language of their community pass through a stage that is closed in just the way gibbon calls

are. A child may have a repertory of several dozen sentences, each of which, in adult terms, has an internal structure, and yet for the child each may be an indivisible whole. He may also learn new whole utterances from surrounding adults. The child takes the crucial step, however, when he first says something that he has not learned from others. The only way in which the child can possibly do this is by blending two of the whole utterances that he already knows.

In the case of the closed call-system of the gibbons or the protohominoids, there is no source for the addition of new

unitary calls to the repertoire except perhaps by occasional imitation of the calls and cries of other species. Even this would not render the system productive, but would merely enlarge it. But blending might occur. Let AB represent the food call and CD the danger call, each a fairly complex phonetic pattern. Suppose a protohominoid encountered food and caught sight of a predator at the same time. If the two stimuli were balanced just right, he might emit the calls ABCD or CDAB in quick sequence, or might even produce AD or CB. Any of these would be a blend. AD, for example, would mean "both food and danger." By

	A	B	C	D
	SOME GRYLLIDAE AND TETTIGONIIDAE	BEE DANCING	STICKLEBACK COURTSHIP	WESTERN MEADOWLARK SONG
1 THE VOCAL-AUDITORY CHANNEL	AUDITORY, NOT VOCAL	NO	NO	YES
2 BROADCAST TRANSMISSION AND DIRECTIONAL RECEPTION	YES	YES	YES	YES
3 RAPID FADING (TRANSITORINESS)	YES, REPEATED	?	?	YES
4 INTERCHANGEABILITY	LIMITED	LIMITED	NO	?
5 TOTAL FEEDBACK	YES	?	NO	YES
6 SPECIALIZATION	YES?	?	IN PART	YES?
7 SEMANTICITY	NO?	YES	NO	IN PART ?
8 ARBITRARINESS	?	NO		IF SEMANTIC, YES
9 DISCRETENESS	YES?	NO	?	?
10 DISPLACEMENT		YES, ALWAYS		?
11 PRODUCTIVITY	NO	YES	NO	?
12 TRADITIONAL TRANSMISSION	NO?	PROBABLY NOT	NO?	?
13 DUALITY OF PATTERNING	? (TRIVIAL)	NO		?

EIGHT SYSTEMS OF COMMUNICATION possess in varying degrees the 13 design-features of language. Column A refers to members of the cricket family. Column H concerns only Western music since the time of Bach. A question mark means that it is

virtue of this, AB and CD would acquire new meanings, respectively "food without danger" and "danger without food." And all three of these calls—AB, CD and AD—would now be composite rather than unitary, built out of smaller elements with their own individual meanings: A would mean "food"; B, "no danger"; C, "no food"; and D, "danger."

But this is only part of the story. The generation of a blend can have no effect unless it is understood. Human beings are so good at understanding blends that it is hard to tell a blend from a rote repetition, except in the case of slips of the tongue and some of the earliest and most tentative blends used by children. Such powers of understanding cannot be ascribed to man's prehuman ancestors. It must be supposed, therefore, that occasional blends occurred over many tens of thousands of years (perhaps, indeed, they still may occur from time to time among gibbons or the great apes), with rarely any appropriate communicative impact on hearers, before the understanding of blends became speedy enough to reinforce their production. However, once that did happen, the earlier closed system had become open and productive.

It is also possible to see how faint traces of displacement might develop in a call system even in the absence of productivity, duality and thoroughgoing traditional transmission. Suppose an early hominid, a man-ape say, caught sight of a predator without himself being seen. Suppose that for whatever reason—perhaps through fear—he sneaked silently back toward others of his band and only a bit later gave forth the danger call. This might give the whole band a better chance to escape the predator, thus bestowing at least slight survival value on whatever factor was responsible for the delay.

Something akin to communicative displacement is involved in lugging a stick or a stone around—it is like talking today about what one should do tomorrow. Of course it is not to be supposed that the first tool-carrying was purposeful, any more than that the first displaced communication was a discussion of plans. Caught in a *cul-de-sac* by a predator, however, the early hominid might strike out in terror with his stick or stone and by chance disable or drive off his enemy. In other words, the first tool-carrying had a consequence but not a purpose. Because the outcome was fortunate, it tended to reinforce whatever factor, genetic or traditional, prompted the behavior and made the outcome possible. In the end such events do lead to purposive behavior.

Although elements of displacement might arise in this fashion, on the whole it seems likely that some degree of productivity preceded any great proliferation of communicative displacement as well as any significant capacity for traditional transmission. A productive system requires the young to catch on to the ways in which whole signals are built out of smaller meaningful elements, some of which may never occur as whole signals in isolation. The young can do this only in the way that human children learn their language: by learning some utterances as whole units, in due time testing various blends based on that repertory, and finally adjusting their patterns of blending until the bulk of what they say matches what adults would say and is therefore understood. Part of this learning process is bound to take place away from the precise situations for which the responses are basically appropriate, and this means the promotion of displacement. Learning and teaching, moreover, call on any capacity for traditional transmission that the band may have. Insofar as the communicative system itself has survival value, all this bestows survival value also on the capacity

E	F	G	H
GIBBON CALLS	PARALINGUISTIC PHENOMENA	LANGUAGE	INSTRUMENTAL MUSIC
YES	YES	YES	AUDITORY, NOT VOCAL
YES	YES	YES	YES
YES, REPEATED	YES	YES	YES
YES	LARGELY YES	YES	?
YES	YES	YES	YES
YES	YES?	YES	YES
YES	YES?	YES	NO (IN GENERAL)
YES	IN PART	YES	
YES	LARGELY NO	YES	IN PART
NO	IN PART	YES, OFTEN	
NO	YES	YES	YES
?	YES	YES	YES
NO	NO	YES	

doubtful or not known if the system has the particular feature. A blank space indicates that feature cannot be determined because another feature is lacking or is indefinite.

for traditional transmission and for displacement. But these in turn increase the survival value of the communicative system. A child can be taught how to avoid certain dangers before he actually encounters them.

These developments are also necessarily related to the appearance of large and convoluted brains, which are better storage units for the conventions of a complex communicative system and for other traditionally transmitted skills and practices. Hence the adaptive value of the behavior serves to select genetically for the change in structure. A lengthened period of childhood helplessness is also a longer period of plasticity for learning. There is therefore selection for prolonged childhood and, with it, later maturity and longer life. With more for the young to learn, and with male as well as female tasks to be taught, fathers become more domesticated. The increase of displacement promotes retention and foresight; a male can protect his mate and guard her jealously from other males even when he does not at the moment hunger for her.

There is excellent reason to believe that duality of patterning was the last property to be developed, because one can find little if any reason why a communicative system should have this property unless it is highly complicated. If a vocal-auditory system comes to have a larger and larger number of distinct meaningful elements, those elements inevitably come to be more and more similar to one another in sound. There is a practical limit, for any species or any machine, to the number of distinct stimuli that can be discriminated, especially when the discriminations typically have to be made in noisy conditions. Suppose that Samuel F. B. Morse, in devising his telegraph code, had proposed a signal .1 second long for "A," .2 second long for "B," and so on up to 2.6 seconds for "Z." Operators would have enormous difficulty learning and using any such system. What Morse actually did was to incorporate the principle of duality of patterning. The telegraph operator has to learn to discriminate, in the first instance, only two lengths of pulse and about three lengths of pause. Each letter is coded into a different arrangement of these elementary meaningless units. The arrangements are easily kept apart because the few meaningless units are plainly distinguishable.

The analogy explains why it was advantageous for the forerunner of language, as it was becoming increasingly complex, to acquire duality of patterning. However it occurred, this was a major breakthrough; without it language could not possibly have achieved the efficiency and flexibility it has.

One of the basic principles of evolutionary theory holds that the initial survival value of any innovation is conservative in that it makes possible the maintenance of a largely traditional way of life in the face of changed circumstances. There was nothing in the make-up of the protohominoids that destined their descendants to become human. Some of them, indeed, did not. They made their way to ecological niches where food was plentiful and predators sufficiently avoidable, and where the development of primitive varieties of language and culture would have bestowed no advantage. They survive still, with various sorts of specialization, as the gibbons and the great apes.

Man's own remote ancestors, then, must have come to live in circumstances where a slightly more flexible system of communication, the incipient carrying and shaping of tools, and a slight increase in the capacity for traditional transmission made just the difference between surviving—largely, be it noted, by the good old protohominoid way of life—and dying out. There are various possibilities. If predators become more numerous and dangerous, any nonce use of a tool as a weapon, any co-operative mode of escape or attack might restore the balance. If food became scarcer, any technique for cracking harder nuts, for foraging over a wider territory, for sharing food so gathered or storing it when it was plentiful might promote survival of the band. Only after a very long period of such small adjustments to tiny changes of living conditions could the factors involved —incipient language, incipient tool-carrying and toolmaking, incipient culture— have started leading the way to a new pattern of life, of the kind called human.

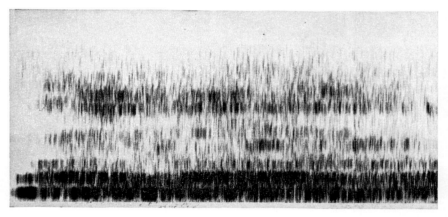

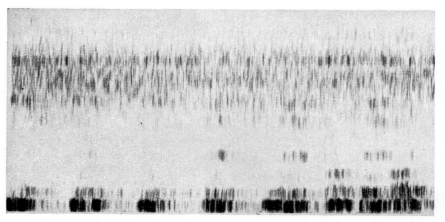

SUBHUMAN PRIMATE CALLS are represented here by sound spectrograms of the roar (*top*) and bark (*bottom*) of the howler monkey. Frequencies are shown vertically; time, horizontally. Roaring, the most prominent howler vocalization, regulates interactions and movements of groups of monkeys, and has both defensive and offensive functions. Barking has similar meanings but occurs when the monkeys are not quite so excited. Spectrograms were produced at Bell Telephone Laboratories from recordings made by Charles Southwick of the University of Southern Ohio during an expedition to Barro Colorado Island in the Canal Zone. The expedition was directed by C. R. Carpenter of Pennsylvania State University.

46

ATTENTION AND THE PERCEPTION OF SPEECH

DONALD E. BROADBENT
April 1962

Paying attention—and not paying attention—are surely two of the most important abilities of human beings. Yet in spite of their crucial role in learning, and in a host of other intelligent activities, psychologists for many years did not consider them proper topics of study. Attention seemed a subjective quality, associated historically with the introspective method of investigation. That method tends to give inconsistent results and so fell into disrepute among experimental psychologists. Correspondingly, most respectable theorists failed to make use of any concept resembling attention; and, since research in psychology tends to be dominated by theory, there was little experimentation along lines that might have revived the idea.

In the past 10 years, however, the concept of attention has begun to force itself on the attention of psychologists in various ways. One is through studies of the efficiency of control systems such as those concerned with the regulation of air traffic at airports. A major cause of failure in these systems is that the human operator has too much information to handle simultaneously, or that he reacts to an unimportant signal when he should be dealing with an important one. These problems require some understanding of phenomena that would commonly be described under the heading of "attention." There is now accumulating a wide variety of experimental results that clarify these phenomena, although the larger part of the work remains to be done. In this article I shall describe some of the research on attention to spoken messages.

One of the earliest findings, and one that agrees with everyday experience, is that it is harder to understand two messages arriving simultaneously than two messages arriving one after the other.

One might be tempted to explain this as a purely physical interference between the two stimuli; for example, the louder passages of one message might drown out the softer passages of the other and vice versa, rendering them both unintelligible. Actually the matter is not so simple. By recording the messages on tape and playing them for different subjects instructed to respond in different ways, the intelligibility is shown to depend on psychological factors. Specifically, either message becomes understandable if the listener is instructed to ignore the other. But the two messages together cannot both be understood, even though the necessary information is available to the ear. Another way of making the same point is to insert the words of one message into spaces between the words from the other: "Oh God say save can our you gracious see Queen." Each message is hard to understand, but each word is spoken separately and is fully audible. The difficulty evidently lies inside the nervous system, which somehow prevents an adequate response to signals that are "heard" satisfactorily.

Further experiments demonstrate that comprehension improves if the two messages differ in certain physical characteristics. For instance, it is better if a man speaks one message and a woman speaks the other; or if the loudspeaker removes the lower tones from one voice but not the other. Spatial separation of the two voices gives the best result of all. The different messages should not come through the same loudspeaker or even from separate speakers mounted one above the other; the two speakers should be separated as far as possible from each other in the horizontal plane. Interestingly enough, a listener also comprehends simultaneous spoken messages

better when they come from a stereophonic system than when they are played over a single loudspeaker. (This effect, rather than the doubtful gain in realism, is for many people the main advantage of stereophonic high-fidelity systems: the listener can pay attention to different musical instruments played at the same time.)

Physical distinctions are most helpful in promoting understanding when one message has no importance for the listener and does not have to be answered. It would seem that the differences allow the brain to filter the incoming sounds and select some for response while ignoring others.

The need to throw away part of the available information can perhaps be understood by comparing the brain with man-made communication systems. Engineers nowadays talk of capacity for transmitting information, by which they mean the number of equally probable messages of which one can be sent in a specified time. Suppose, for example, that two complicated military plans have been prepared and an order is to be sent to carry out one of them. A simple communication system consisting of a red and a green lamp can transmit the message with maximum efficiency by the lighting of a single lamp. If there were four plans instead of two, however, it would be impossible to give the order by lighting one of the two lamps no matter how simple each plan might be. Either there must be more lamps or more time is needed for sending the order. In the most efficient code for two lamps, two successive flashes of the red lamp would mean one plan, a red flash followed by a green flash would mean another, and so on. One of four possible messages can be transmitted with two lamps, but only by taking two units of time. With eight pos-

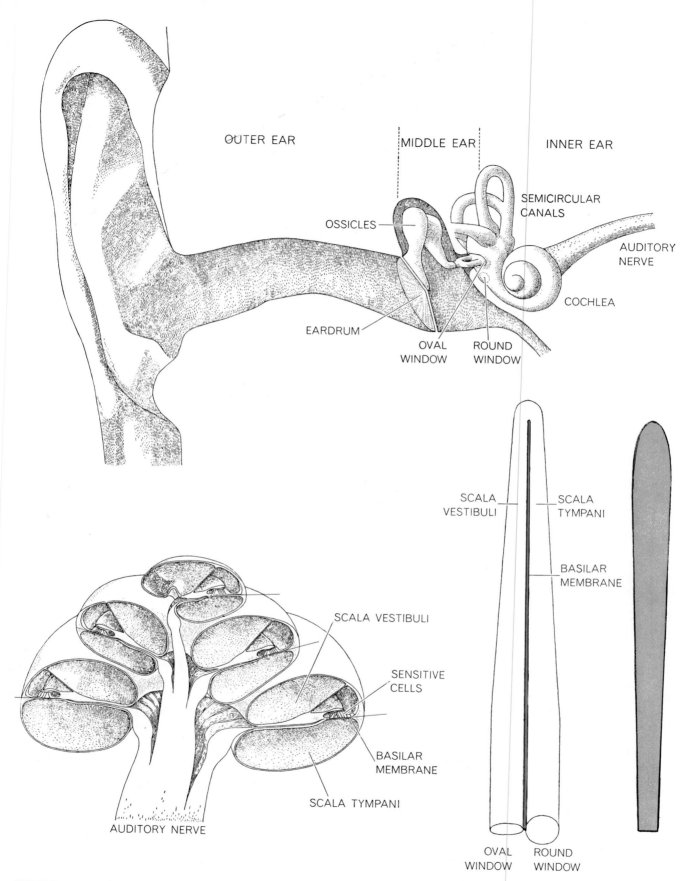

PERCEPTION OF SPEECH begins in the ear, shown at top in simplified cross section. The eardrum transmits sound vibrations to the three small bones called ossicles, which cause waves in fluid in the cochlea. The cochlea, seen in cross section at bottom left, contains the basilar membrane (*color*), on which rest the sensitive cells that excite auditory-nerve fibers. At bottom center cochlea is rolled out, with basilar membrane in side view. Front view of the basilar membrane (*bottom right*) shows that it is wider at one end than the other. The wide region vibrates in response to low frequencies, whereas the narrow region responds to high frequencies.

sible messages the code would call for three flashes of the two lamps, taking three units of time; 16 possible messages would require four flashes, and so forth.

Although the human brain has far more than the two states represented by the red and the green lamp, the number of its possible states is presumably limited. One would expect, then, that there is a limit to the number of different possibilities among which it can distinguish in a given time. Indeed, a number of experiments suggest a close parallel with the two-lamp system: in many cases a man's reaction time in responding to one of several possible signals increases by an equal amount every time the number of possible signals is doubled. Since there is a maximum speed at which one signal can be distinguished from others, the brain limits the number of possibilities being considered at any one time by selecting only part of the information reaching the ears. Therefore the degree of difficulty in dealing with two simultaneous spoken messages depends on the number of other messages that might have arrived instead of the two that did arrive. If only a few other messages are possible, the two messages together may not exceed the capacity of the brain and the listener may understand both. On the other hand, if each message is drawn from a very large range of possibilities, it may be all the listener can do to respond appropriately to one of them.

Several studies support these conclusions. John C. Webster and his associates at the U.S. Navy Electronics Laboratory in San Diego, Calif., observed that control-tower operators in San Diego could sometimes identify two aircraft call signs arriving at the same time but could understand only one of the two messages that followed. The call signs penetrated because the operators knew pretty well which aircraft might call. They did not know what the pilots would say.

An experiment at the Applied Psychology Research Unit in Cambridge, England, required a listener to answer a rapid series of questions while pressing a key in response to an intermittent buzzer. The interference produced by the buzzer in the ability to answer questions increased after the subject had been told that he would also have to respond to a bell. Even when the bell did not ring, the subject found the questions harder to answer than when he was expecting only the buzzer.

These results help to explain why a person can sometimes listen to two things at once and sometimes cannot pay atten-

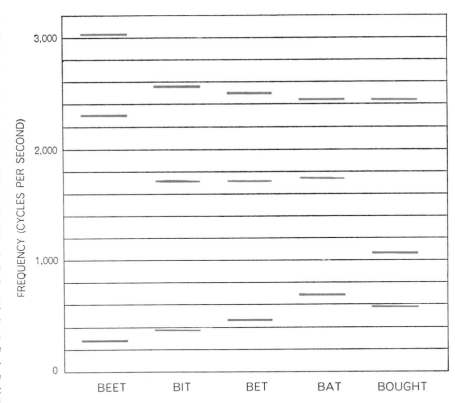

VOWEL FORMANTS, or frequencies that make up each vowel sound, are shown here for five different vowels. The values given are averages for male voices. Actually they differ from person to person. Although three formants are shown here for each sound, quite recognizable vowels can be produced by mechanisms using two filters to make two formants.

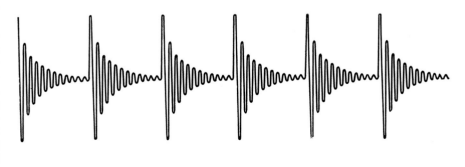

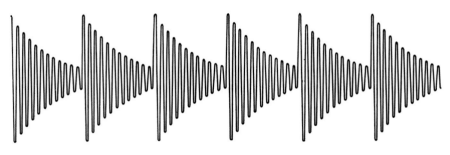

DECAY RATE of pulses from vocal cords affects quality of speech. Waves of highest amplitude mark beginning of each pulse. At top, pulses decay rapidly, helping to give the voice a crisp or sharp sound. At bottom, the decay is much slower, giving the voice a mellow quality. In both cases the frequencies of the pulses and the vibrations are exactly the same.

tion to more than one. When the listener is thoroughly familiar with a situation, so that he knows to within a small number of alternatives what each message will be, he can comprehend two simultaneous messages. But when one or both messages are drawn from a large number of possibilities, the filter in the brain lets only one message come through.

How does the filter work? As yet the answer is not known. Enough is known, however, about the physical characteristics of speech and the physiology of hearing to make possible some reasonable speculation. Human speech is produced by the combined action of the vocal cords and the vocal tract, which consists of the cavities of the throat, mouth and nose. Taut vocal cords produce a buzz when air is forced through them. The buzz consists of brief pulses, or puffs of air, at the rate of 100 or more per second, each pulse containing energy at many frequencies. These pulses excite into vibration the air in the cavities of the throat, nose and mouth. The cavities can be tuned to different frequencies by changing the position of the tongue, cheeks, jaw and lips. What emerges is a train of waves that contains a particular group of frequencies and is pulsed about 100 times per second. Each pulse starts out at full strength and decays rapidly until the sound energy is renewed by the next one [see bottom illustration on preceding page].

Many vowel sounds contain waves at two or more widely separated frequencies. For example, when the greatest energy is at 375 and 1,700 cycles per second, the vowel sound in the word "bit" is produced; frequencies of 450 and 1,700 cycles per second give the vowel in "bet." (These figures apply to a typical male voice. In the voices of women and children the whole range of frequencies may be higher but the listener takes this into account.) On reaching the ear, the sounds stimulate sense organs arranged along the basilar membrane in the cochlea [see illustration on page 424]. Low frequencies stimulate organs at one end of the membrane; high frequencies affect those at the other end. A complex sound made up of several frequencies energizes several different regions of the basilar membrane. Each sense organ on the membrane connects with particular nerve fibers going to the brain; thus the word "bit" stimulates one combination of fibers and the word "bet" another combination.

If both words reach the ear simultaneously, both combinations of fibers would come into play and the brain would have the problem of deciding which belong together. It might seem then that two or more voices would produce so much confusion in the ear that the brain could not select one voice for special attention. Of course, certain obvious features help distinguish one speaker from another: accent, rate of speaking, loudness or softness. But one cannot make use of these features until one knows which frequencies belong to which voice. Thus the problem remains: How does the brain manage to focus attention on one voice? Studies of the artificial generation of speech sounds have begun to throw some light on this problem.

Peter Ladefoged of the University of Edinburgh and I have been experimenting with a device that was developed by Walter Lawrence of the Signals Re-

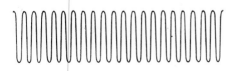

LOW FILTER FREQUENCY

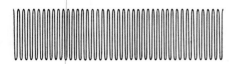

HIGH FILTER FREQUENCY

SPEECH SOUNDS consist of pulses of energy from the voice, shown here as high and

search Development Establishment in England. Our version of the apparatus sends a series of electrical pulses (analogous to pulses from the vocal cords) through two filter circuits, each of which passes primarily one frequency. The waves from one filter circuit, which are like those from the largest human speech cavity, are mixed with waves from the other, which imitate the frequencies produced by the second largest cavity. To-

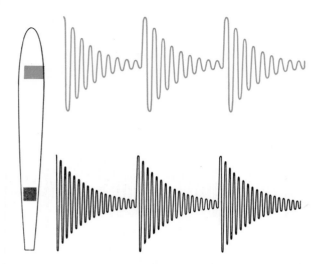

DIFFERENT FILTER FREQUENCIES but same rate of pulsation or modulation from voice excites two different regions of a basilar membrane (left). Listener reports he hears one vowel sound.

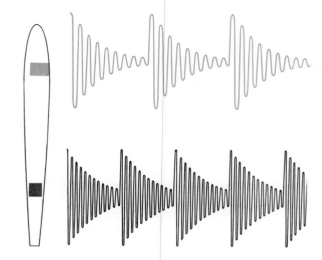

DIFFERENT PULSATION RATES and different filter frequencies make the listener hear two different sounds, even though only one ear or basilar membrane is actually being used for hearing.

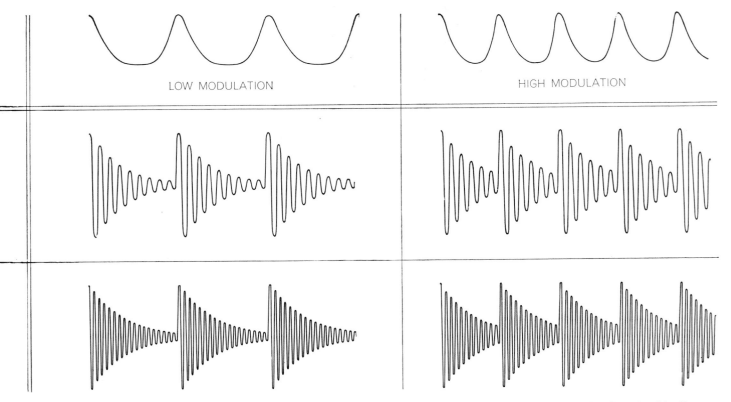

LOW MODULATION   HIGH MODULATION

low modulations (*across top*), and of specific frequencies emitted by the mouth and throat "filters," or cavities (*far left*). These two types of wave combine in patterns like those in this diagram. Effects of such waves are shown across bottom of these two pages.

gether the two wave trains are heard as quite acceptable vowel sounds that can be changed by tuning the filters to different frequencies. Varying the pulse rate used to excite the filters alters the apparent pitch or intonation of the "speech": it rises with faster pulse rates and falls with slower ones.

When the same pulses excite both filters, a listener hears the output as readily identifiable vowel sounds. This is true even when the low frequency is fed into one ear and the high frequency into the other. But if the two filters are pulsed at slightly different rates, the "speech" becomes unacceptable and listeners say that they are hearing two sounds coming from two sources rather than a single vowel sound.

Other experiments on the fusion of sounds at the two ears, conducted by Colin A. Cherry and his colleagues at the Imperial College of Science and Technology in London, also support the idea that when the rate of pulsing, or modulation, is the same for two sounds, the hearer perceives them as one sound. It seems reasonable to suppose, therefore, that a man can listen to one person

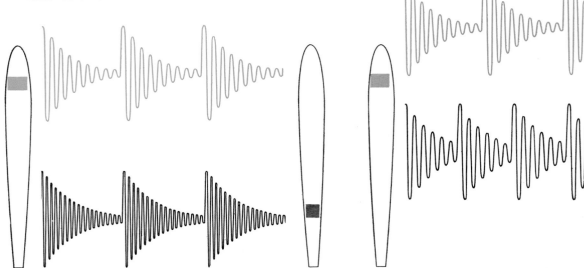

USING BOTH EARS, listener will hear one vowel sound, although right ear hears one filter frequency and left ear hears another. The pulsation or modulation rate has to be the same.

TWO PULSATION RATES, combined with same filter frequency and fed into each ear separately, produce two distinct sounds. The brain evidently focuses its attention on the rate of pulsation.

and ignore another primarily by selecting from the mass of sounds entering his ears all those frequencies that are being modulated at the same rate. Since it is most unlikely that the vocal cords of two speakers would vibrate at exactly the same rate at any moment, modulation would almost always provide an important (if not the sole) means of separating a pair of voices.

It is now a generally accepted principle of neurophysiology that messages traveling along a particular nerve can differ either by involving different nerve fibers or by producing a different number of impulses per second in the fibers. High-frequency and low-frequency sounds stimulate different fibers. It may be that the rate at which the sounds are pulsed controls the rate of firing of the fibers. If so, the brain could pick out one voice from others by focusing its attention on all auditory nerve fibers that are firing at the same rate.

A further indication of the importance of modulation is that it, rather than the frequency of the waves being modulated, seems under certain conditions to determine the pitch of a voice. This can be demonstrated with the artificial speech generator. A filter tuned to, say, 3,000 cycles per second is pulsed at the rate of 100 cycles per second. A listener is asked to match the pitch of the sound with either of two simple sound waves, one at 100 cycles per second and the oth-

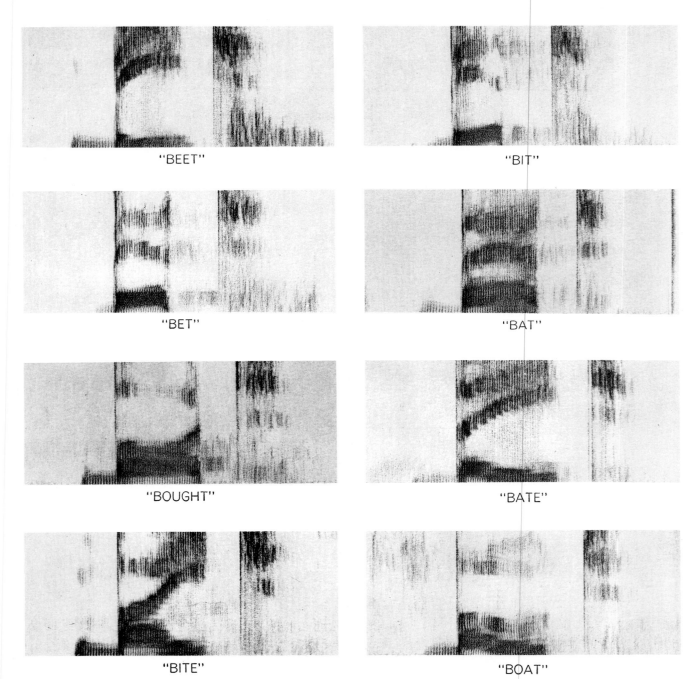

"BEET"   "BIT"

"BET"   "BAT"

"BOUGHT"   "BATE"

"BITE"   "BOAT"

SOUND SPECTROGRAMS show that various vowel sounds are made of several different frequencies. Time is shown horizontally, frequencies vertically and intensity of sound by relative darkness. The "b" of each word appears at lowest frequency. Vowel begins suddenly as lips open. After vowel there is a quiet period followed by a burst of noise primarily at high frequency as the "t" explodes. Frequency shifts in "bate" and "bite" are diphthongs. Spectrograms were made by H. K. Dunn of Bell Telephone Laboratories.

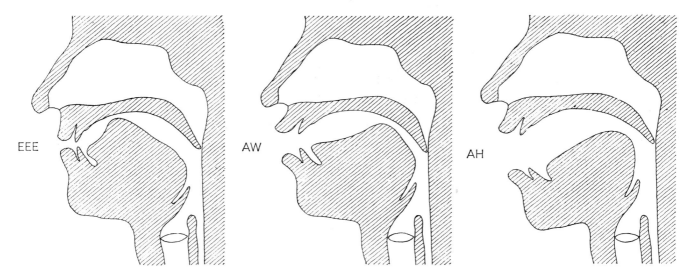

SHAPE OF CAVITIES in the mouth is primarily responsible for the production of different vowel sounds. Three other factors that play a key role in this process are the configuration of the tongue, the size of the opening of the mouth and the position of the lips.

er at 3,000. Usually he selects the 100-cycle sound.

The selection mechanism that has been described is still hypothetical, but I believe that something much like it must exist. There can be no doubt, however, that it is not the only basis for auditory attention. Several experiments have served to make this clear. In one, a listener is equipped with earphones that feed one voice into the right ear and another voice into the left. Normally the subject has no difficulty in understanding the message entering one ear and ignoring the other. But under certain conditions sound from the ear being ignored can break into consciousness. For example, Neville Moray of the University of Oxford has demonstrated that a man fully occupied in listening to speech entering one ear will hear his own name in the other ear even though

he remains quite unresponsive to any other word in that ear. Under similar circumstances Anne M. Treisman of the University of Oxford has found that speech entering the rejected ear can break through to the subject's attention if it consists of words that would probably follow the words that have just been heard by the ear that is receiving attention. In these cases the content of the speech has taken precedence over its physical characteristics.

How the brain focuses attention on meaning or content is as yet an almost complete mystery. One thing is clear. If the method proposed for choosing between voices is correct, there must be two attention mechanisms. Selection on the basis of content involves examining a stimulus for its possible appropriateness to a particular set of responses

rather than for the presence or absence of a physical marker. At one moment, for example, a person might be ready to write down any of the digits one through nine and highly unready to write anything else, or indeed to respond in any other way. If he hears a sound from any direction or in any voice that can be interpreted as the name of one of the digits, he will respond by writing it down; only if the sound cannot be so interpreted will he not respond. At another time he might be ready to write down letters of the alphabet but not numbers, and so on.

Both types of attention are now the subject of intensive research. The next few years should yield more definite clues to the nature of each and at least a tentative answer to the question of whether or not they depend on different mechanisms.

BIBLIOGRAPHIES

I GENETICS AND HUMAN EVOLUTION

1. The Genetic Basis of Evolution

GENETICS AND THE ORIGIN OF SPECIES. Th. Dobzhansky. Columbia University Press, 1937.

2. Tools and Human Evolution

CEREBRAL CORTEX OF MAN. Wilder Penfield and Theodore Rasmussen. Macmillan Company, 1950.

THE EVOLUTION OF MAN. Edited by Sol Tax. University of Chicago Press, 1960.

THE EVOLUTION OF MAN'S CAPACITY FOR CULTURE. Arranged by J. N. Spuhler. Wayne State University Press, 1959.

HUMAN ECOLOGY DURING THE PLEISTOCENE AND LATER TIMES IN AFRICA SOUTH OF THE SAHARA. J. Desmond Clark in Current Anthropology, Vol. I, pages 307-324; 1960.

3. The Distribution of Man

HUMAN ANCESTRY FROM A GENETICAL POINT OF VIEW.

Reginald Ruggles Gates. Harvard University Press, 1948.

MANKIND IN THE MAKING. William White Howells. Doubleday & Company, Inc., 1959.

RACES: A STUDY OF THE PROBLEMS OF RACE FORMATION IN MAN. Carleton S. Coon, Stanley M. Garn and Joseph B. Birdsell. Charles C. Thomas, 1950.

THE STORY OF MAN. Carleton Stevens Coon. Alfred A. Knopf, Inc., 1954.

4. The Present Evolution of Man

EVOLUTION, GENETICS AND MAN. Theodosius Dobzhansky. John Wiley & Sons, Inc., 1955.

MIRROR FOR MAN. Clyde Kluckhohn. McGraw-Hill Book Co., Inc., 1949.

RADIATION, GENES AND MAN. Bruce Wallace and Theodosius Dobzhansky. Henry Holt & Co., Inc., 1959.

II THE EVOLUTION AND DEVELOPMENT OF BEHAVIOR: INSTINCT AND EXPERIENCE

5. The Evolution of Behavior

THE STUDY OF INSTINCT. N. Tinbergen. Clarendon Press, 1952.

6. Early Environment

EFFECTS OF EARLY EXPERIENCE UPON THE BEHAVIOR OF ANIMALS. Frank A. Beach and Julian Jaynes in Psychological Bulletin, Vol. 51, No. 3, pages 239-263; May, 1954.

THE EFFECTS OF EARLY RESTRICTION ON ACTIVITY IN DOGS. W. R. Thompson and W. Heron in Journal of Comparative and Physiological Psychology, Vol. 47, No. 1, pages 77-82. February, 1954.

THE GENESIS OF EMOTIONAL BEHAVIOR: AN EXPERIMENTAL STUDY OF THE DOG. R. Melzack in Journal of Comparative and Physiological Psychology, Vol. 47, No. 2, pages 166-168; April, 1954.

7. The Reproductive Behavior of Ring Doves

CONTROL OF BEHAVIOR CYCLES IN REPRODUCTION. Daniel S. Lehrman in *Social Behavior and Organization among Vertebrates*, edited by William Etkin. The University of Chicago Press, 1964.

HORMONAL REGULATION OF PARENTAL BEHAVIOR IN BIRDS AND INFRAHUMAN MAMMALS. Daniel S. Lehrman in *Sex and Internal Secretions*, edited by William C. Young, Williams & Wilkins Company, 1961.

INTERACTION OF HORMONAL AND EXPERIENTIAL INFLUENCES ON DEVELOPMENT OF BEHAVIOR. Daniel S. Lehrman in *Roots of Behavior*, edited by E. L. Bliss. Harper & Row, Publishers, 1962.

8. The Origin of Form Perception

EFFECTS OF EARLY EXPERIENCE UPON THE BEHAVIOR OF ANIMALS. Frank A. Beach and Julian Jaynes in *Psychological Bulletin*, Vol. 51, No. 3, pages 239-263; May, 1954.

FORM PREFERENCES IN NEWLY HATCHED CHICKS. Robert L. Fantz in *Journal of Comparative and Physiological Psychology*, Vol. 50, No. 5, pages 422-430; October, 1957.

ON THE STIMULUS SITUATION RELEASING THE BEGGING RESPONSE IN THE NEWLY HATCHED HERRING GULL CHICK. N. Tinbergen and A. C. Perdeck in *Behavior*, Vol. 3, Part 1, pages 1-39; 1950.

PATTERN VISION IN YOUNG INFANTS. Robert L. Fantz in *Psychological Record*, Vol. 8, pages 43-47; 1958.

THE PERCEPTION OF THE VISUAL WORLD. James J. Gibson. Houghton Mifflin Company, 1950.

9. Love in Infant Monkeys

THE DEVELOPMENT OF AFFECTIONAL RESPONSES IN INFANT MONKEYS. Harry F. Harlow and Robert R. Zimmermann in *Proceedings of the American Philosophical Society*, Vol. 102, pages 501-509; 1958.

THE NATURE OF LOVE. Harry F. Harlow in *American Psychologist*, Vol. 12, No. 13, pages 673-685; 1958.

III   BRAIN AND CONSCIOUSNESS

10. "The Great Ravelled Knot"

THE PHYSICAL BACKGROUND OF PERCEPTION. E. D. Adrian. Oxford University Press, 1947.

MAN ON HIS NATURE. Charles Sherrington. Macmillan, 1941.

BRAIN AND INTELLIGENCE. Ward C. Halstead. University of Chicago Press, 1947.

AGNOSIA, APRAXIA, APHASIA. J. M. Nielsen. Paul Hoeber, 1946.

11. The Reticular Formation

BRAIN MECHANISMS AND CONSCIOUSNESS. J. F. Delafresnaye. Blackwell Scientific Publications, 1954.

BRAIN STEM RETICULAR FORMATION AND ACTIVATION OF THE EEG. G. Moruzzi and H. W. Magoun in *Electroencephalography and Clinical Neurophysiology*, Vol. 1, No. 4, pages 455-473; November, 1949.

PATTERNS OF ORGANIZATION IN THE CENTRAL NERVOUS SYSTEM. Edited by Philip Bard. The Williams & Wilkins Company, 1952.

SPASTICITY: THE STRETCH-REFLEX AND EXTRAPYRAMIDAL SYSTEMS. H. W. Magoun and Ruth Rhines. Charles C. Thomas, 1947.

12. The Analysis of Brain Waves

COMPUTER TECHNIQUES IN EEG ANALYSIS. Edited by Mary A. B. Brazier. *Electroencephalography and Clinical Neurophysiology*, Suppl. 20; 1961.

THE ELECTRICAL ACTIVITY OF THE NERVOUS SYSTEM. Mary A. B. Brazier. The Macmillan Co., 1960.

PROCESSING NEUROELECTRIC DATA. Communications Biophysics Group of Research Laboratory of Electronics and William M. Siebert. The Technology Press of the Massachusetts Institute of Technology, 1959.

SOME USES OF COMPUTERS IN EXPERIMENTAL NEUROLOGY. Mary A. B. Brazier in *Experimental Neurology*, Vol. 2, No. 2, pages 123-143; April, 1960.

THE WAKING BRAIN. H. W. Magoun. Charles C. Thomas, 1958.

13. The Split Brain in Man

CEREBRAL COMMISSUROTOMY. J. E. Bogen, E. D. Fisher and P. J. Vogel in *Journal of the American Medical Association*, Vol. 194, No. 12, pages 1328-1329; December 20, 1965.

CEREBRAL ORGANIZATION AND BEHAVIOR. R. W. Sperry in *Science*, Vol. 133, No. 3466, pages 1749-1757; June 2, 1961.

LANGUAGE AFTER SECTION OF THE CEREBRAL COMMISSURES. M. S. Gazzaniga and R. W. Sperry in *Brain*, Vol. 90, Part 1, pages 131-148; 1967.

MICROELECTRODE ANALYSIS OF TRANSFER OF VISUAL INFORMATION BY THE CORPUS CALLOSUM. G. Berlucchi, M. S. Gazzaniga and G. Rizzolati in *Archives Italiennes de Biologie*, Vol. 105, pages 583-596; 1967.

OBSERVATIONS ON VISUAL PERCEPTION AFTER DISCONNEXION OF THE CEREBRAL HEMISPHERES IN MAN. M. S. Gazzaniga, J. E. Bogen and R. W. Sperry in *Brain*, Vol. 88, Part 2, pages 221-236; 1965.

IV NEURON AND SYNAPSE: THE BASIS OF INTEGRATION AND PLASTICITY IN THE BRAIN

14. The Nerve Impulse and the Squid

THE CROONIAN LECTURE: IONIC MOVEMENTS AND ELECTRICAL ACTIVITY IN GIANT NERVE FIBRES. A. L. Hodgkin in *Proceedings of the Royal Society,* Series B, Vol. 148, No. 930, pages 1-37; January 1, 1958.

THE NEUROPHYSIOLOGICAL BASIS OF MIND. John Carew Eccles. Clarendon Press, 1953.

THE PHYSIOLOGY OF NERVE CELLS. John Carew Eccles. The Johns Hopkins Press, 1957.

15. The Synapse

EXCITATION AND INHIBITION IN SINGLE NERVE CELLS. Stephen W. Kuffler in *The Harvey Lectures, Series 54.* Academic Press, 1960.

PHYSIOLOGY OF NERVE CELLS. John C. Eccles. Johns Hopkins Press, 1957.

THE PHYSIOLOGY OF SYNAPSES. John Carew Eccles. Academic Press, 1964.

THE TRANSMISSION OF IMPULSES FROM NERVE TO MUSCLE, AND THE SUBCELLULAR UNIT OF SYNAPTIC ACTION. B. Katz in *Proceedings of the Royal Society,* Series B, Vol. 155, No. 961, pages 455-477; April, 1962.

16. Nerve Cells and Behavior

NERVE, MUSCLE, AND SYNAPSE. Bernhard Katz. McGraw-Hill Book Company, 1966.

RESPONSE DECREMENT OF THE FLEXION REFLEX IN THE ACUTE CAT AND TRANSIENT RESTORATION BY STRONG STIMULI. W. A. Spencer, R. F. Thompson, and D. R. Neilson, Jr., in *Journal of Neurophysiology,* Vol. 29, No. 2, pages 221-239; March, 1966.

CELLULAR NEUROPHYSIOLOGICAL APPROACHES IN THE STUDY OF LEARNING. Eric R. Kandel and W. Alden Spencer in *Physiological Reviews,* Vol. 48, No. 1, pages 65-134; January, 1968.

ANALYSIS OF RESTRICTED NEURAL NETWORKS. Donald Kennedy, Allen I. Selverston and Michael P. Remler in *Science,* Vol. 164, No. 3887, pages 1488-1496; June 27, 1969.

THE ROLE OF SYNAPTIC PLASTICITY IN THE SHORT-TERM MODIFICATION OF BEHAVIOR. E. R. Kandel, V. Castellucci, H. Pinsker and I. Kupfermann in *Short-Term Changes in Neural Activity and Behavior,* edited by G. Horn, R. A. Hinde. Cambridge University Press, 1970.

17. Pathways in the Brain

SYNAPTIC DISTRIBUTION OF CENTRIPETAL AND CENTRIFUGAL NERVE FIBRES IN THE OLFACTORY SYSTEMS OF THE RAT: AN EXPERIMENTAL ANATOMICAL STUDY. Lennart Heimer in *Journal of Anatomy,* Vol. 103, Part 3, pages 413-432; November, 1968.

CONTEMPORARY RESEARCH METHODS IN NEUROANATOMY: PROCEEDINGS OF AN INTERNATIONAL CONFERENCE HELD AT THE INSTITUTE OF PERINATAL PHYSIOLOGY. Edited by W. J. H. Nauta and O. E. Ebbesson. Springer-Verlag New York Inc., 1970.

V THE CHEMISTRY OF BEHAVIOR AND EXPERIENCE: HORMONES AND DRUGS

18. Hormones

HORMONES AND BEHAVIOR. Frank A. Beach. Paul B. Hoeber, Inc., 1948.

THE HORMONES IN HUMAN REPRODUCTION. George W. Corner. Princeton University Press, 1943.

THE HORMONES: PHYSIOLOGY, CHEMISTRY AND APPLICATIONS. Edited by Gregory Pincus and Kenneth V. Thimann. Academic Press, Inc., 1955.

HORMONES IN REPRODUCTION. *British Medical Bulletin,* Vol. 11, No. 2; May, 1955.

RECENT PROGRESS IN HORMONE RESEARCH: Vol. 12. Edited by Gregory Pincus. Academic Press, Inc., 1956.

19. Chemical Stimulation of the Brain

CHEMICAL TRACING OF NEURAL PATHWAYS MEDIATING THE THIRST DRIVE. Alan E. Fisher and John N. Coury in *Thirst: Proceedings of the First International Symposium on Thirst in the Regulation of Body Water*, edited by Matthew J. Wayner. Pergamon Press, 1964.

MATERNAL AND SEXUAL BEHAVIOR INDUCED BY INTRACRANIAL CHEMICAL STIMULATION. Alan E. Fisher in *Science*, Vol. 124, No. 3214, pages 228-229; August, 1958.

20. Stress and Behavior

ADRENOCORTICAL ACTIVITY AND AVOIDANCE LEARNING AS A FUNCTION OF TIME AFTER AVOIDANCE TRAINING. Seymour Levine and F. Robert Brush in *Physiology & Behavior*, Vol. 2, No. 4, pages 385-388; October, 1967.

HORMONES AND CONDITIONING. Seymour Levine in *Nebraska Symposium on Motivation: 1968*, edited by William J. Arnold. University of Nebraska Press, 1968.

EFFECTS OF PEPTIDE HORMONES ON BEHAVIOR. David de Wied in *Frontiers in Neuroendocrinology*, edited by William F. Ganong and Luciano Martini. Oxford University Press, 1969.

THE NEUROENDOCRINE CONTROL OF PERCEPTION. R. I. Henkin in *Perception and Its Disorders: Proceedings of the Association for Research in Nervous Mental Disease*, 32, edited by D. Hamburg. The Williams & Wilkins Co., 1970.

21. Marihuana

THE MARIHUANA PAPERS. Edited by David Solomon. The Bobbs-Merrill Company, Inc., 1966.

SOCIAL AND PARA-MEDICAL ASPECTS OF HALLUCINOGENIC DRUGS. William H. McGlothlin in *The Use of LSD in Psychotherapy and Alcoholism*, edited by Harold A. Abramson. The Bobbs-Merrill Company, Inc., 1967.

CLINICAL AND PSYCHOLOGICAL EFFECTS OF MARIHUANA IN MAN. Andrew T. Weil, Norman E. Zinberg and Judith M. Nelsen in *Science*, Vol. 162, No. 3859, pages 1234-1242; December 13, 1968.

22. The Hallucinogenic Drugs

THE CLINICAL PHARMACOLOGY OF THE HALLUCINOGENS. Erik Jacobsen in *Clinical Pharmacology and Therapeutics*, Vol. 4, No. 4, pages 480-504; July–August, 1963.

LYSERGIC ACID DIETHYLAMIDE (LSD-25) AND EGO FUNCTIONS. G. D. Klee in *Archives of General Psychiatry*, Vol. 8, No. 5, pages 461-474; May, 1963.

PROLONGED ADVERSE REACTIONS TO LYSERGIC ACID DIETHYLAMIDE. S. Cohen and K. S. Ditman in *Archives of General Psychiatry*, Vol. 8, No. 5, pages 475-480; May, 1963.

THE PSYCHOTOMIMETIC DRUGS: AN OVERVIEW. Jonathan O. Cole and Martin M. Katz in *Journal of the American Medical Association*, Vol. 187, No. 10, pages 758-761; March, 1964.

VI SENSORY PROCESSES AND PERCEPTION

23. The Perception of Pain

ANATOMIES OF PAIN. K. D. Keele. Blackwell Scientific Publications, 1957.

CORD CELLS RESPONDING TO TOUCH, DAMAGE AND TEMPERATURE OF SKIN. Patrick D. Wall in *Journal of Neurophysiology*, Vol. 23, No. 2, pages 197-210; March, 1960.

EFFECTS OF DISCRETE BRAIN STEM LESIONS IN CATS ON PERCEPTION OF NOXIOUS STIMULATION. Ronald Melzack, W. A. Stotler and W. K. Livingston in *Journal of Neurophysiology*, Vol. XXI, No. 4, pages 352-367; July, 1958.

MEASUREMENT OF SUBJECTIVE RESPONSES. Henry K. Beecher. Oxford University Press, 1959.

PAIN MECHANISMS. W. K. Livingston. The Macmillan Company, 1943.

RESPONSES EVOKED IN THE BRAIN STEM BY TOOTH STIMULATION. D. I. B. Kerr, F. P. Haugen and R. Melzack in *American Journal of Physiology*, Vol. 183, No. 2, pages 253-258; November, 1955.

24. The Ear

THE EARLY HISTORY OF HEARING—OBSERVATIONS AND THEORIES. Georg v. Békésy and Walter A. Rosenblith in *Journal of the Acoustical Society of America*, Vol. 20, No. 6, pages 727-748; November, 1948.

HEARING: ITS PSYCHOLOGY AND PHYSIOLOGY. Stanley Smith Stevens and Hallowell Davis. John Wiley & Sons, Inc., 1938.

PHYSIOLOGICAL ACOUSTICS. Ernest Glen Wever and Merle Lawrence. Princeton University Press, 1954.

25. Retinal Processing of Visual Images

RECEPTIVE FIELDS, BINOCULAR INTERACTION AND FUNCTIONAL ARCHITECTURE IN THE CAT'S VISUAL CORTEX. D. H. Hubel and T. N. Wiesel in *Journal of Physiology*, Vol. 160, No. 1, pages 106-154; January, 1962.

THE MECHANISM OF DIRECTIONALLY SELECTIVE UNITS IN RABBIT'S RETINA. H. B. Barlow and W. R. Levick in *Journal of Physiology*, Vol. 178, No. 3, pages 477-504; June, 1965.

RECEPTIVE FIELDS OF SINGLE OPTIC NERVE FIBERS IN A MAMMAL WITH AN ALL-CONE RETINA. Charles R. Michael in *Journal of Neurophysiology*, Vol. 31, No. 2, pages 249-282; March, 1968.

26. The Visual Cortex of the Brain

DISCHARGE PATTERNS AND FUNCTIONAL ORGANIZATION OF MAMMALIAN RETINA. Stephen W. Kuffler in *Journal of Neurophysiology*, Vol. 16, No. 1, pages 37-68; January, 1953.

INTEGRATIVE PROCESSES IN CENTRAL VISUAL PATHWAYS OF THE CAT. David M. Hubel in *Journal of the Optical Society of America*, Vol. 53, No. 1, pages 58-66; January, 1963.

RECEPTIVE FIELDS, BINOCULAR INTERACTION AND FUNCTIONAL ARCHITECTURE IN THE CAT'S VISUAL CORTEX. D. H. Hubel and T. N. Wiesel in *Journal of Physiology*, Vol. 160, No. 1, pages 106-154; January, 1962.

THE VISUAL PATHWAY. Ragnar Granit in *The Eye, Volume II: The Visual Process*, edited by Hugh Davson. Academic Press, 1962.

27. Eye Movements and Visual Perception

PATTERN RECOGNITION. Edited by Leonard M. Uhr. John Wiley & Sons, Inc., 1966.

CONTEMPORARY THEORY AND RESEARCH IN VISUAL PERCEPTION. Edited by Ralph Norman Haber. Holt, Rinehart & Winston, Inc., 1968.

A THEORY OF VISUAL PATTERN PERCEPTION. David Noton in *IEEE Transactions on Systems Science and Cybernetics*, Vol. SSC-6, No. 4, pages 349-357; October, 1970.

SCANPATHS IN EYE MOVEMENTS DURING PATTERN PERCEPTION. David Noton and Lawrence Stark in *Science*, Vol. 171, No. 3968, pages 308-311; January 22, 1971.

28. Plasticity in Sensory-Motor Systems

MOVEMENT-PRODUCED STIMULATION IN THE DEVELOPMENT OF VISUALLY GUIDED BEHAVIOR. Richard Held and Alan Hein in *Journal of Comparative & Physiological Psychology*, Vol. 56, No. 5, pages 872-876; October, 1963.

NEONATAL DEPRIVATION AND ADULT REARRANGEMENT: COMPLEMENTARY TECHNIQUES FOR ANALYZING PLASTIC SENSORY-MOTOR COORDINATIONS. Richard Held and Joseph Bossom in *The Journal of Comparative and Physiological Psychology*, Vol. 54, No. 1, pages 33-37; February, 1961.

PLASTICITY IN HUMAN SENSORIMOTOR CONTROL. Richard Held and Sanford J. Freedman in *Science*, Vol. 142, No. 3591, pages 455-462; October 25, 1963.

VII DRIVE, MOTIVATION, AND EMOTION

29. Electrically Controlled Behavior

FERNREIZUNG FREIBEWEGLICHER TIERE. W. Jechorek and E. Von Holst in *Die Naturwissenschaften*, Vol. 43, Part 19, page 455; 1956.

VOM WIRKUNGSGEFÜGE DER TRIEBE. Erich von Holst and Ursula von Saint Paul in *Die Naturwissenschaften*, Vol. 47, Part 18, pages 409-422; 1960.

WIRKUNGEN DER REIZUNGEN UND KOEGULATIONEN IN DEN STAMMGANGLIEN BEI STEREOTAKTISCHEN HIRNOPERATIONEN. R. Hassler and T. Riechert in *Der Nervenarzt*, Vol. 32, No. 3, pages 97-109; March, 1961.

ZENTRALNERVENSYSTEM. Erich von Holst in *Fortschritte der Zoologie*, Vol. 11, pages 245-275; 1958.

30. Pleasure Centers in the Brain

THE BEHAVIOR OF ORGANISMS: AN EXPERIMENTAL ANALYSIS. B. F. Skinner. Appleton-Century-Crofts, Inc., 1938.

DIENCEPHALON. Walter Rudolf Hess. Grune & Stratton, Inc., 1954.

PSYCHOSOMATIC DISEASE AND THE "VISCERAL BRAIN": RECENT DEVELOPMENTS BEARING ON THE PAPEZ THEORY OF EMOTION. Paul D. MacLean in *Psychosomatic Medicine*, Vol. 11, pages 338-353; 1949.

31. Curiosity in Monkeys

DISCRIMINATION LEARNING BY RHESUS MONKEYS TO VISUAL-EXPLORATION MOTIVATION. Robert A. Butler in *Journal of Comparative and Physiological Psychology*, Vol. 46, No. 2; April, 1953.

THE GREAT APES. Robert M. Yerkes and Ada W. Yerkes. Yale University Press, 1929.

MICE, MONKEYS, MEN AND MOTIVES. Harry F. Harlow in *Psychological Review*, Vol. 60, No. 1; January, 1953.

32. Attitude and Pupil Size

PUPIL SIZE AS RELATED TO INTEREST VALUE OF VISUAL STIMULI. Eckhard H. Hess and James M. Polt in *Science*, Vol. 132, No. 3423, pages 349-350, August 5, 1960.

PUPIL SIZE IN RELATION TO MENTAL ACTIVITY DURING SIMPLE PROBLEM-SOLVING. Eckhard H. Hess and James M. Polt in *Science*, Vol. 143, No. 3611, pages 1190-1192; March 13, 1964.

33. Social Deprivation in Monkeys

AFFECTIONAL RESPONSES IN THE INFANT MONKEY. Harry F. Harlow and Robert R. Zimmermann in *Science*, Vol. 130, No. 3373, pages 421-432; August 21, 1959.

DETERMINANTS OF INFANT BEHAVIOUR. Edited by B. M. Foss. Methuen & Co., Ltd., 1961.

THE DEVELOPMENT OF LEARNING IN THE RHESUS MONKEY. Harry F. Harlow in *Science in Progress: Twelfth Series*, edited by Wallace R. Brode, pages 239-269. Yale University Press, 1962.

THE HETEROSEXUAL AFFECTIONAL SYSTEM IN MONKEYS. Harry F. Harlow in *American Psychologist*, Vol. 17, No. 1, pages 1-9; January, 1962.

VIII   SLEEP, DREAMING, AND AROUSAL

34. The States of Sleep

ASPECTS ANATOMO-FONCTIONNELS DE LA PHYSIOLOGIE DU SOMMEIL. Edited by M. Jouvet. Centre National de la Recherche Scientifique, 1965.

AN ESSAY ON DREAMS: THE ROLE OF PHYSIOLOGY IN UNDERSTANDING THEIR NATURE. W. C. Dement in *New Directions in Psychology: Vol. II*. Holt, Rinehart & Winston, Inc., 1965.

SLEEP AND WAKEFULNESS. Nathaniel Kleitman. The University of Chicago Press, 1963.

SLEEP AND WAKING. Ian Oswald. American Elsevier Publishing Company, Inc., 1962.

SLEEP MECHANISMS. Edited by K. Akert, C. Bally and J. P. Schadé. American Elsevier Publishing Company, Inc., 1965.

35. Patterns of Dreaming

A COMPARISON OF "DREAMERS" AND "NONDREAMERS": EYE MOVEMENTS, ELECTROENCEPHALOGRAMS AND THE RECALL OF DREAMS. Donald R. Goodenough, Arthur Shapiro, Melvin Holden and Leonard Steinschriber in *Journal of Abnormal and Social Psychology*, Vol. 59, No. 3, pages 295-302; November, 1959.

CYCLIC VARIATIONS IN EEG DURING SLEEP AND THEIR RELATION TO EYE MOVEMENTS, BODY MOTILITY, AND DREAMING. William Dement and Nathaniel Kleitman in *Electroencephalography and Clinical Neurophysiology*, Vol. 9, No. 4, pages 673-690; November, 1957.

THE RELATION OF EYE MOVEMENTS DURING SLEEP TO DREAM ACTIVITY: AN OBJECTIVE METHOD FOR THE STUDY OF DREAMING. W. Dement and N. Kleitman in *Journal of Experimental Psychology*, Vol. 53, No. 5, pages 339-346; May, 1957.

STUDIES IN PSYCHOPHYSIOLOGY OF DREAMS. I: EXPERIMENTAL EVOCATION OF SEQUENTIAL DREAM EPISODES. Edward A. Wolpert and Harry Trosman in *A.M.A. Archives of Neurology and Psychiatry*, Vol. 79, No. 4, pages 603-606; April, 1958.

TWO TYPES OF OCULAR MOTILITY OCCURRING IN SLEEP. E. Aserinsky and N. Kleitman in *Journal of Applied Physiology*, Vol. 8, No. 1, pages 1-10; July, 1955.

36. What People Dream About

THE INTERPRETATION OF DREAMS. Sigmund Freud in *The Basic Writings of Sigmund Freud*. Random House, 1938.

THE INTERPRETATION OF DREAMS, Vols. I and II. Wilhelm Stekel. Liveright Publishing Corp., 1943.

37. Conflict and Arousal

CONFLICT AND THE ORIENTATION REACTION. D. E. Berlyne in *Journal of Experimental Psychology*, Vol. 62, No. 5, pages 476-483; November, 1961.

CONFLICT, AROUSAL AND CURIOSITY. D. E. Berlyne. McGraw-Hill Book Company, Inc., 1960.

EFFECTS OF STIMULUS COMPLEXITY AND INCONGRUITY ON DURATION OF EEG DESYNCHRONIZATION. D. E. Berlyne and P. McDonnell in *Electroencephalography and Clinical Neurophysiology*, Vol. 18, pages 156-161; 1965.

MOTIVATION INHERENT IN INFORMATION PROCESSING AND ACTION. J. McV. Hunt in *Cognitive Factors in Motivation and Social Organization*, edited by O. J. Harvey. The Ronald Press Company, 1963.

38. The Pathology of Boredom

EFFECTS OF DECREASED VARIATION IN THE SENSORY ENVIRONMENT. W. H. Bexton, W. Heron and T. H. Scott in *Canadian Journal of Psychology,* Vol. 8, No. 2, pages 70-76; June, 1954.

THE MAMMAL AND HIS ENVIRONMENT. D. O. Hebb in *American Journal of Psychiatry,* Vol. 111, No. 11, pages 826-831; May, 1955.

VISUAL DISTURBANCES AFTER PROLONGED PERCEPTUAL ISOLATION. Woodburn Heron, B. K. Doane and T. H. Scott in *Canadian Journal of Psychology,* Vol. 10, No. 1, pages 13-18; March, 1956.

IX   LEARNING AND MEMORY

39. Learning in the Autonomic Nervous System

INSTRUMENTAL LEARNING OF HEART RATE CHANGES IN CURARIZED RATS: SHAPING, AND SPECIFICITY TO DISCRIMINATIVE STIMULUS. Neal E. Miller and Leo DiCara in *Journal of Comparative & Physiological Psychology,* Vol. 63, No. 1, pages 12-19; February, 1967.

INSTRUMENTAL LEARNING OF VASOMOTOR RESPONSES BY RATS: LEARNING TO RESPOND DIFFERENTIALLY IN THE TWO EARS. Leo V. DiCara and Neal E. Miller in *Science,* Vol. 159, No. 3822, pages 1485-1486; March 29, 1968.

HOMEOSTASIS AND REWARD: T-MAZE LEARNING INDUCED BY MANIPULATING ANTIDIURETIC HORMONE. Neal E. Miller, Leo V. DiCara and George Wolf in *American Journal of Physiology,* Vol. 215, No. 3, pages 684-686; September, 1968.

LEARNING OF VISCERAL AND GLANDULAR RESPONSES. Neal E. Miller in *Science,* Vol. 163, No. 3866, pages 434-445; January 31, 1969.

40. What Is Memory?

THE ELECTRICAL ACTIVITY OF THE NERVOUS SYSTEM. Mary A. Brazier. The Macmillan Company, 1951.

PSYCHOLOGY OF HUMAN LEARNING. John Alexander McGeogh. Longmans Green, 1951.

HANDBOOK OF EXPERIMENTAL PSYCHOLOGY. S. S. Stevens. John Wiley & Sons, Inc., 1951.

41. Memory and Protein Synthesis

ANTIMETABOLITES AFFECTING PROTEINS OR NUCLEIC ACID SYNTHESIS: PHLEOMYCIN, AN INHIBITOR OF DNA POLYMERASE. Arturo Falaschi and Arthur Kornberg in *Federation Proceedings,* Vol. 23, No. 5, Part I, pages 940-989; September–October, 1964.

CHEMICAL STUDIES ON MEMORY FIXATION IN GOLDFISH. Bernard W. Agranoff, Roger E. Davis and John J. Brink in *Brain Research,* Vol. 1, No. 3, pages 303-309; March–April, 1966.

MEMORY IN MICE AS AFFECTED BY INTRACEREBRAL PUROMYCIN. Josefa B. Flexner, Louis B. Flexner and Eliot Stellar in *Science,* Vol. 141, No. 3575, pages 57-59; July 5, 1963.

42. The Neurophysiology of Remembering

THE PROBLEM OF CEREBRAL ORGANIZATION IN VISION. K. S. Lashley in *Biological Symposia, a Series of Volumes Devoted to Current Symposia in the Field of Biology: Vol. VII, Visual Mechanisms,* edited by Jaques Cattell. The Jaques Cattell Press, 1942.

IN SEARCH OF THE ENGRAM. K. S. Lashley in *Physiological Mechanisms in Animal Behavior: Symposia of the Society for Experimental Biology, No. 4.* Academic Press, 1950.

TOWARD A SCIENCE OF NEUROPSYCHOLOGY (METHOD AND DATA). Karl H. Pribram in *Current Trends in Psychology and the Behavioral Sciences.* University of Pittsburgh Press, 1954.

THE PHYSIOLOGY OF IMAGINATION. John C. Eccles in *Scientific American,* Vol. 199, No. 3, pages 135-146; September, 1958.

SOME DIMENSIONS OF REMEMBERING: STEPS TOWARD A NEUROPSYCHOLOGICAL MODEL OF MEMORY. Karl H. Pribram in *Macromolecules and Behavior,* edited by John Gaito. Appleton-Century-Crofts, 1966.

X COMPLEX PROCESSES: THOUGHT, LANGUAGE, AND ATTENTION

43. Learning to Think

THE NATURE OF LEARNING SETS. H. F. Harlow in *Psychological Review*, Vol. 56, No. 1, pages 51-65; 1949.

THE MENTALITY OF APES. W. Köhler. Harcourt, Brace & Co., 1925.

44. The Functional Organization of the Brain

HIGHER CORTICAL FUNCTIONS IN MAN. A. R. Luria. Basic Books, Inc., 1966.

HUMAN BRAIN AND PSYCHOLOGICAL PROCESSES. A. R. Luria. Harper & Row, Publishers, 1966.

THE CO-ORDINATION AND REGULATION OF MOVEMENTS. N. Bernstein. Pergamon Press, 1967.

TRAUMATIC APHASIA. A. R. Luria. Mouton Publishers, 1969.

45. The Origin of Speech

A COURSE IN MODERN LINGUISTICS. Charles F. Hockett. Macmillan Company, 1958.

ANIMAL "LANGUAGES" AND HUMAN LANGUAGE. C. F. Hockett in *The Evolution of Man's Capacity for Culture*, arranged by J. N. Spuhler, pages 32-38. Wayne State University Press, 1959.

BEES: THEIR VISION, CHEMICAL SENSES, AND LANGUAGE. Karl von Frisch. Cornell University Press, 1950.

LANGUAGE: AN INTRODUCTION TO THE STUDY OF SPEECH. Edward Sapir. Harcourt, Brace & Company, 1921.

46. Attention and the Perception of Speech

CONTEXTUAL CUES AND SELECTIVE LISTENING. Anne M. Treisman in *Quarterly Journal of Experimental Psychology*, Vol. 12, No. 4, pages 242-248; November, 1960.

ON THE FUSION OF SOUNDS REACHING DIFFERENT SENSE ORGANS. D. E. Broadbent and Peter Ladefoged in *The Journal of the Acoustical Society of America*, Vol. 29, No. 6, pages 708-710; June, 1957.

PERCEPTION AND COMMUNICATION. D. E. Broadbent. Pergamon Press, Inc. 1958.

THREE AUDITORY THEORIES. J. C. R. Licklider in *Psychology: A Study of a Science*, edited by Sigmund Koch, Vol. 1, pages 41-144. McGraw-Hill Book Company, Inc., 1959.